Teachers Discovering Computers
INTEGRATING TECHNOLOGY IN A CONNECTED WORLD

SEVENTH EDITION

Gary B. Shelly

Glenda A. Gunter

Randolph E. Gunter

COURSE TECHNOLOGY
CENGAGE Learning·

SHELLY
CASHMAN
SERIES®

Australia • Brazil • Japan • Korea • Mexico • Singapore • Spain • United Kingdom • United States

COURSE TECHNOLOGY
CENGAGE Learning·

Teachers Discovering Computers
Integrating Technology in a Connected World,
Seventh Edition
Gary B. Shelly
Glenda A. Gunter
Randolph E. Gunter

Vice President, Publisher: Nicole Pinard

Executive Editor: Kathleen McMahon

Product Managers: Emma Newsom and
     Aimee Poirier

Associate Product Manager: Caitlin Womersley

Editorial Assistant: Angela Giannopoulos

Director of Marketing: Elisa Roberts

Marketing Manager: Tristen Kendall

Marketing Coordinator: Adrienne Fung

Print Buyer: Julio Esperas

Content Project Manager: Matthew Hutchinson

Development Editor: Pam Conrad

Proofreader: Kim Kosmatka

Indexer: Alexandra Nickerson

Art Director: Marissa Falco

Text Design: Joel Sadagursky

Cover Designer: Lisa Kuhn, Curio Press, LLC

Cover Photo: Thomas Tolstrup/Getty Images

Compositor: GEX Publishing Services

For product information and technology assistance, contact us at
Cengage Learning Customer & Sales Support, 1-800-354-9706
For permission to use material from this text or product, submit all requests online at **www.cengage.com/permissions**
Further permissions questions can be emailed to
permissionrequest@cengage.com

Library of Congress Control Number: 2011936892

ISBN-13: 978-1-133-52655-1

ISBN-10: 1-133-52655-1

Course Technology
20 Channel Center Street
Boston, MA 02210
USA

Cengage Learning is a leading provider of customized learning solutions with office locations around the globe, including Singapore, the United Kingdom, Australia, Mexico, Brazil, and Japan. Locate your local office at:
international.cengage.com/region

Cengage Learning products are represented in Canada by Nelson Education, Ltd.

To learn more about Course Technology, visit **www.cengage.com/course technology**

To learn more about Cengage Learning, visit **www.cengage.com**

Purchase any of our products at your local college store or at our preferred online store **www.cengagebrain.com**

Printed in the United States of America
1 2 3 4 5 6 7 17 16 15 14 13 12 11

Teachers Discovering Computers Integrating Technology in a Connected World
Seventh Edition

Table of Contents at a Glance

Teachers Discovering Computers Integrating Technology in a Connected World

Seventh Edition

Contents

Chapter **3**

Software for Educators   99

Chapter **4**

Hardware for Educators   153

Special Feature

A World without Wires — Tablets, Apps, and More

Chapter **7**

Evaluating Educational Technology and Integration Strategies   351

Chapter 8

Security Issues and Ethics in Education   411

Preface

The Shelly Cashman Series® offers the finest textbooks in computer education. We are proud of the fact that our previous *Teachers Discovering Computers* books have been so well received by instructors and students. The previous edition's popularity was due to (1) the integration of the World Wide Web, (2) the currency of the materials; (3) readability, (4) extensive exercises, (5) supplements, and (6) the ancillaries that allow an instructor to teach the way he or she wants to teach.

This latest edition of *Teachers Discovering Computers: Integrating Technology in a Connected World, Seventh Edition* continues with the innovation, quality, and reliability you have come to expect from this series. In addition to the standard technological updates and appropriate content changes, the seventh edition of *Teachers Discovering Computers* includes these enhancements:

- An increased emphasis on technology integration
- A new emphasis on teaching and reaching today's digital generation, as well as extensive information on using and integrating tablet computers (tablet-based learning) and apps (app-based learning)
- A new section added to Chapter 1 providing students with ideas and suggestions for creating a professional teaching portfolio (ePortfolio)
- A new Chapter 6 that discusses the way education is changing and the skills necessary to teach K-12 students either in a fully online or blended virtual environment

Distinguishing Features

Teachers Discovering Computers: Integrating Technology in a Connected World, Seventh Edition includes the following distinguishing features:

The Proven Shelly Cashman Series Pedagogy

More than five million students have learned about computers using the Shelly Cashman Series computer concepts textbooks. With World Wide Web integration and interactivity, extraordinary visual drawings and photographs, unprecedented currency, and the Shelly Cashman Series approach, this book will make your introductory educational technology course for educators exciting and dynamic — an experience your students will remember as a highlight of their educational careers. Students and course instructors will find this to be the finest textbook they have ever used.

World Wide Web

Teachers Discovering Computers continues the Shelly Cashman Series tradition of innovation with its extensive integration of the World Wide Web. The purpose of integrating the World Wide Web into the book is to (1) offer students additional infomation and currency on topics of importance; (2) make available alternative learning techniques with Web-based curriculum-specific content, learning games, practice tests, and new instructional videos; (3) underscore the relevance of the World Wide Web as a basic information tool that can be used in all facets of K-12 education and society; and (4) offer instructors the opportunity to organize and administer their campus-based or distance education-based courses on the Web. The Computer Concepts CourseMate Web site for Teachers Discovering Computers at *www.cengagebrain.com* works hand-in-hand with the text in three central ways:

- End-of-chapter assignments and many of the Special Features in the book have Web components. While working on an end-of-chapter assignment, students can go to the Computer Concepts CourseMate Web site for *Teachers Discovering Computers* to look up key terms, explore the vast resources the Web has for education, or get an alternative point of view. The Computer Concepts CourseMate Web site for *Teachers Discovering Computers* provides students with thousands of links to additional sources of information on a chapter-by-chapter basis. These sources have been evaluated for appropriateness and are maintained by a team of educators.

- Computer Concepts CourseMate Web site for Teachers Discovering Computers provides a rich multimedia learning experience. Students can watch informational videos to learn about new technologies, reinforce their learning by playing interactive games, and explore new integration concepts like blogs, podcasts, wikis, and screencasts. In addition, an interactive timeline steps students through the major computer technology developments of the past 70 years, including the most recent advances.

- A new Special Feature that follows Chapter 6 titled A World without Wires — Tablets, Apps, and More that provides students with an overview of the wireless revolution with an emphasis on tablet computers and their features, as well as information on apps and app-based learning.

- Located in the margins in all chapters are ePortfolio Idea icons, which identify a topic or technology that students can include in their personal ePortfolio.

Web Info

For more information on the age of convergence, visit the Computer Concepts CourseMate Web site at *www.cengagebrain.com*, navigate to the Chapter 1 Web Info resource for this book, and then click Age of Convergence.

Integration Strategies

To access dozens of integration ideas specific to your classroom curriculum, visit the Computer Concepts CourseMate Web site at *www.cengagebrain.com*, navigate to the Chapter 1 Apps Corner resource for this book, and then navigate to your grade-level corner.

FAQ

Are tablet computers replacing traditional computers in schools?

Yes, numerous computer companies offer tablets and because of their small size and functionality, tablet computers are quickly becoming mainstream with students in both K-12 and higher education.

ePortfolio Idea

- Throughout the text, marginal annotations titled Web Info provide suggestions on how to obtain additional information via the Web about an important topic covered on the page. The Computer Concepts CourseMate Web site for Teachers Discovering Computers at *www.cengagebrain.com* provides links to these additional sources.

This textbook, however, does not depend on Web access to be used successfully. The Web access adds to the comprehensive treatment of topics within the book.

A Visually Appealing Book that Maintains Student Interest

The latest technology, pictures, drawings, and text have been artfully combined to produce a visually appealing and easy–to–understand book. Many of the figures show a step-by-step pedagogy, which simplifies the more complex computer and educational technology concepts. Pictures and drawings reflect the latest trends in computer and educational technology. In addition, three marginal elements are included: Integration Strategies, FAQs, and ePortfolio Ideas. Integration Strategies boxes contain ideas and suggestions for integrating various end-of-chapter segments and special features related to topics presented in the text. Frequently asked questions (FAQ) boxes offer common questions and answers about subjects related to the topic at hand. The ePortfolio Idea icon identifies topics or technologies that students can include in their personal ePortfolio. Finally, the text was set in two columns, which research shows is easier for students to read. This combination of pictures, step-by-step drawings, and tested text layout sets a new standard for education textbook design.

Latest Educational Technology and Computer Trends

The terms and examples of educational technology described in this book are the same ones your students will encounter when using computers, especially tablet computers, in the school setting and at home. The latest educational software packages as well as apps for tablet computers and other mobile devices are shown throughout this book.

Macs and PCs

Unlike many businesses, both Macs and PCs are used in the K-12 school environment. This textbook addresses both computer platforms and describes the appropriateness and use of educational software for both Macs and PCs.

End-of-Chapter Activities

Unlike other books on educational technology fundamentals, a major effort was undertaken in *Teachers Discovering Computers* to offer exciting, rich, and thorough end-of-chapter materials to reinforce the chapter objectives and assist you in making your course the finest ever offered. As indicated earlier, each and every one of the end-of-chapter pages is stored as a Web page on the Computer Concepts CourseMate Web site to provide your students in-depth information and alternative methods of preparing for examinations.

- An updated References page, which contains information about all the references used to write this book.

The content of the textbook and the Computer Concepts CourseMate Web site also have been enhanced to allow for curriculum-specific learning by all K-12 educators. That is, students using the *Teachers Discovering Computers* textbook will be able to learn both how to use, and more importantly, how to integrate technology into their current or future classroom curriculum. In addition, this seventh edition of *Teachers Discovering Computers* has been updated to address the ever-changing learning needs of the digital generation and to provide instructional strategies with techniques to address these needs.

Objectives of This Textbook

Teachers Discovering Computers: Integrating Technology in a Connected World, Seventh Edition is intended for use in a one-quarter or one-semester undergraduate or graduate-level introductory computer course for educators. Students will finish the course with a solid understanding of educational technology, including how to use computers, how to access and evaluate information on the World Wide Web, and how to integrate computers and educational technology into classroom curriculum. This book also can be used for in-service training workshops that train teachers, administrators, and counselors how to use and effectively integrate

educational technology. The objectives of this textbook are to:

- Present practical, efficient ways to integrate technology resources and technology-based methods into everyday curriculum-specific practices
- Provide students with an understanding of the concepts and skills outlined in the new National Educational Technology Standards for Students (NETS-S) and the National Educational Technology Standards for Teachers (NETS-T)
- Present the fundamentals of computers and educational technology in an easy-to-understand format
- Make use of the Web as a repository of the latest information and as an educational resource and learning tool for K-12 education
- Provide information about both Macs and PCs
- Give students an in-depth understanding of why computers are essential to society, the business world, and K-12 education
- Provide students with the knowledge of how to use educational technology with diverse K–12 student populations
- Offer numerous examples of how to use educational technology in various subject areas and with K–12 students who have special needs
- Provide students with knowledge of responsible, ethical, and legal uses of technology, information, and software resources
- Provide students with knowledge of technology to enhance their personal and professional productivity

Visual Walkthrough of the Book

Current. Relevant. Innovative.
Teaching the Significance of Today's Digital World.

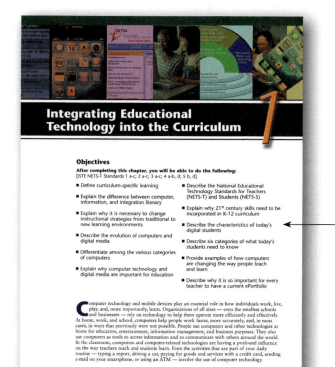

Chapter Objectives

Before reading the chapter, carefully read through the Objectives to familiarize yourself with what you will learn in each chapter.

Step Figures

Step figures present complex computer concepts using a step-by-step pedagogy.

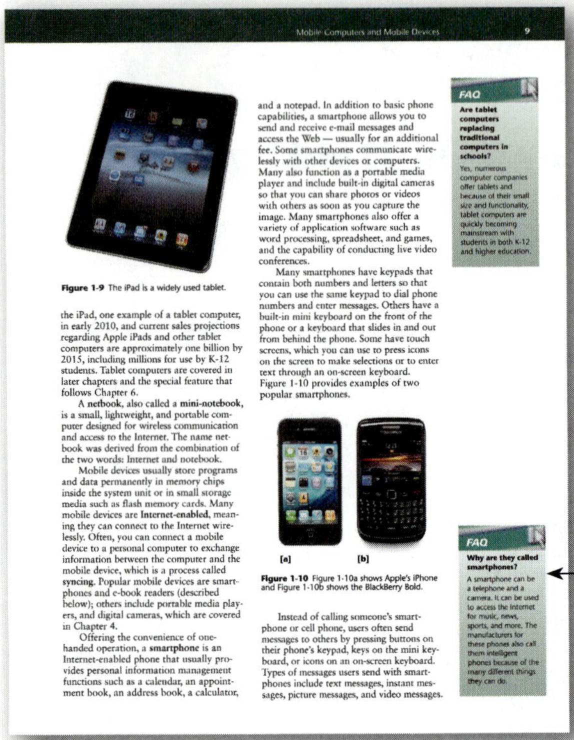

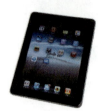

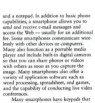

Figure 1-9 The iPad is a widely used tablet.

the iPad, one example of a tablet computer, in early 2010, and current sales projections regarding Apple iPads and other tablet computers are approximately one billion by 2015, including millions for use by K-12 students. Tablet computers are covered in later chapters and the special feature that follows Chapter 6.

A **netbook**, also called a **mini-notebook**, is a small, lightweight, and portable computer designed for wireless communication and access to the Internet. The name netbook was derived from the combination of the two words: Internet and notebook.

Mobile devices usually store programs and data permanently in memory chips inside the system unit or in small storage media such as flash memory cards. Many mobile devices are **Internet-enabled**, meaning they can connect to the Internet wirelessly. Often, you can connect a mobile device to a personal computer to exchange information between the computer and the mobile device, which is a process called **syncing**. Popular mobile devices are smartphones and e-book readers (described below); others include portable media players, and digital cameras, which are covered in Chapter 4.

Offering the convenience of one-handed operation, a **smartphone** is an Internet-enabled phone that usually provides personal information management functions such as a calendar, an appointment book, an address book, a calculator, and a notepad. In addition to basic phone capabilities, a smartphone allows you to send and receive e-mail messages and access the Web — usually for an additional fee. Some smartphones communicate wirelessly with other devices or computers. Many also function as a portable media player and include built-in digital cameras so that you can share photos or videos with others as soon as you capture the image. Many smartphones also offer a variety of application software such as word processing, spreadsheet, and games, and the capability of conducting live video conferences.

Many smartphones have keypads that contain both numbers and letters so that you can use the same keypad to dial phone numbers and enter messages. Others have a built-in mini keyboard on the front of the phone or a keyboard that slides in and out from behind the phone. Some have touch screens, which you can use to press icons on the screen to make selections or to enter text through an on-screen keyboard. Figure 1-10 provides examples of two popular smartphones.

[a] [b]

Figure 1-10 Figure 1-10a shows Apple's iPhone and Figure 1-10b shows the BlackBerry Bold.

Instead of calling someone's smartphone or cell phone, users often send messages to others by pressing buttons on their phone's keypad, keys on the mini keyboard, or icons on an on-screen keyboard. Types of messages users send with smartphones include text messages, instant messages, picture messages, and video messages.

FAQ

Are tablet computers replacing traditional computers in schools?

Yes, numerous computer companies offer tablets and because of their small size and functionality, tablet computers are quickly becoming mainstream with students in both K-12 and higher education.

FAQ

Why are they called smartphones?

A smartphone can be a telephone and a camera. It can be used to access the Internet for music, news, sports, and more. The manufacturers for these phones also call them intelligent phones because of the many different things they can do.

FAQs

FAQ (frequently asked questions) boxes offer common questions and answers about subjects related to the topic at hand.

in virtual classrooms across the world (Figure 1-21). More importantly, students need to learn how to communicate and work collaboratively in the global workplace they will find themselves employed in.

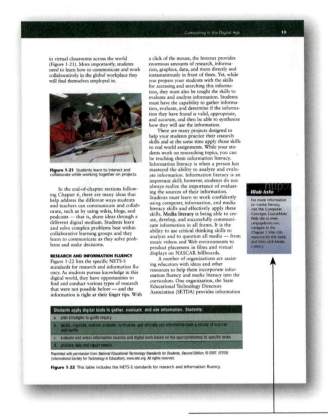

Figure 1-21 Students learn to interact and collaborate while working together on projects.

In the end-of-chapter sections following Chapter 6, there are many ideas that help address the different ways students and teachers can communicate and collaborate, such as by using wikis, blogs, and podcasts — that is, share ideas through a different digital medium. Students learn and solve complex problems best within collaborative learning groups and they learn to communicate as they solve problems and make decisions.

RESEARCH AND INFORMATION FLUENCY

Figure 1-22 lists the specific NETS-S standards for research and information fluency. As students pursue knowledge in this digital world, they have opportunities to find and conduct various types of research that were not possible before — and the information is right at their finger tips. With a click of the mouse, the Internet provides enormous amounts of research, information, graphics, data, and more directly and instantaneously in front of them. Yet, while you prepare your students with the skills for accessing and searching this information, they must also be taught the skills to evaluate and analyze information. Students must have the capability to gather information, evaluate, and determine if the information they have found is valid, appropriate, and accurate, and then be able to synthesize how they will use the information.

There are many projects designed to help your students practice their research skills and at the same time apply those skills to real world assignments. While your students work on researching topics, you can be teaching them information literacy. Information literacy is when a person has mastered the ability to analyze and evaluate information. Information literacy is an important skill; however, students do not always realize the importance of evaluating the sources of their information. Students must learn to work confidently using computer, information, and media literacy skills and effectively apply these skills. **Media literacy** is being able to create, develop, and successfully communicate information in all forms. It is the ability to use critical thinking skills to analyze and to question all media — from music videos and Web environments to product placement in films and virtual displays on NASCAR billboards.

A number of organizations are assisting educators with ideas and other resources to help them incorporate information fluency and media literacy into the curriculum. One organization, the State Educational Technology Directors Association (SETDA) provides information

Students apply digital tools to gather, evaluate, and use information. Students:
a. plan strategies to guide inquiry.
b. locate, organize, analyze, evaluate, synthesize, and ethically use information from a variety of sources and media.
c. evaluate and select information sources and digital tools based on the appropriateness to specific tasks.
d. process data and report results.

Figure 1-22 This table includes the NETS-S standards for research and information fluency.

Web Info

For more information on media literacy, visit the Computer Concepts CourseMate Web site at www.cengagebrain.com, navigate to the Chapter 1 Web Info resource for this book, and then click Media Literacy.

Web Info

These marginal annotations provide suggestions on how to obtain additional information via the Web about an important topic covered on the page.

new learning environments for K-12 students. As you continue to integrate educational technology, mobile devices, and digital media, you will find yourself transitioning from using traditional teaching and learning strategies to using many new and exciting technology-enriched teaching and learning strategies. Refer to Figure 1-1 often as you learn how to integrate technology, mobile devices, and digital media into your curriculum and practice using these new teaching strategies.

Another important issue is that teachers no longer have the time to create their various lesson plans and other documents from scratch, or in other words, constantly reinvent the wheel. The primary reason for extensively eLearning-enhancing this textbook is to provide you with hundreds of outstanding curriculum-specific resources and integration ideas that you can modify for use in your classroom curriculum. These resources are organized so you can choose the best curriculum-specific content to improve your students' learning. We encourage you to interact with the curriculum-specific content that works for you, and then adopt and modify the content and other information, integrating it into your classroom curriculum.

Computer, Information, and Integration Literacy

Today, the vocabulary of computing is all around you. Before the advent of computers, memory was an individual's mental ability to recall previous experiences; storage was a place for all your extra stuff; and communication was the act of exchanging opinions and information through writing, speaking, or sign language. In today's world, these words and countless others have taken on new meanings as part of the vocabulary used to describe computers and their uses.

When you hear the word "computer," initially you may think of computers used in schools to perform activities such as creating flyers, memos, and letters; managing student records and calculating grades; or tracking library books. In the course of a day or week, however, you encounter many other computers. Your home, for instance, contains a myriad of electronic devices, such as wireless telephones, DVRs, DVD players, handheld video games, digital cameras, and mobile devices (such as portable computers, e-book readers, iPads, and so on).

Computers help you with your banking when you use automatic teller machines (ATMs) to deposit or withdraw funds. When you buy groceries, a computer tracks your purchases and calculates the amount of money you owe; it may even generate custom coupons based on your buying patterns. Even your car is equipped with numerous computers that operate the electrical system, control the temperature, run sophisticated antitheft devices, and much more.

Today, most occupations involve the use of computers on a daily basis (Figure 1-2). As the world of computers and computer-related technologies

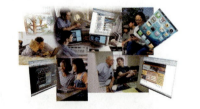

Figure 1-2 Computer technology, digital media, and mobile devices are present in every aspect of daily living — in the workplace, at home, in the classroom, and for entertainment.

Integration Strategies

To access dozens of integration ideas specific to your classroom curriculum, visit the Computer Concepts CourseMate Web site at www.cengagebrain.com, navigate to the Chapter 1 Apps Corner resource for this book, and then navigate to your grade-level corner.

Integration Strategies

These boxes contain ideas and suggestions for integrating various end-of-chapter segments and special features related to topics presented in the text.

ePortfolio Idea

The ePortfolio Idea icon identifies topics or technologies that students can include in their personal ePortfolio.

End-of-Chapter Student Activities

Key Terms

This list of the key terms with page references will aid students in mastering the chapter material. A complete summary of all key terms in the book, together with their definitions, appears in the index at the end of the book.

Checkpoint

Matching and short-answer questions, together with a figure from the chapter that can be labeled, are used to reinforce the material presented within the chapter.

Teaching Today

This section is designed to help students gain an appreciation of the value that technology and the World Wide Web have for K-12 education by visiting exciting educational Web pages and completing suggested curriculum integration tasks. The Web pages provide links to challenge students further on a vast array of interesting teacher-related topics.

Education Issues

The use of computers and other technologies in education are not without controversy. At the end of each chapter, several scenarios are presented that challenge students to critically examine the use of technology in K-12 education and society in general. Other non-technology related scenarios allow students to explore many current controversial issues in education, such as school violence. The corresponding Web page provides links to challenge students further.

Apps Corner

This innovative section provides extensive ideas and resources for integrating apps into your classroom-specific curriculum. Each chapter provides information on applicable iPad, BlackBerry, and Android Apps in the following 4 corners: Early Childhood, Elementary, Middle School, and Secondary.

Software Corner

Today's educators can choose from a variety of high-quality and often inexpensive educational software. Students learn about popular software programs by researching them on the Web and, in many cases, even downloading or ordering a free evaluation copy so they can evaluate a program before buying it.

Digital Media Corner

Today's K-12 digital students need their learning to be meaningful and relevant to their lives. Digital Media Corner provides links to videos, ideas, and examples of how students can use digital media to enhance their teaching as well as the learning of their K–12 students. The Web pages provide links to challenge students further.

Assistive Technologies Corner

This new section provides information on current hardware, software, and peripherals that will assist students using this text in delivering instruction to their K-12 students with physical, cognitive, or sensory challenges. The Web pages provide extensive additional information and links to dozens of current and emerging assistive technologies.

In the Lab

These exercises are divided into two areas: productivity and integration. Students can use the productivity exercises to improve their software-specific skills in using word processing, spreadsheets, database, desktop publishing, curriculum and Web page development, and other productivity software programs. They can use the integration ideas for incorporating these programs into their classroom-specific curriculum.
The Web pages provide links to tutorials, productivity ideas, integration examples and ideas, and more.

Learn It Online

These exercises allow students to improve their computer and integration skills by learning exciting new skills online. This section includes video clips, practice tests, learning games, and much more.

Special Features

Guide to Professional, State, and Federal Web Sites   This special feature following Chapter 1 contains more than 30 popular professional educational organizations, over 25 federal government agencies, as well as links to the departments of educations for all 50 states and the District of Columbia; these links are also updated and described at the Computer Concepts CourseMate Web (*www.cengagebrain.com*) site for this textbook.

Learning Theories and Educational Research   The special feature following Chapter 5 provides information about educational learning theories and research. This feature introduces students to educational terms, learning theories and theorists, educational research, and learning strategies.

A World without Wires — Tablets, Apps, and More   This new and innovative special feature following Chapter 6 presents an overview of the wireless revolution and covers the latest information on and features of tablet computers. Also included is extensive information on apps and app-based learning.

Timeline — Milestones in Computer History   At the Computer Concepts CourseMate Web site (*www.cengagebrain.com*) for this book is an interactive, colorful, and highly informative timeline of the history of computers from 1937 to the present. The timeline contains dozens of links to extensive supplemental information, including historical audio segments, animations, videos, and much more.

Guide to World Wide Web Sites, Searching Techniques, and Search Tools for Education   At the Computer Concepts CourseMate Web site (*www.cengagebrain.com*) for this book is a multi-page listing with updated links and information on more than 150 popular Web sites. These Web sites are organized into general categories, such as Entertainment, Health and Medicine, Government and Politics, Shopping, and more. This feature also provides links to numerous popular education search tools.

Buyer's Guide: How to Purchase Computers and Mobile Devices   At the Computer Concepts CourseMate Web site (*www.cengagebrain.com*) for this book is a multi-page guide that introduces students to purchasing a personal computer, desktop computer, notebook/netbook computer, and tablet computers and other mobile devices.

Appendix   The appendix lists the various books, articles, and other sources of information used in developing Teachers Discovering Computers that are not referenced at the Computer Concepts CourseMate Web site for this book (*www.cengagebrain.com*).

Instructor Resources

Available on the Instructor Companion site and on the Instructor's Resource disc, these Instructor Resources include both teaching and testing aids.

Instructor's Manual Includes lecture notes summarizing the chapter sections, figures and boxed elements found in every chapter, teacher tips, classroom activities, lab activities, and quick quizzes in Microsoft Word files.

Syllabus Easily customizable sample syllabi that cover policies, assignments, exams, and other course information.

Figure Files Illustrations for every figure in the textbook in electronic form.

Solutions to Exercises Includes solutions for all end-of-chapter exercises.

PowerPoint Presentations A multimedia lecture presentation system that provides slides for each chapter. Presentations are based on chapter objectives.

Test Bank & Test Engine Test Banks include 112 questions for every chapter, featuring objective-based and critical thinking question types, and including page number references and figure references, when appropriate. Also included is the test engine, ExamView, the ultimate tool for your objective-based testing needs.

NEW! Computer Concepts CourseMate

The new Computer Concepts CourseMate for *Teachers Discovering Computers* is the most expansive digital site for any computer concepts text in the market today! The content in the CourseMate site is integrated into the pages of the text, giving students easy access to current information on important topics, reinforcement activities, and alternative learning techniques. Integrating the Computer Concepts CourseMate into the classroom keeps today's students engaged and involved in the learning experience.

For each chapter in the text, students can access a variety of interactive quizzes and learning games, exercises, Web links, videos, and other features that specifically reinforce and build on the concepts presented in the chapter. This digital solution encourages students to take learning into their own hands and explore related content on their own to learn even more about subjects in which they are especially interested.

All of these resources on the Computer Concepts CourseMate for *Teachers Discovering Computers* enable students to get more comfortable using technology and helps prepare students to use the Internet as a tool to enrich their lives.

Contact Us

The Shelly Cashman Series is dedicated to providing you with all of the tools you need to make your class a success. For information on any of our product offerings, contact your Cengage Learning representative or call one of the following telephone numbers:

Colleges, Universities, Continuing Education Departments, Post-Secondary Vocational Schools, Career Colleges, Business, Industry, Government, Trade, Retailer, Wholesaler, Library, and Resellers
Call Cengage Learning at 800-354-9706

K-12 Schools, Secondary Vocational Schools, Adult Education, and School Districts
Call Cengage Learning at 800-354-9706

In Canada
Call Nelson Cengage Learning at 800-268-2222

Anywhere
www.cengage.com/coursetechnology

Online Content

Student Edition Labs

Our Web-based interactive labs help students master hundreds of computer concepts, including input and output devices, file management and desktop applications, computer ethics, virus protection, and much more. Featuring up-to-the minute content, eye-popping graphics, and rich animation, the highly interactive Student Edition Labs offer students an alternative way to learn through dynamic observation, step-by-step practice, and challenging review questions. Access the Student Edition Labs from the Computer Concepts CourseMate Web site for Teachers Discovering Computers at www.cengagebrain.com.

SAM 2010: Assessment & Training and Project Grading Solutions

SAM (Skills Assessment Manager) is a robust assessment, training, and project-based system that enables students to be active participants in learning valuable Microsoft Office 2010 skills. A set of testbank questions ties directly to each chapter in this book. Let SAM be an integral part of your students' learning experience!

Content for Online Learning

Course Technology has partnered with the leading distance learning solution providers and class-management platforms today. To access this material, instructors will visit our password-protected instructor resources at www.cengage.com/coursecare/cartridge/. Instructor resources include the following: case projects, test banks, practice tests, custom syllabi, and more. For additional information or for an instructor user name and password, please contact your sales representative. For students to access

this material, they must have purchased a Course Cartridge PIN-code specific to this title and your campus platform. The resources for students may include (based on instructor preferences) but are not limited to the following: topic review, review questions, and practice tests.

CourseCasts Learning on the Go
Always available. . . always relevant.

Our fast-paced world is driven by technology. You know because you are an active participant — always on the go, always keeping up with technological trends, and always learning new ways to embrace technology to power your life. Let CourseCasts, hosted by Ken Baldauf of Florida State University, be your guide to weekly updates in this ever-changing space. These timely, relevant podcasts are produced weekly and are available for download at http://coursecasts.course.com or directly from iTunes (search by CourseCasts). CourseCasts are a perfect solution to getting students (and even instructors) to learn on the go!

CourseNotes — Technology in a Flash!

Course Technology's CourseNotes are six-panel quick reference cards that reinforce the most important and widely used features of a software application in a visual and user-friendly format. CourseNotes serve as a great reference tool during and after the student completes the course. CourseNotes are available for software applications, such as Microsoft Office 2010, Word 2010, Excel 2010, Access 2010, PowerPoint 2010, and Windows 7. Topic-based CourseNotes are available for Best Practices in Social Networking, Hot Topics in Technology, and Web 2.0. Visit www.cengage.com/ct/coursenotes to learn more!

Acknowledgements

For this seventh edition, the authors would like to thank Pam Conrad for her professionalism and remarkable attention to detail in making this edition the best TDC textbook ever. Special thanks also to Brandie Glessner, Laura Coyle, Jessica Levene, Alyssa Pinti and Christine Condis for assisting in the development of Chapters 5/6 and Katie Gusman, Tiffany Swenson, and Jacqueline Lorente-Pico for assisting in the development of the end-of-chapter materials. Our heartfelt thanks to Abby Reip for all her hard work on the photos and permissions for this edition. And finally, a big thank you to the exceptional team at Cengage, especially Emma Newsom and Aimee Poirier, who day after day answer our questions, address our concerns, and keep this book on track and fabulous.

Gary B. Shelly
Glenda A. Gunter
Randolph E. Gunter

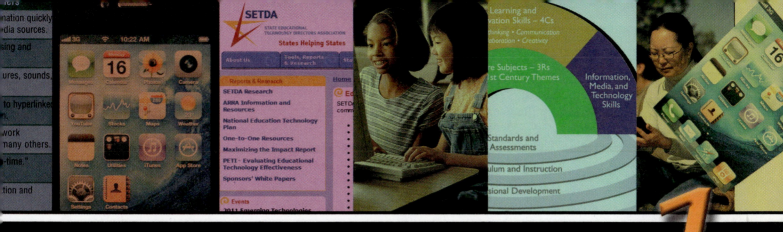

Integrating Educational Technology into the Curriculum

Objectives

After completing this chapter, you will be able to do the following:

[ISTE NETS-T Standards 1 a-c; 2 a-c; 3 a-c; 4 a-b, d; 5 b, d]

- Define curriculum-specific learning

- Explain the difference between computer, information, and integration literacy

- Explain why it is necessary to change instructional strategies from traditional to new learning environments

- Describe the evolution of computers and digital media

- Differentiate among the various categories of computers

- Explain why computer technology and digital media are important for education

- Describe the National Educational Technology Standards for Teachers (NETS-T) and Students (NETS-S)

- Explain why 21st century skills need to be incorporated in K-12 curriculum

- Describe the characteristics of today's digital students

- Describe six categories of what today's students need to know

- Provide examples of how computers are changing the way people teach and learn

- Describe why it is so important for every teacher to have a current ePortfolio

Computer technology and mobile devices play an essential role in how individuals work, live, play, and, more importantly, learn. Organizations of all sizes — even the smallest schools and businesses — rely on technology to help them operate more efficiently and effectively. At home, work, and school, computers help people work faster, more accurately, and, in most cases, in ways that previously were not possible. People use computers and other technologies at home for education, entertainment, information management, and business purposes. They also use computers as tools to access information and to communicate with others around the world. In the classroom, computers and computer-related technologies are having a profound influence on the way teachers teach and students learn. Even the activities that are part of your daily routine — typing a report, driving a car, paying for goods and services with a credit card, sending e-mail on your smartphone, or using an ATM — involve the use of computer technology.

Web Info

For more information about and ideas from teachers integrating technology into their curriculum, visit the Computer Concepts CourseMate Web site at *www.cengagebrain.com*, navigate to the Chapter 1 Web Info resource for this book, and then click Integration Ideas.

As they have for a number of years, computers and related technologies continue to influence the lives of most individuals. Today, teachers in K-12 schools are educating students who will spend all of their adult lives in a technology-rich society. To help schools better educate students, the federal government, state governments, and school districts have spearheaded massive funding efforts to equip classrooms with computers, with connectivity to networks, and with access to the Internet and the World Wide Web. Teachers in these classrooms must be prepared to utilize both current and emerging technologies.

The purpose of this book is to provide you with the knowledge you need to use and integrate technology into your specific classroom curriculum. Chapter 1 introduces you to basic computer concepts and digital media as well as to how teachers and administrators integrate computer technology and digital media into K-12 education. As you read, you also will begin to understand the vocabulary used to describe computer technology, mobile devices, digital media, and educational technology. Remember that this chapter lays the foundation for you to begin to understand how you can modify your teaching strategies to include the skills that your students will need to be successful and productive citizens.

Curriculum-Specific Learning

As you review the materials and concepts presented in this textbook and the accompanying Web site, continuously ask yourself how you can use and integrate the knowledge you are gaining into your specific curriculum interests. Reflect on three ways you can use your newly acquired knowledge: (1) for your own professional development, (2) for using technology as a productivity tool in your classroom, and, most importantly, (3) for extensively integrating technology, mobile devices, and digital media into your instructional strategies, lessons, student-based projects, and student assessments to improve student learning — in other words, throughout the curriculum. By doing this, you will be involved in **curriculum-specific learning** or **discipline-specific learning**, which is when you are learning how to apply teaching principles, knowledge, and ideas to authentic and practical classroom lessons and projects that can benefit your students.

Traditional 20th century educational practices will no longer provide you with the skills you need to teach your students effectively how to become productive citizens in today's high-tech, global workplace. Figure 1-1 lists characteristics representing traditional approaches to learning and corresponding strategies associated with

Establishing New Learning Environments by Incorporating New Strategies

Traditional Learning Environments	→	New Learning Environments
Teacher-centered instruction	→	Student-centered learning
Single-sense stimulation	→	Multisensory stimulation
Single-path progression	→	Multipath progression
Single media	→	Multimedia
Isolated work	→	Collaborative work
Information delivery	→	Information exchange
Passive learning	→	Active/exploratory/inquiry-based learning
Factual, knowledge-based learning	→	Critical thinking and informed decision making
Reactive response	→	Proactive/planned action
Isolated, artificial context	→	Authentic, real-world context

Source: International Society for Technology in Education (ISTE)

Figure 1-1 This chart shows the characteristics that represent traditional approaches to learning and corresponding strategies often associated with new learning environments for K-12 students.

new learning environments for K-12 students. As you continue to integrate educational technology, mobile devices, and digital media, you will find yourself transitioning from using traditional teaching and learning strategies to using many new and exciting technology-enriched teaching and learning strategies. Refer to Figure 1-1 often as you learn how to integrate technology, mobile devices, and digital media into your curriculum and practice using these new teaching strategies.

Another important issue is that teachers no longer have the time to create their various lesson plans and other documents from scratch, or in other words, constantly reinvent the wheel. The primary reason for extensively eLearning-enhancing this textbook is to provide you with hundreds of outstanding curriculum-specific resources and integration ideas that you can modify for use in your classroom curriculum. These resources are organized so you can choose the best curriculum-specific content to improve your students' learning. We encourage you to interact with the curriculum-specific content that works for you, and then adopt and modify the content and other information, integrating it into your classroom curriculum.

Computer, Information, and Integration Literacy

Today, the vocabulary of computing is all around you. Before the advent of computers, memory was an individual's mental ability to recall previous experiences; storage was a place for all your extra stuff; and communication was the act of exchanging opinions and information through writing, speaking, or sign language. In today's world, these words and countless others have taken on new meanings as part of the vocabulary used to describe computers and their uses.

When you hear the word "computer," initially you may think of computers used in schools to perform activities such as creating flyers, memos, and letters; managing student records and calculating grades; or tracking library books. In the course of a day or week, however, you encounter many other computers. Your home, for instance, contains a myriad of electronic devices, such as wireless telephones, DVRs, DVD players, handheld video games, digital cameras, and mobile devices (such as portable computers, e-book readers, iPads, and so on).

Computers help you with your banking when you use automatic teller machines (ATMs) to deposit or withdraw funds. When you buy groceries, a computer tracks your purchases and calculates the amount of money you owe; it may even generate custom coupons based on your buying patterns. Even your car is equipped with numerous computers that operate the electrical system, control the temperature, run sophisticated antitheft devices, and much more.

Today, most occupations involve the use of computers on a daily basis (Figure 1-2). As the world of computers and computer-related technologies

Figure 1-2
Computer technology, digital media, and mobile devices are present in every aspect of daily living — in the workplace, at home, in the classroom, and for entertainment.

Web Info

For more information on information fluency, visit the Computer Concepts CourseMate Web site at *www.cengagebrain.com*, navigate to the Chapter 1 Web Info resource for this book, and then click Information Fluency Ideas.

FAQ

Is data singular or plural?

With respect to computers, it is accepted and common practice to use the word data as either singular and plural as long as you are consistent in how you use it.

advances, it is essential that you gain some level of **computer literacy**; that is, you must have current knowledge and understanding of computers and their uses.

Information literacy, also known as **information fluency**, means knowing how to find, analyze, use, and communicate information. Information literacy is the ability to gather information from multiple sources, select relevant material, and organize it into a form that will allow the user to make decisions or take specific actions.

Students must learn to make informed decisions based on information obtained in all areas of their lives. For example, suppose you decide to move to a new city and need a place to live. You could find a home by driving around the city looking for a house or apartment within your price range that is close to school or work. As an information literate person, however, you might search for a home using the **Internet**, which is a global network of computers that contains information on a multitude of subjects. Using Internet resources to locate potential homes before you leave will make your drive through the city more efficient and focused.

How does computer technology relate to information literacy? They relate because information on housing, cars, and other products, as well as information on finances, school systems, travel, and weather, is increasingly accessible by using computers. For example, with communications equipment, you can use a computer to connect to the Internet to access information on countless topics. After you have accessed the desired information, computers can help you analyze and use that information.

Computer and information literacy are very important for educators because today's teachers also must use computers as a tool to facilitate learning. Teachers must be able to assess technology resources and plan classroom activities using available technologies. These skills are part of **integration literacy**, which is the ability to use computers, mobile devices, digital media, and other technologies combined with a variety of teaching and learning strategies to enhance students' learning. Integration literacy means that teachers understand how to match appropriate technology to learning objectives, goals, and outcomes. A solid foundation of computer

and information literacy is essential to understanding how to integrate technology into the classroom curriculum successfully.

As an educator, technology will affect your work and your life every day — and will continue to do so in the future. Today, school administrators use technology to access and manage information, and teachers use computers to enhance teaching and learning. The computer industry is continually developing new uses for computers, mobile devices, and digital media, while also making improvements to existing technologies. Learning about computers, mobile devices, digital media, and other technologies will help you function effectively in society and become a better facilitator of learning.

What Is a Computer and What Does It Do?

In basic or traditional terms, a **computer** is an electronic device that operates under the control of instructions stored in its memory, accepts data, processes the data according to specified rules, produces results, and stores the results for future use. In other words, a computer is a computational device.

Data is a collection of unorganized facts. Computers manipulate and process data to create information. **Information** is data that is organized, has meaning, and is useful. Examples of information are reports, newsletters, receipts, pictures, invoices, or checks. As shown in Figure 1-3, for example, computers process lots of data to provide a student grade report.

Data entered into a computer is called **input**. The processed results are called **output**. Thus, a computer processes input to create output. A computer can hold data for future use in an area called **storage**. This cycle of input, process, output, and storage is called the **information processing cycle**.

The electronic and mechanical equipment that makes up a computer is called **hardware**. These components are covered in Chapter 4. **Software** is the series of instructions that tell the hardware how to perform tasks. Software is covered in Chapter 3. Without software, hardware is useless; hardware needs the instructions provided by software to process data into information.

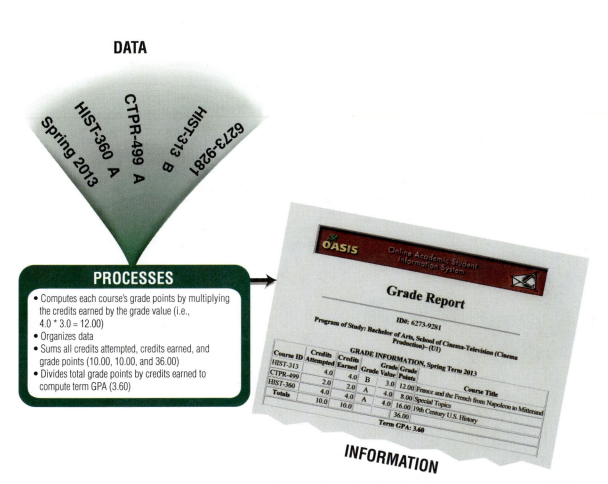

DATA

PROCESSES
- Computes each course's grade points by multiplying the credits earned by the grade value (i.e., 4.0 * 3.0 = 12.00)
- Organizes data
- Sums all credits attempted, credits earned, and grade points (10.00, 10.00, and 36.00)
- Divides total grade points by credits earned to compute term GPA (3.60)

OASIS Online Academic Student Information System

Grade Report

ID#: 6273-9281

Program of Study: Bachelor of Arts, School of Cinema-Television (Cinema Production)–(U1)

GRADE INFORMATION, Spring Term 2013

Course ID	Credits Attempted	Credits Earned	Grade	Grade Value	Grade Points	Course Title
HIST-313	4.0	4.0	B	3.0	12.00	France and the French from Napoleon to Mitterand
CTPR-499	2.0	2.0	A	4.0	8.00	Special Topics
HIST-360	4.0	4.0	A	4.0	16.00	19th Century U.S. History
Totals	10.0	10.0			36.00	

Term GPA: 3.60

INFORMATION

Figure 1-3 A computer processes data into information. In this simplified example, the student identification number, semester, course codes, and course grades all represent data. The computer processes the data to produce the grade report (information).

The Evolution of Computers and Digital Media

The evolution of modern technologies started over 100 years ago, first with the telegraph, then telephones, radios, television, early computers, large and bulky mainframe computers, and, finally, the development of the personal computer in the early 1980s. The enormous popularity of the Internet, in particular the World Wide Web, has resulted in a computer that is more than a simple computational device. In fact, the computer has morphed into a device used for communication, media creation, learning, and so much more.

Recent advancements in technology merge the various forms of communications (the telephone, television, and computers) into effective, interactive, mobile devices. Even though the merging of these technologies into mobile devices continues to evolve, the first decade of the 21st century was known as the **age of convergence**. This age of convergence will continue to evolve in new, exciting, and yet to be determined ways as we live, teach, learn, and work in the second decade of this century. This merging of technologies is possible because significantly faster processors and high-speed wireless networks have been able to capitalize on the advancements made in the areas of digital graphics, video, animation, audio, and online media. Today's personal computer and mobile device architectures take advantage of a computer's individual power, digital media capabilities, and the ability to be interconnected with others in networked environments, also known as social networking. As a result, multimedia technology systems have become increasingly more powerful and better able to handle information rich in visual and aural content.

Web Info

For more information on the age of convergence, visit the Computer Concepts CourseMate Web site at *www.cengagebrain.com*, navigate to the Chapter 1 Web Info resource for this book, and then click Age of Convergence.

Figure 1-4 Common computer hardware components associated with a digital media computer.

The goal of multimedia computing and communications is to assist individuals in organizing and managing vast amounts of information in various types of media. Figure 1-4 above shows the components of a typical digital media computer system that allows the average person to use multiple senses when working and communicating. To see just how far personal computer technology has come in a relatively short period of time, compare this figure to the pictures shown on the next page of personal computers developed by IBM and Apple in the early 1980s.

WHAT IS DIGITAL MEDIA?

Digital media is defined in a variety of ways; however, for the purposes of this book, **digital media** is defined as those technologies that allow users to create new forms of interaction, expression, communication, and entertainment in a digital format. The term digital media has been coined to reflect the evolution of multimedia computing into multisensory communications. The goal of multimedia, and now digital media, is to reproduce as closely as possible the reliability and effectiveness found in face-to-face (f2f) communications, and then emulate that in virtual and online environments, such as social networking, using computers, mobile devices, and other technologies.

In the next few sections, we will briefly review the various categories of computers, including information on mobile computers and mobile devices.

Categories of Computers

Computers can be organized in these general categories: personal computers; mobile computers and mobile devices; game consoles; and servers, supercomputers, and embedded computers. The next few sections briefly cover these categories; all of these types of computers are discussed in detail in later chapters and special features.

Personal Computers

A **personal computer**, or **PC**, is a computer that has the capability to perform input, processing, output, and storage activities. A personal computer contains a processor, memory, and one or more input, output, and storage devices.

Many people associate the term personal computer, or PC, with computers that use Microsoft Windows, which is a popular operating system used on many of today's computers. All personal computers, however, do not use Windows. For example, Apple computers use a different operating system, Mac OS, but they still are a type of personal computer. Why the confusion?

The first Apple computer, available for personal use, was built in 1976. Subsequent versions, the Apple II and later the Apple IIe, were immediate successes. These Apple computers were quickly adopted by elementary schools, high schools, and colleges.

In 1981, the IBM Corporation released its first personal computer, the IBM Personal Computer (Figure 1-5). The IBM Personal Computer was an instant business success and quickly became known by its nickname — the PC. For marketing reasons, IBM allowed other companies to copy its computer design; therefore, many companies started making IBM-compatible computers. These computers originally were called IBM-compatible because they used software that was the same as or similar to the IBM PC software. All subsequent IBM computers and IBM-compatible computers were called PCs.

Three years after the introduction of the first IBM PC, the Apple Computer Company introduced the **Macintosh computer,** now known as **Mac** computers or simply Macs (Figure 1-6). In addition to the Mac, Apple also introduced a pointing device called a mouse. Macs could accomplish many of the same tasks as PCs, but they were very different from each other. Macs were incompatible with IBM PCs because they used operating system software different from the IBM and IBM-compatible computers. As a result, a distinction developed between the terms Mac and PC, even though Macs are personal computers. This distinction and confusion between the two types of computers continues today. To avoid confusion,

Web Info

For more information about Apple computers, visit the Computer Concepts CourseMate Web site at *www.cengagebrain. com*, navigate to the Chapter 1 Web Info resource for this book, and then click Apple.

Figure 1-5 The original IBM Personal Computer was introduced in 1981.

Figure 1-6 Apple Computer Company produced the Macintosh computer in 1984.

users often refer to these two types of personal computers as Windows environment or Mac environment.

Today, businesses, homes, and K-12 schools use dozens of different models of Apple and IBM-compatible personal computers. To avoid confusion in this textbook, personal computers that use Microsoft Windows are referred to as PCs and all Apple personal computers are referred to as Apple or Mac computers (Figure 1-7). When this textbook refers to the terms personal computer, desktop computer, or computer, the subject matter being discussed is applicable to Apple, IBM, and IBM-compatible computers. Most of the concepts and terms covered in this textbook are applicable to all types of personal computers.

Personal computers shown in Figure 1-7 also are called **desktop computers** because they are designed so the system unit, input devices, output devices, and any other devices fit entirely on a desk.

Mobile Computers and Mobile Devices

A **mobile computer** is a personal computer that you can carry from place to place. One popular type of mobile computer is the notebook computer. Other popular types include tablet computers and netbooks. A **mobile device** is a computing device small enough to hold in your hand and usually does not have disk drives.

A **notebook computer**, also called a laptop computer, is a portable, personal computer small enough to fit on your lap. Today's notebook computers are thin and lightweight, yet they can be as powerful as the average desktop computer (Figure 1-8).

The **tablet computer**, or simply **tablet**, is a letter-sized notebook computer that you interact with by touching the screen with your finger (Figure 1-9). If preferred, you can use a wireless keyboard and other accessories with a tablet. Apple introduced

[a]

[a]

[b]

[b]

Figure 1-7 Figure 1-7a shows a typical PC using the Windows OS and Figure 1-7b shows a typical Apple computer using the Mac OS.

Figure 1-8 Notebook computers are available in Windows and Mac environments. Shown in Figure 1-8a is a typical PC notebook using Windows; Figure 1-8b shows a MacBook.

Figure 1-9 The iPad is a widely used tablet.

the iPad, one example of a tablet computer, in early 2010, and current sales projections regarding Apple iPads and other tablet computers are approximately one billion by 2015, including millions for use by K-12 students. Tablet computers are covered in later chapters and the special feature that follows Chapter 6.

A **netbook**, also called a **mini-notebook**, is a small, lightweight, and portable computer designed for wireless communication and access to the Internet. The name netbook was derived from the combination of the two words: Internet and notebook.

Mobile devices usually store programs and data permanently in memory chips inside the system unit or in small storage media such as flash memory cards. Many mobile devices are **Internet-enabled**, meaning they can connect to the Internet wirelessly. Often, you can connect a mobile device to a personal computer to exchange information between the computer and the mobile device, which is a process called **syncing**. Popular mobile devices are smartphones and e-book readers (described below); others include portable media players, and digital cameras, which are covered in Chapter 4.

Offering the convenience of one-handed operation, a **smartphone** is an Internet-enabled phone that usually provides personal information management functions such as a calendar, an appointment book, an address book, a calculator, and a notepad. In addition to basic phone capabilities, a smartphone allows you to send and receive e-mail messages and access the Web — usually for an additional fee. Some smartphones communicate wirelessly with other devices or computers. Many also function as a portable media player and include built-in digital cameras so that you can share photos or videos with others as soon as you capture the image. Many smartphones also offer a variety of application software such as word processing, spreadsheet, and games, and the capability of conducting live video conferences.

Many smartphones have keypads that contain both numbers and letters so that you can use the same keypad to dial phone numbers and enter messages. Others have a built-in mini keyboard on the front of the phone or a keyboard that slides in and out from behind the phone. Some have touch screens, which you can use to press icons on the screen to make selections or to enter text through an on-screen keyboard. Figure 1-10 provides examples of two popular smartphones.

[a]   **[b]**

Figure 1-10 Figure 1-10a shows Apple's iPhone and Figure 1-10b shows the BlackBerry Bold.

Instead of calling someone's smartphone or cell phone, users often send messages to others by pressing buttons on their phone's keypad, keys on the mini keyboard, or icons on an on-screen keyboard. Types of messages users send with smartphones include text messages, instant messages, picture messages, and video messages.

FAQ

Are tablet computers replacing traditional computers in schools?

Yes, numerous computer companies offer tablets and because of their small size and functionality, tablet computers are quickly becoming mainstream with students in both K-12 and higher education.

FAQ

Why are they called smartphones?

A smartphone can be a telephone and a camera. It can be used to access the Internet for music, news, sports, and more. The manufacturers for these phones also call them intelligent phones because of the many different things they can do.

An **e-book reader** (short for electronic book reader), or **e-reader**, is a handheld device that is used primarily for reading e-books (Figure 1-11). An **e-book, ebook,** or **digital book,** is an electronic version of a printed book, readable on computers and other digital devices. In addition to books, users can purchase and read other forms of digital media such as newspapers and magazines. Most e-book readers have a touch screen and are Internet-enabled. Personal computers, tablets, and most smartphones can also display e-books.

Figure 1-11 An e-book reader.

Game Consoles

A **game console** is a computing device designed for single player or multiplayer video games. Standard game consoles use a handheld controller as an input device: a television screen as an output device; and hard disks, optical discs, and or memory cards for storage. Popular models include the Nintendo Wii, Sony PlayStation, and Microsoft Xbox. These models utilize traditional handheld game devices. In addition to supporting game play, many consoles allow users to listen to music, watch movies, and connect to the Internet. Game consoles can cost from around $100 to more than $500.

The Nintendo Wii is one of the newest consoles to hit the market. The Wii console utilizes an interface that permits individuals to play games using normal kinetic motions rather than utilizing buttons and toggle switches (Figure 1-12). In education, the Wii console could be useful in helping students develop psychomotor skills and as a tool to energize students' cognitive domain of learning through interactivity.

Figure 1-12 The technology represented in Nintendo's Wii develops psychomotor skills and has the potential to impact education in yet unseen ways.

Servers, Supercomputers, and Embedded Computers

A **server** manages the resources on a network and provides a centralized storage area for software programs and data. You will learn more about servers and how they are used in education in Chapter 2. A **supercomputer** is the fastest, most powerful computer — and the most expensive. The fastest supercomputers are capable of processing trillions and trillions of instructions in a single second. Supercomputers are used for tasks such as analyzing weather patterns, tracking hurricanes, and identifying safety issues regarding space travel. Although schools do not have supercomputers, teachers do use the output from supercomputers in their lessons.

An **embedded computer** is a special-purpose computer that functions as one component in a larger product. Embedded computers are everywhere — at home, in your car, at work, and at school. These computers perform various functions, depending on the requirements of the product in which they reside.

Why Use Computer Technology in Education?

In any society, educators have the ability to make an enormous positive contribution. Making such a contribution is a challenge, and teachers must willingly embrace new teaching and learning opportunities. Educators are beginning to recognize that they must teach students, the future leaders and citizens of society, using current and emerging technologies so that these students will be comfortable using future technologies.

Technology and digital media are everywhere and integrated into every aspect of individuals' lives. Today's educators must provide students with the skills they will need to excel in a technology-rich society. Parents no longer are urging schools to incorporate technology into the classroom; instead, they are insisting on it. When used appropriately, technology has the potential to enhance students' achievement and assist them in meeting learning objectives.

An extensive body of education research is showing that technology can support learning in many ways. Using technology in the classroom, for example, can be motivational. Teachers have found that using computers, mobile devices, digital media, and other computer-related technologies can capture students' attention and improve students' outcomes. Computers also can provide many unique, effective, and powerful opportunities for teaching and learning. These opportunities include skill-building practice, real-world problem solving, interactive learning, discovery learning, and linking learners to a multitude of instructional resources.

Computers also support communications beyond classroom walls, thus enabling schools and communities to provide an environment for cooperative learning, development of higher-order thinking skills, and solving complex problems. As demonstrated by these examples, technology, when placed in the hands of teachers and students, can provide unique, effective, and powerful opportunities for many different types of instruction and learning.

INTERNATIONAL SOCIETY FOR TECHNOLOGY IN EDUCATION

Several national and international organizations support education and educators in the use of technology. The leading organization is the **International Society for Technology in Education (ISTE)**, which is a nonprofit group that promotes the use of technology to support and improve teaching and learning. ISTE supports all areas of K-12 education, community colleges and universities, and teacher education organizations.

ISTE has been instrumental in developing the National Educational Technology Standards (NETS) for the **National Council for Accreditation for Teacher Education (NCATE)**. NCATE is the official body for accrediting teacher education programs. ISTE has developed standards for K-12 teachers, school administrators, and students.

STANDARDS FOR TEACHERS As you work through this textbook and its related Web site, you will gain an understanding of the concepts and skills outlined in the **National Educational Technology Standards for Teachers (NETS-T)**, which define the fundamental concepts, knowledge, skills, and attitudes for applying technology in K-12 educational settings (Figure 1-13 on the next page).

STANDARDS FOR SCHOOL ADMINISTRATORS ISTE's standards for school administrators **National Educational Technology Standards for Administrators (NETS-A)** (updated in 2009) are organized in five categories: Inspire Excellence Through Transformational Leadership, Establish a Robust Digital Age Learning Culture, Advance Excellence in Digital Age Professional Practice, Ensure Systemic Transformation of the Educational Enterprise, and Model and Advance Digital Citizenship. For information about how to access the most current version of these standards, see the Web Info on this page.

STANDARDS FOR STUDENTS ISTE also provides **National Educational Technology Standards for Students (NETS-S)**. These standards are organized into six important categories: Creativity and Innovation; Communication and Collaboration; Research and Information Fluency; Critical Thinking, Problem Solving, and Decision Making; Digital Citizenship; and Technology Operations and Concepts.

Web Info

For more information about the International Society for Technology in Education (ISTE), visit the Computer Concepts CourseMate Web site at *www.cengagebrain.com*, navigate to the Chapter 1 Web Info resource for this book, and then click ISTE.

Web Info

For more information about ISTE's standards for students, teachers, and administrators, visit the Computer Concepts CourseMate Web site at *www.cengagebrain.com*, navigate to the Chapter 1 Web Info resource for this book, and then click Students, Teachers, or Administrators.

ePortfolio Idea

1. **Facilitate and Inspire Student Learning and Creativity**

    Teachers use their knowledge of subject matter, teaching and learning, and technology to facilitate experiences that advance student learning, creativity, and innovation in both face-to-face and virtual environments. Teachers:

    a. promote, support, and model creative and innovative thinking and inventiveness.

    b. engage students in exploring real-world issues and solving authentic problems using digital tools and resources.

    c. promote student reflection using collaborative tools to reveal and clarify students' conceptual understanding and thinking, planning, and creative processes.

    d. model collaborative knowledge construction by engaging in learning with students, colleagues, and others in face-to-face and virtual environments.

2. **Design and Develop Digital-Age Learning Experiences and Assessments**

    Teachers design, develop, and evaluate authentic learning experiences and assessment incorporating contemporary tools and resources to maximize content learning in context and to develop the knowledge, skills, and attitudes identified in the NETS·S. Teachers:

    a. design or adapt relevant learning experiences that incorporate digital tools and resources to promote student learning and creativity.

    b. develop technology-enriched learning environments that enable all students to pursue their individual curiosities and become active participants in setting their own educational goals, managing their own learning, and assessing their own progress.

    c. customize and personalize learning activities to address students' diverse learning styles, working strategies, and abilities using digital tools and resources.

    d. provide students with multiple and varied formative and summative assessments aligned with content and technology standards and use resulting data to inform learning and teaching.

3. **Model Digital-Age Work and Learning**

    Teachers exhibit knowledge, skills, and work processes representative of an innovative professional in a global and digital society. Teachers:

    a. demonstrate fluency in technology systems and the transfer of current knowledge to new technologies and situations.

    b. collaborate with students, peers, parents, and community members using digital tools and resources to support student success and innovation.

    c. communicate relevant information and ideas effectively to students, parents, and peers using a variety of digital-age media and formats.

    d. model and facilitate effective use of current and emerging digital tools to locate, analyze, evaluate, and use information resources to support research and learning.

4. **Promote and Model Digital Citizenship and Responsibility**

    Teachers understand local and global societal issues and responsibilities in an evolving digital culture and exhibit legal and ethical behavior in their professional practices. Teachers:

    a. advocate, model, and teach safe, legal, and ethical use of digital information and technology, including respect for copyright, intellectual property, and the appropriate documentation of sources.

    b. address the diverse needs of all learners by using learner-centered strategies providing equitable access to appropriate digital tools and resources.

    c. promote and model digital etiquette and responsible social interactions related to the use of technology and information.

    d. develop and model cultural understanding and global awareness by engaging with colleagues and students of other cultures using digital-age communication and collaboration tools.

5. **Engage in Professional Growth and Leadership**

    Teachers continuously improve their professional practice, model lifelong learning, and exhibit leadership in their school and professional community by promoting and demonstrating the effective use of digital tools and resources. Teachers:

    a. participate in local and global learning communities to explore creative applications of technology to improve student learning.

    b. exhibit leadership by demonstrating a vision of technology infusion, participating in shared decision making and community building, and developing the leadership and technology skills of others.

    c. evaluate and reflect on current research and professional practice on a regular basis to make effective use of existing and emerging digital tools and resources in support of student learning.

    d. contribute to the effectiveness, vitality, and self-renewal of the teaching profession and of their school and community.

Source: International Society for Technology in Education (ISTE)

Figure 1-13 The ISTE technology standards and performance indicators provide a framework for implementing technology in teaching and learning.

All educators need to understand these standards and, more importantly, strive to make sure that their students meet these standards. This is important as today's students will have to compete in an increasingly flat world. These standards will be covered in greater detail later in this chapter; however, first let's explain what we mean by a flat world.

The World Is Flat

In his books, *The World Is Flat* and *Hot, Flat, and Crowded*, Thomas Friedman describes how "lightning-swift changes in technology and communications put people all over the globe in touch with each other as never before — creating an explosion of wealth in India and China, and challenging the rest of us to run faster just to stay in place" (Figure 1-14). In other words, the world has become flat in terms of instant communications and global economics. Friedman and others stress that many young people are not prepared to be successful in a global economy, which in turn is impacting how America competes on the world stage. To see how teachers were inspired after reading Thomas Friedman's book, visit the Flat Classroom Project Web site (see the Web Info on this page). Teachers from around the world are teaching their students real world skills so they will be able to work effectively in the global economy.

Our high school graduates must be prepared to enter institutions of higher education, and they must strive to become lifelong learners. As you review the remainder of this chapter, start formulating ways that you can incorporate the ideas, concepts, standards, and initiatives presented in this chapter with your students in your curriculum. Working together, we can equip students with the knowledge and skills they will need to be successful. Many states, the federal government, and organizations are trying to help schools and institutions of higher education learn how to provide students with new and emerging skills; skills for the emerging flat world of the 21st century.

Web Info

For more information on the Flat Classroom Project, visit the Computer Concepts CourseMate Web site at *www.cengagebrain. com*, navigate to the Chapter 1 Web Info resource for this book, and then click Flat Classroom Project.

Figure 1-14 What has emerged as we enter the second decade of the 21st century is a world that is flat, as hundreds of millions of workers from dozens of countries interact seamlessly in a global economy.

Web Info

For more information on the Partnership for 21st Century Skills and its P21 Framework, visit the Computer Concepts CourseMate Web site at *www.cengagebrain.com*, navigate to the Chapter 1 Web Info resource for this book, and then click Partnership or P21 Framework.

21st Century Skills

The Partnership for 21st Century Skills is a national organization that focuses on infusing 21st century skills into education — both K-12 and higher education. The partnership's goal is to ensure that students who graduate from our schools have the skills needed to be effective workers, citizens, and leaders in the new global economy. One of the Partnership's initiatives, the *P21 Framework*, details a vision that can be used as a basic framework to improve our education system and prepare students for their future (Figure 1-15). This framework provides information on both student outcomes and necessary support systems.

21st CENTURY STUDENT OUTCOMES

Student outcomes as represented by the rainbow portion of Figure 1-15 include the following: core subjects and 21st century themes; learning and innovation skills; information, media, and technology skills; and life and career skills.

CORE SUBJECTS AND 21st CENTURY THEMES

Core subjects include English, reading or language arts, world languages, arts, mathematics, economics, science, geography, history, government, and civics. The Partnership's 21st century themes include global and health awareness along with financial and civic literacy.

LEARNING AND INNOVATION SKILLS

The Partnership identifies a number of skills as necessary for students to be able to succeed in the work environment of the increasingly flat world of the 21st century. These skills include the following:

- Creativity and Innovation
- Critical Thinking and Problem Solving
- Communications and Collaboration

INFORMATION, MEDIA, AND TECHNOLOGY SKILLS

Students need to be able to use new and emerging technology to learn 21st century skills and knowledge. These skills also are known as information literacy; media literacy; and information, communications, and technology (ICT) literacy.

LIFE AND CAREER SKILLS

The Partnership stresses that students need more than content and thinking skills. The Partnership recognizes the following specific life and

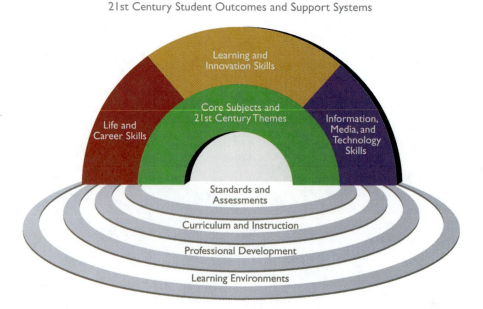

21st Century Student Outcomes and Support Systems

Figure 1-15 This figure shows the vision of the Partnership for 21st Century Skills that can be used to help educators strengthen our education system.

career skills that students need to have in order to be able to compete globally:

- Flexibility and Adaptability
- Initiative and Self-Direction
- Social and Cross-Cultural Skills
- Productivity and Accountability
- Leadership and Responsibility

For additional information on the above student outcomes and information on the Partnership's 21st Century Skills Support Systems represented in the lower portion of Figure 1-15, visit The Partnership for 21st Century Skills Web site (see Web Info on previous page).

Technology, if integrated effectively, holds the promise of helping teachers prepare their students with the necessary skills for employment in our changing world — this theme is what this textbook is all about. Next, you will learn about computing in the digital age, how your digital students learn, and what your students need to know to be successful in the workforce of the 21st century.

Computing in the Digital Age

Digital technology allows greater participation in the creative process, turning viewers into creative producers. Individuals can customize formats, outcomes, and usage of the information presented to them. Today, individuals use digital technology to input, edit, manage, publish, and share all kinds of information that was previously either impossible or too expensive for the average person to create and share. This digital revolution has accomplished in only 50 years that which took hundreds of years to accomplish beginning with the invention of Gutenberg's printing press in the late 16th century — that is, the democratization of information flow, the flow of the production process down to the masses.

DIGITAL STUDENTS: WHO ARE THEY AND HOW DO THEY LEARN?

The digital revolution has resulted in one unintended consequence. Today's youth are much more media-centric than previous generations. In fact, many people believe that the brains of today's youths have actually become rewired to accommodate the thousands of hours they spend in front of computer screens watching and creating video, listening to music, and playing computer and video games. It also has been said that today's youth actually speak digitally.

Today's students play on electronic playgrounds with a variety of powerful media functioning as their recreational equipment. Watch how they read e-mails, send instant messages and text messages over handheld devices, and speak to one another in short sound bites; also notice how visually oriented these students are. You will soon see that something is different about today's youth. Many have called this new generation the **digital generation**.

The world in which today's students live is significantly different from the past. Today's students use different technologies to communicate and to access information from multiple resources. They use computers, smartphones, tablets, netbooks, and laptops to connect to teachers, friends, family, and others in their community and all over the world. A recent National School Boards Association (NSBA) report stated that 96 percent of U.S. teens and tweens (students age 8-12) who have Internet access use social networking to connect with their peers. Digital students now have a virtual world at their fingertips — with all its pitfalls and promises.

Apple Computer defines these **digital students** or **digital kids** as kids who are (1) hypercommunicators who use multiple tools to communicate, (2) multitaskers who do several things at once with ease, and (3) goal oriented as they pursue multiple goals at the same time. Today's digital generation is profoundly different from previous generations and these differences need to be understood by teachers if they are to facilitate effective learning for today's digital students. The stark contrasts and differences between generations become more apparent when they are viewed visually (Figure 1-16 on the next page).

Today's students are essentially different from previous generations in the way they think, in the way they access, absorb, interpret, process, and apply information and, above all, in the way they view, interact, and communicate in this technology-rich and connected world. Today's digital kids like watching TV, listening to music on their

Integration Strategies

To learn more about integrating video with your students, visit the Computer Concepts CourseMate Web site at *www.cengagebrain.com*, and then navigate to the Chapter 1 Digital Media Corner resource for this book.

Understanding Today's Digital Generation

Students from Previous Generations	→	Today's Digital Students
Passive communicators	→	Hypercommunicators
Single taskers	→	Multitaskers
Work oriented	→	Play oriented
Linear thinking	→	Random access
Nonrelevancy learning — relevancy was not critical to learning	→	Learning has to be relevant and fun
Single sensory input	→	Multisensory input
Text-based first	→	Digital and graphics first
Reality-based	→	Fantasy-based learning
Conventional speed	→	Twitch speed

Figure 1-16 This table shows some characteristics of students from previous generations and today's digital students.

iPods, listening to their favorite shows via podcasts, talking on their smartphones, playing games on their iPads, texting or instant messaging their friends, and blogging. Perhaps the most amazing aspect of this scenario is that they often are doing all of these activities while completing their math homework assignment.

Understanding today's digital kids and how they learn has profound implications not only for how teachers teach these digital students, but also, and perhaps more importantly, for how teachers reach them. Educational technology, mobile devices, and digital media can be valuable tools when they are integrated into the curriculum appropriately to achieve learning gains, particularly when they are combined with a 21st century curriculum.

Teachers have to decide whether to try to pull digital students away from their native digital world or to motivate digital students by tapping into their digital world and using their natural inclination and inquisitiveness about all that is digital. A quick look at the school system today, which has been so slow to change, makes it easy to see the disconnect between how teachers teach and how students learn.

Most of the schools today were designed for the Industrial Age and yet, the students attending schools today are living in the digital age. The world in which digital students live has changed drastically and it continues to change in a techno fast-paced manner. Unfortunately, many school environments have not kept up with that change. Marc Prensky stated in 2001 that digital kids are the digital natives and teachers are the digital immigrants. Today's students speak digitally; they are all native speakers of the digital language. Review carefully the information shown in Figure 1-17 as it provides insight into the profound differences between how digital kids learn and how digital immigrant teachers teach.

Digital Native Learners	Digital Immigrant Teachers
Prefer receiving information quickly from multiple multimedia sources.	Prefer slow and controlled release of information from limited sources.
Prefer parallel processing and multitasking.	Prefer singular processing and single or limited tasking.
Prefer processing pictures, sounds, and video before text.	Prefer to provide text before pictures, sounds, and video.
Prefer random access to hyperlinked multimedia information.	Prefer to provide information linearly, logically, and sequentially.
Prefer to interact/network simultaneously with many others.	Prefer students to work independently rather than network and interact.
Prefer to learn "just-in-time."	Prefer to teach "just-in-case" (It's on the exam.).
Prefer instant gratification and instant rewards.	Prefer deferred gratification and deferred rewards.
Prefer learning that is relevant, instantly useful, and fun.	Prefer to teach to the curriculum guide and standardized tests.

Source: Understanding the Digital Generation. Authors Ian Jukes, Ted McCain, Lee Crockett.

Figure 1-17 Differences between digital native learners and digital immigrant teachers.

DIGITAL STUDENTS: WHAT THEY SHOULD KNOW

Now that you have a better understanding of how today's digital kids learn, let's continue to learn more about what your students need to know. As mentioned earlier, ISTE released the updated National Educational Technology Standards for Students (NETS-S): The Next Generation in June of 2007. These specific technology skills complement the key elements for 21st century learning that you explored earlier in this chapter. The NETS-S emphasize "what students should know and be able to do to learn effectively and live productively in an increasingly digital world" and are covered in greater detail here.

CREATIVITY AND INNOVATION   Figure 1-18 lists the specific NETS-S standards for creativity and innovation. These standards will help you teach a generation of students who are different from any other. The digital or net generation is one that has grown up in a world that is constantly changing in terms of the use and ubiquity of computers, mobile devices, and digital media; and you need to be aware of this. For this generation of students to be able to learn effectively and productively in a global society, they must have a different set of skills and have the opportunity to create and generate more original ideas. Most generations in the past were willing to work a lifetime for a large corporation but this digital generation tends to move from job to job, is always thinking of creative ways to develop their own products, and is predicted to be the most entrepreneurial in history. As teachers, you must find ways to nourish this creative thinking process and have students develop original works through individual and group projects, e-portfolios, and other forms of authentic learning.

Research is showing that these students are independent, possess a thoughtful learning style, and are self-motivated by interactive technology and the ability to use it in innovative ways for personal expression. This might explain why even at a young age, students are successful in using computers, exploring a multitude of online sites, communicating in a variety of ways, and playing video games. Today's students learn differently! Different modes of teaching are required to motivate students and empower them to invest in their own learning.

The good news is that there are hundreds of exciting technology tools (such as apps), education software, and Web resources that teachers can use to stimulate student imagination and ingenuity. In addition, a whole new generation of educational applications are emerging — from student-created educational games and simulations to robotics that will empower teachers and students in many positive and far reaching ways.

One way to motivate students to apply existing knowledge in order to generate new ideas or products is to have students create their own video games that demonstrate their understanding of newly acquired information. The creation process should be complex enough that students demonstrate critical problem solving and higher-thinking

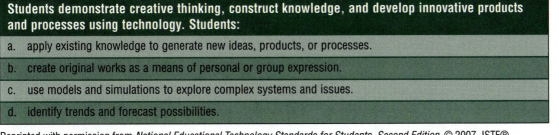

Students demonstrate creative thinking, construct knowledge, and develop innovative products and processes using technology. Students:

a. apply existing knowledge to generate new ideas, products, or processes.

b. create original works as a means of personal or group expression.

c. use models and simulations to explore complex systems and issues.

d. identify trends and forecast possibilities.

Figure 1-18 This table includes the NETS-S standards for creativity and innovation.

Figure 1-19 Gamemaker is an example of a software program that allows students to create video games while fostering opportunities for creativity and innovation.

skills to solve game design problems, yet should still give the students flexibility to modify the characters, scenarios, and settings (Figure 1-19). As you continue to explore the thousands of ideas and resources in this textbook and at the textbook Web site, you will find many ways to foster creativity and innovation with your students.

COMMUNICATION AND COLLABORATION

Figure 1-20 lists the specific NETS-S standards for communication and collaboration. Since the beginning of time, mankind has always attempted to communicate and collaborate with each other; however, the use of technology has never been as pervasive in society as it is today.

In 1492, people thought the world was flat when Christopher Columbus sailed to prove it was round. Thomas Friedman, in his book describes the world as being flat. Both men saw the world differently, but if the world has become flat due to instant communications and global economics, how do we prepare our students for success in a highly connected society where the power to transform the world has changed from major corporations and giant trade organizations to individuals? Your job as educators is to teach your students not only to get along and communicate with the person sitting next to them but also to teach them to work on team projects and to correspond and cooperate with students

Integration Strategies

To learn more about integrating online communications and collaboration tools that your students are using, like blogs, wikis, and podcasts, review Chapter 6.

Students use digital media and environments to communicate and work collaboratively, including at a distance, to support individual learning and contribute to the learning of others. Students:
a. interact, collaborate, and publish with peers, experts, or others employing a variety of digital environments and media.
b. communicate information and ideas effectively to multiple audiences using a variety of media and formats.
c. develop cultural understanding and global awareness by engaging with learners of other cultures.
d. contribute to project teams to produce original works or solve problems.

Figure 1-20 This table includes the NETS-S standards for communication and collaboration.

in virtual classrooms across the world (Figure 1-21). More importantly, students need to learn how to communicate and work collaboratively in the global workplace they will find themselves employed in.

Figure 1-21 Students learn to interact and collaborate while working together on projects.

In the end-of-chapter sections following Chapter 6, there are many ideas that help address the different ways students and teachers can communicate and collaborate, such as by using wikis, blogs, and podcasts — that is, share ideas through a different digital medium. Students learn and solve complex problems best within collaborative learning groups and they learn to communicate as they solve problems and make decisions.

RESEARCH AND INFORMATION FLUENCY
Figure 1-22 lists the specific NETS-S standards for research and information fluency. As students pursue knowledge in this digital world, they have opportunities to find and conduct various types of research that were not possible before — and the information is right at their finger tips. With

a click of the mouse, the Internet provides enormous amounts of research, information, graphics, data, and more directly and instantaneously in front of them. Yet, while you prepare your students with the skills for accessing and searching this information, they must also be taught the skills to evaluate and analyze information. Students must have the capability to gather information, evaluate, and determine if the information they have found is valid, appropriate, and accurate, and then be able to synthesize how they will use the information.

There are many projects designed to help your students practice their research skills and at the same time apply those skills to real world assignments. While your students work on researching topics, you can be teaching them information literacy. Information literacy is when a person has mastered the ability to analyze and evaluate information. Information literacy is an important skill; however, students do not always realize the importance of evaluating the sources of their information. Students must learn to work confidently using computer, information, and media literacy skills and effectively apply these skills. **Media literacy** is being able to create, develop, and successfully communicate information in all forms. It is the ability to use critical thinking skills to analyze and to question all media — from music videos and Web environments to product placement in films and virtual displays on NASCAR billboards.

A number of organizations are assisting educators with ideas and other resources to help them incorporate information fluency and media literacy into the curriculum. One organization, the State Educational Technology Directors Association (SETDA) provides information

Web Info

For more information on media literacy, visit the Computer Concepts CourseMate Web site at *www. cengagebrain.com*, navigate to the Chapter 1 Web Info resource for this book, and then click Media Literacy.

Students apply digital tools to gather, evaluate, and use information. Students:
a. plan strategies to guide inquiry.
b. locate, organize, analyze, evaluate, synthesize, and ethically use information from a variety of sources and media.
c. evaluate and select information sources and digital tools based on the appropriateness to specific tasks.
d. process data and report results.

Figure 1-22 This table includes the NETS-S standards for research and information fluency.

and an extensive toolkit of resources for educators dealing with media literacy (Figure 1-23).

Figure 1-23 The Web contains an abundance of resources that educators can use to help ensure their students are knowledgeable in the areas of media, research, and information fluency.

CRITICAL THINKING, PROBLEM SOLVING, AND DECISION MAKING Figure 1-24 lists the specific NETS-S standards for critical thinking, problem solving, and decision making. Traditionally, educators have defined literacy as the ability to read and write; however, 21st century skills include many different types of literacies, as students are learning. Students not only need to investigate data using critical thinking skills, but they also must be able to figure out what the data really means and be able to synthesize, evaluate, and create new

information and knowledge once they have determined its quality.

Today's students prefer to work in collaborative groups to solve complicated problems rather than to problem-solve individually. Activities must be active with authentic learning experiences rather than be passive requiring reading and regurgitation of facts. Researchers learned long ago that retention is low if students are not able to touch and to perform any skill more than once — they actually need to perform a skill many times through real-life learning experiences before they can master the skill. Imagine listening to a radio versus creating a live radio broadcast. There are schools where the students create live radio broadcasts every morning, reporting the events of the day, lunch menus, testing schedules, and current news; students as young as ten years old are creating the actual broadcast. Teachers must look for the most innovative ways to teach their digital students or teachers may lose them. As Clem and Simpson stated in an eSchools News article, "In the absence of pedagogical innovation, these students may become instructional casualties of how and what we teach inside the school." Teachers need to integrate the technology tools that students adapt so easily to.

In his article, *Information Literacy, Statistical Literacy and Data Literacy*, Milo Schield concludes that information literacy requires both statistical and data literacy. According to Schield, "Students must be information literate: they must be able to think critically about concepts, claims, and arguments: to read, interpret, and evaluate information. Statistical literacy is an

Students use critical thinking skills to plan and conduct research, manage projects, solve problems, and make informed decisions using appropriate digital tools and resources. Students:
a. identify and define authentic problems and significant questions for investigation.
b. plan and manage activities to develop a solution or complete a project.
c. collect and analyze data to identify solutions and/or make informed decisions.
d. use multiple processes and diverse perspectives to explore alternative solutions.

Reprinted with permission from *National Educational Technology Standards for Students, Second Edition*, © 2007, ISTE® (International Society for Technology in Education), www.iste.org. All rights reserved.

Figure 1-24 This table includes the NETS-S standards for critical thinking, problem solving, and decision making.

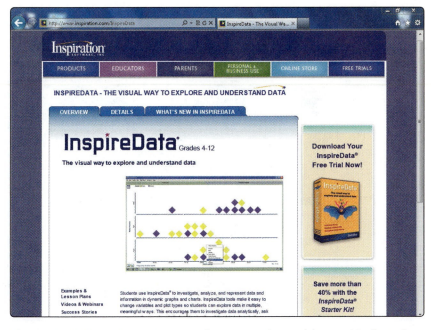

Figure 1-25 Using InspireData, students can solve problems critically and interpret data through visualization.

essential component of information literacy. Students must be statistically literate: they must be able to think critically about basic descriptive statistics. Analyzing, interpreting and evaluating statistics as evidence is a special skill. In addition, students must be data literate."

Data literacy means students need to be able to view, manipulate, analyze, and interpret data. As teachers, we must create instructional strategies that facilitate opportunities for students to become seekers of information in order to develop the ability to interpret and solve complex problems, engage and practice in critical thinking, develop arguments, and then make informed decisions. Teachers need to create

activities for students to promote the use of higher-order thinking skills that can increase students' critical and problem solving skills while reaching a newer audience — digital kids. An example would be students learning to gather their own data, solve problems through inquiry, and explore solutions with visualization and data plots (Figure 1-25).

DIGITAL CITIZENSHIP   Figure 1-26 lists the specific NETS-S standards for digital citizenship. Due to the changes in our society, the list of skills needed by students to be productive citizens in a technology-rich society has grown and changed and will continue to evolve in an increasingly flat world.

Integration Strategies

To learn more about digital citizenship and teaching your students about responsibility, visit the Computer Concepts CourseMate Web site at *www.cengagebrain.com*, and then navigate to the Chapter 1 Education Issues resource for this book.

Students understand human, cultural, and societal issues related to technology and practice legal and ethical behavior. Students:
a.   advocate and practice safe, legal, and responsible use of information and technology.
b.   exhibit a positive attitude toward using technology that supports collaboration, learning, and productivity.
c.   demonstrate personal responsibility for lifelong learning.
d.   exhibit leadership for digital citizenship.

Reprinted with permission from *National Educational Technology Standards for Students, Second Edition*, © 2007, ISTE® (International Society for Technology in Education), www.iste.org. All rights reserved.

Figure 1-26 This table includes the NETS-S standards for digital citizenship.

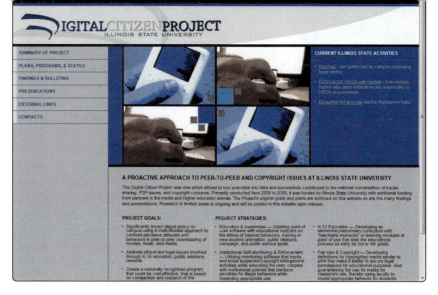

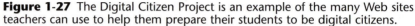

Figure 1-27 The Digital Citizen Project is an example of the many Web sites teachers can use to help them prepare their students to be digital citizens.

While the technology standards cover concepts of abiding by certain ethical and practical ideals with regard to computer and technology usage, it is still essential that students understand and change their attitudes and corresponding habits. A great way to teach students to be digital citizens is to have a debate activity. For example, the side one often takes in a media copyright debate depends on whether one is a producer or a consumer of videos and music. Students often think that if they found it on the Web, then it must be free! Yet, students will understand this debate better as they become producers themselves and they begin to recognize the need to preserve their individual intellectual property. Participating in these kinds of debates, where students are asked to take opposing sides, is a good way for them to begin to value the concepts they are debating and express these values in an active way.

In his book *If They Can Argue Well, They Can Write Well*, Bill McBride supports the use of debating as a way to help students define, explain, and persuade others to understand the critical thinking processes they used to analyze information. It is only after thoughtful reflection and critical thinking on creating a personal plan of action that students will begin to organize and prioritize their behaviors and begin to internalize these issues. Debates are great activities for teachers to help students understand and take responsibility for legal and ethical issues.

Being a good digital citizen includes knowledge and commitment for understanding things like etiquette; communication techniques and standards; issues surrounding media and computers, business, commerce, entrepreneurship, privacy rights and responsibilities; ergonomic issues (which are the physical and/or emotional dangers associated with extended computer usage); and information about security, asset management, and protection from losing data and personal information from computer crashes (backing up files), hackers, and other kinds of intruders. You will learn more about security issues and ethics in Chapter 8. In addition, there are many Web sites that can provide you with information on helping students become digital citizens (Figure 1-27).

TECHNOLOGY OPERATIONS AND CONCEPTS

As you learned earlier, students must possess computer literacy as a basic skill before they can progress to other skill levels with technology. Figure 1-28 lists the specific NETS-S standards for technology operations and concepts.

Students demonstrate a sound understanding of technology concepts, systems, and operations. Students:
a.   understand and use technology systems.
b.   select and use applications effectively and productively.
c.   troubleshoot systems and applications.
d.   transfer current knowledge to learning of new technologies.

Reprinted with permission from *National Educational Technology Standards for Students, Second Edition,* © 2007, ISTE® (International Society for Technology in Education), www.iste.org. All rights reserved.

Figure 1-28 This table includes the NETS-S standards for technology operations and concepts.

Students should have the ability to use computers, technology, and digital media efficiently. They should understand how computers work, and students should understand the different hardware and software that are associated with computers. Most digital students gravitate toward technology very quickly, think they know the technology, and many times jump in without asking any questions; however, many times they do not possess the skills they need. Many business and industry employers report that the students they hire have breadth but not depth of technology skills. Students need a sound foundation of operation and application skills that can be transferred to current, new, and emerging technologies. Without a sound understanding of technology concepts, students cannot compete in a technology rich global society. This knowledge is vital!

Digital media allows teachers to use a combination of technology tools to appeal to an array of learning styles digitally. If integrated properly, digital media also has the capability to stimulate imagination and develop critical thinking skills all while allowing students to take an active role in their own learning. The ARCS Motivational Model, which is discussed next, can help you reflect on ways to modify your teaching techniques and strategies to find innovative ways to motivate today's digital students to learn.

ARCS MOTIVATIONAL MODEL

The **ARCS Motivational Model** was developed by John M. Keller in 1983 and is applicable to learning in the digital age. Keller stressed that even the best designed instructional strategy will fail if students are not motivated to learn. Many students are only performing to pass the test. Without a desire to learn, retention is unlikely. Thus, teachers should strive to create a deeper motivation in learners to gain new skills.

Frustrated that so much of the interest in psychology was concentrated on differences in learner ability, Keller developed a model that would attribute differences in student learning to the amount of effort students were willing to put forth. As a result, he cataloged four specific areas that could account for the differences in student effort. A discussion of these areas follows.

ATTENTION   Effective learning techniques seek to capture students' attention, to eliminate boredom, and to arouse natural curiosity. Lessons should increase students' focus by using novel, surprising, out of the ordinary, and uncertain events. Effective techniques should stimulate the sense of wonder and maintain interest. Most students are not only auditory or visual learners, but also multisensory learners. Digital media has the ability to capture the attention of the learner because it addresses a variety of learning styles. Today's students expect to use digital media devices in their daily lives, so these devices, or similar media technology, should be woven seamlessly into their classroom experiences.

RELEVANCE   When students feel that learning is relevant or important to their lives, they will become motivated to learn. By using digital media to develop lesson concepts, teachers bring familiar technology into the classroom. Concepts

Integration Strategies

To learn more about integrating music in your classroom as an effective and novel learning technique, visit the Computer Concepts CourseMate Web site at *www. cengagebrain.com,* and then navigate to the Chapter 1 Teaching Today resource for this book.

Integration Strategies

To learn more about challenging your students by integrating digital media, visit the Computer Concepts CourseMate Web site at *www.cengagebrain. com,* and then navigate to the Chapter 1 Digital Media Corner or Learn It Online resource for this book.

developed with digital media utilize technologies that students value.

CHALLENGE/CONFIDENCE Students who believe they can achieve often do. Lessons created with digital media allow students to develop confidence by enabling them to succeed. Interactive lessons created with digital media present a degree of challenge that allows for meaningful success through both learning and performance conditions. Content created with digital media can be leveled to challenge multiple skill levels, to generate positive expectations, to provide feedback, and to support internal attributions for success — all of which means students are working at a level at which they can achieve success and gain confidence. Assignments completed using technology allow students to see just how far their imagination can take them. Using technology will be natural for some but a struggle for others because not all students will be at the same skill level when it comes to using digital media. It is important to develop lessons that contain several achievement levels so students can progress at a pace that meets their needs, that is,

that challenges them while building their confidence.

SATISFACTION/SUCCESS Feeling good about one's self is a natural motivator. Technology provides opportunities for students to use newly acquired knowledge or skills in simulated settings successfully. Lessons developed using digital media can be designed to provide feedback that will sustain the desired behavior. Using technology, students can showcase their achievements, allowing them to share their successes with others, which increases their desire for positive peer evaluation.

Figure 1-29 summarizes the key concepts of Keller's ARCS Motivational Model. As you continue to explore the concepts and resources provided in this textbook, use the information to help you transition from being a digital immigrant teacher to one that facilitates students' learning in the digital age. Next, you will learn how to create an ePortfolio and why it is so important to keep your ePortfolio up to date as you enter or continue in the teaching profession.

The ARCS Motivational Model and Digital Students	
Attention	Lessons are designed to gain students' attention using alternative techniques, such as a story, sensory stimuli, thought-provoking questions, and variability in exercises, and using digital media.
Relevance	Students see relevance in the lesson, which, in turn, leads to increased learning. The lesson must be relevant not only to the learner, but also to previously taught lessons.
Challenge/Confidence	Students are challenged to achieve, and they gain confidence as they meet the challenge. Students need to feel that if they put in a good faith effort, they are capable of achieving the objectives. The challenge should properly match the students' abilities.
Satisfaction/Success	Students gain success in achieving their objective, which promotes self-satisfaction from the learning experience. The most powerful reward is that the students find that the learning experience is relevant and useful to their own world or the one they aspire to live and work in.

Figure 1-29 This figure highlights the components of the ARCS Motivational Model.

Creating a Professional Teaching Portfolio

When you apply for a teaching job as a new teacher or if you are applying for a position at a new school/school district, having a professional teaching portfolio is one of the tools that will set you apart from the crowd (Figure 1-30).

Figure 1-30 Having a Professional Teaching ePortfolio can highlight the skills you possess to place you ahead of the competition for a teaching job.

Whether you get a job teaching or are currently teaching face to face (f2f), online, or both, you will want to have a professional teaching portfolio that allows you to highlight your instructional credentials and provide a sampling of your work, such as detailing your accomplishments and showcasing your development of content-specific standards-based lessons. Furthermore, it is important that you keep your professional teaching portfolio up to date, even if you have been teaching for many years. An up-to-date professional teaching portfolio just may be your key to job security, and it is essential when you pursue a new job in a different school, district, or state. The following sections will help you develop your understanding of what you need to do to create and maintain a professional teaching portfolio.

What Is a Professional Teaching Portfolio?

A **professional teaching portfolio**, also known as an **ePortfolio, e-Portfolio,** or **eFolio,** is a collection of evidence to document your development and growth in the teaching profession. This collection includes materials and artifacts to document or provide evidence of your education, background, philosophy, teaching strategies, experience in teaching, lesson plans, your personal achievements, and more. For the purpose of this book, we will refer to a professional teaching portfolio as an ePortfolio.

Throughout this book, you will see starbursts next to text that represent suggestions for items to include in your ePortfolio. Due to increases in technology tools and digital media resources, teachers and many districts and institutions are interested in seeing, not only paper documents, but also digital products, multimedia projects, and other types of items in applicants' portfolios, that reflect the National Educational Technology Standards for Teachers (NETS-T) and other curriculum-specific standards. Many K-12 administrators feel that a traditional paper portfolio cannot provide enough substance about a potential candidate who wants to enter a field that is striving to meet the needs of today's digital learners while addressing teaching 21st century skills.

WHY YOU SHOULD HAVE AN ePORTFOLIO

The emergence of **virtual learning environments (VLEs)** in K-12 schools and universities has led to an increased rationale for ePortfolios. An ePortfolio represents a person's individual background and it should reflect that person's skills, knowledge, and accomplishments. As the result of creating an ePortfolio, many students have a better understanding of their personal philosophy of education and are better able to reflect on their learning and teaching goals throughout their schooling and career. The principal reason for developing your professional ePortfolio is that, as you

Figure 1-31 The many technology tools available today can help you create many different digital items for your ePortfolio.

build your ePortfolio, you learn to tell a story about yourself to others. Another benefit is that by digitizing your work and developing and managing your ePortfolio, you are developing hands-on experience with and demonstrating proficiency with a wide variety of technologies that you can showcase to prospective employers (Figure 1-31).

Similar to traditional paper-based portfolios such as those used in the art world (called a *dossier*), you should provide evidence of your learning and growth through reflection, which leads to a better understanding of learning strategies and students' needs. Your ePortfolio should be an ongoing, living resource that documents your professional growth and development throughout your career, reflects the stages of your progress, and continues to record your achievements in the field of teaching and learning (Figure 1-32).

One thing to consider is that you probably will use the materials in your ePortfolio for multiple purposes and for different audiences, so it is very important that your collection of digital evidence be current and accurately reflect you. Your ePortfolio will change over time as you strengthen your teaching skills, explore new instructional

Figure 1-32 You should always carry printed copies in addition to a DVD/flash drive and a Web link with you to show ePortfolio artifacts to potential employers.

strategies, and evaluate and reflect on student learning results. You also will have an opportunity to demonstrate your development of different teaching approaches and your assessments of instructional techniques. Such an assembly of evidence may consist of many different items and categories; however, for the purposes of this textbook we are going to discuss the more common items included in an ePortfolio. The following section contains ideas and suggestions to help you develop a successful ePortfolio.

What Should Be Included in Your ePortfolio?

An ePortfolio usually opens with your philosophy of education followed by your résumé. It can include reflective essays, presentations, research papers, images, videos, projects, reports, lesson samples, or anything that you feel is relevant to your background story. Letters from students, instructors, and feedback from others make a nice addition to your ePortfolio.

Remember, your ePortfolio should provide a snapshot of you and should help you see your personal development over time. An ePortfolio provides a way to look back and reflect upon what has been accomplished; it provides a way for you to tell a story about yourself. Figure 1-33 lists some general ideas for setting up your ePortfolio.

As discussed throughout this textbook, teachers must meet the NETS-T and your ePortfolio should document that your technology skills meet the NETS-T. You also need to document your understanding and capacity to integrate the National Educational Technology Standards for Students (NETS-S). You should include images, multimedia projects, blogs, Wikis, and lesson plans you developed that meet the NETS-T and NETS-S standards that integrate 21st century learning skills for both you and your students.

Think of your ePortfolio as an ongoing project, and if you do, it will provide you with formal documentation as you transition through the various stages of education and employment and even into retirement. The table in Figure 1-34 provides a number of excellent Web resources that will help you create and maintain your ePortfolio. Finally, you might find the checklist shown in Figure 1-35 on page 29 helpful as you develop your ePortfolio.

ePortfolio Creation Ideas
Be sure the components of your ePortfolio work well together both when viewed online or during a face-to-face (f2f) interview.
Make sure your ePortfolio has a professional appearance with sections clearly defined and divided. Include a table of contents to help users quickly see this organization, as well as navigate easily to sections of interest.
Make sure the content is clear, concise, and easy to follow.
Use a logical organizational structure (e.g. you might organize your content around district, state, and national Standards based on your teacher preparation program's conceptual framework).
Be sure to include a résumé or vita that summarizes your education background, related work experience, multicultural experiences, as well as highlights teaching skills and provides a good vision of accomplishments.
Provide work that demonstrates attainment of ISTE standards, as well as a checklist showing how the ISTE standards correlate to each course or lesson so users can quickly see how you integrate ISTE standards into your instruction.
Provide work that shows you have met the content specific standards in your area of specialization.
Include a rationale for each piece of evidence in your ePortfolio. Remember your ePortfolio should tell a story about you.
Provide essays and other assessments that reveal your growth in teaching strategies and reflect your teaching style.
Include a balance between different types of evidence (e.g., integration digital tools and Web 2.0/Web 3.0). Make sure you cross-reference appropriate evidence.
Have a colleague or someone in the education field review your ePortfolio once it is complete in order to provide constructive feedback. Incorporate the feedback if it helps make your ePortfolio stronger.
Use your ePortfolio as a reflective document by setting aside a designated time each year (or so) to review and update its content, as well as to reflect on your professional growth.

Figure 1-33 This table provides some overarching ideas to consider when putting your ePortfolio together.

Web Resources	URL*
Wichita Teacher Education Portfolio	education.wichita.edu/teportfolio/
Developing Your Teaching Portfolio	http://www.adelaide.edu.au/clpd/teaching/portfolio/t_portfolio.pdf
Creating the Ultimate Portfolio	http://teachnet.com/how-to/employment/portfolios/
Developing a Professional ePortfolio using WordPress	teach.educ.ubc.ca/resources/pdfs/word_press_manual_may_21.pdf
Building Your Professional Teaching Portfolio	www2.scholastic.com/browse/article.jsp?id=3749720
Preparing a Teaching Portfolio	http://ctl.utexas.edu/teaching-resources/advance-your-career/
Portfolio Suggestion List	teachingtoday.glencoe.com/userfiles/file/portfolio_list.pdf
Example of One Teacher's Portfolio and Classroom Management Plan	sitemaker.umich.edu/ckeng/classroom_management_plan
Developing a Teaching Portfolio	http://taproject.rutgers.edu/services_tips/teach_portfolio.pdf
Overview of ePortfolios	net.educause.edu/ir/library/pdf/ELI3001.pdf
Learning about ePortfolios	http://www.coolmath.com/continuing-ed/e-portfolios_about.html
Portfolio Assessment Guide	www.teachervision.fen.com/assessment/resource/5942.html
To locate additional resources, search using your favorite search tool.	

*These links were active at the time the book was written; however, URLs are constantly changing, so if a link does not work, please use your favorite search engine and key term in the left column to find the related content.

Figure 1-34 The Web provides excellent resources that you can explore to help you create and maintain your ePortfolio.

Where Should I Store My ePortfolio?

Many ePortfolios are maintained within a university's VLE and are not easily accessed by people outside the VLE. A well-known product used for maintaining ePortfolios at universities is LiveText. **LiveText** is a flexible management system that provides institutions of higher learning with advanced and user-friendly Web-based tools for developing, assessing, and measuring student learning and more. Universities often do not allow you to have access to the ePortfolio site after you graduate, or your ePortfolio might be archived to an alumni site where, for a fee, you will have access to your ePortfolio but your potential employers will not. LiveText is one of many programs that you can use to create your ePortfolio, your university or college may use a different one; others include Chalk & Wire, TaskStream, and Aurbach & Associates. For recommendations, ask your professor, K-12 administrator, or a colleague; you

also can search the Web. Also, it is very important that you keep backups of all materials you submit to a university-based ePortfolio site.

Create more than one backup of your ePortfolio by saving your materials to another medium, such as your hard drive or a flash drive or both. Remember, each time you update your ePortfolio, such as by adding new artifacts, to update your ePortfolio in all locations where it is stored. Also, keep your backups in different locations to prevent total loss due to fire and unexpected acts of nature. Do not become a victim of Murphy's Law (in this case, if it can be lost or deleted, it will be). Figure 1-35 provides a checklist of important components to include when creating an ePortfolio. Your ePortfolio might include all of the items in the checklist or only some of the items. It also may include other items relevant to you that are not in the checklist. Whatever items you include, be sure they reflect you, your philosophy of education, and your teaching style.

ePortfolio Checklist		
Included	**Date added/ update**	**Item**
☐		Introduction/Personal Information/Personal Statement: information such as career objectives, goals, work (including part time), and military history (if applicable)
☐		Cover Letter
☐		Curriculum Vita or Résumé
☐		Philosophy of Education Statement
☐		Certification Information: education, licenses, certifications, and specialization certificates
☐		Academic Record: a list of relevant courses
☐		Evidence/Artifacts of your Educational Philosophy and Teaching Style: include summaries of clinical experiences, evaluations, student products based on standards, instructional strategies correlated to the standards, and so on
☐		Teaching Evaluations and/or Critiques of Field Experiences with Reflection
		Lesson Plans
☐		• Standards-based activities that document the relationship between knowledge and standards through the development of well-defined lesson plans
☐		• Authentic Learning Activities
☐		• Assessment and Evaluation Activities that provide examples of evaluation strategies, as well as alternative and authentic assessment strategies
☐		• Planning Tools
☐		Examples of Parent-Teacher Correspondence (remove any reference to names)
☐		Technology Integration Proficiencies: include skills and certification
☐		Honors, Awards, Scholarships, and Grants (these also might be listed on your résumé)
☐		Professional Development: include training activities/workshops attended
☐		Research, Publications, and Manuals
☐		Other Evidence/Artifacts: any relevant documentation you want to archive that explain and support your vita or résumé
☐		Letters of Recommendation
Other Important Issues		
☐		All written items included in the ePortfolio have been checked for clarity, spelling, and grammar by someone other than yourself
☐		Create a Web site to showcase your ePortfolio, or better yet, both a Web site and an app
☐		Carry printed copies of your ePortfolio, QR code associated with your ePortfolio, and Web link to your ePortfolio with you to all interviews
☐		Carry DVD/Flash drive backup of your ePortfolio with you to all interviews
☐		Be sure the Web site or app is loaded on your tablet computer and ready to display
☐		Create two or more backup copies of your ePortfolio and keep one at a different location than original
☐		Be sure to make new backup copies each time you update your ePortfolio

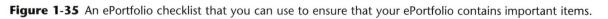

Figure 1-35 An ePortfolio checklist that you can use to ensure that your ePortfolio contains important items.

Impact of Smartphones, Tablet Computers, and Apps on Education

Many experts are predicting that in the near future every student in the United States and the majority of students in many other countries will be using an array of mobile devices, including tablet computers, in their formal and informal educational experiences. There will be no child left behind in this app- and tablet-based changing face of education. Your students' tablet computers will be loaded with digital textbooks, interactive textbook apps, social media apps, and an array of inexpensive curriculum- and grade-specific education apps and games. In addition, all of your students will be taking online and hybrid (face-to-face and online) classes.

As expected, this changing face of education is impacting the teaching profession, making your position as a teacher more important than ever. One underlying reason for all these changes is globalization, which was covered earlier in this chapter. To be competitive in our changing flattening world, our future leaders and workers must be prepared to utilize current and emerging technologies. This is where you come in. As an educator, you will be a driving force in helping prepare today's students for tomorrow's workplace. You will help guide students as they explore and learn to use current and emerging technologies. Students will not only need to learn new technologies but also embrace the idea that they will need to be life-long technology learners in order to keep up with the always changing world of technology and related tools. You will be instrumental in helping students not only meet but exceed the NETS-S. Your influence and impact cannot be overstated.

To help you prepare for this important task, we have written this textbook in order to provide you with a strong technology knowledge-base and related resources. We hope this textbook and its resources will help you understand this technology revolution so you can integrate what you learn into your instructional methods. Because of the myriad of online resources associated with this textbook as well as the technology integration focus of the textbook, we consider this textbook to be an **e-learning enhanced** textbook. As you explore the many features found in this textbook and on this textbook's CourseMate Web site and discussed in the next section, you will gain a deeper understanding of how technology (not just computers) is the driving force in e-learning. To use this textbook and its resources to the fullest extent, we hope you will spend a little time becoming familiar with the Computer Concepts CourseMate Web site for Teachers Discovering Computers 7e.

Accessing the Computer Concepts CourseMate Web Site for Teachers Discovering Computers 7e

The Computer Concepts CourseMate Web site for Teachers Discovering Computers 7e provides a variety of activities, exercises, and other resources. To use the site, you first must create a student account at *www.cengagebrain.com* and then register this book, as described in the following steps:

1. Start your Web browser, type the following Web address *www.cengagebrain.com* in the browser Address bar, and then press the Enter key to display the CengageBrain home page.

2. If you do not have an account, follow the on-screen instructions to sign up for a new account. If you have an account, log in with your user name and password.

3. Register this book by entering its Access Code in the appropriate text box and then clicking the corresponding button.

4. To open the resources for this book, click the button corresponding to the Computer Concepts CourseMate Web site for Teachers Discovering Computers.

As a result of using this textbook and its related resources, including the Computer Concepts CourseMate Web site for Teachers Discovering Computers, you will create a new technology-rich learning environment for your students.

Using the Computer Concepts CourseMate Web Site for Teachers Discovering Computers 7e

Each chapter in this textbook contains 10 end-of-chapter sections, all of which are stored either completely or partially as Web pages on the Computer Concepts CourseMate Web site for this book. In addition, the textbook includes three special features and one References section; which also are located on the Computer Concepts CourseMate Web site for this book. To enhance your learning experience, be sure to view the end-of-chapter materials and special features on the Computer Concepts CourseMate Web site for this book, where you will find curriculum-specific information, integration ideas, interactive exercises, and links to thousands of popular educational sites.

In all eight chapters, annotations in the margins, called Web Info, send you to the Computer Concepts CourseMate Web site for this book, where you will find links to current and additional information about Web Info topics. Also located in the margins are FAQ boxes that consist of frequently asked questions and their answers, as well as Integration Strategies boxes that help you locate integration ideas.

For access to all resources for this, visit *www.cengagebrain.com*. To display an end-of-chapter section, click the desired chapter number and then navigate to any of the end-of-chapter sections; for example, click Chapter 1 and then navigate to Teaching Today. The special features may be accessed at anytime.

INTERACTING WITH END-OF-CHAPTER MATERIALS

The following sections explain how you can interact in a curriculum-specific way with the resources available in the various end-of-chapter materials. This will help you transition to using the new learning environments described in Figure 1-1 on page 2.

KEY TERMS Click any term to see a term definition. Click the Web link to visit a Web page for supplemental information on the term.

CHECKPOINT Use these interactive questions and answers to check your knowledge level of the chapter and to prepare for quizzes and examinations.

TEACHING TODAY This section provides insight into the value that technology and the Web have for K-12 education. Each segment contains one or more links that reinforce the information presented in the segment.

EDUCATION ISSUES Education Issues contains several scenarios that allow you to explore controversial and current issues in education, for example, school violence. Click the links for additional information on the issue.

APPS CORNER This innovative section provides extensive ideas and resources for integrating apps into your classroom-specific curriculum. Each chapter provides information on applicable iTunes, BlackBerry, and Android Apps in the following 4 corners: Early Childhood, Elementary, Middle School, and Secondary. Choose your area and explore the app resources to learn how to integrate apps into your specific classroom curriculum and review comments by other educators and users.

SOFTWARE CORNER Today's educators can choose from a variety of high-quality and often inexpensive educational software programs. You can learn about popular software programs by researching them on the Web and in many cases even downloading or ordering a free trial version so you can evaluate a program prior to buying it.

DIGITAL MEDIA CORNER A recurring theme throughout this book emphasizes that today's teachers need to make learning meaningful and relevant to the lives of today's K-12 digital students. This section provides you with Web resources of selected chapter topics that can be used to supplement your digital lessons.

ASSISTIVE TECHNOLOGIES CORNER This section provides important information on current hardware, software, and peripherals that will assist you in delivering instruction to students with physical, cognitive, or sensory disabilities. Links, strategies, ideas, and more are available at the

Computer Concepts CourseMate Web site for this book.

IN THE LAB   These exercises are divided into two areas: productivity and integration. Use the productivity exercises to improve your software-specific skills in using word processing, spreadsheet, desktop publishing, curriculum and Web page development, as well as other productivity software programs. Use the integration ideas for incorporating these programs into your specific classroom curriculum. Click the links for tutorials, productivity ideas, integration examples and ideas, and more.

LEARN IT ONLINE   These exercises allow you to improve your computer and integration skills by learning exciting new skills online. This section includes interactive lab exercises, software tutorials, scavenger hunts, practice tests, learning games, and much more.

ePORTFOLIO

Located in the margins in all chapters are ePortfolio Idea icons, which identify a topic or technology you might want to include in your personal ePortfolio.

ePortfolio Idea

Timeline — Milestones in Computer History

At the Computer Concepts CourseMate Web site for this book is an interactive, colorful, and highly informative multipage timeline of the history of computers from 1937 to the present. The timeline contains dozens of links to extensive supplemental information, including historical audio segments from National Public Radio, animations, videos, and much more.

To display this interactive special feature, go to the Computer Concepts CourseMate Web site for this book, and then navigate to the Timeline. All of the graphics and pictures contain links to the Web. Explore the special feature with your mouse; to access the interactive links, click when your mouse pointer changes to a hand.

Guide to Professional, State, and Federal Educational Web Sites

The federal government, state governments and institutions, and professional educational organizations provide a multitude of resources for K-12 teachers and students. The special feature that follows this chapter provides links to and information on (1) more than 30 popular professional education organizations, all of which provide educational resources for teachers and students, (2) over 30 federal government agencies, and (3) Departments of Education for all 50 states and the District of Columbia. Updated links to the most current URLs for these resources are located at the Computer Concepts CourseMate Web site for this book.

Summary of Introduction to Integrating Technology in Education

This chapter presented a broad introduction to concepts and terminology related to computers and computers in education. You now have a basic understanding of what a computer is and how it processes data into information. You were introduced to digital media and how today's digital students learn. You learned about the national technology standards for students and explored what your students should know to become productive citizens in an emerging global economy. You also have seen some examples of how computers are being used in K-12 schools and integrated into classroom settings. You should be starting to formulate your own strategies for teaching your digital students and for creating your professional teaching ePortfolio.

Key Terms

INSTRUCTIONS: Use the Key Terms to help focus your study of the terms used in this chapter. To further enhance your understanding of the Key Terms in this chapter, visit the Computer Concepts CourseMate Web site at www.cengagebrain.com, and then navigate to the Chapter 1 Key Terms resource for this book. Read the definition for each term and then access current and additional information about the term from the Web.

age of convergence [5]
ARCS Motivational Model [23]

computer [4]
computer literacy [4]
curriculum-specific learning [2]

data [4]
data literacy [21]
desktop computers [8]
digital book [10]
digital generation [15]
digital kids [15]
digital media [6]
digital students [15]
discipline-specific learning [2]

ebook [10]
ePortfolio [25]
e-book [10]
e-book reader [10]
eFolio [25]
e-Learning-enhanced textbook [28]
e-portfolio [25]
e-reader [10]
embedded computer [10]

game console [10]

hardware [4]

information [4]
information fluency [4]
information literacy [4]
information processing cycle [4]
input [4]
integration literacy [4]
International Society for Technology
    in Education (ISTE) [11]
Internet [4]
Internet-enabled [9]

LiveText [28]

Macintosh computer (Mac) [7]
mini-notebook [9]
media literacy [19]
mobile computer [8]
mobile device [8]

National Council for Accreditation
    for Teacher Education
    (NCATE) [11]
National Educational Technology
    Standards for Administrators
    (NETS-A) [11]

National Educational Technology
    Standards for Students
    (NETS-S) [11]
National Educational Technology
    Standards for Teachers
    (NETS-T) [11]
netbook [9]
notebook computer [8]

output [4]

personal computer (PC) [7]
professional teaching portfolio [25]

server [10]
smartphone [9]
software [4]
storage [4]
supercomputer [10]
syncing [9]

tablet [8]
tablet computer [8]

virtual learning environments
    (VLEs) [25]

1. Label the Figure

Instructions: Identify each element of a digital media system by placing the correct label on its numbered line.

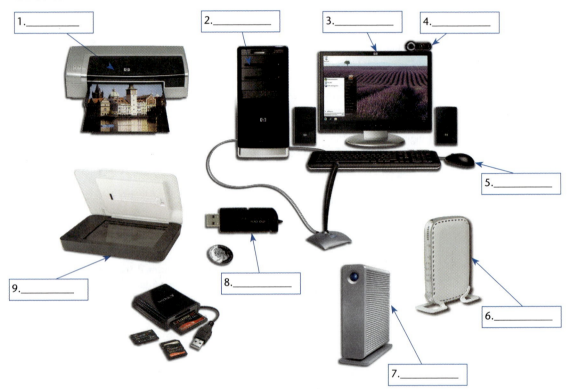

1._____   2._____   3._____   4._____

5._____

9._____   8._____   6._____

7._____

2. Matching

Instructions: Match each term from the column on the left with the best description from the column on the right.

_____ 1. media literacy

_____ 2. digital students

_____ 3. input

_____ 4. digital media

_____ 5. data literacy

a. able to view, manipulate, analyze, and interpret information

b. data entered into a computer

c. allows users to create new forms of interaction

d. hypercommunicators, multitaskers, and goal oriented

e. able to create, develop, and communicate information

3. Short Answer

Instructions: Write a brief answer to each of the following questions.

1. What is the difference between computer literacy, information literacy, and integration literacy?
2. Define digital students. Why are they different from previous generations of students?
3. Briefly summarize the six National Educational Technology Standards for Students (NETS-S).
4. What is the ARCS Motivational Model? What are the four categories of the ARCS Motivational Model?
5. Briefly summarize why computers should be used in K-12 schools.

Teaching Today

INSTRUCTIONS: Teaching Today provides teachers with integration strategies and ideas for teaching and, more importantly, reaching today's digital generation. Each numbered segment contains one or more links that reinforce the information presented in the segment. To display this page from the Web, visit the Computer Concepts CourseMate Web site at www.cengagebrain.com, and then navigate to the Chapter 1 Teaching Today resource for this book.

1. Online vs. Printed Newspapers

Computers have changed the way people access information dramatically. For example, avid newspaper readers can turn to Web sites offered by their favorite newspapers. Some of the more recognizable names include *The Boston Globe*, *Los Angeles Times*, *The Miami Herald*, *New York Times*, *USA TODAY*, and *eSchools*; or you can search a Web site that will allow you to find your hometown newspaper online. You can also download an app for most newspapers. Links to downloadable apps are located on the newspapers' Web sites and at the various app stores for mobile devices and tablet computers (iTunes, for example). How is the online or app rendering of a periodical different from the printed version? How are they similar? What are the advantages and disadvantages of each? Do you see a use for these online or app newspaper resources in your classroom? Why?

2. Online News and Social Networking

Social networking has become a communication phenomenon — allowing individuals to communicate and connect with others in order to share views, interests, and hobbies. Many students use social networking to connect with friends; but the level of social networking has gone beyond friends talking to friends. Today, agencies and television shows, such as CNN, NBC News, and Meet the Press to name a few, are using social networking for discussion and dissemination of information. Meet the Press has been using Twitter, a microblogging social networking tool. Many say tools, like Twitter, help people interact and share with others. What are the advantages and disadvantages of social networking? How likely are you to interact with news agencies through a social networking Web site? What possibilities do you see for using social networking in education? What are the implications of such use?

3. Health-related Information Online

The healthcare industry has made significant breakthroughs during the past few years, and continued advances are expected in many health-related areas. For example, major prescription drug companies currently are developing/testing more than 1,000 new medicines. The Web offers an up-to-date source for information on virtually every area of healthcare. You can locate current information on diseases and other health ailments, such as migraines. People can obtain an abundance of important information in a very short time, such as the latest treatment options. Visit the following medical site and research one specific area of healthcare that is of personal importance to you.

4. mLearning

In the classroom, you often are bombarded with new acronyms as names of things change or evolve. You may or may not be familiar with mLearning, also known as Mobile Learning. This is a new way of teaching that incorporates the use of cost efficient, light-weight, portable devices such as media players and smartphones. Mobile Assisted Language Learning (MALL) is becoming increasingly popular in Language classrooms. Students who often are difficult to reach through traditional methods such as lecture and busy work are interested in lessons that incorporate portable mobile devices that they are using outside of school to communicate with each other and keep up with events in the world. Teachers who are using mLearning are revolutionizing their classrooms into digital powerhouses where students can apply critical thinking and problem solving skills they will need in the future.

Education Issues

INSTRUCTIONS: Education Issues provides several scenarios that allow you to explore controversial and current issues in education. Each numbered segment contains one or more links that reinforce the information presented in the segment. To display this page from the Web, visit the Computer Concepts CourseMate Web site at www.cengagebrain.com, and then navigate to the Chapter 1 Education Issues resource for this book.

1. School Violence

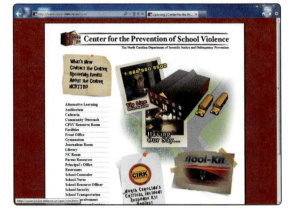

Numerous polls have shown that school safety is now the number-one concern of both parents and teachers. National leaders are calling the increase in school violence a national crisis. What are some of the causes of school violence? Do you agree that school violence should be the main concern of parents? One popular answer to the dramatic increase in the incidences of school violence is to build protective nets around the nation's schools, including fences, metal detectors, high-tech video surveillance, body searches, and armed guards. Do you agree with this solution? Other political and educational leaders stress that turning schools into armed camps is not the solution. Instead, schools and communities must address and attempt to find solutions for the causes of school violence. Do you agree with this solution? What would you suggest to reduce the incidences of school violence?

2. Possible Child Abuse

During your student internship, you notice that one of your nine-year-old students has bruises all over his arms and legs. He has been one of your more inquisitive students, but lately you have noticed that he has become moody, seems uninterested in class, and his grades are falling. The school nurse casually informs you that she has noticed that this student has been losing weight the past couple of months. You suspect that your student may be a victim of child abuse. You ask your supervising teacher what you should do and she says, "Oh! He is the son of a member of the school board; I am sure he is just growing and is at a clumsy age." You really like the school and would like to work there after graduation. Do you tell someone or do you ignore it? If so, whom do you tell? What else could you do?

3. Reality or Fantasy

The space shuttle was first flown in July 1969 and landed on the moon that same year. An ingredient in many popular shampoos has been proven to cause cancer. It is illegal to contact space aliens. None of these statements is true, but each appeared on the Web. In today's society, some people, especially young students, think that anything in print is true, and the Web adds to that because anyone can publish anything on a Web page. Authors with a wide range of expertise, authority, and biases create Web pages. Web pages can be as accurate as the most scholarly journal or no truer than some articles in supermarket tabloids. Ultimately, who is responsible for the accuracy of information on the Web? Why? How can you verify information on the Web? How would you teach your students to make sure information is accurate?

4. Possible Cheating

Today, students are wired for cheating with smartphones, graphing calculators, pagers, tablet computers, notebook computers, iPods, and other electronic devices. During a test, you notice that a student is using a cell phone. As you approach the student, you realize that the student is looking at a smartphone with a picture on the screen. The student puts away the phone and apologizes, indicating that he had forgotten to turn off the phone when a call came in. After class, another student informs you that the student you caught with the phone was making calls to another student in the classroom, and they were taking pictures of the equations. This student was almost positive the two students were cheating by sending each other pictures of the answers over their smartphones. How should you handle this situation? Is there a way to gather proof? What next? Should all mobile devices be banned in classrooms? If so, how? What is your role? Explain.

Apps Corner

INSTRUCTIONS: Apps Corner provides extensive ideas and resources for integrating technology into your classroom-specific curriculum. To display this page from the Web and information on numerous education apps, visit the Computer Concepts CourseMate Web site at www.cengagebrain.com, and then navigate to the Chapter 1 Apps Corner resource for this book.

Apps Corner is designed for teachers and other educators who are looking for innovative ways to integrate apps into their content-specific curriculum. Apps Corner not only provides great apps with current information but also shows how other educators are using and integrating education apps. As a result, Apps Corner is designed with all educators in mind, regardless of their interests or subject area. You can use Apps Corner to expand your resources by reviewing apps outside your curriculum area; remember many apps associated with one curriculum area can be adapted for use and added to lesson plans in a wide variety of other curriculum areas.

Use Apps Corner as a springboard for collaborating and sharing the successes and hurdles of integrating apps in a classroom or an entire school system. Consider Apps Corner a place to locate app integration ideas and resources. Information on educational apps are organized in four Corners (Early Childhood, Elementary, Middle School, and Secondary), and different apps are available for each chapter. Many apps are free, others cost between $1 and $5. Inexpensive site licenses for classrooms, schools, and school districts are available for many apps.

Shown below are a sample app for 1st grade students and an app created by Audubon Middle School, which parents, students, and teachers can use to keep up with what is happening at their school on their smartphone or tablet computer.

Software Corner

INSTRUCTIONS: Software Corner provides information on popular software programs. Each numbered segment discusses specific software programs and contains a link to additional information about these programs. To display this page from the Web, visit the Computer Concepts CourseMate Web site at www.cengagebrain.com, and then navigate to the Chapter 1 Software Corner resource for this book.

1. A.D.A.M. Interactive Anatomy Online

For over a decade, A.D.A.M., Inc. has been dedicated to creating new and innovative tools for teaching anatomy and physiology. A.D.A.M. Interactive Anatomy Online, the most comprehensive interactive anatomy teaching tool is now available online for K-12 students with more features than ever before. A.D.A.M. includes incredibly detailed graphics, precision accuracy, and the most advanced functionality, which are combined with A.D.A.M.'s award-winning Multimedia Encyclopedia—completely new library of 3D images and over 3,000 new illustrations for learning clinical concepts. A.D.A.M. is the perfect resource to enhance your anatomy and physiology studies, and it is ideal for your allied health, nursing, continuing medical education, or other medical-related courses requiring the study of clinical applications and concepts.

2. iRead

It is not a secret any longer that students must possess strong literacy skills. Research is revealing that instructional strategies that strengthen reading performance will also improve overall student achievement. Several teachers in the Escondido Union School District have developed a powerful program and learning tool called iRead. This program works by utilizing digital audio tools (iPods, microphones, Garageband, iTunes, Keynote, etc.) to improve reading processes while providing students with key practice in areas such as reading fluency and comprehension. In addition to providing instructional practice, this application allows for students to self monitor their progress as they practice their skills.

3. Quarter Mile

Quarter Mile is useful in helping students learn math skills from basic math facts to difficult skills such as integers, converting percents and fractions, and advanced equations. Quarter Mile is a super remediation program for the exceptional student classroom as well as a great skills practice program for the regular classroom at all educational levels. What makes this program interesting for students is that they race against their own time, allowing them to see their own progress.

4. Timeliner XE

Timeliner XE allows teachers and students to create, print, and illustrate timelines using pictures or text with ease for any time period. Timeliner XE can be used at the elementary level by having students create timelines of their life using personal events to help them gain an understanding of the concept of time and sequence of important events. Elementary teachers can use this program to teach the concept of decade, century, millennium, and more. At the middle and high school levels, Timeliner XE can be used to help students visualize historical progress of specific time periods, chart world-changing occurrences and causes of important events, or even illustrate the different stages of a novel, like The Red Badge of Courage.

5. WebBlender

If you are looking for a product that can make it easy for you to create a Web site for your class with a combination of text, graphics, and sound, even a class photo and art gallery, then WebBlender is the perfect tool for you. Its user friendly interface lets you focus on the content and easily share your students' work. If you have been interested in adding podcasting to your classroom Web site, look no further because you can share stories, videos, and music in a podcast without knowing how to create RSS feeds — all you do is add the content and WebBlender takes care of the details.

Digital Media Corner

INSTRUCTIONS: Today's K-12 digital students need their learning to be meaningful and relevant to their lives. Digital Media Corner provides videos, ideas, and examples of how you can use digital media to enhance your teaching and your students' learning. To access the videos and links to additional information, visit the Computer Concepts CourseMate Web site at www.cengagebrain.com, and then navigate to the Chapter 1 Digital Media Corner resource for this book.

1. PC or Mac?

Even though there have been numerous enhancements over the years, PCs and Macs are not yet fully compatible. In the meantime users are being asked to decide between these two platforms. Now that choice is easier than ever. In fact, you do not really have to make a choice. Parallels Desktop for Mac is a product that enables you to run Windows side-by-side with Mac OS on any Intel-powered Apple computer. With Parallels, you can use Windows and Mac OS at the same time, providing you the opportunity to utilize either operating system. You can share files and folders between both operating systems by simply dragging them back and forth. You can even open Windows files with Mac programs and vice versa.

2. Prezi

Today, teachers all over are searching for software that will "spice up" their lessons and still meet their learning objectives. Imagine that you are developing another slide show presentation for your class. Your students have been getting antsy in class, and honestly so have you; however, you are tired of PowerPoint and ready for something that is more engaging and full of surprises. Another teacher recently shared with you presentation software that you can use called Prezi that meets these expectations. Prezi incorporates digital media, PowerPoint slides, photographs, Adobe PDF files, and many others. This is a great way to

have all of your resources available in one place, either online or on your classroom computer. Prezi is available online and has free licenses for educators.

3. Audacity

As educators we are always looking for solutions that are cross platform and cost effective for our students — look no further for software to edit audio files. Audacity is free, open source software for recording and editing all kinds of sounds (including voice and music and ambient sound effects) and is available for Mac OS, Microsoft Windows, and other operating systems. With Audacity, you can import audio from outside sources such as QuickTime and export your completed project back to them in many different file formats. The program allows you to perform activities, such as equalize (balance), add effects, remove unwanted noise, generate tones, and convert file formats from one format to another to make them playable using the media player on your computer.

4. Discovery Education Streaming

Video can be a key component of digital media. Video, when used appropriately in your lessons, can help students think for themselves. But before video can be viewed, it has to get to students. Until recently, this has been a daunting task for teachers, but not anymore. Discovery Education Streaming allows teachers and students to access over 71,000 educational video content clips and 9,000 full video titles from The Discovery School easily. Discovery Education Streaming has a huge server network that soaks up most of the work to download or stream video media. As a result, over 35,000,000 students and teachers from many K-12 schools can digitally enhance their lessons, group activities and projects, and much more. Click the Discovery Education Streaming link to learn more.

1. What Is Assistive/Adaptive Technology?

Some people find operating a computer difficult, perhaps impossible because of some physical, cognitive, or sensory disability. Applied to computers, the term assistive/adaptive technology refers to any equipment, modification, or accommodation that can improve a person's capacity to learn, to communicate, to solve a problem, or to complete a task through the use of a computer.

2. Why Learn About Assistive Technologies?

The U.S. Census Bureau reports 11 percent of children ages 6 to 14 (about 4 million children) have some form of disability. An awareness of assistive/adaptive technology is valuable to each teacher committed to providing new learning environments in the classroom. New technologies designed for specific disabilities benefit those who need them, but anyone, at any time, may be in need of such technology as a result of injury or accident. In addition, as the population ages, more users of any technology will require some specialized accommodations in using that technology.

For a student with special needs, a learning environment without assistive/adaptive technology does not meet the requirements of the Individuals with Disabilities Education Act (IDEA). IDEA is a non-discrimination law requiring schools to accommodate the needs of children with disabilities to provide them an equal opportunity to participate in and benefit from the general education curriculum. In the area of technology, the law specifies that computers be accessible to students who use them. In K-12 schools, students with disabilities often have an Individualized Educational Program (IEP). The program may specify that some assistive/adaptive technology be used in the student's learning environment. Teachers are often called upon for advice, or to locate, or to make recommendations for purchase of special technology. As you explore each chapter's Assistive Technologies Corner, you will gain extensive knowledge that will allow your students with disabilities to be all they can be and learn all they can.

3. Do Microsoft and Apple Operating Systems Have Built-In Accessibility Features?

In response to the many computer users who need some accommodation to use a computer, Apple and Microsoft provide accessibility features and assistance at their Web sites as well as built-in accessibility features in their operating systems. These features allow users to customize their computers to meet their needs for computer input and output.

In Windows 7 or Vista, you use the Ease of Access Center to change settings for accessibility options. To open the Ease of Access Center, click the Start button, click Control Panel, and then click the Ease of Access Center icon. Built-in accessibility features for Windows XP are controlled through the Accessibility Wizard. To access the Accessibility Wizard, click the Start button, point to All Programs, point to Accessories, point to Accessibility, and then click Accessibility Wizard.

The Macintosh OS X System Preferences panel provides the Universal Access feature. To access this feature, click the Apple menu and then click System Preferences. When the System Preferences window displays, click the Universal Access icon. In the Universal Access panel, you will find setup instructions for zooming text, visual alerts, and keyboard and mouse modifications.

Follow the Web instructions at the top of this page to display additional information and this chapter's links on assistive technologies, including alternative input devices and other accessibility features.

INSTRUCTIONS: In the Lab provides word processing exercises that are divided into two areas, productivity and integration. To access the links to tutorials, productivity ideas, integration examples and ideas, and more, visit the Computer Concepts CourseMate Web site at www.cengagebrain.com, and then navigate to the Chapter 1 In the Lab resource for this book.

PRODUCTIVITY IN THE CLASSROOM

Introduction: Word processing skills are essential for both teachers and students. Improving your word processing skills will save you time and energy! Many powerful word processing software applications are available today. In addition, many of the major word processing applications have online tutorials. These tutorials can provide fast and easy access to learning new skills such as setting page margins, inserting a graphic, and changing the font, font color, and font size. To learn new word processing skills or improve your current skills, click the following links: Microsoft Word, iWork, Microsoft Works, Pages app, Google Docs app, and Corel WordPerfect.

1. Creating and Formatting a School Activity Flyer

Problem: As the seventh-grade class trip sponsor, you need to create a flyer to notify parents and students of an upcoming informational meeting. Open your word processing software and create a new flyer as described in the following steps. Use the flyer shown in Figure 1-36 on the next page as an example. (*Hint:* If you do not have the suggested font, use any appropriate font.)

Instructions: Perform the following tasks.

1. Select a class trip destination/title for the project. Display the title in the first heading line centered in 36-point, Comic Sans MS font.
2. Select a school name and display the second heading line centered in 22-point, Arial Narrow, bold font.
3. Choose an appropriate picture, image, or clip art graphic and insert it centered on the page.
4. Describe the field trip in three lines of text. Display the text in 14-point, Times or Times New Roman font.
5. Create a bulleted list that provides specific information about the meeting. Display the bulleted list with a one-half-inch margin in 12-point, Arial, bold font. Display a portion of each bulleted phrase in orange.
6. Provide contact information at the bottom of the flyer (your name and e-mail address). Display the information in 14-point, Times or Times New Roman, blue font.
7. Save the document to the location of your choice with a name of your choice. Print the document and then follow your instructor's directions for submitting the assignment.

2. Creating and Formatting a Band Fund-Raiser Flyer

Problem: As the band teacher, you need to create a flyer advertising the fall fund-raiser. Open your word processing software and create a new flyer as described in the following instructions. (*Hint:* If you do not have the suggested font, use any appropriate font.)

Instructions: Display the first heading line in 30-point, Lucinda Sans font. Insert an appropriate picture, image, or clip art graphic centered on the page. Enter a second heading line below the image in 22-point, Verdana, red font. Next enter four lines of text describing the purpose of the fall fund-raiser in 16-point, Times or Times New Roman font. Create a bulleted list with a one and a half-inch margin in 14-point, Times or Times New Roman font listing the dates, items to be sold, and place of the fund-raising event. Enter a closing phrase following the bulleted list in 18-point, Verdana, blue font. Finally, enter two lines of contact information in 12-point, Times or Times New Roman font that includes your name and e-mail address. Display the entire document in bold.

7th Grade Sea Camp Trip

Indian Trails Middle School

The 7th grade class at Indian Trails Middle School has the opportunity to attend Sea Camp April 21 through April 23. This is an exciting educational opportunity! Please join us at the informational meeting to learn more.

- November 19 – Join us at 7:00 p.m. in the Media Center
- Slide show – Watch an informational slide show about Sea Camp
- Application Packet – Packets will be available for distribution

For more information, please contact:
Mr. Mark Allman
m_allman@ssms.k12.ca.us
November 5, 2013

Figure 1-36

After you have typed and formatted the document, save the document to the location of your choice with a filename of your choice. Print the document and then follow your instructor's directions for submitting the assignment.

3. Creating and Formatting an Announcement Flyer

Problem: You have been asked to create a flyer announcing the upcoming school play.

Instructions: Create a document similar to the flyer illustrated in Figure 1-36. Use appropriate fonts styles, font sizes, font colors, and images. Include your name and e-mail address on the bottom of the flyer. After you have typed and formatted the document, save the document to the location of your choice using an appropriate filename. Print the document and then follow your instructor's directions for submitting the assignment.

ePortfolio Idea

INTEGRATION IN THE CLASSROOM

1. Your class is studying geometric shapes in architecture. Students will locate pictures of buildings and identify at least three geometric shapes. They will create a flyer that contains the following information: a heading line, an image of the building, a few lines explaining what they found, and a bulleted list with the three different geometric shapes. Create a flyer to use as an example for your students. Include two final lines listing your name and your school name.

2. Your students are studying various careers. They conduct research on the Internet and gather information about pay scales, educational requirements, and other benefits of their chosen profession. The students then prepare a flyer to share their information with the class. Create a flyer to present as an example for your students. Use appropriate font styles, font sizes, font colors, and images. Include your name and e-mail address on the bottom of the flyer.

3. You are teaching your elementary students about famous painters, including Vincent van Gogh, Pablo Picasso, Henri Matisse, Mary Cassatt, Leonardo da Vinci, Georgia O'Keefe, and Claude Monet. The students work in groups and select their favorite artist. They create a flyer about the life and work of their favorite artist. Create a flyer to present as an example for your students. Use appropriate font styles, sizes, colors, and images. Include your name and e-mail address on the bottom of the flyer.

Learn It Online

INSTRUCTIONS: Use the Learn It Online exercises to reinforce your understanding of the chapter concepts and increase your computer, information, and integration literacy. To access dozens of interactive student labs, practice tests, learning games, and more, visit the Computer Concepts CourseMate Web site at www.cengagebrain.com, navigate to the Chapter 1 resources for this book, and then click the link for the resource you want to review.

1. ISTE Learning — An Online Learning Community

Educators across the world are transforming their classrooms using Web 2.0 project-based learning that is grounded in the NETS. To find out more and access ISTE's anytime, anywhere online community for educators, click the ISTE Learning link.

2. At the Movies

Click the At the Movies link to watch hundreds of videos from the Howstuffworks Web site, including videos from the Discovery Channel, Science Channel, Sharecare, and more. Click the At the Movies 2 link to watch a movie and tour the Digibarn Computer Museum and then answer questions about the movie.

3. Introduction to Macs and PCs

Many software packages provide an introductory tour that offers an overview of the program. These tours usually cover any new features and provide tips on using software; many even use digital media enhancements. To learn more about taking an introductory tour of your personal computer operating system, click the Introduction to Macs and PCs link and complete the exercise that follows.

4. Practice Test

Click the Practice Test link. Answer each question. When completed, enter your name and click the Grade Test button to submit the quiz for grading. Make a note of any missed questions. If required, submit your score to your instructor.

5. Who Wants to Be a Computer Genius?

Click the Who Wants to Be a Computer Genius link to find out if you are a computer genius. When you are ready to play, click the Play button. If required, submit your score to your instructor.

6. Wheel of Terms

Click the Wheel of Terms link to reinforce important terms you learned in this chapter by playing the Shelly Cashman Series version of this popular game. When you are ready to play, click the Play button. If required, submit your score to your instructor.

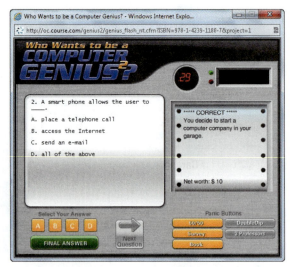

7. Crossword Puzzle Challenge

Click the Crossword Puzzle Challenge link. Complete the puzzle to reinforce skills you learned in this chapter. When you are ready to play, click the Play button. If required, submit the completed puzzle to your instructor.

Special Feature: Guide to Professional, State, and Federal Web Sites

INSTRUCTIONS: To gain World Wide Web access to additional and up-to-date information and links to these sites, visit the Computer Concepts CourseMate Web site for Teachers Discovering Computers at www.cengagebrain.com, and then navigate to the the Professional Sites or the State/Federal Sites resource.

Guide to Professional Educational Organizations

Many public and private nonprofit professional organizations provide educators with a variety of Web resources, assistance with important issues that educators deal with on a daily basis, and much more. Professional educational organizations are dedicated to promoting and supporting improvement in student learning and educational practices, as well as to providing support for professional growth in K-12 education and teacher education. These organizations also provide networking opportunities, information, and leadership in a variety of education areas, including information technology and other technologies integrated into the educational environment. A continually updated Guide to Professional Educational Organizations, which links the most current URLs for a representative cross section of professional organizations, can be found at the the Computer Concepts CourseMate Web site for Teachers Discovering Computers at www.cengagebrain.com.

Professional Educational Organizations

Site Name	Location	Description
Academy for Educational Development (AED)	www.aed.org	This independent nonprofit organization is committed to solving critical social and economic problems in all 50 states and more than 150 countries through education, social marketing, research, training, policy analysis, and innovative program design and management.
American Association of School Administrators (AASA)	www.aasa.org	The AASA, founded in 1865, is the professional organization for more than 13,000 educational leaders throughout the United States. The organization's focus is on supporting and developing effective school system leaders who are dedicated to the highest quality public education for all children.
American Federation of Teachers (AFT)	www.aft.org	The American Federation of Teachers is a national organization committed to teachers' professional interests. The American Federation of Teachers was founded in 1916 to represent the economic, social, and professional interests of classroom teachers. The AFT has more than 3,000 local affiliates nationwide and more than 1.5 million members.
American School Counselor Association (ASCA)	www.schoolcounselor.org	ASCA is a professional organization for licensed school counselors. This organization provides information and resources that support school counselors' efforts to help students focus on academic, personal/social, and career development.
Association for Career and Technical Education (ACTE)	www.acteonline.org	The Association for Career and Technical Education is the largest national education association in the United States. It is dedicated to the advancement of career education for both youth and adults. ACTE offers a wide variety of valuable resources for teachers, counselors, and administrators.
Association for Educational Communications and Technology (AECT)	www.aect.org	The mission of the Association for Educational Communications and Technology, founded in 1923, is to provide leadership in educational communications and technology by linking professionals, who hold a common interest in the use of educational technology and its application, to the learning process.
Association for Supervision and Curriculum Development (ASCD)	www.ascd.org	The ASCD, founded in 1943, is an international, nonprofit, nonpartisan association of professional educators of all grade levels and subject areas; it provides a forum for education issues and shares research, news, and information.
Association for the Advancement of Computing in Education (AACE)	www.aace.org	AACE, founded in 1981, is an international, educational, and professional not-for-profit organization dedicated to the advancement of the knowledge, the theory, and the improvement of the quality of learning and teaching at all levels with information technology.

(continued on next page)

Site Name	Location	Description
Computer-Using Educators (CUE)	www.cue.org	Computer-Using Educators, Inc. was founded in 1978 with the goal to promote and develop instructional uses of technology in all disciplines and at all educational levels from preschool through college. CUE is the largest organization of this type in the western Hemisphere and one of the largest in the United States.
Consortium for School Networking (CoSN)	www.cosn.org	The Consortium for School Networking promotes the use of technology to improve K-12 learning. Members represent state and local education agencies, nonprofits, companies, and individuals. CoSN is dedicated to promoting leadership development, advocacy, coalition building, and emerging technologies.
Council for Exceptional Children (CEC)	www.cec.sped.org	The Council for Exceptional Children is the largest international professional organization dedicated to improving educational outcomes for individuals with exceptionalities, students with disabilities, and/or gifted students.
Education Week on the Web (EdWeek)	www.edweek.org	Education Week is a nonprofit organization based in Washington DC. Its primary mission is to raise awareness and understanding among professionals and the public about important issues in education.
International Society for Technology in Education (ISTE)	www.iste.org	ISTE consists of international leaders in educational technology. The organization promotes appropriate uses of information technology to support and improve learning, teaching, and administration in PK-12 and teacher education.
National Art Education Association (NAEA)	www.naea-reston.org	Founded in 1947, NAEA is a non-profit educational organization for early elementary educators to administrators that promotes art education through professional development, service, advancement of knowledge, and leadership.
National Association for Multicultural Education (NAME)	www.nameorg.org	NAME is an active, growing organization that is working to bring together individuals and groups with an interest in multicultural education at all levels of education, different academic disciplines, and from diverse educational institutions and occupations. Membership includes educators from preschool through higher education and representatives from businesses and communities throughout the United States.
National Association for Music Education (MENC)	www.menc.org	MENC's mission is to advance music education as a profession and to ensure that every child in America has access to a balanced, sequential, high-quality education that includes music as a core subject of study.
National Association for Sport and Physical Education (NASPE)	www.aahperd.org/naspe	The National Association for Sport and Physical Education is a non-profit membership association. Its mission is to enhance knowledge, improve professional practice, and increase support for high-quality physical education, sport, and physical activity programs through research, development of standards, and dissemination of information.
National Association for the Education of Young Children (NAEYC)	www.naeyc.org	Founded in 1926, NAEYC is the world's largest organization working on behalf of young children. It is dedicated to improving the well-being of young children, with focus on the quality of educational and developmental services for all children from birth to age eight.
National Association of Elementary School Principals (NAESP)	www.naesp.org	NAESP was founded in 1921 by a visionary group of principals who sought to advance the profession. The mission of NAESP is to lead in the advocacy and support of elementary school principals, middle school principals, and other education leaders in their commitment to all children.
National Association of Secondary School Principals (NASSP)	www.nassp.org	This professional organization, founded in 1916, includes tens of thousands of middle level and high school principals, assistant principals, and aspiring principals from the United States and other countries around the world. Its mission is to promote excellence in school leadership by offering a wide variety of programs and services.
National Business Education Association (NBEA)	www.nbea.org	The National Business Education Association is the nation's leading professional organization devoted exclusively to serving individuals and groups engaged in instruction, administration, research, and dissemination of information for and about business.

(continued on next page)

Site Name	Location	Description
National Council for the Social Studies (NCSS)	www.socialstudies.org	Founded in 1921, NCSS's mission is to provide leadership, service, and support for all social studies educators. With members in all the 50 states, the District of Columbia, and 69 foreign countries, NCSS serves as an umbrella organization for elementary, secondary, and college teachers of history, civics, geography, economics, political science, sociology, psychology, anthropology, and law-related education.
National Council of Teachers of English (NCTE)	www.ncte.org	NCTE's mission is to improve the teaching and learning of English and the language arts at all levels of education. Since 1911, NCTE has provided opportunities for teachers to continue growing professionally. In addition, it founded a forum to deal with issues that affect the teaching of English.
National Council of Teachers of Mathematics (NCTM)	www.nctm.org	Founded in 1920, NCTM is a recognized leader in efforts to ensure excellent mathematics education for all students and an opportunity for every mathematics teacher to grow professionally. With about 90,000 members, NCTM is the largest association of mathematics educators in the world, providing professional development opportunities by holding annual regional leadership conferences, as well as publishing journals, books, videos, and software.
National Education Association (NEA)	www.nea.org	Founded in 1857, NEA is the nation's largest organization committed to advancing the cause of public education with more than 3.2 million members who work at every level of education, from preschool to university graduate programs. NEA has affiliates in every state dedicated to helping students.
National High School Association (NHSA)	www.nhsa.net	The National High School Association is a nonprofit membership association dedicated to improving the professional knowledge of high school educators so that all high school students may experience academic success. Members include administrators, teachers, parents, policymakers, and others interested in student achievement.
National Middle School Association (NMSA)	www.nmsa.org	The National Middle School Association is dedicated to improving the educational experiences of adolescents by providing vision, knowledge, and resources to all who serve them to develop healthy, productive, and ethical citizens. NMSA has over 30,000 members from across the United States, Canada, and 46 other countries.
National PTA (PTA)	www.pta.org	The National PTA is the largest volunteer child advocacy organization in the United States. It is an association of parents, educators, students, and other citizens who are active leaders in their schools and communities in facilitating parent education and involvement in schools.
National School Boards Association (NSBA)	www.nsba.org	The mission of the NSBA is to foster excellence and equity in public education through school board leadership. The NSBA believes local school boards are the nation's preeminent expression of grass roots democracy and that this form of governance of the public schools is fundamental to the continued success of public education.
National Science Teachers Association (NSTA)	www.nsta.org	Founded in 1944, NSTA is the largest organization in the world committed to promoting excellence and innovation in science teaching and learning. NSTA's current membership of more than 60,000 includes science teachers, science supervisors, administrators, scientists, business and industry representatives, and others involved in science education.
National Staff Development Council (NSDC)	www.nsdc.org	The National Staff Development Council is a national nonprofit association of more than 13,000 educators. NSDC is the largest nonprofit professional association committed to ensuring success for all students through staff development and school improvement.
Phi Delta Kappa (PDK)	www.pdkintl.org	Phi Delta Kappa is an international association of professional educators and was founded in 1906. Since its founding, this member-based association has served more than 500,000 members in communities across the United States and abroad. PDK's mission is to promote quality education, with particular emphasis on publicly supported education.
Rural School and Community Trust	www.ruraledu.org	The Rural School and Community Trust is a national nonprofit organization addressing the crucial relationship between good schools and thriving communities. This organization's mission is to help rural schools and communities get better together.

State and Federal Government Web Sites

The state sites and federal government sites and organizations provide a multitude of Web resources for K-12 teachers and students. The state sites contain pertinent information related to education and education policies in their respective states. These sites often include information such as state standards, curriculum-specific ideas and lesson plans, and additional resources. The federal government sites provide a wealth of information related to their specific agency. These sites often include facts, games, and additional resources. New and exciting education Web resources and apps are continuously added to these sites.

State Departments of Education Web Sites

Site Name	Location
Alabama	www.alsde.edu
Alaska	www.eed.state.ak.us
Arizona	ade.state.az.us
Arkansas	arkansased.org
California	www.cde.ca.gov
Colorado	www.cde.state.co.us
Connecticut	www.sde.ct.gov
Delaware	www.doe.state.de.us
District of Columbia	dcps.dc.gov
Florida	www.fldoe.org
Georgia	www.doe.k12.ga.us
Hawaii	doe.k12.hi.us
Idaho	www.sde.idaho.gov
Illinois	www.isbe.state.il.us
Indiana	www.doe.in.gov
Iowa	www.iowa.gov/educate
Kansas	www.ksde.org
Kentucky	www.education.ky.gov
Louisiana	www.doe.state.la.us
Maine	www.maine.gov/education
Maryland	www.marylandpublicschools.org
Massachusetts	www.doe.mass.edu
Michigan	www.michigan.gov/mde
Minnesota	www.education.state.mn.us
Mississippi	www.mde.k12.ms.us
Missouri	www.dese.mo.gov

Site Name	Location
Montana	mt.gov/education.asp
Nebraska	www.education.ne.gov
Nevada	www.doe.nv.gov
New Hampshire	www.ed.state.nh.us/education
New Jersey	www.state.nj.us/education
New Mexico	sde.state.nm.us
New York	www.nysed.gov
North Carolina	www.dpi.state.nc.us
North Dakota	www.dpi.state.nd.us
Ohio	www.ode.state.oh.us
Oklahoma	sde.state.ok.us
Oregon	www.ode.state.or.us
Pennsylvania	www.pde.state.pa.us
Rhode Island	www.ride.ri.gov
South Carolina	www.ed.sc.gov
South Dakota	www.doe.sd.gov
Tennessee	www.tn.gov/education
Texas	www.tea.state.tx.us
Utah	www.schools.utah.gov
Vermont	www.education.vermont.gov
Virginia	www.doe.virginia.gov
Washington	www.k12.wa.us
West Virginia	wvde.state.wv.us
Wisconsin	www.dpi.state.wi.us
Wyoming	www.k12.wy.us

Federal Government Web Sites

Site Name	Location	Description
Ben's Guide to U.S. Government for Kids	bensguide.gpo.gov	Ben's Guide provides a comprehensive listing of government Web sites for kids.
Bureau of Land Management	www.blm.gov/wo/st/en.html	This site, created by the U.S. Department of the Interior, presents learning opportunities associated with the 262 million acres of public lands that the Bureau of Land Management manages for all Americans; included is extensive information for students, teachers, and adult learners to use in the classroom, informal outdoor settings, or virtual classrooms.
Comprehensive Centers	www.ed.gov/programs/newccp/index.html	ED was created in 1980 to promote student achievement and preparation for global competitiveness by fostering educational excellence and ensuring equal access. Links for students, parents, teachers, and administrators are included.
Department of Defense (DoD)	www.dodea.edu	This Web site provides general information about educational programs sponsored in whole or in part by the Department of Defense. This gateway to education effort is sponsored by the DoD.
Department of Energy	http://www.energy.gov/sciencetech/education.htm	This site, maintained by the Department of Energy Education, provides educational resources in science, technology, energy, math, and more. The site includes an Energy Glossary with more than 4,000 energy definitions, as well as other energy-related terms for middle and secondary students.
EDSITEment	edsitement.neh.gov	This subject-based catalog from the National Endowment for the Humanities provides access to the top humanities sites on the Web. It includes online humanities resources from some of the world's great museums, libraries, cultural institutions, and universities for use directly in your classroom.
Educational Resources Information Center (ERIC)	www.eric.ed.gov	A nationwide information network funded by the U.S. Department of Education that acquires, catalogs, summarizes, and provides access to education information from many sources.
EPA for Students and Educators	www.epa.gov/epahome/students.htm	This U. S. Environmental Protection Agency (EPA) Web site provides fact sheets, interactive games, and more for kids, students, and teachers who want to learn about the environment or share what they know with others. The Web site can help you with all sorts of information about the EPA and the environment.
Federal Bureau of Investigation	www.fbi.gov/fun-games/kids/kids	This Web site is sponsored by the Department of Justice; it is designed for children and parents to learn more about the FBI.
Federal Communications Commission (FCC)	www.fcc.gov/learnnet	The FCC LearnNet Web site provides information about FCC programs that are working to bring every school in America into the information age.

(continued on next page)

Site Name	Location	Description
Federal Resources for Educational Excellence (FREE)	www.free.ed.gov	FREE provides more than 1,500 Internet-based education resources supported by federal agencies available at one great Web site.
FedWorld	www.fedworld.gov	FedWorld is a comprehensive central access point for searching, locating, ordering, and acquiring government information.
FirstGov for Kids	www.kids.gov/k_5/k_5_government.shtml	This U.S. government interagency Kids' Portal provides links to federal kids' sites along with some of the best kids' sites from other organizations all grouped by subject.
Food and Drug Administration (FDA)	www.fda.gov	Learn about the latest FDA developments that will help keep you and your students informed about important health issues.
healthfinder®	www.healthfinder.gov	This Web site is an important source for educators to find reliable consumer, health, and human services information.
Institute of Education Sciences	http://ies.ed.gov	The U. S. Department of Education provides educational research resources funded by Congress at this Web site.
Library of Congress	www.loc.gov	The Library of Congress is an incredible library resource for students and teachers.
National Aeronautics and Space Administration (NASA)	www.nasa.gov	This awesome Web site covers NASA's extensive education program.
National Archives and Records Administration (NARA)	www.archives.gov/education	The NARA site presents the Digital Classroom, which encourages teachers of students at all levels to use archival documents in the classroom.
National Endowment for the Humanities	www.neh.gov	Online projects at this Web site support learning in history, literature, philosophy, and other areas of the humanities.
National Gallery of Art (NGA)	www.nga.gov	The National Gallery of Art (NGA) is home to the world's finest paintings and sculptures. This site offers a wealth of culture. It includes a link to NGA Kids for exciting animation and interactivity.
National Oceanic and Atmospheric Administration (NOAA)	www.noaa.gov	NOAA provides information about the weather, oceans, satellites, fisheries, climates, and more.
National Park Service (NPS)	www.nps.gov/learn	NPS is your one stop for finding education materials about America's national parks; includes zones for teachers and students, games, a gallery, and how to become a junior ranger.
National Register of Historic Places: Teaching with Historic Places (TwHP)	www.cr.nps.gov/nr/twhp	TwHP offers great lesson plans and guidance on using historic places in teaching and learning.
National Science Foundation (NSF)	www.nsf.gov	The NSF Web site promotes the progress of science and health; it is a must stop for science teachers.
Peace Corps	www.peacecorps.gov/wws/	The Peace Corps World Wise Schools education program is designed to help students gain a greater understanding of other cultures and countries.

(continued on next page)

Site Name	Location	Description
Recreation.gov	www.recreation.gov	This is a fantastic Web site for anyone searching for information about recreational opportunities on federal lands.
Regional Educational Laboratories	http://ies.ed.gov/ncee/edlabs	This Web site provides information from research and practice to those involved in educational improvement at the local, state, and regional levels.
Smithsonian Center for Education and Museum Studies	smithsonianeducation.org	This essential source includes lesson plans, resource guides, field trips, and more for all educators.
students.gov	www.students.gov	This Web site contains great links to federal Web site resources for postsecondary students.
The Educator's Reference Desk	www.eduref.org	The Educator's Reference Desk provides high-quality resources and services to the education community; included are more than 2,000 lesson plans, 3,000 plus links to online education information, and more than 200 question archive responses.
The Kennedy Center ARTSEDGE	http://artsedge.kennedy-center.org	The National Arts and Education Network links the arts and education through technology.
United States Department of Agriculture (USDA)	www.usda.gov	The USDA provides extensive research and education resources about many important subjects for all ages.
United States Geological Survey (USGS)	education.usgs.gov	The USGS Learning Web site is dedicated to K-12 education, exploration, and lifelong learning.
USA.gov	www.usa.gov	USA.gov is the U.S. Government's office Web site for information and services. You will find a wide variety of online information, services, and resources.
U.S. Census Bureau	www.census.gov	Through this Web site, expose your students to timely, relevant, and quality data about the people and economy of the United States.
U.S. Department of Education	www.ed.gov	All teachers should make this Web site a first stop as they embark on their teaching careers. The site provides information about student readiness, gives lesson ideas and materials, includes training and development sources, offers guidelines for applying for grants, and much more.
U.S. Department of Energy: Office of Science	www.science.energy.gov	This Web site is dedicated to helping educate America's next generation of scientists.
U.S. Department of Health and Human Services (HHS)	www.dhhs.gov	The HHS offers a wealth of information related to public health, privacy issues, grant programs, and more at this Web site.
U.S. Department of the Interior (DOI)	www.doi.gov	The DOI is dedicated to the internal development of the United States and the welfare of its people.
U.S. Fish and Wildlife Service	www.fws.gov	Learn how to protect the homes and lives of fish and wildlife at this interesting Web site.
USDA Forest Service	www.fs.fed.us	This Web site is a great resource for information about public lands in the United States; it includes a special section just for kids.

(continued on next page)

Site Name	Location	Description
USDA for Educators	*www.usda.gov*, then select Educators and Students in the Information for list	This United States Department of Agriculture Web site includes an "Information for Educators and Students" section that teachers and students can use to locate resources related to agriculture.
Welcome to the White House	*www.whitehouse.gov*	Welcome to the White House provides links to many collections, programs, and products of significant educational benefit; offers a wealth of information and news about the president, government, and history; and includes virtual tours and interactivity of value for all ages.

Communications, Networks, the Internet, and the World Wide Web

2

Objectives

After completing this chapter, you will be able to do the following:
[ISTE NETS-T Standards 1 a-d; 2 a-d; 3 a-d; 4 a-b, d; 5 a-b, d]

- Define communications

- Identify the basic components of a communications system

- Describe how and why computer networks are used in schools and school districts

- Explain how the Internet works

- Describe the World Wide Web portion of the Internet

- Explain how Web documents are linked to one another

- Explain the use of Web browser software

- Explain how to use a Web search tool to find information

- Identify several types of multimedia products available on the Web

- Explain how Internet services such as e-mail, newsgroups, chat rooms, and instant messaging work

- Describe the educational implications of the Internet and the World Wide Web

- Describe different ways to connect to the Internet and the World Wide Web

- Describe the pros and cons of Web 2.0 tools for teachers and students

Communications and networks are the fastest growing areas of computer technology and digital media. Adding tremendously to this growth is the popularity of the Internet and the World Wide Web (also called the Web), which is a service of the Internet that supports graphics and multimedia. Together, the Internet and the World Wide Web represent one of today's most exciting uses of networks. Already, these networks have changed the way people gather information, conduct research, shop, take classes, and collaborate on projects dramatically.

Businesses encourage you to browse their Web-based catalogs, send them e-mail for customer service requests, and buy their products online. The government publishes thousands of informational Web pages to provide individuals with materials such as legislative updates, tax forms, and e-mail addresses for members of Congress. Colleges have virtual tours of their campuses on the Web, accept applications online, and offer thousands of Web-based classes.

Web Info

For more information on how the Web is expanding student learning, visit the Computer Concepts CourseMate Web site at *www.cengagebrain. com*, navigate to the Chapter 2 Web Info resource for this book, and then click Expanding Student Learning.

Today, communications media and networks are breaking down classroom walls, allowing students to view the world beyond where they live and learn. The Internet continues to expand student learning beyond the covers of a textbook to include interactive, up-to-date, Web- and app-based content. Never before has any technology opened so many opportunities for learning.

The future will bring even more exciting applications of these technologies when combined with tablet computing. Federal and state governments, private businesses, and organizations are investing billions of dollars in Internet-related hardware and software for K-12 schools. As a result of this substantial investment, most public schools are equipping their classrooms with multimedia computers and providing teachers and students with access to the Internet. This chapter discusses communications, networks, the Internet, and the World Wide Web; explains how they work; and reviews how students, teachers, and administrators can use these technologies to communicate, obtain almost unlimited educational information, and enhance student learning.

What Is Communications?

Communications, sometimes called **telecommunications**, describes a process in which two or more computers or devices transfer data, instructions, and information. The ability to communicate information instantly and accurately has changed the way people conduct business and interact with each other, and the way students learn. Electronic mail (e-mail), voice mail, facsimile (fax), telecommuting, online services, video-conferencing, the Internet, and the World Wide Web are examples of applications that rely on communications technology.

Communications Networks

Computers were stand-alone devices when they were first introduced. As computers became more widely used, companies designed hardware and software so computers could communicate with one another. Originally, developers created communications capabilities only for large computers. Today, even the smallest computers and handheld devices can communicate with each other. Figure 2-1 shows a sample communications system, which can contain many types of devices.

Integration Strategies

To explore ideas on integrating 21st century communications tools in your curriculum, visit the Computer Concepts CourseMate Web site at *www.cengagebrain. com*, and then navigate to the Chapter 2 Digital Media Corner resource for this book.

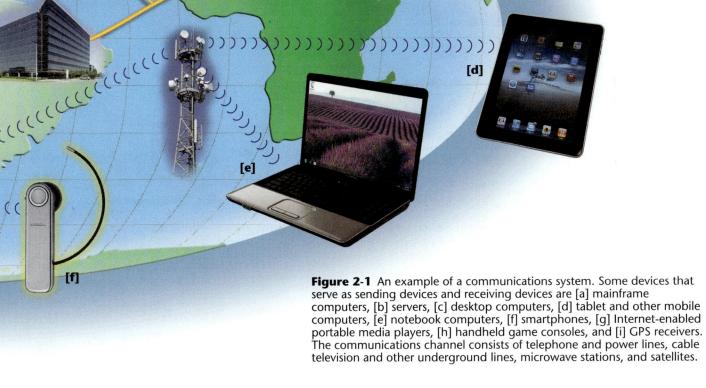

Figure 2-1 An example of a communications system. Some devices that serve as sending devices and receiving devices are [a] mainframe computers, [b] servers, [c] desktop computers, [d] tablet and other mobile computers, [e] notebook computers, [f] smartphones, [g] Internet-enabled portable media players, [h] handheld game consoles, and [i] GPS receivers. The communications channel consists of telephone and power lines, cable television and other underground lines, microwave stations, and satellites.

Web Info

For more information on communications networks, visit the Computer Concepts CourseMate Web site at *www.cengagebrain. com*, navigate to the Chapter 2 Web Info resource for this book and then click Communications Networks.

A **communications network** is a collection of computers and other equipment organized to share data, information, hardware, and software. A basic communications system consists of the following equipment:

- Two computers, one to send and one to receive data

- Communications devices that send and receive data

- A communications channel over which data is sent

This basic model also includes **communications software** — programs that manage the transmission of data between computers.

A **communications channel** is the path that data follows as the data is transmitted from the sending equipment to the receiving equipment in a communications network. Communications channels are made up of **transmission media,** which are the physical materials or other means used to establish a communications channel. The most widely used transmission medium is twisted-pair cable. **Twisted-pair cable**

consists of pairs of plastic-coated copper wires twisted together (Figure 2-2). Standard telephone lines in your home also use twisted-pair cables. Other examples of transmission media include coaxial cable, fiber-optic cable, microwave transmission, communications satellites, and wireless transmissions.

Digital signals are individual electrical pulses that a computer uses to represent data. Telephone equipment originally was designed to carry only voice transmission, which comprises a continuous electrical wave called an **analog signal.** For telephone lines to carry data, a communications device called a **modem** converts digital signals into analog signals.

The word modem comes from a combination of the words modulate, to change a digital signal into sound or analog signal, and demodulate, to convert an analog signal into a digital signal. Computers at both the sending and receiving ends of this communications channel must have a modem for data transmission to occur. At the sending computer, a modem converts digital signals from the computer to analog

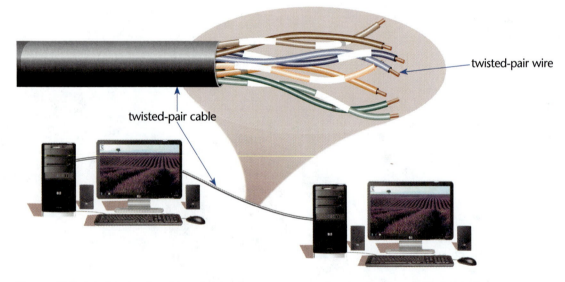

twisted-pair wire

twisted-pair cable

Figure 2-2 A twisted-pair cable consists of one or more twisted pair wires. Each twisted-pair wire usually is color coded for identification. Telephone networks and LANs often use twisted-pair cable.

signals for transmission over regular telephone lines. At the receiving computer, a modem converts analog signals back to digital signals (Figure 2-3a).

Older computers purchased for home use included a dial-up modem that could transmit data at rates up to approximately 56,000 bits per second (56K modem). A **dial-up modem** is a communications device that can convert digital signals to analog signals and analog signals to digital signals so that data can travel along an analog telephone line.

A number of different kinds of modems are in use today. Many home and small business users are using cable modems and DSL modems, also called digital modems, which provide significantly higher data access rates than 56K (Figure 2-3b). Cable modems provide broadband access over a cable television

(CATV) network and DSL modems provide broadband access over telephone lines. These newer types of modems are discussed later in this chapter. Networks are classified as either local area networks (LANs) or wide area networks (WANs).

LOCAL AREA NETWORKS

A **local area network (LAN)** is a communications network that covers a limited geographical area, such as a school, office building, or group of buildings. A LAN consists of a number of computers connected to a central computer, or server. A **server** manages the resources on a network and provides a centralized storage area for software programs and data. A **wireless LAN (WLAN)** is a LAN that uses no wires. Instead of wires, a WLAN uses wireless media, such as radio waves.

[a] digital to analog to digital communications channel

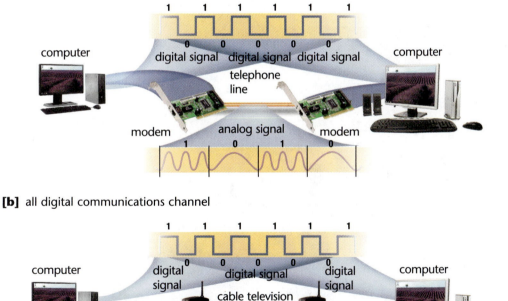

[b] all digital communications channel

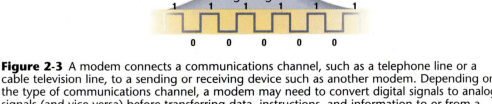

Figure 2-3 A modem connects a communications channel, such as a telephone line or a cable television line, to a sending or receiving device such as another modem. Depending on the type of communications channel, a modem may need to convert digital signals to analog signals (and vice versa) before transferring data, instructions, and information to or from a sending or receiving device.

WIDE AREA NETWORKS

A **wide area network (WAN)** covers a large geographical region (such as a city or school district) and uses regular telephone lines, digital cables, microwaves, wireless systems, satellites, or other combinations of communications channels. A WAN can consist of numerous LANs organized into one larger network. For example, a large school district may establish a WAN that consists of dozens of local area networks, each LAN representing an individual school.

HOME NETWORKS

If you have multiple computers in your home or home office, you can connect all of them together with a **home network.**

Some advantages to having a home network include the following: all computers in the house can be connected to the Internet at the same time, each computer can access files and programs on the other computers, and all computers can share the same peripherals, such as a scanner, printer, or DVD drive.

Home networks can be either wired or wireless. To network computers and devices that span multiple rooms or floors in a home, it may be more convenient to use a wireless network (see Figure 2-4). Local cable and other Internet service providers will help you set up a wireless home network for free or for a minimal installation charge. Monthly fees usually include the rental fee for a wireless modem.

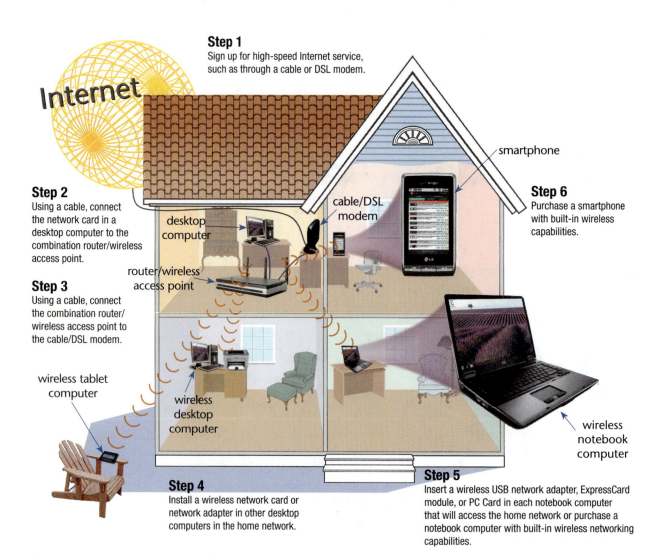

Step 1
Sign up for high-speed Internet service, such as through a cable or DSL modem.

Internet

smartphone

Step 2
Using a cable, connect the network card in a desktop computer to the combination router/wireless access point.

cable/DSL modem

Step 6
Purchase a smartphone with built-in wireless capabilities.

desktop computer

router/wireless access point

Step 3
Using a cable, connect the combination router/wireless access point to the cable/DSL modem.

wireless tablet computer

wireless desktop computer

wireless notebook computer

Step 4
Install a wireless network card or network adapter in other desktop computers in the home network.

Step 5
Insert a wireless USB network adapter, ExpressCard module, or PC Card in each notebook computer that will access the home network or purchase a notebook computer with built-in wireless networking capabilities.

Figure 2-4 An example of a wireless home network.

Networking the Classroom, School, and District

Due to extensive federal, state, and local funding, virtually all schools and school districts in the United States have networked their computers. Schools have installed networks for four reasons (Figure 2-5): (1) to share hardware and software resources, (2) to enable communications among schools and other organizations, (3) to connect students and teachers to the Internet, and (4) use and share information and data.

A school network server connects all of the computers located within a school. A server manages the resources on a network and provides a centralized storage area for software programs and data. Typically, any teachers and students who use the network can access software and data on the server, although school or network administrators can limit access to specific records and software applications.

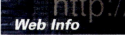

Web Info

For more information about school networks, visit the Computer Concepts CourseMate Web site at *www.cengagebrain.com*, navigate to the Chapter 2 Web Info resource for this book, and then click School Networks.

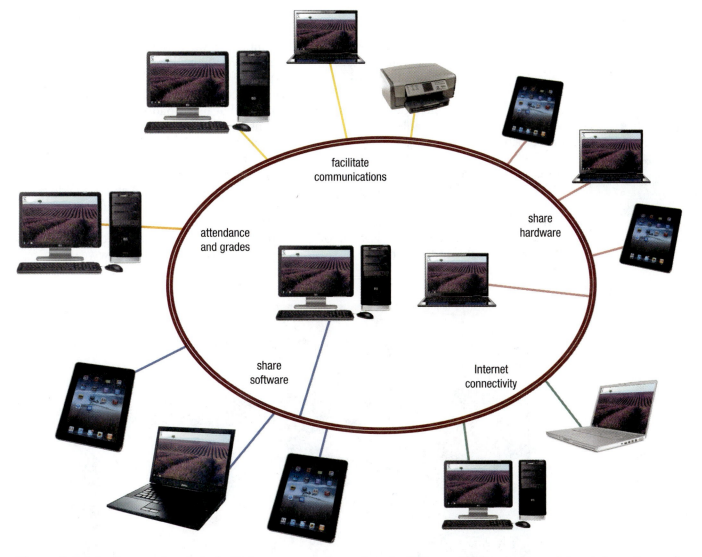

facilitate communications

attendance and grades

share hardware

share software

Internet connectivity

Figure 2-5 Schools use networks to facilitate communications, share hardware and software, use and store information and data like grades and attendance, and connect students and teachers to the Internet. Desktop computers, tablet computers like iPads, and other computing devices can be connected to a network.

WIRELESS SCHOOLS AND CLASSROOMS

Not long ago, teachers used traditional telephones that were connected to a telephone company by cables to communicate with friends, family, and fellow teachers. Today, wireless technology allows teachers to keep in touch with friends and family from anywhere in the world, using a variety of devices: a smartphone, a tablet computer, or a notebook computer with high-speed Internet access.

Teachers and students already are part of the wireless revolution that is taking place in education. Many colleges, universities, and K-12 schools have installed wireless networks and are utilizing wireless computers and other wireless devices. Many experts, including Steve Jobs, CEO of Apple Computers, believe that the future of educational computing, in both K-12 and higher education, is wireless networks, wireless tablet computers, and other wireless devices.

Today, all major computer manufacturers provide wireless network solutions and devices for K-12 schools (Figure 2-6). Devices include wireless keyboards, wireless notebook computers, wireless mobile labs, and many other devices. The use of wireless networks and devices in

K-12 schools and classrooms is discussed in future chapters.

HIGH-SPEED OR BROADBAND ACCESS

Over the past 10 years, school districts have concentrated on installing and upgrading local and wide area networks so that their teachers and students have Internet access in their classrooms or at the point of instruction. Many school networks, however, do not provide their classroom computers with continuous high-speed access to the Internet; access speeds vary greatly. Students and teachers must be provided continuous high-speed access to allow them to find and quickly download complex, content-rich resources. The federal government recognizes this and is spearheading initiatives to provide broadband access to K-12 schools. Networks and media that use **broadband** technologies transmit signals at much faster speeds than traditional network configurations. A recent federal report to the President and Congress stated that the promise of widely available, high-quality, Web-based education is made possible by technological and communications trends that could lead to important digital media-based educational applications over the next few years.

FAQ

What does bandwidth have to do with Internet access?

Bandwidth is a measure of how fast data travels over transmission channels. Thus, higher-speed broadband Internet connections have a higher bandwidth than dial-up connections.

Figure 2-6 An example of a wireless classroom.

The Benefits of Computer Networks in Education

One benefit of networking is that administrators, teachers, and students can share computer hardware, software, and data resources available throughout the school district. For example, administrators can maintain all student records and information securely at one central location. Teachers and administrative staff who have a need for access to student records can access various student information databases from just about any networked computer at any location.

By far, the most important benefit of networking school computers is that administrators, teachers, and students can access the unlimited educational resources available on the Internet and communicate with other educators and students all over the world instantly (Figure 2-7). In brief, networking provides schools with limitless possibilities for teaching and learning. Without question, the introduction of networks and the Internet into today's schools has had and continues to have a dramatic impact on the current generation of teachers and students.

Figure 2-7 The Internet is useful as a tool to hold students' attention.

What Is the Internet?

You have learned that a network is a collection of computers and devices connected via communications devices and media. Recall also that the world's largest network is the **Internet,** which is a worldwide collection of networks that link together millions of businesses, governments, educational institutions, and individuals using modems, telephone lines, and other communications devices and media (Figure 2-8). Each of these networks provides resources and data that add to the abundance of goods, services, and information accessible via the Internet.

Figure 2-8 The world's largest network is the Internet, which is a worldwide collection of networks that link together millions of businesses, governments, educational institutions, and individuals.

Networks that constitute the Internet, also called the **Net,** consist of federal, regional, local, and international networks. Public or private organizations own individual networks that constitute the Internet; no single organization owns or controls the Internet. Each organization on the Internet is responsible only for maintaining its own network.

Today, more than one billion users around the world connect to the Internet for a variety of reasons:

- Explore virtual worlds and social networks.

- Access a wealth of information, news, research, and educational material.

- Conduct business or complete banking and investing transactions.

- Access sources of entertainment and leisure, such as online games, magazines, and vacation-planning guides.

- Shop for goods and services.

- Meet and converse with people around the world through discussion groups, instant messaging, blogs, wikis, or chat rooms.

Web Info

For tips and ideas on using the Internet with digital kids, visit the Computer Concepts CourseMate Web site at *www. cengagebrain.com,* navigate to the Chapter 2 Web Info resource for this book, click Web Info, and then click Internet.

- Access hundreds of thousands of apps for smartphones, tablet computers, and other mobile devices.

- Send messages to or receive messages from other connected users.

- Download and listen to music or download and watch movies.

- Take a course or access educational materials.

To allow you to perform these and other activities, the Internet provides a variety of services, such as the World Wide Web, e-mail, File Transfer Protocol (FTP), newsgroups, mailing lists, instant messaging, chat rooms, and Internet telephony. These services, along with a discussion of the history of the Internet and how the Internet works, are explained in the following sections.

History of the Internet

Although the history of the Internet is relatively short, its growth has been explosive. The Internet has its roots in a networking project of the U.S. Department of Defense's **Advanced Research Projects Agency (ARPA)**. ARPA's goal was to build a network that (1) would allow scientists at different locations to share information and collaborate on military and scientific projects and (2) could function even if part of the network was disabled or destroyed by a disaster, such as a nuclear war. That network, called **ARPANET**, became functional in September 1969, effectively linking together scientific and academic researchers in the United States.

The original ARPANET was a wide area network consisting of four main computers, located at the University of California at Los Angeles, the Stanford Research Institute, the University of California at Santa Barbara, and the University of Utah. Each of these four computers served as the network's host. A **host** is the main computer in a network of computers connected by communications links. A host often stores and transfers data and messages on high-speed communications lines and provides network connections for additional computers.

As researchers and others realized the great benefit of using ARPANET's electronic mail to share information and notes, ARPANET underwent phenomenal growth. By 1984, ARPANET had more than 1,000 individual computers linked as hosts (today, more than 350 million host computers exist on the Internet).

To take further advantage of the high-speed communications offered by ARPANET, organizations decided to connect entire networks to ARPANET. In 1986, for example, the **National Science Foundation (NSF)** connected its huge network of five supercomputer centers, called **NSFnet,** to ARPANET. This configuration of complex networks and hosts became known as the Internet.

Because of its advanced technology, NSFnet served as the major backbone network of the Internet until 1995. A **backbone** is a high-speed network that connects regional and local networks to the Internet (Figure 2-9). Other computers then connect to these regional and local networks to access the Internet. A backbone thus handles the bulk of the communications activity, or **traffic,** on the Internet.

In 1995, NSFnet terminated its backbone network on the Internet to return to its purpose as a research network. Today, a variety of corporations, commercial firms, and other companies operate the backbone networks that provide access to the Internet. These backbone networks, telephone companies, cable and satellite companies, educational institutions, and the government all contribute extensive resources to the Internet. As a result, the Internet is a truly collaborative entity.

Over the years, the total number of computers connected to the original network increased steadily and within the last few years, explosively. Today, experts estimate that hundreds of millions of computers distribute information over the Internet, including those at virtually all K-12 schools.

An emerging Internet, called **Internet2 (I2)**, is an extremely high-speed network that develops and tests advanced Internet technologies for research, teaching, and learning, including those used by Web 2.0 and Web 3.0. Members of Internet2 include more than 200 U.S.

Web Info

For the history of the Internet, visit the Computer Concepts CourseMate Web site at *www.cengagebrain.com*, navigate to the Chapter 2 Web Info resource for this book, click Web Info, and then click History.

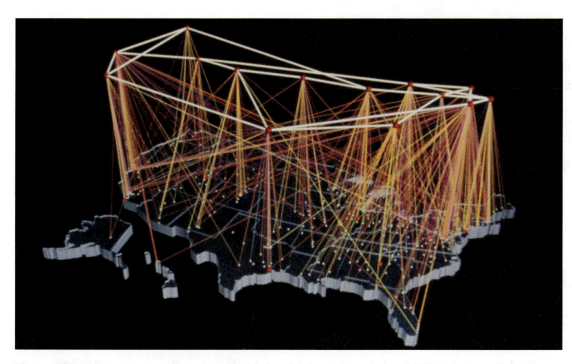

Figure 2-9 This map was prepared by the National Science Foundation (NSF) and shows the major United States Internet connections.

universities in cooperation with 115 leading corporations. Examples of Internet2 projects that are now mainstream include telemedicine, digital libraries (online books, magazines, music, movies, speeches, and so on), and faster Internet services.

How the Internet Works

Computers and other digital devices connected to the Internet work together to transfer data around the world. When a computer sends data over the Internet, the computer's software divides the data into small pieces, called **packets**. The data in a packet might be part of an e-mail message, a file, a document, a graphic, or a request for a file. Each packet contains the data, as well as the recipient (destination), origin (sender), and sequence information needed to reassemble the data at the destination. Packets travel along the fastest path available to the recipient's computer via hardware devices called **routers** (Figure 2-10 on the next page).

If the most direct path to the destination is overloaded or not operating, routers send the packets along alternate paths. Although each packet may arrive out of

sequence, the destination computer uses the sequence information contained in each packet to reassemble the original message, file, document, or request. **Packet switching** is the technique of breaking a message into individual packets, sending the packets along the best route available, and reassembling the data.

For a technique such as packet switching to work, all of the devices on the network must follow certain standards or protocols. A **communications protocol** specifies the rules that define how devices connect to each other and transmit data over a network. The protocol used to define packet switching on the Internet is **Transmission Control Protocol/Internet Protocol (TCP/IP)**.

Data sent over the Internet travels over networks and communications lines owned and operated by many companies. You can connect to these networks in one of several ways. Some users connect to the Internet through an Internet service provider (ISP) or an online service provider (OSP), often using a modem to establish a connection. Organizations such as schools and businesses provide Internet access for students and employees by connecting their own network to an ISP. Some school districts

FAQ

Just how fast is Internet2?

Really fast! Recently, Internet2 researchers broke a speed record by sending data from Los Angeles to Geneva, Switzerland, at a speed that is nearly 10,000 times faster than the average home high-speed Internet connection.

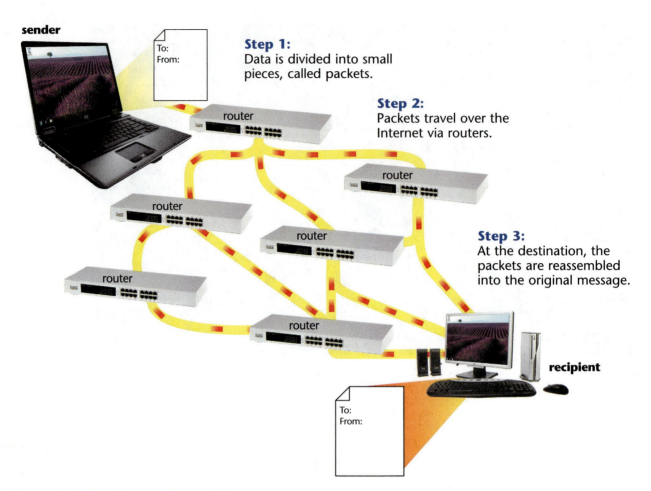

sender

Step 1:
Data is divided into small pieces, called packets.

Step 2:
Packets travel over the Internet via routers.

Step 3:
At the destination, the packets are reassembled into the original message.

recipient

Figure 2-10 How data travels over the Internet.

Integration Strategies

To learn more about digital equity and the differences between the haves and have-nots, as well as how to minimize the impact, visit the Computer Concepts CourseMate Web site at *www.cengagebrain.com*, and then navigate to the Chapter 2 Education Issues resource for this book.

and states also provide Internet services for teachers and administrators so they can access the Internet from their homes.

INTERNET ACCESS PROVIDERS

An **Internet service provider (ISP)** is a regional or national access provider. A **regional ISP** is a business that usually provides Internet access to a specific geographic area. A **national ISP** is a business that provides Internet access in cities and towns nationwide and broadband access in many locations. Because of their size, national ISPs offer more services and generally have a larger technical support staff than regional ISPs.

Like an ISP, an **online service provider (OSP)** provides access to the Internet, but an online service provider also has members-only features that offer special content and a variety of services. Typical content and services include news, weather,

educational information, financial information, hardware and software guides, games, entertainment, news, and travel information. For this reason, the fees for using an online service provider usually are slightly higher than fees for an ISP. Popular OSPs are America Online (AOL) and Microsoft Network (MSN).

A **wireless Internet service provider (WISP)** is a company that provides wireless Internet access to computers with wireless modems or access devices or to Internet-enabled mobile computers or devices. Internet-enabled mobile devices include smartphones, tablet computers, and e-book readers. Some examples of wireless ISPs include AT&T Wireless, T-Mobile, and Verizon Wireless.

Users and schools access the Internet through regional or national ISPs, OSPs, and WISPs using a variety of connection methods. Individual user accounts vary from about $5 to $25 per month for dial-up access to $20 to $75 per month for higher-speed access.

Internet access providers offer services such as news, weather, financial data, games, travel guides, e-mail, photo communities, and online storage to hold digital photos and other files. Some of these services are offered for free, others are offered for a fee.

CONNECTING TO THE INTERNET

There are many ways to connect to the Internet (Figure 2-11). Teachers and students often connect to the Internet through their school network. When connecting from home or from the road while traveling, some individuals use dial-up access to connect to the Internet. With **dial-up access**, you use your computer and a modem to dial into an ISP or online service over regular telephone lines. The computer at the receiving end, whether at an ISP or online service, also uses a modem. Dial-up access has traditionally been an easy way for mobile and home users to connect to the Internet to check e-mail, read the news,

and access other information. Because dial-up access uses standard telephone lines, the speed of the connection is limited.

Because dial-up access is slow-speed technology, many home and business users have opted for higher-speed broadband Internet connections through cable television (CATV) networks, DSL, or satellite.

With more than 100 million homes wired for cable television, it is not surprising that more and more users are getting Internet access from their cable company. Road Runner is a popular high-speed CATV online service provided by AOL Time Warner. CATV uses a high-speed **cable modem** that sends and receives data over the cable television network.

As shown in Figure 2-12 on the next page, CATV (also called cable) service enters your home through a single line and then is split between your television and your cable modem, which, in turn, is connected to your computer. Access speeds using CATV can be significantly faster than access speeds using dial-up, in many cases 20 to 50 times faster.

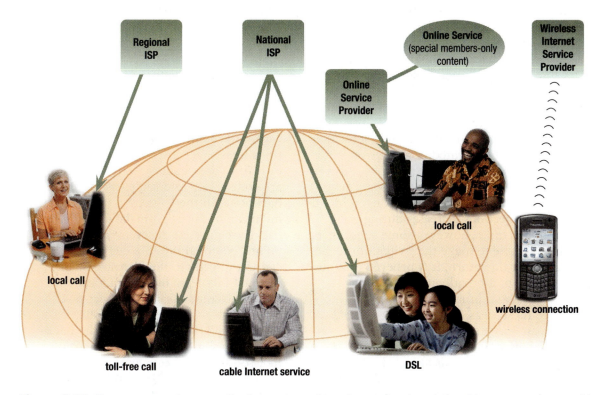

Figure 2-11 Common ways to access the Internet are through a regional or national Internet service provider, an online service provider, or a wireless Internet service provider.

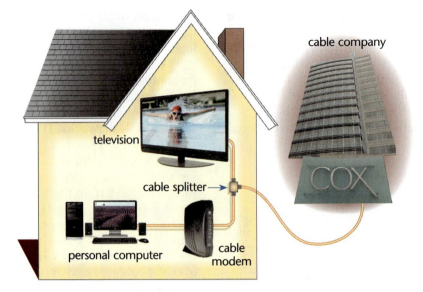

Figure 2-12 A typical cable modem installation.

Another high-speed alternative is a **digital subscriber line (DSL)** that transmits data on existing standard telephone lines. DSL can provide Internet access from 25 to 150 times faster than Internet access using a dial-up connection. A third option is satellite. Similar to a cable or DSL modem, a **satellite modem** provides high-speed Internet connections. It communicates with a satellite via a satellite dish. Installation and monthly access fees for cable, DSL, and satellite services vary.

All three — cable, DSL, and satellite modems — use broadband technologies. In addition to access speed, another advantage of using cable, DSL, and satellite services is that they are dedicated or always-on connections to the Internet, unlike a dial-up connection, which must be reestablished each time it is used. Subscriptions to broadband connections increases during good economic times, however, some subscribers may hesitate to make the switch during an economic downturn. It is believed that once the price of a broadband connection decreases and broadband is available in more rural areas, its popularity will increase further.

Many home users set up a Wi-Fi network, which sends signals to a communications device that is connected to a high-speed Internet service such as cable or DSL. Many hotels and airports provide broadband (often wireless) Internet connections for a usage or per-day fee;

others provide these services for free. In many public locations, people connect wirelessly to the Internet through a **public Internet access point**. Public Internet access points are appearing in airports, hotels, shopping malls, schools, and coffee shops providing wireless Internet access either for a usage fee or for free.

THE INTERNET BACKBONE

The inner structure of the Internet works much like a transportation system. Just as highways connect major cities and carry the bulk of the automotive traffic across the country, the main communications lines that have the heaviest amount of traffic (data packets) on the Internet are collectively referred to as the **Internet backbone**. In the United States, the communications lines that make up the Internet backbone intersect at several different points. National ISPs use dedicated lines to connect directly to the Internet. Smaller regional ISPs lease lines from local telephone companies to connect to national networks. These smaller, slower-speed networks extend from the backbone into regions and local communities like roads and streets extend to major interstates. Figure 2-13 illustrates how all of the components of the Internet work together to transfer data over the Internet from and to your computer using a cable modem connection.

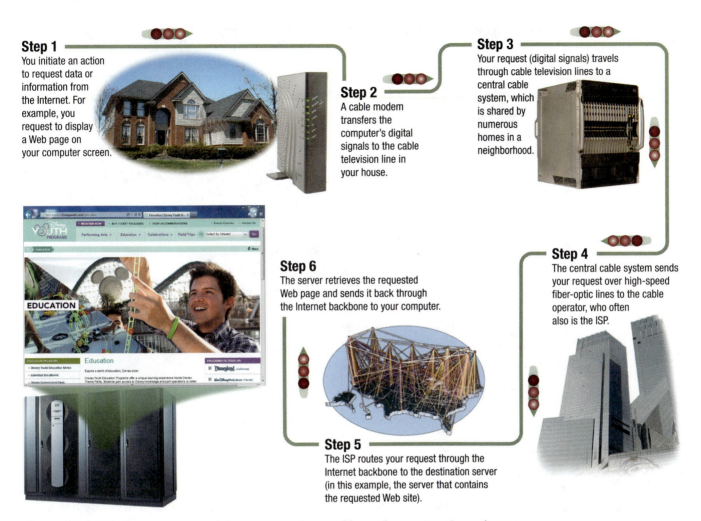

Step 1
You initiate an action to request data or information from the Internet. For example, you request to display a Web page on your computer screen.

Step 2
A cable modem transfers the computer's digital signals to the cable television line in your house.

Step 3
Your request (digital signals) travels through cable television lines to a central cable system, which is shared by numerous homes in a neighborhood.

Step 4
The central cable system sends your request over high-speed fiber-optic lines to the cable operator, who often also is the ISP.

Step 5
The ISP routes your request through the Internet backbone to the destination server (in this example, the server that contains the requested Web site).

Step 6
The server retrieves the requested Web page and sends it back through the Internet backbone to your computer.

Figure 2-13 How data might travel the Internet using a cable modem connection at home.

INTERNET ADDRESSES

The Internet relies on an addressing system much like that of the postal system to send data to a computer at a specific destination. Each computer's location on the Internet has a specific numeric address consisting of four groups of numbers. Because these all-numeric computer addresses are difficult to remember and use, the Internet supports the use of text-based names that represent the numeric address. The text version of a computer address is called a **domain name**. Figure 2-14 shows both the numeric address and the domain name of the CengageBrain Web site. The components of a domain name are separated by periods, each of which is referred to as a dot.

For domestic Web sites, the rightmost portion of the domain name contains a domain type label that identifies the type of organization that maintains the Web site. The rightmost portion of a university Web site, for example, is .edu, which denotes it as a site operated by an educational institution. The domain names for some K-12 school sites include the label .k12 followed by the abbreviation for the school's state. For international Web sites, the domain name also includes a country code, such as .us for the United States and .uk for the United Kingdom. Figure 2-15 on the next page lists common domain type labels, as well as several country code abbreviations.

numeric address

domain name

Figure 2-14 The numeric address and domain name for the CengageBrain Web site.

[a] This table lists domain labels commonly used today.

Domain Label	Type of Organization
com	Commercial organizations, businesses, and companies
edu	Educational institutions
gov	Government institutions
mil	Military organizations
net	Network providers
org	Nonprofit organizations
k12	K-12 schools

[b] A partial listing of country code abbreviations.

Abbreviation	Country	Abbreviation	Country
au	Australia	jp	Japan
aq	Antarctica	nl	Netherlands
ca	Canada	se	Sweden
de	Germany	th	Thailand
dk	Denmark	uk	United Kingdom
fr	France	us	United States

Figure 2-15 Examples of domain labels and country code abbreviations.

Web Info

For an overview of the World Wide Web, visit the Computer Concepts CourseMate Web site at *www.cengagebrain.com*, navigate to the Chapter 2 Web Info resource for this book, click Web Info, and then click WWW.

FAQ

How do I change my Web browser's home page?

To change the home page in Microsoft Internet Explorer, click Tools, click Internet Options, click the General tab in the Home page section, type or paste the URL for the desired Web page, and then click the OK button.

The World Wide Web

Although many people use the terms World Wide Web and Internet interchangeably, the World Wide Web is just one of the many services available on the Internet. The Internet has been in existence since the late 1960s, but the World Wide Web came into existence in the early 1990s. Since then, however, it has grown phenomenally to become the most widely used service on the Internet.

The **World Wide Web**, or simply **Web**, consists of a worldwide collection of electronic documents that have built-in hyperlinks to other related documents. These **hyperlinks**, also called **links**, allow users to navigate quickly from one Web page to another, regardless of whether the Web pages are located on the same computer or on different computers in different countries. A **Web page** is an electronic document viewed on the Web. A Web page can contain text, graphics, sound, and video, as well as hyperlinks to other Web pages. A **Web site** is a collection of related Web pages. Most Web sites have a starting point, called a **home page**, which is similar to a book cover or table of contents for the site and provides information about the site's purpose and content.

Each Web page on a Web site has a unique address, called a **Uniform Resource Locator (URL)**. As shown in Figure 2-16, a URL consists of a protocol, domain name, and sometimes the path to a specific Web page. Most Web page URLs begin with **http://**, which stands for **Hypertext Transfer Protocol**, the communications protocol used to transfer pages on the Web. You access and view Web pages using a software program called a Web browser, or browser.

Some Web pages are static (fixed); others are dynamic (changing). All visitors to a **static Web page** see the same content. In contrast, visitors to a **dynamic Web page** can customize some or all of the viewed content, such as stock quotes, weather for a region, or ticket availability for flights, which means visitors see content unique to their settings. Some industry experts use the terms **Web 2.0** and **participatory Web** to refer to Web sites that allow users to modify Web site content, provide a means for users to share personal information (social networking), and have application software built into the site for visitors to use.

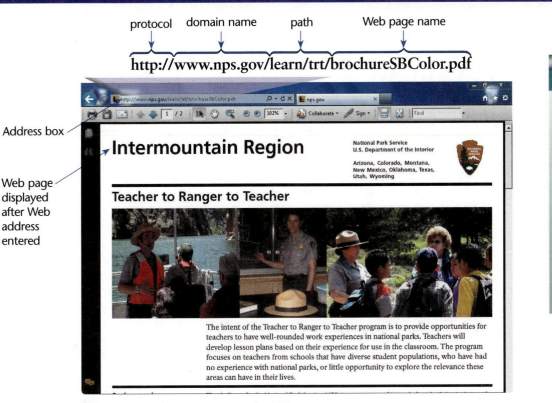

protocol   domain name   path   Web page name

http://www.nps.gov/learn/trt/brochureSBColor.pdf

Address box

Web page displayed after Web address entered

Figure 2-16 The components of a URL.

FAQ

How does a person or company obtain a domain name?

You register for a domain name via a registrar, which is an organization that maintains a master list of names for a particular top-level domain, .com, for example. Some registrars also offer Web site hosting.

The Web has evolved through versions 1.0 and 2.0, and work is underway to develop Web 3.0. **Web 3.0** or **Semantic Web** is when the semantics of information and services on the Web is defined, thus allowing the Web to understand and satisfy the requests of people to use Web content instantly. For example, your computer will be able to scan a Web page for information in much the same way that you do in order to look for specific useful information. If you need the location of the nearest eye doctor and the time when your brother's flight from Chicago actually will land, Web 3.0 first will provide that information and then search your calendar, checking to see if your schedule allows time for the eye doctor appointment before picking up your brother at the airport. In essence, the Web will become one huge searchable database, and automated agents of every type will retrieve the data you request. Some researchers predict that this next generation of the Web will perform practically any task imaginable.

The Web pages that constitute a Web site are stored on a server, called a Web server. A **Web server** is a computer that delivers (serves) requested Web pages. For example, when you enter the URL *www.cengagebrain.com* in your browser's address box, your *browser* sends a request

to the server whose domain name is *cengagebrain.com*. The server then fetches the CengageBrain home page and sends it to your browser. Web servers can store multiple Web sites.

HOW A WEB PAGE WORKS

A Web page is a hypertext or hypermedia document residing on an Internet computer. A Web page can contain text, graphics, video, and sound. A **hypertext** document contains text hyperlinks to other documents. A **hypermedia** document contains text, graphics, video, or sound hyperlinks that connect to other documents.

Three types of hyperlinks exist. **Target hyperlinks** link to another location in the same document. **Relative hyperlinks** link to another document on the same Internet server. **Absolute hyperlinks** link to another document on a different Internet server that could be across the country or across the world.

Hypertext and hypermedia allow students to learn in a nonlinear way. Reading a book from cover to cover is a linear way of learning. Branching off and investigating related topics as you encounter them is a nonlinear way of learning, also known as **discovery learning**. As students' interest inspires them to learn more, the Web allows them to continue to explore for additional sources of information on any given topic. **Web surfing** is displaying pages from one Web site after another.

A **Webmaster** is the person responsible for developing Web pages and maintaining a Web site. Webmasters and other Web page developers create and format Web pages using **Hypertext Markup Language (HTML)**, which is a set of special codes, called **tags**, that define the placement and format of text, graphics, video, and sound on a Web page. Because HTML can be difficult to learn and use, many other user-friendly tools exist for **Web publishing**, which is the development and maintenance of Web pages. Today, many teachers are utilizing user-friendly programs, such as Dreamweaver, WebBlender, Microsoft Word, Publisher, Apple iWork, Wikispaces, and many other programs to publish and maintain their own classroom Web pages (Figure 2-17a).

Figure 2-17 The HTML code (Figure 2-17b) for the top portion of the Web page (Figure 2-17a). Web browser software interprets the HTML tags and displays the text, graphics, and hyperlinks.

WEB BROWSER SOFTWARE

As discussed, you access and view Web pages using a software program called a Web browser. A **Web browser**, or **browser**, is application software that allows users to access and view Web pages or access Web 2.0 programs. Figure 2-17b shows the HTML source document used to create the teacher's Web page shown in Figure 2-17a. Your Web browser translates the source document, which includes HTML tags, into a functional and beautiful Web page with many interactive features. Internet-enabled mobile devices such as smartphones use a special type of browser, called a **microbrowser**, which is designed for their small screens and limited computing power. Many Web sites design Web pages specifically for display on a microbrowser.

Besides HTML, current Web development tools utilize newer languages like **eXtensible Markup Language (XML)** and **eXtensible HTML (XHTML)**. **XML** is a format increasing in popularity that allows Web page authors to create customized **tags** known as **schema**. The tags are stored in libraries and can be used in Cascading Style Sheets. A **Cascading Style Sheet (CSS)** is a simple mechanism for adding style (e.g. fonts, colors, spacing) to Web documents and defines style and formatting properties that are applied to HTML and/or XML-based Web pages. **XHTML** is flexible and also enables Web pages to be displayed on smartphones.

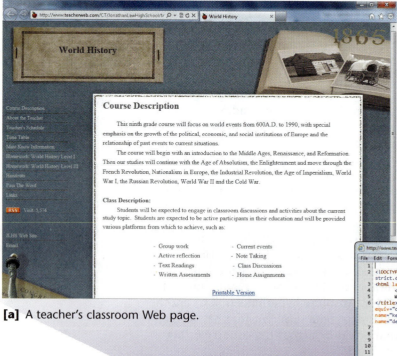

[a] A teacher's classroom Web page.

[b] HTML source document.

The first Web browsers used only text commands and displayed only text-based documents. In 1993, Marc Andreessen, a student at the University of Illinois, created a graphical Web browser called Mosaic. **Mosaic** displayed documents that included graphics and used a graphical interface. The graphical interface made it easier and more enjoyable to view Web documents and contributed to the rapid growth of the Web. Andreessen later developed the Netscape Navigator Web browser.

Before you can use a Web browser to view pages on the World Wide Web, your computer or mobile device has to connect to the Internet through an ISP or online service. When the browser program opens, it retrieves and displays a home page. As discussed earlier, a home page often is used to describe the first page at a Web site. The same term, home page, describes the Web page designated as the page to display each time you start your browser. Most browsers utilize their own Web page as the default home page, but you may change your browser's home page at any time. Many teachers, for example, set their school's home page as their browser's home page so it is the first page they see when they start their browser.

After the browser retrieves a Web page using the page's URL, it can take anywhere from a few seconds to several minutes to display the page on your computer screen. The speed at which a Web page displays depends on the speed of the Internet connection, your computer, and the amount of graphics on the Web page. Many current Web browsers support **tabbed browsing**, where the top of the browser displays a tab (similar to a file folder tab) for each Web page you open (Figure 2-18). Click a tab to move from one open Web page to another.

Browsers display hyperlinks to other documents either as underlined text of a different color or as a graphical image. When you position the mouse pointer over a hyperlink, the mouse pointer changes to a small hand with a pointing finger (Figure 2-18). Some browsers also display the URL of the hyperlinked document at the bottom of the screen. You can display the document by clicking the hyperlink with a pointing device or by typing the URL in the location or Address text box of the Web browser. To remind you that you have seen a document, some browsers change the color of a text hyperlink after you click it.

Two ways to keep track of Web pages you have viewed are a history list and a favorites or bookmark list. A **history list** records the pages viewed during the time you are online, also known as a session. If you think you might want to return to a page in a future session, you can save its location as a favorite or bookmark. A **favorite** or **bookmark** consists of the title and URL of a page. Favorite lists, also called **bookmarks**, are stored on your computer, and may be used in future Web sessions. Favorites, bookmarks, and history lists allow you to display a Web page quickly by clicking the name in the list.

Web page address; also called location or URL

pointer positioned over a hypertext link changes shape to a hand with a pointing finger

tabbed browsing

Figure 2-18 An example of a Web page.

WEB SITE CATEGORIES

Figure 2-19 summarizes popular categories of Web sites. Many Web sites fall into more than one of these categories. Today's digital generation is actively involved and interacting with many newer features of the World Wide Web on a daily basis, including using Web apps on smartphones, podcasting using both audio and video, social networks, wikis, Role-Playing Games (RPG), Massively Multiplayer Online Role-Playing Games (MMORGs), and blogs to name just a few. Understanding the impact of these Web-based technologies on today's digital generation is critically important to your success as a classroom teacher.

Category	Web Site Description
Portal	A **portal** is a Web site that offers a variety of Internet services from a single, convenient location. Most portals offer free services including search engine and/or subject directory, news, sports and weather, and many other services. Many portals have **online communities**, which are Web sites that join specific groups of people with similar interests or relationships.
News	A news Web site contains newsworthy material including stories and articles relating to current events, life, money, sports, and the weather.
Informational	An informational Web site contains factual information. Many United States government agencies have informational Web sites providing information such as census data, tax codes, and the congressional budget.
Business	A business Web site contains content that promotes or sells products or services and most businesses have a business/marketing Web site. Many of these companies also allow you to purchase their products or services online.
Education	An educational Web site offers exciting and challenging avenues for formal and informal teaching and learning. Many of the Web sites included as links at this textbook's companion Web site are educational Web sites.
Entertainment	An entertainment Web site offers an interactive and engaging environment. Popular entertainment Web sites offer music, videos, sports, games, ongoing Web episodes, sweepstakes, chats, and more. Sophisticated entertainment Web sites often partner with other technologies. For example, you can cast your vote about a topic on a television show.
Advocacy	An advocacy Web site contains content that describes a cause, opinion, or idea. These Web sites usually present views of a particular group or association.
Blog	A **blog**, short for **Weblog**, is an informal Web site consisting of time-stamped articles, or posts, in a diary or journal format, usually listed in reverse chronological order. A blog that contains video clips is called a **video blog**, or **vlog**. A **microblog** allows users to publish short messages, usually between 100 and 200 characters, for others to read. Twitter is a popular microblog. Blogs have become an important means of worldwide communications. Teachers create blogs to collaborate with other teachers and students.
Wiki	A **wiki** is a collaborative Web site that allows users to create, add to, modify, or delete the Web site content via their Web browser. Most wikis are open to modification by the general public. A popular wiki is Wikipedia, a free Web encyclopedia.
Online Social Network	An **online social network**, also called a social networking Web site, is a Web site that encourages members in its online community to share their interests, ideas, stories, photos, music, and videos with other registered users. Most include chat rooms, newsgroups, and other communications services. Popular social networking Web sites include Facebook and MySpace. A **media sharing Web site** is a specific type of online social network that enables members to share media such as photos, music, and videos. Flickr, Fotki, and Webshots are popular photo sharing communities; PixelFish and YouTube are popular video sharing communities.
Web Application	A **Web application**, or **Web app**, is a Web site that allows users to access and interact with software through a Web browser on any computer or device that is connected to the Internet. Examples of Web applications include Google Docs (word processing, spreadsheets, presentations), TurboTax Online (tax preparation), and Windows Live Hotmail (e-mail).
Content Aggregator	A content aggregator is a business that gathers and organizes Web content and then distributes, or feeds, the content to subscribers for free or a fee. Examples of distributed content include news, music, video, and pictures.
Personal	A personal Web site that might be a single Web page or a collection of Web pages maintained by a private individual or a family not usually associated with any organization.

Figure 2-19 Popular Web site categories.

SEARCHING FOR INFORMATION ON THE WEB

Searching for information on the Web can be challenging due to the sheer volume of content on the Web. In addition, no central menu or catalog of Web site content and addresses exists. Many Web sites, however, do provide search tools and maintain organized directories of Web sites to help you locate specific information. **Search tools** enable users to locate information found at Web sites all over the world. Two basic types of search tools exist: search engines and subject directories.

A **search engine** is a specific type of search tool that finds Web sites, Web pages, and Internet files that match one or more keywords you enter. Some search engines look for simple word matches and others allow for more specific searches on a series of words or an entire phrase. Search engines do not actually search the entire Internet (such a search would take an extremely long time). Instead, they search an index or database of Internet sites and documents. Search tool companies continuously update their databases. Because of the explosive growth of the Internet and because search engines scan different parts of the Internet and in different ways, performing the same search using different search engines often yields different results. The table in Figure 2-20 lists some operators you can include in your search text to refine your search. Instead of using operators to refine your search text, many search engines have an Advanced Search feature that displays a form that assists with refining your search.

Many search engines also provide subject directories. A **subject directory** is a type of search tool that allows users to navigate to areas of interest without having to enter keywords. Surfing subject directories is a simple matter of selecting topics and following the links for that topic. Subject directories are usually organized in categories such as education, sports, entertainment, or business.

MULTIMEDIA ON THE WEB

Most Web pages include more than just formatted text and hyperlinks. In fact, some of the more exciting Web developments involve **multimedia**, which is the combination of graphics, animation, audio, video, 3-D modeling, and virtual reality (VR). A Web page that incorporates color, sound, motion, and pictures with text has much more appeal than one with text on a plain background. Combining text, audio, video, animation, and sound brings a Web page to life, increases the types of information available on the Web, expands the Web's potential uses, and makes the Internet a more entertaining place to explore. Although multimedia Web pages often require more time to open because they contain large files such as video or audio clips, the pages usually are worth the wait.

Web Info

For links to many popular education-related search engines, visit the Computer Concepts CourseMate Web site at *www.cengagebrain.com*, navigate to the Chapter 2 Web Info resource for this book, click Web Info, and then click Search Tools.

Operator	Keyword Examples	Description
AND (+)	art AND music smoking health hazards fish +pollutants +runoff	Requires both words to be in the page No operator between words or the plus sign (+) are shortcuts for the Boolean operator AND
OR	mental illness OR insane canine OR dog OR puppy flight attendant OR stewardess OR steward	Requires only one of the words to be in the page
AND NOT (–)	auto AND NOT SUV AND NOT convertible computers – programming shakespeare – hamlet – (romeo+juliet)	Excludes pages with the word following AND NOT The minus sign (–) is a shortcut for the Boolean operator AND NOT
( )	physics AND (relativity OR einstein)	Parentheses group portions of Boolean operators together
" "	"harry potter" "19th century literature"	Requires the exact phrase within quotation marks to be in the page
*	writ* clou*	The asterisk (*) at the end of words substitutes for any combination of characters

Figure 2-20 Use search engine operators to help refine a search.

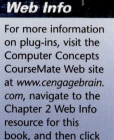

Web Info

For more information on plug-ins, visit the Computer Concepts CourseMate Web site at *www.cengagebrain. com*, navigate to the Chapter 2 Web Info resource for this book, and then click Plug-ins.

Plug-In Application		Description	Web Address
Acrobat Reader	Get ADOBE® READER®	View, navigate, and print Portable Document Format (PDF) files — documents are formatted to look just as they look in print	adobe.com
Flash Player	Get ADOBE® FLASH® PLAYER	View dazzling graphics and animation, hear outstanding sound and music, display Web pages across an entire screen	adobe.com
Java	» Get it Now	Enables Web browser to run programs written in Java, which adds interactivity to Web pages	java.com
QuickTime	Get QuickTime Free Download	View animation, music, audio, video, and VR panoramas and objects directly on a Web page	apple.com
RealPlayer	real RealPlayer DOWNLOAD	Listen to live and on-demand near-CD-quality audio and newscast-quality video, stream audio and video content for faster viewing, play MP3 files, create music CDs	real.com
Shockwave Player	Get ADOBE® SHOCKWAVE® PLAYER	Experience dynamic interactive multimedia, 3-D graphics, and streaming audio	adobe.com
Silverlight	Install Microsoft® Silverlight™	Experience high-definition video, high-resolution interactive multimedia, and streaming audio and video	microsoft.com
Windows Media Player	Windows MediaPlayer	Listen to live and on-demand audio, play or edit WMA and MP3 files, burn CDs, and watch DVD movies	microsoft.com

Figure 2-21 Plug-ins can extend the multimedia capability of Web browsers. Users usually can download them free from the developers' Web sites.

Most browsers have the capability to display multimedia elements on a Web page. Sometimes, however, your browser needs an additional program called a plug-in. A **plug-in** is a program that extends the capability of the browser.

Figure 2-22 The use of colorful graphic designs and images enhances the visual appeal of the Web page and helps to convey the messages.

You can download or copy plug-ins free from many Web sites (Figure 2-21 above). In fact, Web pages that use multimedia elements often include links to Web sites containing the required plug-in. Most browsers include commonly used plug-ins, but users often have to update their browsers as new plug-ins become available. Some plug-ins run on mobile devices as well as computers. Others have special versions for mobile devices.

The following sections discuss Web development in the multimedia areas of graphics, animation, audio, video, and virtual reality.

GRAPHICS A **graphic**, or **graphical image**, is a digital representation of nontext information such as a drawing, chart, or photograph. Graphics were the first medium used to enhance the text-based Internet. The introduction of graphical Web browsers allowed Web page developers to incorporate illustrations, logos, and other images into Web pages. Today, many Web pages use colorful graphical designs and images to convey messages (Figure 2-22).

Abbreviation/ File Extension	Name	Uses
BMP/.bmp	Bitmap	Desktop background, scanned images
GIF/.gif	Graphics Interchange Format	Simple diagrams, shapes, images with a few colors
JPEG/.jpg	Joint Photographic Experts Group	Digital camera photos
PNG/.png	Portable Network Graphics	Web graphics
TIFF/.tif	Tagged Image File Format	Photos used by printing industry

Figure 2-23 The Web uses graphics file formats for images.

Two common file formats for graphical images found on the Web are JPEG (pronounced JAY-peg) and GIF (pronounced jiff or giff). Figure 2-23 above lists these and other file formats used on the Internet.

The Web contains thousands of image files on countless subjects that you can download at no cost and use for noncommercial purposes. Because some graphical files can be time-consuming to download, some Web sites use thumbnails on their pages. A **thumbnail** is a small version of a larger graphical image that usually you can click to display the full-sized image (Figure 2-24).

ANIMATION Animation is the appearance of motion created by displaying a series of still images in rapid sequence. Animated graphics make Web pages visually more interesting and draw attention to important information or links. For example, text that is animated to scroll across the screen, called a **marquee** (pronounced mar-KEE), can serve as a ticker to display stock updates, news, school sports scores and events, or weather.

One popular type of animation, called an **animated GIF**, is a group of several images combined into a single GIF file. An abundance of education-related animations are available on the Web, many that you can download or copy at no cost.

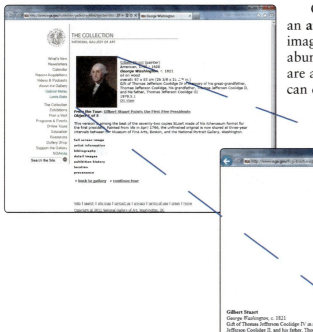

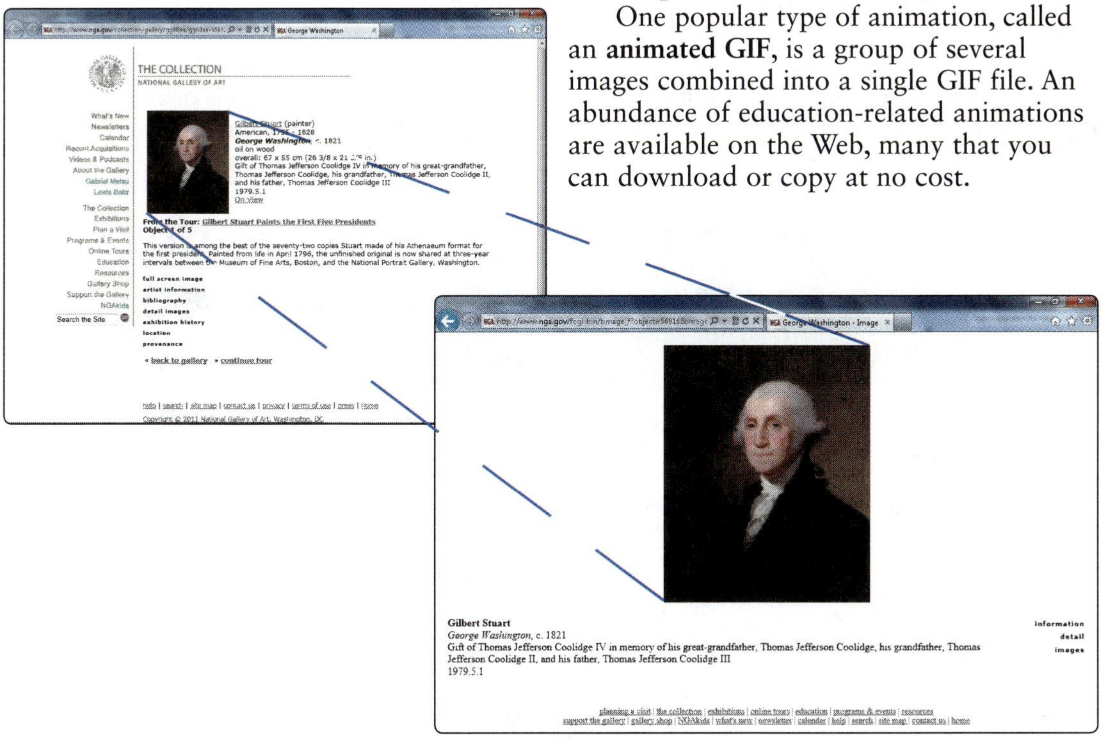

Figure 2-24 After the visitor clicks the thumbnail of the George Washington painting in the top-left screen, a full-sized image of the painting appears in a separate window.

FAQ

How long does it take to download a single song?

Depending on the speed of your Internet connection and the size of the file, a single song can take from 1 to 20 minutes to download.

AUDIO   On the Web, you can listen to prerecorded audio clips and live audio. **Audio** is music, speech, or any other sound. Simple Web audio applications consist of individual sound files that are available for downloading to a computer. After being downloaded, you can play or listen to the contents of these files. Audio files exist in a variety of formats, including MP3, WAV, WMA (Windows Media Audio), RealAudio, and QuickTime. Audio files are compressed to reduce their file sizes. For example, the MP3 format reduces an audio file to about one-tenth of its original size, while preserving the original quality of the sound.

Users can download copyrighted music legally only if the copyright holder of the music has granted permission for users to download and play it. Many music publishers allow users to purchase and download an entire CD of music tracks to their hard disk. However, controversy concerning copyright infringement has surfaced due to the ease with which music can be transferred across the Internet.

Most current operating systems contain a program, called a **player**, that can play audio files on your computer. Windows Media Player, RealPlayer, and iTunes are popular players. If your player will not play a particular audio format, you can download the necessary player free from the Web.

More advanced Web audio applications use streaming audio. **Streaming** is the process of transferring data in a continuous and even flow. Streaming is important because most users do not have fast enough Internet connections to download large audio files quickly. **Streaming audio** enables you to listen to the sound file as it downloads to your computer. Many radio and television stations use streaming audio to broadcast music, interviews, talk shows, sporting events, music videos, news, live concerts, and other segments.

Podcasting is another popular method of distributing audio. A **podcast** is recorded audio, usually an MP3 file, stored on a Web site that can be downloaded to a computer or a portable media player such as an iPod (Figure 2-25). Examples of podcasts include music, radio shows, news stories, classroom lectures, political messages, and television commentaries. Users subscribe to a feed and receive new audio files automatically by using **Really Simple Syndication (RSS)**, which is a protocol that allows users to receive the feeds automatically. In education, podcasting can be very useful for teachers who want to send class content, announcements, and so on to their students automatically. Virtually all students who own iPods or other similar devices are using these digital communications tools on a daily basis.

Figure 2-25 Apple provides extensive podcast-related resources for educators, including podcast tools, tutorials, and even free server space.

VIDEO Video consists of full-motion images that are played back at various speeds. Many Web sites include real-time video to enhance visitors' understanding of information or for entertainment (Figure 2-26).

You can use the Web to watch live and/or prerecorded coverage of your favorite television programs or enjoy a live performance of your favorite vocalist. You can upload, share, or view video clips at a video sharing Web site such as YouTube. Educators, politicians, and businesses are using video blogs to engage students, voters, and consumers.

Like audio, Web video applications consist of individual video files, such as movies or television clips, that a user must download completely before viewing. Because video segments usually are large and take a long time to download, they often are short.

Streaming video allows you to view longer or live video images as the video file downloads to your computer. Windows Media Player, RealPlayer, and Apple QuickTime can play downloaded or streaming video files.

Streaming video is creating new possibilities for teaching and learning and is having a profound impact on today's digital generation. As the speed of the Internet increases dramatically over the next few years, students from even the most remote schools will have access to thousands of full-motion videos from all over the world that cover an almost endless multitude of topics.

VIRTUAL REALITY Virtual reality (VR) is the simulation of a real or imagined environment that appears as a three-dimensional (3-D) space. On the Web, VR involves the display of 3-D images that you can explore and manipulate interactively. Using special VR software, a Web developer can create an entire 3-D site that contains infinite space and depth called a **VR world**. A VR world, for example, might show a room with furniture. You can walk through a VR room by moving your pointing device forward, backward, or to the side. To view a VR world, you may need to update your Web browser by downloading a VR plug-in program.

Games are a popular use of virtual reality by K-12 digital students, but VR has many practical applications as well. Companies can use VR to showcase products or create advertisements. Architects create VR models of buildings and rooms to show their clients how a construction project will look before construction begins. Virtual reality also opens up a world of learning opportunities. Science educators, for example, can create VR models of molecules, organisms, and other

Figure 2-26 Discovery Education is an example of a Web site that provides extensive video resources for educators and students.

structures for students to examine (Figure 2-27). Students also can take virtual tours of historic sites located all over the world. Several schools even use VR to allow parents to take a virtual tour of the school from their home.

Figure 2-27 This instructional software uses VR so students can conduct virtual dissections.

Other Internet Services

Although the World Wide Web is the most talked about service on the Internet, many other Internet services are available. These services include e-mail, FTP, newsgroups and message boards, mailing lists, instant messaging, chat rooms, and Voice over IP (VoIP), also known as Internet telephony. Each of these services is discussed in the following sections.

E-MAIL

E-mail (**electronic mail**) is the transmission of messages and files via a computer network. E-mail was one of the original features of the Internet, enabling scientists and researchers working on government-sponsored projects to communicate with their colleagues at other locations. Today, e-mail enables administrators, teachers, and students to communicate with millions of Internet users all over the world. E-mail has become a primary communications method for both personal and business use.

Using an **e-mail program**, you can create, send, receive, forward, store, print, and delete messages. E-mail messages can be simple text or they can include attachments such as word processing documents, graphics, audio or video clips, and even family pictures (Figure 2-28).

When you receive an e-mail message, your ISP's software stores the message in your personal **mailbox** on its mail server. A **mail server** is a server that contains users' mailboxes and associated e-mail messages. Most ISPs and online services provide an Internet e-mail program and a mailbox on a mail server as a standard part of their Internet access services. You also can use free e-mail services such as Hotmail or Yahoo! Mail.

An **e-mail address** is a combination of a username and a domain name that identifies the user so he can both send and receive messages (Figure 2-29). Your **username** is a unique combination of characters that identifies you, and it must differ from other usernames located on the same mail server. Your username sometimes is limited to eight characters and often is a combination of your first and last names, such as the initial of your first name plus your last name. You may choose a nickname or any combination of characters for your username, but unusual combinations might be harder to remember.

Although no complete listing of Internet e-mail addresses exists, several Internet sites list addresses collected from public sources. These sites also allow you to list your e-mail address voluntarily so others may find it. The site might prompt you for other information, such as the high school or college from which you graduated, so others can determine if you are the person they want to reach.

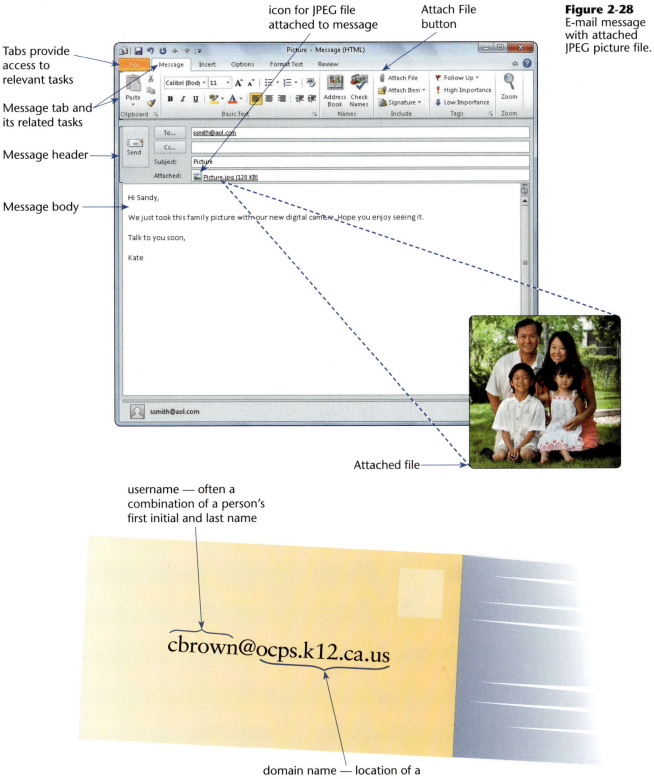

icon for JPEG file attached to message

Attach File button

Figure 2-28
E-mail message with attached JPEG picture file.

Tabs provide access to relevant tasks

Message tab and its related tasks

Message header

Message body

Attached file

username — often a combination of a person's first initial and last name

cbrown@ocps.k12.ca.us

domain name — location of a person's e-mail account

Figure 2-29 An example of an Internet e-mail address. Sometimes, the underscore character or a period separates sections of the user's name; for example, cindy_brown@ocps.k12.ca.us.

FILE TRANSFER PROTOCOL (FTP)

File Transfer Protocol (FTP) is an Internet standard that allows you to exchange files with other computers on the Internet. For example, if you click a link on a Web page in your browser window that begins to download a file to your hard disk, you probably are using FTP.

An **FTP server** is a computer that allows users to upload and download files using FTP. An FTP server contains one or more FTP sites. An **FTP site** is a collection of files, including text, graphics, audio, video, and program files. Some FTP sites limit file transfers to individuals who have authorized accounts (usernames and passwords) on the FTP server. Many corporations, for example, maintain FTP sites for their employees.

Other FTP sites allow **anonymous FTP**, whereby anyone can transfer some, if not all, available files. Many educational sites, for example, have FTP sites that use anonymous FTP to allow educators to download lesson plans and other files. Many program files located on anonymous FTP sites are freeware or shareware programs. Many FTP sites allow users to download educational and other application software for a free 30-day evaluation period (Figure 2-30). This allows teachers, administrators, and other users to evaluate software for content and appropriateness before purchasing.

To view or use an FTP file, first you must **download**, or copy, it to your computer. In most cases, you click the filename to begin the download procedure. Large files on FTP sites often are compressed to reduce storage space and download transfer time. Before you use a compressed file, you must expand it with a decompression program, such as WinZip or Stuffit. Such programs usually are available at the FTP site or are packaged with the file you download.

In some cases, you may want to **upload**, or copy, a file to an FTP site. To upload files from your computer to an FTP site, you use an FTP program. Many ISPs include an FTP program when you subscribe to their service. Several FTP programs also are available on the Web. In addition, many operating systems such as Windows have built-in FTP capabilities.

NEWSGROUPS AND MESSAGE BOARDS

A **newsgroup** is an online area in which users conduct written discussions about a particular subject. To participate in a discussion, a user sends a message to the newsgroup and other users in the newsgroup read and reply to the message. The entire collection of Internet newsgroups is called **Usenet**, which contains thousands of newsgroups on a multitude of topics. Some major topic areas include education, news, recreation, business, and computers.

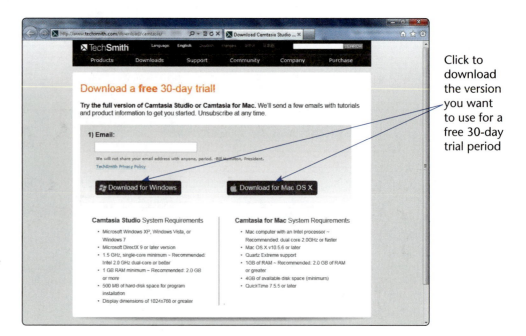

Figure 2-30
To ensure you can find the file when the download is complete, you should write down the file's name and the location where the file is being saved.

Click to download the version you want to use for a free 30-day trial period

A **news server** is a computer that stores and distributes newsgroup messages. Most universities, corporations, ISPs, online services, and other large organizations have a news server. Some newsgroups require you to enter your username and password to participate in the discussion. These types of newsgroups are used when the messages on the newsgroup are to be viewed only by authorized members, such as students taking a college course.

To participate in a newsgroup, you must use a program called a **newsreader**, which is included with most browsers. The newsreader enables you to access a newsgroup to read a previously entered message, called an **article**, and add an article of your own, called a **posting**. A newsreader also keeps track of which articles you have and have not read.

Newsgroup members often post articles as a reply to another article — either to answer a question or to comment on material in the original article. These replies often cause the author of the original article, or others, to post additional articles related to the original article. The original article and all subsequent related replies are called a **thread** or **threaded discussion**. A thread can be short-lived or continue for some time, depending on the nature of the topic and the interest of the participants.

Using the newsreader, you can search for newsgroups discussing a particular subject, such as a type of musical instrument, brand of sports equipment, or educational topic. If you like the discussion in a particular newsgroup, you can **subscribe** to it, which means your newsreader saves the location so you can access it easily in the future.

A popular Web-based type of discussion group that does not require a newsreader is a message board. **Message boards** also are called discussion boards and typically are easier to use than newsgroups. Many Web sites provide message boards for their users (Figure 2-31).

MAILING LISTS

A **mailing list** is a group of e-mail names and addresses given a single name. When a user sends a message to a mailing list, every person on the list receives a copy of the message in her mailbox. To add your e-mail name and address to a mailing list, you subscribe to it; to remove your name, you **unsubscribe** from the mailing list. **LISTSERV** is a popular software program used to manage many educational mailing lists.

Web Info

For more information about message boards, visit the Computer Concepts CourseMate Web site at *www.cengagebrain. com*, navigate to the Chapter 2 Web Info resource for this book, and then click Message Boards.

Web Info

For more information on mailing lists, visit the Computer Concepts CourseMate Web site at *www. cengagebrain.com*, navigate to the Chapter 2 Web Info resource for this book, and then click Mailing Lists.

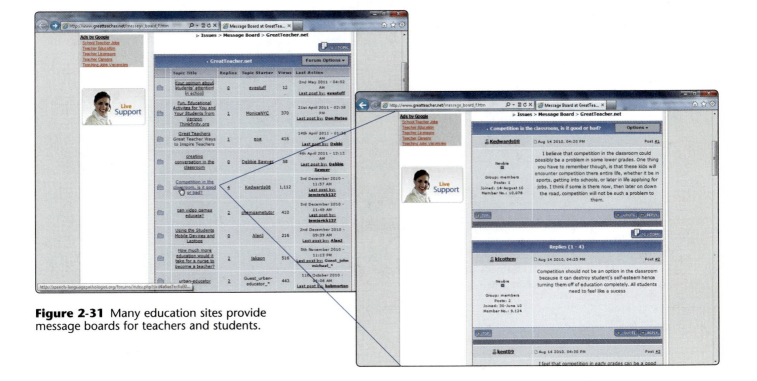

Figure 2-31 Many education sites provide message boards for teachers and students.

The basic difference between a newsgroup and a mailing list is that users on the mailing list discuss topics using e-mail, whereas newsgroup members use a newsreader for discussions. Thousands of mailing lists exist on a variety of topics in areas of entertainment, business, computers, society, culture, health, recreation, and education. To locate a mailing list dealing with a particular topic, you can use your Web browser to search for mailing lists or LISTSERVs.

INSTANT MESSAGING

Instant messaging (IM) is a real-time Internet communications service (Figure 2-32) that notifies you when one or more people are online and then allows you to exchange messages or files, or join a private chat room (discussed next) with them. **Real time** means that you and the people with whom you are conversing are online at the same time. Many IM services can alert you to information, such as calendar appointments, stock quotes, weather, or sport scores. Some IM services support voice and video conversations.

People use IM on all types of computers, including handheld computers and Web-enabled devices. Although popular with all age groups, instant messaging services, such as AOL Instant Messenger, have become a staple of teenage life for tens of millions of middle and high school students from around the world.

While not an Internet service, **text messaging**, known formally as **Short Message Service (SMS)** is a service that permits the sending and receiving of short messages and that is available on most digital mobile phones and other mobile devices. Text messaging is similar to instant messaging, except text messaging is most often associated with cell phones whereas instant messages are usually sent and received using personal computers. The number of text messages sent worldwide has exploded the past few years; experts estimate that the total number of text messages sent daily exceeds the population of the planet, over 10 billion messages daily. Instant messaging and text messaging are the basic forms of communications for the digital generation, that is, between your students and their friends.

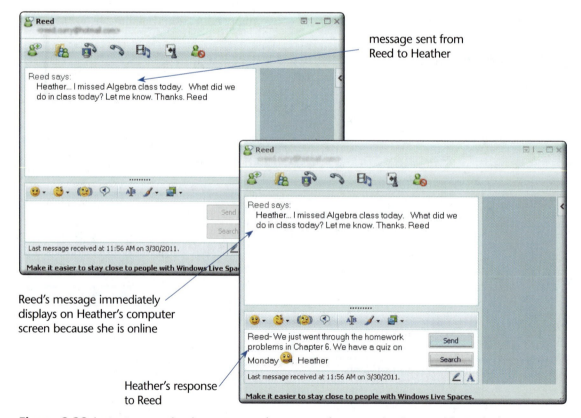

message sent from Reed to Heather

Reed's message immediately displays on Heather's computer screen because she is online

Heather's response to Reed

Figure 2-32 Instant messaging is a very popular means of communication used by today's digital students.

CHAT ROOMS

A **chat** is a real-time typed conversation that takes place on a computer. With chat, when you enter a line of text on your computer screen, your words immediately display on one or more participant's screens. To conduct a chat, you and the people with whom you are conversing must be online at the same time.

A **chat room** refers to the communications medium, or channel, that permits users to chat with each other. Anyone on the channel can participate in the conversation, which usually deals with a specific topic.

To start a chat session, you must connect to a chat server through a **chat client**, which is a program on your computer. Today's browsers usually include a chat client. If yours does not, you can download a chat client from the Web. Some chat clients are text-based only, whereas others support graphical and text-based chats. Some chat rooms support voice or video chats that allow users to hear and see each other.

After you install a chat client, you then can create or join a conversation on a chat server. The channel name should indicate the topic of discussion. The person who creates a channel acts as the channel operator and has responsibility for monitoring the conversation and disconnecting anyone who becomes disruptive. Users can share operator status or transfer operator status to someone else.

Numerous controlled and monitored chat rooms are available for K-12 students and teachers. Several Web sites also exist for the purpose of conducting chats. Some chat sites even allow participants to assume the role or appearance of a character.

VOICE OVER IP (VoIP)

Voice over IP (Internet Protocol), also called **Internet telephony**, enables users to speak to other users over the Internet using their desktop computer, mobile computer, or mobile device. That is, Voice over IP uses the Internet (instead of traditional telephone networks) to connect a calling party to one or more local or long-distance parties.

As you speak into a microphone or telephone connected to your computer, the Internet telephone software and the computer's sound card or the telephone adapter convert your spoken words (analog signals) to digital signals and then transmit the digitized audio over the Internet to the people you are calling. Software and equipment at the receiving end reverse the process so the receiving parties can hear what you said.

Instead of paying a monthly fee for VoIP, one alternative is to use a device, such as a magicJack (Figure 2-33), that provides VoIP for an annual fee of less than $20 (first year cost is $40 which includes the magicJack, a phone number, and first year's service). **magicJack** is a USB device that contains both the software and electronics necessary to place outgoing and receive incoming Internet-based telephone calls using your computer. You can use your traditional telephone simply by plugging it in to the magicJack device, use a headset, or simply use your computer's microphone and speakers. Included in your annual fee are many services, like call waiting, 911 service, voicemail, and more. You also can use your magicJack on multiple computers, simply unplug the magicJack device from one computer and plug into another. To use magicJack, you must have high-speed Internet service and your computer must be turned on.

Figure 2-33 Using a magicJack, you can place and receive Internet calls using your computer, any traditional telephone, and your existing high speed Internet access.

Netiquette

Netiquette, which is short for **Internet etiquette**, is the code of acceptable behaviors users should follow while on the Internet — that is, the conduct expected of individuals while online. Netiquette includes rules for all aspects of the Internet, including the Web, e-mail, FTP, newsgroups and message boards, chat rooms, and instant messaging. Figure 2-34 on the next page outlines the rules of netiquette.

Figure 2-34 The rules of netiquette.

Web Info

For more information about filtering software, visit the Computer Concepts CourseMate Web site at *www.cengagebrain.com*, navigate to the Chapter 2 Web Info resource for this book, and then click Filtering Software.

Web Info

For more information about Acceptable Use Policies (AUPs), visit the Computer Concepts CourseMate Web site at *www.cengagebrain.com*, navigate to the Chapter 2 Web Info resource for this book, and then click AUP.

Netiquette

Golden Rule: *Treat others as you would like them to treat you.*

1. In e-mail, newsgroups, and chat rooms:
   - Keep messages brief using proper grammar and spelling.
   - Be careful when using sarcasm and humor, as it might be misinterpreted.
   - Be polite. Avoid offensive language.
   - Avoid sending or posting **flames**, which are abusive or insulting messages. Do not participate in **flame wars**, which are exchanges of flames.
   - Avoid sending spam, which is the Internet's version of junk mail. **Spam** is an unsolicited e-mail message or newsgroup posting sent to many recipients or newsgroups at once.
   - Do not use all capital letters, which is the equivalent of SHOUTING!
   - Use **emoticons** to express emotion. Popular emoticons include

:)	Smile	:\	Undecided
:(	Frown	:o	Surprised
:|	Indifference	:-D	Laughing

   - Use abbreviations and acronyms for phrases such as

BTW	by the way
FYI	for your information
FWIW	for what it's worth
IMHO	in my humble opinion
TTFN	ta ta for now
TYVM	thank you very much

   - Clearly identify a **spoiler**, which is a message that reveals a solution to a game or ending to a movie or program.

2. Read the **FAQ** (frequently asked questions) document if one exists. Many newsgroups and Web pages have an FAQ.

3. Use your username for your personal use only.

4. Do not assume material is accurate or up to date. Be forgiving of others' mistakes.

5. Never read someone's private e-mail.

Internet Security

Any time a school district or business connects its private network to a public network such as the Internet, it must consider security concerns such as unauthorized access to confidential information. To prevent unauthorized access, schools and businesses implement one or more layers of security. A **firewall** is a general term that refers to both hardware and software used to restrict access to data on a network.

Firewalls deny network access to unauthorized personnel. For example, firewalls restrict students from access to inappropriate materials or sensitive information such as student grades and attendance records.

Even with netiquette guidelines, the Internet still opens up the possibility for inappropriate behaviors and content. For example, amidst the wealth of information and services on the Internet, some content may be inappropriate for certain people. Some Web sites, newsgroups, and chat rooms, for instance, contain content or discussions that are unsuitable for children. Schools need to ensure that students do not gain access to inappropriate or objectionable materials.

To assist schools and parents with these types of issues, many browsers include software that can screen out unacceptable content. You also can purchase stand-alone Internet **filtering software**, which allows parents, teachers, and others to block access to certain materials on the Internet.

Schools help protect students from the negative aspects of the Internet by using filtering software, firewalls, and teacher observation. Most schools also use an **Acceptable Use Policy (AUP)**, which is an outline of user standards that reminds teachers, students, and parents that they are guests on the Internet and that they need to use it appropriately. Most schools require students, teachers, and parents to sign AUPs. Chapter 8 discusses these and other security issues in greater detail.

The Impact of the Internet and the World Wide Web on Education

More than 500 years ago, Johannes Gutenberg developed a printing press that made the written word accessible to the public and revolutionized the way people shared information. The World Wide Web is the Gutenberg printing press of modern times — opening doors to new learning resources and opportunities and allowing the sharing of information and knowledge such as never before. Just a few years ago, most students were unable to visit the Grand Canyon, the White House, the Smithsonian Institution, the National Art Gallery, or the Louvre Museum. Today, students around the world can visit these historic places and thousands of others by exploring these locales using interactive and sometimes even virtual tours on the Web.

Not only does the Internet provide access to extensive text and multimedia resources, it also allows teachers and students to communicate with other teachers and students all over the world. For example, **ePALS** Classroom Exchange is a project designed to enable digital students to develop an understanding of different cultures through student exchanges using many of the Internet-based tools discussed in this chapter (Figure 2-35). The mission of ePALS is to have students creatively write in primary and secondary languages, as well as to do research and gather information about other cultures and individuals. Project ePALS is adaptable for any grade level in any country.

As the Internet expanded and evolved from a text-based communications system into the powerful multimedia communications system of today, educators quickly recognized the tremendous potential of the Internet — and especially the Web — to revolutionize the classroom. By providing a variety of learning tools, the Internet and the Web are transforming the way teachers instruct and the way students learn basic skills and core subjects. These changes have brought the Web to the forefront of instructional strategies in education in a very short period.

Throughout this textbook and its companion Web site accessible via the Computer Concepts Web site at *www.cengagebrain.com*, thousands of links and dozens of exercises will help you understand the incredible possibilities the Web offers for K-12 education in general and your classroom in particular.

The Future of the Internet and the World Wide Web

What is the future of the Internet and the World Wide Web? Without question, the Web will continue to evolve as the primary communications channel for people around the world. As the Web grows in size and operates at higher speeds, it will continue to have a major influence on restructuring K-12 education. Other predictions regarding the future of the Internet and the World Wide Web and its impact on education include the following:

- By 2014, more than two billion communications devices will be in use worldwide, and most of these products will have the ability to access the Web wirelessly.

- Devices that use embedded computers, such as automobiles, will have built-in Internet access capabilities.

- Web search capabilities will be more intelligent and focused. Within a few years, the Web will operate at speeds 10,000 times faster than today.

- The Web will become an integral part of education, revolutionizing the way students learn core subjects.

- The Internet of the future (Web 3.0) will be much larger, helping Web surfers browse more than 250 million anticipated Web sites.

- Use and creation of Web-based video by today's digital generation will continue to grow explosively during the next few years.

- Researchers predict image searches will be common on the Internet in less than 10 years and will include a voice interface, a

Web Info

For more information about ePALS, visit the Computer Concepts CourseMate Web site at *www.cengagebrain. com*, navigate to the Chapter 2 Web Info resource for this book, and then click ePALS.

Integration Strategies

For more information on Your Web, Your Way and Web 2.0, visit the Computer Concepts CourseMate Web site at *www. cengagebrain.com*, and then navigate to the Chapter 2 Digital Media Corner resource for this book.

Figure 2-35 The online project ePALS allows millions of students from all over the world to communicate with each other.

thesaurus, and customized results. For example, facial recognition technology could identify pictures based on facial features, such as blue eyes or dimples. Once an individual is identified, the search engine then could search for other pictures of that person stored on a computer or on the Internet.

■ Many experts believe that separate, proprietary networks used for telephone, television, and radio will merge with the Internet. Eventually, a single, integrated network will exist, made up of many different media that will carry all communications traffic. This is known as **media convergence**, which is a theory in communications in which every mass medium eventually merges into one medium due to the advent of new communications technologies.

APPS AND TABLET COMPUTERS

Two recent technologies have the potential to fundamentally change teaching and learning, do it quickly, and do it in many, many positive and unique ways. Extensive additional information on apps and tablet computers are covered in future chapters and the special feature that follows Chapter 6. Many of the predictions below will be driven by societal issues and could save schools, districts, and states significant funds.

■ Sales of tablet computers will exceed the overall sales of desktop and notebook computers in the next few years. As sales increase, the cost of tablets will continue to decline.

■ Sales of apps will replace many current application software programs as education software quickly morphs into thousands of education apps. These apps will be continuously evaluated by teachers and students; their reviews will drive both real-time improvements and overall sales of successful apps. Decisions on which apps to use in classrooms will be made by users (teachers and students) instead of district level administrators or state/federal bureaucrats.

■ Many schools, districts, and states will create their own standards-based education apps for use by teachers, students, and their parents.

■ Many students will be using note taking apps, like Note Taker HD, which is an app for writing and organizing handwritten notes and diagrams on a tablet computer.

■ Education apps will target specific learning styles, aptitudes, and abilities. Apps will revolutionize the ability of schools to educate students with disabilities.

■ Education apps and tablet computers may indeed measurably increase student achievement (including test scores) and could do it quickly.

Guide to World Wide Web Sites and Search Tools

At the textbook Web site are links to more than 200 popular up-to-date Web sites organized by category and search tools, including education-specific search tools. To display these links, go to the Computer Concepts Web site for this book at *www. cengagebrain.com*, and then navigate to Guide to WWW Sites or Search Tools.

Summary of Communications, Networks, the Internet, and the World Wide Web

Communications will continue to impact how you work, learn, teach, access information, and use computers. Because of communications technology, individuals, schools, and organizations no longer are limited to local data resources; they can obtain information instantly from anywhere in the world. Communications networks are just one way that school districts will use communications technology to meet current instructional and management challenges. In just a few years, the Internet and World Wide Web may redefine education, just as it has transformed modern businesses and today's society. As educators all over the world integrate the Internet and the World Wide Web into their classroom curriculum, their efforts are creating an educational revolution in today's schools — one that is having a significant positive impact on the quality of graduating students.

Integration Strategies

To learn more about integrating apps with your students, visit the Computer Concepts CourseMate Web site at *www. cengagebrain.com*, and then navigate to the Chapter 2 Apps Corner resource for this book.

Key Terms

INSTRUCTIONS: Use the Key Terms list to help focus your study of the terms used in this chapter. To further enhance your understanding of the Key Terms in this chapter, visit the Computer Concepts CourseMate Web site at www.cengagebrain.com, and then navigate to the Chapter 2 Key Terms resource for this book. Read the definition for each term and then access current and additional information about the term from the Web.

absolute hyperlink [69]
Acceptable Use Policy (AUP) [84]
Advanced Research Projects Agency (ARPA) [62]
analog signal [56]
animated GIF [75]
animation [75]
anonymous FTP [80]
ARPANET [62]
article [81]
audio [76]

backbone [62]
bandwidth [60]
blog [72]
bookmark [71]
broadband [60]
browser [70]

Cascading Style Sheet (CSS) [70]
cable modem [65]
chat [83]
chat client [83]
chat room [83]
communications [55]
communications channel [56]
communications network [56]
communications protocol [63]
communications software [56]

dial-up access [65]
dial-up modem [57]
digital signal [56]
digital subscriber line (DSL) [66]
discovery learning [69]
domain name [67]
download [80]
dynamic Web page [68]

e-mail (electronic mail) [78]
e-mail address [78]
e-mail program [78]
emoticon [84]
ePALS [85]

FAQ [84]
favorite [71]
File Transfer Protocol (FTP) [80]
filtering software [84]
firewall [84]
flame [84]
flame war [84]
FTP server [80]
FTP site [80]

graphic [74]
graphical image [74]

history list [71]
home network [58]
home page [68]
host [62]
http:// [68]
hyperlink [68]

hypermedia [69]
hypertext [69]
Hypertext Markup Language (HTML) [70]
Hypertext Transfer Protocol [68]

instant messaging (IM) [82]
Internet [61]
Internet2 (I2) [62]
Internet backbone [66]
Internet etiquette [83]
Internet service provider (ISP) [64]
Internet telephony [83]

link [68]
LISTSERV [81]
local area network (LAN) [57]

magicJack [83]
mail server [78]
mailbox [78]
mailing list [81]
marquee [75]
media convergence [86]
media sharing Web site [72]
message board [81]
microblog [72]
microbrowser [70]
modem [56]
Mosaic [71]
multimedia [73]

national ISP [64]
National Science Foundation (NSF) [62]
Net [61]
netiquette [84]
news server [81]
newsgroup [80]
newsreader [81]
NSFnet [62]

online community [72]
online service provider (OSP) [64]
online social network [72]

packet [63]
packet switching [63]
participatory Web [68]
player [76]
plug-in [74]
podcast [76]
portal [72]
posting [81]
public Internet access point [66]

real time [82]
Really Simple Syndication (RSS) [76]
regional ISP [64]
relative hyperlink [69]
router [63]

satellite modem [66]
schema [70]
search engine [73]

search tool [73]
Semantic Web [69]
server [57]
Short Message Service (SMS) [82]
spam [84]
spoiler [84]
static Web page [68]
streaming [76]
streaming audio [76]
streaming video [77]
subject directory [73]
subscribe [81]

tabbed browsing [71]
tags [70]
target hyperlink [69]
telecommunications [55]
text messaging [82]
thread [81]
threaded discussion [81]
thumbnail [75]
traffic [62]
Transmission Control Protocol/ Internet Protocol (TCP/IP) [63]
transmission media [56]
twisted-pair cable [56]

Uniform Resource Locator (URL) [68]
unsubscribe [81]
upload [80]
Usenet [80]
username [78]

video [77]
video blog [72]
virtual reality (VR) [77]
vlog [72]
Voice over IP (VoIP) [83]
VR world [77]

Web [68]
Web 2.0 [68]
Web 3.0 [69]
Web app [72]
Web application [72]
Web browser [70]
Web page [68]
Web publishing [70]
Web server [69]
Web site [68]
Web surfing [70]
Weblog [72]
Webmaster [70]
wide area network (WAN) [58]
wiki [72]
wireless LAN (WLAN) [57]
wireless Internet service provider (WISP) [64]
World Wide Web (WWW) [68]

XML [70]
XHTML [70]

Checkpoint

INSTRUCTIONS: Use the Checkpoint exercises to check your knowledge level of the chapter. To complete the Checkpoint exercises interactively, visit the Computer Concepts CourseMate Web site at www.cengagebrain.com, and then navigate to the Chapter 2 Checkpoint resource for this book.

1. Label the Figure

Instructions: Identify the components of a communications system.

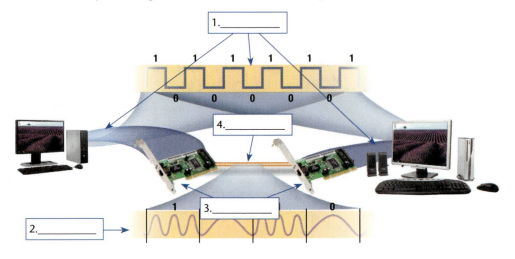

2. Matching

Instructions: Match each term from the column on the left with the best description from the column on the right.

____ 1. e-mail

____ 2. Webmaster

____ 3. network

____ 4. filtering software

____ 5. search tool

a. an individual responsible for developing Web pages and maintaining a Web site

b. a collection of computers and other equipment organized to share data, hardware, and software

c. the transmission of messages and files via a computer network

d. enables users to locate information found at Web sites all over the world

e. allows parents, teachers, and others to block access to certain materials on the Internet

3. Short Answer

Instructions: Write a brief answer to each of the following questions.

1. How are local area networks (LANs) different from wide area networks (WANs)?
2. What is a Web page? What purpose do hyperlinks have on a Web page? What is Hypertext Markup Language (HTML)?
3. Explain the process of streaming over the Web. How are streaming audio and streaming video similar? For what purposes is streaming used?
4. What is a firewall? What is filtering software? What is an Acceptable Use Policy (AUP)? Why is the use of firewalls, filtering software, and AUPs so important for K-12 networks?
5. What is a search tool? Name the two basic types of search tools and describe how each of these works. Which would you use to search for links in the category, Education?

Teaching Today

INSTRUCTIONS: Teaching Today provides teachers with integration strategies and ideas for teaching and, more importantly, reaching today's digital generation. Each numbered segment contains one or more links that reinforce the information presented in the segment. To display this page from the Web, visit the Computer Concepts CourseMate Web site at www.cengagebrain.com, and then navigate to the Chapter 2 Teaching Today resource for this book.

1. Digital Earth

Today's digital students need digital tools that can offer them unique and interactive learning experiences through which they can explore and discover the world using virtual environments. Google Earth is an online, virtual globe, 3D program that allows students to develop critical thinking skills on how everyday decisions affect our environment as they travel and explore the globe, while communicating with other students and teachers through Google Community. There are different levels through which you and your students can get involved in the virtual community, explore the different regions of the world, architecture, terrain, climates, and much more.

2. Search Engines

You have started using the computer lab to work on classroom projects with your digital students, which is a great opportunity for all students to get hands-on experiences with different technologies. Scanners, videos, CDs, DVDs, and many other technologies are available from which to choose. Students also can access the Internet. Managing your students in the lab or your classroom while they explore these different technologies is a challenge. You decide to design a project that requires your students to work in groups to research a famous person in history. Before students begin their research, you reflect on the following questions: Do students need guidance on how to use a search engine to perform a proper search? Do they need help to avoid getting lost using the various technologies? Do they understand that asking the correct question or questions is an important part of the solution for finding the correct answer? What about searching reference materials? Are students using primary and secondary resources? How can I design research projects that go beyond the standard writing of a paper to engage my digital students in using many different types of technologies in a collaborative way? By reflecting upon these questions, you will be able to manage your classroom time more effectively.

3. Interactive Bulletin Boards

Who says that you are limited to one or two bulletin boards in the classroom? Wall Wisher is an option for teachers who are in search of a digital bulletin board to increase communication between parents, students, and faculty. Sometimes it is nice to have a bulletin board for you and your students to leave questions, videos, pictures, poems, homework tips, spelling words, project ideas, and many others. Wall Wisher is a Web-based tool that is easy to update with a few simple clicks.

4. TeacherTube

As educators, we always are looking for Web sites like YouTube — where we can share video content with students or other teachers, but in a safe environment. Look no further, now there is TeacherTube, a Web site that is gaining popularity with educators and many others. This Web site is a community-building Web site like YouTube but offers an educator's version. According to TeacherTube's founders, their goal is to provide an educationally focused, safe place for teachers, schools, and students. This is a super place for educators to upload short or long instructional videos; currently there is no limit on file size or video length. The TeacherTube Web site is a safe location where teachers can post videos designed for students to view in order to learn or administrators can post videos to provide professional development opportunities for their teachers and staff.

Education Issues

INSTRUCTIONS: Education Issues provides several scenarios that allow you to explore controversial and current issues in education. Each numbered segment contains one or more links that reinforce the information presented in the segment. To display this page from the Web, visit the Computer Concepts CourseMate Web site at www.cengagebrain.com, and then navigate to the Chapter 2 Education Issues resource for this book.

1. Skype in the Classroom

Your principal suggests that you begin using Skype in your classroom in order to interact with classrooms around the globe. You have never used Skype and are concerned if you should use it. You do research and find out that Skype is changing the way many classrooms are approaching authentic-learning experiences that are relevant, meaningful, and engaging. No longer is it impossible to invite guest speakers from around the world into your classroom. You can set up a global gateway to the world and conference call with other classrooms, experts, and authors. Should you try Skype? Should you use the video capabilities of Skype? Why or why not?

2. Banning Smartphones in School

Most people would never consider cutting in line at the cafeteria or stealing somebody else's personal parking space in the parking lot. This courtesy seems to elude many people when it comes to cellular phone etiquette. People take calls during class, meetings, doctor appointments, or other inappropriate times. Psychologists have found that it may not be the smartphone users' speech volume that annoys us, but rather that the person is having a seemingly one-way conversation with no one, which is a much more difficult background noise for the brain to filter out. Recently, smartphones have taken on a new personality in schools — some students have been using phones to plan disturbances, fights, and gatherings — students call or text message each other and a situation quickly escalates from involving two students to involving twenty or more students. Many schools have told students they must leave their smartphones in their lockers and only use them during breaks; other schools have completely banned smartphone usage on school campus. Should smartphone use (or just some smartphone apps) be banned or limited in their use in schools? Why or why not?

3. Virtual High Schools

Today, many high schools, especially small rural high schools, have difficulty offering classes such as AP biology, Latin, AP calculus, and other similar classes due to budget constraints, classroom overcrowding, lack of qualified teachers, and other important issues. Currently, many school districts and states are addressing these problems by offering a variety of online classes. In addition, many states are now requiring that students complete at least one online course as a graduate requirement. Most educators agree that the Internet has great potential for education and that online classes need to be part of the K-12 learning environment. Some districts have opened 100 percent online or virtual high schools, which has generated a heated debate among educators about the effectiveness and even appropriateness of such schools. Do you think 100 percent online high schools are an effective solution? Why or why not? Substantiate your answer.

4. Net Censoring

Each day, schools, organizations, and individuals across the country continue in an ongoing debate about Internet censorship. A number of organizations, including the American Library Association (ALA), oppose the use of Internet filtering software programs. Many schools are blocking their students from viewing popular Web sites like Wikipedia, YouTube, and even the Weather Channel. Some people feel that schools are censoring valuable information and that students would be better off with unlimited access, coupled with strict teacher observation and guidelines. Others, however, are very concerned about the use of the Internet in schools and do not want children using the Internet — even if filtering programs and Acceptable Use Policies (AUPs) are in place. Do you think schools should limit or ban Internet usage? How could you use the Internet effectively in your classroom without offending or angering parents?

Apps Corner

INSTRUCTIONS: Apps Corner provides extensive ideas and resources for integrating technology into your classroom-specific curriculum. To display this page from the Web and information on numerous education apps, visit the Computer Concepts CourseMate Web site at www.cengagebrain.com, and then navigate to the Chapter 2 Apps Corner resource for this book.

Apps Corner is designed for teachers and other educators who are looking for innovative ways to integrate apps into their content-specific curriculum. Apps Corner not only provides great apps with current information but also shows how other educators are using and integrating education apps. As a result, Apps Corner is designed with all educators in mind, regardless of their interests or subject area. You can use Apps Corner to expand your resources by reviewing apps outside your curriculum area; remember many apps associated with one curriculum area can be adapted for use and added to lesson plans in a wide variety of other curriculum areas.

Use Apps Corner as a springboard for collaborating and sharing the successes and hurdles of integrating apps in a classroom or an entire school system. Consider Apps Corner a place to locate app integration ideas and resources. Information on educational apps are organized in four Corners (Early Childhood, Elementary, Middle School, and Secondary) and different apps are available for each chapter. Many apps are free, others cost between $1 to $5. Inexpensive site licenses for classrooms, schools, and school districts are available for many apps.

Shown below are two highly rated Apps, one for high school students to practice Algebra 1 concepts and Note Taker HD that allows students to write (with a stylus or their fingers) and organize handwritten notes, diagrams, and much more on an iPad or other tablet computers.

Software Corner

INSTRUCTIONS: Software Corner provides information on popular software programs. Each numbered segment discusses specific software programs and contains a link to additional information about these programs. To display this page from the Web, visit the Computer Concepts CourseMate Web site at www.cengagebrain.com, and then navigate to the Chapter 2 Software Corner resource for this book.

1. Screen Captures with SnagIt

Perhaps you are a Math teacher who is building a PowerPoint presentation for an upcoming unit on Integers. As you know, it can be rather difficult to find images of math problems that allow you to save them as a specific type of file, which you can then incorporate into your presentation. SnagIt is a screen capturing program that allows you to capture a screen easily, and then edit and save it in a variety of file types or simply copy and paste it into your presentation. With this program, you are able to capture or grab any item on the fly such as your entire desktop, a region, a window, or a scrolling window — all with a single click. Try the free download, you just might like it!

2. Jing

Teachers, many times repeat the same set of instructions over and over again, often feeling like a broken record. One innovative approach to this problem is to create your own repository of "how to" videos or instructions. Jing is a simple to use freeware program that allows you to capture screen shots or record screen activities with a couple of clicks! Jing works alone or in combination with Screencast.com, a hosting service offered by TechSmith to store videos and pictures of screens for free! Once you have finished your screen capture or video, you can immediately e-mail it, post it on a blog, or save it to your computer to use later in digital multimedia presentations. A super way to integrate Jing is to have your students create instructional videos on their own or in a group, and share their work with the class.

3. InspireData

As a teacher, you are always looking for ways to improve data literacy by helping your students to make connections between data and real world applications. Through the use of data visualizations, students develop a more meaningful understanding of content knowledge, develop critical thinking skills, strengthen the inquiry process, and learn to analyze data. InspireData applies the proven strategies of visual learning to data literacy, inspiring students to discover significance of data as they collect and explore data in an active inquiry process. One InspireData feature is a Time Series animation, which represents data as it changes over time. This feature assists students in understanding trends and making future predictions.

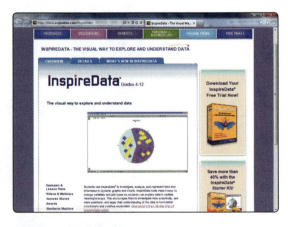

4. Google Apps Education Edition

Google Apps Education Edition is a free suite of hosted communication and collaboration applications designed for schools and universities. With free e-mail, messaging, and shared calendars, everyone on campus is connected. Google states that there is no advertising for students, faculty, and staff. Features include collaboration in real time and access to documents, presentations, spreadsheets, and sites from anywhere, on any device. You also can watch a Google video to learn more about Google Apps Education Edition.

5. Virtual Dissecting Software

High school students and teachers will enjoy using the different virtual dissection software packages being offered as an alternative to former dissection techniques that is not only fun but also clean — no disgusting smell of formaldehyde! Several companies offer teachers and students a complete virtual dissection lab on CD or DVD, which allows dissections including a frog, squid, earthworm, rat, pig, crayfish, perch, and more. You can also see demos and practice your dissections on the Web with online versions.

Digital Media Corner

INSTRUCTIONS: Today's K-12 digital students need their learning to be meaningful and relevant to their lives. Digital Media Corner provides videos, ideas, and examples of how you can use digital media to enhance your teaching and your students' learning. To access the videos and links to additional information, visit the Computer Concepts CourseMate Web site at www.cengagebrain.com, and then navigate to the Chapter 2 Digital Media Corner resource for this book.

1. Your Web, Your Way

Web 2.0 is creating a new set of tools to empower educators, consumers, and businesses. Software producers have long used version numbers to designate upgrades to their products. Using the term "Web 2.0" implies a series of enhancements and the term Web 2.0 derives its meaning from improvements to the basic infrastructure of the programs and servers supporting access to Web content. For all of us using the Web, the result of these enhancements is increased functionality of Web-based applications for use in databases and general computing capabilities needed to make the Web work faster and more efficiently. The exciting news not only for education in particular but also for society as a whole is that these improvements have permitted new technologies for everyday users to create their own products, like classroom Weblogs, media sharing programs, social network Web sites, multiplayer online games, information catalogs, personal radio stations, and bookmark sharing programs.

2. Searching the Web

As you know, helping your students to search the Web efficiently while gaining information literacy can be a daunting task. One of the many benefits of using emerging Web services is the ability for new and advanced search capabilities. So you can go above and beyond basics with greatly improved searches, Google has added customization capabilities to its search engine so your students and you can get better search results.

3. Instant Messaging from Anywhere

Today's digital students use instant messaging (IM) as an essential tool to stay in touch with their friends and to communicate with parents and teachers. People all over the world are using IM because of its quick and synchronous way to communicate with other people. Now, you can even take IM on the road, without the wires. Do you ever wonder what it really means to IM? This article will answer many of those questions. As a teacher, you need to know about the newest technology developments. Click here to see how IM works. Students can spend hours talking to their friends over the Internet. Since we know they enjoy chatting over IM, why not use IM as a classroom reading and writing activity? At this Web site, you will find some great ideas on how to turn instant messaging into an instructional tool for teaching in your classroom.

4. Flash

Most people know about Flash as a plug-in that allows users to view digital media enhancements on the Web. Flash is also a popular software application. It is a dynamic digital media-creation program that can be used to create interactive animations, Web sites, presentations, games, Flash movies, and much more. There are great examples of Web sites using Flash designed for today's digital students that include extensive lessons and other resources for teaching and learning subjects like mathematics, science, and more. The Center for Technology Teacher Education (CTTE) offers a rich catalog of instructional aides that utilize Flash as a part of its programs.

5. TWICE: Two Way Interactive Connections in Education

As you learned in Chapter 1, the majority of U.S. public schools have implemented Discovery Education Streaming's digital video library capabilities, but some schools are at the forefront of utilizing the speedy Internet for interactive education. TWICE, which stands for Two Way Interactive Connections in Education, promotes collaborative connections both nationally and regionally. For example, students sheltered from snowy weather in Detroit can visit NASA for a launch in tropical Cape Canaveral, Florida. While on their virtual field trip, students have the full attention of a NASA employee who receives and answers their questions in real time!

Assistive Technologies Corner

INSTRUCTIONS: Assistive Technologies Corner provides information on current hardware, software, and peripherals that will assist you in delivering instruction to students with physical, cognitive, or sensory challenges. To access extensive additional information, visit the Computer Concepts CourseMate Web site at www.cengagebrain.com, and then navigate to the Chapter 2 Assistive Technologies Corner resource for this book.

1. How Does a Person Who Is Deaf or Hard of Hearing Use the Telephone?

A student who is mildly hard of hearing may choose to use an amplified telephone, one that makes telephone communication louder and more understandable. Persons who are deaf or more severely hard of hearing have used teletypwriter (TTY) or Telecommunication Devices for the Deaf (TDD) for many years. A TTY has a keyboard, a text display, and a coupler. A regular phone connection is established between two users and both users must have a TTY. The phone handset is placed into the coupler fitted for both parts of the handset. One user begins typing. The words appear on the text display for both users and the conversation proceeds. At one time, these were large bulky machines; however, today's TTYs are portable and can connect to cell phones.

Another and newer tool allows high-quality video relay such as that provided by Sorenson Video Relay Service (VRS). The VRS uses a sign language interpreter to translate voice and sign communication. A user connects with the video relay service. The interpreter places the call, and all communication goes through the interpreter. One user with a video display and camera signs to the interpreter, who translates simultaneously to the voice telephone user. When the voice user speaks, the interpreter signs, and the message is viewed on the signer's video display. Wireless communications devices with QWERTY keyboards and the associated services have brought communication freedom to the deaf and hard of hearing. The wireless services of blackberry.com, for example, provide solutions, including instant messaging and wireless e-mail.

2. How Can a Blind or Visually Impaired Person Access the Graphical Web?

The graphical nature of today's Web provides the biggest obstacle to students with a visual disability. We can make accommodations through assistive technology. Visual impairments vary in severity and in type. A slight impairment may be accommodated by activating the built-in accessibility features of the browser. For most browsers, you can increase the size of the text that is viewed on the screen.

Blind users, however, require special software installed on their computers such as a screen reader that renders text to voice. Two popular screen readers are Freedom Scientific's JAWS and GW Micro's Window Eyes. Screen reader programs read all text that appears on the computer screen. Screen reader programs provide equal access for students. Because a blind user does not use a mouse, the screen reader requires keyboard skills. These programs are somewhat expensive. Somewhat less expensive is IBM's Homepage Reader, which is a talking browser. A blind user opens the browser and the Homepage Reader software reads the contents of the Web page aloud. A different voice indicates a link, and the user selects the link using the keyboard.

3. What About Web Page Accessibility?

A screen reader, a talking browser, or any assistive device can work well only with Web pages that are accessible, that is, they meet the criteria for standards that allow smooth integration of technologies. However, many Web sites are not fully accessible because the code used to create them does not follow accessibility guidelines, or they use technologies that are simply not accessible. To determine if a Web page is accessible for the student, a teacher may visit Web Accessibility Initiative, which provides a list of Web accessibility evaluation tools.

Follow the instructions at the top of this page to display additional information and this chapter's links on assistive technologies.

In the Lab

INSTRUCTIONS: In the Lab provides word processing exercises that are divided into two areas, productivity and integration. To access the links to tutorials, productivity ideas, integration examples and ideas, and more, visit the Computer Concepts CourseMate Web site at www.cengagebrain.com, and then navigate to the Chapter 2 In the Lab resource for this book.

PRODUCTIVITY IN THE CLASSROOM

Introduction: All students and teachers need to know how to write a professional cover letter as well as how to develop a résumé. Many of the popular word processing applications provide templates that take users through the steps of creating these special documents. Learning how to use templates will save you time and provide useful guidance.

1. Using a Letter Template to Create a Cover Letter

Problem: As a recent graduate from a Master's program in Educational Technology, you are seeking a position as a technology coordinator at a local middle school. Open your word processing software and create a cover letter as described in the following set of steps. Use the letter shown in Figure 2-36 on the next page as an example. (*Hint:* If you do not have the suggested font, use any appropriate font.)

Instructions: Perform the following tasks.

1. Create a cover letter using a letter template. If possible, use a letterhead style similar to the one shown in Figure 2-36. Insert your own name and address where indicated by placeholder text.
2. Modify the cover letter so the font is 12-point Times or Times New Roman. Use today's date in the date line. Modify the inside address and message by personalizing the information to your specific situation.
3. Create a numbered list highlighting at least two of your qualifications.
4. Check the cover letter for spelling and grammar errors.
5. Save the cover letter to a USB flash drive. Use an appropriate filename.
6. Print the cover letter.
7. Follow your instructor's directions for handing in the assignment.

2. Using a Résumé Template to Create a Résumé

Problem: You have prepared the cover letter in Figure 2-36 and now you are ready to create a résumé similar to the one shown in Figure 2-37 on page 97 to accompany your cover letter. You want your information to be clearly presented and to highlight your qualifications. Use a résumé template.

Instructions: Perform the following tasks.

1. Use a résumé template to create a résumé. Use your name and address information.
2. Personalize the résumé using your specific information.
3. Check the résumé for spelling and grammar errors.
4. Save the résumé to a USB flash drive using an appropriate filename.
5. Print a copy of the résumé.
6. Follow your instructor's directions for handing in the assignment.

INTEGRATION IN THE CLASSROOM

1. As a follow-up activity to career day at your school, you have your students locate job advertisements online. The students select a job they would be interested in and then use a wizard or template to write a cover letter. Students should use the cover letter shown in Figure 2-36 as an example of the type of information they should include in the first two paragraphs. The students also should include a numbered list highlighting two of their accomplishments or qualifications and then a closing paragraph with contact information. Create a cover letter to use as an example for your students. Include today's date, your name, and address.

In the Lab

Jon Marc Bowers

692 East First Street
Chapel Hill, NC 27516
(919) 555-4332
jmbowers@spms.k12.nc.us

August 5, 2013

Dr. Roz Seguero
Superintendent
Chapel Hill City School District
1452 Fort King Street
Chapel Hill, NC 27514

Dear Dr. Seguero,

I am writing to apply for the position of Technology Coordinator at Blue Ridge High
School. After reviewing my enclosed resume, I hope you will agree that my training and
experiences will greatly assist the staff and students to use and integrate technology
effectively.

I have been an educator for the past nine years. I have organized and led numerous staff
development workshops on a variety of software applications. I also have integrated
technology extensively throughout my classroom curriculum.

I would like to mention my most important qualifications:

1. Nationally Board Certified Educator 2009

2. Master's degree in Educational Technology

3. MCAS Certified in Microsoft Word, Excel, and PowerPoint

I look forward to meeting with you to discuss my qualifications for this position further.
Please contact me at (919) 555-4332 or e-mail me at jmbowers@spms.k12.nc.us.

Sincerely,

Jon Marc Bowers

Figure 2-36

In the Lab

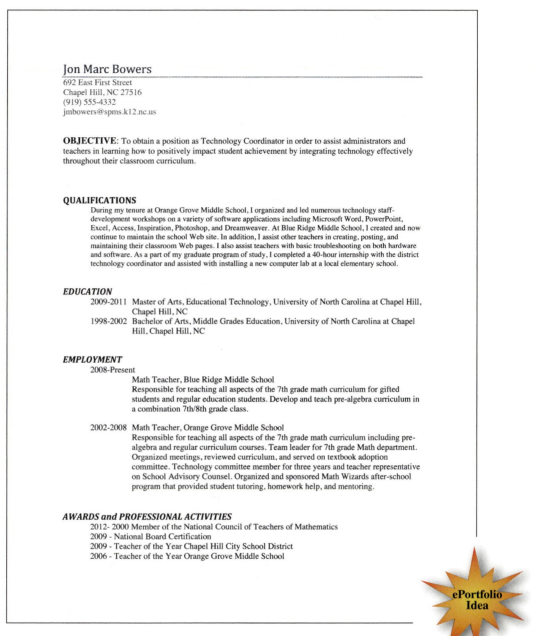

Jon Marc Bowers

692 East First Street
Chapel Hill, NC 27516
(919) 555-4332
jmbowers@spms.k12.nc.us

OBJECTIVE: To obtain a position as Technology Coordinator in order to assist administrators and teachers in learning how to positively impact student achievement by integrating technology effectively throughout their classroom curriculum.

QUALIFICATIONS

During my tenure at Orange Grove Middle School, I organized and led numerous technology staff-development workshops on a variety of software applications including Microsoft Word, PowerPoint, Excel, Access, Inspiration, Photoshop, and Dreamweaver. At Blue Ridge Middle School, I created and now continue to maintain the school Web site. In addition, I assist other teachers in creating, posting, and maintaining their classroom Web pages. I also assist teachers with basic troubleshooting on both hardware and software. As a part of my graduate program of study, I completed a 40-hour internship with the district technology coordinator and assisted with installing a new computer lab at a local elementary school.

EDUCATION

2009-2011   Master of Arts, Educational Technology, University of North Carolina at Chapel Hill, Chapel Hill, NC
1998-2002   Bachelor of Arts, Middle Grades Education, University of North Carolina at Chapel Hill, Chapel Hill, NC

EMPLOYMENT

2008-Present
          Math Teacher, Blue Ridge Middle School
          Responsible for teaching all aspects of the 7th grade math curriculum for gifted students and regular education students. Develop and teach pre-algebra curriculum in a combination 7th/8th grade class.

2002-2008   Math Teacher, Orange Grove Middle School
          Responsible for teaching all aspects of the 7th grade math curriculum including pre-algebra and regular curriculum courses. Team leader for 7th grade Math department. Organized meetings, reviewed curriculum, and served on textbook adoption committee. Technology committee member for three years and teacher representative on School Advisory Counsel. Organized and sponsored Math Wizards after-school program that provided student tutoring, homework help, and mentoring.

AWARDS and PROFESSIONAL ACTIVITIES

2012- 2000 Member of the National Council of Teachers of Mathematics
2009 - National Board Certification
2009 - Teacher of the Year Chapel Hill City School District
2006 - Teacher of the Year Orange Grove Middle School

ePortfolio Idea

Figure 2-37

INTEGRATION IN THE CLASSROOM (continued)

2. Using the job they selected from the Internet, have students create a résumé to accompany their cover letter. Modify the résumé you created previously to create a résumé to use as an example for your students. Change the information in the résumé to match the cover letter in Integration in the Classroom number 1.

3. Your students have just finished reading a book of their choice and they are ready to begin working on their book reports. To make it more interesting, you want the students to select a character from their book, choose a job for the character, and write a cover letter and résumé based on the character's life. Choose one of your favorite characters from a book and create a sample cover letter and résumé for your students. Use today's date and your name and address as the potential employer.

Learn It Online

INSTRUCTIONS: Use the Learn It Online exercises to reinforce your understanding of the chapter concepts and increase your computer, information, and integration literacy. To access step-by-step online tutorials, videos, practice tests, learning games, and more, visit the Computer Concepts CourseMate Web site at www.cengagebrain.com, navigate to the Chapter 2 resources for this book, and then click the link for the resource you want to review.

1. Publishing Your Résumé

Publishing your résumé on the Web is a great way to distribute your résumé to multiple people. To learn how to publish your résumé on the Web, click the Publish Resume link.

2. At the Movies

Click the At the Movies link to review a video about creating your own blog. Click the At the Movies 2 link to see why the Sling Media Slingbox is a great way to beam your favorite shows to any broadband connected computer or Windows mobile device in the world and then answer questions about the movie.

3. Expanding Your Understanding

When you buy a new computer, the computer manufacturer often sets the default home page so the company's Web page displays every time you open your browser. Click the Expanding Your Understanding link to learn how to change your Web browser's home page to display your school district's home page, your Web site, or any other site.

4. Using Favorites

Click the Using Favorites link and complete the exercise that appears on the screen. Print just the first page of this Web site. On the back of the printout, write a brief summary explaining how to organize your favorites or bookmarks. If required, submit your results to your instructor.

5. Search Engine Tutorial

Click the Search Engine Tutorial link and complete the exercise that appears on the screen. Print just the first page of this Web site. On the back of the printout, write a brief summary of three new things that you learned about Web searching. If required, submit your results to your instructor.

6. Practice Test

Click the Practice Test link. Answer each question. When completed, enter your name and click the Grade Test button to submit the quiz for grading. Make a note of any missed questions. If required, submit your score to your instructor.

7. Who Wants to Be a Computer Genius?

Click the Who Wants to Be a Computer Genius link to find out if you are a computer genius. Directions about how to play the game will be displayed. When you are ready to play, click the Play button. If required, submit your score to your instructor.

8. Wheel of Terms

Click the Wheel of Terms link to reinforce important terms you learned in this chapter by playing the Shelly Cashman Series version of this popular game. Directions about how to play the game will be displayed. When you are ready to play, click the Play button. If required, submit your score to your instructor.

9. Crossword Puzzle Challenge

Click the Crossword Puzzle Challenge link. Complete the puzzle to reinforce skills you learned in this chapter. Directions about how to play the game will be displayed. When you are ready to play, click the Play button. If required, submit the completed puzzle to your instructor.

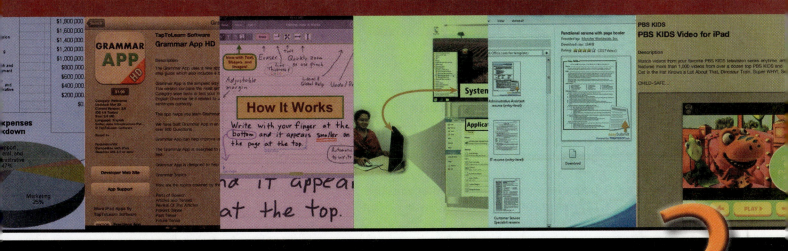

Software for Educators

3

Objectives

After completing this chapter, you will be able to do the following:
[ISTE NETS-T Standards 1 b; 2 a-d; 3 a, d; 4 b; 5 a-c]

- Explain the role of an operating system and list the main operating systems used on today's computers

- Define and describe a user interface and a graphical user interface

- Identify the important features of widely used software applications

- Describe the advantages of software suites

- Explain how to create documents

- Discuss why the use of video authoring and editing software is important for K-12 schools

- Explain the difference between software application, Web application, and app

- Explain how to work with different versions of software applications

An essential aspect of building computer literacy is learning about software, which is the series of instructions that tell computer hardware how to perform tasks. Having a solid understanding of software — especially application software — will help you comprehend how administrators, teachers, students, and other individuals use personal computers in today's society. It also will help you use your computer and other technologies to be more productive, organized, and well informed.

Application software such as word processing, spreadsheet, project planning, and e-mail programs can help you perform tasks such as creating documents, visualizing data, managing projects, and communicating with others. Before discussing various software applications used by teachers and students, however, this chapter provides a basic overview of the operating system and the user interface used on Macs, PCs, and mobile devices. The user interface controls how you work with any software, including application software.

Understanding software can help advance your personal and professional goals by helping you manage student records, teach students with different academic needs, and work more productively. This chapter introduces you to the learning aids and tools available to help you and your students learn to use software applications. You can refer back to this chapter as you learn more about how computers are used today and how they can help you in your teaching career.

The Operating System

As with most computer users, you are probably somewhat familiar with application software. To use any application software, however, your computer must be running another type of software — an operating system.

THE ROLE OF THE OPERATING SYSTEM

Software can be categorized into two types: system software and application software. **System software** consists of programs that control the operations of the computer and its devices. System software serves as the interface between you (the user), your application software, and your computer's hardware (Figure 3-1). One type of system software, the **operating system**, contains instructions that coordinate all of the activities of the hardware devices in a computer. The operating system also contains instructions that allow you to run application software.

Before either a Mac or a PC can run any application software, the operating system must be loaded from the hard disk or other storage location into the computer's memory. Each time you start your computer, the operating system is loaded, or copied, into memory. After the operating system is loaded, it tells the computer how to perform functions, such as processing program instructions or transferring data between input and output devices and memory. The operating system, which remains in memory while the computer is running, allows you to communicate with the computer and other software, such as word processors, gradebooks, and other application programs. The operating system continues to run until the computer is turned off.

USING DIFFERENT OPERATING SYSTEMS

Each new release of an operating system contains new features that make computers more powerful and easy to use. In addition, the newest operating systems provide enhanced integration with the World Wide Web and increase the multimedia capabilities of computers. Due to budget constraints and other factors, however, schools, businesses, and home users do not always upgrade their computers every time a new version of an operating system is released. As a result, a number of different versions of operating systems currently are running on school, business, and home computers.

Figure 3-1 System software is the interface between the user, the application software, and the computer's hardware. In this example, a user instructs the word processing software to print a document, the word processing software sends the print instructions to the system software, and the system software sends the print instructions to the printer.

System Software

Application Software

STAND-ALONE OPERATING SYSTEMS

A **stand-alone operating system** is a complete operating system that works on a desktop computer, notebook computer, or mobile computing device. Examples of currently used stand-alone operating systems are Windows 7 and Mac OS X.

WINDOWS 7 Windows 7 is Microsoft's fastest, most efficient operating system to date, offering quicker program start up, multitasking capabilities, built-in diagnostics, automatic recovery, improved security, enhanced searching and organizing capabilities, and an easy-to-use interface (Figure 3-2). Previous versions of Microsoft Windows still widely in use today include Windows Vista and Windows XP.

MAC OS X Mac OS X is an operating system that supports multitasking and is available only for computers manufactured by Apple. The latest version, **Mac OS X Lion** (released summer 2011), includes features from previous versions of the Macintosh operating system and many new features such as the Mac App Store, which offers endless possibilities for browsing and purchasing apps. Newly purchased apps install in one step and appear right in the new Launchpad, which gives users instant access to apps. Another new powerful feature, Mission Control, provides users with a bird's-eye view of everything, all in one place.

EMBEDDED OPERATING SYSTEMS

The operating system on mobile devices and many consumer electronics, called an **embedded operating system**, resides on an internal chip, rather than a hard drive. Most of today's embedded operating systems support multi-touch, which means they recognize multiple points of contact and allow users to interact using a stylus or finger motions, such as tapping a button on the screen and sliding a finger to drag an object. Embedded operating systems allow users to interact with hundreds of thousands of applications, known as apps. Three popular embedded operating systems include Apple's iOS, Google Android, and Blackberry OS.

iOS Apple's **iOS** (previously known as iPhone OS) is an operating system developed by Apple and used on the iPad, iPod Touch, iPhone, and Apple TV. Apple allows programmers worldwide to design apps specifically for devices supporting this operating system. iOS-based apps are available for download at the Apple App Store.

GOOGLE ANDROID **Google Android** is an operating system designed by Google for mobile devices. Used on more than 20 different types of mobile devices, including tablet computers, Google Android allows programmers to design programs specifically for devices supporting this operating system.

BLACKBERRY OS **BlackBerry OS** is a proprietary operating system developed by Research In Motion for Blackberry's line of smartphones and Playbook tablet computers.

EMERGING OPERATING SYSTEMS

One emerging operating system that has the potential to revolutionize computing is Google's **Chrome OS**. Chrome OS (based on Google Android) is an operating system designed to work exclusively with Web-based and cloud-based applications and to run on Chromebook computers. Chromebook computers are covered in Chapter 4 and Web-based and cloud-based applications are detailed in the special feature that follows Chapter 6, *A World without Wires – Tablets, Apps, and More*.

Figure 3-2 Windows 7 has a new interface, easier navigation and searching techniques, and improved security.

FAQ

Can I simply turn the computer off when I am finished?

No! You must use the operating system's shut-down procedure so various processes are closed in sequence and items in memory are released properly.

THE ROLE OF THE USER INTERFACE

All software, including the operating system, is designed to communicate with the user in a certain way, through a user interface. A **user interface** controls how you enter data or instructions (input) and how information is presented on the screen (output).

One of the more common user interfaces is a graphical user interface. A **graphical user interface**, or **GUI** (pronounced gooey), combines text, graphics, and other visual cues to make software easier to use.

Application Software

Recall that **application software** consists of programs designed to perform specific tasks for users. Application software, also called **application programs**, can be used for the following purposes:

- As a productivity/business tool
- Assisting with graphics and multimedia projects
- Supporting school and professional activities
- Helping with home and personal activities
- Facilitating communications

The table in Figure 3-3 categorizes popular types of application software by their general use. These five categories are not all-inclusive nor are they mutually exclusive; for example, e-mail can support productivity, a software suite can include Web page authoring tools, and tax preparation software can be used by a business. In the course of a day, week, or month, you are likely to find yourself using software from many of these categories, whether you are at school, home, or work. Even though you may not use all of the applications, you should at least be familiar with their capabilities.

Communications applications, such as e-mail, Web browsers, and others, were discussed in Chapter 2. This chapter gives a general overview of each of the other four categories and provides specific examples of applications in each category that are used on both PCs and Macs. Finally, there is a new category of software, called Apps, that has recently exploded in terms of both availability and use over the past two to three years. Apps are covered in each end-of-chapter section called Apps Corner and in the special feature that follows Chapter 6, *A World without Wires – Tablets, Apps, and More.*

A wide variety of application software, such as word processing, is available as packaged software that can be purchased from software vendors in retail stores or on the Web. Many application software programs also are available as shareware, freeware, and public-domain software; these programs, however, usually have fewer capabilities than retail software programs.

Figure 3-3 The five major categories of popular application software. You likely will use software from more than one of these categories.

Categories of Application Software

Productivity/ Business	Graphic Design/ Multimedia	School	Home/Personal	Communications
• Word Processing	• Desktop Publishing	• School/Student Management	• Personal Finance	• E-Mail
• Spreadsheet	• Paint/Image Editing	• Gradebook	• Tax Preparation	• Web Browser
• Presentation Graphics	• Multimedia Authoring	• K-12 Educational Software Applications	• Legal	• Chat Rooms
• Database	• Web Page Authoring	• Special Needs	• Entertainment	• Newsgroups
• Personal Information Management				• Instant Messaging
• Software Suite				• Blogs
				• Wikis

STARTING A SOFTWARE APPLICATION

To use application software, you must instruct the operating system to start the program. Both Mac OS and Microsoft Windows use the concept of a desktop to make the computer easier to use. The **desktop** is an on-screen work area that uses common graphical elements such as icons, buttons, windows, menus, and dialog boxes to make it easy and intuitive for users to interact with the computer. Figure 3-4 illustrates how to start and then interact with the Paint program on a PC using Microsoft Windows.

An **icon** is a small image that represents a program, an instruction, or some other object. A **button** is a graphical element (usually a rectangular or circular shape) that when selected, causes a specific action to take place. Typically you click a button using a pointing device, such as a mouse, to select it. You also can select a button using the keyboard. Icons, text, or a combination of both are used to identify buttons.

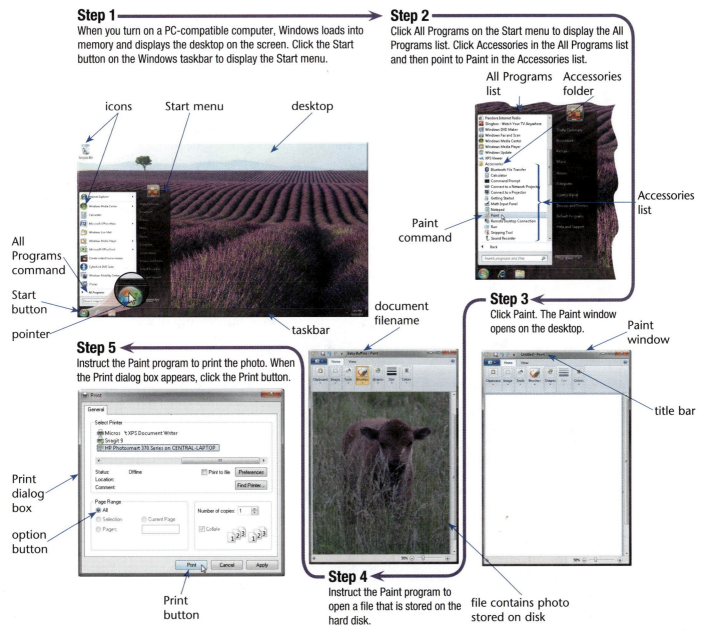

Step 1
When you turn on a PC-compatible computer, Windows loads into memory and displays the desktop on the screen. Click the Start button on the Windows taskbar to display the Start menu.

Step 2
Click All Programs on the Start menu to display the All Programs list. Click Accessories in the All Programs list and then point to Paint in the Accessories list.

Step 3
Click Paint. The Paint window opens on the desktop.

Step 4
Instruct the Paint program to open a file that is stored on the hard disk.

Step 5
Instruct the Paint program to print the photo. When the Print dialog box appears, click the Print button.

Figure 3-4 How to start and interact with an application.

Integration Strategies

To learn more about how to integrate content-specific software applications, such as Kidspiration, Tessellation Exploration, and Thinkology, visit the Computer Concepts CourseMate Web site at *www.cengagebrain. com*, and then navigate to the Chapter 3 Software Corner resource for this book.

The Windows desktop contains a Start button in its lower-left corner, which can be used to start an application. When you click the Start button, the Start menu opens on the desktop. A **menu** is a list of commands from which you can make a selection. **Commands** are instructions that cause a computer program to perform a specific action. For example, as shown in Steps 1 and 2 of Figure 3-4 on the previous page, when you click the Start button and click the All Programs command on the Start menu, the All Programs list is displayed. Clicking the Accessories folder in the All Programs list displays the Accessories list. As shown in the Accessories list, Windows includes several applications, such as Calculator, Paint, and WordPad.

You can start an application by clicking its program name on a menu or in a list. Doing so instructs the operating system to start the application by transferring the program's instructions from a storage medium into memory. For example, if you click Paint in the Accessories list, Windows transfers the program instructions from the computer's hard disk into memory.

Once started, an application is displayed in a window on the desktop. A **window** is a rectangular area of the screen that is used to display a program,

data, and/or information (see Step 3 of Figure 3-4 on the previous page). The top of a window has a **title bar**, which is a horizontal space that contains the window's name.

Any document you are working on or you have saved exists as a file. A **file** is a named collection of data, such as a document that you create, a program, or a set of data used by a program. To distinguish among various files, you assign each file a **filename**, which is a unique set of letters, numbers, and other characters that identifies the file. The title bar of the document window usually displays a document's filename, as shown in Step 4 of Figure 3-4 on the previous page. Also shown in Step 4 of Figure 3-4 is the contents of the file Baby Buffalo displayed in the Paint window. The Baby Buffalo file contains a photograph created with a digital camera.

One of the major advantages of a graphical user interface is that elements such as icons, buttons, and menus, usually are common across applications. After you learn the purpose and functionality of these elements, you can apply that knowledge to several software applications. Many of the features just described also are applicable to the desktop of the Macintosh operating system (Figure 3-5), which is arranged somewhat differently than the desktop of a PC.

The features of a graphical user interface make it easier for users to communicate with a personal computer. You will see examples of these features and how they are used as you learn about various software applications used by schools, businesses, and individuals.

WORKING WITH SOFTWARE APPLICATIONS

While using many software applications, you have the ability to create, edit, format, print, and save documents. A **document** is a piece of work created with an application and saved on a storage medium with a unique filename. Many users think of documents as files created using word processing software. To a computer, however, a

Figure 3-5 The Mac OS X desktop contains features similar to a PC desktop, however, the arrangement of the features is different.

document is nothing more than a collection of characters, so a spreadsheet or graphic is as much a document as a letter or report. During the process of developing a document, you likely will switch back and forth among the following activities.

Creating involves developing the document by entering text or numbers, designing graphics, and performing other tasks using an input device, such as a keyboard or mouse. If you design a map using the graphics tools in Paint, for example, you are creating a document.

Editing is the process of making changes to the document's existing content. Common editing tasks include inserting, deleting, cutting, copying, and pasting items in a document. For example, using Paint, you can **insert**, or add, text to a map, such as the names of key landmarks. When you **delete**, you remove text or objects. To **cut** involves removing a portion of the document and electronically storing it in a temporary storage location called the **Clipboard**. When you **copy**, a portion of the document is duplicated and stored on the Clipboard. To place whatever is stored on the Clipboard into the document, you **paste** it into the document.

Formatting involves changing the appearance of a document. Formatting is important because the overall look of a document can significantly affect its ability to communicate effectively. For example, you might want to increase the size of the text to improve readability.

One often-used formatting task involves formatting text by changing the font, font size, or font style of text. A **font** is a name assigned to a specific design of characters. Arial and Times New Roman are examples of fonts. The **font size** specifies the size of the characters in a particular font. Font size is gauged by a measurement system called **points**. A single point is about 1/72 of an inch in height. The text you are reading in this book is 10.5 pts. Thus, each character is about 10/72 of an inch in height. A **font style** is used to add emphasis to a font. Examples of font styles are **bold**, *italic*, and underline. Examples of these and additional formatting features are shown in Figure 3-6.

While you are creating, editing, and formatting a document, it is held temporarily in memory. As you work, you normally save your document for future use. **Saving** is the process of copying a document from memory to a storage medium, such as a

Figure 3-6 Examples of formatting features available with many productivity programs.

Header Example ← header appears at top of every page　　　date (and time) can appear in header or footer → April 21, 2013

FONT & FONT STYLES *Examples show different typefaces in bold, underline, or italic.*	Courier **Courier Bold**	Helvetica <u>Helvetica Underlined</u>	Times New Roman *Times New Roman Italic*
POINT SIZES *Examples show different point sizes, which can be used to make type larger or smaller.*	6 point　　8 point　　10 point　　**12 point**　　**14 point** 20 point　30 point　50 point		
COLUMNS & ALIGNMENT *Examples show four columns with different alignments.*	This is an example of **left alignment**. Notice how the words at the beginning of each line are aligned with the left column margin.	This is an example of **justified alignment**. The spacing between words is adjusted so the words at the beginning and the end of the lines are aligned with the left and right column margins.	This is an example of **center alignment**. The words are centered in the column.　　This is an example of **right alignment**. Notice how the words at the end of each line are aligned with the right column margin.
TABLES & GRAPHICS *Example shows a three-column table, which can be moved as a single object, shading applied to every other row, and a border around the table.*			

Part Number	Description	Price
A101	widget	$ 9.95
B202	gizmo	$ 14.95
C303	thingee	$ 19.95
D404	doodad	$ 24.95

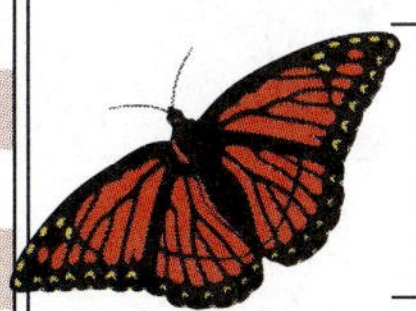

Example shows that a graphic can be placed anywhere on page.

USB flash drive or hard disk. You should save the document frequently while working with it so your work will not be lost if the power fails or the computer crashes. Many applications also have an optional **AutoSave** feature that automatically saves open documents at specified time periods. You should save your work frequently, however, and not rely on the AutoSave feature.

After you have created a document, you can print it many times, with each copy looking just like the first. **Printing** is the process of sending a file to a printer to generate output on a medium, such as paper. You also can send the document to others electronically, if your computer is connected to a network.

In some cases, when you instruct a program to perform an activity such as printing, a dialog box opens. A **dialog box** is a special window displayed by a program to provide information, present available options, or request a response using command buttons, option buttons, text boxes, and check boxes (Figure 3-7). A Save As dialog box, for example, gives you many save options, such as saving a file to a different location or in a different file format.

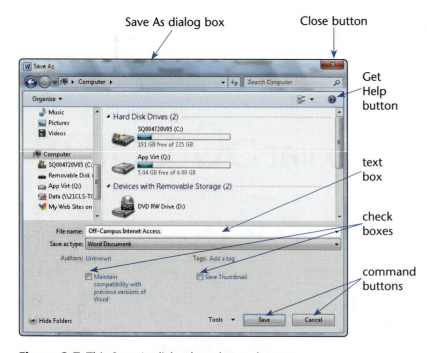

Figure 3-7 This Save As dialog box shows elements common to many dialog boxes, such as text boxes, check boxes, and command buttons.

VOICE RECOGNITION

Many software applications support voice recognition. **Voice recognition**, also called **speech recognition**, is the computer's capability of distinguishing spoken words. You speak into the computer's microphone and watch your words display on your screen as you talk. You also can edit and format a document by speaking or spelling instructions.

NOTE TAKING SOFTWARE

Did you ever experience the frustration of not being able to read your written notes before a test? Have you looked through page after page of your written notes for answers to specific questions but couldn't find them? These problems may be a thing of the past for today's digital kids. In fact, note taking software for this digital generation may be a perfect solution both inside and outside the classroom.

Note taking software is application software that enables users to enter typed text, handwritten comments, graphs, drawings, or sketches anywhere on a page and then save the page as part of an electronic notebook. The software can convert handwritten comments to typed text or store the notes in a handwritten form. Users also can include audio recordings as part of their notes.

After notes are captured (entered and saved), users can organize them, reuse them, and share them easily. The software allows the users to search through saved notes for specific text. Users can search through an entire notebook. Users can flag important notes with color, highlight, and shapes. On a desktop or notebook computer, users enter notes primarily via the keyboard or microphone. On a tablet computer, however, the primary input device is your finger or a stylus. Students may find note taking software more convenient and easier to use during class lectures, in libraries, and in other settings that previously required a pencil and tablet of paper for recording thoughts and discussions.

Note taking software incorporates many of the features found in word processing software, such as checking spelling, changing fonts and font sizes, adding colors, recognizing voice input, inserting audio and video files, providing research capabilities, and so much more. By using note taking software (Figure 3-8), students can have digital documents that are legible, searchable, and editable; however, most students are still taking notes the traditional way, with paper and pencil. Although more and more K-12 students are bringing their laptops to class and typing their notes, many of these students cannot type as fast as they can write. With the power of note taking software, students can increase their comprehension and capture more of the content.

Many experts are predicting that as tablet computers and other mobile note taking devices become mainstream, printed school and college textbooks will become obsolete. Instead, digital students will interact with digital versions of their textbooks (Figure 3-9). In fact, several publishers are perfecting various ways of providing their content via the Web, tablet computers, and traditional printed versions of their textbooks to determine which one is successful with students.

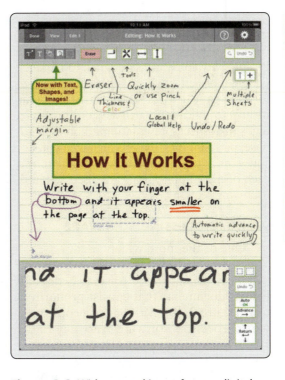

Figure 3-8 With note taking software, digital students and other mobile users can handwrite notes, draw sketches, type text, send handwritten e-mails, and more. Shown is NoteTaker HD on an iPad.

Integration Strategies

To learn more about how to use and integrate Microsoft's note taking software, OneNote, visit the Computer Concepts CourseMate Web site at *www.cengagebrain.com*, and then navigate to the Chapter 3 Digital Media Corner resource for this book.

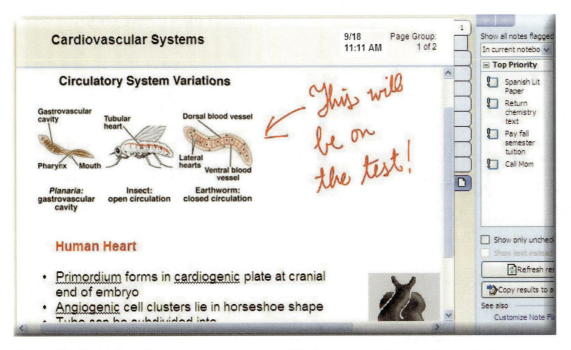

Figure 3-9 Education will reap many benefits as tablet computers and the multitude of software products being developed for them become mainstream.

Productivity Software

Productivity software is designed to make people more effective and efficient while performing daily activities. Productivity software includes applications such as word processing, spreadsheet, presentation graphics, database, personal information management, and software suites. The features and functions of each of these applications are discussed in the following sections.

WORD PROCESSING SOFTWARE

One of the more widely used application software is **word processing software**, which is used to create, edit, and format documents that consist primarily of text (Figure 3-10). Millions of people use word processing software every day to create documents such as letters, memos, reports, fax cover sheets, mailing labels, and newsletters. The more popular word processing programs used in schools today are Microsoft Word and the word processing applications included with Apple iWork (formally called AppleWorks) and Microsoft Works. By acquiring solid word processing skills, teachers can increase their productivity significantly by using word processing software to create written documents, such as lesson plans, handouts, parent communications, and student tests.

In addition to supporting basic text, word processing software has many formatting features to make documents look professional and visually appealing. When developing a newsletter, for example, you can change the font and font size of headlines and headings, change the color of characters, or organize text into newspaper-style columns. Any colors used for characters or other formatting will print as black or gray unless you have a color printer.

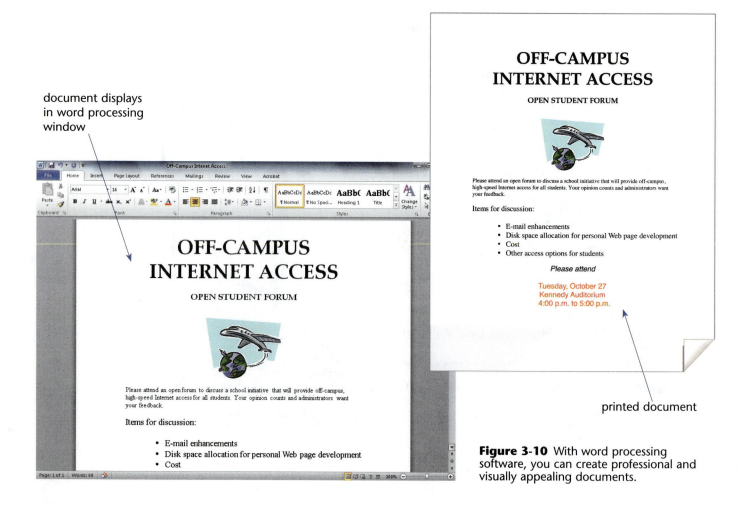

document displays in word processing window

printed document

Figure 3-10 With word processing software, you can create professional and visually appealing documents.

Most word processing software also can incorporate many types of graphics. For example, you can enhance a document by adding a **border**, which is a decorative line or pattern along one or more edges of a page or graphic. One type of graphic commonly included with word processing software is **clip art**, which is a collection of drawings, diagrams, and photographs that can be inserted in other documents. **Clip art collections**, which can contain several hundred to several thousand images, usually are grouped by type, such as buildings, people, or nature (Figure 3-11). If you want to use clip art not included in your word processing software package, you **import** (bring into) the clip art into a word processing document from another source such as a purchased CD collection or from a Web site. You can also create graphics using Paint and other image editing software. You can import these graphics into your document too. Paint and image editing software are discussed later in this chapter. After you insert, or import, a clip art image or other graphic into a document, you can move, resize, rotate, crop, and adjust its color.

All word processing software provides basic capabilities to help you create, edit, and format documents. For example, you can define the size of the paper on which to print, as well as the **margins** — that is, the portion of the page outside the main body of text, on the top, bottom, left, and right sides of the paper. The word processing software automatically readjusts any text so it fits within the new margin settings.

If you type text that extends beyond the page margin or window boundary, the word processor uses **wordwrap** to automatically position text at the beginning of the next line. Wordwrap allows you to type words in a paragraph continually without pressing the Enter key at the end of each line.

In some instances, for example if you create a multipage document, you can view only a portion of a document on the screen at a time. The top portion of the document moves upward, or scrolls, off the screen as you type more lines of text than can be displayed on the screen. **Scrolling** is the process of moving different portions of the document into view on the screen.

A major advantage of using word processing software is that you can change easily what you have written. You can insert, delete, or rearrange words, sentences, or entire sections. You can use the **find** or **search** feature to locate all occurrences of a particular character, word, or phrase. This feature can be used in combination with the **replace** feature to substitute existing characters or words with new ones. Current word processing software packages even have a feature that automatically corrects errors and makes word substitutions as you type text.

To review the spelling of individual words, sections of a document, or the entire document, you can use a **spelling checker**, also called a **spell checker**.

Web Info

For samples of clip art available on the Internet, visit the Computer Concepts CourseMate Web site at *www.cengagebrain. com*, navigate to the Chapter 3 Web Info resource for this book, and then click Clip Art.

Web Info

For details about spelling bees, visit the Computer Concepts CourseMate Web site at *www.cengagebrain. com*, navigate to the Chapter 3 Web Info resource for this book, and then click Spelling.

Lion 1

Iris

Puppy

Puffin

Conch 1

Trout

Mammoth

Figure 3-11 Clip art consists of previously created illustrations that can be added to documents. Clip art collections include graphic images that are grouped by type. These clip art examples are from an animals and nature collection.

A spelling checker compares the words in the document with an electronic dictionary that is part of the word processing software (Figure 3-12). You can customize the electronic dictionary by adding words, such as names of companies, schools, streets, and cities, and personal names, so the software can spell check those words as well. Many word processing software packages allow you to check the spelling of a whole document at one time or check the spelling of single words as you type.

You also can insert headers and footers into a word processing document. A **header** is text you want at the top of each page; a **footer** is text you want at the bottom of each page. Page numbers, as well as company and school names, report titles, or dates are examples of items frequently included in headers and footers.

Many word processing programs make it quick and easy for teachers and students to create personalized documents using templates and special programs called wizards. A **template** is a document that contains the formatting necessary for a specific document type. A **wizard**, or **assistant**, is an automated tool that helps you complete a task by asking you questions and then automatically performing actions based on your answers. Many software applications include wizards. Word processing software, for example, uses wizards and templates to help you create blogs, memos, résumés, meeting agendas, letters, and other professional looking documents (Figure 3-13).

In addition to these basic features, most current word processing packages provide many other features, some of which are listed in the table in Figure 3-14.

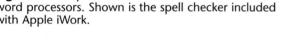
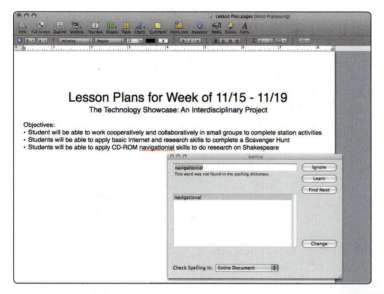

Figure 3-12 Spell checkers are included with most word processors. Shown is the spell checker included with Apple iWork.

[a] Apple iWork

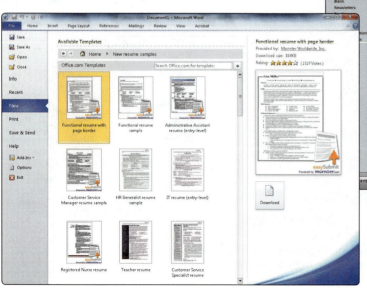

[b] Microsoft Word

Figure 3-13 Templates allow teachers and students to create personalized flyers, newsletters, certificates, résumés, and more quickly. Figure 3-13a shows some of the templates available in Apple iWork, and Figure 3-13b shows some of the templates available in Microsoft Word.

Some Word Processing Features	
AutoCorrect	As you type words, the AutoCorrect feature corrects common spelling errors. AutoCorrect also corrects capitalization mistakes.
AutoFormat	As you type, the AutoFormat feature automatically applies formatting to the text. For example, it automatically numbers a list or converts a Web address to a hyperlink.
Collaboration	Collaboration includes discussions and online meetings. Discussions allow multiple users to enter comments in a document and read and reply to each other's comments. Through an online meeting, users share documents with others in real time and view changes as they are being made.
Columns	Most word processing software can arrange text in two or more columns to look like a newspaper or magazine. The text from the bottom of one column automatically flows to the top of the next column.
Grammar Checker	The grammar checker proofreads documents for grammar, writing style, sentence structure errors, and reading statistics.
Ink Input	Ink input supports input from a digital pen. Word processing software that supports ink input incorporates a user's handwritten text and drawings in a word processing document. Ink input is popular on tablet computers.
Macros	A *macro* is a sequence of keystrokes and instructions that a user records and saves. When you want to execute the same series of instructions, execute the macro instead.
Mail Merge	Mail merge creates form letters, mailing labels, and envelopes.
Reading Layout	For those users who prefer reading on the screen, reading layout increases the readability and legibility of an on-screen document by hiding unnecessary toolbars, increasing the size of displayed characters, and providing navigation tools.
Research	Some word processing software allows you to search through various forms of online and Internet reference information — based on selected text in a document. Research services available include a thesaurus, English and bilingual dictionaries, encyclopedias, and Web sites that provide information such as stock quotes, news articles, and company profiles.
Smart Tags	*Smart Tags* automatically appear on the screen when you perform a certain action. For example, typing an address causes a Smart Tag to appear. Clicking this Smart Tag provides options to display a map of the address or driving directions to or from the address.
Tables	Tables organize information into rows and columns. In addition to evenly spaced rows and columns, some word processing programs allow you to draw tables of any size or shape.
Templates	A *template* is a document that contains the formatting necessary for a specific document type. Templates usually exist for memos, fax cover sheets, and letters. In addition to templates provided with the software, users have access to many online templates through the software manufacturer's Web site.
Thesaurus	With a thesaurus, a user looks up a synonym (word with the same meaning) for a word in a document.
Tracking Changes	If multiple users work with a document, the word processing software highlights or color-codes changes made by various users.
Voice Recognition	With some word processing programs, users can speak into the computer's microphone and watch the spoken words appear on the screen as they speak. With these programs, users edit and format the document by speaking or spelling an instruction.
Web Page Development	Most word processing software allows users to create, edit, format, and convert documents to be displayed on the World Wide Web.

Figure 3-14 Some of the features included with word processing software.

SPREADSHEET SOFTWARE

Another widely used software application is **spreadsheet software**, which allows you to organize numeric data in rows and columns. These rows and columns collectively are called a **spreadsheet**, or **worksheet**. Manual spreadsheets created using pencil and paper have long been used to organize numeric data. The data in an electronic spreadsheet is organized in the same manner as it is in a manual spreadsheet (Figure 3-15 on the next page).

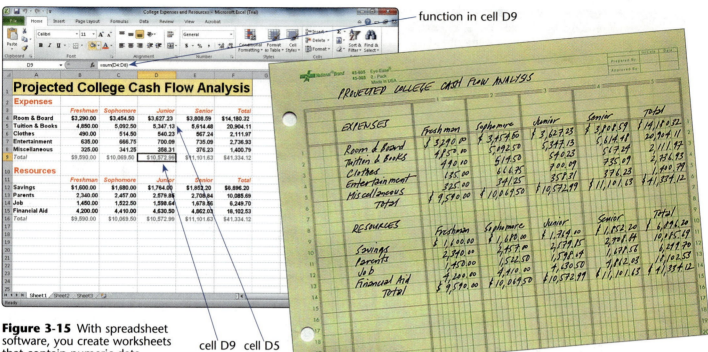

function in cell D9

Figure 3-15 With spreadsheet software, you create worksheets that contain numeric data arranged in rows and columns.

cell D9   cell D5

Individuals who frequently work with numbers, such as financial statements and payroll, use spreadsheets. Many teachers interact with spreadsheet programs on a daily basis. Every time teachers enter students' grade or attendance information into a computer, they are entering information into a special spreadsheet program, called an electronic gradebook. K-12 gradebook programs are discussed later in this chapter.

As with word processing software, most spreadsheet software has basic features to help you create, edit, and format electronic spreadsheets. These features, which are included in several popular spreadsheet packages, are described below. Spreadsheet software included in Microsoft Works and Apple iWork, as well as Microsoft Excel that is packaged with Microsoft Office, are the programs typically used in schools.

Spreadsheet files normally have thousands of columns and rows. Each column is identified by a letter, and each row is identified by a number. The column letters begin with A and row numbers begin with 1. Only a small fraction of these columns and rows are displayed on the screen at one time. You can scroll to view different parts of a worksheet on your screen.

The intersection of a column and row is called a **cell**. Cells are identified by the column and row in which they are located. For example, the intersection of column D and row 5 is referred to as cell D5. In Figure 3-15 above, cell D5 contains the number 5,347.13, which represents Junior year Tuition & Books expenses.

Cells may contain three types of data: labels (text), values (numbers), and formulas. The text, or **label**, entered in a cell is used to identify the data and help organize the spreadsheet. Using descriptive labels, such as Room & Board, Tuition & Books, and Clothes, helps make a spreadsheet more meaningful.

Many of the spreadsheet cells shown in Figure 3-15 contain a number, or a **value**. Other cells, however, contain formulas that are used to generate values. A **formula** performs calculations on the numeric data in the spreadsheet and displays the resulting value in the cell containing the formula.

In Figure 3-15, for example, cell D9 contains a special formula called a function, which is used to calculate the projected total expenses for the student's junior year. A **function** is a predefined formula that performs common calculations, such as adding the values in a group of cells. For example, instead of using the

line chart   column chart

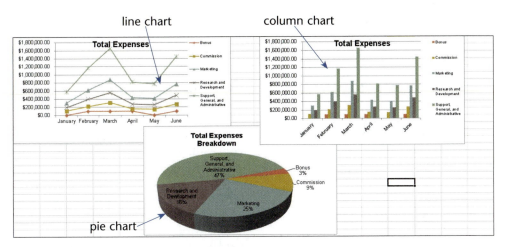

pie chart

Figure 3-16 Three basic types of charts provided with spreadsheet software are line charts, column charts, and pie charts. The line chart, column chart, and pie chart shown were created from the data in the worksheet in Figure 3-15.

formula =D4+D5+D6+D7+D8 to calculate the projected total expenses for the student's junior year, you should use the function =sum(D4:D8), which adds, or sums, the contents of cells D4, D5, D6, D7, and D8.

Another standard feature of spreadsheet software is the capability of turning numeric data into a **chart** that graphically illustrates the relationship of the numeric data. Visual representation of data in charts often makes it easier to analyze and interpret information. Most charts are variations of three basic chart types — line charts, column charts, and pie charts, as shown in Figure 3-16. It is important to pick the chart type that provides the best visualization for your data. To improve their appearance, most charts can be displayed or printed in a three-dimensional format.

As with word processing software, you can create professional looking spreadsheets quickly using wizards. Using the wizards in most popular spreadsheet packages is easy and allows you to create gradebooks, classroom and school schedules, charts, and more. Spreadsheet software also incorporates many of the features of word processing software, such as a spelling checker, font formatting, and the capability of converting an existing spreadsheet document into the standard document format for the World Wide Web. Because individual rows, columns, cells, or any combination of cells can be formatted, school districts and businesses often use spreadsheet programs to create their standardized forms.

DATABASE SOFTWARE

A **database** is a collection of data organized in a manner that allows access, retrieval, and use of that data. In a manual system, information is recorded on paper and stored in a filing cabinet (Figure 3-17). In a computerized database, such as the one shown in Figure 3-20 on page 115, data is stored in an electronic format on a storage medium. **Database software** allows you to create a computerized database; add, change, and delete data; sort and retrieve data from the database; and create forms and reports using the data in the database.

Database software is used extensively by businesses and other organizations to organize data and information about customers, employees, equipment, product

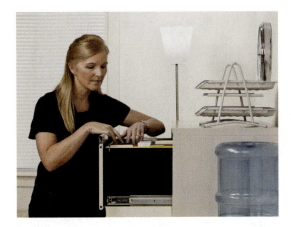

Figure 3-17 A database is similar to a manual system in which related data items are stored in files.

inventory, sales information, and more. Schools use databases to organize data and information about students, staff members, school policies, equipment inventories, book inventories, purchases, and more. Database programs typically used in schools include Microsoft Access, FileMaker Pro, and the database software included in Microsoft Works.

When you use a database, you need to be familiar with the terms file, record, and field. Just as in a manual system, a **database file** is a collection of related data that is organized in records. Each **record** contains a collection of related facts called fields. A **field** is the smallest unit of information you can access in a database. For example, a student database file might consist of records containing names, address information, and parental or guardian information. All of the data that relates to one student is considered a record. Each fact in a record, such as the street address or telephone number, is called a field.

Figures 3-18 through 3-20 present the development of a database containing basic information about students enrolled in

Ms. Eileen Tanner's second grade class at Martin Luther King Elementary School. This simple database contains the following information about each student: first name, last name, guardian's address, name, and telephone number.

Before you begin creating a database, you should make a list of the data items you want to organize (Figure 3-18). Each set of related information will become a record. Each item will become a field in the database. A field entry screen from Microsoft Works is shown in Figure 3-19. To identify the different fields, assign each field a unique name that is short, yet descriptive. For example, the field name for a student's last name could be Last Name, the field name for a student's first name could be First Name, and so on. Database programs differ slightly in how they require the user to enter or define fields.

After the database structure is created by defining the fields, data for individual database records can be entered. After data for all records is entered, the database can be used to produce information. Figure 3-20 shows the database after the information about the students has been entered.

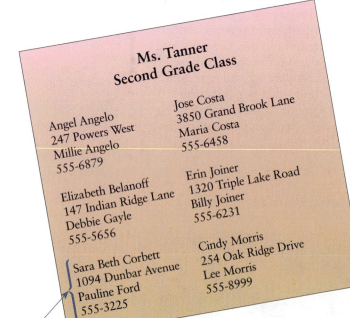

one record

Figure 3-18 This figure shows a partial list of the student information Ms. Tanner will be entering in her student database.

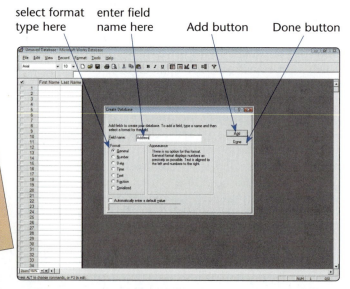

Figure 3-19 To create database fields in Microsoft Works, you simply type each field name, select the format associated with each field, and then click the Add button. After entering all the fields and clicking the Done button in the Create Database dialog box, you are ready to enter the data in the new database.

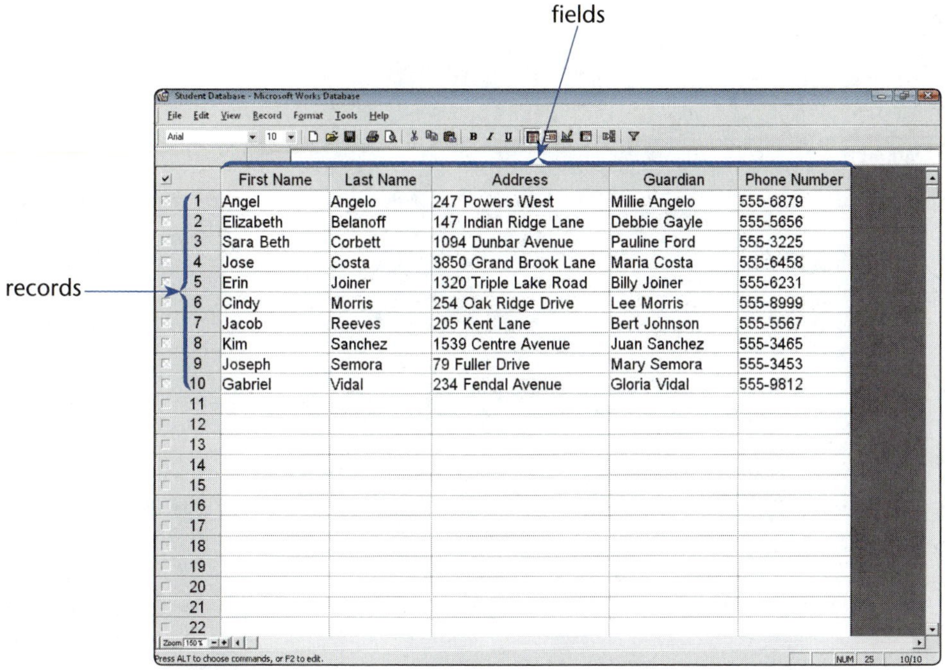

fields

Figure 3-20 After data has been entered into a database, the records can be arranged in any order specified by users. In this example, the records have been organized alphabetically based on students' last names.

As with word processing and spreadsheet software, database software includes wizards that allow teachers and students to create databases for use as address books, directories of parents and students, equipment and book inventories, and so on.

PRESENTATION GRAPHICS SOFTWARE

Using **presentation graphics software**, you can create documents called **presentations**, which you then use to communicate ideas, messages, and other information to a group, such as a class or people in an auditorium. The presentations can be viewed as **slides** that are displayed on a large monitor or projected onto a screen. Slides also can be made into traditional overhead transparencies or printed and given to students as a handout (Figure 3-21 on the next page).

Presentation programs typically used in schools are the presentation software included with Apple iWork, Keynote, and Microsoft PowerPoint packaged with Microsoft Office.

Presentation graphics software typically provides an array of predefined presentation formats that define complementary colors for backgrounds, text, and other special effects. Presentation graphics software also provides a variety of layouts for each individual slide so you can create a title slide, a two-column slide, a slide with clip art, and slides with other formats. Any text, charts, and graphics used in a slide can be enhanced with 3D and other effects such as shading, shadows, and textures.

With presentation graphics software, you can incorporate objects from the clip art/image gallery into your slides to create multimedia presentations. A **clip art/image gallery** includes clip art images, pictures, videos, and audio files. A clip art/image gallery can be stored on a hard disk, a CD, or a DVD; you can also access clip art/image galleries on the Web. As with clip art collections, a clip art/image gallery typically is organized by categories, such as academic, business, entertainment, and transportation. For example, the transportation category may contain a clip art image of a bicycle, a photograph of a locomotive, a video of an airplane in flight, and an audio of a Model T car horn.

Web Info

For more information on Apple's Keynote, visit the Computer Concepts CourseMate Web site at *www. cengagebrain.com*, navigate to the Chapter 3 Web Info resource for this book, and then click Keynote.

screen display

handout

Figure 3-21 Teachers and students use presentation graphics software to create electronic slides. The slides can be displayed on a computer, projected on a screen, printed and handed out, or made into transparencies.

When building a presentation, you can set the slide timing so the presentation automatically displays the next slide after a predetermined delay. You also can apply special effects to the transition between each slide. For example, one slide might slowly dissolve as the next slide comes into view.

To help organize the presentation, you can view small versions of all the slides in a slide sorter. A **slide sorter** presents a screen view similar to how 35mm slides look

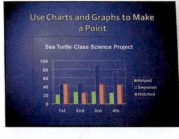

transparency

For tips on using graphics effectively in a presentation, visit the Computer Concepts CourseMate Web site at *www. cengagebrain.com*, navigate to the Chapter 3 Web Info resource for this book, and then click Presentation.

Web Info

on a photographer's light table. The slide sorter allows you to arrange the slides in any order or display them one at a time by clicking the mouse or pressing a key on the keyboard (Figure 3-22 on the next page).

Presentation graphics software also incorporates some of the features provided in word processing software, such as spell checking, formatting, and converting an existing slide show into a format that can be viewed on the World Wide Web.

Presentation graphics programs are important software programs for K-12 schools. Teachers can create and integrate electronic presentations into any classroom curriculum as an exciting

FAQ

Is PowerPoint hard for young students to use?

No, students as young as six and seven years old are creating PowerPoint presentations.

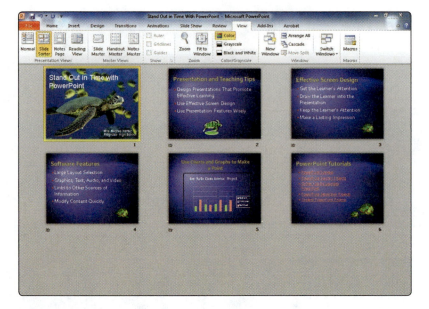

Figure 3-22 This slide sorter screen shows a small version of each slide. Using a pointing device or the keyboard, users can rearrange the order of the slides.

alternative to the traditional lecture-only teaching style (Figure 3-23). Students take great pride in creating their own presentations using presentation graphics software. Later chapters provide real-life examples of how teachers integrate presentation graphics software into their instruction and curriculum. A unique feature of presentation graphics software is

that it allows you to create a presentation that presents information in a nonlinear format. When using overhead transparencies, teachers traditionally show one transparency after another in a predetermined order — that is, linear teaching and learning.

With presentation graphics software programs, teachers and students can create

Figure 3-23 Electronic slide presentations are an exciting alternative to the traditional lecture-only teaching style.

presentations easily with links to a variety of information sources. Teachers and students, for example, can create presentations with links to other slides, other presentations, other files and software programs, animations, videos, audio files, and even sites on the World Wide Web (Figure 3-24) if the presentation computer is connected to the Internet. Using these links, teachers and students can branch off in a nonlinear fashion at any point in a presentation, to display or access additional information.

The ability to modify presentation content according to student interest makes presentation graphics software a powerful teaching and learning tool. The In the Lab end-of-chapter section in Chapter 5 discusses using and integrating Microsoft PowerPoint in more depth.

Figure 3-24 By clicking a hyperlink in a PowerPoint presentation, teachers and students can access another slide, slide presentation, sound files, videos, or a Web site if connected to the Internet.

PERSONAL INFORMATION MANAGERS

A **personal information manager (PIM)** is a software application installed on smartphones that includes an appointment calendar, address book, notepad, and other features to help you organize personal information such as appointments, task lists, and more. A PIM allows you to take information that you tracked previously in a weekly or daily calendar, and organize and store it on your computer or smartphone. PIMs can manage many different types of information, such as telephone messages, project notes, reminders, task and address lists, and important dates and appointments (Figure 3-25).

An **appointment calendar** allows you to schedule activities for a particular day and time. With an **address book**, you can enter and maintain names, addresses, and telephone numbers of coworkers, family members, and friends. Instead of writing notes on a piece of paper, you can use a **notepad** to record ideas, reminders, and other important information.

Most smartphones contain many other features and built-in software programs in addition to those shown in Figure 3-25, including Web browsing, instant messaging, and more. One of these features allows users to **synchronize**, or transfer, information and programs from the smartphone to a personal computer and vice versa—a process known as syncing.

WEB APPLICATIONS

A **Web application**, or **Web app**, is an application that allows users to access and interact with software from any computer

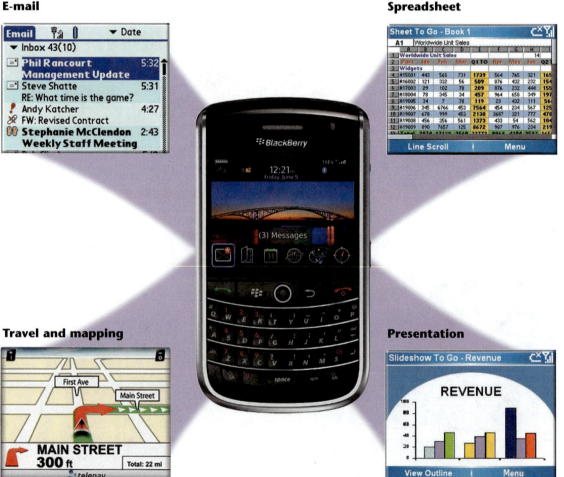

Figure 3-25 In addition to an appointment calendar, an address book, and a notepad, current smartphones include business and other software such as e-mail, spreadsheet, presentation, and travel and mapping.

or device that is connected to the Internet — which is sometimes called **cloud computing**. Users often interact with Web applications, directly at the Web site (referred to as the host) through their Web browser. Some Web sites, however, require you to download the software to your local computer or device. Web application hosts often store users' data and information on their servers. Some Web applications provide users with an option of storing data locally on their personal computer or mobile device.

Many of the previously discussed types of application software are available as Web applications. In addition, thousands of games are available as Web applications. Some Web application hosts provide free access to their software, such as Google Docs, while others, such as Google Earth, offer part of their Web application free but charge for access to more features. Some Web applications, such as online tax preparation programs, allow you to use the Web application free but require you to pay a fee when a certain action occurs. For example, you can prepare your tax return free, but if you elect to print it or file it electronically, you pay a minimal fee.

Experts often use the term Web 2.0 to describe Web applications. Recall that Web 2.0 refers to Web sites that provide users with a means to facilitate participatory environments by sharing personal information and collaborating. Web 2.0 also allows users to modify Web site content and/or have application software built into the site for visitors to use.

IS AN APP DIFFERENT FROM A WEB APPLICATION OR AN APPLICATION SOFTWARE PROGRAM?

As discussed earlier in this chapter, Web applications and application software programs are usually multipurpose programs. Users can purchase application software from a software vendor, retail store, or Web-based business. Users typically install purchased application software on a computer before they run it. There are advantages and disadvantages to using installed software. Advantages include faster processing time because the application is on your computer and access to the program even when Internet access is not available. Disadvantages include disk space is required on your computer to store the software and it can be costly to upgrade as vendors release new versions. As an alternative, some users opt to access Web applications described earlier. With Web applications, users pay a fee to use the application via the Internet but it is not installed locally.

Today, virtually all mobile device users download and use apps on their smartphones, tablet computers, and other mobile devices. So what is an app? In 2011, the American Dialect Society voted app the word of the year. An **app**, also called a **mobile app**, is a program you can download and use primarily on your mobile device. Apps often are single purpose programs, such as a weather app, a coupon app, and so on. There are thousands of apps available to meet your needs and all can be purchased and downloaded via your computer, smartphone, or mobile device.

Apple created and marketed the concept of an app as a free or $1–$5 unit and offered apps for download from their App Store. What Apple did for apps is similar to what they did for music (i.e., iTunes) — they made single purpose software programs available at their user-friendly App Store. Today, over 500,000 apps are available from Apple's App Store for use on iPads, iPhones, and the iPod Touch. Hundreds of thousands of additional apps are available from other vendor apps stores for smartphones and tablet computers. To explore hundreds of education apps (like the one shown in Figure 3-26 on the next page), access each chapter's end-of-chapter section, Apps Corner.

While apps, Web applications, and application software programs are all computer programs that help users accomplish a task, apps are generally single purpose programs whereas Web applications and application software programs are usually multipurpose programs.

Figure 3-26 There are apps for everyone at Apple's App Store, including a wide variety of apps for PK-12 teachers, administrators, and students.

SOFTWARE SUITES

A **software suite** is a collection of individual application software packages sold as a single package. The most popular software suite used in businesses, universities, and K-12 schools is Microsoft Office available both for PCs and Macs (Figure 3-27). Microsoft Office 2010, the latest version of Office, is available in a number of versions including Home and Student, Home and Business, and Professional.

For many school, home, and some business users, the capabilities of a less expensive software suite more than meet their needs. Popular inexpensive software suites include **Microsoft Works** for PCs and **Apple**

iWork, formerly AppleWorks, for Macs (Figure 3-28). Microsoft Works contains word processing, spreadsheet, database, and communications software. Apple's iWork contains word processing, spreadsheet, paint, and presentation software. In addition, individual programs included with iWork are available at Apple's App Store; for additional information, see this chapter's Apps Corner on page 145.

When you install a suite, you install the entire collection of applications at once, rather than installing each application individually. At a minimum, comprehensive suites, like Microsoft Office, typically include word processing, spreadsheet, database, and

Figure 3-27 Microsoft Office is available in versions for both PCs and Macs.

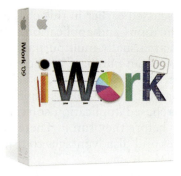

Figure 3-28 Apple iWork is available for Macs.

presentation graphics. Each application in a software suite is designed specifically to work as part of a larger set of applications and to share common features.

Software suites offer two major advantages: lower cost and ease of use. Typically, buying a collection of software packages in a suite costs significantly less than purchasing the application packages separately. Software suites provide ease of use because the applications within a suite normally use a similar interface and have some common features. Thus, after you learn how to use one application in the suite, you are familiar with the interface of other applications in the suite. For example, after you learn how to print using the suite's word processing program, you can apply the same skill to the spreadsheet, database, and presentation graphics programs in the suite.

Graphics and Multimedia Software

In addition to productivity software, many individuals also work with software designed specifically for their fields of work. For example, engineers, architects, publishers, and graphic artists often use powerful software that allows them to work with graphics and multimedia. Types of graphics and multimedia software include desktop publishing software, paint/image editing software, clip art/image gallery, multimedia authoring tools, video and audio editing software, Web page authoring software, and many others. The features and functions of some of these applications are discussed in the following sections.

DESKTOP PUBLISHING SOFTWARE

Desktop publishing (DTP) software allows you to design, produce, and deliver sophisticated documents that contain text, graphics, and brilliant colors. Although many word processing packages have some of the capabilities of DTP software, professional designers and graphic artists use DTP software because it is designed specifically to support **page layout**, which is the

process of arranging text and graphics in a document. DTP software is ideal for the production of high-quality color documents, such as newsletters, marketing literature, catalogs, and annual reports. In the past, documents of this type were created by slower, more expensive traditional publishing methods, such as typesetting. Today's DTP software also allows you to convert a color document into a format for use on the World Wide Web.

Many home, school, and small business users use a simple, easy-to-understand DTP software program (such as Microsoft Publisher), which is designed for individual desktop publishing projects. Using this DTP software, you can create newsletters and brochures, postcards and greeting cards, letterhead and business cards, banners, calendars, logos, and other such documents (Figure 3-29). Personal DTP software guides you through the development of these documents by asking a series of questions, offering numerous predefined layouts, and providing standard text you can add to documents. As you enter text, the personal DTP software checks your spelling. You can print your finished publications on a color printer or place them on the Web.

FAQ

I cannot open some files on the Web, including brochures, applications, education articles, and reports. Why?

To open a file, you must have the same application the file was created with unless the file has been saved using the Adobe PDF format. The PDF format allows readers to view a document even when they do not have the same program used to create the original document. To view and print a PDF file, simply download the free Adobe Acrobat Reader software from the Adobe Web site (*adobe.com*).

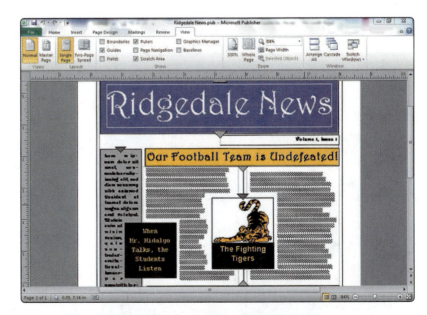

Figure 3-29 Teachers and students use desktop publishing software, such as Microsoft Publisher, to create flyers, certificates, newsletters, and other types of documents.

PAINT/IMAGE EDITING SOFTWARE

Graphic artists, multimedia professionals, desktop publishers, and many others use paint software and image editing software to create and modify graphics (Figure 3-30), such as those used in DTP documents and Web pages. **Paint software** allows you to draw pictures, shapes, and other graphics using various tools on the screen, such as a pen, brush, eye dropper, and paint bucket. **Image editing software** provides the capabilities of paint software as well as the capability of modifying existing graphics. For example, you can retouch photographs, adjust or enhance image colors, and add special effects such as shadows and glows.

Many home, school, and small business users opt for personal paint/image editing software. Personal paint/image editing software provides a much easier-to-use interface and usually has simplified capabilities, with functions tailored to the needs of the home and small business user. Personal paint/image editing software includes various simplified tools that allow you to draw pictures, shapes, and other graphics. Professional paint/image editing software provides more sophisticated tools for drawing and modifying pictures, shapes, and other images.

One popular type of image editing software, called **photo editing software**, allows you to edit digital photographs by removing red-eye, adding special effects, or creating electronic photo albums. When the photograph is complete, you can print it on labels, calendars, business cards, and banners; or place it on a Web page. Popular photo editing programs used by educators include Photo Story and iPhoto.

CLIP ART/IMAGE GALLERY

Although many applications include clip art, you may find that you want a wider selection of graphics. One way to obtain them is to purchase a clip art/image gallery, which is a collection of clip art and photographs. In addition to clip art (Figure 3-31), many clip art/image galleries provide fonts, animations, sounds, videos, and audio files. You can use the images, fonts, and other items from the clip art/image gallery in all types of documents, such as letters, flyers, and class projects.

MULTIMEDIA AUTHORING SOFTWARE

Multimedia authoring software is used to create electronic presentations, simulations, and software demonstrations that can include text, graphics, video, audio, animation, and screen captures. While many multimedia authoring software programs are available, two popular programs used by educators are Camtasia Studio and Adobe Captivate. These easy to use multimedia authoring programs help

Figure 3-30 With image editing software, users can create and modify a variety of graphic images. Shown is Corel Painter.

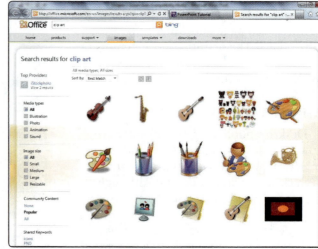

Figure 3-31 Clip art/image galleries provide thousands of clip art images and photographs for use in documents such as letters, newsletters, greeting cards, class projects, and presentations.

Figure 3-32 With video and audio editing software, teachers and students can edit their home and school movies.

Integration Strategies

To learn more about using and integrating various multimedia authoring software programs, visit the Computer Concepts CourseMate Web site at *www.cengagebrain. com*, and then navigate to the Chapter 3 Digital Media Corner resource for this book.

educators create video presentations. Educators can use these programs even if they do not have programming knowledge or multimedia skills.

VIDEO AND AUDIO EDITING SOFTWARE

Video consists of full-motion images played back at various speeds. With video editing software, you can modify a segment of a video, called a clip (Figure 3-32). For example, you can add and remove clips, or add special effects like sounds, banners, credits, and more. Video editing programs normally allow you either to edit or add audio components. Current PC and Macintosh computers include extensive audio and video editing capabilities; you and your students can even make your own videos. Popular programs used by educators include iMovie, iLife, Movie Maker, and Final Cut.

WEB PAGE AUTHORING SOFTWARE

Web page authoring software is designed specifically to help you create Web pages, in addition to organizing, managing, and maintaining Web sites. As noted in previous sections, many application software packages include Web page authoring features that you can use to create Web pages and Web sites or that you can use to save a document as a Web page. For

example, Figure 3-33 shows you how to convert a word processing document into the standard document format for the World Wide Web automatically by saving it as a Web page. After being saved, the document can be published to the Web and viewed in any Web browser. Word processing programs, for example, contain enough features to satisfy the formatting and layout needs of teachers and students for building resource pages and other Web documents.

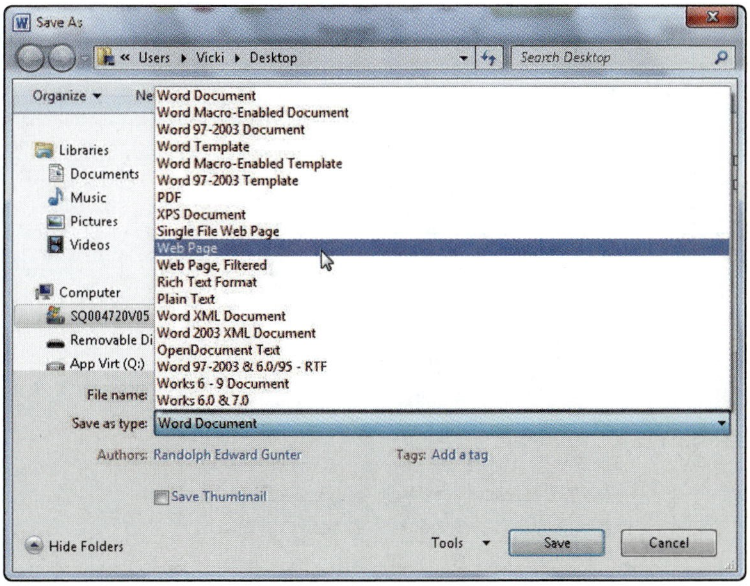

Figure 3-33 The figure shows how to convert a word processing document into a Web page.

Software for School Use

Many school districts have undergone a period of transition in how they maintain student records and other pertinent information. An important factor driving this transition is the installation of networks.

Having networks in schools allows schools to manage and maintain information about students and teachers in a centralized way. At the lower technological end, some schools still maintain all student records manually or in software programs on individual computers. Teachers and other school personnel then periodically input student records manually into student management software that stores grades and attendance records. At the higher technological end, some schools maintain district-wide student management programs.

SCHOOL AND STUDENT MANAGEMENT SOFTWARE

Schools that have networked at least one computer in each classroom usually install school and student management software. When standardized throughout the school district, these programs can improve a school's ability to manage and analyze daily operations, budgets, and student information dramatically.

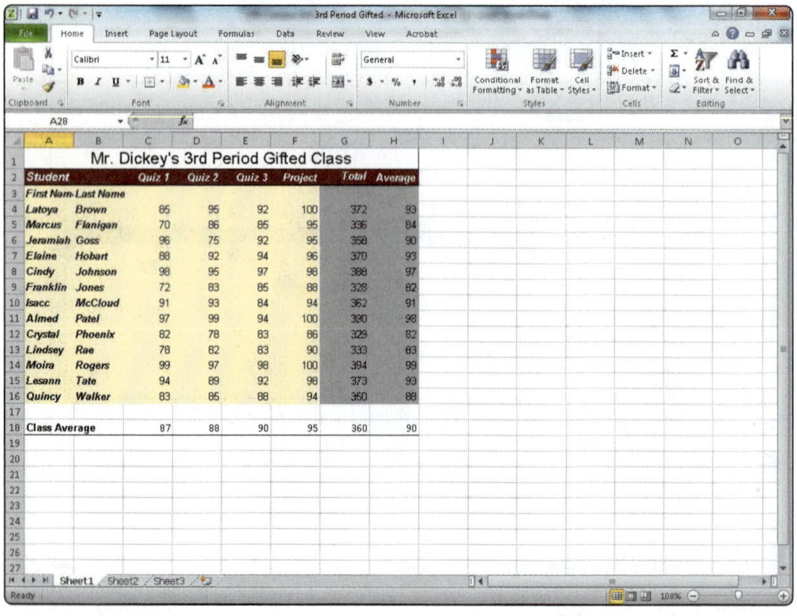

School management software is a centralized program that allows district and school personnel to manage the school district operations, such as budgeting, inventory, technology, and expenses. Most school management software packages allow a school district to keep a database of all district assets, salaries and benefits, and food services inventory; manage other school and department budgets; and track transportation vehicle maintenance and use. Some school management software also includes databases for attendance and other student information and has other functions similar to student management software. **Student management software** is a centralized program that allows administrators, teachers, and other staff to manage and track information about students, which includes attendance and academic records.

GRADEBOOK SOFTWARE

Gradebook software allows teachers to track and organize student tests, homework, lab work, and other scores. Most gradebook software allows you to track thousands of students and hundreds of assignments within the same gradebook and sort students by name, student number, or current average. Most programs allow teachers to weight various scores automatically, apply grading curves, adjust letter grade cutoffs, or use a customized grading scale, such as Fair, Good, Excellent, and so on. Grades can be displayed and entered as points, percentages, letter grades, or in a customized grading scale.

At some schools, teachers enter attendance and student grades into the same gradebook program, which is installed on all district computers. Not all schools have one district-wide gradebook program for teachers to use, however, so many teachers choose their own gradebook program. Numerous outstanding gradebook and attendance programs are available for teachers. Some of these are shareware programs; others have trial versions that you can download from the Web for evaluation purposes. Popular gradebook programs include Engrade, MicroGrade, GradeQuick, WebGrader, Easy Grade Pro, and Gradebook Plus. You also can create a basic gradebook using the wizards and templates in Microsoft Excel (Figure 3-34), Apple iWork, and other programs.

Figure 3-34 An example of a gradebook that teachers can create using Microsoft Excel.

K-12 Educational Software Applications

An **educational software application** refers to computer software products used to support teaching and learning of subject-related content. Interactive digital media applications enrich the learning process by providing individualized instruction and exploration; allowing students to examine their skills in a risk-free environment; and providing instant feedback, testing, and review. Many educational software applications now are correlated to common core state standards.

The number and quality of educational software applications designed specifically for the K-12 learning environment have increased dramatically in the past few years. Educational software applications are available in many different designs, forms, and curriculum levels, as shown in Figure 3-35. The math program shown in Figure 3-35a allows students to interact with video lessons on math concepts created by an award-winning teacher. There are an abundance of grade-specific science applications, such as an app called Molecules (see Figure 3-35b) that

[a] Video Calculus app

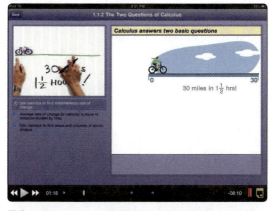

[b] science app called Molecules

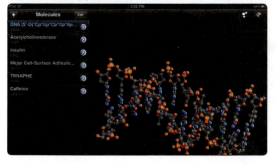

Figure 3-35 Digital media apps are great tools to help teach difficult math and science concepts.

allows students to view three-dimensional renderings of molecular structures and then manipulate them using their fingers.

The next sections discuss computer-assisted instruction, drill-and-practice, educational games, tutorials, educational simulations, integrated learning systems, and curriculum-specific educational software applications. Chapters 5 through 7 provide you with ways to integrate these types of software programs into your classroom curriculum.

COMPUTER-ASSISTED INSTRUCTION (CAI)

Computer-assisted instruction (CAI) has been used in education for more than two decades. Computer-assisted instruction is software designed to help teach facts, information, and/or skills associated with subject-related materials. At its most basic level, computer-assisted instruction is using a computer to enhance instruction. Most educators, however, do not feel that the term computer-assisted instruction accurately describes the many different computer-based educational software programs available today. With the growth of educational technology, other names used to refer to education software have emerged, such as computer-based instruction (CBI), computer-based learning (CBL), and computer-aided learning (CAL). For the purposes of this textbook, the term educational software applications is used as an umbrella term that emcompasses the other terms and that refers to computer software products, including apps, that support teaching and learning of subject-related content (Figure 3-36).

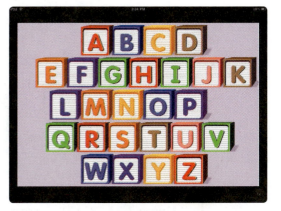

Figure 3-36 Starfalls ABCs allows younger students to see, hear, and interact with letters and sounds in words, sentences, and games.

DRILL-AND-PRACTICE SOFTWARE

Drill-and-practice software is software that first supplies factual information and then through repetitive exercises allows students to continue to work on specific materials to remember or memorize the information. Another name for this type of software is **skills-reinforcement software**. Drill-and-practice software is effective for learning basic skills and for remediation. **Remediation** is reviewing content many times and using alternative means to help a student grasp the concepts being taught.

One of the important features of drill-and-practice software and other educational software is that students receive instant feedback on correct and incorrect answers. Using drill-and-practice software can increase students' performance in areas that are weak. Drill-and-practice software usually has built-in features that allow the computer to move the student to the next level automatically when she masters a level. Drill-and-practice software is effective when used with students who require extra assistance in content instruction.

EDUCATIONAL GAMES

Today, the majority of educational games are available on DVDs and the Web. An **educational game** usually includes a set of rules, and students can compete against other students or the game itself. Games can be an effective way to teach content through repetition and practice.

Many students find educational games a fun way to learn. Various educational games create problem-solving environments forcing students to use higher-order thinking skills, for example, problem solving skills, to find solutions.

In his book *What Video Games Have to Teach Us About Learning and Literacy*, James Gee discusses how video games (especially those in which the player takes on a role of a fantasy character moving through an elaborate world) teach many things, regardless of specific content. Dr. Gee has identified up to 36 learning principles, most of them taken in a social learning context (what he refers to as "social achievement skills"), that are present in well-developed games. Video games promote and facilitate problem solving and students gladly accept the challenge, even without any lengthy introductory instruction.

Many games are provided for free to students and teachers. For example, *Ready To Learn* is an innovative learning partnership between PBS and the U.S. Department of Education. *Ready To Learn* integrates free and universally available children's educational television and online resources with community outreach to help parents and educators prepare today's digital kids for success in school. Figure 3-37 shows the PBS KIDS Web site where digital kids

Web Info

To access PBS Parents, PBS KIDS, PBS KIDS GO!, and PBS Teacher, visit the Computer Concepts CourseMate Web site at *www. cengagebrain.com*, navigate to the Chapter 3 Web Info resource for this book, and then click Ready To Learn.

Figure 3-37 PBS KIDS is a great and safe Web resource for today's young digital kids up to 8 years old.

up to 8 years old can learn and play with all of their favorite characters through games, music, and more.

PBS also provides a Web site, PBS KIDS GO!, for digital kids ages 6–12, where they can share their opinions and stories, play games, solve puzzles, and much more (Figure 3-38). The *Ready to Learn* partnership also provides a Web site for parents (PBS Parents) and for teachers (PBS Teacher). To access all of these *Ready To Learn* Web sites, see the Web Info on the preceding page.

TUTORIALS

A **tutorial** is a teaching program designed to help individuals learn to use a product or concepts. Tutorials are designed to tutor, or instruct. Many software products contain built-in tutorials to teach the user how to use the software. Developers create computer-based educational tutorials that cover an entire instructional area so students can work their way through the tutorial to learn content without any additional or outside help or materials. The teaching solutions provided by tutorials range from a structured linear approach with specific content objectives to a non-linear approach, called **branching**, that offers alternative paths through the lesson based on students' responses. Branching reflects classroom learning theory by allowing students to excel at their own pace, providing feedback and remediation when needed. Figure 3-39 provides some of the features of effective educational tutorials.

EDUCATIONAL SIMULATIONS

An **educational computer simulation** or a **video game** is a computerized model of real life that represents a physical or simulated process. These programs are unique because the user can cause things to happen, change the conditions, and make decisions based on the criteria provided to simulate real-life situations. These interactive programs model some event, reality, real-life circumstances, or phenomenon. Simulations offer learners the opportunity to manipulate variables that affect the outcomes of the experience. Using simulation is not a new teaching strategy.

Figure 3-38 The PBS KIDS GO! Web site provides games, digital storytelling, and much more for digital kids ages 6–12.

Tutorial Features

- User-friendly
- Easy to navigate
- Available on both PC and Mac platforms
- Student-centered interactivity throughout software
- Learner control over delivery of content
- Active instructional techniques
- Innovative learning strategies
- Real-life learning experiences
- Motivational and appropriate for grade level
- Contains valid testing
- Appropriate scope and sequence of content
- Evaluated by educators

Figure 3-39 Features of effective educational tutorials.

Interest is growing in programs, such as SimCity, Sim Theme Park, and Sim Coaster, that let students design, interact, and provide more accurate explanations and examples of real life. **SimCity** is a very popular simulation program for education (Figure 3-40). Students design cities, communities, neighborhoods, and businesses, including the infrastructure, such as telephone lines, buildings, and more. As the cities grow in size and complexity, and as natural disasters and other realistic problems occur continuously, students find they must use all available city resources, including financial resources, to keep the cities running.

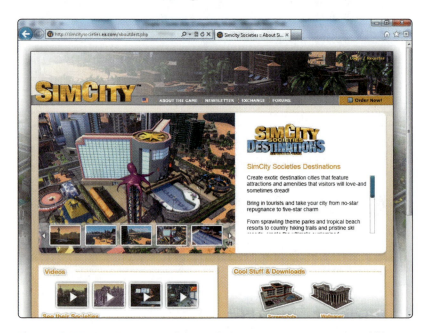

Figure 3-40 SimCity, a popular simulation program, creates a real-life environment for development of problem-solving skills.

Figure 3-41 Classworks from Curriculum Advantage is a popular open learning system.

The availability of educational computer simulations on the Web is experiencing dramatic growth. A student can learn how a building is demolished, how to dissect a frog, see how a human heart works, and more.

INTEGRATED LEARNING SYSTEMS

An **integrated learning system (ILS)** is a sophisticated software program usually developed by an established educational software corporation as a complete educational software solution in one package. These software solutions provide individual student diagnostic data through pretests, instruction based on the diagnostic data, continuous monitoring of student performance with automatic adjustments in instruction when needed, a variety of formats for teaching content, and content available at multiple levels.

Most integrated learning systems also offer a comprehensive management solution for maintaining the software and for tracking student use and progress. Although expensive, integrated learning systems are praised as a comprehensive software solution for low-achieving schools. Integrated learning systems are appealing to school administrators, school boards, and principals because they offer a full, flexible solution in one package. Popular programs include CompassLearning, Renaissance Learning, Pearson Digital Learning, and PLATO Learning.

A type of software application has evolved that is similar to an ILS, called an open learning system or an advanced learning system. An **open learning system** or an **advanced learning system** is an integrated learning system that includes software titles from leading publishers. What makes this type of learning system different from a traditional ILS is the number of different software titles and activities these packages include. In addition, many ILS applications prescribe the solution for the student while the new open learning systems make the teacher the key player in determining and prescribing the appropriate assessment, choosing the ideal activities, matching the software to objectives and standards, and integrating the software into their curriculum. A popular open learning system is Classworks from Curriculum Advantage (Figure 3-41).

CURRICULUM-SPECIFIC EDUCATIONAL SOFTWARE

Today, hundreds of high-quality interactive and educational software programs are available for use by K-12 educators. Most of these programs are available on CD and DVD or they are installed on school networks; others are available for download from the Web. Many of these educational software applications are designed for curriculum-specific teaching and learning and can be organized in categories as described in the following sections. These major categories are by no means inclusive, as many software programs are available for K-12 educators that can be used in dozens of curriculum areas.

CREATIVITY Creativity applications often have students start with a blank canvas, which allows them to use their imagination and ingenuity. Students can control the design of their projects completely, using the tools provided by the software application. Some applications provide students with ideas and premade backgrounds and images. Students typically have complete control over the design, graphics, and path they create. A number of popular software programs are available that fit in this category. Creativity software applications include JumpStart Artist (Figure 3-42), iLife, Inspiration, Kidspiration, Ultimate Writing and Creativity Center, StoryWeaver, Microsoft Publisher, PaintShop Photo Pro, Photoshop, Disney Magic Artist Online, Kid Works Deluxe, MediaWorks, Kid Pix, and Adobe Creative Suite.

CRITICAL THINKING Critical-thinking applications stimulate students to use critical-thinking skills. Students often are presented with a problem and a variety of ways to solve the problem. They must use critical-thinking skills to obtain the correct solution to the problem. Critical-thinking software applications include I SPY; Classroom Jeopardy; Building Thinking Skills; The New Way Things Work (Figure 3-43); Kidspiration; Inspiration; Thinkin' Things collections; Clifford Thinking Adventures; Zoombinis collection; SimCity; Decisions, Decisions series; and Thinkology.

Figure 3-43 Dozens of critical-thinking applications are available for students of all ages. Shown is a popular program called The New Way Things Work.

EARLY LEARNING Early learning applications are designed to provide students in grades PreK-3 with a developmental head start in reading, language arts, math, science, and other curriculum areas. Students are presented with engaging graphics, a variety of paths, and a wide variety of activities. These fun and interactive programs include Kidspiration (Figure 3-44 on the next page), Bailey's Book House, Millie's Math House, Trudy's Time & Place House, Sammy's Science House, the JumpStart

Figure 3-42 JumpStart Artist is an example of creativity software that helps young students express themselves artistically.

Figure 3-44 Early learning software applications are designed primarily for grades PreK-3 and provide students with a developmental head start. Displayed is a popular program called Kidspiration.

series of software titles, Reader Rabbit's Reading series, Sticky Bear, and many more outstanding programs.

ESL/FOREIGN LANGUAGE   ESL and foreign language applications provide K-12 students with assistance in learning English and other languages (Figure 3-45 below). These applications enable students to practice their skills in a nonthreatening environment. These language-specific programs include Rosetta Stone, JumpStart

Spanish, Heartsoft Bestsellers ESL and ELL, English for Kids, Instant Immersion series, Phonics Tutor, Rocket French, and dozens of other language programs designed for students in all grades. You also can download free translation software that lets your computer talk from the ReadPlease Web site.

LANGUAGE ARTS   Language arts applications, available for all grade levels, support student learning throughout the

Figure 3-45 ESL and foreign language applications include software programs for Spanish, English, French, and many other languages. Shown is Rosetta Stone.

Figure 3-46 Language arts software is available for all grade levels. Shown is Reader Rabbit, a software designed for preschool and kindergarten students.

reading and writing process (Figure 3-46 above). These applications try to engage students, encouraging them to learn critical skills in a fun and creative environment. Popular language arts programs include Edmark Reading Program series, StoryWeaver, That Spelling is Right, Clicker 5, the Reader Rabbit series, Clifford Phonics, Amazing Writing Machine, Reading for Meaning, Reading Blaster series, Read 180, Simon Sounds It Out, Chuck Wagon Bill's Language Skills, and dozens more.

MATH Math applications help students master basic and complex mathematics and are available for all grade levels (Figure 3-47 below). Many applications provide students with skill practice and problem-solving activities. Math programs include the Math Advantage series, Destination Math, Go Solve series, Geometer's Sketchpad, Math Blaster, Math Workshop Deluxe, MathXpert, the Mighty Math series, FASTT Math, Math Companion, Tessellation Exploration, Wild West Math, InspireData, and many more.

[a] Math Advantage - Algebra

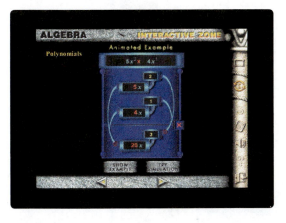

[b] MathXpert

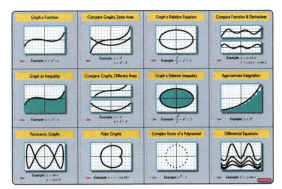

Figure 3-47 Math software engages and motivates students to learn basic and complex concepts. Figure 3-47a shows a Math Advantage Algebra 1 title, and Figure 3-47b displays MathXpert software. MathXpert is designed for high school students and covers hundreds of math concepts, including graphing.

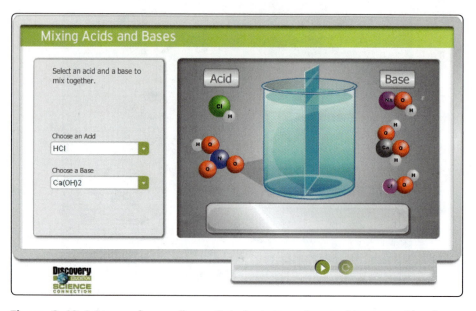

Figure 3-48 Science software allows all students to explore and interact with science concepts. Shown is an interactive sample from Discovery Education Science.

SCIENCE   Science applications are available for all grade levels and assist students in learning a wide variety of science concepts. Digital media science applications can assist students in mastering difficult or abstract concepts by providing visual representations.

Science applications include Thinkin' Science, Sammy's Science House, My Amazing Human Body, I Love Science, Discovery School series, Magic School Bus series, A.D.A.M. Interactive Anatomy, BBC Science Simulations, Discovery Education

Science (Figure 3-48 above), Squibs Science, Science Court series, and numerous others.

SOCIAL STUDIES   Social studies applications encourage higher-order thinking skills, provide reinforcement of facts, and allow students to define their own path. A few social studies programs include the Carmen Sandiego series, Oregon Trail, Amazon Trail, TimeLiner, Liberty's Kids, 3D World Atlas, Chronicle Encyclopedia of History (Figure 3-49 below), and the Discovery Education series.

Figure 3-49 Interactive digital media software, such as the Chronicle Encyclopedia of History, allows students to understand social studies concepts.

SPECIAL NEEDS SOFTWARE

Special needs software, also called **assistive technologies software**, is designed specifically for students with physical impairments or learning disabilities to assist them in completing school assignments and everyday tasks (Figure 3-50). Special needs software includes such programs as **speech synthesis software**, text enlargement programs, talking calculators, and more.

Today, teachers have many software options available to use as tools to enhance teaching and learning of students with special needs. Many software applications discussed in this chapter and other chapters also can be used to assist students with special needs. When students use these software programs in combination with assistive devices, such as touch screens and adaptive keyboards, their ability to succeed increases. These and other special input and output devices designed for use by students with special needs are discussed in Chapter 4 and in each chapter's Assistive Technologies Corner.

Recall that the textbook Web site includes an end-of-chapter section called Apps Corner. Included with Apps for each chapter is information on special needs apps and information on how other teachers are integrating apps to help special needs students. Finally, the Assistive Technologies Corner at the end of this chapter and on the Web provides extensive information and links to special needs software programs.

Figure 3-50 Using assistive technologies software, teachers help students with disabilities learn subject-related content.

Software for Home and Personal Use

Many software applications are designed specifically for home or personal use. Personal software includes personal finance software, tax preparation software, legal software, entertainment software, and more. Most of the products in this category are relatively inexpensive, often priced at less than $25–$50. The features and functions of some of these applications are discussed in the following sections. In addition, many of these programs are now available as apps for use on mobile devices. To explore a wide variety of personal use apps, visit your favorite apps store.

PERSONAL FINANCE SOFTWARE

Personal finance software is a simplified accounting program that helps you pay bills, balance your checkbook, track your personal income and expenses, such as credit card bills, track investments, evaluate financial plans, and maintain a home inventory (Figure 3-51 on the next page). Popular personal finance software includes Quicken and Microsoft Money.

Using personal finance software can help you determine where, and for what purpose, you are spending money so you can manage your finances. Reports can summarize transactions by category (such as dining), by payee (such as the electric company), or by billing period (such as the last two months). Bill-paying features include the ability to print checks on your printer or have an outside service print your checks.

Personal finance software packages usually offer a variety of online services, which require access to the Web. For example, you can track your investments online, compare insurance rates from leading insurance companies, and even do your banking online. **Online banking** offers access to account balances, provides bill payment services, and allows you to download transactions and statements from the Web directly to your computer.

Web Info

For more information about a popular and free text-to-speech software program, visit the Computer Concepts CourseMate Web site at *www. cengagebrain.com*, navigate to the Chapter 3 Web Info resource for this book, and then click ReadPlease.

FAQ

How many people bank online?

The number of people banking online is approaching 75 million, with that number expected to continue growing.

Figure 3-51 Many home users work with personal finance software to assist them with tracking personal expenses, paying bills, maintaining a home inventory, and more.

In addition, with online banking, you can transfer money electronically from your checking to savings or vice versa. To obtain current credit card statements, bank statements, and account balances, you download transaction information from your bank using the Web.

Financial planning features include analyzing home and personal loans, preparing income taxes, and managing retirement savings. Other features in many personal finance packages include budgeting and tax-related transactions.

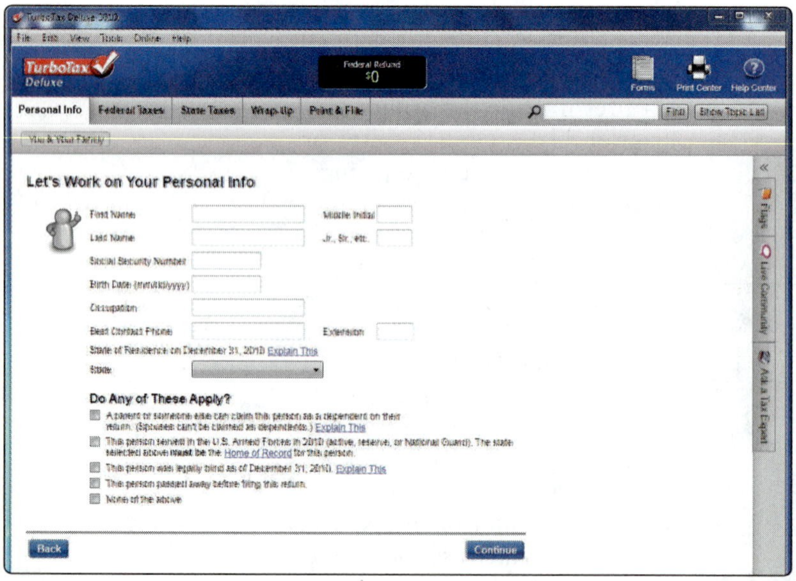

TAX PREPARATION SOFTWARE

Tax preparation software guides individuals, families, or small businesses through the process of filing federal taxes (Figure 3-52). Popular tax preparation software includes TurboTax, TaxACT, and TaxCut. These software packages offer money-saving tax tips, designed to lower your tax bill. After you answer a series of questions and complete basic forms, the tax preparation software creates and analyzes your tax forms to search for potential errors and missed deduction opportunities. After the forms are complete, you can print any necessary paperwork. Most tax preparation software packages allow you to file your tax forms electronically for a small fee — an increasingly popular option. In addition, most tax preparation packages are now available as Web applications.

Figure 3-52 Tax preparation software can assist you in preparing your federal and state tax returns efficiently and accurately. You can prepare your return completely online or even file your return electronically.

LEGAL SOFTWARE

Legal software assists in the preparation of legal documents and provides legal advice to individuals, families, and small businesses. Legal software provides standard contracts and documents associated with buying, selling, and renting property; estate planning; and preparing a will (Figure 3-53). By answering a series of questions or completing a form, the legal software tailors the legal document to your needs.

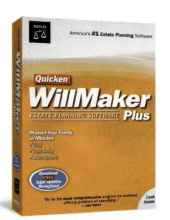

Figure 3-53 Legal software provides legal advice to individuals, families, and small businesses and assists in the preparation of legal documents.

After the legal document is created, you can file the paperwork with the appropriate agency, court, or office; or you can take the document to your attorney for her review and signature.

ENTERTAINMENT SOFTWARE

Entertainment software includes interactive games, videos, and other programs designed to support a hobby or just provide amusement and enjoyment. For example, you can use entertainment software to play games, make a family tree, compose music, or simulate flying an aircraft.

Learning Aids and Support Tools

Learning how to use an application software package effectively involves time and practice. To aid you in that learning process, your school may offer professional development classes or in-service workshops. In addition

to these learning opportunities, many software applications and Web sites provide Help, tutorials, and FAQs. Thousands of printed and digital books also are available to help you learn specific software packages. Many tutorials are packaged with software or are available free on the Web.

USING ONLINE HELP

Online Help is the electronic equivalent of a user manual; it usually is integrated into an application software package (Figure 3-54). Online Help provides assistance that can increase your productivity and reduce your frustrations by minimizing the time you spend learning how to use an application software package.

In most programs, a function key or a button on the screen starts the Online Help feature. When using a program, you can use the Online Help feature to ask a question or access the Online Help topics in subject or alphabetical order. In most cases, Online Help has replaced the user manual altogether, which means software developers no longer include user manuals with the software.

Most Online Help also links to Web sites that offer **Web-based Help**, which

Figure 3-54 Online Help provides assistance from within your application or by connecting to the Internet and accessing Web-based help if the computer is connected to the Internet.

Web Info

For more information on legal software, visit the Computer Concepts CourseMate Web site at *www.cengagebrain.com*, navigate to the Chapter 3 Web Info resource for this book, and then click Legal Software.

provides updates and more comprehensive resources in response to both technical and non-technical issues about software. You can often search Help Web sites for answers to your questions, which you can enter in complete sentences or simply by using keywords. Some Help Web sites contain chat rooms, in which a user can talk directly with a technical support person or join a conversation with other users who may be able to answer questions or solve problems.

OTHER LEARNING RESOURCES

If printed documentation is included with a software package, often it is organized as reference material rather than structured for learning. This makes it helpful after you know how to use a package, but difficult to use when you are first learning. For this reason, many **trade books** (digital and printed) are available to help you learn to use the features of software application packages. These books are available where software is sold, in regular bookstores, or online. Web pages that contain an **FAQ** (**frequently asked questions**) section about application software abound on the Internet and help you find answers to common questions.

Tutorials are step-by-step instructions using real examples that show you how to use an application. Some tutorials are printed manuals (Figure 3-55); others are software-based or Internet-based, thus allowing you to use your computer to learn about an application software package.

Many colleges and K-12 school districts provide training on many of the applications discussed in this chapter. If you want more direction than is provided in Help, trade books, FAQs, and tutorials, contact your college or school district for a list of workshops and continuing education courses that they offer.

In addition to those discussed here, many other software programs are available for use in schools, homes, and businesses. In the following chapters, you will learn more about other types of educational software, including how-to guides, computer-assisted instructional software, educational games, tutorials, educational simulations, multimedia authoring software, as well as multimedia applications.

Figure 3-55 Many programs provide extensive Web-based help, including tutorials, videos, and more.

Software Versions and Upgrades

Software programs, including operating systems, usually are designated by a **version** number. A new version of a software product designed to replace an older version of the same product is called an **upgrade**. As software manufacturers develop a newer version of a software package, the newer version usually is assigned higher numbers.

Most manufacturers designate major software releases by increasing the version number by a whole number, for example, version 4.0 to 5.0. To designate minor software improvements, manufacturers usually change the version number by less than a whole number change, such as version 4.0 to 4.2.

Sometimes manufacturers switch their naming convention. For example, Microsoft Office 2003 was replaced with Office 2007, which in turn was replaced with Office 2010. Similar versions of software can have different designations when used on Macs and PCs. Microsoft Office 2011 for Macintosh computers, for example, is basically the same as Microsoft Office 2010 for Windows computers.

If not prompted automatically by your operating system or software program, you should check periodically for critical updates to your operating system and other software programs. Most critical updates and minor software upgrades are usually free of charge.

USING DIFFERENT SOFTWARE VERSIONS

Because of the cost of software, most schools do not upgrade their software each time a manufacturer releases a new version. When schools purchase new computers, however, the latest versions of operating systems and application software often are preinstalled on the computers.

Teachers and students should know which versions of software applications are installed on their school, classroom, and home computers. Many software programs include an About or Information command on the Help menu to indicate the software version. Often, teachers and students have different versions of the same software on their home and classroom computers; a teacher might have PowerPoint 2003 on an older classroom computer and PowerPoint 2007 or PowerPoint 2010 on a new home computer.

When working with different versions of the same software, two general rules can help make your work easier. First, an older version of a software package may not open a file created in a newer version of the software. Second, newer versions usually open files created in older versions.

To help alleviate the first problem, most software programs allow you to save a document in a format compatible with earlier versions of the same software or in a different file format that can be read by another software program.

MICROSOFT OFFICE 2007/2010 Microsoft Office 2007 introduced new file formats called **Microsoft Office Open XML Formats**. These formats are based on XML. The new file formats are applied to Word 2007/2010, Excel 2007/2010, and PowerPoint 2007/2010. Figure 3-56 summarizes some of the benefits of the Office Open XML Formats. File extension names also are different in Office 2007/2010. For example, earlier versions of Word saved files with a .doc extension; the default extension for most Word 2007/2010 files is .docx, where the "x" designates an XML file.

Benefit	Description
Compact Files	Files are automatically compressed and can be up to 75 percent smaller in some cases. The Office Open XML Formats use zip compression technology to store documents, offering potential cost savings as it reduces the disk space required to store files and decreases the bandwidth needed to send files via e-mail, over networks, and across the Internet. When you open a file, it is automatically unzipped. When you save a file, it is automatically zipped again.
Improved Damaged File Recovery	Files are structured in a modular fashion that keeps different data components in the file separate from each other. This allows files to be opened even if a component within the file (for example, a chart or table) is damaged or corrupted.
Better Privacy and More Control Over Personal Information	Documents can be shared confidentially because personally identifiable information and business-sensitive information, such as author names, comments, tracked changes, and file paths can be easily identified and removed using the Document Inspector feature.

Figure 3-56 Some of the many benefits of Microsoft Office 2007/2010 Open XML Formats.

Figure 3-57 summarizes the common file extension differences between Office 2007/2010 and earlier versions of Office.

Program	Office 2007/2010 Files	Office 97-2003 Files
Word	.docx	.doc
Excel	.xlsx	.xls
PowerPoint	.pptx	.ppt

Figure 3-57 This figure shows the basic file extensions for Word, Excel, and PowerPoint 2007/2010 compared to earlier versions of these programs.

Because of the new XML formats, earlier versions of Office will not automatically open Word, PowerPoint, and Excel files created in 2007/2010 XML format. There are two options to solve this compatibility issue.

■ You can save your Office 2007/2010 file in the format that was used by earlier versions of Office. Figure 3-58 shows how to save a Word 2007/2010 file in the earlier Word 97-2003 document or .doc format.

■ You can open and edit a file created using Office 2007/2010 in an earlier version of Word, Excel, or PowerPoint by downloading the necessary file converters. On the computer with an earlier version of Office, go to the Microsoft download center and download the Microsoft Office Compatibility Pack for Word, Excel, and PowerPoint File Formats. Important Note: For the converters to work, your version of Microsoft Office must already be updated with the latest service pack. You can check to see if your version of Office is current at the Microsoft download center and if not, you can download the latest service pack.

Summary of Software for Educators

In this chapter, you learned about user interfaces and several software applications used in schools, businesses, and homes. You also read about some of the learning aids and support tools that are available for application and other software. Understanding these software applications increases your computer literacy and helps you to understand how personal computers can help in your career as a teacher, in your classroom instruction, and at home. The next chapter introduces you to computer hardware; future chapters provide information on additional software applications used by educators and show you how to integrate various software applications into your classroom curriculum.

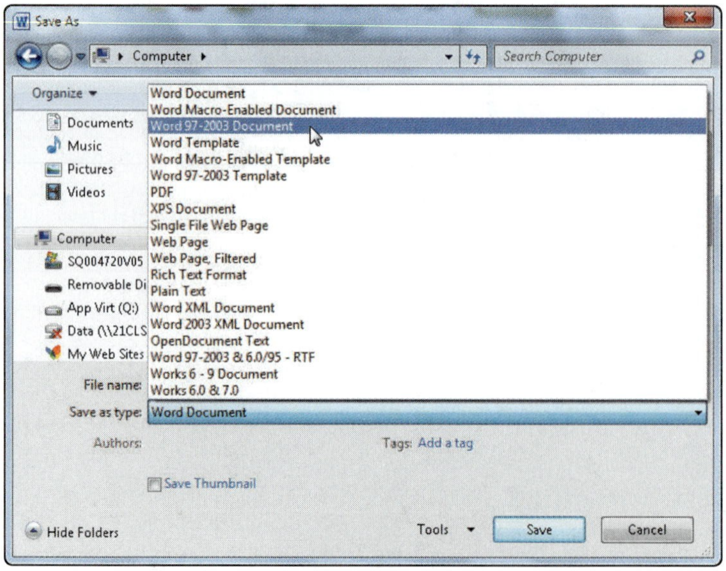

Figure 3-58 Using Microsoft Word 2007/2010, you can save a Microsoft Word 2007/2010 file in the format that was used by earlier versions of Word.

Key Terms

INSTRUCTIONS: Use the Key Terms to help focus your study of the terms used in this chapter. To further enhance your understanding of the Key Terms in this chapter, visit the Computer Concepts CourseMate Web site at www.cengagebrain.com, and then navigate to the Chapter 3 Key Terms resource for this book. Read the definition for each term and then access current and additional information about the term from the Web.

address book [120]
advanced learning system [130]
app [121]
Apple iWork [122]
application program [102]
application software [102]
appointment calendar [120]
assistant [110]
assistive technologies software [135]
AutoSave [106]

BlackBerry OS [101]
border [109]
branching [129]
button [104]

cell [112]
chart [113]
Chrome OS [101]
clip art [109]
clip art collection [109]
clip art/image gallery [115]
Clipboard [105]
cloud computing [121]
command [104]
computer-assisted instruction (CAI) [127]
copy [105]
creating [105]
creativity applications [131]
critical-thinking applications [131]
cut [105]

database [113]
database file [114]
database software [113]
delete [105]
desktop [103]
desktop publishing (DTP) software [123]
dialog box [106]
document [104]
drill-and-practice software [128]

early learning applications [131]
editing [105]
educational computer simulation [129]
educational game [128]
educational software application [127]
embedded operating system [101]
entertainment software [137]
ESL and foreign language applications [132]

FAQ (frequently asked questions) [138]
field [114]
file [104]
filename [104]
find [109]
font [105]
font size [105]
font style [105]
footer [110]
formatting [105]
formula [112]
function [112]

Google Android [101]
gradebook software [126]
graphical user interface (GUI) [102]

header [110]

icon [103]
image editing software [124]
import [109]
insert [105]
integrated learning system (ILS) [130]
iOS [101]

label [112]
language arts applications [132]
legal software [137]

Mac OS X [101]
Mac OS X Lion [101]
math applications [133]
margin [109]
menu [104]
Microsoft Office Open XML Formats [139]
Microsoft Works [122]
mobile app [121]
multimedia authoring software [124]

note taking software [106]
notepad [120]

online banking [135]
online help [137]
open learning system [130]
operating system [100]

page layout [123]
paint software [124]
paste [105]
personal finance software [135]
personal information manager (PIM) [120]
photo editing software [124]

point [105]
presentation [115]
presentation graphics software [115]
printing [106]
productivity software [108]

record [114]
remediation [128]
replace [109]

saving [105]
school management software [126]
science applications [134]
scrolling [109]
search [109]
SimCity [129]
skills-reinforcement software [128]
slide sorter [116]
slide [115]
social studies applications [134]
software suite [122]
special needs software [135]
speech recognition [106]
speech synthesis software [135]
spell checker [109]
spelling checker [109]
spreadsheet [111]
spreadsheet software [111]
stand-alone operating system [101]
student management software [126]
synchronize [120]
system software [100]

tax preparation software [136]
template [110]
title bar [104]
trade book [138]
tutorial [129]

upgrade [138]
user interface [102]

value [112]
video [125]
video game [129]
voice recognition [106]

Web applications [120]
Web apps [120]
Web-based Help [137]
Web page authoring software [125]
window [104]
Windows 7 [101]
wizard [110]
word processing software [108]
wordwrap [109]
worksheet [111]

Checkpoint

1. Label the Figure

Instructions: Identify each component of the Save As dialog box.

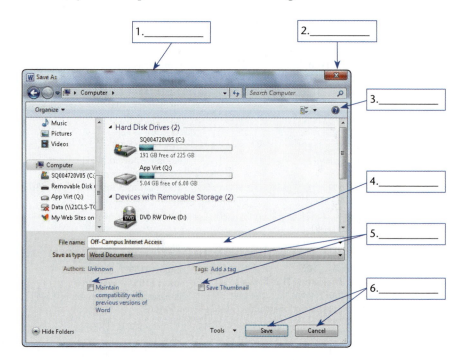

2. Matching

Instructions: Match each term from the column on the left with the best description from the column on the right.

____ 1. Clipboard   a. collection of related fields

____ 2. database   b. instructions that cause software to perform specific actions

____ 3. record   c. temporary storage location

____ 4. command   d. where a column and row meet

____ 5. cell   e. collection of data organized in a manner that allows access, retrieval, and use of that data

3. Short Answer

Instructions: Write a brief answer to each of the following questions.

1. What is a graphical user interface? Describe some common features of both the Windows and Macintosh graphical user interface.
2. Name and describe four different types of productivity software used by K-12 teachers. Which productivity software program do you use the most? Why?
3. What are the advantages of software suites? Describe three popular software suites used in K-12 schools.
4. What is a database? How are databases used in K-12 schools?
5. What are the advantages of using presentation graphics software programs? What are the disadvantages? How are teachers and students using presentation graphics programs?

Teaching Today

INSTRUCTIONS: Teaching Today provides teachers with integration strategies and ideas for teaching, and more importantly, reaching today's digital generation. Each numbered segment contains one or more links that reinforce the information presented in the segment. To display this page from the Web, visit the Computer Concepts CourseMate Web site at www.cengagebrain.com, and then navigate to the Chapter 3 Teaching Today resource for this book.

1. Software Suites

Your school uses Macintosh computers. Your principal is considering purchasing Apple iWork for all new classroom and lab computers. You have never used Apple iWork; however, you are familiar with Microsoft Office for the Macintosh. Your principal also is interested in open source software, for example Google Docs or Open Office. He has asked you to compare the different software programs and make a presentation to the school's teachers. How are the programs the same? How are the programs different? What type of support does each software program offer? Is one easier to use than the other? Why or why not? Is one easier to learn than the other? Why or why not?

2. Build Interdisciplinary Projects

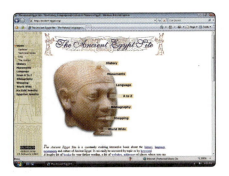

As an elementary teacher, you must teach all subjects to your students. You have decided to teach a variety of your grade-level skills using a project that is interdisciplinary, combining language arts, social studies, math, and science. You also have decided to integrate technology throughout the project not only to do research but also to help students learn to become better researchers, writers, and presenters. The topic of your project is Ancient Egypt. You start by using the Media Center to gather books, CDs, DVDs, reference materials, Web sites, and more. Develop a project focused on Ancient Egypt that uses the Internet, reference software, apps, word processing software, your curriculum-specific software, and presentation graphics software. Where could you locate sample lesson plans to help you get started? Explain your plan to integrate these software applications into an interdisciplinary project that includes two or more curriculum areas.

3. Cloud Computing

Cloud computing is a growing trend in technology; it is like having your personal computer in the clouds. The best way to describe cloud computing is to think of a place in the clouds that not only stores information that was once stored on your computer but also hosts software programs you can use to work with that information. In the classroom, cloud computing offers many benefits such as increased productivity since documents are available from any computer with an Internet connection (no more losing documents or leaving the most up-to-date version at home), increased communication opportunities between students, parents, and teachers (who can all have access to the same documents), and cost (cloud computing is often free!). There are multiple resources that utilize cloud computing such as GoogleDocs, VoiceThread, Microsoft Cloud Power, and Animoto. Are cloud-based computing applications changing the way you process and communicate information on a daily basis? How is your school organization embracing the robust capabilities of cloud-based computing?

4. Software Vendors

Most state Departments of Education negotiate one-year or multiyear contracts with various vendors for educational software products. This enables schools to acquire software products at substantial discounts. Contact a school in your district or access your state's Department of Education Web site and find out about a few of the software products available through the state purchasing program. Compare these prices with purchasing the same software either online or at a local computer store. What kind of discounts are the schools receiving? How many titles are available through the state catalog? What procedures does a teacher have to go through to purchase software not in the catalog?

Education Issues

INSTRUCTIONS: Education Issues provides several scenarios that allow you to explore controversial and current issues in education. Each numbered segment contains one or more links that reinforce the information presented in the segment. To display this page from the Web, visit the Computer Concepts CourseMate Web site at www.cengagebrain.com, and then navigate to the Chapter 3 Education Issues resource for this book.

1. Wikis and Education

Some wikis are tightly controlled with a limited number of contributors and expert editors, these usually focus on narrowly-defined, specialized topics. Large online wikis, such as Wikipedia, often involve thousands of editors, many of whom remain anonymous. Recently, an entry on Wikipedia was maliciously altered to suggest that a prominent journalist was involved in the assassination of John F. Kennedy. As the number of wikis has grown and the source of the content is often unknown, some educators and librarians have shunned wikis as valid sources of research. Many wikis provide information stating they have adequate controls to correct false or misleading content. Citizendium, is a wiki project started by a founder of Wikipedia that aims to improve the credibility of wikis by requiring contributors to use their real names; although anyone still can change content. Should you allow your students to use wikis as valid sources for academic research? Why or why not? Would you allow your students to submit a paper to you that cites a wiki as a source? Why or why not? What policies could wikis enforce that could garner more confidence from the public?

2. Reading Problems

You teach middle school, and this year you have the most challenging group of students you have ever had. Many of your students seem completely uninterested in learning or even in coming to school for that matter. As a result, you have continuous discipline problems and spend a lot of time sending students to the principal's office. After a few days, you become convinced that a deeper problem must exist, so you do a little research and find out that many of the students are below the 30th percentile in reading. You wonder how these students got this far without knowing how to read. Traditional reading programs obviously have not worked for these students. Using the Internet and other sources, do research to find out whether reading software programs and educational technology might be able to help them. Continue your research to investigate alternative techniques using technology that might motivate these students and help them to learn to read. Try this reading Web site to locate appropriate software. Where could you locate additional software and innovative teaching strategies that could help you help these students learn to read?

3. Software Adoption and Adaptation

You come into your classroom after a long weekend to find new content-specific, learner-centered, and standards-based software has been loaded on your classroom computers and in the media center. You decide to ask around and see if anyone knows about this software — no one knows. You are aware that software designed to be learner-centered focuses on the needs of individuals and provides a valuable tool for creating instructional strategies, especially when teaching digital students. You are also aware of the fact that teachers are one of the single most important factors in adoption and effective integration of software in the classroom. What steps would you take to learn more about the software that was installed without your knowledge or prior input? How would you successfully implement the installed software in a content-specific area? What about teacher training? Do you think these kinds of decisions, such as software purchases, should be made with no teacher input? How can you work with the administration to make sure teachers are in the decision-making process? Think of ways you could help in changing the antiquated decision-making top-down process and alter the process to a bottom-up process — letting teachers have more say in what is purchased.

4. Computer Use in the Classroom

With the explosion of educational software, multimedia, digital media, and the Internet, educators still are learning the best use for computers in the classroom. Drill and practice? Problem solving? Games? A growing number of educators feel that students should be taught the software applications they will have to know to succeed in the workplace. From the applications presented in this chapter, make a list of five applications you think every student should learn, from more important to less important. Explain your ranking. At what level do you think each application should be taught? Why?

Apps Corner

INSTRUCTIONS: Apps Corner provides extensive ideas and resources for integrating technology into your classroom-specific curriculum. To display this page from the Web and information on numerous education apps, visit the Computer Concepts CourseMate Web site at www.cengagebrain.com, and then navigate to the Chapter 3 Apps Corner resource for this book.

Apps Corner is designed for teachers and other educators who are looking for innovative ways to integrate apps into their content-specific curriculum. Apps Corner not only provides great apps with current information but also shows how other educators are using and integrating education apps. As a result, Apps Corner is designed with all educators in mind, regardless of their interests or subject area. You can use Apps Corner to expand your resources by reviewing apps outside your curriculum area; remember many apps associated with one curriculum area can be adapted for use and added to lesson plans in a wide variety of other curriculum areas.

Use Apps Corner as a springboard for collaborating and sharing the successes and hurdles of integrating apps in a classroom or an entire school system. Consider Apps Corner a place to locate app integration ideas and resources. Information on educational apps are organized in four Corners (Early Childhood, Elementary, Middle School, and Secondary), and different apps are available for each chapter. Many apps are free, others cost from $1 to $5. Inexpensive site licenses for classrooms, schools, and school districts are available for many apps.

There are hundreds of productivity software programs that are available as apps for use on tablet computers. Shown below are three apps that are iPad app versions of the main productivity applications included with Apple's iWork software suite: Pages (word processing), Numbers (spreadsheets), and Keynote (presentations). These apps are sold individually for $9.99 each and are available for volumn discounts.

Software Corner

INSTRUCTIONS: Software Corner provides information on popular software programs. Each numbered segment discusses specific software programs and contains a link to additional information about these programs. To display this page from the Web, visit the Computer Concepts CourseMate Web site at www.cengagebrain.com, and then navigate to the Chapter 3 Software Corner resource for this book.

1. PrimeTime Math

Teachers will find the PrimeTime Math series excellent support software for the math curriculum. PrimeTime Math engages students by providing stories about real-world professionals using math in real-life situations and includes titles like Adrift!, Cliffbound!, Fire!, Lost!, Emergency!, and Stakeout! This software meets the National Council of Teachers of Mathematics (NCTM) standards by building mathematical understanding through use of stories about crimes, medical emergencies, fires, and wilderness search and rescues, while at the same time assisting students in realizing the importance of math in the world in which they live.

2. Adobe Photoshop Elements

Adobe Photoshop Elements allows you and your students to edit pictures from resources, such as those downloaded from digital cameras and the Internet. You can use these edited pictures to create multimedia digital projects, unique reports, personalized calendars, student bulletin boards for classroom instruction, posts to blogs, and much more. Using Adobe Photoshop Elements helps your classroom photos have a professionally finished look without a lot of hassle and the price is perfect for education!

3. Thinkology

Developing students' critical thinking skills and creating learning opportunities that engage higher-order thinking skills always have been a struggle for teachers. Thinkology by Heartsoft helps K-3 students master essential critical thinking skills while having fun! Students are guided through a critical-thinking-skills journey with a cast of clever animated characters. Students learn to reason through concepts and are asked questions such as, does this make sense?

4. Kidspiration

Ever had trouble getting young learners to organize their thoughts and develop their great ideas into understandable concepts? Kidspiration is an excellent visual learning tool for teaching K-5 students to organize and express those great ideas through visual learning! Created for inexperienced readers and writers, Kidspiration helps students increase their confidence as they learn to understand concepts, organize information, write stories, and convey and share their thoughts. Brainstorming, visual mapping, thought webs, and other visual tools are used to enhance students' comprehension of concepts and information.

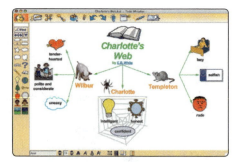

5. Tessellation Exploration

Do you want to make teaching tessellations to your 4th grade and up students fun and easy? One piece of software that makes the concept of tessellations easier to teach and allows students to practice is Tessellation Exploration by Tom Snyder Productions. The software includes an extensive tutorial on the concept of tessellations. Teachers can use the software as a tool to present the concept of tessellations. Next, students use Tessellation Exploration to construct their own tessellations, by selecting a base shape and moves, such as slides, flips, and turns; students watch their tessellation form before their eyes. Students can create slide shows with the tessellations or print them out.

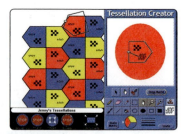

Digital Media Corner

INSTRUCTIONS: Today's K-12 digital students need their learning to be meaningful and relevant to their lives. Digital Media Corner provides videos, ideas, and examples of how you can use digital media to enhance your teaching and your students' learning. To access the videos and links to additional information, visit the Computer Concepts CourseMate Web site at www.cengagebrain.com, and then navigate to the Chapter 3 Digital Media Corner resource for this book.

1. Windows Live Movie Maker

Movie Maker is a free Windows-based video editing software program that provides tools you and your students can use to create, edit, and publish movies. You can edit and produce a movie from video clips, pictures, and audio files by dragging and dropping various digital media components into timelines and then adding special effects, transitions, and voice-overs. Movie Maker is a great product for creating digital storytelling projects with your students. Review this Movie Maker tutorial to learn how to create a movie that can be published in a variety of ways, including to the Web, on a CD or DVD, or downloaded to a camera for playback on a TV.

2. Microsoft Photo Gallery and Windows Live SkyDrive

Photo Gallery, also a free download for Windows, brings your digital photos to life. You can add stunning special effects, soundtracks, and your own voice narrations and much more to your photos and your digital storytelling projects. Import photos and videos from your camera, organize them into albums, and edit them so they look their best. Use powerful photo tools to create stunning panoramas, movies, slide shows, and more. When you are ready to share, publish your photos and videos to your favorite social networking Web sites like YouTube, Facebook and Flickr directly from Photo Gallery. Using Windows Live SkyDrive, you get 25 GB of free online storage, enough space to upload and share thousands of photos. Once you upload photos and movies, you can share them with anyone you choose.

3. iLife

One of the true values of digital media in education is its ability to empower teachers and students to develop stories using various forms of self-expression. This is evident if you look at the iLife software suite that is loaded free on all Apple computers. iLife is an integration software application suite that includes support for telling stories using photographs (iPhoto), music (iTunes and GarageBand), and video (iMovie).

4. Adobe Software

A popular digital media production software application package is Adobe Creative Suite. The Adobe Creative Suite includes the widely used image editing program Photoshop, the illustration creator Illustrator, the page publisher InDesign, Adobe Acrobat, and a number of other applications. Adobe's popularity is due in part to its high performance on both Windows and Macintosh platforms as well as its industry standard Portable Document Format or .pdf file format.

5. OneNote

Microsoft's OneNote is an easy-to-use note taking and information management program that is a natural fit for today's digital generation. You and your students can use OneNote to capture your handwritten thoughts and ideas in electronic notebooks. OneNote allows you to organize, search, and share your notes. You can share your notes, even with people who do not have OneNote. You can e-mail notes pages or publish entire notebooks to a Web site. Using a Tablet PC and OneNote, you can convert your handwritten notes to Word files. OneNote comes with a variety of templates to help you customize your pages and sections. You can choose from decorative backgrounds, watermarks, and more that you can easily customize.

Assistive Technologies Corner

INSTRUCTIONS: Assistive Technologies Corner provides information on current hardware, software, and peripherals that will assist you in delivering instruction to students with physical, cognitive, or sensory challenges. To access extensive additional information, visit the Computer Concepts CourseMate Web site at www.cengagebrain.com, and then navigate to the Chapter 3 Assistive Technologies Corner resource for this book.

1. Should Special Needs Software Be Available for All Teachers?

Yes! The educator's primary concern is to fit the software to the learner, and not the other way around. You can choose the appropriate assistive technology software when you consider the particular disability of the learner, the learner's strengths, and the learner's academic needs. A challenged student may need assistance with reading, or with communication, or with organizing and processing new information.

In the Chapter 1 Assistive Technologies Corner, you learned that operating systems have built-in accessibility features. Some of these features may be further enhanced with system software that affects the behavior of the computer across all other programs. You may choose to add new voices to the speech software built into the operating system of the computer or to add new large mouse pointers, for example, which will display whether your students are using Microsoft Word or Internet Explorer. To change the size of the mouse pointer in Windows 7, click the Start button on the Windows taskbar and then click Control Panel. When the Control Panel window opens, double-click the Ease of Access Center link, and then click the Change how your mouse works link. When the Make the mouse easier to use dialog box opens, select the mouse pointer settings to meet your needs. Numerous mouse pointer options are available.

2. What Is Speech Synthesis Software?

Many application tools are available to increase student productivity. Speech synthesis software allows students with speech and vocal muscle disorders to participate in classroom discussions. Students assign shortcut keys to reproduce specific, frequently used phrases. Then, they use the shortcut keys to type in a response quickly; the word processing software reads the response in a computerized voice. Students with visual impairments may use software with text enlargement features. Other helpful software applications include an on-screen talking calculator that features big, colorful number buttons and high-quality speech synthesis.

3. What Is Speech-to-Text Software?

Speech-to-text software is used by many nondisabled users to control computers and produce documents. In the classroom, this type of software assists learners with disabilities to produce a printed document. There is speech-to-text dictation software for both Windows (Nuance Dragon Naturally Speaking) and Macintosh (IBM ViaVoice) environments. As the student speaks, the software types. These software packages "learn" to respond to the voice of the user. iCommunicator puts the speech-to-text program in an enhanced environment that also provides sign language. Although not a substitute for a sign language interpreter, this software provides an alternative for students with unique communication challenges.

4. What Is Text-to-Speech Software?

Software programs that read text aloud are called text-to-speech software. Kurzweil is a robust system available for struggling learners. With the Kurzweil system, any text from books or documents can be scanned and read aloud to the student. In addition to this enhanced text-to-speech feature, the Kurzweil system allows students to complete tests and worksheets. A built-in word processor displays the test or worksheet, and the student types in responses. In addition, many freeware and shareware text-to-speech programs are available on the Internet.

Follow the instructions at the top of this page to display additional information and this chapter's links on assistive technologies.

In the Lab

INSTRUCTIONS: In the Lab provides spreadsheet exercises that are divided into two areas, productivity and integration. To access the links to tutorials, productivity ideas, integration examples and ideas, and more, visit the Computer Concepts CourseMate Web site at www.cengagebrain.com, and then navigate to the Chapter 3 In the Lab resource for this book.

PRODUCTIVITY IN THE CLASSROOM

Introduction: Spreadsheets have many uses for both students and teachers in the classroom. Spreadsheets are a great teacher productivity tool. Gradebooks, lesson plans, rubrics, classroom inventory, textbook inventory, and many other time-saving documents can be created in a spreadsheet. Students can creatively display data using a spreadsheet's charting feature, in addition to sorting and manipulating data, thereby using higher-order thinking skills.

Many of the productivity software suites have spreadsheet programs. Excel is a part of the Microsoft Office suite. Microsoft Works and Apple iWork also have a spreadsheet program. Lotus 1-2-3 and Quattro Pro also are popular spreadsheet programs.

Spreadsheets are not just for math class. It is possible to integrate spreadsheets effectively into many different curriculum areas in ways that excite students and empower their learning.

1. Building a Gradebook Spreadsheet

Problem: Keeping a gradebook by hand can be a tedious task. To save time, you have created your gradebook in a spreadsheet program so you can calculate percentages and grades quickly, as shown in Figure 3-59. Open your spreadsheet software and create the gradebook as described in the following steps. Use the gradebook shown in Figure 3-59 as an example. (*Hint:* Use the program's Help feature to better understand the steps. If you do not have the suggested font, use any appropriate font.)

Instructions: Perform the following tasks.

1. Use the names and numbers displayed in Figure 3-59 (cells A2:F16) to create a spreadsheet, then complete the remaining steps to format the spreadsheet.
2. Calculate the total and average for each student and for the entire class.
3. Personalize the spreadsheet title by inserting your name and curriculum area. Format the spreadsheet title in 16-point, Arial Black font and centered over columns A through H.
4. Format cells A2:H16 so they look similar to Figure 3-59. The numbers appear in the Number format with 0 decimal places.
5. Bold the Class Average label in cell A18, and then verify that the column headings in row 2 are bold and italic. Add a solid black border to the bottom of cells A18:H18.

	A	B	C	D	E	F	G	H
1	colspan Mr. Radcliff's 4th Period Language Arts Class							
2	Student		Book Report	Vocab Quiz	Poem	Essay	Total	Average
3	First Name	Last Name						
4	Jenny	Carlson	98	100	100	97	395	99
5	Leah	Chambers	80	70	85	90	325	81
6	Brittany	Cook	70	80	75	75	300	75
7	Oliver	Flint	78	80	90	95	343	86
8	Maria	Gomez	94	80	85	92	351	88
9	Ema	Granger	100	90	95	100	385	96
10	Chelsea	Jackson	85	100	75	90	350	88
11	Cho	Ling	92	90	85	95	362	91
12	Devon	McBride	75	90	85	90	340	85
13	Justin	Pillman	95	100	92	95	382	96
14	Carlos	Ramirez	93	90	95	95	373	93
15	Harry	Rollins	96	90	95	100	381	95
16	Juan	Sanchez	88	80	90	85	343	86
17								
18	Class Average		88	88	88	92	356	89

Figure 3-59

In the Lab

6. Create a custom header to show your name left-aligned, course number or title center-aligned, and the current date right-aligned.
7. Save the spreadsheet to the location of your choice using an appropriate filename.
8. Print the spreadsheet.
9. Follow directions from your instructor for turning in the assignment.

2. Building a Student Council Fund-Raiser Spreadsheet

Problem: You are the teacher sponsor of the student council at your high school. To raise money, student council members sell various items throughout the day and at special school functions. You want to see which items are the most profitable for the group and what time of day is the most successful, so you keep track of sales for four weeks. Using a spreadsheet program, prepare the spreadsheet and chart shown in Figures 3-60 and 3-61. (*Hint:* Use Help to better understand the steps. If you do not have the suggested font or color, use any appropriate font or color.)

Instructions: Perform the following tasks.

1. Create the spreadsheet shown in Figure 3-60 using the numbers as displayed.
2. Calculate the total sales for the four weeks for each period and each item.
3. Personalize the spreadsheet title by inserting the name of your school. Add a gray, solid pattern to the foreground of cells A1:E1. Format the title in row 1 as 16-point, Arial, bold, purple font and centered over columns A through E.
4. Format the subtitle, Student Council Fund-Raisers (Feb 1 – Feb 28), as 11-point, Arial, bold, black font and centered over columns A through E. Add a thick aqua top and bottom border around cells A2:E2.
5. Format the remaining portion of the spreadsheet to look similar to Figure 3-60. Display the numbers using the Currency format with two decimal places.

	A	B	C	D	E
1			Ridgedale High School		
2		Student Council Fund-Raisers (Feb 1 - Feb 28)			
3	*Item*	*Before School*	*Lunch*	*After School*	*Total*
4	Lollipops	$100.00	$25.00	$175.00	$300.00
5	Flowers	$175.00	$250.00	$75.00	$500.00
6	Pizza	$0.00	$0.00	$450.00	$450.00
7	Pencils	$300.00	$100.00	$50.00	$450.00
8	**Total**	$575.00	$375.00	$750.00	$1,700.00

Figure 3-60

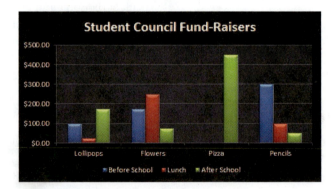

Figure 3-61

6. Create a custom header to show your name left-aligned, course number or title center-aligned, and the current date right-aligned.
7. Print the spreadsheet.
8. Create the 3D Column chart from the spreadsheet data, as shown in Figure 3-61. Add the title, Student Council Fund-Raisers, to the chart. Place the legend below the chart.
9. Apply the chart style shown in Figure 3-61. Print the 3D Column chart.

In the Lab

ePortfolio
Idea

10. Save the spreadsheet and chart to the location of your choice using an appropriate filename.
11. Follow directions from your instructor for turning in the assignment.

INTEGRATION IN THE CLASSROOM

1. You are working on the concept of categorizing with your third-grade students. To meet state technology standards for students and to assist them with understanding this concept, you introduce spreadsheets and charts. Together with the class, you create a spreadsheet to show your students' favorite colors. You then create a 3D Column chart to show their favorite colors graphically. Create a sample spreadsheet and 3D Column chart to demonstrate the project for the students. Before submitting this assignment, include a custom header to show your name left-aligned, course number or title center-aligned, and the current date right-aligned.

2. As a part of your Health Education class, you decide to have your students keep track of the total fat grams they consume daily during breakfast, lunch, dinner, and snacks for one week. You encourage students to examine the labels on products and nutrition tables for all foods consumed, including fast food. The students will create a spreadsheet including totals for each day of the week and each meal of the week to determine which days and meals are the healthiest. The students will also include a bar chart to illustrate their data. Create a sample spreadsheet and bar chart to demonstrate the project for the students. Before submitting this assignment, include a custom header to show your name left-aligned, course number or title center-aligned, and the current date right-aligned.

3. Now that the students are aware of their total fat grams consumed, you want them to explore exercise options and burning calories. Students will select three types of aerobic exercise that they will participate in for 30 minutes, three times a week. They will need to determine how many calories each type of exercise will burn. (*Hint:* Have the students search the World Wide Web.) The students will prepare a spreadsheet to record the total minutes spent exercising weekly and chart the number of calories each type of exercise burned over a one-week period. Create a sample spreadsheet and pie chart to demonstrate the project for the students. Include a custom header to show your name left-aligned, course number or title center-aligned, and the current date right-aligned.

Learn It Online

INSTRUCTIONS: Use the Learn It Online exercises to reinforce your understanding of the chapter concepts and increase your computer, information, and integration literacy. To access dozens of interactive student labs, practice tests, learning games, and more, visit the Computer Concepts CourseMate Web site at www.cengagebrain.com, navigate to the Chapter 3 resources for this book, and then click the link for the resource you want to review.

1. Windows Exercises

Click the Windows 7 exercises link to learn about locating information about your computer, customizing the keyboard, using the mouse and keyboard to interact with a Web application, using the mouse keys, and using the on-screen keyboard.

2. At the Movies

Click the At the Movies link to review a video about creating your own wiki. Click the At the Movies 2 link to review a video about creating your own videos using Camtasia.

3. Expanding Your Understanding

Click the Expand Your Understanding link to expand your understanding of Microsoft products and their use in K-12 classrooms. Microsoft seeks to help teachers and students use its products by maintaining an extensive array of user-friendly resources. Research this Web site and write a report summarizing your findings. If required, submit your report to your instructor.

4. Practice Test

Click the Practice Test link. Answer each question. When completed, enter your name and click the Grade Test button to submit the quiz for grading. Make a note of any missed questions. If required, submit your score to your instructor.

5. Who Wants to Be a Computer Genius?

Click the Who Wants to Be a Computer Genius link to find out if you are a computer genius. Directions about how to play the game will be displayed. When you are ready to play, click the Play button. If required, submit your score to your instructor.

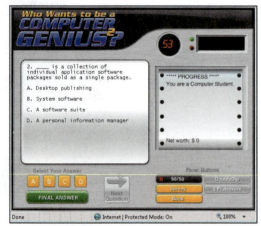

6. Wheel of Terms

Click the Wheel of Terms link to reinforce important terms you learned in this chapter by playing the Shelly Cashman Series version of this popular game. Directions about how to play the game will be displayed. When you are ready to play, click the Play button. If required, submit your score to your instructor.

7. Crossword Puzzle Challenge

Click the Crossword Puzzle Challenge link. Complete the puzzle to reinforce skills you learned in this chapter. Directions about how to play the game will be displayed. When you are ready to play, click the Play button. If required, submit the completed puzzle to your instructor.

Hardware for Educators

4

Objectives

After completing this chapter, you will be able to do the following:
[ISTE NETS-T Standards 2 b, c; 3 a-d]

- Describe the system unit

- Define the term bit and describe how a series of bits are used to represent data

- Identify the major components of the system unit and explain their functions

- Explain how the CPU uses the four steps of a machine cycle to process data

- Describe the four types of input as well as various input devices and pointing devices

- List the characteristics of a keyboard and identify various types of keyboards

- Differentiate among the four types of output

- Identify different types of output devices

- Explain differences among various types of printers

- Differentiate between storage and memory

- Identify types of storage media and devices

- Differentiate between CDs, DVDs, and BDs

During your teaching career or personal endeavors, you most likely will decide to purchase a new computer or upgrade an existing one. To be effective in this decision-making process and to be an informed teacher, you should possess a general knowledge of major computer components and how various computer components interact. In addition, the International Society for Technology in Education (ISTE) has developed a series of K-12 National Educational Technology Standards (NETS) and skills that K-12 students need to learn throughout their education. One of these technology standards recommends that graduating K-12 students demonstrate a sound understanding of technology concepts, systems, and operations. To help you better understand these concepts, so that you in turn can help your students understand them, this chapter presents a brief look at some of the hardware components used for input, processing, output, and storage. Because Macs and PCs use similar, and in many cases identical, hardware components, the majority of information presented in this chapter applies to both computer platforms. In instances in which Macs and PCs use slightly different hardware, these differences are explained.

The System Unit

The **system unit** is a boxlike case that houses the electronic components a computer uses to process data. All types and sizes of computers (such as desktop computers and notebook computers) and mobile devices (such as tablet computers like the iPad and smartphones like the iPhone) have a system unit (Figure 4-1). The system unit is made of metal or plastic and protects the electronic components from damage. On a personal computer, the electric components and most storage devices reside inside the system unit; other devices, such as a keyboard and monitor, usually are located outside the system unit. Notebook computers, netbooks, smartphones, tablet computers, and other mobile devices contain almost all of their components in the system unit, including the keyboard and monitor or display.

The following explanation of how data is represented in a computer will help you understand how the components housed in the system unit process data.

Data Representation

To understand fully how the various components of the system unit work together to process data, you need a basic understanding of how data is represented in a computer. Human speech is **analog**, meaning that it uses continuous signals to represent data and information. Most computers, by contrast, are **digital**, meaning that they understand only two discrete states: on and off. Computers are electronic devices powered by electricity, which has only two states: on or off. These two states

Figure 4-1 All types and sizes of computers and mobile devices have a system unit.

are represented by electronic circuits using two digits; 0 is used to represent the electronic state of off (absence of an electric charge) and 1 is used to represent the electronic state of on (presence of an electric charge) (Figure 4-2).

BINARY DIGIT (BIT)	ELECTRONIC CHARGE	ELECTRONIC STATE
0		OFF
1		ON

Figure 4-2 A computer circuit represents the binary digits 0 or 1 electronically by the absence or presence of an electronic charge.

When people count, they use the digits 0 through 9, which are digits in the decimal system. Because a computer understands only two states, it uses a number system that has just two unique digits, 0 and 1. This numbering system is referred to as the **binary** system. Using just these two binary numbers, a computer can represent data electronically by turning circuits off or on.

Each off or on digital value is called a **bit** (short for **bi**nary dig**it**). A bit represents the smallest unit of data the computer can handle. By itself, a bit is not very informative. When eight bits are grouped together as a unit, they are called a **byte**. A byte is informative because it provides enough different combinations of 0s and 1s to represent 256 individual characters, including numbers, uppercase and lowercase letters of the alphabet, and punctuation marks (Figure 4-3).

The combinations of 0s and 1s used to represent characters are defined by patterns called a coding scheme. The most widely used coding scheme to represent data on many personal computers is the **American Standard Code for Information Interchange**, also called **ASCII** (pronounced ASK-ee). Coding schemes, such as ASCII, make it possible for humans to interact with digital computers that recognize only bits. When you press a key on a keyboard, the keyboard converts that action into a scan code, which in turn is converted into a binary form the computer understands. That is, every character is converted to its corresponding byte. The computer then processes that data in terms of bytes, which actually is a series of off/on electrical states. When processing is finished, the computer converts the bytes back into numbers, letters of the alphabet, or special characters to be printed or displayed on a screen (Figure 4-4 on the next page). All of these conversions take place so quickly that you do not even realize they are occurring.

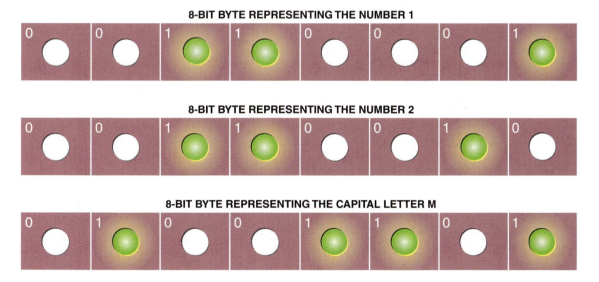

8-BIT BYTE REPRESENTING THE NUMBER 1

0 0 1 1 0 0 0 1

8-BIT BYTE REPRESENTING THE NUMBER 2

0 0 1 1 0 0 1 0

8-BIT BYTE REPRESENTING THE CAPITAL LETTER M

0 1 0 0 1 1 0 1

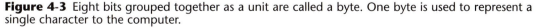

Figure 4-3 Eight bits grouped together as a unit are called a byte. One byte is used to represent a single character to the computer.

Step 1

A user presses the capital letter **T** (SHIFT+T keys) on the keyboard, which in turn creates a special code, called a scan code, for the capital letter **T**.

Shift key

Step 2

The scan code for the capital letter **T** is sent to the system unit.

Step 4

After processing, the binary code for the capital letter **T** is converted to an image and displayed on the output device.

Step 3

The system unit converts the scan code for the capital letter **T** to its ASCII binary code (01010100) and stores it in memory for processing.

Figure 4-4 Converting a letter to its ASCII binary code form and then back to its letter form.

The Components of the System Unit

The major components of the system unit discussed in the following sections include the motherboard, CPU, memory, expansion slots and expansion cards, removable memory devices, and ports and connectors.

THE MOTHERBOARD

Many of the electronic components in the system unit reside on a circuit board called the **motherboard**. Figure 4-5 shows a photograph of a motherboard used in a personal computer and identifies some of its components, including several different types of chips. A **chip** is a small piece of semiconducting material usually no bigger than one-half-inch square and is made up of many layers of circuits and microscopic components that carry electronic signals. These circuits are also called integrated circuits. An integrated circuit contains millions of electronic components, as well as many microscopic pathways that carry electical current. The motherboard in the system unit contains many different types of chips. Of these, one of the most important is the central processing unit (CPU).

expansion cards

CPU (processor)

memory module
(RAM chips)

expansion slots
for adapter cards

memory slots

motherboard

Figure 4-5 The motherboard in a personal computer contains many chips and other electronic components.

THE CPU

The **central processing unit (CPU)** interprets and carries out the basic instructions that operate a computer. The CPU, also called the **processor** or **microprocessor**, manages most of a computer's operations. Most of the devices that connect to a computer, such as a monitor, keyboard, mouse, printer, scanner, and digital camera, communicate with the CPU to carry out tasks (Figure 4-6).

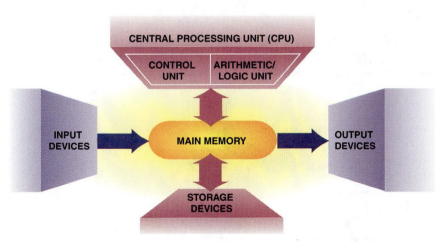

Figure 4-6 Most of the devices connected to a computer communicate with the CPU to carry out a task. The arrows in this figure represent the flow of data, instructions, and information.

In a personal computer, the CPU (also called the processor) is a single chip (Figure 4-7). Several processor chip manufacturers now offer dual-core and multi-core processors. A **dual-core processor** is a single chip that contains two separate processors. Similarly, a **multi-core processor** is a single chip with more than two separate processors.

A processor contains a number of components, including a control unit, an arithmetic/logic unit, and a system clock. The following sections describe how these components work together to perform processing operations.

THE CONTROL UNIT   The **control unit**, one component of the CPU, directs and coordinates most of the operations in the computer. The control unit has a role much like a traffic cop. The control unit interprets each instruction issued by a program and then initiates the appropriate action to carry out the instruction. For every instruction, the control unit operates by repeating a set of four basic operations: (1) fetching an instruction, (2) decoding the instruction, (3) executing the instruction, and (4) storing the result. The stored result is displayed on the monitor and can be saved and/or printed if requested.

Fetching is the process of obtaining a program instruction or data item from memory. **Decoding** is the process of translating the instruction into commands the computer understands. **Executing** is the process of carrying out the commands. **Storing** is the process of writing the result to memory. Together, these four instructions comprise the **machine cycle** or instruction cycle (Figure 4-8).

Xeon

Celeron

Core i7

Athlon X2

Core i7 Extreme

Figure 4-7 Most high-performance PCs use Core i7 processors. Basic PCs often use a Celeron processor. Newer Macintosh computers use the Dual 2 Core or the Xeon processor.

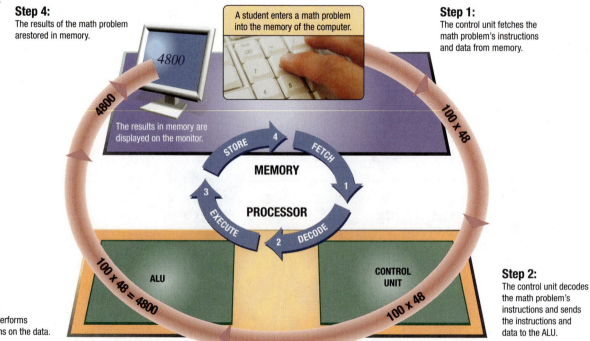

Step 4:
The results of the math problem arestored in memory.

Step 1:
The control unit fetches the math problem's instructions and data from memory.

A student enters a math problem into the memory of the computer.

The results in memory are displayed on the monitor.

Step 3:
The ALU performs calculations on the data.

Step 2:
The control unit decodes the math problem's instructions and sends the instructions and data to the ALU.

STORE FETCH EXECUTE DECODE MEMORY PROCESSOR ALU CONTROL UNIT 4800 100 x 48 100 x 48 = 4800 100 x 48

Figure 4-8 This figure shows the steps involved in a machine cycle.

THE ARITHMETIC/LOGIC UNIT The arithmetic/logic unit (ALU), another component of the CPU, performs the execution part of the machine cycle. Specifically, the ALU performs arithmetic, comparison, and logical operations.

Arithmetic operations include addition, subtraction, multiplication, and division. **Comparison operations** involve comparing one data item with another to determine if the first item is greater than, equal to, or less than the other. Depending on the result of the comparison, different actions may occur. For example, to determine a student's letter grade, the student's numeric grade is compared with a set of numbers corresponding to various letter grades (for instance, a numeric grade equal to or greater than 90 equates to a letter grade of A). If the student's numeric grade is equal to or greater than 90, then a letter grade of A is given; if the numeric grade is less than 90, a letter grade of A is not given and more comparisons are performed until a letter grade can be assigned. **Logical operations** work with conditions and logical operators such as AND, OR, and NOT. For example, if you wanted to search a job database for part-time work in the admissions office, you would search for any jobs classified as part-time AND listed under admissions.

THE SYSTEM CLOCK The control unit relies on a small chip called the **system clock** to synchronize, or control the timing of, all computer operations. Just as your heart beats at a regular rate to keep your body functioning, the system clock generates regular electronic pulses, or ticks, that set the operating pace of components in the system unit. Think of the components of the CPU as members of a marching band that take their steps to the beat of the system clock drummer.

Clock speed is the speed at which a processor executes instructions and is measured in **gigahertz (GHz)**. Giga is a prefix that stands for one billion, and a hertz is one cycle per second. Thus, one **gigahertz** equates to one billion ticks of the system clock in one second. A computer that operates at 4 GHz has 4 billion clock cycles, or ticks, in one second. The faster the clock speed, the more instructions the CPU can execute per second.

MEMORY

While performing a processing operation, a processor needs a place to store data and instructions temporarily. A computer uses **memory** to store data and information. The memory chips on the circuit boards in the system unit perform this and other functions.

Memory stores three basic items: (1) the operating system and other system software that control the computer equipment; (2) the application software designed to carry out a specific task, such as word processing; and (3) the data being processed by the application software. When a computer transfers program instructions and data from a storage medium into memory, the computer stores them as bytes. The computer stores each byte in a precise location in memory, called an address. An **address** is simply a unique number identifying the location of the byte in memory. The illustration in Figure 4-9 shows how seats in a stadium are similar to addresses in memory: (1) a seat holds one person at a time and an address in

Figure 4-9 This figure shows how seats in a stadium are similar to addresses in memory: (1) a seat holds one person at a time and an address in memory holds a single byte, (2) both a seat and an address can be empty, and (3) a seat has a unique identifying number and so does an address.

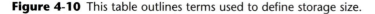

Term	Abbreviation	Approximate Memory Size	Exact Memory Amount	Approximate Pages of Text
Kilobyte	KB or K	1 thousand bytes	1,024 bytes	1/2
Megabyte	MB	1 million bytes	1,048,576 bytes	500
Gigabyte	GB	1 billion bytes	1,073,741,824 bytes	500,000
Terabyte	TB	1 trillion bytes	1,099,511,627,776 bytes	500,000,000

Figure 4-10 This table outlines terms used to define storage size.

memory holds a single byte, (2) both a seat and an address can be empty, and (3) a seat has a unique identifying number and so does an address. To access data or instructions in memory, the computer references the addresses that contain bytes of data.

Recall that a computer stores a character as a series of 0s and 1s, called a byte. A byte is the basic storage unit in memory. Because a byte is such a small amount of storage, several terms have evolved to define storage size related to memory and storage devices (Figure 4-10 above). A **kilobyte** of memory, abbreviated **KB** or **K**, is equal to 1,024 bytes, but is usually rounded to 1,000 bytes. A **megabyte**, abbreviated **MB**, is equal to approximately 1 million bytes. A **gigabyte**, abbreviated **GB**, is equal to approximately 1 billion bytes. A **terabyte** (**TB**) is equal to approximately 1 trillion bytes.

The system unit contains two types of memory: volatile and nonvolatile. The contents of **volatile memory** are lost (erased) when the computer's power is turned off. The contents of **nonvolatile memory**, on the other hand, are not lost when a computer is turned off or power to the computer is interrupted. RAM (random access memory) is an example of volatile memory. ROM (read-only memory) and flash memory are examples of nonvolatile memory. The following sections discuss each of these types of memory.

RANDOM ACCESS MEMORY (RAM)   Some memory chips in the system unit are **random access memory** (**RAM**). When the computer is powered on, certain operating system files, such as the files that determine how your desktop is displayed, are loaded from a storage device, such as a hard disk, into RAM. As long as the power remains on, these files remain in RAM. Because RAM is volatile, the programs and data

stored in RAM are erased when the power to the computer is turned off. Any files or data created by a user that will be needed for future use must be copied from RAM to a storage device, such as a hard disk, before the power to the computer is turned off.

The most common form of RAM used in personal computers is **synchronous dynamic RAM**, or **SDRAM**. Today, most RAM is installed by using a **dual inline memory module (DIMM)**. A DIMM is a small circuit board that contains multiple RAM chips (Figure 4-11). Common DIMM modules can hold 1, 2, or 4 gigabytes of memory. DIMM chips are installed in special sockets on the motherboard and can be removed and replaced easily with higher-capacity RAM chips or with additional RAM chips. The amount of memory a computer can handle depends on the motherboard.

dual inline   memory
memory   chip
module

Figure 4-11 This photo shows a dual inline memory module (DIMM).

The amount of RAM a computer requires often depends on the types of applications to be used on the computer. Remember that a computer can manipulate only data that is in memory. RAM is similar to the workspace you have on the top of your desk. Just as a desktop needs a certain amount of space to hold papers, pens, and your computer, a computer needs a certain amount of memory to store programs and files.

The more RAM a computer has, the more programs and files it can work on at once. Having sufficient RAM (2–4 GB or higher) is important for memory-intensive tasks, such as manipulating graphics; downloading music, videos, and movies; and creating and editing sound, digital images, and video.

A software package usually indicates the minimum amount of RAM and other system requirements. For an application to perform optimally, you usually need more than the minimum specifications on the software package.

READ-ONLY MEMORY (ROM) Read-only memory (ROM) chips store information or instructions that do not change. Manufacturers permanently record

instructions and data on ROM chips. Unlike RAM, ROM memory is nonvolatile because it retains its contents even when the power is turned off. In addition to personal computers, manufacturers install ROM chips in automobiles, home appliances, toys, educational games, and thousands of other items used by people everyday.

FLASH MEMORY Flash memory is a type of nonvolatile memory that can be erased electronically and rewritten to. Most computers use flash memory to hold startup instructions because it allows the computer to update its contents easily. For example, when the computer changes from standard time to daylight saving time, the contents of a flash memory chip (and the real-time clock chip) change to reflect the new time. Flash memory chips are also used to store data and programs on many mobile computers and devices, such as smartphones, printers, digital cameras, and digital voice recorders. When you enter names and addresses in a smartphone, a flash memory chip stores the data. Some portable media players store music on flash memory chips (Figure 4-12); others store music on tiny hard disks or flash memory cards.

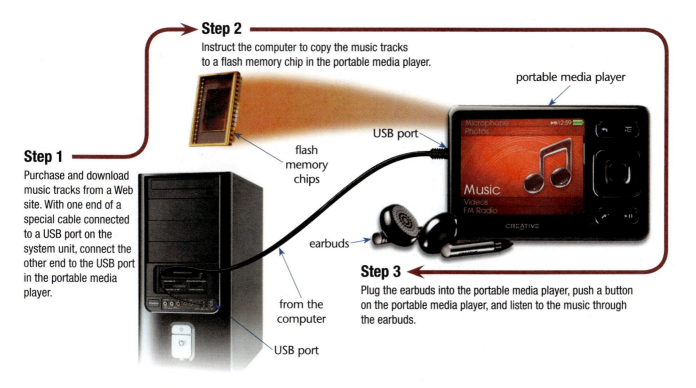

Step 2
Instruct the computer to copy the music tracks to a flash memory chip in the portable media player.

portable media player

USB port

flash memory chips

Microphone
Photos
pm12:59
Music
Videos
FM Radio
CREATIVE

Step 1
Purchase and download music tracks from a Web site. With one end of a special cable connected to a USB port on the system unit, connect the other end to the USB port in the portable media player.

earbuds

from the computer

USB port

Step 3
Plug the earbuds into the portable media player, push a button on the portable media player, and listen to the music through the earbuds.

Figure 4-12 How a portable media player might store music in flash memory.

EXPANSION SLOTS AND EXPANSION CARDS

An **expansion slot** is a socket on the motherboard that can hold an expansion card. An **expansion card**, sometimes called an **adapter card**, is a circuit board that enhances functions of a system component and/or provides connections to peripherals. A **peripheral** is a device that connects to the system unit and is controlled by the processor in the computer. Most of today's computers support **Plug and Play**, which means the computer can configure devices automatically as they are installed.

REMOVABLE MEMORY DEVICES

Four widely used types of removable flash memory devices include flash memory cards, USB flash drives, PC Cards, and ExpressCard modules. You can change a removable flash memory device without having to open the system unit or restart the computer. This feature, called **hot plugging**, allows you to insert and remove the removable flash memory while the computer or mobile device is running.

A **flash memory card** is a removable flash memory device that you insert and remove from a slot in a computer or mobile device. Many consumer devices, such as smartphones and digital cameras use these memory cards. Some printers and computers have built-in slots that read flash memory cards. Flash memory cards are available in a variety of shapes and sizes (Figure 4-13).

Integration Strategies

To learn more about how to integrate portable media storage into your classroom, visit the Computer Concepts CourseMate Web site at *www. cengagebrain.com*, and then navigate to the Chapter 4 Teaching Today resource for this book.

Storage capacities of flash memory cards range from 256 MB to more than 100 GB.

A **USB flash drive** is a flash memory storage device that plugs in to a USB port on a computer or portable device. USB flash drives are available in a variety of shapes and sizes with storage capacities ranging from 2 GB to 32 GB (see Figure 4-13) to more than 64 GB. USB flash drives with up to 8 GB in storage are available at stores for less than $30.

A **PC Card** is a thin, credit card-sized removable flash memory device that is used primarily to enable notebook computers to access the Internet wirelessly. An **ExpressCard module**, which can be used as a removable flash memory device, adds memory, communications, multimedia, and security capabilities to computers. Many computers have a **PC Card slot** or an **ExpressCard slot**, which is a special type of expansion slot that holds a PC Card or an ExpressCard module, respectively (Figure 4-14).

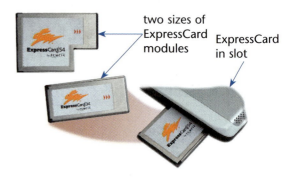

two sizes of ExpressCard modules

ExpressCard in slot

Figure 4-14 An ExpressCard module slides into an ExpressCard slot on a computer and is available in two sizes.

PORTS AND CONNECTORS

Cables are often used to attach external devices, such as a keyboard, monitor, printer, mouse, and microphone, to the system unit. A **port** is the point of attachment to the system unit. Most computers contain ports on the back as well as the front of the system unit (Figure 4-15).

Ports use different types of **connectors** that come in various sizes and shapes and that are usually male or female. Male connectors have one or more exposed pins, like the end of an electrical cord you plug into the wall. Female connectors have

memory cards

USB flash drive

Figure 4-13 Removable flash memory devices are inserted in a slot in a computer or mobile device; a USB flash drive plugs into a USB port.

built-in memory card readers

microphone port

headphones port (or jack)

keyboard port

digital audio (or S/PDIF) out port

serial port

FireWire ports

USB ports

side surround sound port

microphone port

speaker port

digital audio (or S/PDIF) in port

network port

rear surround sound port

center surround sound/subwoofer port

audio in port

S-video port

HDMI port

DVI port

Figure 4-15 Most computers have ports on the front and back of the system unit. Shown are the ports available on a PC. Macs have similar ports.

matching receptacles to accept the pins, like an electrical wall outlet.

A **USB port,** short for **universal serial bus port** can connect up to 127 different peripheral devices with a single connector type. Devices that connect to a USB port include the following: mouse, printer, digital camera, scanner, speakers, portable media player, optical disc drive, smartphone, game console, and removable hard disk. Personal computers typically have four to eight USB ports on the front and/or back of the system unit (see Figure 4-15 above). The **USB 2.0 port** is more advanced and faster, with speeds 40 times faster, than the original USB port. The latest version, **USB 3.0 port** is more than 10 times faster than USB 2.0.

Similar to a USB port, a **FireWire port** can connect devices that require faster data transmission speeds, such as digital video cameras, digital VCRs, color printers, and DVD drives to a single connector type. The FireWire port is found on more expensive PCs and most Macs.

Bluetooth technology uses radio waves to transmit data between two devices. If you have a computer that is not Bluetooth enabled, you can purchase a Bluetooth wireless port adapter that will convert an existing USB port into a Bluetooth port (Figure 4-16). Many computers, peripheral devices, smartphones, cars, and other consumer electronics are Bluetooth-enabled, which means they contain a small chip that allows them to communicate with other Bluetooth-enabled computers and devices. Bluetooth headsets allow smartphone users to connect their telephone to a headset wirelessly.

Figure 4-16 A Bluetooth wireless port adapter converts a USB port into a Bluetooth port.

a computer. As soon as input is in memory, the CPU can access it and process the input into output. Input can be categorized into four types: data, programs, commands, and user responses (Figure 4-17).

■ **Data** is a collection of unprocessed items. A computer manipulates and processes data into information that is useful, such as words, numbers, pictures, sounds, and so on. Although a single item of data should be referred to as datum, the term data commonly is used and accepted as both the singular and plural form of the word.

■ A **program** is a series of instructions that tells a computer how to perform the tasks necessary to process data into information. Programs are kept on storage media such as a hard disk,

to a computer program. Commands can be issued by typing keywords or pressing special keys on the keyboard. A **keyword** is a special word, phrase, or code that a program understands as an instruction. Many programs also allow you to issue commands by selecting graphical objects. Today, most programs have a graphical user interface that uses icons, buttons, and other graphical objects to issue commands.

■ Sometimes a program asks a question, such as "Do you want to save the changes you made?", that requires a **user response**. Based on your response, the program performs specific actions. For example, if you answer Yes to this question, the program saves your file to a storage medium.

Web Info

To search for a solution to a specific hardware problem for a PC, visit the Computer Concepts CourseMate Web site at *www. cengagebrain.com*, navigate to the Chapter 4 Web Info resource for this book, and then click Hardware.

Figure 4-17
Input can be categorized as data, programs, commands, and user responses.

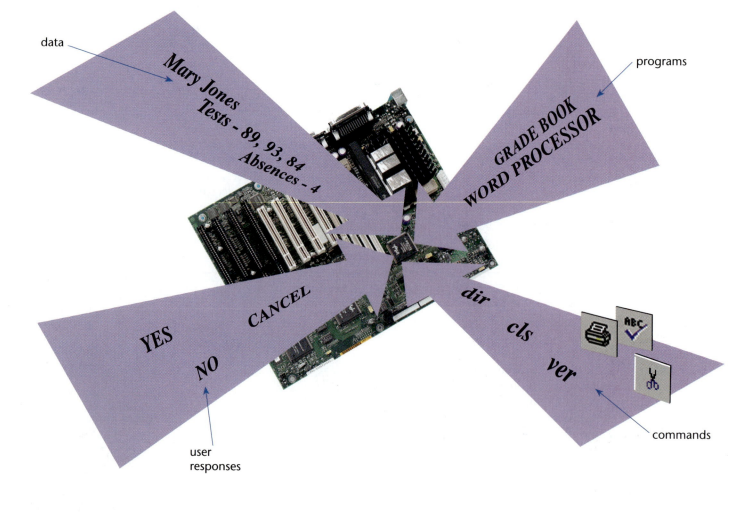

What Are Input Devices?

An **input device** is any hardware component that allows you to enter data, programs, commands, and user responses into a computer. Input devices include keyboards, pointing devices, optical scanners and reading devices, digital cameras, audio and video input devices, smartphones, media players, and input devices for students with special needs. Many of these input devices are discussed on the following pages.

THE KEYBOARD

One of the primary input devices used with a computer is the keyboard. A **keyboard** is an input device that contains keys users press to enter data and instructions into a computer. Most keyboards are similar to the ones shown in Figure 4-18. You enter data, commands, and other input into a computer by pressing keys on the keyboard.

Personal computer keyboards usually contain from 101 to 105 keys; keyboards for smaller computers, such as notebook and netbook computers, contain fewer keys. A keyboard includes keys that allow you to type letters, numbers, spaces, punctuation marks, and other symbols such as the dollar sign ($) and the asterisk (*). A keyboard also contains special keys that allow you to enter data and instructions into the computer.

All computer keyboards have a typing area that includes the letters of the alphabet,

number keys

typing area

arrow keys

[a] Apple Wireless Keyboard

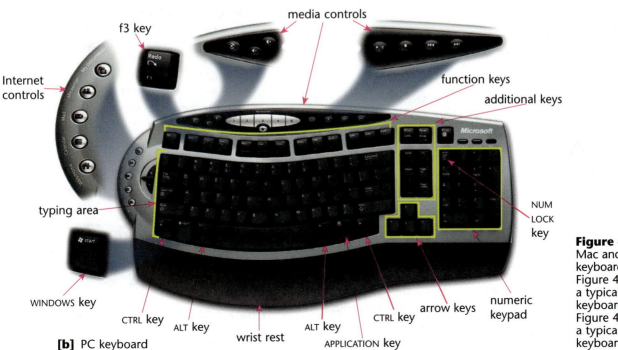

f3 key

media controls

Internet controls

function keys

additional keys

typing area

NUM LOCK key

WINDOWS key

CTRL key   ALT key

wrist rest

ALT key

CTRL key

APPLICATION key

arrow keys

numeric keypad

[b] PC keyboard

Figure 4-18
Mac and PC keyboards are similar. Figure 4-18a shows a typical Mac keyboard and Figure 4-18b shows a typical PC keyboard.

numbers, punctuation marks, and other basic keys. Because of the layout of its typing area, a standard computer keyboard sometimes is called a QWERTY keyboard, pronounced KWER-tee. This keyboard layout is named after the first six letters on the top-left alphabetic line of the keyboard.

Many desktop computer keyboards also have a numeric keypad located on the right side of the keyboard. A **numeric keypad** is a calculator-style arrangement of keys representing numbers, a decimal point, and some basic mathematical operators. The numeric keypad is designed to make it easier to enter numbers.

Keyboards also contain arrow keys that can be used to position the insertion point on the screen. The **insertion point**, or **cursor**, is a symbol that indicates where the next character you type will appear on the screen. Depending on the program, the symbol may be a vertical bar, a rectangle, or an underline. These arrow keys allow you to move the insertion point right, left, up, or down. Most keyboards also contain keys such as HOME, END, PAGE UP, and PAGE DOWN that you can press to move the insertion point to the beginning or end of a line, page, or document.

Most keyboards also include toggle keys, which can be switched between two different states. The NUM LOCK key, for example, is a toggle key found on computer keyboards. When you press it once, it locks the numeric keypad so you can use it to type numbers. When you press the NUM LOCK key again, the numeric keypad is unlocked so the same keys serve as arrow keys that move the insertion point. The CAPS LOCK key is another example of a toggle key and is used on both PCs and Macs. Many keyboards have status lights in the upper-right corner that light up to indicate that a toggle key is activated.

Keyboards often include specialized buttons that allow you to access and use your CD/DVD drive, adjust speaker volume, open your e-mail program, start your Web browser, and more. Most keyboards attach to a serial port on the system unit via a cable. On notebook and netbook computers, the keyboard often is built onto the top of the system unit (Figure 4-19). Tablet computers (like the Apple iPad) and some mobile devices have onscreen keyboards.

Figure 4-19 Notebook computers, tablet computers, and mobile devices use a variety of keyboard types.

A popular keyboard used in K-12 classrooms is a **wireless keyboard,** also called a **cordless keyboard**. A wireless keyboard is a battery-operated device that transmits data using wireless technology, such as radio waves or infrared light waves (Figure 4-20). Wireless keyboards are standard on all new Macs and available for most PCs. Some wireless keyboards come packaged with a wireless pointing device.

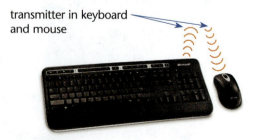

transmitter in keyboard and mouse

Figure 4-20 Wireless keyboards and mice can be passed easily from student to student while they work on group projects.

POINTING DEVICES

A **pointing device** is an input device that allows you to control a pointer on the screen. In a graphical user interface, a pointer, or mouse pointer, is a small symbol on the monitor's screen. A pointer often takes the shape of a block arrow (), an I-beam (I), or a pointing hand (☝). Using a pointing device, you can position the pointer to move or select items on the screen. For example, you can use a pointing device to move the insertion point; select text, graphics, and other objects; and click buttons, icons, links, and menu commands. Common pointing devices include the mouse, touchpad and pointing stick, trackball, joystick and wheel, and touch screen.

MOUSE A mouse is the most widely used pointing device because it takes full advantage of a graphical user interface. Designed to fit comfortably under the palm of your hand, a **mouse** is an input device used to control the movement of the pointer on the screen and to make selections from the screen. The top of the mouse usually has one or two buttons; some have a small wheel. The mouse used with PCs usually is a two-button mouse (Figure 4-21); newer Macs use the Magic Mouse (Figure 4-22). The first type of mouse was a mechanical mouse. The bottom of a mechanical mouse is flat and contains a multidirectional mechanism, usually a small ball, which senses movement of the mouse.

The mouse often rests on a **mouse pad**, which usually is a rectangular rubber or foam pad that provides better traction for the mouse than the top of a desk. The mouse pad also protects the ball mechanism from a build up of dust and dirt, which could cause it to malfunction.

An optical mouse or a wireless mouse (also called a cordless mouse) can be used with most new computers. An **optical mouse** has no moving mechanical parts; instead, it emits and senses light to detect the mouse's movement. A **wireless mouse** or **cordless mouse** is a battery-powered device that transmits data using wireless technology, such as radio waves or infrared light waves. Many wireless keyboards come packaged with a separate wireless mouse.

As you move the mouse across a flat surface or a mouse pad, the pointer on the screen also moves. For example, when you move the mouse to the left, the pointer moves left on the screen. When you move the mouse to the right, the pointer moves right on the screen, and so on.

By using the mouse to move the pointer on the screen and then pressing, or **clicking**, the buttons on the mouse, you can perform actions such as selecting commands on tabs, making menu selections, editing a document, and moving, or **dragging**, data from one location in a document to another. To press and release a mouse button twice without moving the mouse is called **double-clicking**. Double-clicking can be used to

FAQ

What can I do to reduce chances of experiencing repetitive strain injuries?

Do not rest your wrist on the edge of a desk; use a wrist rest. Keep your forearm at wrist level so your wrist does not bend. Do hand exercises every fifteen minutes. Keep your shoulders, arms, hands, and wrists relaxed while you work. Keep your feet flat on the floor, with one foot slightly in front of the other.

FAQ

How do I use a wheel on a mouse?

Roll it forward or backward to scroll up or down. Tilt it to the right or left to scroll horizontally. Hold down the CTRL key while rolling the wheel to make the text on the screen bigger or smaller. These scrolling and zooming functions work with most software, including Web browsers.

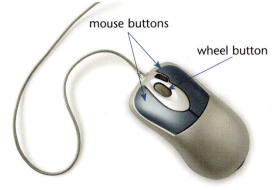

mouse buttons

wheel button

Figure 4-21 A typical two button optical mouse with a wheel.

Figure 4-22 All new iMacs come with the wireless (Bluetooth) Magic Mouse, which is based upon Apple's multi-touch technology used on the iPad.

perform actions such as starting a program or opening a document. The function of the buttons on a two-button mouse can be changed to accommodate right- and left-handed individuals.

TOUCHPAD AND POINTING STICK A **touchpad** is a small, flat, rectangular pointing device that is sensitive to pressure and motion. Most touchpads have one or more buttons near the pad that work like mouse buttons. Touchpads often are found on notebook computers (Figure 4-23). A **pointing stick** is a pressure-sensitive pointing device shaped like a pencil eraser that is positioned between keys on the keyboard (Figure 4-24).

To avoid using both a keyboard and a mouse with desktop computers, some schools purchase special keyboards that include a touchpad. Some notebook computers contain both touchpads and pointing sticks.

Figure 4-23 Many notebook computers have a touchpad that can be used to control the movement of the pointer.

Figure 4-24 Some notebook computers use a pointing stick to control the movement of the pointer.

TRACKBALL Some users opt for pointing devices other than a mouse, such as a trackball. Whereas a mouse has a ball mechanism on the bottom, a **trackball** is a stationary pointing device with a ball mechanism on its top (Figure 4-25).

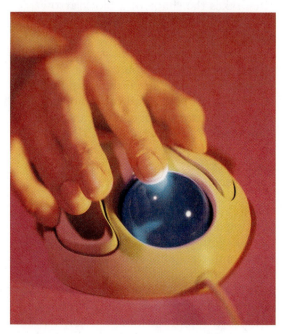

Figure 4-25 A trackball is like an upside-down mechanical mouse. You rotate the ball with your thumb, fingers, or palm to move the pointer.

The ball mechanism in a larger trackball is about the size of a Ping-Pong ball; notebook computers have small trackballs about the size of a marble. To move the pointer using a trackball, you rotate the ball mechanism with your thumb, fingers, or palm of your hand. Around the ball mechanism, a trackball usually has one or more buttons that work just like mouse buttons.

A trackball requires frequent cleaning because it picks up oils from fingers and dust from the environment. If you have limited desk space or use a notebook computer, however, a trackball is a good alternative to a mouse because you do not have to move the entire device.

JOYSTICK AND WHEEL Users running game software, such as driving or flight simulation software, may prefer to use a joystick, wheel, or other device as their pointing and control device (Figure 4-26). A **joystick** is a vertical lever mounted on a base. You move the lever in different directions to control

gamepad

joystick

guitar

dance pad

pedal

balance board

wheel

motion-sensing game controller

light gun

B

DANCE

A

Figure 4-26 A variety of pointing devices and game controllers.

the actions of a vehicle or a player. The lever usually includes buttons, called triggers, that you can press to activate certain events. Some joysticks also have additional buttons that you can set to perform other actions.

A **wheel** is a steering-wheel type input device. You turn the wheel to simulate driving a car or other vehicle. Most wheels also include foot pedals for acceleration and braking action. A joystick and wheel typically attach via a cable to the game port on a sound card or game card, or to a USB port.

TOUCH AND MULTI-TOUCH SCREENS

A monitor that has a touch-sensitive panel on the screen is called a **touch screen,** which is a touch-sensitive display device. You interact with the computer by touching areas of the screen with your finger (Figure 4-27). With a touch screen, the screen is the input device.

To enter data, instructions, and information, you touch words, pictures, numbers, or locations identified on the screen. Some touch screens also respond to finger motions, such as sliding your finger to drag an object or pinching your fingers to zoom in or out. Touch screens that recognize multiple points of contact at the same time are known as **multi-touch.**

Some models of desktop computers (see Figure 4-28) and notebook computers, all tablet computers, and many mobile devices have touch screens. With many smartphones, portable media players, and

touch screen on tablet computer

touch screen on smartphone

Figure 4-27 Computers and mobile devices have touch screens.

multi-touch touch screen on desktop computer

Figure 4-28 When fingers touch the display, it senses them using electrical fields, and then the operating system instantly transforms taps, swipes, and pinches into lifelike actions.

Figure 4-29 This traveler checks in using an airport kiosk.

other mobile devices, for example, you can touch the screen to perform tasks such as dialing phone numbers, entering text using a pop-up keyboard, and making on-screen selections. Increasingly, handheld game consoles, like Wii U, also have touch screens.

In addition, a touch screen often is used as the input device for a **kiosk**, which is a freestanding computer that provides information to the user. Visitors at museums, for example, can use a kiosk to access and print maps, facts on tours and exhibits, and other information. Travelers often use touch screens to check in, print their boarding passes, and indicate the number of bags they will be checking (Figure 4-29 above).

OPTICAL SCANNERS

An optical scanner, usually called a **scanner**, is an input device that captures an entire page of text or images, such as photographs or artwork electronically. A scanner converts the text or image on the original

document into digital data that can be stored on a storage medium and processed by the computer. The digitized data can be printed, displayed separately, or merged into another document for editing. Handheld devices that scan only a portion of a page at a time also are available.

PEN INPUT

Mobile users often enter data and instructions with a pen-type device. With pen input, users write, draw, and tap on a flat surface to enter input. The surface may be a monitor, a screen, or a special type of paper. Two devices used for pen input are the stylus and digital pen. A **stylus** is a small metal or plastic device that looks like a tiny ink pen but uses pressure instead of ink (Figure 4-30). A **digital pen**, which is slightly larger than a stylus, typically provides more functionality than a stylus, featuring electronic erasers and programmable buttons.

Figure 4-30 You use a stylus or a pen to write, draw, or make selections, for example, on a smartphone screen, a signature capture pad, or a graphics tablet.

DIGITAL CAMERAS

A **digital camera** allows you to take pictures and store the photographed images digitally instead of on traditional film (Figure 4-31). After you have taken a picture or series of pictures, you download, or transfer a copy of, the pictures to your computer. As soon as the pictures are stored on your computer, they can be edited with photo editing software, printed, posted on a Web site, and more.

Figure 4-31 A digital camera is used to take pictures so images can be stored on a computer.

AUDIO AND VIDEO INPUT

Although characters (text and numbers) still are the primary forms of computer input, individuals are increasingly using other types of input, such as images, audio, and video. In the previous sections, you learned about a variety of ways to input image data. The next sections discuss methods used to input audio and video data into a computer. Audio and video data often are stored on a computer's hard disk.

Audio input is the process of entering any sound into the computer, such as speech, music, and sound effects. Most personal computers sold today are equipped with a sound card that is needed to record high quality sound. Recorded sound is input via a device, such as a microphone or a CD/DVD player. The most popular way to input recorded sounds today is to download audio files from the Web.

With a microphone plugged into the microphone port on the sound card, you can record sounds using the computer. After you save the sound as a file, you can play it, add it to a document, or edit it using audio editing software.

Another use for a microphone is speech recognition. **Speech recognition**, also called **voice recognition**, is the capability of a computer to distinguish spoken words. Speech recognition programs do not understand speech, but they can be trained to recognize certain words. The vocabulary of speech recognition programs can range from two words (such as Yes and No) to more than two million words. Experts agree that voice recognition capability eventually will be added to all software programs.

Video input is the process of capturing or downloading full-motion images and storing them on a computer's storage medium, such as a hard disk or DVD. To capture video, you plug a digital video camera, Web cam, or similar device directly into a USB or FireWire port. To download music videos, TV shows, and movies directly from the Web, you use your Web browser. There are a variety of Web sites, for example iTunes, that provide access to videos, usually for a fee. After the video is saved, you can play or edit it using video editing software.

Recent advances in audio and video technologies are allowing users to create and edit audio files and video easily. The creation, use, and integration of audio and video in K-12 education are helping teachers address the needs of today's digital generation. Creating and editing audio and video on both Macs and PCs is covered in greater detail in the Digital Media and Software Corners at the end of each chapter.

SMARTPHONES AND MEDIA PLAYERS INPUT

Increasingly more people, including many teachers and students, are using a variety of devices, such as smartphones and media players. A large variety of input alternatives are available for these devices. Figure 4-32 on the next page provides examples of devices that can be used to input data into a smartphone.

Voice is the traditional method of input for smartphones. Today, however, text messaging, instant messaging, and picture messaging have become popular methods of entering input into a smartphone.

Web Info

For an explanation of speech recognition, visit the Computer Concepts CourseMate Web site at *www.cengagebrain.com*, navigate to the Chapter 4 Web Info resource for this book, and then click Speech Recognition.

Web Info

To learn more about iTunes, visit the Computer Concepts CourseMate Web site at *www.cengagebrain.com*, navigate to the Chapter 4 Web Info resource for this book, and then click iTunes.

obtain maps and directions on the phone by attaching this navigation receiver to your vehicle's window

speak into the microphone that wirelessly communicates with the phone

take a picture using the digital camera built into the back of the phone

use one end of the stylus to write on the phone's screen and the other end as a ballpoint pen

transfer data and instructions to and from the computer and phone by connecting it to the computer with a cable

enter text-based messages via a wireless keyboard

Figure 4-32 Users have many options for inputting data into a smartphone.

Portable media players that do not have touch screens typically have a **touch-sensitive pad**, which is an input device that enables users to scroll through and play music, view pictures, watch videos or movies, adjust volume, and/or customize settings. Touch-sensitive pads typically contain buttons and/or wheels that are operated with a thumb or finger(s). For example, users rotate a **Click Wheel** to browse through the portable media player's song, picture, or movie lists; and they press the Click Wheel's buttons to play or pause media, display a menu, and perform other actions (Figure 4-33).

Additional input devices used in businesses, homes, and schools are described in Chapters 5 through 7. Input devices for students with special needs are covered in this chapter's Assistive Technologies Corner.

Click Wheel

Figure 4-33 You use your thumb to rotate or press buttons on a Click Wheel.

What Is Output?

Output is data that has been processed into a useful form called information. That is, a computer processes input into output. Computers generate several types of output, depending on the hardware and software being used and the requirements of the user. Four common types of output are text, graphics, audio, and video (Figure 4-34).

- **Text** consists of characters that are used to create words, sentences, and paragraphs. A character is a letter, number, punctuation mark, or any other symbol that requires one byte of computer storage space.

- **Graphics** are digital representations of nontext information, such as images, drawings, charts, pictures, and photographs. Displaying a series of still graphics creates an animation — a graphic that has the illusion of motion. Many of today's software

programs support graphics; others are designed specifically to create and edit graphics. Graphics programs, called image editors, allow you to alter graphics by including enhancements, such as blended colors, animation, and other special effects.

- **Audio** is any music, speech, or other sound that is stored and produced by the computer. Recall that sound waves, such as the human voice or music, are analog. To store such sounds, a computer converts them from a continuous analog signal into a digital format.

- **Video** consists of photographic images that are played back at speeds that provide the appearance of full motion in real time. Software and Web sites often include videos to enhance understanding. Vodcasts and vblogs, for example, add a video component to the traditional podcast and blog.

FAQ

What can I do to ease eyestrain while using my computer?

Blink your eyes every five seconds. Use a glare screen. Adjust the room lighting. Use larger fonts or zoom the display. Take an eye break every 10 to 15 minutes. If you wear glasses, ask your doctor about computer glasses.

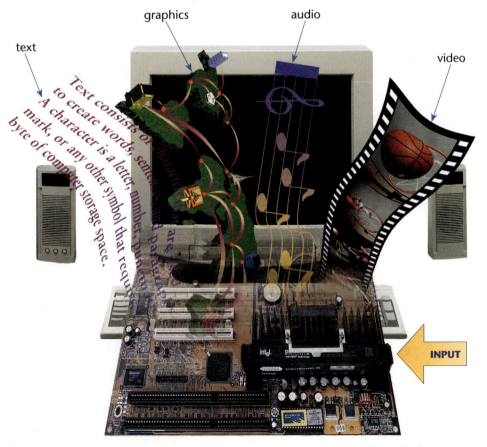

Figure 4-34 Four common types of output are text, graphics, audio, and video.

What Are Output Devices?

An **output device** is any computer component capable of conveying information to a user. Commonly used output devices include display devices, printers, data projectors, facsimile (fax) machines, multifunction devices, interactive whiteboards, speakers, headphones, and earphones. Each of these output devices is discussed on the following pages.

DISPLAY DEVICES

A **display device** is an output device that displays text, graphics, and video information. A **monitor** is a display device that is packaged as a separate peripheral. Information shown on a display device often is called **soft copy** because the information exists electronically and is displayed for a temporary period.

Monitors for personal computers are available in a variety of sizes, with the more common sizes being 19, 20, 22, 24, 26, 27, and 30 inches. The size of a monitor is measured diagonally, from corner to corner, in the same way that television screens are measured. The monitor size and the viewable size do not always match. For example, a monitor listed as a 17-inch monitor may have a viewable size of only 15.7 inches. Determining what size monitor to use depends on what the monitor will be used for. A larger monitor allows you to view more information at once, but it is usually more expensive. If you work on the Web or use multiple applications at one time, however, you may want to invest in at least a 22-inch or larger monitor.

Most monitors have a tilt-and-swivel base that allows users to adjust the angle of the screen to minimize neck strain and reduce glare from overhead lighting. Monitor controls permit users to adjust the brightness, contrast, positioning, height, and width of images. Some have integrated speakers. Most mobile computers and devices integrate the display and other components into the same physical case.

Two types of display devices are older CRT monitors and flat-panel displays, which include LCD monitors and screens, as well as plasma monitors. The following sections discuss each of these display devices.

Web Info

For more information about display devices, visit the Computer Concepts CourseMate Web site at *www.cengagebrain.com*, navigate to the Chapter 4 Web Info resource for this book, and then click Display Device.

CRT MONITORS   Like an older television set, the core of some monitors is a large glass tube called a **cathode ray tube (CRT)** (Figure 4-35). The screen, which is the front of the tube, is coated with tiny dots of phosphor material that glow when electrically charged. The CRT moves an electron beam back and forth across the back of the screen, causing the dots to glow, which produces an image on the screen. CRT monitors are still found in many homes and schools, although all new desktop computers now come with flat panel displays.

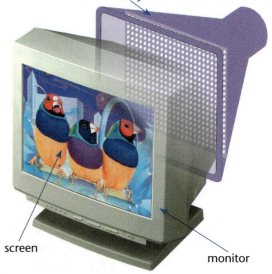

cathode ray tube

screen

monitor

Figure 4-35 The core of most older PC monitors is a cathode ray tube.

Each dot, called a **pixel** (short for picture element), is a single point in an electronic image (Figure 4-36). Monitors consist of hundreds, thousands, or millions of pixels arranged in rows and columns that can be used to create pictures. The pixels are so close together that they appear connected.

Figure 4-36 A pixel is a single dot of color, or point, in an electronic image.

FLAT-PANEL DISPLAYS A flat-panel display is a lightweight display device with a shallow depth and flat screen that typically uses LCD (liquid crystal display) or gas plasma technology. Types of flat-panel displays include LCD monitors, LCD screens, and plasma monitors.

LCD MONITORS AND LCD SCREENS An **LCD monitor**, also called a **flat panel monitor,** is a desktop monitor that uses a liquid crystal display to produce images (Figure 4-37). These monitors produce sharp, flicker-free images and do not take up much desk space. Most are **widescreen,** which means they are wider than they are tall (Figure 4-37).

speakers

Figure 4-37 This widescreen LCD monitor has built-in speakers.

Mobile computers (such as notebook computers and netbooks) and mobile devices (such as tablet computers, portable media players, and smartphones) often have built-in **LCD screens** (Figure 4-38). Notebook computer screens are available in a variety of sizes, with the more common being 14, 15, 17, and 20 inches. Tablet screens range from 7 to 10.1 inches and netbooks range from 7 to 12.1 inches. Portable media players usually have screen sizes from 1.5 to 3.5 inches. On smartphones, screen sizes range from 2.5 to 4.1 inches. Digital camera screen sizes usually range from 2.5 to 4 inches.

LCD monitors and screens use a technology called **liquid crystal display (LCD)**, which uses a liquid compound to present information on a display device. The quality of an LCD monitor or LCD screen depends primarily on its resolution, response time, brightness, dot pitch, and contrast ratio.

PLASMA MONITORS Some businesses, universities, and schools use plasma monitors, which often measure more than 150 inches wide (Figure 4-39 on the next page). A **plasma monitor** is a display device that uses gas plasma technology, which sandwiches a layer of gas between two

handheld game console

smartphone

notebook computer

digital camera

portable media player

Figure 4-38 Many mobile devices, such as notebook and tablet computers, digital cameras, portable media players, and smartphones have built-in LCD screens.

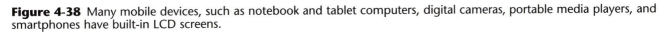

Figure 4-39 Large plasma monitors can measure more than 150 inches wide.

Figure 4-40 Many users are using programs such as Apple's AirPlay (shown here) to stream video from an iPad to a HDTV.

glass plates. When voltage is applied, the gas releases ultraviolet (UV) light. This UV light causes the pixels on the screen to glow and form an image. Plasma monitors offer larger screen sizes and richer colors than LCD monitors but are more expensive. Like LCD monitors, plasma monitors can hang directly on a wall.

RESOLUTION Resolution is the number of horizontal and vertical pixels in a display device. For example, a monitor that has a 1600 × 1200 resolution displays up to 1600 pixels per horizontal row and 1200 pixels per vertical column, for a total of 1,920,000 pixels to create a screen image. A higher resolution uses a greater number of pixels and thus provides a smoother, sharper, and clearer image. As you increase the resolution, however, some items on the screen appear smaller. With LCD monitors and screens, resolution generally is proportional to the size of the device. For example, a widescreen 19-inch LCD monitor typically has a resolution of 1440 × 900, while a 22-inch LCD monitor has a resolution of 1680 × 1050.

TELEVISIONS Because home users often prefer their larger television displays for game playing, watching movies, and browsing the Internet, they are using their high definition television (HDTV) more and more as a display device. For example, iPad users can stream their music, photos, and videos (including feature length movies) wirelessly to their HDTV using Apple TV and an iPad feature called AirPlay (Figure 4-40). You can stream the movies you own or access others using provider's apps.

Subscribers to Netflix, HBO, and other providers can download a free app, such as Netflix or HBO GO, to their tablet computer, smartphone, and other mobile devices in order to stream video to those devices. With game consoles, such as Microsoft's Xbox 360, Nintendo's Wii, and Sony's PlayStation 3, the output device often is a television. Users plug one end of a cable into the game console and the other end into the video port on the television.

PRINTERS

A **printer** is an output device that produces text and graphical information on a physical medium, such as paper or transparency film. Printed information is called **hard copy** because it is a more permanent form of output than that presented on a monitor. Users can print a hard copy of a file in either portrait or landscape orientation. A page with **portrait orientation** is taller than it is wide, with information printed across the shorter width of the paper. A page with **landscape orientation** is wider than it is tall, with information printed across the wider part of the paper.

Because printing requirements vary greatly among users, manufacturers offer printers with varying speeds, capabilities, and printing methods. Until a few years ago, printing a document required connecting a computer to a printer with a cable via a USB or parallel port on the computer. Although many users today continue to print using this method, a variety of printing options are available, as shown in Figure 4-41.

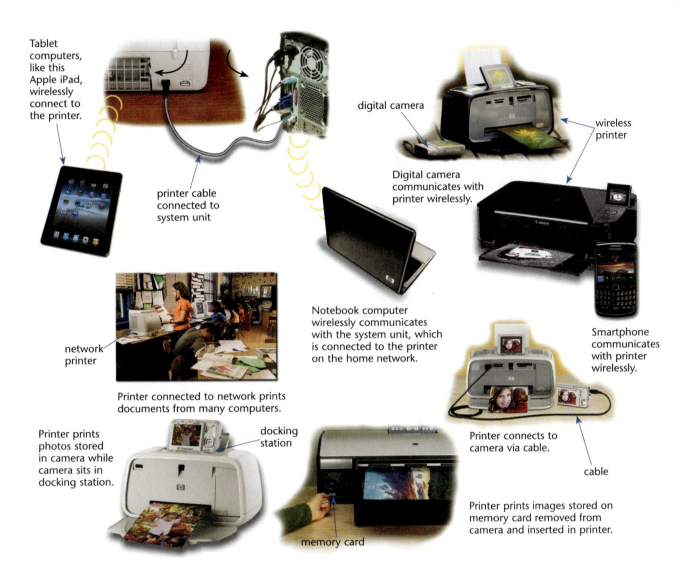

Tablet computers, like this Apple iPad, wirelessly connect to the printer.

printer cable connected to system unit

digital camera

wireless printer

Digital camera communicates with printer wirelessly.

Notebook computer wirelessly communicates with the system unit, which is connected to the printer on the home network.

Smartphone communicates with printer wirelessly.

network printer

Printer connected to network prints documents from many computers.

docking station

Printer prints photos stored in camera while camera sits in docking station.

Printer connects to camera via cable.

cable

memory card

Printer prints images stored on memory card removed from camera and inserted in printer.

Figure 4-41 Users print documents and pictures using a variety of printing methods.

NONIMPACT PRINTERS A nonimpact **printer** forms marks on a piece of paper without actually striking the paper. Two common types of nonimpact printers are ink-jet and laser printers.

Because of their reasonable cost and print quality, ink-jet printers often are used in homes and schools. An **ink-jet printer** is a type of nonimpact printer that forms marks by spraying tiny drops of liquid ink onto a piece of paper. Ink-jet printers can produce high-quality text and graphics in both black-and-white and color on a variety of media such as paper, envelopes, labels, or transparencies. Ink-jet printers use small ink cartridges that are replaced easily or may be refilled using inexpensive ink-jet refill kits. In addition, many ink-jet printers include software to help you create items such as announcements, banners, cards, and so on.

A **photo printer** is a color printer that produces photo lab quality pictures (Figure 4-42). Many photo printers use ink-jet technology and can print photos in various sizes.

Figure 4-42 Ink-jet photo printers are a popular type of color printer used at home.

A **laser printer** is a high-speed, high-quality nonimpact printer (Figure 4-43 above). Operating in a manner similar to a copy machine, a laser printer uses powdered ink, called toner, which is packaged in a cartridge. When electrically charged, the toner sticks to a special drum inside the printer and then is transferred to the paper through a combination of pressure and heat. When the toner runs out, you simply replace the cartridge.

Web Info

For more information about data projectors and how they are used in K-12 classrooms, visit the Computer Concepts CourseMate Web site at *www. cengagebrain.com*, navigate to the Chapter 4 Web Info resource for this book, and then click Data Projectors.

Figure 4-43 A laser printer operates similarly to a copy machine. Electrically charged toner sticks to a special drum inside the printer and then is transferred to the paper through a combination of pressure and heat.

Laser printers, in a manner similar to ink-jet printers, usually use individual sheets of letter and legal-size paper stored in a removable tray that slides into the printer

case. Most printers also have a manual feed slot where you can insert individual sheets, transparencies, and envelopes.

Although laser printers cost more than ink-jet printers, laser printers print very high-quality black-and-white text and graphics quickly. While color laser printers are available, replacement color ink cartridges are expensive and rarely found in K-12 classrooms.

Other nonimpact printers include thermal printers, portable printers, label and postage printers, plotters, and large-format printers.

DATA PROJECTORS

A **data projector** projects the image that displays on a computer screen onto a large screen so that an audience, such as a classroom or school assembly, can see the image clearly (Figure 4-44). Data projectors range in size from large devices attached to a ceiling or wall in an auditorium to smaller portable devices. Two types of smaller lower-cost units are LCD projectors and DLP (digital light processing) projectors. An LCD projector, which also uses liquid crystal display technology, attaches directly to a computer and uses its own light source to display the information shown on the computer screen. A digital light processing (DLP) projector uses tiny mirrors to reflect light, producing crisp, bright, colorful images that remain in focus and can be seen clearly even in a well-lit room.

Figure 4-44 Data projectors produce sharp, bright images.

FACSIMILE (FAX) MACHINES

A **facsimile (fax) machine** is a device that transmits and receives documents over telephone lines. The documents (called faxes) can contain text, graphics, or photos, or can be handwritten. A fax machine scans the original document, converts the image into digitized data, and transmits the digitized image (Figure 4-45). A fax machine at the receiving end reads the incoming data, converts the digitized data into an image, and prints or stores a copy of the original image.

Figure 4-45 A stand-alone fax machine.

The fax machine just described is a stand-alone fax machine. You also can add fax capability to your computer via a fax modem. A fax modem is a communications device that allows you to send and receive electronic documents as faxes. A fax modem transmits electronic documents, such as a word processing letter or digital photo. A fax modem is like a regular modem except that it transmits documents to a fax machine or to another fax modem. When you receive a fax on your computer, you can view the document on the screen or print it using special fax software.

MULTIFUNCTION DEVICES

A **multifunction device** (**MFD**), also called an **all-in-one device**, is a single piece of equipment that provides the functionality of a printer, fax machine, copier, and scanner. The features of multifunction devices vary widely. For example, some use color ink-jet printer technology, while others use a black-and-white laser printer. Small businesses, home offices, and school administrative offices use multifunction devices because they take up less space and cost less than a separate printer, scanner,

copy machine, and fax machine (Figure 4-46). Quality multifunction devices are available for less than $150.

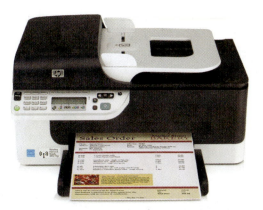

Figure 4-46 This multifunction device is an all-in-one device that includes a color printer, scanner, fax, and copy machine.

INTERACTIVE WHITEBOARDS

An **interactive whiteboard** (**IWB**) is a large interactive display that resembles a dry-erase board. An IWB connects to a computer and projector, which gives it the ability to project the interactivity of the computer desktop to the display. An IWB is touch-sensitive when connected to a computer. A device driver and software must be installed on the connected computer so that the interactive whiteboard can be used as an interactive learning tool. Front projection and rear projection interactive whiteboards, which are hung on the wall or mounted on a stand, range in size from 48 to 94 inches.

Interactive whiteboards have recently become very popular in K-12 classrooms as a teaching tool. Because, unlike a projection screen, the interactive whiteboard provides teachers and students with the ability to use multiple input devices in order to create active learning environments. A teacher controls the computer program used to display the image by clicking a remote control, touching the whiteboard, drawing on or erasing the whiteboard with a special digital pen and eraser, stylus, or writing on a special tablet (Figure 4-47 on the next page). IWBs are used in a variety of settings, including classrooms at all levels of education, in business, and in training rooms for professional development. Integrating IWBs into your curriculum is covered in greater detail in Chapter 5.

Figure 4-47 Teachers and students can write directly on an interactive whiteboard, or they can write on a wireless slate that communicates with the whiteboard.

SPEAKERS, HEADPHONES, AND EARPHONES

Electronically produced voice output is growing in popularity. **Voice output** occurs when you hear a person's voice or when the computer talks to you through the speakers on the computer. In some programs, the computer can speak the contents of a document through voice output. On the Web, you can listen to (or download and then listen to) interviews, talk shows, sporting events, news, recorded music, and live concerts from many radio and television stations. Some Web sites dedicate themselves to providing voice output, where you can hear songs, quotes, historical lectures, speeches, and books. In order to take advantage of voice output, users need an audio output device connected to their computers.

An **audio output device** is a component of a computer that produces music, speech, or other sounds, such as beeps. Three commonly used audio output devices are speakers, headphones, and earphones.

Most personal computers have a small internal speaker that usually emits only low-quality sound. For this reason, many personal computers are sold with stereo speakers. **Speakers** can be separate devices placed on either side of the monitor or they can be built into the monitor or the system unit. Stereo speakers are connected

to ports on the sound card. Most speakers have tone and volume controls. Some users add surround sound speakers to their computers to generate a higher-quality sound for playing games, interacting with multimedia presentations, listening to music CDs, and viewing DVDs.

When using speakers, anyone within listening distance can hear the output. Speakers are not always practical in classrooms and computer labs. Often, teachers and students use headphones or earphones that can be plugged into a port on the sound card, on a speaker, or on the front of the system unit. The difference is that **headphones** cover or are placed outside the ear (Figure 4-48), whereas **earphones**, or **earbuds** (shown in Figure 4-53 on page 183) rest inside the ear canal. By using headphones or earphones, students can concentrate better on the sound from their computers and they will not be disturbed by sounds on nearby computers or disturb other students.

Figure 4-48 Headphones or earphones are used in lab settings to help with noise control.

What Is Storage?

Storage refers to the media on which data, instructions, and information are kept, as well as the devices that record and retrieve these items. To understand storage, you should understand the difference between how a computer uses memory and how it uses storage. As discussed earlier in this chapter, RAM temporarily stores data and programs that are being processed. RAM is volatile because data and programs stored in memory are lost when the power is turned off or a power failure occurs.

Storage stores data, instructions, and information when they are not being processed. Think of storage as a filing cabinet used to hold file folders, and think of memory as the top of your desk (Figure 4-49). When you need to work with a file, you remove it from the filing cabinet (storage) and place it on your desk (memory). When you are finished with the file, you return it to the filing cabinet (storage). Storage is nonvolatile, which means that data, instructions, and information in storage are retained even when power is removed from the computer.

Figure 4-49 Think of storage as a filing cabinet used to hold file folders and memory as the top of your desk.

Storage Media and Devices

A **storage medium** (media is the plural), also called **secondary storage,** is the physical material on which data, instructions, and information are kept. One commonly used storage medium is a **disk,** which is a round, flat piece of plastic or metal on which items such as data, instructions, and information can be encoded. A **storage device** is the mechanism used to record and retrieve these items to and from a storage medium. Examples of storage media are hard disks, solid state drives, CDs and DVDs, PC Cards and ExpressCard modules, flash memory cards, USB flash drives, and smart cards.

Storage devices can function as sources of input and output. For example, each time the CPU transfers data, instructions, and information from a storage medium into memory — a process called reading — the storage device functions as an input source. When the CPU transfers these items from memory to a storage medium — a process

called writing — the storage device functions as an output source.

The size, or capacity, of a storage device is measured by the amount of bytes (data) it can hold. Storage capacity usually is measured in megabytes or gigabytes. Some devices can hold thousands of bytes, whereas others can store trillions of bytes. For example, a reasonably priced USB flash drive can store up to 4 GB of data (approximately 4 billion bytes) and a typical hard disk has 750 GB (approximately 750 billion bytes) of storage capacity.

Storage requirements among users vary greatly. A teacher, for example, might have a list of names, test scores, and average grades for 30 students that requires several hundred bytes of storage. Users of larger computers, such as banks or libraries, might need to store trillions and trillions of bytes worth of historical data or records. To meet the needs of a wide range of users, numerous types of storage media and storage devices exist, many of which are discussed in the following sections.

MAGNETIC DISKS

A **magnetic disk** uses magnetic patterns to store data, instructions, and information on the disk's surface. Depending on how the magnetic particles are aligned, they represent either a 0 bit or a 1 bit. Recall that a bit (binary digit) is the smallest unit of data a computer can process. Most magnetic disks are read/write storage media; that is, you can read data from and write data to a magnetic disk any number of times.

Before data can be read from or written to a magnetic disk, the disk must be formatted. **Formatting** is the process of preparing a disk for reading and writing by organizing the disk into storage locations called tracks and sectors (Figure 4-50 on the next page). A **track** is a narrow storage ring around the disk — similar to the annual rings on a tree. A **sector** is a pie-shaped section of the disk, which breaks the tracks into small arcs. A **cluster** is the smallest unit of disk space that stores data and information.

Three types of magnetic disks are 3.5-inch disks, Zip disks, and hard disks. From the early 1980s through the first few years of the 21st century, the most common form of inexpensive portable magnetic

Integration Strategies

To learn more about storing digital data so you can help your students understand how to transfer current knowledge to learning of new technologies, visit the Computer Concepts CourseMate Web site at *www.cengagebrain.com,* and then navigate to the Chapter 4 Education Issues resources for this book.

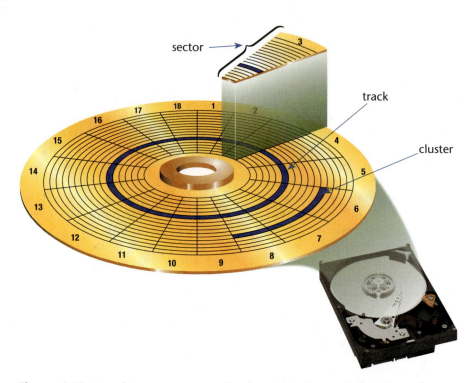

Figure 4-50 A track is a narrow recording band that forms a full circle on the surface of a disk. The disk's storage locations then are divided into pie-shaped sections, which break the tracks into small arcs called sectors.

disks for home and school use were floppy disks (first 5.25-inch and then 3.5-inch) and the more expensive and greater capacity Zip disks. While these magnetic disks are still used by some users and in some schools, USB flash drives have quickly replaced them as the preferred portable storage medium.

HARD DISKS

When personal computers were introduced, software programs and their related files required small amounts of storage and files fit easily on floppy disks. As software became more complex and included graphical user interfaces and multimedia, file sizes and storage requirements increased. Today, hard disks, which provide for larger storage capacities, are the primary media for storing software programs and files. Current personal computer hard disks can store from 320 GB to 1.5 TB or more of data, instructions, and information.

A **hard disk** usually consists of several inflexible, circular disks, called platters, on which items, such as data, instructions, and information, are stored electronically. A **platter** in a hard disk is made of aluminum,

glass, or ceramic and is coated with a material that allows data to be magnetically recorded on its surface. Although removable hard disks do exist, the hard disks in most personal computers are housed permanently inside the system unit and are enclosed in an airtight, sealed case to protect the platters from contamination (Figure 4-51).

hard disk mounted inside system unit

close-up of hard disk; top of case removed

Figure 4-51 The hard disk in a personal computer normally is housed permanently inside the system unit.

current or new location
of the data.

Step 1
The circuit board controls
the movement of the head
actuator and a small motor.

Step 4
The head actuator positions the
read/write head arms over the
correct location on the platters
to read or write data.

Figure 4-52 How a hard disk works.

Recall that a hard disk is a magnetic disk that stores data, instructions, and information using magnetic patterns. Hard disks also are read/write storage media; that is, you can both read from and write to a hard disk any number of times. Figure 4-52 above shows how a hard disk works. Before you can write data, instructions, or information to a hard disk, the hard disk must be formatted. Usually, hard disk manufacturers format hard disks before they are installed in computers. Typically, a hard disk is designated drive C on PCs and as the HD Disk on Macs.

For many years, PC computers came standard with two floppy disk drives, one for 5.25-inch disks that was designated drive A and one for 3.5-inch disks that was designated drive B. Computer hard drives were normally designated as drive C. Although floppy disk drives are no longer installed on PCs, computer manufacturers have retained the designation of drive C for the hard drive so as to not confuse users. The drive A and drive B designations are no longer used.

MINIATURE HARD DISKS Many mobile devices and consumer electronics include miniature hard disks, which provide users with greater storage capacities than flash memory. These tiny hard disks are found in devices, such as media players, digital cameras, and other small devices. Miniature hard disks have storage capacities that range from 1 GB to 320 GB or more (Figure 4-53).

earbuds for portable
media player

Figure 4-53 Miniature hard disks are used in a variety of electronic devices.

PORTABLE HARD DISKS Two types of portable hard disks are external hard disks and removable hard disks (Figure 4-54 on the next page). An **external hard disk** is a separate hard disk that connects to a USB or FireWire port by a cable. External hard disks

insert into a special bay in the system unit.

Sale prices for medium-capacity portable hard drives have dropped to $50 or less. Many teachers and other users have purchased a portable hard drive to supplement their home and school internal hard drives and to back up their home and school files.

external hard disk

Web Info

For more information about DVDs, visit the Computer Concepts CourseMate Web site at *www.cengagebrain. com,* navigate to the Chapter 4 Web Info resource for this book, and then click DVD.

one type of removable hard disk

removable hard disk drive

Figure 4-54 Example of large-capacity portable hard disks.

SOLID STATE DRIVES

A **solid state drive (SSD)** is a storage device that typically uses flash memory to store data, instructions, and information and contains no moving parts. Solid state drives range in size from 16 GB to 512 GB and more. SSDs are being used in all types of computers including servers, desktop computers, mobile computers, and devices such

and consuming less power. As the price of SSDs continues to decrease, experts predict that SSDs (Figure 4-55) will eventually replace traditional magnetic hard drives described earlier in this chapter.

Figure 4-55 An example of a solid state drive found inside newer computers and other devices.

OPTICAL DISCS

An **optical disc** is a type of storage medium that consists of a flat, round, portable disc made of metal, plastic, and lacquer that is written to and read from using a laser. Optical discs used in personal computers are 4.75 inches in diameter. Smaller computers, game consoles, and mobile devices, however, use mini discs that have a diameter of 3 inches or less.

CDs AND DVDs

CDs and DVDs are one type of optical storage media that consists of a flat, round, portable, plastic disc with a protective metal coating. The term *disk* is used for magnetic media and *disc* is used for optical media.

CDs and DVDs primarily store music, movies, digital photographs, and software programs. Just about every personal computer today includes some type of CD or DVD drive. Some CD and DVD drives are read only, meaning you cannot write (save) to the media. Others are read/write, which allows users to save to the disc in much the same way as they would save to a hard disk.

On personal computers, the drive designation of a CD or DVD drive usually follows alphabetically after that of the hard disk. For example, if your hard disk is drive C, then the CD or DVD drive usually will be drive D. When you place a CD or DVD in a Mac, an icon that looks like a CD appears on the computer desktop.

CHARACTERISTICS OF CDs AND DVDs

DVDs are optical media that store data, information, music, and video in microscopic pits on the bottom portion of the disc. A high-powered laser light creates the pits. A lower-powered laser light reads items from the disc by reflecting light off the bottom of the disc, which usually is either gold or silver in color. The reflected light is converted into a series of bits the computer can process. Most manufacturers place a silk-screened label on the top of the disc.

CARE OF OPTICAL DISCS Manufacturers guarantee that a properly cared for CD or DVD will last five years, but could last up to 100 years. Exposing discs to extreme temperatures or humidity could cause them to warp. Stacking discs, touching the underside of discs, or exposing them to any type of contaminant may scratch the discs. If a disc becomes warped or if its surface is scratched, data on the disc may be unreadable. Always place a CD or DVD in a protective case, such as a jewel box or disc storage case, when you are finished using it.

CDs and DVDs are available in a variety of formats. The following sections discuss many of these formats.

TYPES OF OPTICAL DISCS

Many different formats of optical discs exist today. Two general categories are CDs and DVDs, with DVDs having a much greater storage capacity than CDs. Specific formats include CD-ROM, CD-R, CD-RW, DVD-ROM, DVD-R, DVD+R, DVD-RW, DVD+RW, DVD+RAM, and BD. Figure 4-56 identifies each of these optical disc formats and specifies whether a user can read from the disc, write to the disc, and/or erase the disc. The following sections describe characteristics unique to each of these disc formats.

CD-ROM Compact disc read-only memory (CD-ROM; pronounced SEE-DEE-rom) is a type of optical disc that uses the same laser

Web Info

For more information about CDs, visit the Computer Concepts CourseMate Web site at *www.cengagebrain.com*, navigate to the Chapter 4 Web Info resource for this book, and then click CD.

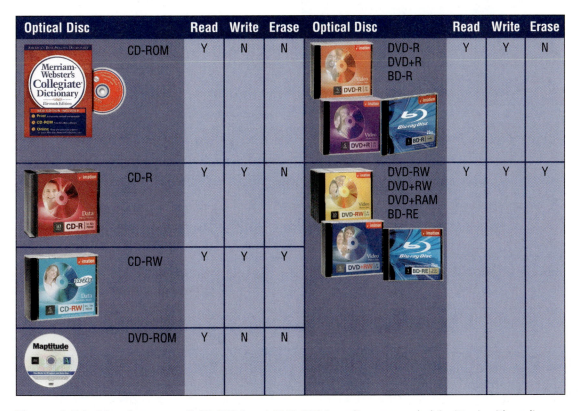

Optical Disc		Read	Write	Erase	Optical Disc		Read	Write	Erase
	CD-ROM	Y	N	N		DVD-R DVD+R BD-R	Y	Y	N
	CD-R	Y	Y	N		DVD-RW DVD+RW DVD+RAM BD-RE	Y	Y	Y
	CD-RW	Y	Y	Y					
	DVD-ROM	Y	N	N					

Figure 4-56 Manufacturers sell CD-ROM and DVD-ROM media prerecorded (written) with audio, video, and software. Users cannot change the contents of these discs. Users, however, can purchase the other formats of CDs and DVDs as blank media and record (write) their own data, videos, and information to these discs.

Integration Strategies

To learn more about removing minor scratches from your CDs and teaching your students the ins and outs of making CD copies, visit the Computer Concepts CourseMate Web site at *www.cengagebrain. com*, and then navigate to the Chapter 4 Digital Media Corner resources for this book.

technology that audio CDs use for recording music. Unlike an audio CD, a CD-ROM can contain text, graphics, animation, and video, as well as sound. The contents of standard CD-ROMs are written, or **recorded**, by the manufacturer and only can be read and used; that is, they cannot be erased or modified — hence, the name read-only. Because audio CDs and CD-ROMs use the same laser technology, you can use your CD drive to listen to an audio CD while working on your computer.

A CD-ROM can hold from 650 MB to 1 GB of data, instructions, and information. Because CD-ROMs have such high storage capacities, they are used to store and distribute today's complex software, such as, education, game, reference, and children's programs (Figure 4-57). Most of today's software programs are sold on CDs or DVDs, or they can be downloaded from the Web after purchase. Some programs even require that the disc be in the drive each time you use the program.

Figure 4-57 Encyclopedias, games, simulations, and many other programs are distributed on CD-ROM.

CD-R AND CD-RW Many computers today include either a CD-R or a CD-RW drive as standard equipment. Unlike standard CD-ROM drives, these new drives allow y ou to record your own data onto a CD-R or CD-RW disc.

A **compact disc-recordable (CD-R)** is a compact disc onto which you can record your own information, such as text, graphic, and audio. With a CD-R, you can write to part of the disc at one time and another part at a later time. You can write to each part only one time, and you cannot

erase the disc's content. To write to a CD-R disc, you must have CD-R software and a CD-R drive.

A **compact disc-rewritable (CD-RW)** is an erasable disc you can write to multiple times. With a CD-RW, the disc acts like a 3.5-inch disk or hard disk. You can easily write and rewrite data multiple times. To write to a CD-RW disc, you must have CD-RW software and a CD-RW drive.

DVD AND BD Although CDs have large storage capacities, even these are not large enough for many of today's complex programs. To meet the tremendous storage requirements of today's software, the **digital video disc read-only memory (DVD-ROM)**, which is a high-capacity optical disc capable of storing from 4.7 GB to 17 GB (Figure 4-58), was developed. Not only is the storage capacity greater than a CD, but the quality of a DVD far surpasses that of a CD. To read a DVD-ROM, you must have a **DVD drive**. Most computers now are sold with DVD drives that will read both CDs and DVDs, including audio CDs.

DVDs are available in a variety of formats, including one which stores motion pictures. Many computers that contain a DVD drive allow you to connect your computer directly to your television. Users also can purchase recordable (DVD-R) and rewritable (DVD+RW) versions of DVDs, which are similar to CD-R and CD-RW in the way they operate.

Many new computers come with a standard combination DVD-ROM/CD-RW drive or optional DVD-R/CD-RW drive.

Figure 4-58 A DVD-ROM is a high-capacity optical disc.

The DVD-R/CD-RW drive is called a SuperDrive on newer Macs.

A newer, more expensive DVD format is called Blu-ray Disc (BD) which has a higher capacity and better quality than standard DVDs. A **Blu-ray Disc (BD)** has storage capacities of 100 GB, with expectations of exceeding 200 GB in the future. Blu-ray drives and players are backward compatible with DVD and CD formats. Some game consoles include a Blu-ray drive.

A mini-DVD that has grown in popularity is the UMD, which works specifically with the PlayStation Portable handheld game console. The UMD (Universal Media Disc), which has a diameter of about 2.4 inches, can store up to 1.8 GB of games, movies, or music.

MINIATURE MOBILE STORAGE MEDIA

Miniature mobile storage media allow mobile users to transport digital images, music, or documents to and from computers and other devices easily (Figure 4-59). Most computers, netbooks, Tablet PCs, smartphones, digital cameras, and media players have built-in slots or ports to read from and write to miniature mobile storage media. For computers or devices without built-in slots, users insert the media in separate peripherals, such as a card reader/writer which typically plugs into a USB port.

Digital cameras, media players, smartphones, and many other devices use miniature mobile storage media. The following sections briefly discuss the widely used miniature storage media: flash memory cards, USB flash drives, and smart cards.

FLASH MEMORY CARDS A **flash memory card** is a type of solid-state media, which means it consists entirely of electronic components and contains no moving parts.

Common types of flash memory cards are shown in Figure 4-60 on the next page, which compares storage capacities and uses of these media. Depending on the device, manufacturers claim miniature mobile storage media can last from 10 to 100 years. Flash memory cards are quite expensive compared to other storage media.

To view, edit, or print images and data stored on miniature mobile storage media, you transfer the contents to a computer or other device. Most newer computers and printers have slots to read flash memory cards. If your computer or device does not have a built-in slot, you can purchase a **card reader/writer**, which

FAQ

Is it legal to copy songs onto a CD?

It is legal to copy songs from an audio CD that you purchase, as long as you use the copied music for your own personal use. It is not legal to download copyrighted music unless the song's copyright holder has granted permission; normally you must pay a fee to download songs legally.

Web Info

For more information about flash memory cards, visit the Computer Concepts CourseMate Web site at *www.cengagebrain.com*, navigate to the Chapter 4 Web Info resource for this book, and then click Flash Memory Cards.

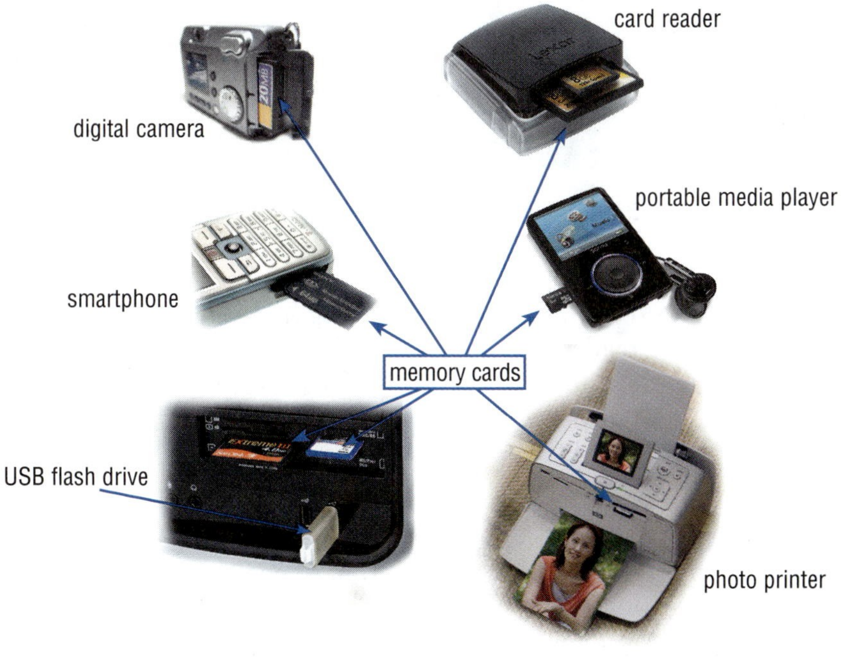

Figure 4-59 Many types of computers and devices use miniature mobile storage media.

Media Type		Storage Capacity	Use
CompactFlash (CF)		512 MB to 100 GB	Digital cameras, smartphones, photo printers, portable media players, notebook computers, desktop computers
Secure Digital (SD)		512 MB to 8 GB	Digital cameras, digital video cameras, smartphones, photo printers, portable media players
SDHC		4 to 32 GB	Digital cameras
microSD		1 to 2 GB	Smartphones, portable media players, handheld game consoles, handheld navigation devices
microSDHC		4 to 16 GB	Smartphones, portable media players, handheld game consoles, handheld navigation devices
xD Picture Card	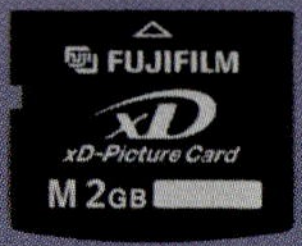	256 MB to 2 GB	Digital cameras, photo printers
Memory Stick PRO Duo	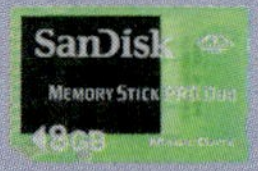	1 to 16 GB	Digital cameras, smartphones, handheld game consoles
Memory Stick Micro (M2)		1 to 16 GB	Smartphones

Figure 4-60   A variety of flash memory cards.

is a device that reads and writes data, instructions, and information stored on flash memory cards. Card reader/writers usually connect to a USB port on the system unit or printer. The type of card you have determines the type of card reader/writer you need.

USB FLASH DRIVES   A USB flash drive, sometimes called a pen drive or thumb drive, is a flash memory storage device that plugs into a USB port on a computer or mobile device. USB flash drives are convenient to use because they are small and

lightweight enough to be transported on a keychain or in your pocket (see Figure 4-13 on page 162). With a USB flash drive, you and your students can transfer documents, pictures, music, and videos from one computer to another easily. Current USB flash drives have storage capacities ranging from 512 MB to 100 GB. USB flash drives have become the primary portable storage device because USB flash drives have large storage capacities, are convenient to carry, and are the preferred portable storage device for students and other computer users.

SMART CARDS A smart card, which is similar in size to a credit card or an ATM card, stores data on a thin microprocessor embedded in the card. Smart cards contain a processor and have input, process, output, and storage capabilities. When you insert the smart card in a specialized card reader, the information on the smart card is read and, if necessary, updated.

Uses of smart cards include storing medical records, vaccination data, and other healthcare and identification information; tracking information such as customer purchases or employee attendance, storing a pre-paid amount of money, such as for student purchases on campus; and authenticating users, such as for Internet purchases. In addition, smart cards can double as an ID card.

CLOUD STORAGE

Cloud storage is a rapidly growing Internet service that provides storage to computer users. Some cloud storage providers offer storage for specific types of files, such as photos and music, whereas others store any type of file. Many cloud storage providers offer additional services such as encryption, passwords, Web applications and services. Cloud storage fee arrangements vary, depending on the user, business, or school's storage requirements; many are free. For example, Apple's **iCloud** service provides 5 GB of storage free to all users of Apple computers and mobile devices (iPhones, iPads, and iPods) for their videos, photos, music, apps, documents, iBooks, and other files (Figure 4-61).

Figure 4-61 Apple's iCloud, released in fall 2011, is an example of computer and software manufacturers allowing users to remotely access, store, and share their photos, movies, and much more.

Today, tens of millions of users and a growing number of businesses and schools are storing their files "in the cloud." Google Chromebook computer is basically a laptop computer except it has no hard drive, instead most software and user files are stored in the cloud and accessed almost instantly via the Web when a user needs them. With Microsoft Windows7 Cloud and Windows Live, users can create, connect, and share movies, photos, and Office documents.

Buyer's Guide

Visit the Computer Concepts CourseMate Web site for Teacher's Discovering Computers at *www.cengagebrain.com*, and then navigate to a highly informative multipage special feature titled *Buyer's Guide: How to Purchase Computers and Mobile Devices*.

Summary of Hardware for Educators

In this chapter, you learned about the various hardware components used in schools, businesses, and homes. First, you learned about some of the major components of the system unit. Next, you learned how to identify several types of input devices and how they operate. Third, you reviewed various output devices and learned how to identify and use them. Finally, you learned about storage devices.

After reading this chapter, you should have a good understanding of the information processing cycle and how various hardware devices are used in education. Now that you have a good working knowledge of computer hardware, you can use your newly gained knowledge to help your students understand technology concepts, systems, and operations. Because technology changes so quickly, you also need to stress to your students the importance of being able to transfer current knowledge when learning new technologies, which is one of the core national technology standards for students.

adapter card [162]
address [159]
all-in-one device [179]
American Standard Code for
    Information Interchange
    (ASCII) [155]
analog [154]
arithmetic/logic unit (ALU) [159]
arithmetic operation [159]
audio [173]
audio input [171]
audio output device [180]

binary [155]
bit [155]
Bluetooth [163]
Blu-ray Disc (BD) [187]
byte [155]

card reader/writer [187]
cathode ray tube (CRT) [174]
central processing unit (CPU) [157]
chip [156]
Click Wheel [172]
clicking [167]
clock speed [159]
cloud storage [189]
cluster [181]
command [164]
compact disc read-only memory
    (CD-ROM) [185]
compact disc-recordable (CD-R) [186]
compact disc-rewritable
    (CD-RW) [186]
comparison operation [159]
connector [162]
control unit [158]
cordless keyboard [166]
cordless mouse [167]
cursor [166]

data [164]
data projector [178]
decoding [158]
digital [154]
digital camera [171]
digital pen [170]
digital video disc read-only memory
    (DVD-ROM) [186]
disk [181]
display device [174]
double-clicking [167]
dragging [167]
dual inline memory module
    (DIMM) [160]
dual-core processor [158]
DVD drive [186]

earbuds [180]
earphones [180]
executing [158]
expansion card [162]

expansion slot [162]
ExpressCard module [162]
ExpressCard slot [162]
external hard disk [183]

facsimile (fax) machine [179]
fetching [158]
FireWire port [163]
flash memory [161]
flash memory card [162, 187]
flat panel monitor [175]
flat-panel display [175]
formatting [181]

gigabyte (GB) [160]
gigahertz (GHz) [159]
graphics [173]

hard copy [176]
hard disk [182]
headphones [180]
hot plugging [162]

iCloud [189]
ink-jet printer [177]
input [164]
input device [165]
insertion point [166]
interactive whiteboard (IWB) [179]

joystick [168]

keyboard [165]
keyword [164]
kilobyte (KB or K) [160]
kiosk [170]

landscape orientation [176]
laser printer [178]
LCD monitor [175]
LCD screen [175]
liquid crystal display (LCD) [175]
logical operation [159]

machine cycle [158]
magnetic disk [181]
megabyte (MB) [160]
memory [159]
microprocessor [157]
monitor [174]
motherboard [156]
mouse [167]
mouse pad [167]
multi-core processor [158]
multifunction device (MFD) [179]
multi-touch [169]

nonimpact printer [177]
nonvolatile memory [160]
numeric keypad [166]

optical disc [184]
optical mouse [167]
output [173]
output device [174]

PC Card [162]
PC Card slot [162]
peripheral [162]
photo printer [177]
pixel [174]
plasma monitor [175]
platter [182]
Plug and Play [162]
pointing device [167]
pointing stick [168]
port [162]
portrait orientation [176]
printer [176]
processor [157]
program [164]

random access memory (RAM) [160]
read-only memory (ROM) [161]
recorded [186]
removable external hard disk [184]
resolution [176]

scanner [170]
secondary storage [181]
sector [181]
smart card [189]
soft copy [174]
solid state drive (SSD) [184]
speakers [180]
speech recognition [171]
storage [181]
storage device [181]
storage medium [181]
storing [158]
stylus [170]
synchronous dynamic RAM
    (SDRAM) [160]
system clock [159]
system unit [154]

terabyte (TB) [160]
text [173]
touch screen [169]
touch-sensitive pad [172]
touchpad [168]
track [181]
trackball [168]

universal serial bus (USB) port [163]
USB 2.0 port [163]
USB 3.0 port [163]
USB flash drive [162, 188]
user response [164]

video [173]
video input [171]
voice output [180]
voice recognition [171]
volatile memory [160]

wheel [169]
widescreen [175]
wireless keyboard [166]
wireless mouse [167]

INSTRUCTIONS: Use the Checkpoint exercises to check your knowledge level of the chapter. To complete the Checkpoint exercises interactively, visit the Computer Concepts CourseMate Web site at www.cengagebrain.com, and then navigate to the Chapter 4 Checkpoint resource for this book.

1. Label the Figure

Instructions: Identify these areas or keys on a typical desktop computer keyboard.

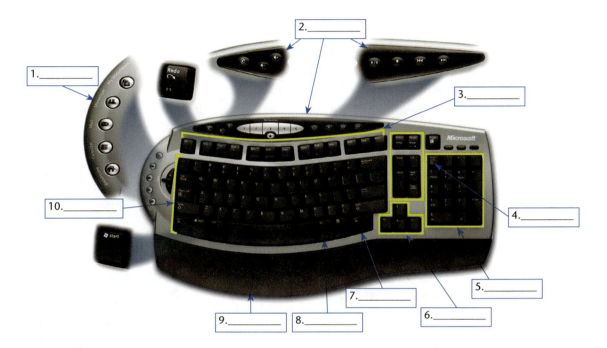

2. Matching

Instructions: Match each term from the column on the left with the best description from the column on the right.

_____ 1. byte
_____ 2. scanner
_____ 3. output
_____ 4. smart card
_____ 5. chip

a. small piece of semiconducting material usually no bigger than one-half-inch square
b. eight bits grouped together as a unit
c. data that has been processed into a useful form, called information
d. an input device that can capture an entire page of text electronically
e. stores data on a thin embedded processor

3. Short Answer

Instructions: Write a brief answer to each of the following questions.

1. What are the components of the system unit? What is the purpose of the central processing unit and system clock?
2. How are RAM and ROM similar? How are they different? What terminology is used to describe the storage capacity of RAM chips?
3. Which type of printer is used commonly in schools? What are some differences between ink-jet and laser printers?
4. What is the main difference between the way you input data into a notebook computer and the way you input data into a tablet computer? What kind of screen does a tablet computer have? Describe one way to stream video from a tablet computer to a TV.
5. What is an optical disc? What are the general categories of optical discs? Which optical disc has the largest storage capacity?

INSTRUCTIONS: Teaching Today provides teachers with integration strategies and ideas for teaching and, more importantly, reaching today's digital generation. Each numbered segment contains one or more links that reinforce the information presented in the segment. To display this page from the Web, visit the Computer Concepts CourseMate Web site at www.cengagebrain.com, and then navigate to the Chapter 4 Teaching Today resource for this book.

1. Graphing Calculators

Teachers are always looking for new technology tools to integrate into their classrooms. Math teachers have known for years that graphing calculators are excellent tools for teaching math. Students can use them not only to solve math problems but also to see the solutions more graphically. Providing graphing calculators also can help students solve problems related to other areas, such as geometry, algebra, and art. Use the Internet to research other ways to integrate graphing calculators into non-math teaching areas. Write a list of ideas that you discover in your research.

2. Portable Storage Media

Because of the need to move files from location to location, various portable storage media are used by students in K-12 schools and in universities. One advantage to using these devices is that you and your students can take all of your files with you. This means students can be working on projects in groups in the media center, in your class, and at home and still keep all their files on one device. These devices' biggest advantage, small size, may also be their biggest disadvantage — they can be easily lost. What can you do help your students keep from losing their portable storage devices? Besides USB flash drives, are there other portable storage devices that you and your students might use in your classroom? Can you think of ways to use portable storage devices in your classroom? What are the advantages of using them?

3. Exergaming

As a physical education teacher, you may sometimes feel neglected when it comes to the technology improvements and digital media. In less than a half decade, well-stocked gym classes could feature rows of TV screen-equipped treadmills on which students race against one another in a massive multiplayer world, running faster to speed up the avatar, and thinking thoughts that the EEG (electroencephalogram) headset can translate into jumping or direction-changing movements; however, there are new ways to combat childhood obesity through Exergaming. From stationary bikes with built-in screens and video games that simulate car racing (the

faster you pedal, the faster your Ferrari goes) to Dance Dance Revolution sessions. Exergames are spreading to public school physical education classes and private youth-targeted gyms, at a rate unseen since the introduction of the hula-hoop. What are some benefits that you can think of from using Exergaming in your curriculum? What are some drawbacks of Exergaming?

4. 3D SpaceNavigator

The 3D SpaceNavigator makes movement within 3D software feel like actual flight. One of the many advantages of 3D SpaceNavigator over a mouse is the ease of doing complex adjustments to views and models without repeatedly stopping to change directions, zoom, or rotate model representations. You also can use 3D SpaceNavigator to rotate your view up, down, left, and right much like you would with a flight simulator joystick. This interactive tool increases the learning potential of software like Google Earth and Google Maps by adding enhancements that are not possible with a regular mouse. Can you see ways that this type of technology could add to your instruction? Could it increase student comprehension of key concepts? What subjects can you see using this tool with and how?

1. Integration Dilemmas

You are excited because you and your students can use the recently updated technology in the school's computer lab. You decide you will create an interactive participatory learning project so your students can create their own products while developing in-depth social studies content. After weeks of work, your class goes to the lab for the final day of working on the projects and all the software and student files have been deleted. Then, you realize the students cannot use their "backup" flash drives because the computer's USB drives no longer work. You ask the technology facilitator what happened and he says, "Sorry, new district policy — no files can be saved to flash drives or the server because of virus issues in the district." What ways can you find to work around these problems? What can you do to try and make district administrators understand how their decisions impact student learning?

2. Digital Age Learners

Research suggests that what many of us refer to as Attention Deficit Disorder (ADD) is really nothing more than a skill developed by some children that have been raised in the digital age. As a result, these research findings are revealing that the learning environment these students are placed in does not match their cognitive or digital learning style, which then affects motivation and achievement. Have some of these students rewired their brains to multitask? Can they read e-mails, send instant messages and text messages over handheld devices, speak to one another in short sentences, and continue to watch movies and participate in multiple conversations, all while fin-

ishing their homework? When we try to place these students in the traditional learning environment, are we working against their cognitive or digital learning style? What are your thoughts about this theory for this new generation of digital kids? Do you see the differences in their learning? What suggestions do you have for reaching them? Give some suggestions and defend your answer.

3. Classroom Observation & Webcams

Chances are that you have been evaluated or done a self evaluation using a video/digital camera of some nature. Almost every aspect of society is being captured in some way through reality television and Webcams. However, it may not be long until everything we do in the classroom is captured on video for viewing by the public. Several politicians have even made proposals for creating pilot programs that involve wiring every classroom in a handful of schools with Internet-connected video and audio equipment, i.e. Webcams. The connection would allow parents to log on to the World Wide Web using a computer or smartphone and then watch their children real time in their classes; similar to the way parents can watch their kids at a childcare center. How would you feel about having every moment of your school day broadcast live online via Webcams? What problems and/or benefits do you foresee with using a Webcam in the classroom? What about safety concerns?

4. Digital Data Doesn't Last Forever

Up to 75% of today's data never existed on paper. Historical data from thousands of years ago still exists because it was written down. Although written documents can be read hundreds of years after they were created, rapid changes in computer technology can make digital records inaccessible. Loss of access to data that is stored on aging media threatens the integrity of data retrieval. A major state university recently admitted that almost 3,000 student and school files could not be accessed due to lost or outdated software. Is the potential unavailability of digital data a problem? What can be done to keep today's digital information available for future generations?

Apps Corner

INSTRUCTIONS: Apps Corner provides extensive ideas and resources for integrating technology into your classroom-specific curriculum. To display this page from the Web and information on numerous education apps, visit the Computer Concepts CourseMate Web site at www.cengagebrain.com, and then navigate to the Chapter 4 Apps Corner resource for this book.

Apps Corner is designed for teachers and other educators who are looking for innovative ways to integrate apps into their content-specific curriculum. Apps Corner not only provides great apps with current information but also shows how other educators are using and integrating education apps. As a result, Apps Corner is designed with all educators in mind, regardless of their interests or subject area. You can use Apps Corner to expand your resources by reviewing apps outside your curriculum area; remember many apps associated with one curriculum area can be adapted for use and added to lesson plans in a wide variety of other curriculum areas.

Use Apps Corner as a springboard for collaborating and sharing the successes and hurdles of integrating apps in a classroom or an entire school system. Consider Apps Corner a place to locate app integration ideas and resources. Information on educational apps are organized in four Corners (Early Childhood, Elementary, Middle School, and Secondary), and different apps are available for each chapter. Many apps are free, others cost from $1 to $5. Inexpensive site licenses for classrooms, schools, and school districts are available for many apps.

Shown below are two highly rated Apps. The first is a free app that takes advantage of the iPad smart cover and allows you to create curriculum-specific flash card type quizzes, tests, and much more for your students. The second is an interactive and free science app from the National Science Foundation, Science360 for iPad.

Software Corner

INSTRUCTIONS: Software Corner provides information on popular software programs. Each numbered segment discusses specific software programs and contains a link to additional information about these programs. To display this page from the Web, visit the Computer Concepts CourseMate Web site at www.cengagebrain.com, and then navigate to the Chapter 4 Software Corner resource for this book.

1. The Graph Club

The Graph Club, by Tom Snyder Productions, is an easy-to-use graphing tool every elementary classroom should have! You can create activities in which your students conduct research and graph their findings. The Graph Club allows students to construct and interpret pie, line, picture, and bar graphs. Students learn to use graphs to analyze data and solve problems, as well as write about graphs they create. Graphs can be printed by the page or even made in poster size for classroom use. The Graph Club is an innovative way to help your students understand and interpret graphs, and it is an excellent resource for standardized test preparation.

2. VoiceThread

Through IM, texting, and Web conferencing, digital conversation has become a major part of the daily life of today's digital students. Relationships that used to be fostered through face-to-face interaction in schools are now developed on MySpace, Facebook, and other social networks. While the method may be different, the underlying principle is still the same — students' need to connect and communicate with each other. As teachers, we need to find new ways to use connection tools for learning. Building that bridge between motivation and required curriculum elements is key, and one way to help may be to utilize a tool like VoiceThread. VoiceThread is a free tool that allows teachers and students to learn with the world, rather than about the world. Known as a "group project audio blog," VoiceThread allows users to record text and audio comments about content specific topics, photos, images, and more.

3. Storytelling Alice

You can have your students create their own animated stories with a program called Storytelling Alice. This program is free and is the result of extensive research by Caitlin Kelleher from Carnegie Mellon. Her goal is to increase female students' interest in computer programming with fun software that is suitable for both middle school and high school students. Your students can choose from a range of custom animations to assist the characters' interaction with one another by giving them commands. No programming knowledge is needed, but some basic programming skills are helpful. This is an excellent software program for your female students to develop computer-related skills.

4. RCampus

Are you looking for a new place to host your class Web site, build rubrics, create ePortfolios, manage your classes, build communities of learners, and connect with peers? RCampus tools are available for free and allow students and faculty to collaborate in many different ways. As long as you use RCampus, you will never lose access to your work from anywhere. In addition, you can build cross-campus clubs and groups, teach or learn at multiple schools using a single system, exchange books with students and find tutors at other campuses and schools around you, and much more.

5. Geometer's Sketchpad

With Geometer's Sketchpad by Key Curriculum Press, your students can explore and analyze geometric figures and concepts they are learning in the classroom. While preserving the geometric relationships of the shapes, students can manipulate the geometric figures created in Geometer's Sketchpad. You can use Geometer's Sketchpad for presentations or your students can use it to work alone or in groups. The software comes with an instructional video and documentation, which includes tutorials and sample classroom activities. Extensive Internet resources also are available.

1. Buying the Right Digital Camera

If you are buying your first digital camera to get started in the world of digital photography or to replace your old camera, a single digital camera that is perfect for every user simply does not exist. When making the decision about which model of digital camera to purchase, you must consider how and where you will use the camera, what results you would like, and what you can afford. What options are important to consider? To learn more about buying the right digital camera and how digital cameras work you should always do your research and learn what is best for you or your classroom needs.

2. Camtasia Studio

Are you looking for great ways to enhance your classes with digital media resources, tutorials, and videos? With Camtasia Studio you create the content exactly the way that you want it to be. Camtasia Studio is an easy-to-use video program that you can use to record your PowerPoint presentations, instructional videos, screencasts, and audio tracks without ever leaving your desk! You can significantly increase student learning and retention by combining visuals with auditory and textual information. With the power of interactive Camtasia Studio videos, you can deliver high-quality video content anytime and anywhere even to remote students. A key feature of Camtasia Studio is the ability to record, edit, and share high-quality screen video on the Web, DVD, and mobile devices like iPods and iPads.

3. Maintaining Your CDs

Just because your favorite CD has a few annoying skips is not enough reason to discard it. A few options are available to help you continue to use those scratched CDs. How do you remove minor scratches from CDs? When a CD skips it may not always be the fault of the CD itself. In fact, it may not have a scratch on it at all. Sometimes just playing the CD in an alternate player will remedy the situation. Another way to get rid of annoying skips is to make a copy of the CD. A series of instructions and an FAQ on the Ins and Outs of making CD copies can be found on the Computer Support Website.

4. ARKive Education Resources

If you are a science teacher, you may spend a lot of time searching for videos, images, and other digital resources. ARKive Education has thousands of wildlife videos, images, and fact files that are appropriate for teaching many key science concepts. Teachers can use the ARKive Education multimedia materials to engage their classes in key biology topics, such as variation and adaptation, habitats or life cycles, or they can use the materials as creative inspiration for art and design projects. All of ARKive Education's photos, video clips, and authenticated fact files are free for teachers to incorporate into classroom activities and presentations to differentiate instruction.

1. Why Have Specialized Hardware in the Classroom?

The growing presence of computers in everyone's lives has generated an awareness of the need to address computing requirements for those with physical limitations. Today, the Americans with Disabilities Act (ADA) requires that all schools ensure that students with all types of special needs are not excluded from participation in, or denied access to, educational programs or activities. In addition to speech recognition, which is ideal for students who are visually impaired or who have physical or cognitive limitations, other input devices are available.

2. Are There Alternatives to Keyboards?

Students with limited hand mobility who want to use a keyboard have several options. One option is to use a keyguard. A keyguard, when placed over the keyboard, prevents the student from inadvertently pressing keys and provides a guide so the student strikes only one key at a time. Another option is a screen-displayed keyboard, which is a graphic of a standard keyboard displayed on the student's screen. Students then use a pointing device to press the keys on the screen-displayed keyboard.

Another type of input device is a touch window, or a touch screen. This is a device that attaches to the front of a monitor that allows students to select items by touching instead of using a keyboard. Yet another alternative input device is the Intellikeys keyboard. This powerful tool has a flexible design permitting teachers to customize the keyboard with special overlays or templates that fit over the keyboard. Using Intellikeys, students with mobility issues or with cognitive disabilities can participate independently in classroom learning activities.

3. What Other Input Devices Can Benefit Students with Special Needs?

A variety of input devices are available for students with motor disabilities. Joysticks and small trackballs that can be controlled with a thumb or one finger can be attached to a table, mounted to a wheelchair, or held in a student's hand. Students with limited hand mobility can use a head-mounted pointer to control the pointer or insertion point. A switch is used much as a mouse button is used. Switches are made in a vast array of colors, shapes, and sizes. They can be operated by a tap, a kick, a swipe, or a puff, and they integrate well with other devices such as Intellikeys.

Many of these input devices now are connected to computers by USB. The computer recognizes them instantly, which means setup time is minimal. Learning how to integrate software programs and hardware devices into your curriculum that allow students with special needs to use computers as tools for learning is covered in Chapters 5 through 7.

Follow the instructions at the top of this page to display additional information and this chapter's links on assistive technologies.

ePortfolio Idea

PRODUCTIVITY IN THE CLASSROOM

Introduction: Desktop publishing provides teachers with effective and efficient ways to communicate with students, parents, faculty, and others in a professional manner. Many word processing applications, such as Microsoft Word, Apple iWork, and Microsoft Works, provide templates enabling users to create newsletters and many other documents with ease. Many excellent desktop publishing software applications also are available. Microsoft Publisher and Adobe PageMaker are two popular programs used by educators. Exciting and innovative ways exist that allow teachers to integrate desktop publishing effectively into the curriculum. Students enjoy creating professional looking documents and finding creative ways to exhibit what they have learned.

1. Creating and Formatting a Parent Newsletter

Problem: As a kindergarten teacher, you believe it is important to send home monthly newsletters to keep parents informed of what is happening in the classroom. Open your word processing or desktop publishing software application and create a newsletter as described in the following list. Use the newsletter shown in Figure 4-62 as an example. If you are using a template, modify the newsletter design to accommodate the template. If you are using Microsoft Word, consider using tables, columns, section breaks, and text boxes to create the newsletter. (*Hint:* Use Help to understand the steps better.)

Instructions: Perform the following tasks.

1. Personalize the newsletter by inserting your name instead of Ms. Erhart's name and the grade level or subject you teach. Format the first and second heading lines in 16-point Times or Times New Roman font centered on the page.

2. Personalize the newsletter by using the current month and year. Enter the month and year (using the format Month, Year) right-aligned in 16-point Times or Times New Roman font.

3. Choose an appropriate picture, image, or clip art graphic, and then insert it on the page in line with its associated text.

4. Create an opening paragraph with a heading and at least three lines of text. Format the heading line in 14-point Times or Times New Roman font. Format the text in 12-point Times or Times New Roman font.

5. Create the body of the newsletter in two columns. Format section headings centered in uppercase 12-point Times or Times New Roman bold font.

6. Create a closing paragraph at the bottom of the newsletter. Format the text in 12-point Times or Times New Roman font.

7. Choose an appropriate picture, image, or clip art graphic and then insert it on the lower-right side of the newsletter.

8. Save the document to the location and with a filename of your choice. Print the document and then follow your instructor's directions for handing in the assignment.

Ms. Erhart's
Kindergarten Class Newsletter

February, 2013

Winter Wonders

January passed quickly for our class! February holds many fun activities and lots of good learning. Please be sure to join us for our Valentine's Day party and mark February 23 on your calendar for our special Black History event!

COME OUT AND READ

Our class is hosting a Come Out and Read night! Students can wear pajamas and get comfy on big pillows as they enjoy a good book with a parent or sibling. We also will have a special storyteller coming in to share some exciting stories with the group. Be sure to join us for the fun!

WHAT'S HAPPENING IN CLASS

We continue to focus on letter recognition and letter sounds during February. We also are studying the seasons and reading stories about winter. These are the stories we will use in class. Check them out from the library to reinforce these concepts at home!

A Snowy Day, by Ezra Jack Keats
The Mitten, by Jan Brett
Little Polar Bear, by Hans de Beer
Mama, Do You Love Me?, by Barbara M. Joosse

BLACK HISTORY MONTH

February is Black History Month, and students will learn about the contributions of inspirational African-Americans. To continue our focus on reading during February, we will be using the following books:

The Story of Ruby Bridges, by Robert Coles
Under the Quilt of Night, by Deborah Hopkinson
Sweet Clara and the Freedom Quilt, by Deborah Hopkinson
Martin's Big Words: The Life of Dr. Martin Luther King, Jr., by Doreen Rappaport
Amazing Grace, by Mary Hoffman

The class will work together and create an exciting presentation for their families on February 23! Look for more information in our next newsletter.

Reading is such an important skill, and together we can prepare your children to be successful readers and lifelong learners. Please do not hesitate to contact me if you have any questions or comments. Remember, you are always welcome to come into our classroom and be a part of the learning experience!

Figure 4-62

2. Creating and Formatting a Department Newsletter

Problem: You are a member of your high school's Foreign Language Department. Your responsibility is to communicate information to the rest of the Foreign Language Department. You decide the easiest way to share new information is by creating a newsletter. Use the newsletter shown in Figure 4-63 as an example. (*Hint:* Use Help to understand the steps better.)

Instructions: Format the first and second heading lines in 14-point Arial bold font. Insert your name in place of Mr. Schatz in 12-point Times or Times New Roman bold font. Enter the current month and year (in the format Month, Year) in 14-point Arial bold font. Create the body of the newsletter in three columns. Personalize the information in the newsletter to reflect the grade level or subject that you teach. Format the section headings in 12-point Arial bold font. Format the text in 12-point Arial font. Format the country names in 11-point Arial bold font. Enter the Web site titles in 11-point Arial font. Format the Web site addresses in 10-point Arial font. Enter the quote in 12-point Times or Times New Roman italic font. Insert appropriate pictures, images, or clip art graphics.

After you have typed and formatted the newsletter, save the newsletter to a location and with a filename of your choice. Print the newsletter and then follow your instructor's directions for handing in the assignment.

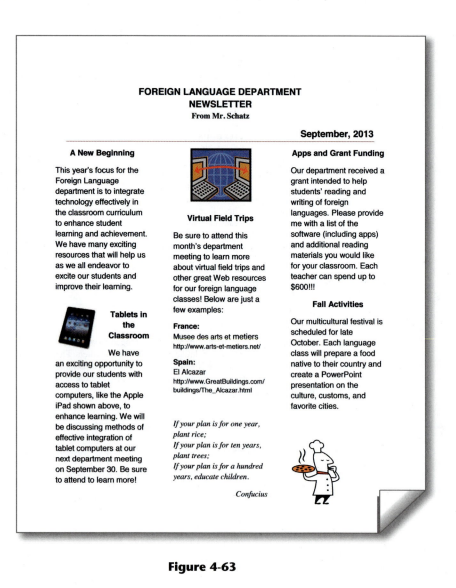

Figure 4-63

3. Creating and Formatting a Newsletter for a State Organization

Problem: You are the secretary for your subject area state organization. It is your responsibility to create a newsletter summarizing your state convention, providing information for the upcoming year's convention, and any other pertinent information.

Instructions: Create a newsletter similar to the newsletter illustrated in Figure 4-63. Use an appropriate layout, and then select font types and styles, font sizes, and clip art images for the newsletter. Include the current date, your name, and e-mail address. Save the newsletter to a location of your choice using an appropriate filename. Print the newsletter and then follow your instructor's directions for handing in the assignment.

INTEGRATION IN THE CLASSROOM

1. In honor of Black History Month, you have planned a cross-curricular project You will divide students into groups and assign each group one of the following curricular areas: science, society and culture, math, art, music, or literature. Each group will choose one famous African-American to research who has made a significant contribution in the group's assigned field. Students then will create a newsletter outlining their findings. They will discuss the person's place of birth, family history, educational background, interests, and contributions to their particular field. Students will include at least one image in the newsletter. Select a famous African-American and create a sample newsletter for your students. Include your name and the current date in your sample newsletter.

2. Your high school Spanish class is studying cities in Spain. To reinforce reading and writing Spanish while learning about the country, students will create a newsletter written in Spanish. Students will work in groups and research three different cities in Spain. They will access and read online newspapers from the cities they select, gather travel and tourist information, obtain appropriate graphics that illustrate aspects of their chosen cities, and then create a newsletter in Spanish that presents the information they learned. Students will present their newsletter to the class and distribute a copy of it to each class member. Create a sample newsletter for your students. If you are not fluent in Spanish, select another foreign language. If you are not fluent in a foreign language, research three cities in Spain and create a newsletter presenting travel and tourist information written in English. Include your name, the current date, Web resources, and graphics in your sample newsletter.

3. While teaching the American Revolution, you team up with an English teacher to provide your students with a constructivist learning activity. Students will select one event that led up to the American Revolution and create a newsletter using information and images they locate from print resources and the Internet. Students will conduct their research in the history classroom and the English teacher will assist students with the layout, design, and writing techniques. Using the ideas and techniques you have learned in this In the Lab, create a sample newsletter for your students. Include your name, the current date, the course number, and course title in your newsletter.

INSTRUCTIONS: Use the Learn It Online exercises to reinforce your understanding of the chapter concepts and increase your computer, information, and integration literacy. To access step-by-step online tutorials, videos, practice tests, learning games, and more, visit the Computer Concepts CourseMate Web site at www.cengagebrain.com, navigate to the Chapter 4 Learn it Online resource for this book, and then click the link for the resource you want to review.

1. Make a Video and Upload It to YouTube

Click the YouTube Video link to learn how to transfer a video from your digital video camera to a computer using Windows Live Movie Maker, logging into YouTube, and then uploading your video.

2. At the Movies

Have you ever wondered how a computer works? Click the At the Movies link to view a video about how RAM, optical drives, video cards, and other computer components work. Click the At the Movies 2 link to learn more about Apple's latest operating System, Mac OS X Lion.

3. Purchasing and Installing Memory in a Computer

One of the less expensive and more effective ways to speed up a computer, that is make it capable of processing more programs and, at the same time, enable it to more effectively handle graphics, gaming, and other high-level programs, is to increase its amount of memory. Click the Purchasing and Installing Memory link to learn how to purchase and install new memory in your computer. Print just the first page of this Web page. On the back of the printout, write a brief summary explaining how to purchase and install memory in a computer. If required, submit your results to your instructor.

4. Expanding Your Understanding

Every computer today contains a sound card and associated hardware and software that allow you to play and record sound. Click the Expanding Your Understanding link to learn how to adjust the sound on your computer.

5. Practice Test

Click the Practice Test link. Answer each question. When completed, enter your name and click the Grade Test button to submit the quiz for grading. Make a note of any missed questions. If required, submit your score to your instructor.

6. Who Wants to Be a Computer Genius?

Click the Who Wants to Be a Computer Genius link to find out if you are a computer genius. When you are ready to play, click the Play button. If required, submit your score to your instructor.

7. Wheel of Terms

Click the Wheel of Terms link to reinforce important terms you learned in this chapter by playing the Shelly Cashman Series version of this popular game. When you are ready to play, click the Play button. If required, submit your score to your instructor.

8. Crossword Puzzle Challenge

Click the Crossword Puzzle Challenge link. Complete the puzzle to reinforce skills you learned in this chapter. When you are ready to play, click the Play button. If required, submit the completed puzzle to your instructor.

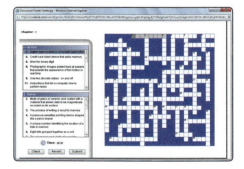

Technology, Digital Media, and Curriculum Integration

5

Objectives

After completing this chapter, you will be able to do the following:
[ISTE NETS-T Standards 1 a-d; 2 a-d; 3 a-d; 4 b, c, d; 5 a-d]

- Name and define the elements of digital media

- Define and explain curriculum standards and learning benchmarks

- Explain technology integration, also called curriculum integration

- Describe the use of computers in computer labs and media centers versus classroom instruction

- Identify ways in which technology can positively influence learning

- Identify ways to plan for technology integration

- Explain various planning tools and instructional models

- Describe the steps of the ASSURE Model

- Identify ways to get started using technology at a new school

- Describe the use of learning centers and interactive whiteboards

Throughout this textbook, you have learned about computers and other educational technologies, and you have seen the impact technology has on schools, classrooms, and people's lives. Every day, computers help many individuals accomplish job-related tasks more efficiently and effectively. For educators, computers and other technologies serve as the tools needed to implement new and evolving teaching strategies.

Chapter 1 of this textbook introduced educational technology and covered the digital generation — how they learn and what they should know. The next three chapters focused on building digital and information literacy skills. The first part of this chapter covers the concept of digital media and how digital media has evolved to allow for individualized instruction and exploration, both of which enrich the educational experience. This chapter then provides you with a basic understanding of how to integrate technology across the curriculum. As you learned in Chapter 1, integration literacy is the ability to use computers and other technologies combined with a variety of teaching and learning strategies to enhance students' learning. Integration literacy means that teachers can determine how to match appropriate technologies to curriculum standards, benchmarks, and learning outcomes. Integration literacy relies on a solid foundation of digital and information literacy, both of which are essential for helping you integrate technology into your classroom curriculum.

What Is Digital Media?

The terms technology, multimedia, and digital media are not mutually exclusive. In fact, in common usage, these terms overlap and are often used interchangeably. A brief discussion of each term follows to put each term in its historic perspective.

Technology was the term first associated with computer use in the classroom. Early on, computers that found their way into schools were used in specialized training programs such as graphic arts, in applied sciences such as auto mechanics, in vocational and production education, and in the office for administrative tasks. Using the term technology to describe this use of computers was a logical step.

The term **multimedia** by definition means "more than one media." Multimedia incorporates a variety of elements, including text, graphics, audio, video, and animation. Originally, a multimedia presentation did not have to be digital. For example, multimedia might have incorporated a slide show for visuals, a tape recorder for audio, and an overhead projector for text. But as software and hardware became capable of and adept at handling more than one media, the term multimedia was coined to define computer software applications and presentations that utilized more than one media.

Recall from Chapter 1 that **digital media** is defined as those technologies that allow users to create new forms of interaction, expression, communication, and entertainment in a digital format. Digital media uses all the elements of multimedia but in a digital format. The term digital media has not superseded or outdated the usefulness of the terms multimedia or technology. The term digital media simply underlines the pervasiveness of the use of digital formats for multimedia elements. Many applications previously defined as multimedia have seamlessly made the transition to digital media because they encompass all the elements of multimedia and digital media. The term digital media continues to evolve; especially now with the emerging and interactive digital enhancements of tablet- and app-based computing (Figure 5-1). **Interactivity** is an essential

Figure 5-1 Interactive digital media, apps, and tablet computers allow students to explore the world's knowledge in ways unheard of just a generation ago and just by using their fingers.

feature of digital media applications because it allows for individualized instruction and exploration, both of which enrich the educational experience.

Have your students watched a rocket blast into orbit in person, viewed the Mona Lisa in the Louvre Museum, traveled to Egypt, or visited this nation's capital and explored its history? With digital media, your students can interact with and become part of these learning adventures and much more without ever physically setting foot outside of the classroom. Never before have students been able to explore the world in so many visual and interactive ways. Digital media has changed the way people work, learn, and play. Extensive research conducted over a period of more than 20 years confirms that the effective integration of multimedia applications, and now digital media, into the classroom curriculum can revolutionize the way today's digital students learn core and other subjects.

Digital media software refers to any computer-based presentation or application software that uses multimedia elements. By definition, digital media includes interaction, so some, but not all digital media software is also considered interactive digital media. **Interactive digital media** allows users to move through information at their own pace. Interactive digital media also describes a digital media application that accepts input from the user by means of a keyboard, voice, finger taps and movements, or a pointing device such as a mouse, and performs an action in response. A well-designed application provides feedback in the form of responses as the user progresses through the application or completes certain tasks.

The digital media application shown in Figure 5-2, for example, allows students to interact with and learn about the human body. The ability of users to interact with a digital media application is perhaps the most unique and important feature of digital media — a feature that has the potential to change dramatically the way digital students learn. Interactive digital media allows students to define their own learning paths, investigate topics in depth, and get immediate feedback from their exploration activities. Digital media applications also tend to engage and challenge students, thus encouraging them to think creatively and independently.

With many digital media applications, you navigate through the content by clicking or tapping links. In a digital media application, links serve a similar function, allowing users to access information quickly and navigate from one topic to another in a nonlinear fashion. For example, while reading about Marco Polo, you might tap or click the keyword Travels to display a menu allowing you to interact with a map of Marco Polo's journeys or listen to a reading from his travel journals.

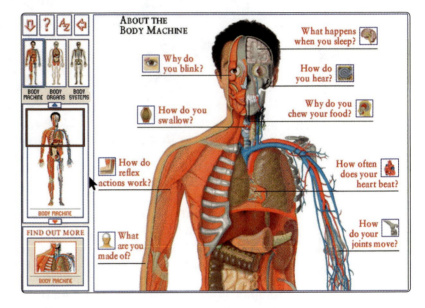

Figure 5-2 The Ultimate Human Body by Dorling Kindersley is a popular educational program that allows students to interact with and learn about the human body. Clicking the heart, for example, allows students to see and hear a video of a human heart in action.

In a digital media application, any clickable or tapable object — text, graphics, animation, and even videos — can function as a link. Figure 5-3 on the next page shows a digital media application that uses text, graphics, and animations as links to additional sources of information. Every object is a link to discovery learning. Digital media applications contain text, graphics, and animation, and often audio and video.

Text consists of characters that are used to create words, sentences, and paragraphs and is a fundamental element used in all multimedia and digital media

barometer
image link

Figure 5-3 The figure to the left shows one page from a popular nature encyclopedia. When a user clicks or taps the barometer, an enlarged barometer (top figure) opens, which provides additional links to other information.

applications. Multimedia and digital media applications not only use ordinary text to convey basic information, they also use a variety of textual effects to emphasize and clarify information. A different font size, color, or style, for example, often is used to emphasize certain words or phrases. A **graphic** is a digital representation of non-text information, such as a drawing, chart, or photograph. A graphic, also called a picture or image, contains no movement or animation. Graphics play an important role in the learning process: many individuals — who are **visual learners** — may learn concepts faster or retain a higher percentage of material if they *see* the information presented graphically.

Displaying a series of still graphics played back at the proper frame rate creates an **animation**, which is a graphic that has the illusion of motion. Animations range in scope from a basic graphic with a simple motion (for example, a blinking icon) to a detailed image with complex movements (such as a simulation of how an avalanche starts). As with graphics, animations can convey information more vividly than text alone. An animation showing the up-and-down movement of pistons and engine valves, for example, provides a better illustration of the workings of an internal combustion engine than a written explanation.

Audio is any music, speech, or other sound. As with animation, audio allows digital media developers to provide information in a way that brings a concept or concepts to life. The vibration of a human heartbeat or the melodies of a symphony, for example, are concepts difficult to convey without the use of sound. Using audio in a digital media application to supplement text and graphics enhances understanding.

Video consists of visual frames that are played back at speeds of 15 to 60 fps (frames per second) and provide full motion in real time. The integration of video into the classroom curriculum has significantly influenced the way that students learn core subjects. Videos can reinforce lectures and readings, provide a common base of knowledge, and show things that students would not otherwise experience. For example, after reading the text of one of Martin Luther King's speeches, students can watch a video of King delivering that same speech to an enthusiastic crowd (Figure 5-4).

Figure 5-4 Interactive encyclopedias and many other Web sites offer students opportunities to hear the words and passages of great historical events and literary works, such as speeches made by Martin Luther King, Jr.

Why Are Digital Media Applications Important for Education?

Digital media applications (including apps for mobile devices) are changing the traditional dynamics of learning in classrooms. As previously noted, interactivity is one of the major features of digital media applications. The ability of users to interact with a digital media application is perhaps the single most critical feature of digital media because it has enormous potential to improve teaching and learning in K-12 schools.

As mentioned earlier, extensive research conducted over a period of more than 20 years has shown that digital media applications are highly effective teaching tools when properly evaluated and integrated into teaching at the point of instruction. Studies indicate that students retain approximately 20 percent of what they see, 30 percent of what they hear, and 50 percent of what they see and hear. When students have a chance to hear, see, and interact with a learning environment, they can retain as much as 80 percent of the information. Digital media applications provide that interactive learning environment, which makes them powerful tools for teaching and learning.

One of the main reasons for teachers to utilize digital media software in the classroom is that it appeals to a variety of learning styles. Helping every student learn in his or her unique way ensures success for all students. Digital media software applications assist teachers in meeting diverse learning styles by combining interactive software integrated with teaching strategies to enhance the learning process. Furthermore, digital media software is engaging and motivational for today's digital students.

Another important reason for students' increased retention is that they become active participants in the learning process instead of passive recipients of information. Interactive digital media applications engage students by asking them to define their own paths through an application, which often leads them to explore many related topics.

Many teachers have noted that students are motivated by and enjoy the process of creating their own interactive digital media presentations using digital media authoring software. Many students enjoy conducting research and writing when their writing projects involve the creation of digital media presentations. In addition to building skills, the completion of a digital media project is a self-esteem and confidence booster for many students.

Teachers can use digital media software both as a productivity tool and as an integration tool. You can use digital media software applications such as PowerPoint or Keynote to introduce new concepts, present lectures, as well as demonstrate effective screen design and presentation techniques. In addition, teachers can create digital media presentations to present new concepts and then provide students access to the presentations so they can easily review new information and interact directly with the software.

When teachers effectively use digital media software as a productivity tool, they are modeling for their students how to use this powerful software. This can be the first step in learning to integrate digital media software effectively into the curriculum. Teachers can have students demonstrate their learning by creating their own digital media presentations and presenting them to the class.

Using and integrating digital media can also help you manage today's digital kids in your classroom. Studies have shown that an increase in student outcomes and reduced dropout rates is linked to highly motivated students who are engaged in their learning. So it follows that keeping students interested in learning increases student achievement. Students' engagement and motivation in school drops as they get older, making it even more important for us as educators to find innovative ways to keep students motivated to learn. Technology offers this opportunity, however technology can be a disruption if you do not organize, manage, and match it to your instructional objectives and strategies. The good news is technology can also assist you with classroom management if you use it correctly. Figure 5-5 covers some teaching strategies to help you manage your students in the digital classroom. The next few sections introduce the importance of understanding curriculum and curriculum standards, as well as discuss other areas specific to technology integration and discusses how to integrate digital media and other tools into your content-specific curriculum.

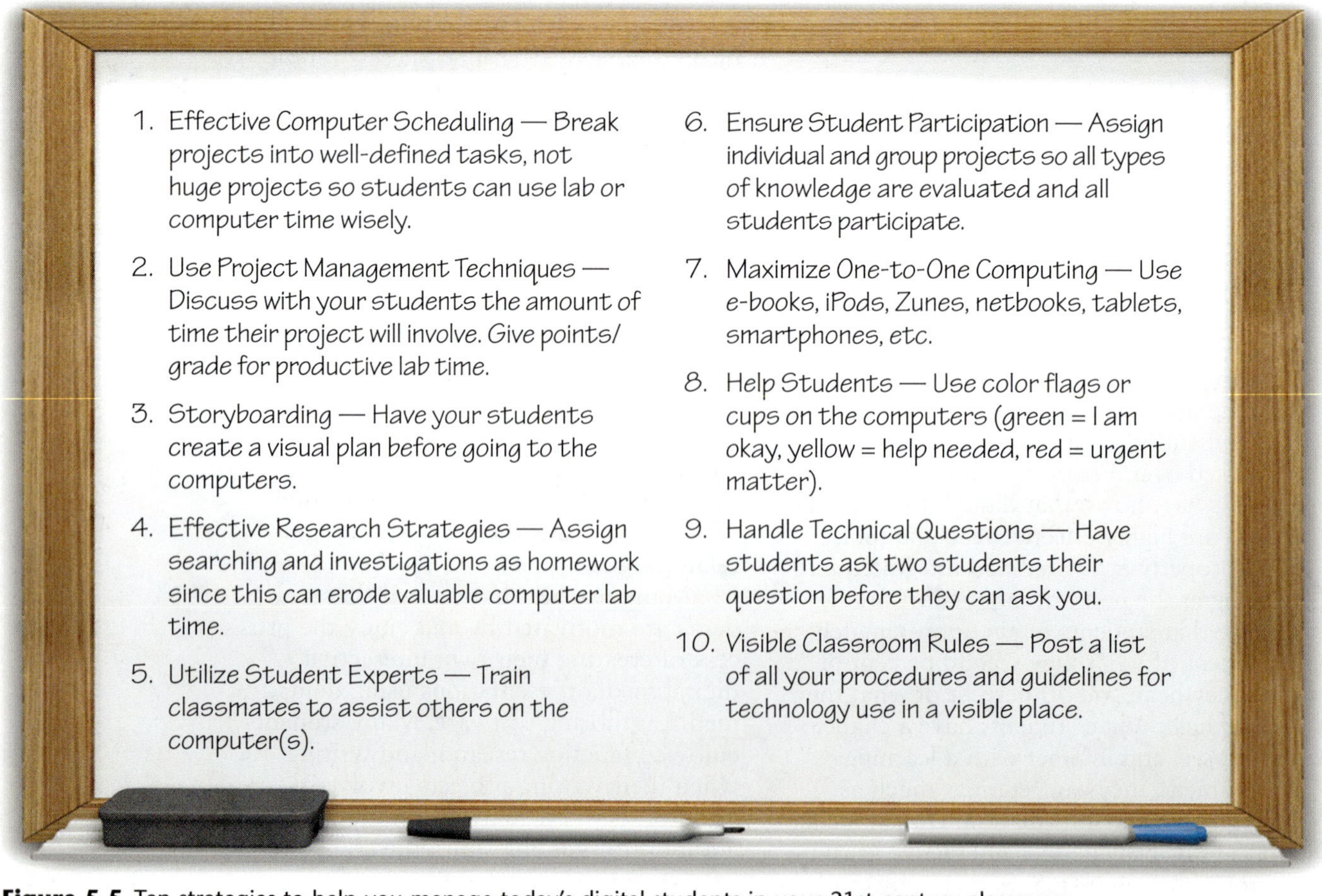

1. Effective Computer Scheduling — Break projects into well-defined tasks, not huge projects so students can use lab or computer time wisely.

2. Use Project Management Techniques — Discuss with your students the amount of time their project will involve. Give points/grade for productive lab time.

3. Storyboarding — Have your students create a visual plan before going to the computers.

4. Effective Research Strategies — Assign searching and investigations as homework since this can erode valuable computer lab time.

5. Utilize Student Experts — Train classmates to assist others on the computer(s).

6. Ensure Student Participation — Assign individual and group projects so all types of knowledge are evaluated and all students participate.

7. Maximize One-to-One Computing — Use e-books, iPods, Zunes, netbooks, tablets, smartphones, etc.

8. Help Students — Use color flags or cups on the computers (green = I am okay, yellow = help needed, red = urgent matter).

9. Handle Technical Questions — Have students ask two students their question before they can ask you.

10. Visible Classroom Rules — Post a list of all your procedures and guidelines for technology use in a visible place.

Figure 5-5 Ten strategies to help you manage today's digital students in your 21st-century classroom.

What Is Curriculum?

Education can be defined as all the experiences, knowledge, and skills a learner gains from both school and society. Education literature defines the term "curriculum" in many ways. Often, curriculum is defined simply as that which is taught.

For the purposes of this textbook, **curriculum** is defined as the knowledge, skills, and performance standards students are expected to acquire in particular grade levels, or through sequences or clusters based on subject matter units of instruction, such as language arts, mathematics, science, English, history, physical education, and others (Figure 5-6). Curriculum often is designed at the state or school district level by a team of curriculum specialists, instructional leaders, and other experts. For curriculum to be implemented properly, teachers must not only understand the curriculum but also be empowered to adapt the curriculum in such a way as to meet the instructional needs of their students.

Many countries have Departments of Education or educational organizations that serve as the governing association for educational regulations and reform. Agencies in the United States include the federal Department of Education (DOE), and each state has its own Department or Board of Education (Figure 5-7 on the next page).

The federal Department of Education is the governing body for public education in the United States and it is responsible for coordinating initiatives to improve and monitor our education system. The **Common Core State Standards Initiative** is a national effort to create state standards that provide a well-defined, reliable framework to prepare our students for their future endeavors. Many states are adopting the **Common Core State Standards**, which were established in June 2010 to ensure that the K-12 curriculum standards are consistent across all states and with the goal that every student is adequately prepared to enter college or the workforce upon graduation from high school.

State education departments provide their school districts with documents that describe curriculum standards and benchmarks for learning. These documents often are called **curriculum frameworks, curriculum guides,** or **curriculum maps.** Although curriculum frameworks usually include subject-specific standards, they often also include direction for specific content areas, learning expectations, performance indicators, benchmarks, activities, and forms of evaluation.

School curriculum frameworks include not only standards but also examples that teachers can use to develop curriculum-based lesson plans. They usually are organized by subject and grade level. Curriculum frameworks can include specific curriculum and performance standards, learning goals, and grade level expectations to assist teachers in meeting curriculum benchmarks.

Figure 5-6 Integrating technology in the classroom helps teachers achieve the learning outcomes defined by the curriculum.

[a]

[b]

Figure 5-7 This figure shows the home page of [a] the U.S. Department of Education and [b] Texas Education Agency. The U.S. government and state education agencies provide parents, educators, and students with a multitude of resources and information.

Many states refer to frameworks as blueprints for implementing content standards.

Many school districts are drafting their own interpretations of state curriculum standards to improve learning and meet the needs of students. Many districts also are creating guides to help teachers teach curriculum standards by providing examples and mastery-level checklists with curriculum performance standards. Teachers usually have to include these documents with their lesson plans to show how students are mastering the skills necessary to be promoted to the next level. All states and districts are incorporating **Performance Guides,** also called **Performance Standards, Expectations,** or **Indicators** into their curriculum, which provide clear expectations for instruction, assessment, and student work. They define the level of work that demonstrates achievement of the standards, they show the content and skills that students are expected to master for each subject area, and they assist teachers in making sure students meet the content standards for a particular subject area. A **Mastery Objective Checklist** identifies skills that must be mastered by a specific grade level and either have or are being developed by many school districts. These skills are usually listed on a grid or table for easy reference.

CORE CURRICULUM STANDARDS AND BENCHMARKS

A **curriculum standard**, also called a **curriculum goal**, defines what a student is expected to know at certain stages of education. Curriculum standards for K-12 education are a collection of general concepts that school districts expect students to learn as they progress through the grade levels. Curriculum standards vary from state to state and usually cover core subjects, such as language arts, mathematics, science, social studies, physical education, art, health, and foreign languages. A **benchmark, learning objective,** or **learning expectation** is a specific, measurable outcome or indicator that usually is tied to a curriculum standard. Figure 5-8 shows one sample curriculum standard and its associated, measurable benchmarks and grade level indicators for the same standard at different grade levels.

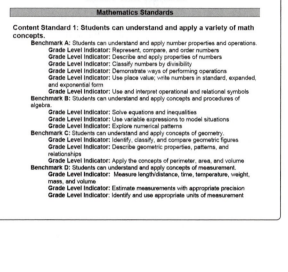

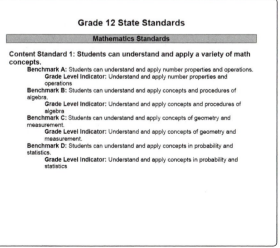

Figure 5-8 One Iowa content standard and its associated benchmarks and indicators for grades 7 and 12.

What Is Technology Integration?

Defining curriculum is easy when compared to defining technology integration. First, **integration** by itself is defined as bringing different parts together into a whole. Therefore, **technology integration,** also called **curriculum integration,** is the combination of all technology parts, such as hardware and software, together with each subject-related area of curriculum to enhance learning. Furthermore, technology integration is using technology to help meet the curriculum standards and learner outcomes for each lesson, unit, or activity.

Mastering the integration of technology into the curriculum is not easy. Extensive formal training and practical experiences are imperative for successful integration of technology at all levels of K-12 education. Technology cannot enhance learning unless teachers know how to use and integrate technology into curriculum-specific or discipline-specific areas.

First and foremost, teachers must remember that technology is only a tool to enhance or support instructional strategies. Educators should take steps to integrate technology throughout classroom experiences, activities, and projects, as well as find ways to use technology to teach curriculum-specific content while establishing connections between those subjects and the real world (Figure 5-9). This chapter assists you in learning the basics necessary to integrate technology into your classroom and provides the understanding needed to promote integration literacy.

Figure 5-9 When teachers integrate multiple technologies into their classroom curriculum, students are introduced to many unique and positive learning experiences.

A critical issue related to technology integration is that technology should not drive the curriculum. The curriculum, rather, should drive the technology; that is, teachers should use the appropriate technologies to enhance learning at the appropriate times and to teach to the standards (Figure 5-10).

In the next section, you will learn the pros and cons of using computers located in a centralized computer lab or media center and in individual classrooms.

Figure 5-10 Many Web sites provide teachers with curriculum integration activities and strategies related to specific standards.

CLASSROOM INTEGRATION VERSUS COMPUTER LABS AND MEDIA CENTERS

Many educators have become advocates of integrating computers into content areas. For years, teachers and administrators have focused their efforts on getting technology or computer labs into schools. A **computer lab,** or **technology lab,** usually is a designated classroom filled with computers and technology for students to use individually or in groups (Figure 5-11). Lab computers usually are connected to the school's local area network (LAN) and provide many resources in a centralized area.

Figure 5-11 Computer labs, such as the one shown here, give students access to computers and other technologies.

Teachers can schedule time in computer labs for an entire class period and use the labs for many purposes, such as whole-group instruction, small-group activities, or individual student-centered learning. In addition to computer labs, school **media centers** contain computers and other relevant technologies; they also can be scheduled for use by classroom teachers. Computer labs and media centers are a popular approach to getting technology into K-12 schools. The primary reasons administrators usually opt for computer labs or media centers are related to cost and location. When computers are installed in the same location, they are easier to maintain and connect to a school network. Popular uses for networked school computer labs and media centers are for students to work on projects and work through tutorial software and integrated learning systems software.

Computer labs and media centers clearly provide solutions to some educational dilemmas and are an excellent addition to any school. Research shows that computers and related technologies,

however, are more effective when integrated into subject content and placed in the classroom — at the point of instruction. **Point of instruction** is having the technology in the classroom at the teachers' and students' fingertips (Figure 5-12), ready for use any time it is needed.

Figure 5-12 This teacher knows that by using computers at the point of instruction he can enhance the students' learning experiences.

If technology is readily available, teachers and students will use the technology more. An example is an elementary teacher presenting a lesson on frogs. Students want to see and learn more about frogs, so they start asking questions. Teachers can turn to the technologies in their classrooms, such as digital media software programs or the Web, to show how a frog jumps, where frogs live, and more. Many educators refer to this as a teachable moment. When students are interested and ready to learn more about a topic, teachers have a **teachable moment,** which is an open window of opportunity for the information to be comprehended in greater detail by students (Figure 5-13 on the next page).

Computers, when placed in the hands of students and teachers, provide unique, effective, and powerful opportunities for many different types of teaching and learning by engaging the students in learning experiences. Research is revealing that students retain knowledge longer when they are

Integration Strategies

To learn more about how to integrate hardware, software, and peripherals with students who are challenged, visit the Computer Concepts CourseMate Web site at *www.cengagebrain.com,* and then navigate to the Chapter 5 Assistive Technologies Corner resource for this book.

Figure 5-13 A teacher often can identify a teachable moment just by looking in the faces of excited students who are motivated to learn!

actively involved in using digital media to meet learning objectives and related benchmarks. In order for learning to take place, technology needs to be available at the time of instruction. As you learned in Chapter 3, an emerging and exciting trend is cloud computing. Cloud computing is rapidly becoming popular in our schools and classrooms where teachers and students can access and share a multitude of resources.

The Classroom in Action

To illustrate the benefits of using technology at the point of instruction, this section takes you into Mr. Balado's fifth-grade classroom at Martin Luther King Elementary School. Just as Mr. Balado finished reading his class

a fictional story about a mouse that barely escaped being swallowed whole by a barn owl, several students raised their hands to ask questions. "How did the barn owl see the mouse in the dark?" asked one student. Another student inquired, "Can an owl really scan the entire barn without moving off of its perch?" "What was the pellet that flew from the owl's mouth?" asked a third student. Mr. Balado smiled because he expected these types of questions and knew they would open the door to a wonderful opportunity for learning. The questions clearly led to a teachable moment, which he could maximize by using his classroom technologies.

Mr. Balado's classroom contains four student computers and two iPads networked to the school's local area network and the World Wide Web. Both tablets contain numerous apps, some were purchased by his school district, others he purchased to improve his teaching. In addition, Mr. Balado has an instructional computer with access to the Web that is connected to an interactive whiteboard (similar to the classroom shown in Figure 5-14). Using a computer to display the images on an interactive whiteboard is an excellent way to allow all students to see what displays on the instructional computer's monitor, to see and hear interactive digital media applications, and to interact with the Web and educational software, while at the same time asking questions. These questions create enthusiasm and a desire for additional knowledge among the students.

Figure 5-14 Teachers easily can connect a computer to an interactive whiteboard to display a computer monitor's image to the entire class.

Mr. Balado had planned and prepared for the integration of various technologies into his interdisciplinary lesson. First, he had searched the Web for sites that would be appropriate for the fifth-grade curriculum and would provide detailed information and research about different owl species and their environment, their food and hunting behaviors, their anatomy, and more. Locating the Web sites in advance allowed him to identify several excellent sites and eliminated the need to waste time searching for Web sites during class instruction time. In addition, Mr. Balado evaluated all of the Web sites in advance for their content and appropriateness for his fifth-grade students. Evaluation of technology resources is an important element in technology integration and is covered in detail in Chapter 7.

While interacting with the Web sites, students asked more questions, such as the following: Where do owls fall on the food chain? What specific foods do owls eat? How do owls gather food? What happens to the food after the owls swallow it whole? Why do owls hoot? Are owls mean animals that are always on the attack? What makes owls different from other birds? This was all part of Mr. Balado's instructional plan, and his students' questions continued as Mr. Balado actively engaged them in exploration and discovery learning at selected owl Web sites (Figure 5-15). The students were genuinely excited while exploring Web sites about these birds of prey; they were discovering new concepts while Mr. Balado guided their learning.

With computers in his classroom for use at the point of instruction, Mr. Balado had his students' full attention. Together they explored interesting Web sites and live Web cams while traveling through interactive virtual field trips as wildlife biologists. **Virtual field trips** allow you to walk through doorways, down halls, enter the forest, and let you see everything in a three-dimensional world via a computer as if you were there.

Mr. Balado's students were no longer only hearing a story about a fictional owl; they were now seeing, hearing, and interacting with a variety of owl species. After they looked at many owl facts, pictures, and video clips, Mr. Balado asked his students to storyboard their narrative stories about owls, the owls' prey, and the food chain. Later, he will

Figure 5-15 The Web provides access to a live Web cam that allows students and teachers to discover innovative ways to enhance learning.

take his students to a computer lab where they will use their storyboards to create narratives with text and visuals.

Integrating Technology into the Curriculum

As this example illustrates, computers and other technologies can provide unique, effective, and powerful opportunities for many different types of teaching and learning. Educators recognize that technology can serve as an extremely powerful tool that can help alleviate some of the problems of today's schools. Motivating students to learn is one area that all educators constantly are trying to achieve. Technology has the potential to increase student motivation and class attendance.

Using technology tools with students of varying abilities has helped to address different learning styles and to reach diverse learners. With the right approach, educators can integrate technologies such as computers, CDs, DVDs, digital cameras, application software, digital media applications and devices, e-books and electronic references, netbook computers, iPods, and the Web into almost any classroom situation. For technology to enhance student learning, however, it must be integrated into the curriculum.

The key to successful technology integration is identifying what you are trying to accomplish within your curriculum. First, you must consider what the standards and related learning objectives are, and then you must identify an appropriate technology tool that will help you accomplish your instructional goals. Although this process sounds simple, complete integration of technology in all subject areas is complex and takes a great deal of planning. A later section of this chapter discusses how to plan for technology integration.

After you have determined specific standards and related learning objectives and you have identified technologies appropriate for areas of the curriculum, you then can begin to develop innovative ways to teach a diverse population of learners with different learning styles. A **learning style** refers to how individuals learn, including how they prefer to receive, process, and retain information. Learning styles vary among individuals. For example, some people learn better alone, while others learn better in groups. Many different types of learning styles exist and most individuals learn using a combination of several styles. The use of technologies, such as digital media tools and the Web, can help address the learning styles and the needs of today's digital generation.

By engaging students in different ways, technology encourages them to take a more active role in the learning process. To learn more about learning styles and theories, read the special feature that follows this chapter: Learning Theories and Educational Research.

Changing Instructional Strategies

When students play a more active role in the learning process, the teacher's role must change. Teachers need to transition from the conventional lecture-practice-recall teaching methods — often called the sage on the stage — to a classroom in which teachers engage students in activities that allow them opportunities to construct knowledge — a new role called the guide on the side. That is, teachers should shift from being the dispenser of knowledge to being the facilitator of learning (Figure 5-16). Rather than dictating a learning process, a **facilitator of learning** motivates students to want to learn, guides the student learning process, and promotes a learning atmosphere and an appreciation for the subject.

Two main assumptions must be considered as teachers become facilitators of learning. The first is that students can create their own learning and that the teachers' role is to assist their students in this process. The second is that academic work

Figure 5-16 Technology is a tool that allows a teacher to be a facilitator of learning and creates valuable learning experiences for many different types of learners.

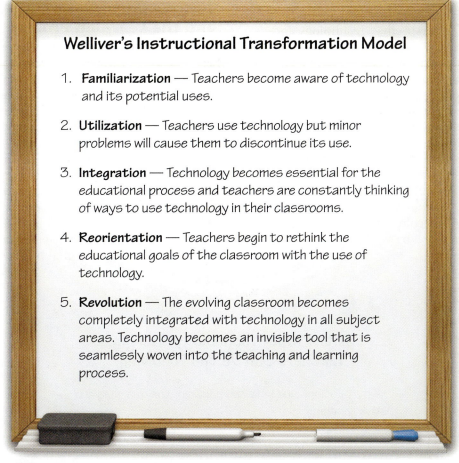

Welliver's Instructional Transformation Model

1. **Familiarization** — Teachers become aware of technology and its potential uses.

2. **Utilization** — Teachers use technology but minor problems will cause them to discontinue its use.

3. **Integration** — Technology becomes essential for the educational process and teachers are constantly thinking of ways to use technology in their classrooms.

4. **Reorientation** — Teachers begin to rethink the educational goals of the classroom with the use of technology.

5. **Revolution** — The evolving classroom becomes completely integrated with technology in all subject areas. Technology becomes an invisible tool that is seamlessly woven into the teaching and learning process.

Figure 5-17 Welliver's Instructional Transformation Model describes five hierarchical stages for technology integration through which all teachers must progress in order to integrate technology effectively.

extends beyond the mere storage of information. Instead, teachers want their students to be able to assimilate information and become problem solvers.

As teachers become facilitators of learning and incorporate technology into their instructional strategies, they will progress through several developmental stages. **Welliver's Instructional Transformation Model**, for example, describes five hierarchical stages of technology integration through which all teachers must progress to integrate technology effectively (Figure 5-17 above).

Barriers to Technology Integration

With all change comes barriers, and technology integration is no exception. Bill Gates stated in a speech, "In all areas of the curriculum, teachers must teach an information-based inquiry process to meet the demands of the information age. This is the challenge for the world's most important profession. Meeting this challenge will be impossible unless educators are willing to join the revolution and embrace the new technology tools available." Even after many years, these words still are true.

For more than two decades, several barriers have hindered technology integration in many schools. Such barriers include a lack of teacher training, security constraints that impede instructional strategies, lack of administration support, limited time for teacher planning, computer placement in remote locations making access difficult, budget constraints, lack of high-speed school networks, and basic resistance to change by many educators.

Web Info

For more information about barriers to technology integration, visit the Computer Concepts CourseMate Web site at *www.cengagebrain.com*, navigate to the Chapter 5 Web Info resource for this book, and then click Barriers.

Every educator looks at the integration of technology — and its challenges — from a different perspective. Technology coordinators view the problems of insufficient hardware, software, and training as major obstacles. Teachers consider the lack of time to develop technology-based lessons a concern. Administrators identify teachers' lack of experience using technology in instruction as yet another challenge. Teachers and administrators, however, can and are beginning to overcome these barriers with effective leadership, proper training, planning, and a commitment to enhancing teaching and learning using technology (Figure 5-18).

Technology Integration and the Learning Process

Before teachers can begin to develop integration skills, they must realize and understand how the integration of technology can enhance teaching and learning. Research shows that using technology in the classroom motivates students, encourages them to become problem solvers, and creates new avenues to demonstrate creative thinking. Teachers also have found that using computers or computer-related technologies can capture and hold students' attention. Interactive technologies, such as software applications, digital media tools,

Web Info

For more information about technology training, visit the Computer Concepts CourseMate Web site at *www.cengagebrain.com*, navigate to the Chapter 5 Web Info resource for this book, and then click Technology Training.

With Proper Technology Training, Teachers Can Do the Following:

- Create relationships between participatory learning and active teaching.

- Develop an appreciation for and an understanding of the potential of technology.

- Learn to be creators of digital media for self-expression.

- Develop leadership skills and become role models for successful integration.

- Understand the power of technology integration.

- Design integrated curriculum activities that develop critical thinking and problem solving skills.

- Develop ownership of the technology through authentic experiences.

- Learn to motivate students with digital media and other technologies.

- Achieve success by becoming informed and reflective decision makers.

- Become advocates for technology integration.

Figure 5-18 With proper training and planning, educators can overcome many of the barriers to effective technology integration.

reference guides, tutorials, animations, simulations, and the Web, are especially engaging as they allow students to determine the flow of information, review concepts, practice skills, do in-depth research, and more.

Technologies that provide interactivity, learner control, and student engagement are a natural choice for improving instruction. When used properly, technology is extremely beneficial in the learning process.

THE LEARNING PROCESS

For learning to take place, learners must be engaged in the process of education. One way to engage learners is to motivate them through authentic learning experiences. **Authentic learning** experiences are instructional activities that demonstrate real-life connections by associating the concept being taught with a real-life experience or event (Figure 5-19). For authentic learning to take place, teachers must involve students in the process of gathering, analyzing, and using information to make informed decisions that relate to real life. More than any previous generation, today's digital students look for revelancy in the content of the various subjects they are learning.

When possible, teachers should promote **participatory learning,** also referred to as **secondary learning,** which is a type of learning that occurs when students become engaged in inquiring, investigating, reflecting, solving problems, and formulating and answering questions. Participatory learning also involves the process of students discussing, brainstorming, explaining, and debating issues with each other and with their teacher, both to determine solutions as well as to identify their own questions. Participatory learning makes learning more relevant by promoting the retention of information, motivating students to extend their learning, and giving students a sense of ownership of the information they are presenting. Participatory learning is especially appropriate when teaching to a wide variety of learning styles.

A lesson on the human digestive system, for example, presents concepts that are difficult for students to understand. Students have never seen the digestive system, nor can they feel or touch it. For students to understand these new concepts, they must have background information or a knowledge base on which to build. Providing a knowledge base on which students can build is called **anchored instruction.** Through anchored instruction, learning and teaching activities are designed around an anchor (or situation) that provides a scenario or problem enhanced with curriculum materials that allow exploration by the learner. Anchored

Web Info

For more information about authentic learning experiences, visit the Computer Concepts CourseMate Web site at *www.cengagebrain. com,* navigate to the Chapter 5 Web Info resource for this book, and then click Authentic Learning.

Figure 5-19 Learners are motivated to learn through authentic, real-life experiences.

Figure 5-20 Britannica has an educational Web site that allows students to interact with a myriad of subjects. In this example, students see and hear how the human heart works.

instruction also includes the component of **problem-based instruction,** in which students use the background (anchor) information to begin to solve and understand complex problems or concepts.

Providing students with opportunities to expand their knowledge base allows them to experience visionary exploration or discovery learning. Recall from Chapter 2 that discovery learning is a nonlinear learning process that occurs when you investigate related topics as you encounter them. Discovery learning also is an inquiry-based method of teaching and learning where students interact with their surroundings by exploring and manipulating objects, investigating and solving problems through inquiry, or performing hands-on exercises and experiments. When students discover and explore meaningful concepts on their own, they are more likely to understand and retain information. Discovery learning also helps students become better critical thinkers.

TECHNOLOGY AND THE LEARNING PROCESS

Technology can provide numerous tools to support many types of instruction and learning. To teach students about the human heart, for example, a teacher could integrate an educational software application such as Primal 3D or A.D.A.M. into the lesson, both of which are digital media products used for teaching related concepts about the human body. **Britannica** is an interactive multimedia encyclopedia. These applications provide working visual models of how the various parts of the human heart interact (Figure 5-20). These applications allow students to see and experience clearly things they could never experience by only reading a textbook. Applications such as these also allow students to build a **cognitive scaffold,** which is a mental bridge for building an understanding of complicated concepts.

Another benefit of integrating educational applications is that they encourage students to think not only in words and pictures, but also in colors, sounds, animations, and more. When people think, their thoughts are filled with sounds, images, colors, and movements. A young child, for example, will describe a fire engine by indicating its color and demonstrating the sounds and movements of fire engines going to a fire (Figure 5-21). Most traditional instruction, however, uses words and pictures only, often in two-color textbooks. Digital media tools allow students to have learning experiences in which concepts are brought to life with a variety of representations — videos, sounds, colors, pictures, simulations, and animations.

Figure 5-21 People think in colors, images, sounds, and animations. A young child, for example, will describe a fire engine by imitating the sounds of a siren, indicating its color, and visualizing the movements of fire engines going to a fire.

Technology helps teachers promote interactive participatory learning and create authentic learning experiences by allowing students to conduct Web-based research, explore concepts in a digital media presentation, create a slide show for a history presentation, create a wiki with results from a group science project, and more. Technology also provides opportunities for anchored instruction. Students can watch a Web-based video clip of a Himalayan mountain-climbing expedition, for example, and then move on to examine the history of Tibet, the Sherpa culture, the physical effects of climbing in high altitudes, or how avalanches start.

Computers, digital media, and especially the Web create numerous opportunities for discovery learning. Many students may never be able to visit an extraordinary museum, such as the Smithsonian Institution. The Web, however, can transport them to a world beyond their own, filled with infinite amounts of information — visually, audibly, and even virtually. Using discovery learning, you can break down classroom walls with technology, the Web, and most importantly — open doors for imagination. Properly integrated technology allows students to understand concepts more clearly and learn no matter who or where they are.

The Internet and the World Wide Web have been called the **educational equalizer** — that is, they give students of all backgrounds, socioeconomic levels, learning styles, geographic locations, academic levels, and learning abilities access to the same information. Figure 5-22 illustrates how the Web brings these elements together to provide valuable learning experiences.

The Web allows students to experience educational opportunities previously not available. Students can publish their work, meet students with similar interests across the globe, and participate in shared learning experiences with classrooms worldwide. The Internet and Web also support projects in which students interact with authors, elected officials, or scientists conducting research. E-mail, blogs, wikis, podcasts, and Web-based projects are ideal for teacher-monitored school projects that involve language arts, cultural learning, history, geography, social studies, science, or communications with friends around the world (Figure 5-23 on the next page).

As illustrated by these examples, computers can provide many unique, effective, and powerful opportunities for teaching and learning. Such opportunities include skill-building practice, interactive

Figure 5-22 The Web, which provides access to a seemingly infinite amount of information, has the capability of addressing learner differences, and, thus, leveling the playing field for all students.

Figure 5-23 Using computers and the World Wide Web, students can join various projects to learn about other cultures and communicate with other students around the world.

learning, and linking learners to instructional technology resources. In addition, computers support communication beyond classroom walls, thus enabling schools and communities to provide an environment for cooperative learning and the development of innovative opportunities for learning.

Cooperative learning refers to a method of instruction in which students work collaboratively in groups to achieve standards and related learning objectives. Instead of working alone on activities and projects, students share ideas, learn teamwork skills, and begin to help one another to accomplish tasks or achieve objectives. **Cooperative classroom activities** are student-centered, with the teacher serving as a facilitator and the students as information seekers. **Higher-order thinking skills** are the abilities to solve problems, engage in critical thinking, and interpret and solve complex issues. Teachers need to create activities for students to promote the use of higher-order thinking skills throughout their educational experiences (Figure 5-24).

By promoting new and enhanced learning experiences, properly integrated technology offers limitless possibilities for instruction and learning. Computers, digital media, the Web, and other technologies help students to understand concepts more clearly and help teachers develop unique activities that maximize every teachable moment. Students become knowledge seekers and participatory learners who acquire knowledge and find different ways to interpret what they discover. Finally, technology can help improve students' abilities as independent thinkers and encourage them to become lifelong learners.

Figure 5-24 Computers support communication beyond classroom walls, thus providing an environment that allows for cooperative learning, development of higher-order thinking skills, and solving complex problems.

Strategies for Integrating Technology into Teaching

The best strategy for curriculum integration is to put the technology into the hands of trained teachers, make it easily accessible, and let them decide how best to use it at the point of instruction in their classrooms. Teachers then can use an array of teaching strategies to develop a learning environment in which students are encouraged to be independent learners and take responsibility for their own learning.

The main goal of such teaching strategies is to provide a consistent application of technology tools to support instructional curriculum areas. Also, it is important to give every student the opportunity to work with computers and related technologies. When proper strategies are used for technology integration, students enjoy learning to use technology as well as the content in the subject-related curriculum areas.

Already, many experienced educators are integrating technology into subject-specific instruction — and have seen the benefits technology integration can bring to the learning experience. One critically important element in effective technology integration is continuous planning. For technology integration to be successful, careful planning is required at all levels, which involves district-level planning, school-level planning, and classroom-level planning. Each level must plan systematically so that technology is integrated effectively and seamlessly into all facets of education.

The Role of the School District

Effective curriculum integration cannot take place if support for technology integration does not come from several sources within the school district. School district administrators must plan carefully for every aspect of curriculum integration, from purchase to installation to teacher and staff training and technical support. Almost every school district has a detailed technology plan for technology integration. A **technology plan** is an outline that specifies the school district's goals and strategies for using and maintaining equipment and software, and training teachers to use and then integrate technology

into their classroom curriculum. Because of emerging and changing technologies, many school districts update their technology plans every three to five years. Many individual school technology committees review their technology plans every couple of years to make sure they meet their district's plans.

To prepare educators to use the technology after it is implemented, administrators provide technology training with mentorship programs and follow-up staff development after training (Figure 5-25). A **mentorship program** teams new or novice teachers with experienced teachers to encourage new teachers to learn to integrate technology resources. Collaboration is promoted by sharing planning time and by exchanging e-mails with other teaching professionals inside and outside the district. Experienced teachers guide new teachers by providing information and suggestions. In-house workshops are provided so teachers learn to use and integrate the available technologies in their schools and classrooms.

Figure 5-25 Mentorship programs allow teachers to learn computer and technology integration concepts from experienced teachers in a nonthreatening environment.

Today, many federal, public, and state grant funding sources are requiring that part of the funding be spent on teacher training. This funding has increased the number of teachers using and integrating technology.

In addition, numerous Web sites are dedicated to mentoring new and experienced teachers in everything from how to get started with technology to classroom management. These sites provide wonderful resources for teachers and offer an avenue for teachers to find ideas, advice, and support. Mentors can help new teachers become more effective in the classroom.

Integration Strategies

To learn more about mentoring and how mentorship programs can help teachers increase their integration literacy skills, visit the Computer Concepts CourseMate Web site at *www.cengagebrain.com*, and then navigate to the Chapter 5 Teaching Today resource for this book.

Web Info

To view a school district's technology plan, visit the Computer Concepts CourseMate Web site at *www.cengagebrain.com*, navigate to the Chapter 5 Web Info resource for this book, and then click Technology Plan.

Web Info

For additional strategies and applications for one-computer classrooms, visit the Computer Concepts CourseMate Web site at *www.cengagebrain*.com, navigate to the Chapter 5 Web Info resource for this book, and then click One Computer.

Web Info

For more information about curriculum planning with technology, visit the Computer Concepts CourseMate Web site at *www.cengagebrain*.com, navigate to the Chapter 5 Web Info resource for this book, and then click Curriculum Planning.

Planning for Technology Integration in the Classroom

Teachers must plan carefully for the use and integration of computers and technologies in the classroom. Just as planning is essential for effective instruction, it is required for effective use and integration of technology in the classroom. One important consideration is deciding on the most appropriate technology to achieve the desired learner outcomes. Teachers must plan how they will teach the curriculum, what areas they need to cover for content, and where they can use technology to meet curriculum standards and related learning objectives.

Another important consideration in the planning stage is preparing the classroom environment (Figure 5-26). The way in which you integrate technology into the curriculum will depend largely on how much technology is in your classroom or in your school. Whether you use one computer, two computers, or thirty computers, you must plan how and when you will use those computers, which might be desktop, notebook, netbook, or tablet computers, and how you will enable your students to use those computers. The amount of planning will vary according to the arrangement of computers

Figure 5-26 Teachers must prepare their classrooms carefully for the integration of computers and other technologies.

in your classroom and school and the scope of your lesson. Chapters 6 and 7 discuss these and other planning issues.

ONE-COMPUTER CLASSROOM

In classrooms with only one computer, teachers must plan to maximize the effectiveness of that one computer. In such classrooms, the computer most commonly is used for teacher administrative use and can be used to create letters, worksheets, puzzles, handouts, lesson plans, tests, forms, newsletters, data collection (such as electronic grade book, attendance, student information, mail merge), and more.

To gain full instructional benefits, you need to use your single computer in different ways. For example, you can use it for record keeping, knowledge acquisition by searching the Web, and classroom presentations. To allow students to view the presentations or demonstrations, you can project the monitor's content with a projector onto a projection screen, classroom wall, or interactive whiteboard, as discussed later in this chapter. If your school has only a few of these devices, you will have to plan ahead to schedule them for use in your classroom.

A good instructional strategy for the classroom computer is to introduce students to various types of software and create learning paths before taking the class to the computer lab or the media center. Using this instructional strategy optimizes the time students spend on computers while in the lab. Rather than spending time learning basic software skills, students can devote time to interacting with the computer to experience discovery learning.

You can turn your computer into an activity or production center and let your students use the computer as a creation tool for production and publishing when working on word processing, database, spreadsheet, graphics, and multimedia projects. You can create opportunities for group presentations created by the students to be made to the class. You can add other handheld technologies to your classroom to extend the use of your single computer.

In addition, teachers in a one-computer classroom can use the computer for the same purposes as described in the next sections on two or more computer classrooms. Many ways exist to enhance teaching and learning in the one-computer classroom. With only one computer available, however, additional planning might be required.

TWO-COMPUTER CLASSROOM

In classrooms with two computers, teachers must develop a strategy to manage their use. One computer could be used mainly for research on the Internet, presentations, Web-based projects, and e-mail. The other computer might be used as a writing center or for students to create digital media projects.

Regardless of how you use the classroom computers, you should develop a strategy for how you will allocate computer use and how students' computer time will be managed. Questions that can assist with planning follow:

- Will both computers have the same hardware, software, and network access?
- Will one or both computers be connected to the Web?
- Will students rotate through using one or both computers on a daily basis?
- How much time will each student be allowed on each computer?
- Is it better to have the students work together on projects?
- How are you going to observe your students using the Internet?
- How will you evaluate student learning?

CLASSROOM WITH MORE THAN TWO COMPUTERS

Teachers who have several computers and mobile devices may find that arranging their classrooms in a single learning center or several learning centers, through which groups of students can rotate as they complete projects or activities, provides an environment for productive use of the computers. Other technologies also can be organized into learning centers, such as a video center in which students can use digital video cameras to record and watch themselves performing plays, creating and telling stories, or role-playing; a CD/DVD center where students can conduct research and learn new skills by interacting with instructional CDs and DVDs; a listening or reading center; a digital media production center where students can create their own digital media projects, and much more.

Before setting up a computer center or centers, teachers should ask the planning questions previously cited, in addition to considering how many computers will be in each center and what other technologies, if any, might be included in the center. As indicated, the technologies a teacher utilizes will depend on the curriculum standards and learning objectives. Furthermore, part of preparing the classroom environment is being aware of the prerequisite skills necessary for students to be successful.

USING A COMPUTER LAB OR A MEDIA CENTER

Because few classrooms include a computer for every student, using a computer lab or a media center allows teachers to provide learning opportunities that are not possible in a one-, two-, or even five-computer classroom. The most important advantage of using a computer lab or a media center is that all students are provided hands-on experience with the computer technology (Figure 5-27). Computer labs and media centers can be used successfully by teachers and students for one-to-one computing, tutorials, remediation, cooperative learning, computer skill instruction, digital production projects, Internet research, whole class instruction, and integrated learning systems (ILSs).

Figure 5-27 By using networked computers with Internet access, students can work on different projects at the same time.

Integration Strategies

To access dozens of integration ideas that you can use with one, two, or more than two classroom computers, visit the Computer Concepts CourseMate Web site at *www.cengagebrain.com*, navigate to the Chapter 5 Apps Corner resource for this book and then navigate to your grade level corner.

Strategies for computer lab or media center use
Work with the computer lab or the media center teacher; you will need his or her help and expertise.
Teach the lesson yourself or encourage the curriculum resource teacher to teach with you.
Set up clear lab management rules.
Provide well-thought-out lessons, with clear instructions.
Make sure to use the available software, Internet, and other technologies to support your curriculum and follow your school's Acceptable Use Policies (AUP).
Always, always have a backup plan for unexpected technology problems.
Alternate between whole-group, small-group, and individual instruction and assignments.

Figure 5-28 Suggestions that will assist teachers in the computer lab or the media center to make the instructional lessons a successful learning experience for students.

Most computer labs and media centers have an added benefit of allowing students to interact with technology and software that is student centered. Taking your class to a computer lab or a media center, however, requires careful planning and scheduling to use the allocated time efficiently and effectively. Managing instruction in a lab environment also requires that teachers carefully plan their learning strategies for this multicomputer environment.

The advantage of using a computer lab or a media center for instructional purposes is that all students have access to computers, the Internet, and software. Many times, other available technologies allow students to work on projects and develop additional technology skills, such as video production and much more. Figure 5-28 above lists some suggestions to help make your time in the computer lab or the media center a successful learning experience.

USING A WIRELESS MOBILE LAB

Today's wireless digital technology represents an evolution of products and services for businesses and education. Many innovative technologies have evolved and are being used in K-12 and higher education classrooms; these technologies provide teachers with new and exciting integration possibilities.

One use of wireless technology is a **wireless mobile lab**, also called a **computer lab on wheels** or **computers on wheels (COW)**. A wireless mobile lab is a portable cart with wireless notebook computers that can be transported from one classroom to another (Figure 5-29). As you learned in previous chapters, wireless communications make technology more accessible and flexible. The wireless mobile lab uses all the advantages of wireless technology, bringing technology to digital students without having to take them to a dedicated computer lab or media center. These rolling digital learning centers can be moved almost anywhere and shared among classrooms. These mobile labs allow for expanded network capabilities and offer many instructional opportunities for teachers.

Figure 5-29 A wireless mobile lab transports computers to the students instead of the students going to a computer lab or media center.

Wireless mobile labs consist of wireless notebook, netbook, and tablet computers that can be purchased in configurations from just a few to as many as 36 computers. The notebook computers are stored and transported on a special cart. The cart serves many purposes, such as moving the computers from classroom to classroom, storing the computers at night, charging the computers, and keeping the computers secure. Each company that has developed mobile labs has its own unique configuration and ways you can charge the computers and external batteries.

Teachers and students both benefit from this access to technology. By bringing technology to the classroom at the point of instruction, wireless mobile labs effectively integrate technology into the classroom. Because of the many possibilities that wireless mobile labs, especially those created with netbooks and tablets, can and are providing, many experts believe that wireless mobile labs will replace traditional, wired computer labs, until such times as all students can carry netbooks and tablets.

Planning Lessons with Technology

One of the more important parts of technology planning is developing classroom lessons and activities that utilize technology. Students begin school having varying degrees of knowledge about computers and technology. Students should, at some point, be taught basic computer concepts and operations, but they will learn many basic computer skills just from everyday use. For the digital generation, technology has always been in every aspect of their lives. Educators need to realize that by integrating digital media and related technologies, students develop their own digital literacy, while at the same time, they are given new reasons to get excited and motivated about content and learning.

When planning lessons that use technology, teachers must consider the skills and knowledge level required for students to start and complete the lesson successfully.

If technology is part of the lesson, teachers need to consider student technology skills. Many different tools are available to assess students' skill levels, such as a skill assessment survey. A **skill assessment survey** is designed to identify individual students' academic and technology skill levels and then create a starting point for developing instructional strategies.

KWL CHARTS

Another simple and effective tool to help in the planning process is a KWL chart. A **KWL chart** is an instructional planning chart to assist a teacher in identifying student understanding of curriculum standards and related objectives by having students state what they already **K**now, what they **W**ant to know, and then, based on that information recording what students **L**earned, as shown in Figure 5-30 on the next page. A KWL chart is a very helpful planning tool in determining skill and knowledge levels of students before beginning almost any project. After a teacher has established the learning objectives, the KWL chart can be used as a survey tool to determine what students already know about a topic and what technology skills they will need for a project. The teacher and students then can determine what they will learn from the project and the technologies best suited to mastering the objectives.

As the project progresses, students are encouraged to list what they have learned on the KWL chart. Not only will students be learning subject-related matter, they will be learning new and different types of technology skills when using technology to accomplish tasks.

An alternative version of the KWL chart is a KWHL chart. A **KWHL chart** also is an instructional planning tool, but adds an additional component — How students will learn. This additional component creates an opportunity for students and teachers to plan for how the learning experiences will occur.

A great way to create participatory learning opportunities for your students is to let them create KWL and KWHL charts when you introduce a new topic or project.

Web Info

For another example of how to use a KWL chart, visit the Computer Concepts CourseMate Web site at *www.cengagebrain.com*, navigate to the Chapter 5 Web Info resource for this book, and then click KWL Chart.

ePortfolio Idea

Know/Want to Know/Learned

KNOW	WANT TO KNOW	LEARNED
Owls live in barns.	Do owls have any other natural environments?	Owls live and hunt in woodlands and grasslands as well as in parks and large gardens.
Owls eat mice.	What other prey do owls hunt?	Owls eat insects, spiders, earthworms, snails, crabs, fish, reptiles, amphibians, birds, and small mammals.
Owls swallow their prey whole.	What happens after owls swallow their prey?	The owls' food passes directly into the digestive system and after a few hours the indigestible parts are compressed into a pellet.
Owls have large eyes.	What other adaptations do owls have that help them survive?	Owls have excellent vision, a sharp sense of hearing, powerful talons and beak, as well as the ability to fly silently.
An owl's neck can turn farther than a human's neck.	Can an owl's neck spin in a complete circle?	An owl can spin its neck 270°.
Owls fly quietly.	Why do owls fly so quietly?	Owls fly slowly and quietly so that they can hunt ground dwelling prey.
Some owls are very small.	How many different species of owls are there?	There are more than 200 known species of owls belonging to two different families. 18 of these species are found in North America.
Owls make a hooting sound.	What do the sounds that owls make mean?	Owls make many sounds including hooting, screeching, whistling, and screaming. These sounds are territorial, related to mating, or a defense.
	How often do owls eat?	About 10 hours after a pellet is formed, the owl regurgitates it and then the owl can eat again.
	Where do owls fall on the food chain?	Owls are predators that are at the top of the food chain because very few animals prey on them.

Figure 5-30 A KWL chart is an instructional planning tool that assists teachers in creating curriculum-specific objectives based on the knowledge of their students.

You can conduct this exercise as a large group activity in which the whole class participates, or you can separate the class into small groups and then let the groups share their results. KWL and KWHL charts can be used in all subjects from kindergarten through university-level classes.

Instructional Models

Before you start a lesson, you plan the lesson, which is a process that involves using an instructional design or model. Effective teaching with technology also involves using an instructional model. An **instructional model** is a systematic guide for planning instruction or a lesson.

When using and integrating technology, an instructional model and the planning take on a more important role. Which technology you use is not the critical issue; what is important is that you integrate the technology effectively and the technology is appropriate to the learning objectives. Many instructional models are available from which you can choose. For the purpose of this textbook, the popular educational instructional model called the ASSURE Model is described.

THE ASSURE MODEL

The **ASSURE Model** developed in the late 1990s by Heinich, Molenda, Russell, and Smaldino is a procedural guide for planning and delivering instruction that integrates technologies and media into the teaching process (Figure 5-31). The ASSURE Model is a well-known guide for developing any instructional lesson. The following is a description of the steps of the ASSURE Model and an explanation of how to use the model in your classroom.

ANALYZE THE LEARNER Knowing your learner's skill level is important. Some students may come into your classroom with academic and technology skills that others do not possess. Teachers should plan for this situation. Know your audience and consider the diverse differences in the student population you are teaching.

STATE OBJECTIVES Student objectives are statements of the type of skills and knowledge you expect students to be able to demonstrate at the end of instruction. When you have clear student objectives, you can select your materials and determine the focus and purpose of the lesson or project more wisely. Be sure to match student objectives to curriculum standards and learning objectives.

ASSURE Model	
Analyze the Learner	• Who are the learners? • What are their skill levels? • What are their learning styles?
State Objectives	• What do you want the learners to gain knowledge of? • What are the specific learner outcomes?
Select Methods, Media, and Materials	• What methods of instruction will you use? • Which media are appropriate? • Which materials will you need?
Utilize Methods, Media, and Materials	• How will you use the methods and media? • How will you use the materials? • What is your instructional strategy?
Require Learner Participation	• What will the learners be required to do? • How will the learners engage in participatory learning?
Evaluate and Revise	• Did the lesson meet the objectives? • How will you evaluate content and technologies used? • How will you revise and improve?

Figure 5-31 The ASSURE Model is an instructional model used by educators to develop technology-enriched lessons.

SELECT METHODS, MEDIA, AND MATERIALS
Selection of methods, media, and materials includes three steps, which are (1) decide on the method of instruction, (2) choose the media format that is appropriate for the method, and (3) select, modify, update, or design materials for the instruction. Media and materials, such as print, technology, information resources, and related components, include all items you choose to meet the curriculum standard. Media can take many forms, including CD, DVD, the Internet or the Web, a video, an LCD projector, digital cameras, Web cams, special technology devices for learning, software, digital media, or any combination of these and other items (Figure 5-32).

The first step is to decide which method best meets your needs, such as lecture, discovery, tutorials, demonstration, or creation of student projects. Next, you need to decide on the media, how you are going to use the media, and what you want the learners to do. Make sure the materials you identify are available and list what you are planning to use them for. Finally, determine if you need to modify any of the media or materials or design new media or materials.

UTILIZE METHODS, MEDIA, AND MATERIALS
Teachers should preview all media and materials they are planning to use, including videos, digital media applications, and Web sites. Although a software company may advertise that a particular software product contains the correct content for your objectives, you, as the teacher, must evaluate the content of all software. Again, refer to your learning objectives to assist you in determining this step. Next, you will need to prepare the classroom environment. Use these questions to guide you in making preparations:

- What equipment, software, or devices are required to use the media?
- Do you need to reserve extra equipment that you might not have in your classroom?
- How do you prepare your classroom to use the equipment?
- How do you prepare the students to use the media and materials?
- Do you need to schedule a computer lab or the media center?

Figure 5-32 Teachers must choose which media to use and when it is appropriate to use the technology.

REQUIRE LEARNER PARTICIPATION As previously discussed, the most effective learning situations are those that require participatory learning and ask learners to complete activities that build mastery toward the learning objectives. Classroom lessons should motivate students to be participatory learners who are involved in the process of learning, such as practicing, performing, solving, building, creating, and manipulating. As you develop these lessons, you must decide what information to include in the activities. If students are doing a research project using the Web, for example, they need guidelines of what to incorporate and how you will assess the outcome of the project. Chapter 7 discusses assessment tools in more detail.

EVALUATE AND REVISE At the end of a project or lesson, it is important to evaluate all aspects of the lesson, instruction, or learning experience. **Evaluation** is the method of appraising or determining the significance or worth of an item, action, or outcome. This **evaluation process** includes assessing learning objectives, reviewing, critiquing the learners' work or works based on specific standards, and evaluating reviews of the media and materials used. Teachers should conduct thoughtful reflection on all aspects of the instructional process. **Reflective evaluation** is thinking back on the components of the teaching and learning process and determining the effectiveness of the learning objectives and the use of technology during the process (Figure 5-33). Students also should be asked to reflect on their learning experiences, their perceptions on the content learned, and their evaluation of the learning process. The lesson should be revised based on the evaluations.

The ASSURE Model is one popular educational model that teachers can use to plan for technology integration into instruction. Emerging technologies will expand teachers' potential to communicate effectively, to convey ideas, and to motivate, encourage, and educate students. As you revise your lesson plans, you will need to evaluate and consider using new and emerging technologies.

As you can see, planning is important on all levels — from the district, to the classroom, to individual lessons. As a new teacher, planning for technology integration will present its challenges. The next section provides information on creating and presenting digital media presentations.

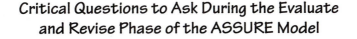

Critical Questions to Ask During the Evaluate and Revise Phase of the ASSURE Model

- Did students learn what you wanted them to learn?

- Can students demonstrate understanding of the content?

- Was the chosen technology effective in achieving the learning objectives?

- Were the learning objectives met using the technology?

- Would these learning objectives be better taught without technology or with another technology?

- Should learning objectives be taught in a different format?

- Can students work cooperatively with a partner on this lesson?

- Would parts of the content be better understood if students worked individually?

- What would you change?

- What would you keep the same?

- How will you revise this lesson?

5-33 Questions teachers should consider during the evaluation and revision phase.

Creating and Integrating Digital Media Presentations

In Chapter 3, you learned about presentation software, and at the beginning of this chapter, you learned about digital media, the various elements that make up digital media, and why digital media is important for education. Now that you have learned about curriculum integration, planning, and an instructional model, you will learn about creating and integrating **digital media presentations,** which involves producing various digital media elements, defining the elements' relationships to each other, and then sequencing them in an appropriate order. Many options are available for you and your students to use digital media authoring software and to present digital media presentations.

Digital media authoring software, also called **multimedia authoring software,** lets you create the application or presentation by controlling the placement of text and graphics and the duration of sounds, video, and animations. Recall that a digital media presentation is interactive, meaning you can decide the amount and order of the material it contains. Digital media authoring software allows you to create interactivity by defining places in the program that respond to user input. In a digital media presentation, for example, you might include a screen where users can click or tap buttons to play a video or skip the video and move to the next screen.

As discussed throughout this textbook, today's youth are very well connected to all that is digital. Technology is a tool they use without fear and they gravitate to it. Popular digital media authoring tools used in K-12 schools are Microsoft PowerPoint and Photo Story, and Apple iLife and Keynote.

Microsoft **PowerPoint** and Apple **Keynote** allow teachers and students to create digital media presentations that can incorporate text, graphics, animation, audio, video, links, and, most importantly, interactivity. You can learn how to use and integrate PowerPoint in your classroom by completing the In the Lab activities at the end of this chapter. In addition, review Chapter 3's Digital Media Corner for more information on Windows Live Essentials suite, which will include Microsoft programs that can help you and your students easily capture, synchronize, and publish audio, video, and digital images in your PowerPoint presentations.

Keynote, which is part of Apple's iWork suite of products, includes many easy-to-use tools and dazzling effects that let you and your students add elements such as tables, charts, media, and shapes to your presentation. Keynote is also available as an app for an iPad, iPhone, or iPod touch. To show their presentations, students simply connect their iPads to a projector, an interactive whiteboard, or an HDTV, or stream their presentations using numerous wireless devices. To learn more about the Keynote app, see this chapter's Digital Media Corner.

The **iLife** integrated suite, included on all new Apple computers, is designed for the digital media revolution (Figure 5-34). Included in iLife are photo editing and manipulation, music and voice-overs, video production, DVD creation, and much more. Many of the programs included in iLife are available as iPad apps, including iMovie and GarageBand. To learn more about the iMovie app and the GarageBand app, see this chapter's Apps Corner.

The digital media capabilities of PowerPoint, Keynote, and iLife are integrated seamlessly and so easy to use that even younger students can begin producing personalized digital media projects almost immediately. The integration makes organizing projects easier because all digital elements (photos, music, video clips, and so on) interlink. These tools help you, as the teacher, become a facilitator who guides the learning, rather than the lecturer who imparts knowledge.

These programs provi of opportunities for stude richly mediated stories, s

Figure 5

Figure 5-34 Apple's iLife was created for today's digital generation.

live scenes from plays as they are performed; creating interactive electronic portfolios; designing and developing videos and/or slide shows of documentaries, political speeches, or historical moments; producing public service announcements that show their understanding of sensitive public policies; taking a stand by debating a topic; and/or demonstrating otherwise complex abstract concepts visually. The topics are endless, the possibilities without limits.

Presenting your digital media presentations, as well as having your students present their digital media projects, normally requires a projection system or electronic whiteboard so your students can see and hear the presentations and projects clearly. You also can copy students' projects to more than one computer so students can watch the presentations in small groups.

DATA PROJECTORS

Recall that a **data projector** is a device that projects the image that appears on a computer screen onto a large screen so an audience, such as students in a classroom or school assembly, can see the image clearly. Data projectors have come down in price significantly over the past couple of years and are now an affordable option for K-12 schools to use in their classrooms. Most new schools and retrofitted schools include installed digital data projectors in the ceilings of their classrooms, labs, and media centers. Older schools usually have data projectors that teachers can share (Figure 5-35). Some schools are adopting a new generation of 3-D projectors. Similar to the technology used to show 3-D movies at theaters, a classroom **3-D projector** provides 3-D content that engages students and enhances the learning experience.

Figure 5-35 Data projectors are used to project a computer's image onto a large screen.

INTERACTIVE WHITEBOARDS

A popular teaching tool with educators is the **interactive whiteboard (IWB)**, also called an **electronic whiteboard**, which turns a computer and data projector into a powerful tool for teaching and learning. One IWB, called a **SMART Board** and produced by Smart Technologies, is more than a presentation system (Figure 5-36). With a computer image projected onto the SMART Board, you can press on its large, touch-sensitive surface to access and control any computer application. The **ActivBoard**, produced by Promethean, is another type of IWB being utilized in classrooms across the world; however, the ActivBoard is not activated by touch, but rather by an electromagnetic pen. In addition to operating computer applications, you can write notes, draw diagrams, and highlight information

Figure 5-36 An electronic whiteboard is an interactive presentation system that turns a computer and data projector into a powerful tool for teaching and learning.

on top of any application. You then can save and print your notes and hand them out to students or make them available on your school's network.

Other companies that have developed interactive whiteboards for schools are Mimeo, eInstruction, and Brightlink. Brightlink now offers an Interactive Projector, an innovative and versatile option for educators in any classroom environment. The **Brightlink Interactive Projector** turns any surface into an interactive surface, such as a table, wall, or traditional dry-erase whiteboard. This is a great option for educators with limited space or who wish to have students working in different locations with the interactive materials. A neat solution for younger students is a SMART Table (Figure 5-37) from Smart Technologies. The **SMART Table** is a multi-touch, multi-user interactive learning center designed to encourage collaboration, discussion, and consensus building. The SMART Table provides students a gathering place to explore digital lessons, read eStories, play educational games, and work together on interactive learning activities. The unique design allows groups of students to simultaneously touch and manipulate objects on the surface and enjoy a playful kind of learning.

Figure 5-37 Young students are drawn to the SMART Table surface, where work and play come together in hands-on collaborative activities.

CLASSROOM INTEGRATION WITH IWBS In the classroom of today, it is crucial to use technology as a tool to enhance instruction and make learning meaningful for students, and this is especially true when using interactive whiteboards. When you find yourself with an IWB at your disposal, it is important to know that you can begin using it right away. Anything you can do with a computer, you can do with an IWB. So, take your PowerPoint presentations, Web activities, videos, and any other content-based activities you have already created, and display it for your students via the IWB. You can then have students use either their finger or pointer device on the IWB to move through the content and interact with it rather than simply viewing it. This gives students the ability to participate in even the smallest aspect of a lesson (such as turning the page or tapping a button), thus creating a more active learning experience. The list that follows provides suggestions for integrating IWBs into your curriculum and to assist you with classroom collaboration, communication, and even classroom management.

- Develop lessons to support your curriculum and lesson objectives
- Develop and practice interactive lessons prior to using them in class
- Evaluate all educational resources (Web sites, apps, videos, educational games, etc.)
- Create and test all links to outside resources and Web sites
- Incorporate multimedia into lessons, such as animation, sound, and video
- Connect with other teachers to form a user-group, participate in forums
- Adapt previously created content and use it with an IWB
- Do not recreate the wheel, gather interactive lessons from other teachers and sources
- Take students on virtual field trips to create collaborative learning experiences
- Create hands-on activities for students to interact with the content and the board, not just the teacher

Each interactive whiteboard comes with its own software that allows users to create unique activities that meet their students' needs. Promethean and SMART

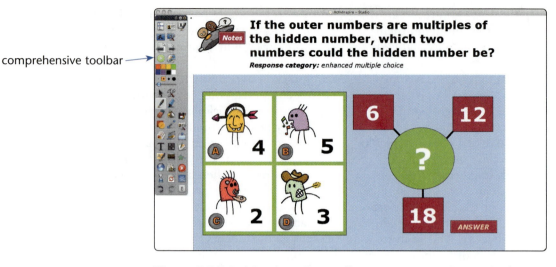

comprehensive toolbar →

Figure 5-38 ActivInspire software allows you to create interactive lessons using a comprehensive toolbar directly related to your specific curriculum and can be used across all content areas.

technologies come with award-winning software and have completed interactive lessons available for free download from the Internet. Both the Promethean ActivInspire and SMART Board software provide users with the tools needed to handwrite in a given blank space, type text, highlight text, create shapes, and insert images.

In addition, as users become more advanced they are able to insert audio and video, build in immediate feedback, and annotate over any Web site or computer program. Access to the software is often a major selling point of an IWB, and many educators download a version of the software on their personal computers so they can build curriculum specific lessons at home to teach content and add interactivity tools to their lessons (Figure 5-38).

Educators' benefit from the ability to enhance their lessons by creating customized activities specific to their students' needs and interests using this software. In addition, teachers are able to use the software with their students as an alternative to PowerPoint for project creation. The ability to build in interactivity with ease gives teachers the opportunity to share student presentations with the class and have other students complete content-specific activities created by their peers (Figure 5-39).

Figure 5-39 Using IWBs, teachers can let students work in teams to develop digitally-enhanced projects in order to gain a deeper understanding of standards-based content.

Company/Web Site	Educator Resources
DYMO/Mimio *www.mimio.dymo.com*	MimioConnect *www.mimioconnect.com*
eBeam *www.e-beam.com*	eBeam Education *www.e-beam.com/education*
Promethean *www.prometheanworld.com*	Promethean Planet *www.prometheanplanet.com*
Smart Technologies *smarttech.com*	Smart Exchange *exchange.smarttech.com*
TeamBoard *teamboard.info*	TeamBoard Content and Resources *content.eganteamboard.com*

Figure 5-40 Interactive whiteboard manufacturers provide tools, software, lesson plans, and other resources for teachers.

STUDENT INTERACTION When students regularly interact with various forms of technology outside of the classroom, it is unreasonable to ask them to "power-down" when they come to school. This means not simply exposing students to available educational technologies, but providing opportunities for student inter-action with these technologies on a regu-lar basis. To make these interactions as meaningful as possible, educators should use the IWB software to create custom-ized activities in each subject area that enhance students' learning experiences. To ensure you are effectively integrating all technology resources with the IWB and lesson content, you should use a planning strategy such as the ASSURE Model discussed earlier in this chapter. This will help you plan exactly how the content will be delivered and the resources you will use to deliver it. This is crucial when implementing new technologies.

Lesson materials can be created by the teacher using custom software pro-vided with the interactive whiteboard, they can be downloaded from educator Web sites where other teachers have pub-lished lessons they created, or they can be purchased from education software com-panies. Figure 5-40 lists content providers and companies creating IWBs. Lessons can also be created using standard application software, such as PowerPoint and Inspiration.

The expense of typical high-end inter-active whiteboard configurations has prompted some budget-constrained schools to implement a low-cost configuration devised by researcher Dr. Johnny Chung Lee. By using a Wii remote (which is essen-tially an infrared camera), an infrared pen constructed from readily available materi-als for minimal cost, and free software downloaded from Dr. Lee's Web site, an interactive whiteboard can be created so it is available to any teacher with access to a computer and projector. The next section provides information on where to go for guidance and materials to help you plan for technology integration in your classroom.

Getting Started at a New School

Suppose you are a new teacher and it is the first day of the preplanning week for teachers. You are excited to get that first glimpse of your new classroom. When you finally do, you discover you have two new networked computers and a color ink-jet printer in your classroom. Fortunately, you learned about Macs and PCs during your teacher education courses. Although you are comfortable using computers, you immediately wonder how to get started.

Web Info

To learn more about Dr. Chung Lee's system, visit the Computer Concepts CourseMate Web site at *www.cengagebrain.com*, navigate to the Chapter 5 Web Info resource for this book, and then click Dr. Chung Lee.

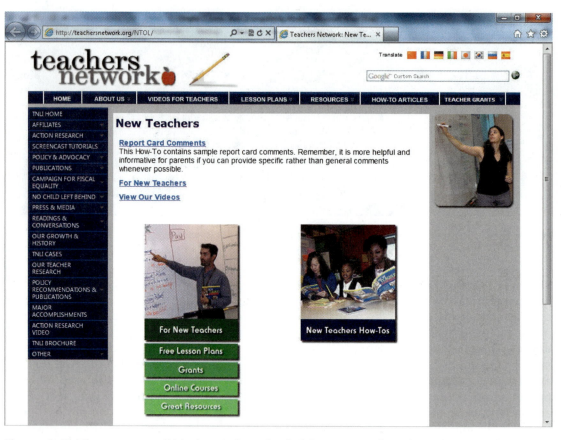

Figure 5-41 There are many Web sites dedicated to helping new teachers through online support and mentoring.

There are many Web sites, like the one shown in Figure 5-41, that can help you as you get started finding ways to integrate these computers into your classroom curriculum. As you start to plan for technology integration, you will need to consider many issues related to technology information and support, technology training, hardware, software, other technologies, and technology supplies.

INFORMATION ABOUT TECHNOLOGY

One of the first items to investigate is who else in the school is using technology in their classrooms. Individuals to consult are your principal, media specialist, curriculum resource teacher, technology committee members, or other teachers, especially those who teach the same grade level and subjects that you teach. These educators will know who else is integrating technology actively in their classrooms. Check to see if your school has a mentorship program.

Ascertain if your school has a technology committee and who the members are. You can get this information from your principal or assistant principal. Consult your teacher's manual for a list of various school committees and their members. A **technology committee** consists of teachers, administrators, and staff who consider, investigate, advise, and make recommendations to the principal and technology coordinator about technology-related issues. A **teacher's manual** contains information, rules and regulations, rights and responsibilities, and policies and procedures, including those related to all aspects of technology in the district. It should provide answers to many of your questions. Most manuals are located on the school or school district Web site.

Finally, you should determine where you should go to get technology support. The principal, media specialist, school or district technology coordinator, and other teachers who use technology can offer you support or guide you to where you can find support.

TECHNOLOGY TRAINING

Take time to find out if your school offers any professional development or in-service training for using and integrating technology. Most schools and school districts offer free training for teachers. **In-service** means training teachers after they have entered the profession of teaching. Your principal, curriculum resource teacher, technology coordinator, or district instructional technology coordinators are able to provide information on in-service training opportunities. Sometimes, school secretaries also will be up to date on this information.

For information about technology workshops, talk with your principal, curriculum resource teacher, other teachers, or district technology coordinator. Let these people know you are interested in any technology or other training that becomes available. If you have students with learning disabilities in your classroom, check with the district exceptional student education program specialist about training opportunities. Many school districts post the dates and times of in-service training and workshops on the district's Web site and other Web resources.

HARDWARE

Determining how you can upgrade your classroom computers or obtaining additional hardware is another item to consider. As soon as you can, join your school's technology committee. Technology committees help make the decisions on what new technologies will be purchased, where these new technologies will be placed, and how the technology plan for the school is implemented. You also may need to look into **educational grants** for additional funds. Your principal and curriculum coordinator usually receive notification of grant opportunities. Let them know you are interested in writing a grant and they will provide you with the information. If your district has a person responsible for grant writing for the district or county, he can serve as a good source of information. In addition, you will find numerous grant opportunities on the Internet. Chapter 7 provides more information on locating and writing educational grants.

A question to consider is what type of equipment you can purchase if you receive grant funds. Before you write a grant, determine what kind of equipment you can purchase. Your principal, technology coordinator, curriculum coordinator, or members of the technology committee should be able to provide you with this information. If your school is networked, also check with the network administrator at the district level.

SOFTWARE

With hardware requirements decided, you will need to determine what kind of software is available to you and where you can find it. First, you should check your classroom computer for installed software. To learn more about the software available at your school or on the school's network, ask the school media specialist, curriculum resource teacher, technology facilitator, or district technology coordinator. If you are a special education teacher, check with your district exceptional student education coordinator, who should know what software is available for students with disabilities.

Next, determine the procedure for purchasing additional software. The school secretary or other teachers can direct you to the right person for this information. If your school is networked, it is important to check with the network coordinator before purchasing software so you can avoid buying software that already may be installed on the network or may conflict with the network. Many schools install computer-assisted instructional software programs on their network servers for use by all teachers.

Finally, you need to determine if your school district or state Department of Education has an adopted state bid list for purchasing software. Many states contract with companies to purchase specific software applications at reduced prices, and these are included on a **state bid list**. Be sure to find out if your state has a special Web catalog of software titles that they have adopted (Figure 5-42 on the next page). Curriculum resource teachers, technology coordinators,

FAQ

Can teachers borrow technologies for their classrooms from other locations?

Yes, public libraries, universities, some businesses, and curriculum resource centers will let teachers check out all types of technologies for use in their classroom.

Figure 5-42 Many states provide online access to state-approved electronic learning resources.

Integration Strategies

To learn more about writing grants to obtain various technologies for your classroom, visit the Computer Concepts CourseMate Web site at *www.cengagebrain.com,* and then navigate to the Chapter 5 Teaching Today resource for this book.

or media specialists are good sources for this information. Your district office should maintain this information as well.

OTHER TECHNOLOGIES

Consider other technologies and where you can find them, such as a VCR, DVD player, digital camera, digital video camera, scanner, projector, or an electronic whiteboard. A school's media center can be scheduled for use by teachers and students (Figure 5-43). Reserve early because allocation is usually based on a first-come, first-served basis. In addition, your media specialist usually handles scheduling and distribution of DVD players, digital cameras, tablet computers, and other equipment. Ask about the length of time that you are allowed to keep checked-out equipment.

You also should ask where you can find a listing of educational software programs offered throughout the school or district for

Figure 5-43 A school's media center can be scheduled for teachers and students.

use in the classroom. The media specialist usually has a list of software programs available on CDs, DVDs, and the school network for teachers to use in the classroom.

A listing of instructional television programs and broadcast times, and any videos the school has or that are available to the school through interlibrary loan programs, usually is maintained by the media specialist. She can inform you of the procedures for checking out CDs, DVDs, VCR tapes, and other equipment.

TECHNOLOGY SUPPLIES

A basic, but often overlooked, question to consider is how you can obtain additional supplies for use with computers and other technologies. If the bulb in your overhead projector burns out, for example, or you need paper or ink cartridges for your printer, how do you go about replacing these supplies? Generally, the media specialist can replace burned-out bulbs and solve other supply problems with projectors. In many schools, the school secretary usually handles orders for general supplies. A good starting point is to talk to the media specialist or technology coordinator and they will direct you to the appropriate person.

Now that you have some basic knowledge of where to go for guidance and materials to help you integrate technology into your classroom, consider how one teacher is putting it all together.

Putting It All Together

As described earlier in this chapter, Mr. Balado is well aware that technology can make a difference in his fifth-grade students' learning — and he has been using technology to enhance his classroom lessons. After the students completed their narratives, Mr. Balado planned a highly integrated classroom strategy for teaching the science curriculum to his fifth graders. As part of the integrated learning environment, he provided carefully planned centers, which enabled him to divide his classroom for group activities and inquiry learning through these interdisciplinary lessons.

CREATING AN INTEGRATED LEARNING ENVIRONMENT

Mr. Balado had an instructional plan for how the students would work through the centers in his classroom. In Mr. Balado's Owl Exploration project, students took on the role of explorer and learned what it would be like to have a career as a wildlife biologist. In order to do this, he created an integrated learning environment that included classroom computers, library resources, cooperative grouping, and more.

Mr. Balado had four computers and two tablet computers in his classroom for student use. He divided his 22 students into groups of two and three; these students would work together throughout the levels of the project. Mr. Balado then assigned each group a North American species of owl to research.

Students were excited and surprised because most did not even know that there was more than one species of owl. Their assignment was twofold. First, they were to find out as much as possible about their owl species. Second, they would use their newly acquired knowledge to help inform the public on what needs to be done to ensure the safety of North American owls and to prevent them from becoming extinct. Instead of writing a report, students would create a research-based interactive digital media project, models, and more.

Mr. Balado gave each group the same guidance and questions to think about for their project, such as the following: What does a wildlife biologist really do? Where might a wildlife biologist have to travel? What kind of education would you need to be a wildlife biologist?

Mr. Balado also instructed his students to conduct research on their species of owl, in a manner similar to the way wildlife biologists would conduct research, by answering questions such as the following: What does your owl look like? In what ecosystem would you find your owl? What does your owl eat? How large is your owl expected to grow and what is its average weight? He also asked each group to gather all the information the group wanted others in the class to understand about their particular species of owl.

Many educators teach their students to use an **essential questioning technique**, which is looking for the most important or

Web Info

To learn how to order technology and other school supplies online, visit the Computer Concepts CourseMate Web site at *www.cengagebrain. com*, navigate to the Chapter 5 Web Info resource for this book, and then click Supplies.

fundamental part of a topic. In this process, students develop their own questions, find their own answers, and develop their own meaning from the information they collect. By using this essential questioning technique, students discover insight and are motivated to learn more. When students have learned how to ask the appropriate questions, they have learned how to learn. Mr. Balado knows that the ability to ask good questions leads to concrete learning opportunities; so he asked the students to formulate their own questions and find answers to them.

THE CLASSROOM CENTERS

Centers, or **learning centers,** give you the opportunity to break your classroom into many different types of learning environments without ever leaving the room. Just as an office building has different offices in which work is accomplished, learning centers allow students to rotate around the classroom to complete projects or activities (Figure 5-44). For his lesson on North American owls, Mr. Balado set up seven learning centers in his classroom. The centers included a discovery computer center, a Web search center with lots of resource books and other materials for locating pictures as well as a computer connected to the Internet, a modeling center, the great explorers' library center, a scanning and photo center with a computer set up for scanning pictures and other objects, a science center, and a digital media project center.

ePortfolio Idea

Figure 5-44 Learning centers are a great way to organize a classroom to optimize learning opportunities.

The discovery computer center included one computer, one iPad, and different CDs and DVDs that Mr. Balado had checked out from the media center. These cover predator and prey relationships, the food chain, and wildlife of North America. He purchased four apps, including a virtual dissection app at his own expense. The Web search center has one computer and an iPad that students can use to investigate various Web sites. Mr. Balado has provided links to these Web sites on his curriculum resource page. To locate these Web sites and other available media, Mr. Balado worked with the media specialist at his school. After he had collected and evaluated a list of sites for the students to conduct their research, Mr. Balado created a curriculum resource page so students would not be wasting time surfing the Web without supervision (Figure 5-45). Mr. Balado is quite aware of the dangers of inappropriate or inaccurate information available at some Web sites.

The modeling center included all types of modeling tools, modeling clay, paper, rocks, and more. This center was for students to create a three-dimensional model of their owls and other objects related to the project. At the next center, the great explorers library center (Figure 5-46), Mr. Balado provided a collection of ebooks, journals, and magazines for students to use to research owls and become great research scientists. The media specialist was instrumental in locating books and print materials through the state's interlibrary loan program, which was established by the state to assist teachers in obtaining resources from media centers throughout the state.

The scanning and photo center had a computer set up with a scanner and digital editing software that students could use to scan and manipulate pictures from books, magazines, and other sources for their projects. The science center had real owl pellets, owl pellet dissection data sheets, and bone sorting charts that Mr. Balado obtained from an Internet science company. This center also included two digital microscopes that the students could use to closely investigate their findings and take digital photographs of their discoveries. Mr. Balado set up this center like a real

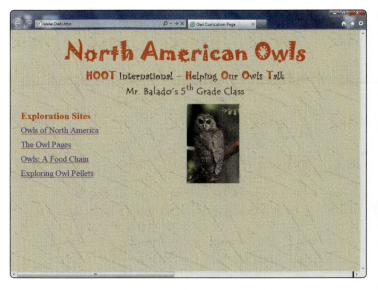

Figure 5-45 Teacher-created curriculum resource pages allow students to link directly to appropriate Web sites.

had now learned to create their own digital video story about an owl.

Having students create the content makes the learning more memorable in two ways. First, they are learning by creating both text-based and visual content that addresses the dual coding theory as suggested by Paivio (you will learn more in the Learning Theories Special Feature at the end of this chapter). Second, because when students are involved in discovery and constructivist learning, the content becomes personalized, and thus more relevant to them.

science lab. He wanted to give his students authentic, hands-on experience to help them gain some understanding of what it takes to work as a scientist.

The last center was the digital media project center, which had one computer set up for students to create their digital media projects using either PowerPoint, Keynote, or iLife. Because the school had site licenses, PowerPoint and iLife were installed on all of the classroom computers and Keynote was installed on the tablet computers so students could work on their projects as they progressed through the various centers. Students took the storyboard with narratives they had written about owls and combined true facts they

Figure 5-46 This learning center contains a variety of print resources for students to use to develop their research projects.

THE RESULTS OF TECHNOLOGY INTEGRATION

Students worked though the centers and created some of the most interesting and creative projects Mr. Balado had ever seen (Figure 5-47 on the next page). One group had located a picture of an owl soaring above its prey in a field, so for their model, they decided to create an owl flying above a field.

Most students could describe in detail all of the information they had learned about their species of owl — and, interestingly, each group had personalized its learning by giving its owl a nickname. The projects were outstanding; most of them contained many pictures and owl stories with research and details about North American owls and field wildlife biology.

Mr. Balado knew that his students were involved actively in their own learning and had interacted with numerous resources, Web sites, and software programs. By using participatory learning at each center and using higher-order thinking skills, Mr. Balado's students, with his assistance, created their own questions, found their own answers, and created their own digital media projects. As a result of this process, Mr. Balado's students created new paths of knowledge that enhanced their learning, while achieving the unit learning objectives, and addressing curriculum standards.

Web Info

For more information about the benefits of technology integration, visit the Computer Concepts CourseMate Web site at *www.cengagebrain.com*, navigate to the Chapter 5 Web Info resource for this book, and then click Benefits.

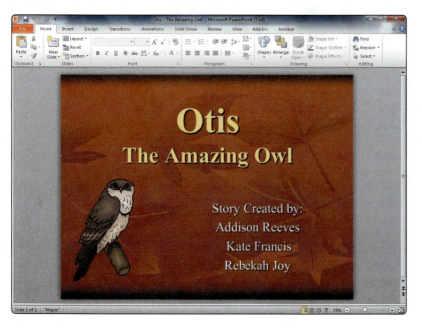

Figure 5-47 Students can use PowerPoint to create digital media projects.

Integration Strategies

To learn more about integrating storytelling with your students, visit the Computer Concepts CourseMate Web site at *www. cengagebrain.com*, and then navigate to the Chapter 5 Teaching Today resource for this book.

As Mr. Balado and his students learned, technology can make a difference in the classroom if used appropriately and integrated into the curriculum. In addition, Mr. Balado noticed that, like the students in Figure 5-48, his students' self-esteem, self-confidence, and writing skills improved as a result of creating projects. Students had prepared for the unit by reflecting on what they knew and what they wanted to know about owls (refer again to the KWL chart in Figure 5-30 on page 228). At the end of the unit, students reflected on their learning by articulating what they learned about owls. This reflection process helped Mr. Balado with his own reflective evaluation.

Figure 5-48 Students feel an amazing sense of pride and ownership when they complete their own projects.

Learning Theories and Educational Research

At the end of this chapter is a special feature that provides information on educational learning theories and theorists. This special feature introduces you to educational terms, learning theories, educational research, and learning strategies that you should understand and apply to your own instructional strategies.

All teaching strategies have learning theories and educational research embedded within the instructional framework. Learning theories help teachers form instructional strategies and technology integration techniques by providing a basic framework for teaching and learning. Teachers learn to combine the different strategies and integration methods that are most suitable and appropriate for teaching their students.

Summary of Technology and Curriculum Integration

As you have learned in this chapter, the best strategy for technology integration is to place technology into the hands of students and trained teachers, make it easily accessible, and let them decide how best to use it in their classrooms at the point of instruction. Teachers are the content experts who should evaluate all resources used in classrooms.

This chapter first discussed digital media, curriculum, and technology issues as they apply to technology integration, and then provided teachers with ideas, an instructional model, and effective planning strategies. The chapter then provided an introduction to the concept of technology integration that will help you build your integration literacy skills. Finally, this chapter showed you how one teacher, Mr. Balado, fully integrated technology into an interdisciplinary project. In Chapters 6 and 7, you will build upon the skills you have learned in this chapter and increase your integration literacy skills by learning implementation strategies and integration activities that are curriculum directed.

INSTRUCTIONS: Use the Key Terms to help focus your study of the terms used in this chapter. To further enhance your understanding of the Key Terms in this chapter, visit the Computer Concepts CourseMate Web site at www.cengagebrain.com, and then navigate to the Chapter 5 Key Terms resource for this book. Read the definition for each term and then access current and additional information about the term from the Web.

3-D projector [233]

ActivBoard [234]
anchored instruction [219]
animation [206]
ASSURE Model [229]
audio [206]
authentic learning [219]

benchmark [211]
Brightlink Interactive Projector [235]
Britannica [220]

centers [242]
cognitive scaffold [220]
Common Core State Standards Initiative [209]
Common Core State Standards [209]
computer lab [213]
computer lab on wheels [226]
computers on wheels (COW) [226]
cooperative classroom activity [222]
cooperative learning [222]
curriculum [209]
curriculum framework [209]
curriculum goal [211]
curriculum guide [209]
curriculum integration [212]
curriculum maps [209]
curriculum standard [210]

data projector [233]
digital media [204]
digital media authoring software [232]
digital media presentations [232]
digital media software [205]

education [209]
educational equalizer [221]
educational grant [239]
electronic whiteboard [234]
essential questioning technique [241]
evaluation [231]
evaluation process [231]

facilitator of learning [216]

graphic [206]

higher-order thinking skills [222]

iLife [232]
in-service [239]
instructional model [229]
integration [212]
interactive whiteboard (IWB) [234]
interactivity [204]
interactive digital media [205]

Keynote [232]
KWHL chart [227]
KWL chart [227]

learning centers [242]
learning expectation [211]
learning objective [211]
learning style [216]

Mastery Objective Checklist [210]
media center [213]
mentorship program [223]
multimedia [204]
multimedia authoring software [232]

participatory learning [219]
Performance Expectations [210]
Performance Guides [210]
Performance Indicators [210]
Performance Standards [210]
point of instruction [213]
PowerPoint [232]
problem-based instruction [220]

reflective evaluation [231]

secondary learning [219]
skill assessment survey [227]
SMART Board [234]
SMART Table [235]
state bid list [239]
student objective [229]

teachable moment [213]
teacher's manual [238]
technology [204]
technology committee [238]
technology integration [212]
technology lab [213]
technology plan [223]
text [205]

video [206]
virtual field trip [215]
visual learners [206]

Welliver's Instructional Transformation Model [217]
wireless mobile lab [226]

1. Label the Figure

Instructions: Identify the five hierarchy stages of the Welliver's Instructional Transformation Model.

Welliver's Instructional Transformation Model

1. _____ is when teachers become aware of technology and its potential uses.

2. _____ is when teachers use technology but minor problems will cause them to discontinue its use.

3. _____ is when technology becomes essential for the educational process and teachers are constantly thinking of ways to use technology in their classrooms.

4. _____ is when teachers begin to rethink the educational goals of the classroom with the use of technology.

5. _____ is the evolving classroom that becomes completely integrated with technology in all subject areas. Technology becomes an invisible tool that is seamlessly woven into the teaching and learning process.

2. Matching

Instructions: Match each term from the column on the left with the best description from the column on the right.

____ 1. ASSURE Model

____ 2. authentic learning

____ 3. curriculum standards

____ 4. mentorship program

____ 5. KWL chart

a. lessons connected to real-life events

b. instructional planning tool to assist teachers in identifying curriculum objectives

c. procedural guide for planning and delivering instruction that integrates technology

d. collection of general concepts that school districts expect their students to learn

e. when new teachers team with experienced teachers

3. Short Answer

Instructions: Write a brief answer to each of the following questions.

1. What is the difference between a curriculum standard and a benchmark? Are both curriculum standards and benchmarks measurable? Why or why not?

2. What are learning styles? How can a teacher be a facilitator of learning and address various students' learning styles at the same time?

3. Name five barriers to technology integration. In your opinion, which barrier is the most detrimental? Why?

4. Name three people who can help teachers find information on available technologies in their schools. Describe other sources that can assist teachers in locating technology resources.

5. Name three areas teachers must address when planning for technology integration in a one-computer classroom. Can these same planning strategies also work for a two-computer classroom?

INSTRUCTIONS: Teaching Today provides teachers with integration strategies and ideas for teaching and, more importantly, reaching today's digital generation. Each numbered segment contains one or more links that reinforce the information presented in the segment. To display this page from the Web, visit the Computer Concepts CourseMate Web site at www.cengagebrain.com, and then navigate to the Chapter 5 Teaching Today resource for this book.

1. Lesson Plans

After using technology in your classroom, you are beginning to understand that using technology is different from integrating technology. You want to begin integrating technology into your social studies curriculum. Where do you begin? Are resources available on the Internet that can help you? Where can you locate examples of lesson plans that integrate technology but still support your curriculum? Can you modify these lessons to use in your classroom?

2. Grant Opportunities

Your school is located in a rural area, and technology funds are limited. You have used technology with students before and were encouraged by the results. You have one computer in your classroom and want to provide your students with greater access to technology. You have decided to explore possible grant opportunities. Your district is small, however, and does not have any grant programs. Very few businesses in your community offer grant opportunities. Where can you learn about other grant opportunities? Are there grants available specific to your circumstances? What are some other funding options? What other organizations in your community could you contact?

3. Mentoring

You want to integrate technology into your curriculum, but you do not know where to start. You want to provide the students with authentic learning activities and you need ideas. You consider talking to a teacher who integrates technology, but you do not know anyone. You have heard of a Web site where teachers can receive mentoring from other teachers as well as ask for advice and receive ideas. What are some advantages to finding assistance online? What are some disadvantages? Could you use this type of assistance for any subject? Why or why not? Could your students benefit from this type of interaction? Why or why not? How can you locate more resources such as this for yourself and for your students?

4. Storytelling

As a teacher, you know that by putting the technology in the hands of students you can create innovative learning experiences and increase motivation, all while teaching curriculum-specific content. You heard about an innovative project designed to get students writing stories about themselves called digital storytelling. The project is based on the principles of telling personal stories. Getting students to write is the crucial step in achieving many curriculum standards and is often one of the learning objectives associated with a standard. Getting students writing, especially about themselves, family, or community, is one way to encourage writing while strengthening writing skills. What kind of lesson plans can you develop using storytelling? What questions could you ask your students to get them thinking? What is a story circle? Could you find ways to weave a story throughout all curriculum areas? How?

Education Issues

INSTRUCTIONS: Education Issues provides several scenarios that allow you to explore controversial and current issues in education. Each numbered segment contains one or more links that reinforce the information presented in the segment. To display this page from the Web, visit the Computer Concepts CourseMate Web site at www.cengagebrain.com, and then navigate to the Chapter 5 Education Issues resource for this book.

1. Bilingual Education

A recent survey of state education agencies indicates that more than seven million students with Limited English Proficiency (LEP) are enrolled in public schools and that this number is growing — dramatically, in many locations — every year. This trend poses unique challenges for educators who want to ensure that these students have the same opportunities as English-proficient students. In transitional bilingual education programs, instruction is provided for some subjects in the students' native language and part of the school day is spent on developing English skills. Bilingual education's critics argue that this approach keeps students in a cycle of native-language dependency that ultimately prevents them from making significant progress in English-language-acquisition and leads to lower test scores. These critics argue that these students must spend 100 percent of their time on task in English to master proficiency in English. What do you think? What Web site resources provide teachers with practical material for culturally diverse classrooms? What other technologies and teaching strategies can you use to enhance LEP student learning?

2. Integrated Learning System

Your school district has spent a significant amount of money on an integrated learning system that is available for all teachers throughout the district to use. This software generates tests and automatically tracks student progress. The software also includes thousands of interactive student assignments, data-driven decision-making capabilities, and the ability to create customized learning paths for your students so they can progress through the content at their own pace and path. What are some of the benefits of this type of software? What are some advantages/disadvantages? Does this type of software appeal to different learning styles? How could students with learning disabilities use this type of software?

3. Levels of Integration

It is the second month of the semester, and you are teaching seventh-grade science. The parents of one of your students contact you. They are upset because when their son was in elementary school, the majority of teachers were using technology in their classrooms. At your middle school, however, their son has not had the same opportunities. The parents are very concerned about the lack of technology. What can you do about this situation? To whom can you refer the parents? Do greater barriers to technology integration exist in middle schools than in elementary or high schools? Why or why not? How could you integrate technology into your seventh-grade science curriculum?

4. Tablet Computing

Around the country and the world, local and national governments are supplying students with tablet computers. School districts and state education agencies are reducing their printed textbook costs by providing digital copies of textbooks on tablet computers, which students can carry back and forth to school. Researchers like Richard Clark feel that technology does not influence learning outcomes when used to deliver content. Others claim that when students use computers, instructors tend to lecture less, requiring students to engage in more research and independent study. Many people oppose plans to equip every student with a computer because they say that the technology detracts from traditional educational subjects, such as basic reading and math. Should schools supply or mandate that parents provide tablet computers to all students? Why or why not? What is the appropriate grade level to mandate tablets for all students?

INSTRUCTIONS: Apps Corner provides extensive ideas and resources for integrating technology into your classroom-specific curriculum. To display this page from the Web and information on numerous education apps, visit the Computer Concepts CourseMate Web site at www.cengagebrain.com, and then navigate to the Chapter 5 Apps Corner resource for this book.

Apps Corner is designed for teachers and other educators who are looking for innovative ways to integrate apps into their content-specific curriculum. Apps Corner not only provides great apps with current information but also shows how other educators are using and integrating education apps. As a result, Apps Corner is designed with all educators in mind, regardless of their interests or subject area. You can use Apps Corner to expand your resources by reviewing apps outside your curriculum area; remember many apps associated with one curriculum area can be adapted for use and added to lesson plans in a wide variety of other curriculum areas.

Use Apps Corner as a springboard for collaborating and sharing the successes and hurdles of integrating apps in a classroom or an entire school system. Consider Apps Corner a place to locate app integration ideas and resources. Information on educational apps are organized in four Corners (Early Childhood, Elementary, Middle School, and Secondary), and different apps are available for each chapter. Many apps are free, others cost from $1 to $5. Inexpensive site licenses for classrooms, schools, and school districts are available for many apps.

Shown below are two example digital media productivity Apps. The first is the very popular and highly rated iMove app from Apple, which was designed specifically for the iPad. The second is Apple's GarageBand, which was also designed from the ground up for iPads and turns your iPad into a full-featured recording studio.

Software Corner

INSTRUCTIONS: Software Corner provides information on popular software programs. Each numbered segment discusses specific software programs and contains a link to additional information about these programs. To display this page from the Web, visit the Computer Concepts CourseMate Web site at www.cengagebrain.com, and then navigate to the Chapter 5 Software Corner resource for this book.

1. Destination Series

Destination Math and Reading series by Riverdeep are comprehensive software programs that provide authentic experiences when teaching mathematics and reading. Destination Math provides a curriculum that makes the connection between real world and mathematics while teaching basic skills, math reasoning, conceptual understanding, and problem solving. The Destination Reading series, for Grades 4-8, is a stimulating reading courseware that builds understanding for all learners. Destination Reading provides careful sequencing of reading and writing skill development so that each new skill builds upon prior knowledge. The Destination Series is aligned with state and national curriculum standards and is grounded in current scientific research.

2. Model ChemLab

Would you like to create experiences to let your students become scientists through challenging, authentic simulations that can be conducted in the computer lab, in the media center, or online? Model Science Software has several software classroom solutions that are perfect alternatives to dangerous, expensive, or environmentally hazardous labs. Model ChemLab is a unique product that integrates observations, practice, and theory with interactive simulations and a lab notebook workspace to create a working lab environment. Frequently used lab equipment and procedures are used to simulate the steps involved in performing an experiment. Students step through the actual lab procedure while interacting with equipment in a way that is similar to the real lab experience. The software has predesigned curriculum with lab experiments and activities for general chemistry for high school and college students.

3. MathType

Design Science is a world leader in developing and supporting software for scientific, mathematical, and technical communication. Their products provide users with the tools to author and publish mathematical notations in print and online documents. One of their products, MathType is a powerful interactive equation editor for PCs and Macs that lets you create interactive math content containing mathematical notation for word processing documents, Web pages, desktop publishing, presentations, and more. MathType works with hundreds of applications and Web sites, allowing you to put equations in all your instructional lessons and presentations.

4. MOLO Molecular Workbench

The goal of the MOLO Molecular Logic project, developed under a National Science Foundation grant, is to improve the ability of all students to understand fundamental biological phenomena in terms of the interactions of atoms and molecules. The Molecular Logic project aims to do this by enhancing biology courses with guided explorations of powerful atomic and molecular computational models. Molecular Workbench is free, open-source software that enables upper level high school biology/chemistry courses to utilize technology for visualizing atoms and molecules. These models are embedded in an easily implemented database linked to both typical textbooks and standards. Along with  dynamic molecular models, the Molecular Workbench engine can display text, images, and questions. Teachers can use the editing environment for creating dynamic model pages since it is modeled after a typical word processor, and does not require any programming knowledge for the authoring of these types of pages.

Digital Media Corner

1. Massively Multiplayer Online Role-Playing Game

A Massively Multiplayer Online Role-playing Game (MMORPG) is a game in which an unlimited number of players can participate. Players assume the fictional role of one of a select number of characters that interact within the fantasy setting initiated within the game. Players have limited control over the actions of their characters. MMORPGs are different from small multiplayer or single player games not only because of the number of participants but also because the game's virtual world persists and evolves, even when the player is absent. The player base for MMORPGs is over 15 million, which shows their popularity worldwide. Players are not limited to children and teens. In fact, the age of players ranges from 18 to 45 years and is expanding on both ends of the scale each year.

2. Windows Live and Windows Live SkyDrive

As teachers, we are always looking for free software sites that offer features and services like Microsoft Windows Live. Microsoft describes Windows Live as a super extension of the Windows operating system. Included with Windows Live are services like Windows Live SkyDrive, which offers 25 GB of free storage space to store your Web pages, photos, files, and more so it is easy to store and share your files with others. When Windows 7 becomes mainstream, users will see applications such as Windows Mail, Windows Photo Gallery, and Windows Movie Maker replaced with the Windows Live Essentials suite, a software that allows the downloading and installation of current and future offerings from Windows Live.

3. Web Publishing with WordPress

WordPress is a free Web publishing package. It traces its roots back to a team of programmers trying to develop a blog writing system that would be exceptionally easy for its users to manage. It shares some features that are similar to other open-source programs. Open-source software permits users to use, change, and improve the software. Besides its ease of use as a Web page editing system and blog writing system, WordPress capabilities are often extended through the use of ancillary programs and scripts called plug-ins. These plug-ins allow bloggers to include pictures, video, sound, etc. in their blogs, which extends what visitors usually expect to find in a blog. WordPress is also a content management system (one that helps developers keep track of content, images, and other media). WordPress is an outgrowth of the Web 2.0 features in which developers are looking to combine static Web pages with products that easily permit and support multiple author and end-user changes and modifications.

4. UB the Director

How do you encourage students to be interested in a book that does not relate directly to them? One technique is to use booktalking, a concept that means telling stories about the context and background in which the book is written. Digital booktalking allows students to read the content as if they were going to make a movie out of the book. Digital booktalking utilizes digital media to tell the story. Students are taught text-to-screen techniques and then learn how to pull important details from a book to create a book trailer. A book trailer is a short 2–3 minute video that encapsulates the essence of the book, main characters, metaphors, and so on. Using easy-to-use video editing software like Apple's iMovie, or Microsoft's Photo Story or Movie Maker, students can easily build their own movies. Examples of trailers can be found at Digital Booktalk. In fact, this Web site accepts student-produced work.

5. Keynote

Keynote is a digital media presentation application that comes with Apple's iWork suite. Keynote includes features such as cinema-like transitions, preset animated text and titling effects, photo masking, and the ability to seamlessly add video clips. Keynote is easy to use, allowing today's digital students to transition to learning the essence of digital storytelling. Keynote works seamlessly with iLife applications such as iPhoto and GarageBand.

Assistive Technologies Corner

INSTRUCTIONS: Assistive Technologies Corner provides information on current hardware, software, and peripherals that will assist you in delivering instruction to students with physical, cognitive, or sensory challenges. To access extensive additional information, visit the Computer Concepts CourseMate Web site at www.cengagebrain.com, and then navigate to the Chapter 5 Assistive Technologies Corner resource for this book.

1. Will Assistive Technology Help My Teaching? Yes!

Just as with students in a typical classroom, students with special needs must also attain curriculum standards. The teacher sets clear learning objectives based on the curriculum standards, and plans for all students to attain those objectives, including those students with special needs. Technology helps engage all students in the learning process; however, technology can greatly enhance the learning process for students with special needs. Reminding educators that curriculum is central to instruction, the Center for Applied Special Technology (CAST) has developed the Universal Design for Learning, a theoretical curriculum design approach providing the fewest barriers to learning.

In their book, *Teaching Every Student in the Digital Age: Universal Design for Learning*, Rose and Meyer remind teachers that access to information is not synonymous with access to learning, and that teachers must plan for learning, and not simply provide accessible information. Like all technology, assistive technologies need to be used at the right time and with the appropriate curriculum goals in mind to provide access to learning.

2. What Are Some Ways to Use Assistive Technology to Help Students Learn?

To better answer this question, let's read about two teachers who are using assistive technologies. Ms. Daniels at Fourth Street Elementary School has two students with dyslexia in her classroom. The class is reading *Island of the Blue Dolphins*. Ms. Daniels uses the classroom Smart Board to present an Inspiration concept map that introduces students to the story's setting and provides them with background information. She will use the same program later to illustrate plot development as the story proceeds. Her dyslexic students depend on this organization to help them comprehend the whole story.

Strengthening of reading skills for many students is challenging, but especially for those students with dyslexia. Her students with dyslexia struggle through decoding and comprehension of the text during reading class, but with the graphical map they have a framework from which to proceed. In science class, these same students often use Kurzweil 3000, their text reader, to complete assigned classroom readings. Using a text reader helps them grasp science concepts quickly, and return to the printed text as needed.

Mr. Kamla's third grade class is studying energy. One of his students, Carla, who has cerebral palsy, finds it difficult to navigate the online tutorial with captioned video clips that Mr. Kamla created for the classroom learning center. Mr. Kamla used Intellitools' Overlay Maker to create a specialized template with large navigation keys that he places over the Intellikeys keyboard. Now, Carla is able to access the same tutorial as her classmates. Because the video clips he created are captioned, they provide all students with multisensory learning opportunities.

Mr. Kamla and Ms. Daniels often collaborate on their accessibility ideas. Last year, they adapted two WebQuests for a class with several students with emotional disturbances. They located a WebQuest on the Web that would meet their curriculum goals, but realized that the special needs students would not be able to participate fully. Following Bernie Dodge's suggestions for adapting existing WebQuests, they used more prompts and more details in the directions and in the accompanying printed materials. They structured the student interaction carefully and with tasks clearly focusing on the learning objectives. Making sure the WebQuest met accessibility standards, they published the WebQuest. Planning for learning by all students is simply good practice in any classroom. Choosing the right technology tool helps instructors explore a myriad of ways to engage all learners!

Follow the instructions at the top of this page to display additional information and this chapter's links on assistive technologies.

In the Lab

ePortfolio Idea

INSTRUCTIONS: In the Lab provides Microsoft PowerPoint exercises that are divided into two areas, productivity and integration. To access the links to tutorials, productivity ideas, integration examples and ideas, and more, visit the Computer Concepts CourseMate Web site at www.cengagebrain.com, and then navigate to the Chapter 5 In the Lab resource for this book.

PRODUCTIVITY IN THE CLASSROOM

Introduction: Chapter 5 introduces digital media software applications and the positive impact they have on learning. Most schools today have a variety of digital media applications, including Microsoft PowerPoint. Both teachers and students can use PowerPoint to create effective and interesting presentations. Students also can use PowerPoint as an authoring tool to create original stories and book reports. PowerPoint is an excellent tool for creating excitement, interest, and motivation in learning.

After working through these In the Lab activities, visit the Computer Concepts CourseMate Web site at www.cengagebrain.com, and then navigate to the Chapter 5 In the Lab resource for this book to learn new skills or to improve your current skills by clicking the following links: Learning Microsoft PowerPoint; PowerPoint FAQ; PowerPoint Tips for Windows and Mac OS.

1. Back to School Open House

Problem: To prepare for Parent Night at your school's Open House, your principal has asked all of the teachers at your school to create a short digital media presentation outlining classroom rules, homework policies, and necessary student supplies specific to their class.

You decide to create your presentation in Microsoft PowerPoint. You create the presentation shown in Figure 5-49. (*Hint:* Use Help to understand the steps better.) If you do not have a suggested template or font, use any appropriate template or font.

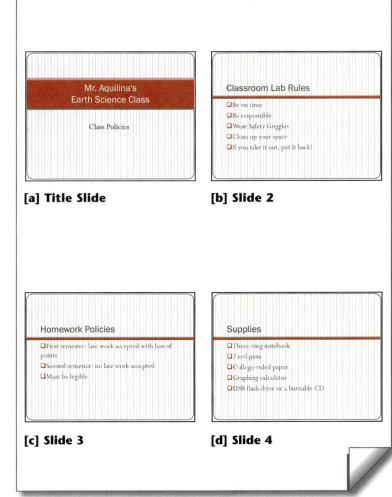

[a] Title Slide

[b] Slide 2

[c] Slide 3

[d] Slide 4

Figure 5-49

Instructions: Perform the following tasks.

1. Create a new presentation using an appropriate design template.
2. Create the title slide shown in Figure 5-49[a] on the previous page, using your name in place of Mr. Aquilina and the subject you teach, or intend to teach, in place of Earth Science. Increase the font size of the text, Class Policies, to 36 point.
3. Create the three bulleted list slides as shown in Figure 5-49 on the previous page, personalizing the lists to your specific subject area or grade level.
4. Correct any spelling errors.
5. Save the presentation to a location of your choice using an appropriate filename.
6. Print the presentation.
7. Follow the directions from your instructor for handing in this assignment.

2. Adding Clip Art and Animation Effects to a Presentation

Problem: You decide to enhance your open house presentation from In the Lab 1 by adding clip art, as shown in Figure 5-50, and slide transitions. You also decide to change to a different design template. (*Hint:* Use Help to understand the steps better.) Use any appropriate clip art image.

Instructions: Use the presentation created in In the Lab 1 for this assignment. Perform the following tasks.

1. Open the presentation you created for In the Lab 1.
2. Change the design to a new design, such as Ocean or Flow.
3. Insert appropriate clip art on three slides.
4. Resize the clip art as necessary. Resize and relocate the text boxes as needed.
5. Apply the Dissolve slide transition effect to Slides 2, 3, and 4.
6. Save the presentation with a different filename to a location of your choice.
7. Print the presentation as a handout with four slides per page.
8. Follow directions from your instructor for handing in the assignment.

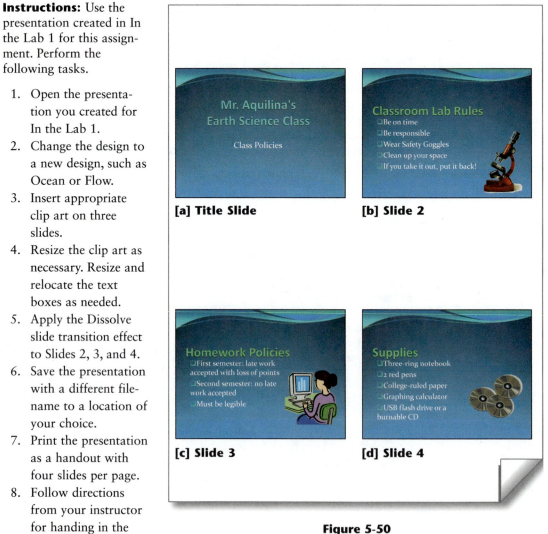

Figure 5-50

3. Classroom Presentation

Problem: On the first day of school, you want to welcome your students to class and have them participate in an introduction activity. You decide to create a PowerPoint presentation to introduce yourself and provide examples of the type of information they might want to share in the activity.

ePortfolio Idea

Instructions: Create a PowerPoint presentation similar to the presentation illustrated in Figure 5-50. Use an appropriate template, attractive font style, size, and clip art images. Include the current date, your name, and e-mail address on the title slide. After you have created the presentation, save it to a location of your choice using an appropriate filename. Print the presentation and then follow your instructor's directions for handing in the assignment.

INTEGRATION IN THE CLASSROOM

1. Your fourth grade students are learning about the life cycle of a butterfly. The students will work in groups to create a research project about one species of butterfly. They will start by gathering the following information: species scientific name, common name, range, four interesting facts, stages in the life cycle, eating habits and favorite flowers or plants, one predator, and one defense against predators. Students also will locate at least two images of the butterfly. Then, they will create a digital media presentation using PowerPoint that contains a title slide and at least four additional slides. Students will use bulleted lists to present their findings. They also will include at

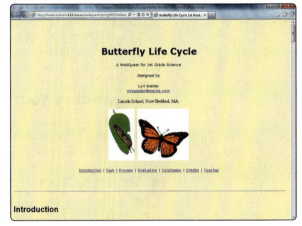

least two images of their butterfly in their presentation, as well as other suitable clip art. Select a species of butterfly and create a sample presentation. Enter the appropriate information to demonstrate the project for the students. Include the name of the butterfly you select, your name, and the current date on your title slide.

2. Your middle school geography class is studying different countries. For a culminating project, each student selects a country and researches its economy, land formations, temperature and climate, population, and places of interest or historic significance. The students then create PowerPoint presentations to share their research with the class. The presentation should consist of a title slide and at least three other slides containing bulleted lists and images. Students need to include sound, transitions, graphic images, and Internet hypertext links in their presentations. The last slide of each presentation should list references. Prepare a PowerPoint presentation to present as an example for your students. Create a title slide and at least three additional slides with bulleted lists, graphic images, sounds, and transitions. Include your name, the current date, and the name of the country on the title slide. Include a list of references on the last slide.

3. William Shakespeare continues to influence modern theater. You want your high school drama students to understand the contributions of the past to theater and drama today. Students will be divided into four groups. Each group will research one of the following topics: the style and construction of the Globe Theater, forms of entertainment, customs of the theater, and costuming during the time of Shakespeare. Groups will create PowerPoint presentations to present their findings. The presentation should consist of a title slide, slides with bulleted lists, and images. Students also may include Internet hyperlinks. Remind students the hyperlink will only work if the computer they are using for their presentation has an active Internet connection. Prepare a presentation to present to the students as an example. Create a title slide and at least three additional slides with bulleted lists and graphic images. Include your name, the current date, and the topic on the title slide.

Learn It Online

INSTRUCTIONS: Use the Learn It Online exercises to reinforce your understanding of the chapter concepts and increase your computer, information, and integration literacy. To access dozens of interactive student labs, practice tests, learning games, and more, visit the Computer Concepts CourseMate Web site at www.cengagebrain.com, navigate to the Chapter 5 resources for this book, and then click the link for the resource you want to review.

1. Integrating Tablet Computers and Apps

Click the Integrating Tablets link to review an article about integrating tablet computers. After reading the article, write a one page summary of the article and list five ways you might integrate tablet computers or apps in your current or future classroom. You can also learn more about using and integrating tablet computers and apps in the special feature that follows Chapter 6.

2. Maintaining Your PC's Hard Disk

You computer's hard disk is used for the majority of your storage requirements. Maintaining your hard disk can help prevent the loss of data. In addition, it is important that your hard disk operates at peak efficiency. Click the Maintaining Your PC's Hard Disk link to learn how to maintain your PC's hard drive by detecting and repairing disk errors using the Check Disk utility, removing unused files and folders using the Disk Cleanup utility, and consolidating the way data is stored using the Disk Defragmenter utility.

3. Expanding Your Understanding

When you print using a computer, you control printing at two different points: first, before the printing actually begins, and second, after the document has been sent to the printer. Click the Expanding Your Understanding link to learn how to set the parameters for printing.

4. Practice Test

Click the Practice Test link. Answer each question. When completed, enter your name and click the Grade Test button to submit the quiz for grading. Make a note of any missed questions. If required, submit your score to your instructor.

5. Who Wants to Be a Computer Genius?

Click the Who Wants to Be a Computer Genius link to find out if you are a computer genius. When you are ready to play, click the Play button. If required, submit your score to your instructor.

6. Wheel of Terms

Click the Wheel of Terms link to reinforce important terms you learned in this chapter by playing the Shelly Cashman Series version of this popular game. When you are ready to play, click the Play button. If required, submit your score to your instructor.

7. Crossword Puzzle Challenge

Click the Crossword Puzzle Challenge link. Complete the puzzle to reinforce skills you learned in this chapter. When you are ready to play, click the Play button. If required, submit the completed puzzle to your instructor.

Special Feature: Learning Theories and Educational Research

A great deal of discussion has taken place about the definition of learning by educational theorists, researchers, and practitioners; yet, no universal definition of learning has been accepted. As a result, numerous definitions exist, and they vary greatly in describing the exact nature of learning. For this textbook, **learning** is defined as the process of gaining knowledge or skills acquired through instruction or study, or to modify behavior through exposure to a type of conditioning or form of gaining experience. A **theory** is a scientific set of principles presented to clarify or explain a phenomenon. **Learning theories** provide frameworks for interpreting the conditions and observations of teaching and learning and provide the bridge between education and research.

Educational research builds the foundation for the development of sound instructional strategies; however, it takes practice and moving the theory into practice to create the bridge that evolves into technology integration. Each new lesson you present to your students should be based on learning theory and educational research. Learning theories have been shown to enhance learning and increase motivation and student achievement. Which learning theory you use depends on what you want to teach, how you want to teach it, and who you are teaching. The latter is very important because today's kids are totally different. The way they learn also is different.

In Chapter 1, you learned some of the characteristics of today's digital generation. In addition to describing who these kids are and how they think, their traits have implications on teaching and learning. Today's students tend to process information at what Prensky refers to as a "twitch speed." In other words, students today often fail to spend time reflecting and processing information at what Craik and Lockhart refer to as **deep processing levels**. Research has found that deep processing is necessary for students to make sense out of information, to give meaning to the information, and to remember things for a longer period of time. Today's students' prefer graphics over text-based communications. This learning preference ties to Clark and Paivio's ideas on dual coding and how pictures interface with a person's abilities to recall information.

Today's students like to live, work, and play with others in digital social settings; this interaction is known as their **social network** (Figure 1). Even though digital students pride themselves on being individuals, they prefer instruction that involves interaction for themselves and with others. This learning preference ties directly to the work of Lev Vygotsky, Albert Bandura, and others. Recall the ARCS Motivational Model described in Chapter 1 and the ASSURE Model described early in Chapter 5 and how both of these models are relevant to discussions about learning theories. Most models, including these, underline how important it is to know one's audience before developing class content and deciding how to mediate the instructional activities.

Figure 1 Today's digital students interact digitally in what is known as their social network, which is in total contrast to the way in which any previous generation interacted socially.

This special feature highlights some of the theories that will help you better integrate technology into your curriculum. For more information about specific learning theories and researchers, including reference materials, access the Web Info annotations located in the margins throughout this special feature. The first section discusses behaviorism.

Behaviorism

Behaviorism is the prediction and control of human behavior in which introspection and/or independent thinking play no essential part of its teaching methods. Behaviorism came into vogue during a period of time that coincided with the industrial revolution called **modernism** in which everything of value (including learning) was measured solely in terms of science. To a behaviorist, human learning is purely an objective and experimental branch of natural science. There is no internal cognitive processing of information.

The behaviorist recognizes no dividing line between man and animal — both learn to behave solely through a system of positive and negative rewards. For some students, this type

of conditioning works very well. Behaviorists such as Pavlov, Skinner, and Bandura have contributed a great deal to the understanding of human behavior, and an overview of their contributions are described in the following sections.

Ivan Pavlov

Ivan Pavlov (1849 – 1936) became famous for his behavioral experiments with dogs, and he won the Nobel Prize in Physiology in 1904 (Figure 2). Pavlov used conditioning to teach dogs to salivate when he rang a bell. When he provided the stimulus (food) and he achieved his desired reflex (salivation), he rang a bell. Eventually, the dogs associated the bell with food and they began to salivate when Pavlov rang the bell even if food was not present. This process was termed **classic conditioning** and refers to the natural reflex that occurs in response to a stimulus. Pavlov was a scientist, and he conducted these experiments to study digestion, but as a result, other behaviorists studied his work as an example of stimulus response. Some behaviorists felt this technique of stimulus response had human applications as well.

Web Info

For more information about Behaviorism, visit the Computer Concepts CourseMate Web site at *www.cengagebrain.com*, navigate to the Chapter 5 Web Info resource for this book, and then click Behaviorism.

Web Info

For more information about Ivan Pavlov, visit the Computer Concepts CourseMate Web site at *www.cengagebrain.com*, navigate to the Chapter 5 Web Info resource for this book, and then click Pavlov.

Figure 2 Ivan Pavlov's research into the physiology of digestion led him to create a science based on conditioned reflexes that won him the Nobel Prize in 1904.

B.F. Skinner

B.F. Skinner (1904 – 1990) describes another form of conditioning that is labeled as behavioral or operant conditioning (Figure 3). **Operant conditioning** describes learning that is controlled and results in shaping behavior through the reinforcement of stimulus-response patterns. Skinner conducted experiments with pigeons and rewarded them when he saw them behaving in a desired manner. When a stimulus-response pattern occurs, such as a pigeon turning (the stimulus), a reward is given (the response). Eventually, Skinner was able to teach pigeons to dance using this technique. Ultimately, he taught pigeons to engage in complex tasks such as bowling in a specially constructed bowling alley.

Skinner believed that people shape their behavior based on the rewards or positive reinforcement they receive. Skinner believed human behavior, even the language development of children, is based on stimulus-response theory. He observed that when children made attempts at sounds, parents smiled and reinforced that behavior. Eventually, the child learns to say the word correctly as parents and others reinforce her efforts.

In his experiments, Skinner found that reinforcement was a powerful motivator. He conducted experiments with people as well and he even used his own infant daughter. Skinner felt that when a child produces a desirable behavior and is rewarded for it, that behavior will be repeated. In contrast, if a response is negative, the behavior will be extinguished. Many classroom management techniques are based on these principles. Figure 4 compares classic and operant conditioning.

Web Info

For more information about B.F. Skinner, visit the Computer Concepts CourseMate Web site at *www. cengagebrain.com*, navigate to the Chapter 5 Web Info resource for this book, and then click Skinner.

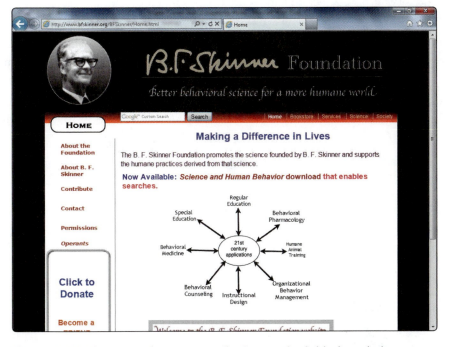

Figure 3 B.F. Skinner made many contributions to the field of psychology, including the theory of behavioral or operant conditioning.

Classic Conditioning Pavlov	Operant Conditioning Skinner
Classic conditioning introduces the stimulus and then reinforces the reflex. A neutral stimulus (the bell) becomes analogous with a reflex (salivation).	Operant conditioning begins with a stimulus (behavior) and then is reinforced with a response (reward). A bond is established between the operant (stimulus/behavior) and the reward.

Figure 4 Classic versus operant conditioning.

Web Info

For more information about Albert Bandura, visit the Computer Concepts CourseMate Web site at *www. cengagebrain.com,* navigate to the Chapter 5 Web Info resource for this book, and then click Bandura.

Many forms of computer-based instruction and educational software are based on Skinner's operant conditioning. They provide positive reinforcement when a desired behavior occurs and negative reinforcement when the student does not provide the desired behavior. For instance, when the correct answer is given, the software program provides positive verbal and visual feedback for the student's correct response. As Figure 5 shows, even young children enjoy learning and getting positive feedback.

Figure 5 Many software and hardware developers are designing products to reinforce learning for younger students.

Albert Bandura

Albert Bandura (1925 –) has studied and is famous for his ideas on **social learning,** which he renamed **Social Cognitive Theory** (Figure 6). Bandura focuses on those motivational factors and self-regulatory mechanisms that contribute to a person's behavior, rather than just environmental mechanisms, which differentiates his theories from Skinner's operant conditioning.

Bandura believes that people acquire behaviors, first, through the observation of others and then, by using those observations to imitate what they have observed. Several studies involving television commercials have supported this theory of observational modeling. **Observational modeling** is watching something and then mimicking the observed behavior. For example, when a person purchases a product advertised on TV based on claims made in the commercial (such as the idea that using a specific shampoo will increase popularity) and then uses the same mannerisms seen in the commercial (such as flipping one's hair while looking coyly over a shoulder), then that person is modeling the behavior shown in the commercial.

Social learning has been applied extensively in the context of behavior modification, which is widely used in training programs.

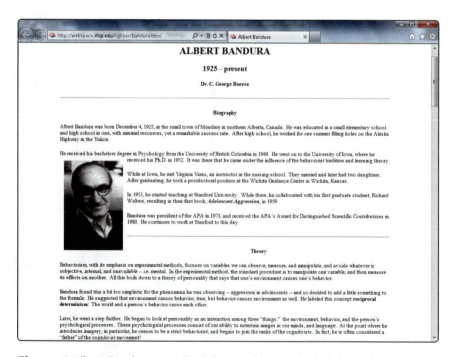

Figure 6 Albert Bandura contributed many ideas to both behaviorist and cognitive learning theories.

More recently, Bandura has focused his work on the concept of self-efficacy, which ties to motivation and cognition. **Self-efficacy** is a personal observation about one's perceived ability to feel, think, and motivate oneself to learn.

As he furthered his research, Bandura began to analyze a person's personality through the interaction of three things: the environment, the behavior, and the person's psychological processes. Bandura then started to consider a person's ability to retain information through images in the mind, called **imagery**. It was at this time that he stopped being a strict behaviorist and began to join the position of the cognitivists, a new movement that was just beginning to take root. So significant were his contributions to this movement, that he often has been called the father of the cognitivist movement. In the next section, you will learn more about cognitive theory and cognitivists like Paivio, Gagne, Gardner, and Bloom.

Cognitivist

Cognitive theory is an offshoot of traditional psychological concepts of thinking, deciding, remembering, and so on. The cognitive psychologist views these activities in terms of how they underlie behavior. According to **cognitive theory**, activities like thinking and remembering seem

like a behavior, thus providing an avenue to use behavior analysis to measure their effect on learning. Because cognitivist theory came about as a reaction to behaviorist thinking that was in vogue at the time, there has always been a certain amount of tension between behaviorist and cognitivist approaches to learning.

Cognitivists objected to behaviorists because they felt that behaviorists thought learning was simply a reactionary phenomenon and ignored the idea that thinking plays a role. Paivio, Gagne, Gardner, and Bloom are just a few of the cognitivists who have contributed a great deal to the understanding of cognitive theory; their contributions are discussed in the sections that follow.

Allan Paivio

Allan Paivio (1925 –) proposed that presenting information in both visual and verbal form enhances recall and recognition. He developed a considerable amount of research to support what has become referred to as the dual coding theory. **Dual coding theory** assumes that people process information in two distinctly different ways: (1) processing of images and (2) processing of language (Figure 7). This research supports the theory that today's visual learners learn in different ways depending on the medium. Dual coding theory identifies

Web Info

For more information on dual coding theory, visit the Computer Concepts CourseMate Web site at *www. cengagebrain.com*, navigate to the Chapter 5 Web Info resource for this book, and then click Dual Coding Theory.

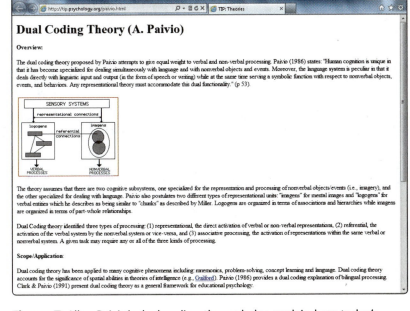

Figure 7 Allan Paivio's dual coding theory helps explain how today's digital students process information.

three subprocesses: (1) representational, in which verbal or nonverbal representations are directly influenced, (2) referential, in which the verbal system is activated by nonverbal communication forms or vice-versa, and (3) associative, in which both text-based systems and graphic representations can trigger mental associations. A given task may require any or all of the three kinds of processing and form the basis for the study of such things as learning a second language.

One of the shortcomings, according to some, is the fact that Paivio placed equal importance on verbal and nonverbal processing. Many theorists have since disputed these findings, in which they have shown that graphics tend to endure longer in one's memory but are not processed as economically. Even with its distracters, the dual coding theory formed the basis of subsequent educational theories.

Robert Gagne

Robert Gagne (1916 – 2002), a psychologist and educator, developed his learning theories based partially on the behaviorist's and information-processing point of view. Gagne is known for his contributions in the area of cognitive learning hierarchies, which involves the development of skills based on a building-block principle. Gagne identified five major categories of learning: verbal information, intellectual skills, cognitive strategies, motor skills, and attitudes (Figure 8). He made an enormous contribution to learning theory and instructional systems design. While in the Air Force, he began to develop some of his ideas for his comprehensive learning theory. He incorporated characteristics of both behavior modification theory and performance education.

Gagne developed three principles that he viewed as integral for successful instruction: (1) providing instruction on the set of component tasks that build toward a final task, (2) ensuring that each component task is mastered, and (3) sequencing the component tasks to ensure optimal transfer to the final task. In other words, a teacher must teach alphabet recognition so that her students can read words. After students can read words, they can read a sentence, and then two sentences, and then a paragraph, and so on. This process reflects a hierarchy of components.

Careful planning must take place so that learning is optimal and instruction can be broken down into meticulously planned lessons. Gagne believed that a variety of internal and external conditions must be present for learning to occur and he also believed that learning results in observable behavior. The internal conditions can be described as states that include attention, motivation, and recall. The external conditions are the factors surrounding a person, such as timing and place. The observable behavior is the result of the internal process of learning. Further, Gagne discussed that learners must go through a hierarchy of skills from simple to complex. Finally, he identified five areas of learning outcomes (Figure 8).

Web Info

For more information about Robert Gagne, visit the Computer Concepts CourseMate Web site at *www.cengagebrain.com*, navigate to the Chapter 5 Web Info resource for this book, and then click Gagne.

Categories of Learning Outcomes	Examples of Outcomes
1. Verbal information	Learner can state what has been learned.
2. Intellectual skills: composed of concrete and defined concepts	Learner can discriminate between facts, can identify colors, and can follow directions.
3. Cognitive strategies	Learner reads books.
4. Motor skills	Learner can use a mouse or joystick.
5. Attitudes	Learner prefers reading to watching TV.

Figure 8 Gagne's five areas of learning outcomes.

Gagne sought to understand what conditions were necessary for students to learn. Instruction is an external condition for learning that leads to the internal process of learning. To maximize the potential for the internal process of learning to occur, Gagne identified **nine events of instruction** (Figure 9). Teachers who incorporate Gagne's nine events of instruction into their lesson plans improve the internal process of learning for their students.

Nine Events of Instruction
1. Gain attention of the learners
2. Inform learners of the objective
3. Stimulate recall of prior learning
4. Present the stimulus or lesson
5. Provide learning guidance and instruction
6. Elicit performance
7. Provide feedback
8. Assess performance
9. Enhance retention and transfer

Figure 9 Gagne's nine events of instruction can help teachers develop technology-enriched lesson plans.

Howard Gardner

Many researchers have focused on understanding and defining intelligence. They believe that intelligence is a key to understanding how students learn. **Intelligence** is the ability to gain knowledge, apply knowledge, manipulate one's environment, and think abstractly. Howard Gardner (1943 –) developed what he called the theory of multiple intelligences.

Gardner (Figure 10), a professor at Harvard University, has conducted years of research on regular and gifted students, as well as adults with brain damage. In those who had been injured, he wanted to correlate what part of the brain had been injured and how the physical injury affected learning and other physical abilities. Through his original research, he concluded that individuals use eight different intelligences to perceive and understand the world. Since then, he has modified the eight to eleven; however, his eight intelligences have withstood the test of time and stand on their own merit. Gardner believes that individuals might have all of the intelligences, yet one, two, or more intelligences may be more dominant than others for each individual. Gardner's eight intelligences and suggested integration strategies are described in Figure 11 on the next page.

Figure 10 Howard Gardner is a professor at Harvard Graduate School of Education and is best known for his theory of multiple intelligences.

Web Info

For more information about Howard Gardner, visit the Computer Concepts CourseMate Web site at *www.cengagebrain. com,* navigate to the Chapter 5 Web Info resource for this book, and then click Gardner.

Intelligence	Description	Technology Integration
Linguistic–verbal	Ease in using language; think in words; sensitivity to rhythm and order; enjoy writing, reading, telling stories, and doing crossword puzzles	Word processing programs, prompted programs, label-making programs, word game programs, and programs that require the student to read and answer questions
Logical–mathematical	Ability to engage in inductive and deductive reasoning; use numbers effectively and to categorize, infer, make generalizations, and test hypotheses	Database programs, spreadsheet programs, problem-solving software, simulations that allow students to experiment with problems and observe results, and strategy game formats
Spatial–visual	Ability to visualize objects and spatial dimensions, think in images and pictures, like to draw and design, and enjoy puzzles	Draw and paint programs; graphic production software; reading programs that use visual clues such as color coding, desktop publishing, multimedia, concept mapping, and atlas programs
Body–kinesthetic	Ability to move the body with skill and control, expertise in using the body to express ideas and feelings	Software requiring alternate input such as joystick, touch window, or graphics tablet; keyboarding/word processing programs; graphics programs that produce blueprints for making 3D models; and software that includes animated graphics and/or requires physical engagement
Musical	Ability to recognize patterns and sounds; sensitivity to pitch and rhythm; the capacity to perceive, express, transform, or discern musical forms; think in tones, and learn through rhythm and melody	Programs that combine stories with songs; reading programs that associate letters/sounds with music; programs that use music as a reward; programs that allow students to create their own songs, hypermedia, and multimedia
Interpersonal	Ability to understand and communicate effectively with others, understand them, and interpret their behavior	Telecommunications programs, programs that address social issues, programs that include group participation or decision making, programs that turn learning into a social activity, and games that require two or more players
Intrapersonal	An awareness of oneself, goals, and emotions; the capacity for self-knowledge of one's own feelings; and the ability to use that knowledge for personal understanding	Tutorial software, programs that are self-paced, instructional games in which the opponent is the computer, programs that encourage self-awareness or build self-improvement skills, and programs that allow students to work independently
Naturalist	An awareness of the natural world around them; can identify people, plants, and other environmental features; can develop a sense of cause and effect in relation to natural occurrences, such as weather; can formulate and test hypotheses	Problem-solving software, simulations that allow students to experiment with problems and observe results, strategy game formats, database software, concept mapping software, and weather probeware

Figure 11 Using Gardner's original eight multiple intelligences and technology integration, teachers can find ways to reach all students.

Gardner also believes that the intelligences are influenced by biological predispositions and learning opportunities in an individual's cultural context. So while the teacher-directed instructional method appeals strongly to the linguistic-verbal and logical-mathematical intelligences, Gardner suggests that instructional methods should include a variety of activities that support other intelligences, such as physical education, role-playing, arts, cooperative learning, reflections, and creative play.

A variety of assessment methods should be incorporated to accommodate the wide variety of student learning styles more accurately. An important observation Gardner made was identifying the need that educators take into account the differences in students' multiple intelligences and use them as a guide to personalize instruction and assessment, which results in the ability to design appropriate instructional strategies.

Benjamin Bloom

Benjamin Bloom (1913 – 1999), an educational psychologist, focused his research on students' learning domains (Figure 12). Bloom and a group of psychologists sought to classify learning behaviors to better understand how knowledge is absorbed. Bloom classified learning into three domains: cognitive, affective, and psychomotor. Bloom defined the **cognitive domain** as a student's intellectual level, in other words, what students know and how they organize ideas and thoughts. He defined the **affective domain** as a student's emotions, interests, attitude, attention, and awareness. Finally, he categorized the **psychomotor domain**, which includes a student's motor skills and physical abilities. All of these domains can overlap in learning activities and are integrated throughout learning experiences.

Bloom wanted to develop a practical means for classifying curriculum goals and objectives. Many educators today develop their curriculum goals and objectives with these three domains in mind. Educators are responsible for planning curriculum activities that support what students already should know and what they should learn. Teachers create their instructional plans based on state standards, learning objectives, and learning theories. Teachers often arrange skills they want students to acquire using a scaffolding effect from simple to complex. Within the cognitive domain, Bloom identified six levels that can be used to acquire knowledge about a topic.

Web Info

For more information about Benjamin Bloom, visit the Computer Concepts CourseMate Web site at *www. cengagebrain.com*, navigate to the Chapter 5 Web Info resource for this book, and then click Bloom.

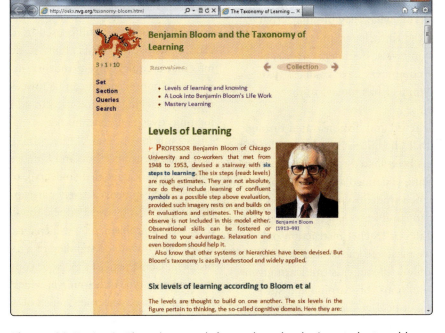

Web Info

For more information about Bloom's Taxonomy, visit the Computer Concepts CourseMate Web site at *www.cengagebrain. com*, navigate to the Chapter 5 Web Info resource for this book, and then click Bloom's Taxonomy.

Figure 12 Benjamin Bloom's research focused on developing student problem-solving abilities and higher-order thinking skills. He was the creator of the concepts of Mastery Learning and Bloom's Taxonomy.

Competencies	Skills
Knowledge Learner can recall information.	Arrange, repeat, recall, define, list, match, name, order, narrate, describe
Comprehension Learner can explain and predict.	Summarize, classify, explain, discuss, give examples, identify, translate
Application Learner can solve problems and use information.	Apply, demonstrate, solve, change, discover, experiment, interpret, show, present
Analysis Learner can see patterns, organize parts, and recognize hidden meanings.	Analyze, experiment, examine, compare, contrast, associate, dissect, conclude, test
Synthesis Learner can use previous ideas to create new ones, and relate ideas from several areas.	Collect, assemble, compose, develop, design, invent, create, plan, revise, role-play, theorize
Evaluation Learner can compare and discriminate between ideas, judge, and value ideas.	Compare, assess, contrast, criticize, debate, judge, value, predict, estimate, appraise

Figure 13 The six levels of Bloom's Taxonomy move from simple to complex.

The levels move from simple to complex and are designed to increase a student's comprehension. These levels commonly are referred to as **Bloom's Taxonomy** (Figure 13 above).

Many teachers may not realize they are creating instructional plans that only challenge students within the first two levels. For instance, if students are learning about computers and then are asked to name only the parts and describe what they do, the activity has stayed in the Knowledge and Comprehension levels. If students are asked to propose how computers have changed their lives, the assignment has moved to the Analysis level.

Bloom believed and demonstrated through his research that all children can learn. Bloom's Taxonomy has been linked to mastery learning. **Mastery learning** is defined as a model for learning in which students continue to gain information and knowledge, working through modules or teacher instruction only after they have mastered the content of the previous modules. All students can learn given the correct conditions for learning and sufficient time. The critical ingredient is changing instructional methods so students can master the content.

Web Info

For more information about Constructivism, visit the Computer Concepts CourseMate Web site at *www. cengagebrain.com*, navigate to the Chapter 5 Web Info resource for this book, and then click Constructivism.

Constructivism

Extensive research has been conducted to assist educators in better understanding which instructional strategies will increase students' motivation to learn and determine their comprehension of a subject. Many researchers agree that traditional teacher-directed or lecture-based instruction often is limited in its effectiveness to reach today's learners. Teacher-directed instruction, however, still is used in many classrooms because of its ability to deliver information quickly; yet, students' understanding and comprehension can be low when this is the only teaching method used to address learning objectives and benchmarks.

Confucius once said, "I hear and I forget. I see and I remember. I do and I understand." Constructivists agree that students learn by doing. When students actively participate in the learning process by using critical-thinking skills to analyze a problem, they will create, or construct, their own understanding of a topic or problem. **Constructivist** theory, or **constructivism**, is based on a type of learning in which the learner forms, or constructs, much of what he or she learns or comprehends. The following sections describe four leading theorists of constructivism.

Jean Piaget

The theories of Jean Piaget (1896 – 1980) profoundly influenced the constructivist movement (Figure 14). Piaget was a psychologist who developed the cognitive learning theory after he observed children for many years. Piaget perceived that children think very differently from adults. He felt children were active learners and did not need motivation from adults to learn. Piaget believed that children were constructing new knowledge as they moved through different cognitive stages or schema, building on what they already knew. Furthermore, children interpret this knowledge differently as they progress through different stages.

Piaget defined four cognitive stages (Figure 15). The first stage **sensorimotor** is when learning takes place primarily through the child's senses and motor actions. The second stage **preoperational** is when children begin to use symbols and images. They use language symbols and play pretend games. An object such as a cardboard box can be a container, but it also can represent a house.

Next, children move from the two egocentric stages into the third stage **concrete operational**.

Web Info

For more information about Jean Piaget, visit the Computer Concepts CourseMate Web site at *www. cengagebrain.com,* navigate to the Chapter 5 Web Info resource for this book, and then click Piaget.

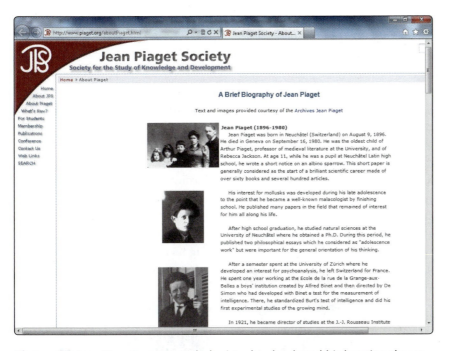

Figure 14 Jean Piaget was a psychologist who developed his learning theory after many years of observing children.

Cognitive Stages	Ages (Approximate)	Characteristics of Learning
Sensorimotor	Birth to 2 years	Imitation, learn through senses and motor activities, do not understand the world around them, and egocentric
Preoperational	2 to 6/7 years	Egocentric, pretend play, drawing ability, speech and communication development, concrete thinking, and intuitive reasoning
Concrete operational	6/7 to 11/12 years	Classification, logical reasoning, problem solving, and beginnings of abstract thinking
Formal operational	11/12 years through adulthood	Comparative reasoning, abstract thinking, deductive logic, and test hypotheses

Figure 15 Piaget's four cognitive stages.

In this stage, beginning about age 7, children begin to think logically. This is the stage when children are beginning to learn many facts. They also can begin to understand other points of view besides their own. Piaget called his last cognitive stage **formal operational**. During this stage, which begins at about age 12, children transition from concrete thinking to more abstract. They can formulate a hypothesis and understand cause and effect. Children or adolescents begin to formulate their own beliefs and morals.

Piaget felt that children are working cognitively toward equilibrium as they move through the four different cognitive stages. While they are learning, children create what Piaget called adaptation. **Adaptation** is their cognitive understanding or development at any given time. Piaget concluded that children assimilate new knowledge as they experience new things and learn new information, which Piaget called **assimilation**. Children fit this information or these experiences into their lives to change their knowledge base and to make sense of their environment and the world around them. Piaget called this process **accommodation**.

Through the insightful work of Piaget and others, researchers believe it is important to provide a rich learning environment for children to explore. Children learn by actively investigating a topic. Piaget's theories support the use and integration of technology because of the opportunities technology supplies to reach a diverse population of learners with different learning styles. Using Web Quests, scavenger and treasure hunts, curriculum resource pages, and many other educational technologies, teachers can create student-centered activities that actively engage students in the learning process.

Jerome Bruner

An American psychologist and educator, Jerome Bruner (1915 –) proposed that learning is an active process in which the learner constructs new ideas or concepts based on his current or past knowledge (Figure 16). Bruner believes that constructivist learners are participatory learners; they are actively engaged in the learning process. Constructivism emphasizes an integrated curriculum where students learn a subject in various ways or through many different activities.

Technology offers many strategies for the constructivist learning environment. When using the constructivist approach, students may complete a variety of activities while learning about a topic. For example, if students are studying endangered species, they may research this topic by using books, videos, and other digital media in the media center, as well as informational Web sites.

Web Info

For more information about Jerome Bruner, visit the Computer Concepts CourseMate Web site at *www.cengagebrain.com*, navigate to the Chapter 5 Web Info resource for this book, and then click Bruner.

Figure 16 Jerome Bruner's constructivist theory stresses that teachers should actively engage their students in their own learning.

They can then use a tablet to write up their findings in a word-processing document, study vocabulary words with electronic flash cards, create a drawing about endangered species in a paint program, create a spreadsheet to graph population changes over time, build a model with clay, and even learn songs about saving endangered animals or species.

Bruner's constructivist theory provides a framework for instruction based on the study of cognition. The theoretical concept of **cognition** suggests that an individual progresses through different intellectual stages. In constructivist theory, the learner selects and changes information to understand and make decisions, relying on higher-order thinking skills to solve a problem. An individual creates in her mind mental models that provide meaning and association to experiences that allow the individual to go beyond the given information. Bruner felt the teacher's role should be to encourage students through exploration and inquiry; in other words, learning should be discovery (Figure 17).

As far as instruction is concerned, teachers should try to encourage students to discover concepts by themselves. Teachers should engage students by providing activities that guide students and create opportunities for discussion or for using the Socratic method of learning. The **Socratic method** is when students learn how to analyze problems, to think critically about their own point of view and the opinions of others, as well as to articulate and defend their position. This method assists students in solving problems through questioning and answering techniques, which engages them in discussion. The task of the teacher is to take the materials to be learned and translate the information into a form appropriate for the learners' current level of understanding. Bruner felt that the curriculum should be organized in a spiral manner so that students continually build upon what they already have learned; this approach is called the **spiral curriculum**.

Lev Vygotsky

Lev Vygotsky (1896 – 1934), a Russian educational psychologist, also was interested in children's cognitive development (Figure 18 on the next page). He developed what is known as **social cognition**. Although his ideas overlap in many ways with the traditional constructivists' point of view, Vygotsky believed that learning was influenced significantly by social development. He theorized that learning took place within the

Figure 17 Many schools, such as Crossroads School in Santa Monica, California, believe students should discover their own learning paths through interactive learning in areas such as intuition, imagination, artistic creativity, and physical expression.

Web Info

For more information about Lev Vygotsky, visit the Computer Concepts CourseMate Web site at *www. cengagebrain.com*, navigate to the Chapter 5 Web Info resource for this book, and then click Vygotsky.

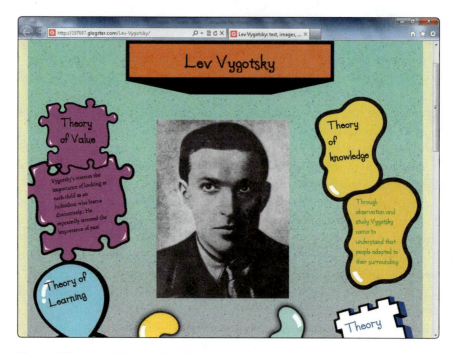

Figure 18 Using Glogster (a Web 2.0 social development tool), students can create a social development project about theorists like Lev Vygotsky, a Russian psychologist who believed that learning is influenced significantly by social development.

context of a child's social development and culture. For instance, when children vocalize, they learn that sounds have meanings and sounds become language. They learn that spoken language becomes the inner language that children use to think or develop cognitively. They also learn that gestures have meaning and are used to communicate and interact with others.

As stated earlier, Piaget believed children progressed through different stages of cognitive development and that achieving higher levels of thinking was not accomplished easily. Lev Vygotsky believed that a child's social environment could positively or negatively affect the child's cognitive development. Vygotsky proposed that children have a **zone of proximal development**, which is the difference between the problem-solving ability that a child has learned and the potential that the child can achieve from collaboration with a more advanced peer or expert, such as a teacher.

If some form of expertise challenges a child, then greater cognitive development can occur. Vygotsky theorized that if a 9-year-old child worked on a problem with an adult or another child who was advanced, the 9-year-old would be

able to learn the concept or ideas that were more complex than the 9-year-old could understand on his own; this is known as **collaborative learning**. With practice, the child then would be able to apply the new cognitive skills to other situations. Vygotsky felt students should work collaboratively to share their different perspectives with each other; then they could negotiate a solution and come to a much deeper understanding of a problem or tasks (Figure 19).

Figure 19 Vygotsky believed students should work collaboratively to share their different perspectives with each other. Here, students use mobile devices to work together to solve math problems.

Furthermore, Vygotsky proposed that teachers should discover the level of each child's cognitive/social development, and build or construct their learning experiences from that point. He referred to this process as **scaffolding**. In education, a scaffold is the altering of the **schemata**, which is an organized way of creating or providing a cognitive mental framework for understanding and remembering information. As teachers and other students provide information and different perspectives for each other, these sources can become a scaffold, a temporary source of knowledge. Then students assimilate this knowledge and build their own, thus removing the need for a scaffold.

Building on constructivist theory and Vygotsky's scaffolding, the Cognition and Technology Group at Vanderbilt (CTGV) developed **anchored instruction**. Anchored instruction is a model for technology-based learning and is a form of instruction where the student already has learned concepts and information, which form a basis for other information to connect to and build upon, and which is called the **anchor**. The CTGV wanted to create complex, realistic problems that students could explore and then develop potential solutions for those problems based on their exploration. When challenged with a problem, anchored instruction motivates students to build new ideas and anchor them to what they already have learned.

John Dewey

John Dewey (1859 – 1952) has influenced American education significantly (Figure 20). He was an educational psychologist, philosopher, and political activist who was an advocate for child-centered instruction. He believed that learning should engage and expand the experiences of the learners. He encouraged educators to reflect on their strategies and create activities that combine concrete and practical relevance to students' lives.

Like Vygotsky, Dewey believed that education was a social process. He viewed school as a community that represented a larger picture. In 1896, Dewey began the University Elementary School, or Laboratory School. Many educators called this school the Dewey School. The school prospered and earned national attention. Dewey felt that school should be viewed as an extension of society and students should play an active role in it, working cooperatively with each other. Dewey viewed learning as student-directed with a teacher serving as a guide for resources.

Web Info

For more information about John Dewey, visit the Computer Concepts CourseMate Web site at *www. cengagebrain.com*, navigate to the Chapter 5 Web Info resource for this book, and then click Dewey.

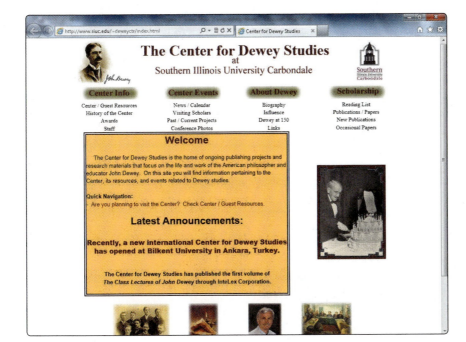

Figure 20 John Dewey, an educational psychologist and philosopher, believed that learning should engage and expand the experiences of the learners.

He believed students learn by doing and should be allowed to construct, create, and actively inquire. Dewey theorized that this type of learning truly prepared students to function well in society.

Dewey was part of a movement in the early 1900s that was called **progressive education**. Progressive education focused on educating the whole child, physically, mentally, and socially, and not on just the dispensation of facts and information. John Dewey's name also has been linked to other early movements, such as **pragmatism**. Pragmatists believed that the truth of a theory could be determined only if a theory worked. In other words, theory is valuable only for its practical application.

Dewey founded several schools in addition to his Laboratory School. He advocated educational reform, pursued philosophy, and supported many political issues, such as women's suffrage. Through his observations, he proposed that education begins with experience. He has been called, by some, the Father of American Education. His influence can be seen in American classrooms today — where children explore the curriculum, conduct science experiments, use manipulatives for math, and search the Internet for information.

Connecting with Today's Kids Through Game-Based Learning

This special feature has presented some, but not all, of the educational theories and theorists — helping you develop a foundation and understanding of the principles of teaching and learning. As we have stated throughout this

textbook, there is a new generation of learners — a digital generation.

Video games have been the center of considerable controversy and discussion in recent years. Many believe that the excessive use of video games has led to a general decline in the academic achievement by today's digital generation, especially those who are gamers. In some ways, they are correct. Peter Moore suggests that some digital students are prone to powering down at school to conserve energy — energy they will need for after-school gaming activities in which the players are called upon to react and interact in a highly developed and fast-paced virtual world. Why are students willing to spend hours in front of a computer screen or using a tablet computer interacting with a game that requires using search and problem-based learning techniques to wind their way through the various encounters, but these same students are not interested in using those same skills in a more traditional learning environment? Does presentation matter? Does content matter? Several studies have reported a link between supposed antisocial behaviors and violent games; however, there have not been any study results that can confirm cause and effect.

Further, stating or implying that playing games, regardless of their aggressiveness, actually promotes antisocial behaviors, has not been shown to be true. In fact, James Gee has identified 36 learning principles that can be found in all successful video games, regardless of content. The meta-learning principles are built into the makeup of video games and are supported by current research on human learning and cognition. Figure 21 lists six of these principles.

Web Info

For more information about game-based learning, visit the Computer Concepts CourseMate Web site at *www.cengagebrain.com*, navigate to the Chapter 5 Web Info resource for this book, and then click Game-Based Learning.

Learning Principles Found in Successful Video Games
1. How players form an identity to buy into the content
2. How players learn to connect different symbol systems (words, symbols, artifacts)
3. How players choose between various methods to solve a problem
4. How players identify, filter, and utilize different nonverbal cues
5. How players leverage their knowledge to reapply solutions learned from one situation to newly discovered ones
6. How players identify and develop a sense for story

Figure 21 This table lists just a few of the learning principles that James Gee suggests are based on human learning and cognitive science.

Games have become an important social trend. Many educators also believe that games have become an important teaching tool because they can provide a compelling context by the way they invoke interactive, engaging, and immersive activities (Figure 22). The fact is, however, that games have yet to effectively and continuously help classroom teachers teach subject-specific content. Yes, there have been successes in some content areas, such as science and history, but there is still room for growth in the gaming industry as it relates to education.

Simulation games have been successful in the military, business, and industry. For example, flight simulators have been very successful in increasing cost-efficient ways of teaching skills to pilots. Educators like James Gee suggest that while most games teach something, most of the positive outcomes of games used in instructional settings center on motivation, social skill-building, simulations, and changing attitudes, rather than on content-related skills. These outcomes are hard to measure and so this has caused considerable confusion among game evaluators. Evaluators often confuse the popularity of games, which is based on gameplay and interactivity (which does foster positive, intrinsic, and social learning) with their educational value. Just because a game is fun to play does not mean it teaches subject-specific content or meets the

curriculum standards that all students must meet each year to progress.

Several outside factors contribute to the lack of success in integrating games into the curriculum. First, many teachers feel pressure to use them despite their lack of content because their students play games so much and they receive funding to have them in their schools. Because many teachers do not play games regularly, they do not understand games and how games became so successful in the market place. Game developers also contribute to this situation because many times they are pressured to add educational content as an afterthought; and as a result, the game often does not follow good educational practices.

It is important to know what makes games successful, both commercially and as instructional aides. Certainly, one might infer that process learning or scaffolding takes place in most commercially successful games as players move from one level to another by recalling rules, game mechanics, and processes from previous levels. A few games promote these processes to some extent to ensure they enforce higher-order learning or critical problem solving skills. Hints (or cheats, which is what they are referred to by the game industry and which is a problem term in education) are provided and can be a great form of feedback for the players/learners, but few of them are written clearly enough to ensure that they effectively resemble feedback needed in lesson situations.

So, as a teacher, how do you go about deciding whether to use a game in your classroom? How do you evaluate the game's content and play process so you can be assured that your students actually are learning what you intend them to be learning? One way is to use a rubric to evaluate the education value of a game.

Many feel educational games have the potential to revolutionize classroom instruction, so three university researchers (Gunter, Kenny, & Vick) created an evaluation rubric based upon their RETAIN (Relevance, Embedding, Transfer, Adaptation, Immersion, Naturalization) model

Figure 22 Student learning comes alive when teachers integrate games and other apps on tablet computers into their classroom curriculum.

Web Info

To learn more about evaluating games, visit the Computer Concepts CourseMate Web site at *www. cengagebrain.com*, navigate to the Chapter 5 Web Info resource for this book, and then click Evaluating Games.

that is shown in Figure 23. The RETAIN rubric correlates to instructional methods and learning theories that are closely aligned with generally accepted game design principles and theories, including Keller's ARCS Model and Gagne's Events of Instruction. The rubric incorporates Bloom's hierarchical structure for knowledge acquisition and Piaget's ideas on schema.

Recently, educators have been looking into games and research has been published that outlines some of the more important and credible aspects of games — those aspects that make games stand out academically. Essentially, it boils down to this: games need to be engrained and based on educational best practices or learning theories.

	Level 0	Level 1	Level 2	Level 3
Relevance	*Limitations*	*Limitations/Features*	*In addition to overcoming limitations and/or adding to Level 1 features, the following are also present:*	*In addition to overcoming limitations and/or adding to Level 1 & 2 features, the following are also present:*
	The story/fantasy creates little stimulus for learning and is in a format that is of little interest to the players/learners nor does it utilize advanced organizers.	The story/fantasy is age/content appropriate or it has a limited educational focus and little a progression.	Specific didactic content is targeted and learning objectives are clearly defined.	Is relevant to players'/learners' lives (real or imagined) and/or the world around them using characters and themes familiar to them.
	The players/learners do not know the state of the game or the required learning content based on the choices presented.	The pedagogic elements are somewhat defined but occasionally players/learners are allowed by the embedded fantasy to become engaged in inappropriate content or contexts.	Creates interest in what is to be learned and a natural stimulus and desire to learn more.	Matches the players/learners to their appropriate developmental level by providing adequate cognitive challenges.
Embedding	*Limitations*	*Limitations/Features*	*In addition to overcoming limitations and/or adding to Level 1 features, the following are also present:*	*In addition to overcoming limitations and/or adding to Level 1 & 2 features, the following are also present:*
	The "teachable" moments disrupt the players'/learners' gameplay, that is, flow of the game.	Didactic elements are present but are not cohesively integrated — one or the other is added as an afterthought to the first.	Allows for extended experiences with problems and contexts specific to the curriculum.	Involves the players/learners both mentally and emotionally in such a way that they are conditioned to accept change and invest in the belief.
	Has no interactive focus/hook either on the emotional, psychological, physical, or intellectual level.	Content to be learned is exogenous to the fantasy context of the game.	Intellectual challenges are presented to players/learners of sufficient level to keep them interested in completing the game.	Educational content is fully endogenous to the fantasy context.
Transfer	*Limitations*	*Limitations/Features*	*In addition to overcoming limitations and/or adding to Level 1 features, the following are also present:*	*In addition to overcoming limitations and/or adding to Level 1 & 2 features, the following are also present:*
	Offers no anchored or scaffolded levels of challenge, no evidence of using integrated content from previous levels, or little challenges at an increasing level of difficulty.	Offers levels of challenge that emphasize similar lines of thought and problem analysis to be applied to other implied contexts.	Players/learners are able to progress through the levels easily. Active problem solving is required to move to the next level.	Includes authentic real life experiences that reward meaningful "post-event" knowledge acquisition.
	Process knowledge is not mapped to targeted academic content.	Contains 3D cues and interactive animation that facilitate the transfer of knowledge during pedagogic events.	Players/learners can progress through instructional elements that are introduced in a hierarchical manner so that knowledge gained during gameplay can be transferred to other situations.	Contains "after action reviews" that offers players/learners an opportunity to teach other players/learners what they have learned (conceptual or actual).

Figure 23 A comprehensive rubric you can use to evaluate the educational value of games.

	Level 0	Level 1	Level 2	Level 3
Adaptation	*Limitations* Fails to involve the players/learners in an interactive context. Information is not structured in a way that can be at least partially grasped by the learner. Does not sequence the material that is to be learned.	*Limitations/Features* Builds upon the players'/learners' existing cognitive structures. New content is sequenced based on the principle of cognitive dissonance — as a result players/learners need to interpret events in order to determine what about the new content contradicts what they already know.	*In addition to overcoming limitations and/or adding to Level 1 features, the following are also present:* Instruction is designed to encourage the players/learners to go beyond the given information and discover new concepts for themselves. Content sequenced in such a way as to require players/learners to identify old schema and transfer it to new ways of thinking.	*In addition to overcoming limitations and/or adding to Level 1 & 2 features, the following are also present:* Makes learning an active, participatory process in which the players/learners construct new ideas based upon their prior knowledge. Presents information that focuses on external or internal characteristics that enable the learner to associate new information with previous learning.
Immersion	*Limitations* Provides no progressive, formative feedback during each unit of gameplay. Presents little or no opportunity for reciprocal action and active participation for players/learners.	*Limitations/Features* Elements of play are not directly involved with the didactic focus, but they do not impede or compete with pedagogic elements. Presents some opportunity for reciprocal action in a defined context, that is, a context that is meaningful, repeatable, and interactive, but players/learners do not feel fully interactive in the learning.	*In addition to overcoming limitations and/or adding to Level 1 features, the following are also present:* Requires the players/learners to be involved cognitively, physically, psychologically, and emotionally in the game content. The use of mutual modeling creates a shared responsibility for learning among the participants.	*In addition to overcoming limitations and/or adding to Level 1 & 2 features, the following are also present:* Presents opportunity for reciprocal action and active participation for players/learners. Presents both the environment and the opportunity for belief creation.
Naturalization	*Limitations* Presents little opportunity for the mastery of facts or a particular skill. Target content/skills are rarely revisited. Little opportunity is given to build upon previous knowledge and/or skills in a logical and sequential manner.	*Limitations/Features* Replay is encouraged to assist in retention and to remediate shortcomings. Improves the speed of cognitive response, automaticity, and/or visual processing.	*In addition to overcoming limitations and/or adding to Level 1 features, the following are also present:* Encourages the synthesis of several elements and an understanding that once one skill is learned it leads to the easier acquisition of later elements. Requires the players/learners to make judgments about ideas and materials.	*In addition to overcoming limitations and/or adding to Level 1 & 2 features, the following are also present:* Causes players/learners to be aware of the content in such a way that they become efficient users of that knowledge. Causes the players/learners to spontaneously utilize knowledge habitually and consistently.

Figure 23 A comprehensive rubric you can use to evaluate the educational value of games.

One of the games in the Carmen Sandiego series, *Where in the World is Carmen Sandiego?*, is a game intended to teach geography. The game was originally created by Broderbund Software in the late 1980s with many updates since. The goal of the game is to track and arrest Carmen and her villains, who travel around the world. The game was not designed originally for the classroom, but when it was adopted by so many schools, the creators broadened its appeal by adding other academic content, such as math and science. The latest releases have returned to its original geographical and historical focus. Figure 24 is an example of how to evaluate the value of games, such as those in the Carmen Sandiego series, using the RETAIN rubric in Figure 23 on pages 274 and 275.

Question	Explanation	Sample Evaluation
Is the game relevant?	In addition to presenting learning materials in a way that is relevant to your students, their needs, and their learning styles, the instructional units in the game should be relevant to one another and set in context with previously learned materials, using introductory materials that contain advanced organizers.	All games in the Carmen Sandiego series have mechanics that make them relevant to the learner. For example, the games' clues build on one another providing scaffolding content as players' progress through the games. Each level builds on previous deductions, which students use as they complete the game. A few places where relevance could be improved include the introduction to each geographic region, which is brief, and the game development, which does little to build on prior content knowledge. At the beginning of play there are no building blocks for the player to learn how to track geographic locations.
Is the content embedded into the story/fantasy?	Research has shown that the closer the learning is tied to the fantasy context the better the learning. The intent is to integrate the educational content in such a way as to make it intrinsic to the fantasy context of the game so that learning and gameplay function together seamlessly.	Each game in the Carmen Sandiego series has a compelling story line that includes geography content and vocabulary placed strategically through the story line. Throughout the game, players are attempting to track down Carmen Sandiego. Students must use the clues they gather to assess where to go next in the game. The geography content is embedded in each story in the Carmen Sandiego series.
Does knowledge transfer?	The game should cause a circumstance in which the targeted knowledge is transferred to similar or new and unique situations so players/learners are able to assimilate and accommodate it. The idea of transfer is well known in education circles as critical to higher-order learning.	Content, especially geography content students learn as they play the games, can be transferred, but the knowledge gained may not result in long term retention. Why? A player collects clues in an area, which are used for figuring out the identity of the thief being tracked and for deciding where to go next. Once those decisions are made, the player has to focus on using the next set of clues to find a new location. Students often forget the previous knowledge gained as they focus on the new content and progressing through the game.
Does the game provide for extended practice?	Extended practice creates an opportunity for what educators call automaticity or spontaneous knowledge. The game needs to be analyzed to assess whether students are able to use what they have learned habitually and whether they are able to consistently monitor their progress without thinking about it and having to devote significant mental resources to the new knowledge.	During the game, players seek out clues and new information in order to track down the thief. In the Carmen Sandiego series, clues build on an identity and solving a crime. The only way to gain more knowledge about a particular geographic area is to play the game again and see if that geographic area is part of the journey. If the thief does not go to that same geographic area, then the student will not encounter background information about that area. This will impact how much a student can learn about a particular geographic area while playing the game.

Figure 24 This figure provides an example of how to evaluate a game using components of the RETAIN rubric.

When using the questions and explanations in Figure 24 to evaluate the Carmen Sandiego series, you can see that the games do not embed content well. The series does permit considerable opportunity for players/learners to become immersed in the background and environment of each game. It also provides good levels of naturalization as well because it allows for repetitive play through its varied content and fantasy context. The second and following times one plays a game in the series, the situations in the game vary greatly, which reduces the boredom often found in games that encourage repetitive practice. Games that do not vary the content often cause the player/learner to lose interest.

There are no manuals to teach players how to play the games. Players do not seem to need them or want them. The construct of the games needs to be such that the process is self-revealing. As these learning principles are implied in the construct of the games, they actually provide better opportunities to teach things to students than most of what is being used to develop lesson activities in today's classroom — classrooms being occupied by digital, game-playing students. Perhaps educators should take a look at how games are constructed and utilize many of these same principles in their own school's curriculum. The results just may be surprising for educators and education. What we are looking for are games that not only stimulate the learner but also teach content in a meaningful way — making the learning and the experience fun and successful!

Putting Theory into Practice

The next two Classroom in Action sections explore how teachers utilize learning theories in their classrooms to facilitate learning and achieve curriculum standards, while at the same time find ways to reach today's digital students. The first story, *Teaching Kids to Think – The Thinking Ladder*, shows how an elementary teacher integrates technology and Bloom's Taxonomy to help her students develop higher-order thinking skills. The second, *Digital Kids – The Sam Schugg Story*, shows how the integration of technology with learning theory can inspire today's digital generation.

The Classroom in Action
Teaching Kids to Think — The Thinking Ladder

This section explores how one teacher puts learning theories into action. Nirsa Gautier, a fourth-grade teacher, was busy working on a simple spelling rule that her class was having difficulty remembering. Suddenly, she thought of a great idea using Bloom's Taxonomy that might enhance her lesson and assist her students' learning.

Mrs. Gautier stopped her spelling lesson and drew a ladder on the whiteboard (Figure 25). She listed the six thinking levels on the ladder and then explained each level in simple terms. She told her students that for them to be successful thinkers, they needed to progress to each level. The new class goal was to get to the highest level!

Mrs. Gautier then went back to the spelling lesson. She asked her students to identify what thinking level they were operating at on the thinking ladder. Some of the students were able to tell her immediately that they were at the Knowledge level. She explained that they could not move to higher levels of thinking

Figure 25 Mrs. Gautier's thinking ladder is based on Bloom's Taxonomy.

success without mastering this basic knowledge. Now she had their attention! The class all agreed they had to remember the rule to move up the ladder.

Mrs. Gautier asked her students to work in groups collaboratively for five minutes to help each other remember the rule. She knew this was a great constructivist learning strategy. After five minutes, she randomly called on students to see if their group strategy had worked. To her amazement, every student she called on knew the rule! She congratulated the class on a job well done and then challenged them to move up to the next level of the thinking ladder.

To encourage higher-order thinking skills, Mrs. Gautier had her students develop questions based on a reading selection. The students responded in their journals and wrote three questions for the selection. Each question had to come from a different thinking level. She found that by asking students to write or construct their own thinking questions from different levels, they first must be able to think on that level. She then would have a student ask a question, another student answer the question, and a third student identify the thinking level. Mrs. Gautier found that often students created better thinking questions than she did! In addition, many of the students were thrilled to know that they were able to answer questions that required higher-order thinking skills. They liked the challenge.

After these experiences, Mrs. Gautier created a large thinking ladder using a word processing program and placed it in the center of the classroom for her students to view. She wanted to make sure that she was integrating the thinking-ladder learning strategy into every class lesson. Mrs. Gautier printed the thinking levels on cardstock, glued magnets on the back, and placed each thinking level on a rung of the ladder. This gave the students colorful visual cues as they moved along the thinking continuum to a higher thinking level. Mrs. Gautier also created a PowerPoint presentation using pictures that illustrated how the students move up the thinking ladder to thinking success (Figure 26). In the presentation, she explained in more detail each

Figure 26 Mrs. Gautier uses PowerPoint to teach her students how to use higher-order thinking skills to move up the thinking ladder.

thinking level and how to apply it when the students read, solve problems, and answer questions. Mrs. Gautier had her students discuss which questions were more difficult to answer. The students began to realize that higher-order thinking involves more time and thought. Consequently, Mrs. Gautier also realized that she must give her students more time to think before answering questions. She decided to call this *think time*.

Mrs. Gautier works her thinking ladder into every subject. When the students create multimedia research projects, she makes sure to include an aspect of each thinking level in the assessment rubric used for evaluation. This guides the students to find information, analyze and evaluate what they read, and then apply it in a meaningful way. After introducing Bloom's Taxonomy into the class, Mrs. Gautier noticed a real excitement as students began to strive to move up the ladder of thinking success.

Teaching students thinking skills using Bloom's Taxonomy revolutionized the way Mrs. Gautier teaches and the way her students learn. Her students became more focused because not only were they thinking, but they were consciously developing the thinking process! They became more confident, taking more responsibility for their learning, and realizing that they must do the thinking to learn.

The Classroom in Action
Digital Kids — The Sam Schugg Story

Sam Schugg is your typical high school kid. He does not like going to high school and when he is there he does not pay attention for very long. It is almost like he is powering down in most of his classes; however, put him in front of a computer and he will pay attention for hours. He shines in his technology class in spite of the fact that he is very reserved and does not speak much. He goes to English class and cannot relate. He wants to be a game developer when he grows up and he feels that reading and writing will not be very important for him to enter that profession. He does okay in math and science but, once again, he does not see their relevance to his plans for the future. As a result, he struggles with his grades in all subjects except for his technology class. What makes matters worse is that all attempts to help remediate his weaknesses have yielded little results because previous efforts mostly centered on requiring him to read more books, to solve more word problems, and/or to conduct more experiments.

Things are about to change. His technology teacher, Bob Phelan, was just completing his studies in instructional design and felt that perhaps a new direction was needed. Banking on Sam's fondness for computers and gaming, Mr. Phelan decided to try a new way to reach Sam and many other students just like him in his technology class (Figure 27).

Figure 27 One technique to motivate today's students to read and write is for teachers to create lessons that integrate digital media.

Mr. Phelan met with Sam's English teacher, Rita Rivera, to discuss his plan. When discussing Sam's situation, Ms. Rivera said that Sam reacted like many of her students when she assigned books to be read, they always wanted to know why they had to read and not simply be allowed to watch the movie! This was frustrating to Ms. Rivera. Mr. Phelan suggested that the students produce a movie about a book. Mr. Phelan had heard of a project called Digital Booktalk. Not only would this activity utilize the students' strengths but it also could be based on many of the learning theories and ideas that Mr. Phelan wanted to put into practice. Mr. Phelan also knew that all students enjoyed stories and if he based the lessons on the premise of bringing out the concept of storytelling, this would be motivating to the students. They decided to combine their classes and teach together. Ms. Rivera could teach about storytelling and Mr. Phelan would teach them digital video editing. Mr. Phelan's students could mentor on the technical aspects of the project and learn about storytelling from the English teacher and her students.

First, they knew that most of their students were visual learners. Both teachers agreed that, even though technology would be the entry point, the activity had to result in making students better readers and writers. After the videos were created, students would write about their experiences and include related vocabulary words. The idea seemed simple — use Robert Doman's ideas about teaching to students' strengths and then remediate the weaknesses. Student learning would be reinforced because they would be working with both images and texts, which was supported by Paivio's ideas about dual coding and Craik and Lockhart's and Bloom's ideas about levels of processing.

Producing their own videos fits the constructivists' ideas about students creating their own meaning while, at the same time, students would be encouraged to retain information because they would be learning by doing and that would also ensure deeper processing of their skills. The instructional plan also follows Gagne's building-block principles.

Web Info

For more information on digital storytelling, visit the Computer Concepts CourseMate Web site at *www.cengagebrain.com*, navigate to the Chapter 5 Web Info resource for this book, and then click Digital Storytelling.

Web Info

For more information on creating movie trailers, visit the Computer Concepts CourseMate Web site at *www.cengagebrain.com*, navigate to the Chapter 5 Web Info resource for this book, and then click Digital Booktalk.

The Digital Booktalk curriculum stated that everyone in the class would read the same book. They would start with the basic premise of the story, then learn text-to-screen techniques of making movies, and move into visual storytelling techniques using a camera and/or photos and a video editor. Students would discuss how to read the selected book as if they were going to make a movie out of it. The two teachers realized that making a full length movie would result in a very large project so they looked at a curriculum that has students create a video trailer about the book. **Video trailers** are short, 2–3 minute summaries of the book (similar to the movie previews shown for upcoming attractions in movie theaters). Using summarizing principles similar to what is done for book talks, the two teachers helped the students come up with their concepts. After the video trailers were produced, the teachers showed the projects, providing students the opportunity to see how others view the content of the same books. The other students would review and evaluate each other's video trailers using a rubric the teachers designed that focused on content. When they were done, students were asked to write the essence of their video trailer in narrative style using vocabulary words that the teachers required.

When the projects were presented, Sam Schugg's project was the best in the class. The students evaluated his project with great feedback and he scored high on the rubric. He did not even complain during the writing portion of the assignment and on reflection said, "I was so surprised that I could do so well on this. I enjoyed this assignment!" The teachers could tell Sam had pride in his work.

This activity was successful because it was founded on sound instructional practices that incorporated many of the learning theories described earlier in this special feature. Students were motivated to read because they were focused on doing something with the information they obtained from the book. Now, instead of the reading being a passive activity, students are reading for a purpose and are involving themselves in the outcomes using a communication medium they are attracted to and one that is already a large part of their digital lives.

Summary of Learning Theories and Educational Research

Learning is a complex task. Understanding how students learn is an internal process that is difficult to observe. Educators can provide instruction and information, and assess how much information has been retained. Educational research and learning theories are important because they help educators to understand how students learn. From learning theories and research, teachers can improve their instruction and the way they provide information to learners, and they can improve teaching and learning environments.

Integrating technology into teaching is a very powerful way to weave these learning theories throughout the curriculum. Digital media technology appeals to a variety of learning styles and learning intelligences (Gardner). Students are more actively engaged in their learning when teachers effectively integrate technology (Bruner). Technology is effective with group projects or when students work in teams (Vygotsky and Dewey), and when students are engaged in problem-solving activities requiring higher-order thinking skills that allow students to build new ideas from their current knowledge base (Bloom). Teachers even have used computer time effectively as part of a behavior management system (Pavlov and Skinner).

Learners are dynamic and no two will be the same. Theorists help teachers understand how to adapt instruction, information, and the environment for different learners. So, much is to be gained by understanding learning theories and what each theorist has contributed. Their ideas can help educators piece together the complex task of teaching all learners. Integrating learning theories and technology into classroom instructional strategies can make a difference in student motivation and also can increase student achievement in your classroom!

For information on the references used in the creation of this special feature, see the References section; for more information about the learning theories presented in this special feature, access this special feature's Web Info segments.

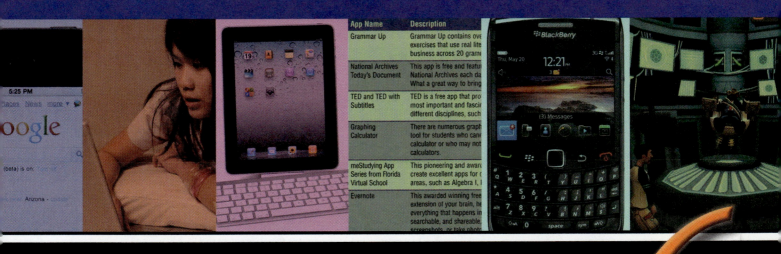

The Changing Face of Education — Teaching Online

6

Objectives

After completing this chapter, you will be able to do the following:
[ISTE NETS-T Standards 1 a-d; 2 a-d; 3 a-d; 4 b-d; 5 a, c-d]

- Describe online learning and virtual environments

- Describe how online and mobile technologies are changing the ways we teach and learn

- Explain the differences between 100 percent online and blended learning

- Explain the skills and strategies you need to know as an online teacher

- List characteristics of a virtual school

- Explain how apps, Web pages, blogs, wikis, and screencasts can be used as tools to enhance teaching and learning

- Distinguish instructional strategies for differentiated online learning experiences

- Identify online assessment or eAssessment techniques

Throughout this textbook, you have learned about ways to integrate technology into your curriculum, as well as many different techniques to engage students in a traditional classroom. This chapter focuses on the changes in teaching and learning that are taking place in all areas of education. This chapter introduces you to the world of online learning and provides you with strategies to begin creating your own online learning content and activities. The late 1990s saw a movement toward online courses in higher education and a few forward thinking virtual high schools. Throughout the first decade of this century, the availability of online courses in higher education exploded; as a result, most states and many school districts started K-12 virtual school programs. During this period, extensive and informative research was conducted on many aspects of online learning culminating in thousands of published articles and books.

Today, this movement toward online learning is revolutionizing education, not just at the college level but at all levels. In fact, online education has become an important long-term strategy for many schools and institutions of higher learning. As technology continues to progress and new mobile tools become more and more readily available, you will see a steady movement in K-12 toward embracing some form of online learning. To have quality online courses and programs, colleges of education and school districts must make sure that teachers have the knowledge and skills to teach online. This chapter provides you with the basic terminology, understanding, and skills to assist you in establishing instructional strategies for the changing face of education, which involves eLearning.

Tipping Point — A Moment in History

For centuries, the PK-12 educational community has used the time-tested face-to-face (F2F) instructional model for teaching students. In a F2F classroom environment, an experienced educator is the teacher and students are grouped by grade levels or by content area. In more recent years, the traditional F2F teaching model is being transformed as educators develop new strategies to create innovative opportunities to educate students along any path, at any time, at any pace, and from any place.

The 21st century has seen many advances in instructional technologies. More importantly, Web 2.0 and communications tools have brought a renewed interest in changing the dynamics of instruction by creating new paths for change and growth. As a result, educational practices are at a **Tipping Point**, which is defined by Malcolm Gladwell as "the levels at which the momentum for change becomes unstoppable." These new educational technologies are spreading rapidly as teachers become more comfortable with the tools that their students already embrace.

Students who have grown up with ubiquitous technology at their fingertips have acquired a certain comfort-level with technology integrated into everyday tasks. Technologies such as DVDs, iPads, iPods, tablets, flash drives, GPS devices, and smartphones, as well as an array of apps, Web 2.0 social networking tools, and games (Figure 6-1) have become a mainstay in our everyday lives, and now, in K-12 education, especially distance education. But what is distance education and why are these tools so important to its success?

Figure 6-1 iPhones and other smartphones, iPads and other tablet computers, apps, and Web 2.0 tools have become mainstream in K-12 education.

Distance Education

Distance education, also called **distance learning**, and **distributed learning**, is defined as the delivery of instruction from one location to another, which means the teaching takes place in one location and the learning takes place at another location. Distance education supports the notion that students could learn with alternative methods of delivery in a different location. The beginning of distance education dates back to the early 1700s. During most of the 18th, 19th, and 20th centuries, distance education was conducted primarily by mail (often called correspondence courses). Over the years, distance education has transformed and moved to different delivery methods. Perhaps the biggest changes in distance education occurred in the last few years of the 20th century and continue to happen as we move through the second decade of the 21st century.

Today, businesses, colleges and universities, K-12 schools, federal and state governments, and many types of organizations are utilizing online environments for classes, courses, training, and all types of professional development. Worldwide, tens of billions of dollars are spent annually on distance education. The distance education courses and programs offered by these institutions are usually in the form of Web-based or Web-enhanced courses. A **Web-based course**, often called an **online course** or **eLearning course** (Figure 6-2), is a course delivered via the Web, rather than in a traditional classroom or via the mail. Many college and university professors Web-enhance their classes. As a result, students have online access to supplemental course information.

DELIVERY OF DISTANCE EDUCATION

As already stated, most distance education is conducted over the Internet, usually, via the Web. Online education may be synchronous, asynchronous, instructor-led, self-paced, or a combination of all of these. **Synchronous** is a direct form of communication, in which communication happens in real time where parties involved are present at the same time, such as a phone call or a face-to-face conversation. Examples of online synchronous activities include live Web conferencing, Web chat, and instant message. **Asynchronous** is when communications occur at different times, and it does not require that parties be present at the same time. Examples of online asynchronous activities include e-mail, discussion posts, or text messaging. **Instructor-led** refers to courses in which the instruction is directed by an instructor teaching the class online, whereas **self-paced** refers to courses in which the learner goes through the content at his or her own pace.

In addition to the previously stated characteristics, delivery of distance learning courses can take on different forms, such as

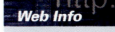
Web Info

For more information about distance education, visit the Computer Concepts CourseMate Web site at *www.cengagebrain.com*, navigate to the Chapter 6 Web Info resource for this book, and then click Distance Education.

Figure 6-2 Shown is an example of an online undergraduate technology integration course, *Technology for Educators*, at the University of Central Florida (UCF).

Web-based training, Webinars, online tutorials, and online workshops. **Web-based training (WBT)** is one approach to distance education that uses the technologies of the Internet and the World Wide Web. Because it is delivered via the Web, WBT has the advantage of being able to offer up-to-date content on any type of computer platform. As a result, Web-based training already has replaced many traditional computer-based instruction (CBI) applications that use stand-alone traditional computers. Web-based training is morphing into tablet- and app-based training. The potential of these new tablet- and app-based technologies, along with new and emerging tools, are covered in detail in the special feature that follows this chapter, *A World without Wires — Tablets, Apps, and More.*

A major component of Web-based training is the tutorial. As you'll recall from Chapter 3, a tutorial provides step-by-step instructions on a specific topic. Today, anyone with access to the Web can take advantage of tens of thousands of online tutorials. Training tutorials cover a range of topics, ranging from how to change a flat tire to how to use Microsoft Office (Figure 6-3). Many of these tutorials are free; others are part of a comprehensive Web-based training course. When that is the case, you may be asked to register

and pay a fee to take the complete Web-based training course.

One of the newer ways to obtain training via the Web any time and any place is through **Web conferencing**, which refers to a type of service that allows meeting events to be shared with individuals in different locations. During a Web conference, one person signs into a computer and identifies that computer as the host, and then others can sign in from remote locations to view the content on the host computer and listen to the presenter. Sometimes, a Web conference is live and individuals can participate as the event is in session; other times, there is a recorded copy of an event and individuals can view the conference at their convenience. If the Web conference is live there are technologies that allow information to be shared simultaneously, across geographically dispersed locations in real time. Web conferencing is often used for meetings, training events, lectures, or short presentations.

Most Web conferencing events require additional software to be downloaded and installed on your computer before you can participate in the event. This software is usually provided by the company providing the Web conferencing services. Most Web conferencing services also provide e-mail and online calendars so participants can receive notifications, help plan the event, and share information about it.

There are many names for Web conferencing: two popular terms are Webinar or Webcast. The term **Webinar** is short for **Web-based seminar**, which is a presentation, lecture, workshop or meeting that is transmitted over the Web. Some Webinars are mainly one-way communication, that is, from the speaker to the audience with limited audience interaction. This type of one-way Webinar broadcast is usually called a **Webcast**.

In order to make Webinars more collaborative, they may include polling or question and answer sessions in order to allow broader participation by the participants. In some cases, the presenter may speak over a standard telephone line while pointing out information being presented on screen, and the audience can respond over their telephones. There are some Web conferencing technologies on the market

Figure 6-3 Shown is an example of the multitude of training tutorials available on the Web.

Figure 6-4 Many states, school districts, and companies use professional development Webinars to train and inform administrators, teachers, and staff.

Web Info

For more information about upcoming education Webinars, visit the Computer Concepts CourseMate Web site at *www.cengagebrain.com*, navigate to the Chapter 6 Web Info resource for this book, and then click Upcoming Webinars.

that have incorporated the use of voice over Internet protocol (VoIP) audio technology in order to allow for a completely Web-based communication. When you use a conventional phone to participate in a Webinar, consider using a speaker phone or a headset for comfort and convenience while participating in the Webinar.

Some developers refer to a Webinar as an **online workshop**. There are thousands of Webinars available either for free and for a fee. For example, Webinars are offered by many different types of training and education organizations, businesses, and school districts. Webinars are used by many school districts for professional development (Figure 6-4 above).

IMPACT ON GOVERNMENT, BUSINESSES, AND ORGANIZATIONS

Over the past few years, the number of government agencies, businesses, and organizations using distance education has exploded. Today, all federal and state governments, most local governments, as well as many businesses and organizations in the United States, provide employees with some type of Web-based training in order to teach new skills or upgrade current skills. Why this unprecedented interest in distance education? Because the government, many businesses, and many organizations know they must invest a great deal of time and effort in training and updating their employees' skills. Currently, much of that training takes place online and provides employees with on-demand, any time, remote learning opportunities. Distance education, especially Web-based training, is a cost efficient and effective way to keep their employees up to date. Employers know that the benefits are endless if their employees are well trained and kept up to date with many evolving training needs.

IMPACT ON COLLEGES AND UNIVERSITIES

As discussed, the availability of Web-based courses has exploded in the past few years. Today, thousands of online classes are available in virtually all disciplines and millions of undergraduate and graduate students take online classes every term. Web-based courses offer many advantages for students who live far from a college or university campus, work full-time, or have scheduling conflicts. Web-based courses allow students to attend class from home or other locations at any time that fits their schedule. In addition to taking online

Figure 6-5 An example of the hundreds of distance learning opportunities available to students enrolled in colleges and universities nationwide.

Web Info

For more information about Walden University, visit the Computer Concepts CourseMate Web site at *www.cengagebrain. com*, navigate to the Chapter 6 Web Info resource for this book, and then click Walden University.

courses (see Figure 6-5 above), many colleges and universities now offer advanced degrees, including doctorate degrees, in which all required courses are offered online. Other colleges and universities offer advanced degrees in which the majority of required courses are offered online but with an **in-residence requirement,** which mean that students must spend a certain percentage of their time on a traditional campus.

A number of fully accredited universities no longer provide traditional courses; instead, 100 percent of their courses and degrees are provided online. For example, **Walden University** is one of the leading fully accredited 100 percent online universities in the world (Figure 6-6). Walden

Figure 6-6 Walden University is an example of a 100% online university that offers undergraduate, masters, and doctoral degrees in multiple disciplines.

University provides online courses and graduate degrees in education, psychology, health and human services, management, engineering, computer science, business administration, and many other curriculum areas.

IMPACT ON K-12 SCHOOLS

Most, if not all, states are now providing Web-based or online courses for their PreK-12 school students. At this educational level, the majority of Web-based courses are offered to help provide an alternative learning solution and instruction for homebound students. In some cases, Web-based courses also allow less-populated districts and schools in rural areas to share teachers and to provide access to courses they would not otherwise be able to offer their students. For example, by using the Web, these schools can offer specialized classes in French, Latin, calculus, and many other core and advanced subjects. By pooling resources and linking students from more than one school into a Web-based course, school districts can expand the number and type of classes they offer and at a reduced cost per student.

In addition to fully Web-based courses, many teachers are Web-enhancing their classes. Teachers **Web-enhance** their classes by creating tools such as class Web sites and curriculum resource pages. These Web-enhanced tools provide students with resources to enrich their learning experience. They also provide parents with access to tools to help their children, for example, a teacher-created Web site might provide links so parents can check on homework assignments, activities, student expectations, and more.

Many schools are looking into online solutions because research is reporting that online teaching has been found not only to improve teaching practices in both virtual and face-to-face settings but also to improve teacher and student relations. The majority of teachers felt that they had a more positive impact on their F2F teaching when they added online teaching components. This has also increased the interaction between teachers and their students. Teachers have reported that their interactions with students, parents, and colleagues were more often focused on teaching and learning in online courses than in the traditional setting. With more interaction, schools are seeing increased learning gains.

Another benefit of using the Web in the classroom is having students interact with subject area experts. For example, many scientists want to increase educational science opportunities for students in the hope that these experiences will inspire some students to become scientists. To help scientists provide these experiences, the Smithsonian Institution, for example, permits teachers and students to interact via the Web with scientists who work for the Smithsonian (Figure 6-7).

An emerging trend in the area of distance education and Web-enhanced learning is for school districts, individual schools, and teachers to app-enhance their online and F2F classes. This concept is covered later in this chapter and in the special feature that follows this chapter.

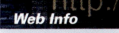

Web Info

For more information about the Ask an Expert Lecture series, visit the Computer Concepts CourseMate Web site at *www.cengagebrain.com*, navigate to the Chapter 6 Web Info resource for this book, and then click Ask an Expert.

Figure 6-7 Shown is the *Ask an Expert Lecture Series* provided by the Smithsonian Air and Space Museum.

IMPACT ON PROFESSIONAL DEVELOPMENT TRAINING

Until recently, in-service professional development training for teachers and administrators has remained basically unchanged for decades. Schools use professional development in order to improve teachers' instructional strategies, keep them current, and provide knowledge of content and standards. Traditional in-service training involves teachers being trained in classrooms or labs and normally is conducted before or after school, on weekends, during in-service days, or during the summer. Schools often have to provide substitutes when teachers are required to be out of the classroom in order to participate in extensive professional development training. Professional development should be targeted, ongoing, and embedded into specific content areas; however, the ultimate goal of teacher professional development is to improve student outcomes.

The traditional model of professional development training is undergoing a revolution — a Web-based or online revolution. Professional development training programs are being redefined in many school districts and state programs. States and school districts are adopting online training as a way to train their teachers in many areas, from technology, to English as a Second Language (ESL), to meeting recertification requirements, to a series of online courses leading to alternative certification. As a result of this professional development revolution, hundreds of thousands of K-12 teachers and administrators are involved in some type of online professional development training, and this is only the beginning. A number of school districts and most states have developed online portals for their teachers to enroll in professional development courses, access resources, and receive assistance (Figure 6-8).

Many companies and universities now work with school districts to provide graduate courses and online professional development training for teachers and administrators. Online professional development training can be self-paced or instructor-led. Most online professional development training available for teachers is self-paced. In **self-paced training**, teachers typically sign up for a specific course or module and, after completing all the requirements, they receive credit for the training. Some self-paced training courses provide access to a Help desk or teachers and staff who can provide assistance. In contrast, **instructor-led training** involves continuous interaction with an instructor and the courses are more structured, often including assignments with due dates. Instructor-led training normally is more effective and has fewer drop-outs than self-paced training, but is often more expensive and time consuming to implement.

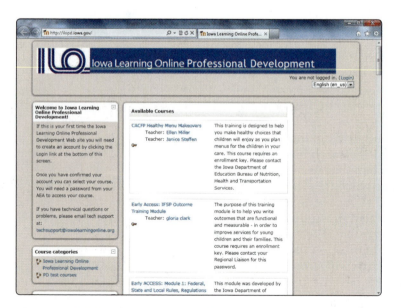

Figure 6-8 All states and many school districts provide extensive online professional development training for their administrators, teachers, and staff.

The K-12 eLearning Environment

eLearning is a fast growing and an ever-expanding component of K-12 education. eLearning, which involves virtual teaching and learning, has made its way not only into the K-12 classroom but also into every aspect of our lives. **eLearning**, also referred to as **electronic learning, online learning, distributed learning, virtual learning**, and **distance learning**, utilizes a local network (such as a school network) or the Internet for delivery of content and interaction between students and teachers, as well as content. eLearning makes it possible for students to become life-long learners.

What makes eLearning classes unique is that they are convenient, flexible, and accessible from any computer with an active network connection (Figure 6-9). This allows students to learn from any place and at any time. In addition, these classes take place in a **virtual classroom environment** or **virtual learning environment**, which is using a network (such as the Internet or school network) to get assignments, discuss topics, work on team projects, and check grades. eLearning has everything you would ordinarily do in a traditional classroom, but without the desks and chairs arranged in rows as they often are in a traditional classroom.

Integration Strategies

To learn more about eLearning issues impacting students, visit the Computer Concepts CourseMate Web site at *www.cengagebrain.com*, and then navigate to the Chapter 6 Education Issues resource for this book.

Figure 6-9 The traditional K-12 classroom is morphing in new and exciting ways.

Growth of Online Schools and Programs

Many schools and universities use terms such as **eLearning, online,** and **virtual** to define classes that are delivered completely online and terms like **blended, hybrid,** or **mixed mode** to define classes that are a combination of both F2F and online. A **100 percent online course,** also called a **Web-based course** or **virtual course,** is a course or class taught completely on the Web, rather than in a traditional classroom. In what direction is education heading — traditional classroom learning in brick-and-mortar schools or eLearning in virtual environments? **Brick-and-mortar school** refers to a traditional school with physical buildings for teachers and students to gather.

Experts predict that over the next five years the majority of K-12 students will continue to take most of their courses in brick-and-mortar schools. However, research revealed that in 2011 over 500,000 K-12 students attended some type of virtual school or online charter school full-time and three million additional K-12 students were enrolled in some type of education offered online, usually taking one or more online classes. Forecasters project that, by 2014, over 13 million K-12 students, including elementary students, will take at least one online class (Figure 6-10). Many millions more will be in blended classes.

Originally, universities and K-12 schools began offering online courses for convenience and cost-effective reasons, but many online courses were also offered for academic reasons. Some online courses were offered to assist in meeting the specific needs of a range of students — from home-schooled, to homebound due to illness, to those with disabilities. Other online classes are geared toward struggling or at-risk students. Still other online courses offer students classes that their schools do not have the resources to offer, such as advanced placement and college-level courses or foreign language courses.

Another variable contributing to the growth of eLearning is the pervasiveness of mobile devices, especially tablet computers. These Internet-ready, interactive mobile devices are making the any time, any place, any path, and any pace learning of eLearning a reality.

Figure 6-10 Millions of K-12 students, including elementary students, are taking online and blended classes.

Figure 6-11 Using an iPad, teachers, students, and parents have instant and always on access to a wealth of information. Shown is the Tennessee Electronic Learning Center which provides multiple eLearning resources.

All forms of virtual and online learning are transforming education (Figure 6-11 above). Online school programs have the potential to dramatically expand the educational opportunities of American students, largely overcoming geographic and demographic restrictions. Many educators feel that virtual learning also has the potential to improve the quality of instruction, while increasing productivity and lowering costs, ultimately reducing the burden on taxpayers. Most states are creating policies that mandate that all students are offered online classes and are creating funding to facilitate online learning. Many states have also mandated that all graduating students complete one or more online classes.

There are various types of online school programs that run from fully online schools to those that are partially online. For many small rural school districts, online programs are a lifeline that makes it possible for them to provide their students with a broad range of course options and, in some instances, the basic courses that their students must take in order to meet the standards-based curriculum. Lastly, when surveyed, college students and even some high school students report they need a more flexible learning environment, which is why the any path, any place, any time, any pace learning exemplified by online education is very popular.

Experienced online teachers are inundated with many questions that range from the curious, the skeptical, the misinformed, and the awe-struck when they tell people what it is that they do — teach online. Questions like: What is a virtual school? How does a virtual school work? What is an online school program? What is blended learning? How does that work? How do you implement instructional strategies online? In addition to questions, you will also hear everyone's opinions on the matter of online learning. Opinions like: Online can never be as good as face-to-face. That's not real teaching. I bet you have to be a computer programmer to be able to teach online.

These are all questions and comments worth addressing as you transition to being an online teacher or even as you prepare to Web-enhance your course in order to provide your students access to course materials online. The following few sections provide answers to the questions listed above as well as other questions you might have about teaching online.

FAQ

What is the primary reason for the dramatic increase in K-12 online schools, programs, and classes?

The explosive expansion in online K-12 education is being driven primarily by economic realities and shrinking K-12 school budgets.

WHAT IS A VIRTUAL SCHOOL?

A **virtual school**, also called a **virtual charter school**, **cyber school**, or **cyber charter school**, refers to an institution not bound by brick-and-mortar buildings. A virtual school differs from the traditional school by offering all student services, instruction, activities, communications, and courses online using Internet technology. Virtual schools use the Internet to link the complete school organization. This includes the connections between administrators, teachers, parents, and students (Figure 6-12).

There are many virtual schools in the U.S. Some are publicly funded, some are privately funded, and some are chartered (and usually funded through a mix of public and private funds). Most states require that virtual schools employ certified teachers to facilitate student learning. Like F2F teachers, virtual teachers coordinate daily lessons, interact with the students, and teach core content. Like brick-and-mortar schools, virtual schools have a system in place to support teachers and students; this system includes principals, guidance counselors, attendance and assessment tools, and programs that track student progress.

In addition to this support system, teachers can use an array of eLearning teaching tools and strategies designed to enhance a student's online learning experience. By integrating various technology devices, interactive software solutions, and the Internet into the learning process, teachers can address the needs of a wide range of students. The resources listed in Figure 6-13 provide additional information about virtual schools.

Figure 6-12 In a virtual school, all resources and interactions between students, teachers, and others are done totally online.

Web Resources	URL
10 Myths about Teaching Online	*courses.csusm.edu/resources/webct/asa/myths.html*
Florida Virtual School	*www.flvs.net*
Georgia Virtual School	*www.gavirtualschool.org*
International Association for K-12 Online Learning	*inacol.org/*
Tips for Teaching Online	*www.onlineteachingtips.org/*
Virtual High School — Global Consortium	*www.govhs.org/*
Connections Academy	*www.connectionsacademy.com/home.aspx*
Illinois Virtual School	*ilvirtual.org/*
K-12 Inc.	*www.k12.com*
Michigan Virtual School	*www.mivhs.org/*
Texas Virtual School	*www.texasvirtualschool.org/*
Virtual School Symposium	*www.virtualschoolsymposium.org/*
eLearners	*www.elearners.com*

All links were accurate at the time this book was printed but pages on the Web are always changing and being updated. If the link does not produce the page you were expecting, use your favorite search engine and key words on the topic to find the page.

Figure 6-13 The Web provides excellent resources that you can explore to increase your knowledge of virtual teaching and learning.

HOW DO VIRTUAL SCHOOLS WORK?

Virtual schools can work in a manner that is similar to a brick-and-mortar school with set time schedules and courses that are fully instructor-led. But in a way, that undermines the beauty of a virtual school, which allows for any time, any place, any path, and any pace instruction. So, most virtual schools are very flexible in how they address students' learning needs and schedules but their content is still standards-based and performance-driven. When it comes to the curriculum, virtual schools and brick-and-mortar schools hold the same high standards.

There are many tools available to help meet the more flexible needs of the virtual school. First and foremost, all virtual schools must provide a secure Internet experience. This is true for stand-alone online courses, Web-enhanced materials, and student information. Teachers, students, and parents must all feel confident that the information stored about them as a result of taking a course, enrolling in a school, or visiting a curriculum resource page is secure.

To help with ensuring security (as well as with curriculum content and logistics), commercial systems called learning management systems or content management systems are available. (See Figure 6-14.) A **Learning Management System (LMS)**, also called **Content Management System (CMS)**, is a secure,

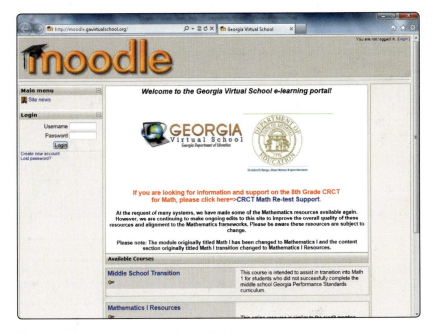

Figure 6-14 Some states and school districts are using an open source LMS, for example, Moodle, which is shown here being used by the Georgia Virtual School.

restricted, Internet-based comprehensive package that includes instructional tools for school administrators, documentation, student tracking, online courses and classes content, and training content. The LMS supports the benefits associated with interactive and participatory learning, and it includes the use of examples, observations, discussions, experiences, situations, rules, interactive games, content-based concepts, and instructional techniques that assist in a comprehensive eLearning system. Figure 6-15 covers the benefits of some of these tools and concepts.

There are a number of commercial LMS software packages available, including Blackboard, eCollege, UCompass Education, eClassroom, and Angel. Open source choices include Moodle (refer again to Figure 6-14 on the previous page), Drupal, and others. Many of these were developed for use at the college level and have been adapted for use in K-12.

As the need for these types of tools expands in the K-12 market over the next few years, a wider offering will become available, including LMS apps for use on mobile devices.

WHAT ARE VITRUAL SCHOOL PROGRAMS?

Virtual school programs are created by school districts or commercial eLearning companies and are school programs that contain an online component. Due to the demand for K-12 online learning, there has been a great deal of growth in eLearning commercial companies that create online curriculum and other resources for K-12 schools. These companies provide options for both public and private schools that allow their students to enroll in online classes in a secure virtual environment. Many school districts contract with an eLearning company that allows its students to enroll in online classes without charge

Tools and Concepts	Benefit
Virtual learning environment	Supports any path, any time, and any place learning
Asynchronous computer mediated communication (e.g., e-mail, discussion groups)	Supports collaboration and increased communication
Synchronous computer mediated communication (e.g., chats, desktop video conferencing, groupware)	Supports interactive eLearning
Electronic documents/learning resources for students (e.g., lecture notes, readings, PDF files, videos)	Provides sharable resources and learning objects
Reusable content	Supports increased consistency and productivity
Functionality	Provides for flexible and convenient delivery of content
Online games	Supports interactive and participatory learning
Applications built for handheld devices	Meets a diversity of learning styles and needs (such as those of homebound students)
Links to external resources	Variety of instructional events
Access to continually updated standards-based (District, State, ISTE) curriculum	Supports individualized learning, which is learner-controlled curriculum
Social networking	Creates an online community of learners
Interactive multimedia	Provides engaging content for digital learners
Podcasts/vodcasts	Provides immediate delivery of updated programming/content
Complete student activity tracking system	Provides individual, peer, and time-based data on student activities
Online assessment	Creates reports and data tools for evaluating learning

Figure 6-15 This figure shows some of the many tools and concepts available through LMSs, as well as the benefits of these tools and concepts when used in an online environment.

to the student. Parents who homeschool their children have the option of purchasing the curriculum they use to homeschool their children in an online format from an eLearning company. Parents who homeschool their children also have the option of enrolling their children in online courses offered through the school district at no additional cost.

When students enroll in an online course or an online school, they are able to work at their own pace with the support of a teacher, sometimes referred to as a learning coach, and their parent/guardian. A **learning coach** is a teacher or instructor who creates individualized lessons and engages with the learner through effective personal communication, feedback, and assessment, as well as provides support and encouragement.

The teacher often conferences with the students via telephone and conducts online communications using programs such as **Blackboard Collaborate**, which allows teachers and students to engage in the learning process using Web conferencing and other technologies as if they were F2F. When students enroll in an online class, they receive student materials such as textbooks or ebooks that they will need for the class. Also included with the materials are answer keys with explanations so that parents/guardians can provide assistance to students. Each student has an online account to the LMS where she logs in to view content and her daily/monthly schedule, submit assignments, contact the teacher, and take online assessments.

In the traditional classroom setting, students have opportunities to socialize and participate in clubs and organizations based on their interests. These virtual school programs provide similar opportunities for students by offering online meetings and courses based on students' interests. For example, students can enroll in photography and video courses where they not only learn more about the topic but also discuss their common interest in the topic with their online classmates by using the chat feature that is available in most LMSs.

In the traditional school setting, parents have options for participating in the Parent-Teacher Associations (PTA) meetings and other after-school events. Many online school programs provide similar opportunities to meet and socialize with other online parents through newsletter and online forums that connect parents. Parents also receive surveys so they can provide feedback to the teachers about their child's progress and experience. Throughout the year, school districts using an LMS program may organize events that are free for enrolled students and their parents to meet at local venues. In addition, online students can meet their teachers and other administrators virtually and in real time using Skype, FaceTime, and other similar technologies. All teachers involved in virtual school programs can connect with students and parents using today's social media tools, such as Twitter and Facebook, or using other communications tools such as blogs or wikis. There are many different virtual K-12 programs gaining popularity because of the services they provide. We will look at two specialized online programs next: Dual Enrollment and Credit Recovery.

DUAL ENROLLMENT   Because online learning has become so popular in colleges and universities, some high school virtual school programs have developed joint relationships with colleges and universities so their students can do dual enrollment. In a **dual enrollment** program, students can enroll in one or more online undergraduate courses at the participating college or university while they are still in high school. Dual enrollment allows high school students to begin acquiring college-level credit. This is particularly helpful for students who want an accelerated path through college or for students who want to pursue a double major in college.

CREDIT RECOVERY   Credit Recovery is one K-12 online school program gaining popularity. A **Credit Recovery** program provides a student with a way to regain credit toward graduation for a course that

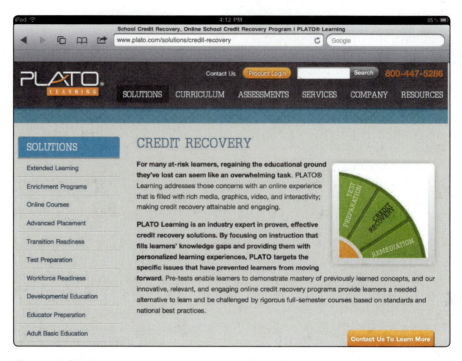

Figure 6-16 Many private companies provide credit recovery solutions for states and school districts.

the student was previously unsuccessful in earning academic credit (Figure 6-16 above). These online courses cannot be taken by students to gain credit on their first attempt at a course, but instead, these online courses focus on helping students complete the failed competency of the content standards for the part(s) of the course they did not pass. The focus of credit recovery programs is providing students a way to stay in school and graduate on time.

WHAT IS BLENDED LEARNING?

As mentioned earlier, most students stay enrolled in a brick-and-mortar school while they take one or more online classes. This is an option sometimes referred to as **blended schooling**. Many parents prefer this option because they like their children to attend both a traditional brick-and-mortar school with all the advantages it has to offer and a virtual school with all the advantages it has to offer. This is one type of **blended learning**. Due to budget cuts and other issues, it is predicted that, in the next few years, some school districts will keep their physical schools open for three or four days a week, yet teachers will still

be required to teach the other one or two days online. This is another type of blended learning or blended schooling.

The SLOAN Consortium (see Figure 6-17) has adopted a definition for blended learning that states: "courses that integrate online content and activities with traditional F2F class activities in a planned, pedagogically valuable manner, and where a portion of the F2F course time is actually replaced by online activity." One example of blended learning is a college course that has a class that meets F2F once per week instead of the usual three-times per week format. Then, the activities that would otherwise be taught in the other two F2F meeting times are taught online. In this situation, the college has created a blended course by using both F2F meeting time and online meeting time.

As just discussed and as shown in Figure 6-18, **blended learning**, also called **hybrid learning** or **mixed mode learning**, combines traditional classroom-based (F2F) courses with some type of eLearning instruction. While there are many different types of blended learning, all combine some F2F instruction with eLearning instruction. Some educators prefer the term

Figure 6-17 The SLOAN Consortium (SLOAN-C) has been instrumental in efforts to integrate quality online education into higher education.

hybrid learning or **hybrid classes** for blended courses because of the variety of instructional strategies used to mix teaching, facilitation of instructional methods, and Web-based activities. Hybrid learning may include the use of videos, virtual field trips, Webcast and Webinars, curriculum-specific apps, mobile devices, collaborative software packages, social media, broadcasting, multimedia projects, and more.

Blended learning is increasing in many areas of education and is one of the fastest growing uses of technologies in the world. Researchers and education leaders predict that by the year 2013, 40 percent of K-12 schools will be offering blended education, including some elementary schools. There are many practical reasons that blended learning is gaining acceptance, such as budget cuts, cost effectiveness,

Figure 6-18 K-12 blended learning programs use the best of both worlds, F2F and online.

instructional offerings, and gains in student learning. Clearly, blended learning offers many powerful and appealing benefits not only to school districts but also to students and teachers.

WHAT ARE THE BENEFITS OF BLENDED LEARNING?

The goal of a blended learning environment is to combine researched best practices with instructional techniques of both traditional F2F and online instruction. The ratio of how much time is spent in-class and how time is spent online is different depending on the course or class. One unique advantage of combining in-class learning and online instruction is that this blended approach encompasses the best of both worlds. Most blended classes combine in-class learning with online activities and discussions. Blended courses meet in a classroom part of the time, and then they integrate online learning in between F2F class meetings. Figure 6-19 summarizes the differences between the different modalities currently being utilized in education, including blended learning.

In-class time can be used to engage students in advanced interactive experiences and to conduct assessments, like tests. The online portion can provide students with multimedia-rich content at any time and any place the student can connect to the Internet. Each provides the learner with different types of learning experiences. The different combination of instructional methods can provide a great deal of flexibility in the scheduling for students and teachers. In addition to flexibility and convenience for students, according to many research studies, there is evidence that using a blended instructional approach can result in increased learning outcome gains and retention of students.

Another benefit of blended learning is it gives teachers the ability to assess students promptly, and then provide quick feedback and individualized instruction based on the assessments. Teachers can use the assessment results to make sure students are on a pathway with individualized learning experiences for their specific needs, which is called differentiated instruction. **Differentiated instruction,** also referred to as **differentiated learning,** involves providing students with different opportunities and ways to master content. For example, a teacher might create a project that produces different avenues for students to learn the same objectives. Research has shown that many of the difficulties students experience during the learning process diminish when their educational environments are modified to their pace and levels of learning. What adds to this type of teaching and learning is the technology component inherent in a blended learning environment, where technology is not a distraction from learning, but rather it is an integral part of the learning process. Creating high-quality blended learning presents considerable opportunities and challenges for both teachers and students.

Integration Strategies

To learn more about integrating blended learning resources, visit the Computer Concepts CourseMate Web site at *www. cengagebrain.com,* and then navigate to the Chapter 6 Teaching Today resource for this book.

Course Category	Course Description
In-class/F2F or Traditional	Has no online technology or components used for content delivery; instructor and students are in the same location for content delivery.
Web-enhanced	Uses Web-based technology to facilitate what is essentially an F2F course; may use a course management system (CMS) or a learning management system (LMS), and/or Web pages to post the syllabus, schedule, and assignments.
Blended/Hybrid or Mixed Mode	Blends online and F2F instructional techniques; substantial proportion of the content is delivered online; typically uses online tools; and has a reduced number of F2F meetings.
100% Online	All of the content is delivered online; if there are F2F meetings, they are optional.

Figure 6-19 These are the different formats or modalities in which content is currently being offered in K-12 and higher education.

Transitioning to Teaching Online

Picture this scenario: During your teaching internship, you learn that, due to new state mandates, diverse student needs, ever-changing learning opportunities, and budget cuts, the school district you are interested in teaching at is telling their teachers that they will have to offer at least one of their classes as either completely online or blended during the upcoming school year. You really have very little background in teaching at a distance, and you did not take any courses or receive any training while studying for your degree that focused on teaching online.

During your undergraduate degree, you did take a few online courses but this is a completely different situation — you are now going to be the teacher, not the student — and you have never taught online. What do you do and what do you need to know to teach in this emerging and changing face of teaching and education — distance education?

WHAT DO I NEED TO KNOW TO TEACH ONLINE?

There are many myths and truths about teaching online; and there are excellent Web resources that can help you learn how to become a virtual teacher. As teachers create and implement online courses, they need to adjust their teaching approach to accommodate the differences between teaching in a virtual environment and teaching F2F in a classroom. They need to update their virtual instructional skills constantly, and they need to self-evaluate their successes and failures frequently so they can offer students the best instruction possible in a virtual environment. A multitude of resources available on the Web can help you meet the often-demanding requirements of teaching virtually. As you familiarize yourself with strategies for online teaching, you will find that many of the strategies you use in your F2F classroom are the same or similar to your online strategies. Before we explore a number of topics concerning you as an online teacher, reviewing the tips in Figure 6-20 on the next page will provide you with additional insight into being an effective online teacher.

In the future, all teachers will teach online — maybe 100 percent online or maybe partially online — but, rest assured, all teachers will teach online. As a result, teachers will need experience and skills for teaching in the evolving eLearning world. What do you need to do to prepare to teach students in eLearning environments. What kind of technology experience do you have to have? Do you have to be a techie to teach online?

DO I HAVE TO BE A COMPUTER GENIUS?

While you do have to possess many basic technology skills to teach online, you do not have to be an expert in technology. More importantly, everything you have learned about integrating technology in your F2F classroom transfers to your online classroom.

The daily tools you will use as an online teacher include a course administration and/or learning management system (LMS), a word processor program, a presentation program, a calendar program, an e-mail program, a spreadsheet program, different Web browsers, your favorite Web 2.0 tools, a screencast recording program, and a plagiarism detection service. Keep in mind that when using an LMS, teachers can see everything a student sees, but teachers also have additional instructor rights, which allow them to create or modify curriculum content and to track student performance. The other tools are used to create content, track progress, or manage time. Your school or district may provide most of the tools you need, although the Web 2.0 tools may be up to you to choose. Some of the fun and creative part of being an online instructor is using these tools to provide your students with online options for creating, developing, and presenting their understanding of content. You will learn more about Web 2.0 tools later in this chapter. And remember to include samples of online course content that you develop in your ePortfolio.

ePortfolio Idea

Tip	Description
Do Unto Others	Imagine how you would want to be treated as a student. When you have a question, you like to receive a helpful and friendly answer, right? If a student writes to you online three different times asking again for the instructions on how to complete an assignment, what do you do? Do you keep e-mailing back telling him to re-read the instructions, call him, send an example, or create a quick screencast to walk them through the assignment? There is no perfect answer, but you must always choose what is best for your student. You will find the same questions get asked over and over. A good idea might be to develop FAQs, perhaps even video-based FAQs to respond to those recurring questions.
Be Positive	This is a very different learning environment and you cannot give students those usual F2F encouragements like a nod of the head or a smile. It is very important to support your students and provide self-assurance by making positive suggestions and corrective assessments. You should always make an effort to encourage students throughout their online experiences. This positive attitude will also help students feel positive self-worth, as well as motivate them to work on correcting and redoing assignments when needed.
Communication is Key	Online coursework can be isolating and frustrating, especially for students new to this method of learning. Your students need to know you are very much "there for them" even though you are not physically there. In this situation, online communication is the key. Fortunately, online instructors have a wide variety of tools available to them to help them communicate and make their presence felt. For example, you can communicate with your students by phone, text, e-mail, instant message, Skype, Blackboard Collaborate sessions, Voki, Jing, and other online communications tools. The key is to leverage these tools and establish that you want to communicate with them and that you are there to support your students.
Just Ask	Whether you are new to your organization or just new to the task of instructing students in an online environment, there are likely to be many new policies, procedures, and tools to learn. Hopefully your virtual school or online program will provide you with training, mentoring, and reference materials to help you acclimate to your new position and role. In addition, proactively find answers on your own. For example, you might find teachers who have experience teaching the same course or content that you are teaching or have a similar type of class. If you do not know the questions to ask, then simply ask these teachers what they wish they had known when they began teaching online. Ask for resources, Web sites, apps, productivity tools, or anything that they are using to improve their instructional practice that might benefit your teaching.
Be Flexible	Online education is ever-changing. The tools and platforms you work with in your online classroom, the needs of your students, the policies of the workplace, as well as state or federal government requests or mandates are all subject to change. There may not always be a clear-cut, right-or-wrong, black-or-white solution to a problem with a process, system, or product in place. Be prepared to handle this kind of constant variability and be adaptable to changes.
Stay Current	As the teacher, the responsibility for delivering effective instruction that is also current is yours. The sheer number of tools available can be daunting. Find a few to test, and evaluate them to see if they are providing the return on your time investment needed to use them. For example, you might send out a simple survey to ask your students if they found the tool helpful. Then, use their feedback to determine if you will continue to use the tool or seek a replacement tool. So, while it is always important to explore and implement new tools to keep your content interesting and up to date, remember that not every new tool is a better tool. Use only tools that benefit both you and your students.
Go Live	One of the most valuable aspects of online instruction is its asynchronous aspect. This provides the instructor and the student flexibility. However, don't overlook the benefits of direct instruction in a synchronous setting, which is a great way to keep students motivated and to convey a sense of your presence and personality as an instructor. You can enhance the participation and interactivity of your instruction with audio, video, chat, and whiteboard functions to facilitate collaborative, personalized learning experiences.
Make Time for You	Balancing work and life is a much-discussed topic in the present-day workplace. There are many books and articles devoted to finding ways to maximize your work effort, to have more time for family and personal growth, and to improve you health and wellness while working demanding and multiple careers. Many new or prospective online instructors underestimate the time commitment that the work can require. Be sure to build balance between your professional life and your personal life into your schedule. Both you and your students will benefit from this balance.

Figure 6-20 Shown are tips to help you become a more effective online teacher.

Technology is always changing, and so, to stay current, you should be interested in learning educational tools and technology. For instance, in the same way that you need to keep up with content knowledge relative to your curriculum area, you also need to stay up to date with current educational technologies (Figure 6-21). In the constantly shifting realm of educational technology, it is important to pay attention to new developments. Although being an early adopter of technology tools and devices is not required, it helps to learn new techniques, software, and apps that might help you teach your students. For example, you should work on reviewing new software and apps that are applicable to your online courses, perhaps even taking online tutorials to help you become familiar with new software and apps.

In addition, you will need to learn the ins and outs of your online classes as well as the management of grades, contact information, and data regarding student and instructor goals. It is helpful for you to feel comfortable using text messaging, e-mail, and social media tools. These tools are staples for many K-12 online instructors. Also, you should know your way around smartphones and tablet computers, and you should stay current on mobile apps, especially ones that will be useful to your students or that relate to your content area. So, while you do not need to be a computer genius, you do need to be actively engaged in the ever changing world of technology in order to be a successful online instructor.

Figure 6-21 Until recently, technologies (like iPads and BlackBerrys) and apps shown in this figure, did not exist. Teachers who teach online need to stay abreast of new technologies that can assist them in engaging today's students.

Web Info

For more information on working for a virtual school, visit the Computer Concepts CourseMate Web site at *www.cengagebrain. com*, navigate to the Chapter 6 Web Info resource for this book, and then click Virtual School Careers.

I Am Ready — Sign Me Up!

Whether you are a brand new teacher taking the plunge or an experienced teacher considering moving to a virtual school — are you ready? The following strategies and tools will help prepare you with the skills you need to get hired, and then, once hired, to facilitate learning in a virtual environment in order to ensure a successful teaching experience for you and learning experience for your students.

Imagine this: You have submitted your application to be considered for an online or blended teaching position. Now what? As you wait for the call to be interviewed, you should use your time to prepare productively for what you will say during the interview. Think about what you should know, what you should say, and how you will show them that you can teach online when you have not done it before. Get ready to tell your story and make your case for why you are the best candidate for the job!

PREPARE FOR THE HIRING PROCESS

First, you should be well informed about the organization where you have applied to work. This goes without saying,

but the field of virtual education is growing rapidly and there are many different types of schools serving students. Some are considered independent cyber charter schools, some are independent public entities, others are university extensions, still others are for-profit corporations, or they might be franchises or affiliates of one of these types. Be familiar with the mission statement, history, and other information available that will help you understand whether the culture of the organization is aligned with your teaching and work philosophies. Is there information from other teachers about life as a virtual teacher on the site? Review the job posting for important keywords that will help you match the skills and proficiencies the employer is seeking with your skill set and experience (Figure 6-22). Like any interview, you should come prepared with questions you have about your potential employer based on your review of the information for the interview.

Whether you are applying to teach online or at a brick-and-mortar school, you will be asked about your technology experience and proficiency during the interview process, and, in fact, you may even be asked to complete a hands-on technology inventory to ascertain your

Figure 6-22 Virtual schools often have hiring information and other pertinent details on their Web sites for teachers and administrators interested in applying for an online position.

skills. You will likely be asked about how you have shown leadership, overcome adversity, or adapted to change in your previous teaching assignments or student teaching. How do you communicate and support your learners in a differentiated manner? How committed are you to your work in helping all learners to succeed? Does your family understand the commitment that you are making to be available during non-traditional teaching hours for your learners?

Before the interview, be sure to take an inventory of your greatest strengths and of your areas for improvement as a teacher, a leader, or a team member. With this information in hand, you will be well on your way to feeling prepared to convey why you are the right person for the job.

TAKE TRAINING AND ASK QUESTIONS

After your interview, you may be asked to begin very soon or it may take some time to receive an offer. Do not be discouraged if you are not immediately offered a position. Many employers like to keep a pool of potential candidates on hand, and schools are no different. In either case, when you do receive your offer, the next step is hopefully training to help you acclimate to your new position. Be an active and attentive participant in your training. Ask questions and take good notes to refer to later.

In addition to training, one of the best ways to prepare for your new job is to ask questions. If you have the opportunity, try to make contact with teachers who work in the organization and ask them about their work. Ask them the real, day-to-day questions that you have. Be sure to ask about your required work hours and availability to students, as these will vary from school to school. Be clear about performance goals and how you will be evaluated as a teacher. Inquire about the opportunities for professional learning and development. Specifically, what support systems are in place for induction or mentoring of new teachers (Figure 6-23). It is important to identify the structures and resources in place so that you will have the best chance of success in your new classroom. And finally, sometimes, when you are trying something new, you do not have enough information about the situation to know

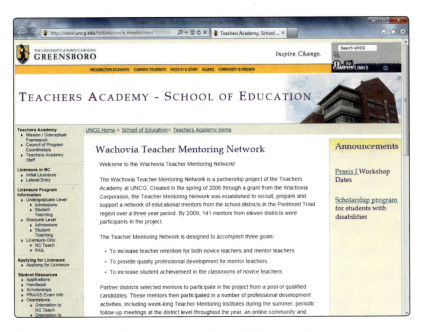

Figure 6-23 Many Web sites and school districts provide mentoring for online teachers.

what questions to ask. In this case it is a good idea to ask an experienced teacher what they wish they would have known when they first began teaching online.

PREPARE FOR THE JOB

There is a lot of preparation that goes into being an online teacher. The curriculum for each of your online courses may be given to you by the school district, or you may find yourself on the design team working to create course content and develop learning activities. Even if your course content and activities have been created for you, you will still need to create supplemental materials that can be used to assist students with challenging assignments or activities or to prepare presentations for use in live instruction sessions. You will also need to compose letters to welcome students to your courses, remind students of learning goals and deadlines, and give feedback and praise to students for a job well done. You can draft these letters ahead of time and then use the draft as a template that you customize to meet each new situation.

You might want to create a screencast (discussed here briefly and in more detail later in this chapter) to show students how to navigate the course or lesson or how to take notes to highlight the most salient points of a concept or lesson, or you might

Integration Strategies

To learn more about integrating eLearning tools in online courses, visit the Computer Concepts CourseMate Web site at *www.cengagebrain.com*, and then navigate to the Chapter 6 Software Corner or Digital Media Corner resource for this book.

want to use a screencast to provide examples that model for students the work product that is expected. Screencasts can be created through the use of programs like Jing, which is available for free. You will also want to create notes that you can send to your students. These notes might be frequently used reminders, feedback, animations, or contact information to send to students. Many online teachers find Web 2.0 tools such as Google Docs, Opera Notes, Evernote, or Ubernote to be helpful in easily storing and accessing notes.

Many virtual schools use Blackboard Collaborate (formally Elluminate/Wimba) or another program to support students during the use of live sessions (Figure 6-24). For some sessions, you may go straight into the course content to share your desktop or a Web site with students. In many cases, you will want to create an interactive and engaging presentation that enhances the lesson content perhaps by including ideas or resources that extend the lesson content. You can use an online whiteboard to display graphic organizers or questions about the subject content that you wish to cover with students. An **online whiteboard**, also known as an **eLearning whiteboard**, is similar to IWBs used in face-to-face classrooms that you learned about in Chapter 5, except

these are 100 percent online and do not have as many features.

Throughout your work with online students, you will find it necessary to create and send reminders to students to keep them on track. You may be sending a gentle reminder that they need to submit their work or checking in to see if they need assistance with their lessons. Sending positive feedback to students and regular praise is very important. One way to be creative and keep your students viewing your messages is to create a colorful, cheerful presentation slide. You can easily include this slide in an e-mail message to brighten the students' day and keep them feeling positive about their hard work. For example, if you have a high school student who has just successfully completed a major assignment or completed a course, you could send that student positive feedback via e-mail. The e-mail might include one of your colorful presentation slides, such as one showing a frosty white cake with Congratulations written on it and a personal note in the body of the e-mail congratulating the student on a job well done (Figure 6-25 on the next page). Or, maybe all your students would like to know when they are doing something well. In this case, you can create virtual greeting cards to share with students on a regular basis.

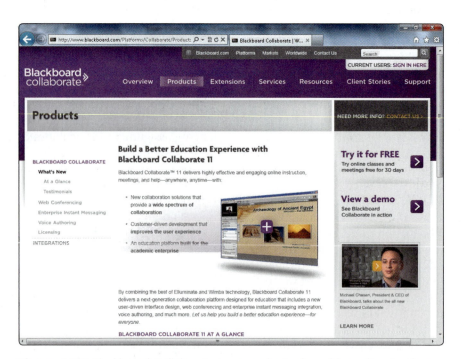

Figure 6-24 Blackboard Collaborate is a popular tool used by online teachers to maximize student engagement and learning.

Figure 6-25 Shown is a PowerPoint slide that could be added to a congratulatory type e-mail message or blog post. Like all students, online students need to receive positive feedback.

KNOW YOUR CONTENT

Some people are under the mistaken impression that since all answers are available online, it is no longer necessary for the teacher to be a content expert. This could not be further from the truth. You are the teacher, whether online or F2F. You are the supplier of information and the facilitator of knowledge. You are the guiding light in the darkness of a student's online course experience. Your students want to trust you and they depend on you. You must do your best to help students meet their needs. Be prepared to do your homework as a teacher and be ready to facilitate for your students. This is especially important as course content, readings, questions, or activities change and you must be clear and current on what students are expected to produce and how you will evaluate their work.

The ideal situation is to really know the course content and assignments well beforehand. Are there novels in your course that students must read? If so, be sure you not only read them but also fully understand their themes, imagery, and all the skills associated with the reading beforehand. Are there lab experiments that students must perform at home? If so, perform them in your kitchen before you ask students to do so. Testing any learner experience will help you understand what can go wrong or right and assist in the learning process. Invest the time to know your content so that you can answer simple questions automatically. Having deep knowledge of your content will also help you delve deeper into the

content with your students. And, knowing your content will help you build deeper relationships with your students and manage your instructional time with them effectively. Teachers with in-depth content knowledge can find multiple ways to present the material, which helps students with different background knowledge, skills, and ways of learning grasp the new content. As a result, students respect teachers who have deep content knowledge. So, just like a teacher in a F2F classroom, you need to know your content.

USE QUESTIONING AS AN INSTRUCTIONAL STRATEGY

Remember we learned about Bloom's Taxonomy in the Special Feature on Learning Theories following Chapter 5 and how important it is for teachers to ensure that they are asking questions that move students through the levels of higher-order thinking skills. An established curriculum should have been developed to rigorous standards and include age, grade, and content appropriate questions. As you get to know your course content, you may find that you'll need to rephrase questions for your students from time to time or that you may need to push your students to the next level of thinking (Figure 6-26).

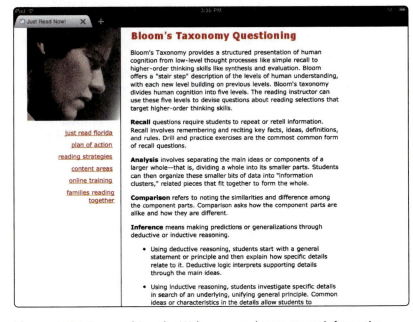

Figure 6-26 By searching the Web, you can locate many informative resources on using Bloom's Taxonomy to help improve your techniques for asking questions.

You should present Bloom's Taxonomy to students so they can understand and strive for higher levels of learning. Develop sample questions for students at a given level, and then ask students to create additional questions at that same level. Help students learn to dissect the questions that you ask by helping them understand this language of questioning.

Many diverse learners come through our virtual doors just as they come through the doors of brick-and-mortar schools. It is the work of the teacher to enable the success of all students to the best of their ability. To that end, it is important to be aware of the cultural biases that may be present in your content. Understand that when asking students questions seeking opinions about "our society" or "our culture", you may receive some surprising responses if students have a limited knowledge of American popular culture or American history depending on their background knowledge and experiences or cultural identity. Students who are still working to acquire English may need significant support in navigating a course that is primarily text-based or writing-intensive. If you do not feel that you have a solid knowledge of literacy or ESL strategies, then it is incumbent upon you to seek out resources to acquire it. There are wonderful ways to use multimedia and Web 2.0 tools to help fill in the gaps and make content more accessible to online learners.

As previously stated, each student brings different prior knowledge, skills, and aptitudes to his or her learning experience. Uncertainty or assumptions about what students understand and their skill level when entering your class could provide a frustrating experience for the learner and the teacher. Whenever possible aim to be specific about the concept or desired outcome. For instance, if a student is required to write a paragraph using sensory details and he or she does not understand the term sensory details, then odds are he or she will not write a paragraph that meets your learning objectives. However, if the question is rephrased to instruct students to write a paragraph that includes sensory details like the smells, sounds, and tastes of an experience, it is

more than likely your students will understand this clue and be able to follow through on the task. As the teacher, you need to be clear in understanding each lesson objective. For example, in the scenario just given, is the objective to see if they know the term sensory details, to see if they are able to write the descriptive paragraph, or both? Your answer to this question should determine how you design and present the lesson.

CREATE A SCHEDULE

As schools add more distance learning opportunities, administrators must also think about the needs of their teachers as they prepare to teach virtually. Teachers must be given the time they need to rethink their teaching strategies and to reorganize their lessons for the online learning environment and the integration of new digital tools. **Time management** is the process you develop and tools you use to organize your day to be more efficient and productive. Time management is important in every job you do but, when you teach online, it is crucial.

One of the most challenging aspects of working in a virtual environment is transitioning from an environment where you are ruled by a set schedule (with bells signaling the start and end of a class period, the completion of a planning or grading period, the end of passing period and the use of the restroom, and snack or meal time) to an environment that requires more flexibility. For example, if you ask ten different online teachers how they schedule their work and personal life tasks, you would likely receive ten completely different responses. While each teacher has the same ultimate goal, successfully facilitating instruction for his or her students, the myriad ways in which this can be accomplished could leave you struggling to find balance or in completing the many different tasks a virtual schoolteacher must undertake.

You may work in an online school that has specific requirements to which you must adhere. For example, you may need to provide virtual office hours at a set time so you are always available for students and parents during that time, or

Web Info

For more information on time management, visit the Computer Concepts CourseMate Web site at *www.cengagebrain.com,* navigate to the Chapter 6 Web Info resource for this book, and then click Time Management.

you may need to establish your own with a particular frequency or during particular hours. There is tremendous variety in how online institutions structure their programs to meet the needs of students, so you need to be sure to understand clearly what the expectations are in your situation.

Whether you are working at a brick-and-mortar school, from home, or from a combination of the two, it is important to have a schedule for your work. When you establish your schedule, be sure to know the expectations of your school and district. Are you required to have evening office hours on particular days or are you required to have office hours at particular times during the week? When are team and professional development meetings typically held? Are you required to be available or to have office hours on the weekends? Should you do virtual office hours? These are important points to be clear on so that you can craft a schedule that works for your students, for you, and for your family. To help establish your schedule, you can use planner or calendar programs such as Outlook, Google Calendar, or **Flash Appointments** (Figure 6-27).

Crafting a schedule that works takes time and, once created, your schedule will require constant adjustments. In fact, your schedule needs to allow for some amount of flexibility so that as meetings or professional development opportunities arise, you can work them into your schedule. While traditional schools generally recess for the summer, many virtual schools are open all year. This will be a big adjustment for teachers who are used to having their summers off in order to design curriculum materials or to pursue professional development and advanced degrees.

Everyone's schedule is different and you need to set hours for yourself and hours to connect to your student. Students in F2F classrooms and brick-and-mortar schools have consistency built into their daily schedules, but surprisingly students who take online courses like a sense of consistency, too. They need to know that they can count on you to be available when you say you will be available. You need to communicate your availability and online course protocols clearly. **Protocols** are a set of guidelines or ground rules that define the teacher and student expectations in an online course experience and help things run smoothly.

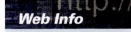
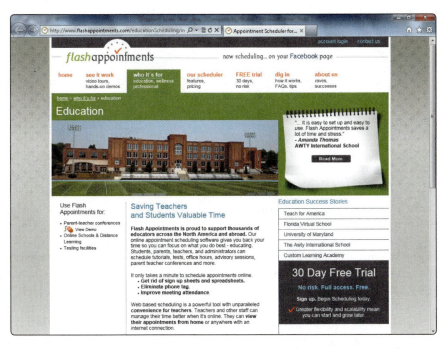

Figure 6-27 Effective time management and scheduling are important for online teachers. Shown is a popular scheduling program for educators.

As you develop your schedule, you will need to set aside specific time to work on grading, making calls, completing professional development activities, or volunteering with a committee or club. You will want to break down your day and create a daily *to do list* of what you need to do and what you want to accomplish. You can include both your work-related goals and personal tasks as well. Also if you are team teaching, your schedule will have to adjust to accommodate your duties and responsibilities associated with your team teaching assignment. **Team teaching** is a method of instruction in which two or more teachers work together to combine their individual talents into one class or course.

Calendar and planner programs can help not only you but also your students, parents, other teachers, and administrators to schedule tutorials, tests, office hours, advisory sessions, parent teacher conferences, and more. If you all use the same scheduling program, you can see one another's calendars, which will allow you all to find joint meeting times and to collaborate more easily.

ESTABLISH A HOME OFFICE

Whether you teach in a brick-and-mortar school, you teach online, or you teach a blended course, you should establish a home office. While you need a home office more if you are teaching online or blended courses, a home office is still a good idea if you teach at a brick-and-mortar school. A home office helps you establish a place where you can accomplish tasks specific to your profession, such as grading papers or contacting students. Consider the following when setting up your home office.

- If you have limited space, set up your home office in part of your bedroom or living room. If you have an extra bedroom or basement, choose that space. The important thing is to have a place away from household noises and a door for privacy.
- Minimally, you need a desk, a chair, a computer with always-on Internet access, a printer, and a phone line with voicemail or an answering machine.
- If possible, have two computers, one primary and one that you can use as a backup in case the primary computer fails. For example, you could use a desktop computer as your primary computer and a portable computer, like a notebook, netbook, or tablet computer, as your backup.
- If you are using a desktop computer, consider investing in a high-quality monitor, preferably 22 inches or larger. A large monitor with more viewing area is well worth the added expense.
- If your school does not provide you with a tablet computer similar to the ones your students are using, buy one.
- Install virus and spyware protection on all your computers. Always update your software and run virus scans weekly. Additional information on security threats and preventing them are covered in Chapter 8.
- Consider an ergonomic keyboard to save your hands and tendons from carpal tunnel syndrome, a headset to keep your hands free while you are on the telephone, and an office chair of sufficient comfort and quality for more than casual use. Additional information and suggestions dealing with health issues and ergonomics in the workplace are covered in Chapter 8.
- Be prepared for **Murphy's Law**, which states that "anything that can go wrong will go wrong."
  - Have a backup computer
  - Backup your files weekly on a flash drive, portable hard drive, or use Cloud storage
  - Have a backup phone service; consider having a traditional wired home phone along with your smartphone cellular service
  - Have a backup plan in case your Internet connection quits working, such as a personal mobile hotspot, which is covered in the special feature following this chapter

Web Info

For more information on setting up a home office, visit the Computer Concepts CourseMate Web site at *www.cengagebrain. com*, navigate to the Chapter 6 Web Info resource for this book, and then click Home Office.

Tools for Online Learning

To teach, and, more importantly, to reach today's digital generation, you need to be able to integrate digital tools into your online classroom curriculum. In the next few sections, you will learn about mobile learning, apps, as well as about creating and using Web pages, blogs, wikis, podcasts, and screencasts. In addition, you will learn how to add video and audio to your creations. You will learn about multimedia authoring programs, such as Camtasia Studio — a user-friendly program that you can use to develop student-centered video creations. Finally, you will explore a number of other strategies that you can potentially use in your online classroom.

MOBILE LEARNING IN THE ONLINE ENVIRONMENT

Throughout this book, you learned about mobile devices and their pervasiveness in our society. As a result of this growth in mobile devices, there has been an explosion of new learning opportunities and tools for education, which makes for a perfect match for the eLearning environment and student. Recall a mobile device is a computing device small enough to hold in your hand that usually does not have disk drives. The important thing for education is that as the use of these devices increases you will see more and more mobile learning or mLearning being used in your online classes. **mLearning** is a type of learning that incorporates the use of cost efficient, lightweight, portable devices such as smartphones or tablet computers. The ongoing growth of the use of mobile devices will only continue to increase the opportunities in online learning because mLearning will increase student collaboration, project-based learning, and the use of Web 2.0 tools. All of these tools add to the potential to increase student achievement. mLearning has been very effective in extending the demand for distance education. As the demand grows, more and more devices, apps, and other tools will be created for the multiple mobile formats and for content delivery to support mLearning.

USING CURRICULUM-SPECIFIC APPS

With this increase in mobile devices also has emerged an amazing array of apps. Recall that apps, also called mobile apps, are software used on tablet computers and other mobile devices and many are being developed for specific curriculum areas. Today, there are over 50,000 apps that were created specifically for educational purposes, including thousands for K-12 teachers and students. Because learning occurs formally and informally throughout a student's day, the potential of the multitude of mobile apps is tremendous. To provide just a sampling of available apps for you to explore, Figure 6-28 lists eight teacher reviewed and

App Name	Description
Grammar Up	Grammar Up contains over 1,800 grammar questions and exercises that use real literature and real examples from business across 20 grammar categories.
National Archives Today's Document	This app is free and features a different document from the National Archives each day. It is searchable and interactive. What a great way to bring history to life!
TED and TED with Subtitles	TED is a free app that provides talks from some of the world's most important and fascinating people, associated with many different disciplines, such as from education to music legends.
Graphing Calculator	There are numerous graphing calculator apps that are a super tool for students who cannot afford an expensive graphing calculator or who may not be able to check out the school's calculators.
meStudying App Series from Florida Virtual School	This pioneering and award winning virtual school continues to create excellent apps for different grade levels and curriculum areas, such as Algebra I, history, and many others.
Evernote	This award-winning free app turns your mobile device into an extension of your brain, helping you remember anything and everything that happens in your daily life. Evernote is indexed, searchable, and shareable, and allows you to take notes, capture screenshots, or take photos, and then organize all your information in digital notebooks.
Flashcards	A free, five-star rated app that allows educators and students to create stacks of flashcards as study materials for quizzes, tests, and more. Also allows users to download quiz material from Quizlet.com, a leading online study site.
Dictionary.com Dictionary and Thesaurus	Another great free app that provides you and your students with reference content from Dictionary.com and Thesaurus.com. The app contains over 2 million words, definitions, synonyms, and antonyms. Included are audio pronunciations, voice-to-text search, and much more.

To evaluate these and thousands of other apps, read reviewer comments, see star ratings, and more, search for the app name or curriculum area at your favorite app store.

Figure 6-28 The apps in this table are just a sampling of the thousands of apps that can supplement both formal and informal student learning.

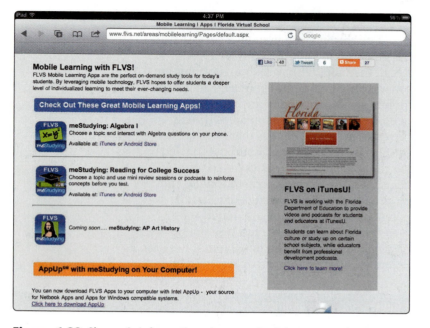

Figure 6-29 Shown is information about meStudying apps, which are created by teachers at Florida Virtual School and used to supplement their online curriculum.

courses (Figure 6-29), while teachers in other virtual schools are using teacher-reviewed apps and incorporating them into their online classroom. You also can use many productivity apps as tools to create interactive quizzes, mobile study guides, interactive presentations, games, and questionnaires, as well as to add audio and video to your online classroom. You can use apps in so many ways to enhance your online or blended classroom. Throughout this textbook, you have learned about the potential of mobile devices and apps to fundamentally change the way you teach and your students learn — app-based learning is just in its infancy with a truly unlimited potential.

CREATING A TEACHER'S WEB PAGE

As you learned in Chapter 2, Web publishing is the development and maintenance of Web pages. Today, teachers and students do not have to learn programming skills to create Web pages and Web sites. Instead, user-friendly Web development programs allow teachers, students, and other users to create their own Web resource pages using basic word processing skills. Popular Web development tools and editors used by educators include Google Sites, WebBlender 2 (Figure 6-30), Apple's iWeb, and TeacherWeb to name just a few.

suggested apps that are available for use on smartphones and tablet computers.

A rapidly emerging trend is the use of curriculum-specific apps on mobile devices or **mobile learning apps** to supplement online teaching and learning, a concept called **app-based learning** or **app-enhanced learning**. Teachers and some virtual schools are creating apps specifically for use with their online

Figure 6-30 Web Blender is a popular program used by teachers to create their classroom Web site.

Creating well-designed Web pages takes a little practice, but once you get the hang of it, it is a lot of fun. The first step is to decide what you want to publish on your Web pages. If you've been teaching for any length of time, you have already collected a great deal of material. Maybe you want to publish stories your students have written, share student projects, promote the activities of an after-school club, communicate with parents, or create an electronic magazine or e-book for the grade level you teach. Be sure to check and follow your school's and your district's policies regarding posting student work.

The first step is to plan the design of your Web pages carefully. The success of your Web pages depends not only on their content but also on their appearance. Web pages that take too long to load will turn visitors away. Web pages that are hard to navigate will frustrate visitors. Web pages with spelling and grammar errors will impact the ability of your visitors to take the content seriously. Figure 6-31 provides tips for designing and organizing your Web pages.

As you have learned, there are many software programs available to help you create Web resources, so you really do not need to have a lot of technical skills to get your class Web page up and running. In fact, there are many Web sites that offer free space and make it easy for you to create customized content in a few minutes. One of these sites is called Google Sites. By registering at sites/google.com for an account, you can create a class page in a matter of minutes. **Google Sites** is

Tip	Details
Web pages should be easy to read.	Make sure font types and colors are easy to read. Choose your background color and designs so they work well with fonts you use and so they make the text easy to read. Avoid flashy effects since these can distract the visitor from the purpose of your Web page.
Web pages should be easy to navigate.	Navigation is very important! If your hyperlinks are not clear to your visitors, they can quickly get lost navigating your Web site. Always be sure visitors can return to your Home page easily. Graphic images, such as buttons or tabs, should be clearly labeled and easy to read. Navigation bars should appear in the same place on each page of your Web site for ease of use. Do not underline text for emphasis because underlined text usually denotes a link.
Web pages should be well-organized.	Organization is the key to good content delivery! A well-organized Web page leads to a well-organized Web site, and that is important. Limit graphics and links per page, use only what is essential, and do not have too much white space. Messy Web pages will take away from your content instead of adding to it. Avoid lengthy, run-on content that requires visitors to scroll. If a long article is part of the Web page, provide a list of topic links at the start of the article so visitors can quickly jump to a topic of interest in the article. Also, once a visitor starts reading an article, provide links throughout the article that allow visitors to get back to the list of topic links at the beginning of the article.
Layout and design should be consistent on all Web pages in a Web site.	Consistency and unity will make your Web pages look more professional. All graphic images and elements, typefaces, headings, theme elements, navigation elements, and so on should remain consistent from Web page to Web page.
Web sites should be easy to locate.	Web sites are located by search engines using keywords. Usually, the developer of the Web site determines the keywords associated with the Web site — the words the search engine uses to find your site. Be sure to associate keywords visitors might use to find your Web site. Also, make your contact information easy to find on the Home page.
Graphics on Web pages should be small files.	Make sure graphics are small in file size. The larger a graphic file size, the longer it takes for the image to appear in your Web site. Readers get frustrated waiting for the graphics to load, and they may not stick around long enough to see your graphics load.
Web pages should be interactive.	Good interactivity engages the user and makes your Web site memorable. Try to find ways to make the Web site engaging. Be sure to update the content often.
Web pages should be quick to download.	Studies have shown that most visitors lose interest in a Web site if it does not load quickly. If you must include a file you know will take a long time to load, provide a warning at the top of the Web page so visitors know why the page is taking so long to load. Also consider providing a way for visitors to by-pass the download.

Figure 6-31 Some tips for creating Web pages.

Figure 6-32 Google Sites provides templates for teachers to use to create their Web pages.

ePortfolio Idea

a user-driven way of presenting content to others online. The example in Figure 6-32 above shows a classroom template that you can use to add all kinds of classroom related information to your Web site.

With the emergence of Web 2.0 tools, an increasing amount of Web sites allow users to group, chunk, and organize bits of information to share with others. Today's

digital students are accustomed to seeing information presented this way. Google Sites and many others are so simple to use, you can create your own Web site for your students in just a few minutes.

CREATING BLOGS

This section is about blogging and how to create classroom blogs for you and your students. Using a Web-based blogging program, like Blogger or EduBlogs, you can create a class blog in minutes! Recall from Chapter 2 that a blog, short for Weblog, is an informal Web site consisting of time-stamped articles, or posts, in a diary or journal format, usually listed in reverse chronological order. Recall also that a blog that contains video clips is called a video blog, or vlog. Blogs can be subject specific, open to the public or private, and entertaining or educational.

Because a blog entry is like a traditional journal or diary entry, it typically includes a date, ideas on a topic of interest, and a signature. Students can use blogs to practice writing and communication skills. Teachers can use them to post daily or weekly assignments, generate thoughts, stimulate classroom discussion, connect with parents, and much more. There are many sites that you can use to create blogs similar to the ones shown in Figure 6-33.

Figure 6-33 Blogs can be an effective integration tool in virtually all areas as shown in this high school teacher's blog for her English students.

BENEFITS OF USING BLOGS IN EDUCATION

There are many benefits to using classroom blogs with your students. In short, blogs can bring today's students into the world of writing and many other curriculum areas. Below are just some of the many benefits of classroom blogging. Using blogs, your students can do the following:

- Keep a diary on their reading, projects, or classroom discussions

- Embed links in their blogs as they research subjects and then report on their findings

- Keep track of project-related tasks that need to be completed

- Write up their findings on scientific experiments daily

- Copy and paste ideas or quotes from other sources, making sure to quote or link to their source, and then personally reflect on the topic

- Create cross-classroom prompts, thus being part of a network of readers and writers

- Create classroom storyboards with ongoing storytelling

- Log chronological events for social studies and research projects

- Learn math and mentor other students having difficulties with math concepts and assignments

- Ask others, such as friends, family members, librarians, and even local business professionals, to edit their blogs, or provide feedback

BLOGGING DO'S   Blogging, like many other technologies you use and integrate into the curriculum, has some risks. Although you cannot review all blog entries before they are published, you can take steps to lessen the risks of inappropriate entries.

- Do know your school's and district's Acceptable Use Policies (AUPs) and convey them to your students.

- Do get parental permission before allowing students to blog if blogging is not part of your school's Acceptable Use Policy (AUP).

- Do avoid blogging sites that require students to include their full names or e-mail addresses.

- Do avoid sites that request personal information from students.

- Do review what is permissible and appropriate with your students.

- Do remind students of the importance of netiquette and being respectful.

- Do have rules of appropriate behavior and consequences of misbehavior.

- Do provide examples of model blogs for students to review.

- Do remind your students that blogging is a privilege and appropriate behavior will ensure continued use.

- Do find out if your school district allows teachers to create classroom blogs that reside on the school or district server, which, in turn can be evaluated in a safe environment using peer evaluation.

LEARNING MORE ABOUT BLOGGING

Blogging is exciting. You can use blogging to engage your digital students in powerful learning activities using the Web-based tools, such as Blogger, that they relate to. Figure 6-34 lists additional resources that you can use to review examples of blogs, to learn more about blogging, and to help you in your blogging adventure.

> **Integration Strategies**
>
> To learn how to create your own classroom blog, refer to the In the Lab section, Creating a Class Blog, on page 334.

BLOG	URL
Blog.com	blog.com
Blogger	blogger.com
Blogstream	blogstream.com
EduBlogs	www.edublogs.org
Google Blog Search	www.google.com/blogsearch
TypePad	www.typepad.com
Weblogg-ed	www.weblogg-ed.com
WordPress	wordpress.org
WorldPress	www.worldpress.org/blogs.htm

All links were accurate at the time this book was printed but pages on the Web are always changing and being updated. If the link does not produce the page you were expecting, use your favorite search engine and key words on the topic to find the page.

Figure 6-34 Popular blog sites

ePortfolio Idea

CREATING A WIKI

Recall from Chapter 2 that a wiki is a collaborative Web site that allows users to create, add to, modify, or delete the Web site content via their Web browser. Most wikis are open to modification by anyone, and wikis are especially suited for collaborative writing. Wikis also allow for linking among any number of pages. This ease of interaction and operation makes a wiki a great tool for group authoring — a powerful tool for use in teaching students team work, writing skills, and so much more.

The term wiki also can refer to the collaborative software itself, called a **wiki engine**, which facilitates the operation of wiki sites. A popular online wiki is Wikipedia (Figure 6-35). A single page in a wiki is referred to as a **wiki page**, while the entire body of pages, which are usually highly interconnected via hyperlinks, is the wiki. A wiki is actually a very simple, easy-to-use, user-maintained database for creating, browsing, and searching for information.

You can integrate wikis in virtually any curriculum. For example, you can use wikis to build collaboration skills and to encourage brainstorming. A wiki is an easy way to create a Web site where students can showcase their work and projects. A wiki can be used to record and organize data, storyboard and plan, and ultimately create projects and other classroom activities. Wikis are great tools for journalism and collaborative writing. The bottom line about wikis is that anyone can edit anything at any time and add to the content of a wiki.

WIKI USES In addition to the ways already discussed, the following are just a few other ways that wikis can be used in education:

- to help create an easy, simple student-centered Web site

- to facilitate group authoring and collaboration

- as a repository for content, which can be viewed at any time from any place with an Internet connection by any student in your class

- to provide storage for data collection, which can be accessed as needed

- to display student projects

- to provide a vehicle for sharing reviews

- to share presentations, which students can view again for clarification or for the first time if they missed the class when a presentation was made

Figure 6-35 Wikipedia is a free encyclopedia used daily by millions of people.

Figure 6-36 Wikispaces is a popular site for creating classroom wikis.

WIKI CREATION SITES Creating your own wiki is as easy as 1-2-3! Wikis are fun, engaging, and powerful teaching and learning tools! There are numerous Web sites that will walk you through creating a wiki and will even host your wiki for free. In fact, numerous wiki sites are dedicated to helping teachers and students create their own wikis (Figure 6-36 above). Figure 6-37 lists popular wiki creation sites and sample classroom wikis.

When using and creating wikis, be sure to evaluate wiki hosting sites carefully before making a decision regarding which one to use. Some free wiki hosting sites require banner ads to be placed on your wiki, which, in most cases, are not appropriate for wikis you create for use with your students.

Integration Strategies

To learn how to create your own classroom wiki, refer to the In the Lab section, Creating a Class Wiki, on page 333.

Wiki Tools	URL
MediaWiki	www.mediawiki.org/wiki/MediaWiki
PBworks	pbworks.com
Wikis in Education	wikisineducation.wetpaint.com/
Wiki Search Engine	www.wiki.com
Wikispaces	www.wikispaces.com
Wiki-Teacher	wiki-teacher.com/
Voicethread	voicethread4education.wikispaces.com/
Sample Education Wikis	**URL**
8th Grade Social Studies Wiki	http://gps8socialstudies.pbwiki.com/
Bud the Teacher Wiki	www.budtheteacher.com/wiki/index.php?title=Main_Page
High School Online Collaborative Writing	schools.wikia.com/wiki/Main_Page
Neighborhood School Wiki	tnsny.org/
Tim Fredrick's ELA Teaching Wiki	timfredrick.pbworks.com/

All links were accurate at the time this book was printed but pages on the Web are always changing and being updated. If the link does not produce the page you were expecting, use your favorite search engine and key words on the topic to find the page.

Figure 6-37 Popular wiki tools and sample education wikis.

Web Info

For more information on podcasting, visit the Computer Concepts CourseMate Web site at *www. cengagebrain.com*, navigate to the Chapter 6 Web Info resource for this book, and then click Podcast.

CREATING A PODCAST

Podcasts are a popular way people share information on the Web using audio. The term podcast is derived from Apple's portable music player, the iPod (Figure 6-38). A **podcast** is recorded audio stored in a file on a Web site. The host or author of a podcast is often called a **podcaster**. A video podcast, or **vodcast**, is a podcast that contains video and usually audio. The term podcast refers to the content; the term podcasting refers to downloading or uploading a podcast.

Basically a podcast is an Internet-based radio show. Examples of podcasts include music, radio shows, news stories, classroom lectures, political messages, and television commentaries. Some Web sites, such as the popular podcast.com, specialize in podcast distribution while others incorporate links to podcasts on their existing Web site. You can often find a link to a podcast feed on your favorite news Web sites.

A podcast can be downloaded to a computer or many mobile devices, such as smartphones and iPods. A podcast can be downloaded automatically using programs capable of reading feed formats, such as RSS or Atom, and programs called feed readers or aggregators. When you want to download podcasts automatically, you subscribe to a feed associated with that podcast. When you subscribe, you supply a link to the podcast feed. Then, on a regular basis, the reader program checks the feeds you subscribe to in order to see if any of those feeds have new content since the last time it checked, and if so, retrieves that content and stores it on the computer or mobile device. Then, at a convenient time and location, you can listen to the downloaded podcast or watch the downloaded vodcast.

To create a podcast, you need a computer with a microphone to capture the audio input, software that allows you to export the audio file in the MP3 file format, software that lets you create an RSS feed, and a site to upload your podcast to. Once you have recorded and exported your podcast in the MP3 file format, you are ready to create your RSS feed and then upload your podcast to a server for others to download and listen to. Be sure to add tags to your file. The tags will be used by search engines to find your podcast. Finally, you want to be sure to submit your podcast with its tags to a search engine so that others will find your podcast when searching the Internet.

There are many sites devoted to podcasting. One to consider that can help you create podcasts is podcast.com, which allows you to record, publish, and upload your podcast directly from the Web site.

Figure 6-38 Apple introduced the concept of a podcast for use on the Apple iPod.

IMPLICATIONS FOR TEACHING Podcasting is a Web 2.0 tool that has become popular in education and popular with your digital students. Podcasts enable students and teachers to share all kinds of information with anyone at any time. In education, podcasts typically are produced (1) by students for use by other students or their friends, (2) by teachers for use by their students, and (3) by universities, corporations, education consortiums, and the government to provide resources and professional development for teachers and students.

You can create podcasts of a lesson or a block of instruction and your students can download the podcast of the recorded lesson. Teachers or administrators can create podcasts to communicate curriculum, assignments, sample tests, and other information to parents. Using podcasts, teachers and students can create book talks, vocabulary or foreign language lessons, international pen pal letters (podcast pals!), music performances, interviews, student presentations, debates, and so many other things — the uses are limitless. To help you learn more about podcasts, refer to Figure 6-39, which lists a number of popular podcast sites and education podcast sites.

MULTIMEDIA AUTHORING SOFTWARE

As you have already learned, multimedia authoring software is used to create electronic presentations, simulations, and software demonstrations that can include text, graphics, video, audio, animation, and screen captures. Some of these software programs, sometimes called video editing programs, are free and others must be purchased. Many of these software programs are covered in other parts of this textbook, especially in the Digital Media and Software Corners that follow each chapter.

A number of software programs help teachers and students easily create video screencasts and then add enhancements like Web cam videos and music tracks. A **screencast** is a digital recording of a computer's screen output, often containing audio. Just as a screenshot is a picture of a computer screen, a screencast is a movie

Podcast Sites	URL
Apple Podcasting	www.apple.com/itunes/podcasts/
Directory of Podcast Sites	www.podcast.com/
Education and Professional Podcast Directory	www.learnoutloud.com/Podcast-Directory/Education-and-Professional
Education Podcast Network	www.epnweb.org/
TruMix	trumix.com/genre/podcasts/Education
Yahoo Education Podcasting	groups.yahoo.com/group/Podcasting-Education/

All links were accurate at the time this book was printed but pages on the Web are always changing and being updated. If the link does not produce the page you were expecting, use your favorite search engine and key words on the topic to find the page.

Figure 6-39 Popular podcast sites.

of what a user sees on the monitor. For example, you can use a program like Camtasia Studio to record anything you do on your computer, including mouse movements, which allows you to show students how to perform activities, such as how to use the software program Inspiration or how to search the Web. The following are just some of the ways you and your students can use screencasts as digital representations of traditional printed materials:

- create digital student-centered and student-created tutorials

- teach lessons using PowerPoint presentations with voice-over and digital enhancements so the presentation becomes a video presentation

- develop short how-to-do videos and video-based, narrated demonstrations

- create digital storytelling projects

- provide digital reviews of software, rubrics, classroom rules, school policies, and so on

- present an explanation of detailed content-specific materials that students can watch over and over again from any place using a variety of media devices

- create animated whiteboard-type presentations

Web Info

For more information on Camtasia, visit the Computer Concepts CourseMate Web site at *www.cengagebrain.com*, navigate to the Chapter 6 Web Info resource for this book, and then click Camtasia.

CAMTASIA STUDIO Camtasia Studio (Figure 6-40) is a powerful, yet easy to use solution for you and your students to record, edit, and share high-quality instructional videos, student-created video-based projects, and more on the Web, via CDs, via DVDs, and via mobile devices, including tablets, smartphones, and iPods. Camtasia provides many powerful features. For example, you can

- Use the Record the Screen feature in Camtasia to record your screencast and

include audio (music and/or narration) if desired. You can even record yourself along with the screen video using an inexpensive Web cam and display yourself as a picture in a picture.

- Use the Record PowerPoint feature to create a narrated presentation literally with two clicks of your mouse. To stop the recording, you press the Esc key on your keyboard, save the file as you would any file, edit the video if necessary, and then produce the video as learning supplements for your students.

- Use Camtasia to create a podcast or vodcast. For example, you can create an audio podcast using your computer's microphone or an inexpensive USB microphone. You can edit your podcast if necessary, and then produce and upload your podcast. You can even upload your podcast using Camtasia's hosting service, Screencast.com.

Figure 6-40 Camtasia Studio allows teachers and students to easily create all types of screencasts and videos, and it has a 30-day free trial.

Camtasia Studio makes it easy to produce and distribute your videos in a number of different formats (see Figure 6-41). Your students can view your videos and their videos truly any time and any place, using the following ways:

- on any computer using the storage medium on which the video is stored, such as the hard drive, a USB flash drive, a CD, or a DVD

- streaming from the Web; even users that have dial up access can view your videos if you save them as Flash (.swf) files, which are significantly smaller than other video formats

- on any TV using a DVD player, a portable media player such as an iPod connected to the TV, or wirelessly from your PC, Macintosh computer, or portable media player using Apple TV or similar device connected to a TV

- on mobile devices, such as tablet computers (including the iPad), smartphones, and iPods, which allows students to watch your videos on the bus, during lunch, after school, or for that matter from just about any location and at any time they choose

Camtasia Studio is one example (there are many others) of new or recently

Figure 6-41 Using the Camtasia Production Wizard, you can produce and distribute your videos in a number of different formats.

updated software programs that allow you to easily and quickly create and distribute true digital instructional solutions to meet the needs of today's digital generation.

As you continue to learn more about online teaching and learning, you will develop many other strategies that will enhance your online classroom. The table in Figure 6-42 lists a number of additional strategies for you to explore. As you know, even with all great tools and educational improvements, you still must assess the learners. The next section focuses on this important area of assessment.

Strategy	Description
Skill Assessment Inventory	Start each class, course, or school year with an assessment tool that measures your students' content knowledge level and creates a baseline or starting point. The skills assessment process is critical in determining the skills and needs of your students before you get started delivering your content. Let students assist in creating the online assessment or survey development for lessons so they understand the learning expectations.
Differential Instruction	Create a variety of lessons and activities for different types of learners — this creates individualized instructional approaches that can be adapted based on the individual student and his or her diverse learning needs. As students learn, you can create activities to help reinforce the skills that contribute to educational success and to prepare them for upcoming assignments. Plus, you can create multiple ways for parents to participate and get involved in their children's learning.
Asynchronous Discussions	This is a very good strategy for getting students to interact (especially since students don't have to be online at the same time but can interact with comments in a discussion any time and any place) and to facilitate participatory learning. To maximize student interaction, discussions can be instructor-led or student-led and structured or unstructured. Discussions are easy to set up and allow students to demonstrate problem solving and critical thinking skills while they are learning from each other. Discussions can be used to create a social presence and interaction between the content and students.
Peer Review	Peer review is a wonderful assessment tool that provides students with an opportunity to coach each other. Research has also shown that peer review provides an excellent way for students to connect with and support each other and removes some of the *distance* from online education. When working with large enrollments, this strategy can make a significant difference in student satisfaction and help reduce the time needed for grading. Before using peer review as a tool, students need to be instructed on peer review techniques including how to effectively provide feedback.
Virtual Field Trips and Virtual Simulations	Online education opens up a virtual world to students — from visiting art museums in Rome to visiting Gettysburg virtually — virtual field trips can enhance almost any curriculum area. Virtual simulations let the student interact in a hands on way with curriculum-specific content, such as performing a virtual dissection, virtual chemistry experiments, virtual math problems, and more. In addition, an amazing number of apps have opened a new dimension for using these virtual tools and making it easier and more enjoyable for students to learn and meet core curriculum standards while having engaging and interactive experiences.
Authentic Learning Activities	Students of all ages are motivated by authentic learning activities. Making learning practical and applicable is key to keeping students engaged in an online class. Case studies are frequently used in higher education for this type of learning activity. You can create a bridge with these activities to your instructional goals. Use one or more case studies that present a central theme or question to prompt and guide you and your students on how to dig deeper into topics.
Interview an Expert	There are many experts willing to expand on your content. Your students can interact with and interview experts to get first-hand accounts of information beyond the classroom. Using video products that allow conferencing such as FaceTime for the iPad, Skype, and many other communication tools, students can meet F2F in real-time with these experts. These tools also help educators meet with students to discuss problems, clarify concepts, or provide individual feedback and support.
Role Playing	This is a super technique to get students of all ages engaged in the learning process and, surprisingly, this is easy to do virtually. Through the use of media, e-mail, synchronous and asynchronous communications, your students can effectively engage in role-playing.
Team Assignments	Well-designed team assignments are usually positively received by students. Working in virtual teams is a good strategy for building social presence and a sense of connectedness. Team projects need to be well structured and students need the opportunity to evaluate team members. One strategy for addressing those students that do not contribute is to place them on their own team! In addition, it is important to provide students with the tools to be successful working in a virtual team, such as access to wikis and chat tools.
WebQuest and/or Scavenger Hunts	WebQuests and Scavenger Hunts can be a great independent learning activity or a good group project as well. Just like any good learning activity, they take some time to set up but students enjoy the "quest" and exploration. This is also an example of problem-based learning. WebQuests increase student motivation, incentives, and interest in topics. When students are motivated, they are likely to put in more effort and are more likely to make learning associations. WebQuests and scavenger hunts create tasks that are designed to address problems or issues that exist in the real world, which makes the task authentic.

Figure 6-42 Shown are a number of additional strategies that you can use to enhance the learning experiences for your online students.

Assessing Online Learning

Are your students learning what they are supposed to be learning and if they are, how do you know? Is there a better way to teach subject-specific content online and promote a higher level of learning? Did I teach what I thought I taught? As an educator, you have probably asked these questions many times. These questions indicate the importance of assessment in all types of instruction.

Any instructional or supplemental materials should include an appraisal or assessment tool. The assessment tool should help students understand how a project or essay is going to be evaluated and it should help the teacher evaluate all projects or essays in a consistent manner. One example of an assessment tool is a rubric. A **rubric** is an explicit set of criteria that the student can use to self-evaluate his or her work prior to submission and that the teacher can use to provide feedback to the student. The feedback should include information about where the student successfully completed the assignment as well as areas that require further development, if any. A rubric can be created easily using the table feature in any word processing program. A rubric can be teacher-generated, student-generated, or a collaborative effort by both teacher and students.

Knowing that you are satisfying the needs of the students by offering appropriate feedback and keeping the lines of communications open is essential for making improvements and keeping students actively learning in your online class. While assessment tools are most often thought of as being used to determine students' grades, they can also be used to evaluate a number of areas, such as student placement, student advancement, differentiated student instructional needs, curriculum, and school standing. Developing fair and accurate assessments that provide feedback, information on what your students learned, how well they learned it, and how well you facilitated it, are vital to the process of education. The development of online assessments is no different.

Recall that assessment is any method used to understand the current knowledge a student possesses. It can range from a teachers' subjective judgment based on a single observation, to a student's performance on a quiz, to a state mandated standardized test results. **Alternative assessment** uses non-traditional methods to determine whether students have mastered the appropriate content and skill level. Teaching online also requires that you assess student learning. **eAssessment**, also called **Online assessment**, is the assessment of online teaching strategies, technology resources, online communications, eLearning activities, and online assignments in which technology and Web 2.0 tools are used.

There are two specific types of assessment that can be utilized in any type of learning: formative assessments and summative assessments. **Formative assessment** is the evaluation of student learning based on a specific time span at multiple points by gathering various activities and assignments to make sure the learner is developing the knowledge, skills, and ability to master the content. **Summative assessment** is the process of evaluating the student learning at any given point in time, for example, a quick quiz to assess student understanding of a concept after a lab has been completed or a test to assess the collective sum of the knowledge at the end of a unit, class, or course, and it is usually completed before moving onto other content.

Students as well as teachers can assess learning. Student assessments can be classified as **self-assessment**, which is the process of critically reviewing the quality of one's own performance, or as **peer-assessment**, which is the process of evaluating the work and activities of another individual or group. Examples of student assessments are participation in discussions, group consensus, as well as short tests and quizzes that encourage students to synthesize information.

As discussed in the special feature following Chapter 5, mastery learning is an instructional strategy that has been used for many years in the traditional classroom as well as in distance education. Supporting student learning through student mastery of content or other techniques like online quizzes, tests, and projects demonstrates student understanding of the online content and standards. eAssessment is an integral part of online evaluation, as it determines whether or not the goals of instruction are being met.

In the online environment, there are many ways to assess learning using various communications tools. One advantage of eAssessment is that it may provide immediate feedback; when this is the case, you can update or change online materials "just in time" to meet student needs. Which type of eAssessment you use to assess student learning will depend on the learning goals, objectives, and performance indicators you have specified in each lesson. Figure 6-43 provides several online activities and assessment techniques that you can explore to use in your online classroom.

Online Activity	Pre-Assessment	Post Assessment
WebQuest or Scavenger Hunt	KWL — The teacher creates a WebQuest or scavenger hunt that includes content-specific questions as well as a list of Web sites where students can go to research the answers. K - students fill in what they already know. W - students fill in what they want to learn.	KWL — Using a rubric created before the project, the teacher assesses student learning of the content by reviewing the student information in the answers they provided on their WebQuest or Scavenger Hunt. Students fill out the **L** section of the KWL to show what they learned.
Glogster	The teacher sends a Glogster with content-specific questions as an interactive survey to evaluate students' understanding of the content.	Using a rubric created before the project, the teacher assesses student learning of content by reviewing student content on their Glogster.
Google Sites	The teacher creates a wiki at Google Sites Web site for students to discuss what they already know or what they want to learn about the content presented in the wiki.	Using a rubric created before the project, the teacher assesses student learning of content by reviewing their responses on the wiki Web site. Students revisit wiki and discuss what they learned.
Google Doc Presentation or PowerPoint	The teacher creates a Google Doc or PowerPoint presentation to create a shared document for the class. The document might include a shape or an area in which a student can write a question he or she has about the content area.	Using a rubric created before the project, the teacher assesses student learning of content by reviewing the Google Doc or PowerPoint presentation. Students revisit the Google doc or PowerPoint presentation and answer the question they originally posted.
Google Doc Table/ Graph or Excel	The teacher uses a pretest-timed quiz to evaluate students' knowledge of content.	Using a rubric created before the project, the teacher assesses student learning of content by reviewing the Google Doc table or Excel table or graph.
Podcast using Audacity	The teacher creates an audio-based guide with questions for students. The teacher gives students a list of statements about content and asks them to write down whether they agree or disagree with the statements.	Using a rubric created before the project, the teacher assesses student learning of content by reviewing podcast. Students review anticipation guide and change answers as needed. Students explain their answers.
Digital Story using Photo or Video Software	Students create a story-based video based on curriculum-specific content using graphics, photos, and screens with text about what they know about the content.	Using a rubric created before the project, the teacher assesses student learning of content by reviewing the story-based video.
Voice Thread	Students create a Voice Thread by creating, collaborating, and communicating about curriculum-specific content; their Voice Thread includes content-specific questions for their classmates to respond to and interact with.	Using a rubric created before the project, the teacher assesses student learning of content by reviewing the Voice Thread content.
Journal or Reflection Blog	The teacher creates a right angle graphic organizer. Students write a fact about the content on the horizontal line and then write any feelings they have about it on the vertical line. They can add additional facts and feelings by adding additional lines.	Using a rubric created before the project, the teacher assesses student learning of content by the students reviewing journal blogs. Students finish their right angle graphic organizers by adding facts and feelings to it.
Wikispaces	The teacher sets up content-specific questions and assignments in a wiki. The students use the wiki to create, collaborate, and communicate throughout the learning process by contributing to the wiki.	Using a rubric created before the project, the teacher assesses student learning of content by reviewing student collaboration and their wikis.

Figure 6-43 Shown are a few pre- and post-assessment ideas matched to online activities.

Putting It All Together: The Florida Virtual School

Florida Virtual School (FLVS) was the first virtual school in the nation and it has had a major influence in the explosion, success, and recognition of K-12 online learning (Figure 6-44). Currently, FLVS is an established leader in the United States and the world in developing and providing virtual K-12 education solutions that meet the diverse needs of today's students. FLVS is a nationally recognized eLearning solution that provides media rich courses and instructional practices that engage students in ways they learn best.

Florida Virtual School was founded in 1997 as a cooperative effort involving the Alachua County and Orange County School Districts. It was originally funded by the Florida state legislature. The original funding was a Break the Mold grant from the Florida Department of Education for $200,000. Today, funding is based on the number of students who complete a course as part of the state public school funding program.

According to the Florida Virtual School Executive Summary, FLVS began with 77 completions its first year (1997) and has grown to more than 259,000 completions over a 14 year period (Figure 6-45). FLVS provides virtual education solutions for students in all 67 Florida school districts, 49 states, and 46 countries. FLVS's main goal is based on one philosophy — to help all students succeed and the mission is to deliver a high-quality, technology-based education that provides the skills and knowledge students need for success. Their vision is to transform education worldwide — one student at a time. The Florida Virtual School is dedicated to individual learning, which is the focus of all its learning activities and instruction.

Beyond the online course content, which is offered in many different formats, teachers interact with students regularly through multiple communication modes such as chat, discussion and forums, e-mail, voice mail, telephone conversations, video conferencing, and instant messaging. Teachers are readily available for students to ask questions and get help on assignments — a usual day is from 8 a.m. to 8 p.m., as well as during weekend hours. One requirement is that teachers speak via telephone with students and their parents at least once per month. These multiple modes of communication not only focus on but also meet the learning needs of students.

In addition to these multiple modes of communication, FLVS has been developing

Figure 6-44 Florida Virtual School is an established leader in the virtual schools movement both in the U.S. and in the world.

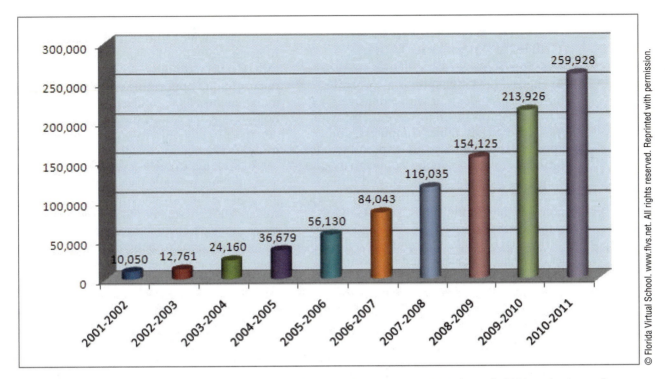

Figure 6-45 This chart shows the amazing growth that FLVS has had from 2001 through 2011 and mirrors the explosive growth of K-12 students taking online courses across the U.S.

education games to teach standards-based curriculum such as history, reading, and much more. The *Conspiracy Code*, an interactive 3D American History adventure game, is a very innovative conceptual framework for teaching that FLVS employs to bring history to life. Students learn while doing in a virtual environment (Figure 6-46).

Another effective strategy used by FLVS teachers is the use of virtual reality. A well-known virtual reality technology is **Second Life for Educators**, which is a

Figure 6-46 Florida Virtual School uses many interactive learning tools to enhance student learning, shown is *Conspiracy Code*, an interactive 3D adventure game.

virtual world used for communication, social networking, presenting, sharing content, and collaborating. Many experts refer to these programs as a multi-user virtual environment (MUVE). The users interact in these online worlds in real time and users create everything in this virtual world. The International Society for Technology in Education (ISTE) endorses the use of Second Life for Educators and has become a very active member in using Second Life.

Remember from earlier in this chapter that **app-based learning** is the use of curriculum specific apps to supplement online teaching and learning and that some virtual schools are creating their own apps because they are perfect solutions for on-demand learning tools for today's online digital students. In fact, teachers and administrators at FLVS are creating a series of apps titled meStudying Apps (see Figure 6-29 on page 310). Teachers at FLVS use meStudying apps to engage students and supplement their online curricula. By leveraging mobile technology, FLVS is offering students another learning tool to gain a deeper level for individualized learning to meet the student's ever-changing needs.

A World without Wires — Tablets, Apps, and More

At the end of this chapter is a special feature that provides you with extensive information on the innovative use of wireless technologies, tablet computers, and apps in education. First, this special feature introduces you to wireless connectivity and explains the characteristics of and differences between three common wireless technologies, Bluetooth, Wi-Fi, and 3G/4G cellular networks.

Next, you will be introduced to the tablet computer revolution and the profound impact this transformation is having on the way you teach and your students learn. Experts are predicting that most students in the U.S. will have their own tablet computer loaded with ebooks and curriculum-specific apps by the start of the 2014/2015 school year. While Apple's iPad as well as many of the features available on the iPad, such as FaceTime, video mirroring, AirPrint, iCloud storage, iTunes U, MobileMe, ebooks, note taking, and accessibility, is highlighted throughout the special feature, this information is transferrable to any tablet you might be using.

Summary and Implications for Education

Distance education is changing the face of education and the way teachers teach and students learn. For example, imagine being a student with an illness such as cancer; one of the many complications of this illness is that you cannot attend school. A virtual school offers so many opportunities for these students to continue their studies on their time and at their own pace, often allowing these students to stay on track with their classmates so, when they are ready to return to school, they can do so seamlessly. This example is just one of the many ways the face of education is changing.

K-12 education is moving toward a more global, technology-rich environment that is designed to meet the changing needs of students and society. The Internet has shifted from being a static communication mode of text-only information into a powerful two-way interactive communications system with applications that are revolutionizing teaching and learning. The Internet removes all obstacles related to time, place, and physical limitations, which opens unique opportunities for teachers and students. The popularity of these technologies has increased the necessity to create and provide online content to students in K-12 and higher education.

In addition to brick-and-mortar buildings, all states are now using online technologies and creating virtual schools for teaching students using different modalities. The instructional strategies of teachers are undergoing major transformations as more and more students are taught using eLearning or virtual learning environments. The changes include the way we think about the role of both teacher and student. Both teachers and students are facing new standards that focus on a student-centered curriculum, increased interactive learning, integration of technology into the educational system, and collaborative learning activities. Basic to these changes needs to be an examination of the critical principles of what determines quality instructional interaction. These principles should guide decisions made that impact the long-term and potential benefit to student learning and that are based on the merits of the technology or the methodologies.

As we progress through this second decade of the 21st century, we are likely to see an explosion of K-12 online blended school programs that will merge the best of both worlds — F2F and online opportunities. Many educators believe blended courses are the best instructional model for preparing today's K-12 digital kids for higher education and employment in an ever-changing global economy. This belief is supported by a major research study conducted by the U.S. Department of Education, *The Evidence on Online Education*, which found that in higher education "students who took all or part of their instruction online performed better, on average, than those taking the same course through face-to-face instruction." The report further stated that courses "that combined elements of online learning and face-to-face instruction appeared to be best of all."

As you continue to grow in your teaching profession, you will need to stay abreast of eLearning and its impact on the changing face of education.

Key Terms

INSTRUCTIONS: Use the Key Terms to help focus your study of the terms used in this chapter. To further enhance your understanding of the Key Terms in this chapter, visit the Computer Concepts CourseMate Web site at www.cengagebrain.com, and then navigate to the Chapter 6 Key Terms resource for this book. Read the definition for each term, and then access current and additional information about the term from the Web.

100 percent online course [290]

alternative assessment [320]
app-based learning [323]
app-enhanced learning [310]
asynchronous [283]

Blackboard Collaborate [295]
blended [290]
blended learning [296]
blended schooling [296]
brick-and-mortar school [290]

Camtasia Studio [318]
Content Management System (CMS) [293]
Credit Recovery [295]
cyber charter school [292]
cyber school [292]

differentiated instruction [298]
differentiated learning [298]
distance education [283]
distance learning [283]
distributed learning [283]
dual enrollment [295]

eAssessment [320]
eLearning [289]
eLearning course [283]
elearning whiteboard [304]
electronic learning [289]

Flash Appointments [307]
formative assessment [320]

Google Sites [311]

hybrid [290]
hybrid classes [297]
hybrid learning [296]

in-residence requirement [286]
instructor-led [283]
instructor-led training [288]

learning coach [295]
Learning Management System (LMS) [293]

mixed mode [290]
mixed mode learning [296]
mLearning [309]
mobile learning apps [310]
Murphy's Law [308]

online [290]
online assessment [320]
online course [283]
online learning [289]
online whiteboard [304]
online workshop [285]

peer-assessments [320]
podcast [316]
podcaster [316]
protocols [307]

rubric [320]

screencast [317]
Second Life for Educators [323]
self-assessment [320]
self-paced [283]
self-paced training [288]
summative assessment [320]
synchronous [283]

team teaching [308]
time management [306]
Tipping Point [282]

virtual [290]
virtual charter school [292]
virtual course [290]
virtual learning [289]
virtual classroom environment [289]
virtual learning environment [289]
virtual school [292]
vodcast [316]

Walden University [286]
Web-based course [283]
Web-based seminar [284]
Web-based training (WBT) [284]
Web conferencing [284]
Web-enhanced [287]
Webcast [284]
Webinar [284]
wiki engine [314]
wiki page [314]

Checkpoint

INSTRUCTIONS: Use the Checkpoint exercises to check your knowledge level of the chapter. To complete the Checkpoint exercises interactively, visit the Computer Concepts CourseMate Web site at www.cengagebrain.com, and then navigate to the Chapter 6 Checkpoint resource for this book.

1. Label the Figure

Instructions: Identify the four different formats or modalities in which content is being offered in K-12 and higher education.

Course Category	Course Description
1. _____	Has no online technology or components used for content delivery; instructor and students are in the same location for content delivery.
2. _____	Uses Web-based technology to facilitate what is essentially an F2F course; may use a course management system (CMS) or a learning management system (LMS), and/or Web pages to post the syllabus, schedule, and assignments.
3. _____	Blends online and F2F instructional techniques; substantial proportion of the content is delivered online, typically uses online discussions, and has a reduced number of F2F meetings.
4. _____	All of the content is delivered online; if there are F2F meetings, they are optional.

2. Matching

Instructions: Match each term from the column on the left with the best description from the column on the right.

_____ 1. distance education	a.	evaluation of student online work
_____ 2. asynchronous	b.	delivery of instruction from one location to another
_____ 3. synchronous	c.	communications occur at different times
_____ 4. podcast	d.	recorded audio stored in a file on a Web site
_____ 5. eAssessment	e.	communication happens in real time

3. Short Answer

Instructions: Write a brief answer to each of the following questions.

1. Explain the differences between 100 percent online and blended learning. Why are both approaches important for K-12 education?

2. List and describe characteristics of a virtual school. What are the differences between a virtual school and a virtual school program?

3. Describe how tablet computers and apps are impacting online learning. Why is it important for teachers and administrators to incorporate apps in their online and blended classes?

4. Explain how Web pages, blogs, wikis, and screencasts can be used as tools to enhance teaching and learning. Why are these tools important tools for K-12 education?

5. Why is eAssessment important for online and blended classes? List and describe three online assessment or eAssessment techniques.

Teaching Today

INSTRUCTIONS: Teaching Today provides teachers with integration strategies and ideas for teaching and, more importantly, reaching today's digital generation. Each numbered segment contains one or more links that reinforce the information presented in the segment. To display this page from the Web, visit the Computer Concepts CourseMate Web site at www.cengagebrain.com, and then navigate to the Chapter 6 Teaching Today resource for this book.

1. Technology Rich Environment

We live in an ever growing and evolving environment where technology is available for us to use everywhere we go. The availability of technology has increased the potential and quality of education. Students no longer have to carry around heavy textbooks; instead, they can access their textbooks electronically via tablet computers, ebook readers, and other mobile devices. Teachers and students are not restricted to paper and pencil activities. Students can download content to many different devices, as well as interact with content from many Web sites. For example, when completing a lesson on air pollution, students can complete an e-lesson on air pollution rather than simply listen to a traditional lecture. What are the benefits of having student's textbooks on mobile devices and activities online? What technology do you have access to that can help your students' motivation and learning?

2. Virtual Field Trips

As a social studies teacher, you know that students learn best through experiences. For this reason field trips are always very beneficial to the growth of your students' academics. As you know, field trips require planning, paper work, funds, and volunteers. Whether you are teaching F2F or a blended online course, you know that going on a field trip to museums or historical sites would be great but it could also be unrealistic. You have decided to teach a unit on World War II. What if you could travel in time and take your students on a virtual field trip to historical places? Your virtual tour could have a presenter who conducts a video chat with your students and shares important historical facts. Locate a virtual field trip that will match a topic that you want your students to experience virtually. What are some advantages? What are some disadvantages?

3. Kids Connected

Students today are always finding ways to get connected. For example, children of all ages know how to use a smartphone. In fact, research has shown that even at the age of three some children learn how to use their parents' and grandparents' smartphones. Often they know how to use these devices even better than their parents and grandparents! These children are always finding ways to connect with the Internet and Web. Why? Because it just seems to be natural to them. To extend this connectedness into the classroom, some teachers are using blogs and other tools to create a connected classroom. Many teachers are setting up online class discussions and assignments using a classroom blog, like KidBlog. How could you use a blog in your classroom? Think about content areas and ways you might want to integrate that content into blogs. Describe some ways you can use this Web 2.0 tool to connect your students and create collaborative activities.

4. Blended Classrooms Using Edmodo

Are you prepared to Tweet with your students? Well, most teachers would be a little leery of this idea; if this is you, then Edmodo is your answer. Edmodo is a teacher-created, private, secure social platform, with a Twitter-type networking tool for teachers and students to share ideas, files, events, and assignments. As you know teaching current events is very important in most grades. A social network tool like Edmodo could help you create an In the News: Current Events Group, which would allow students to post articles and blogs that are relevant to classroom curriculum. Teachers can use Edmodo to develop chat rooms where students can collaborate with one another in real time. Teachers can use Edmodo to instruct, assign, and communicate with their students online and in real time in their blended classrooms. Think of ways you could use Edmodo in a lesson or unit for your students. What are the benefits of using Edmodo in a blended virtual classroom? What are the disadvantages?

Education Issues

INSTRUCTIONS: Education Issues provides several scenarios that allow you to explore controversial and current issues in education. Each numbered segment contains one or more links that reinforce the information presented in the segment. To display this page from the Web, visit the Computer Concepts CourseMate Web site at www.cengagebrain.com, and then navigate to the Chapter 6 Education Issues resource for this book.

1. Cyberbullying

In January 2010, the Boston Herald reported that several Massachusetts high school students were questioned and suspended from school following the suicide of a teenage girl at their school. Friends and school officials reported the 15-year-old girl had been bullied by several male students at school and online since moving to Massachusetts from another country. The bullies allegedly reported they taunted the teen through text messages, Facebook, and other social networking sites. It is not clear why the young girl committed suicide but you have to consider the horrible influence of bullying and cyberbullying. The news reported that, even after her death, the bullies continued cyberbullying by posting disparaging messages on her Facebook memorial page. Cyberbullying continues to be a growing problem in F2F and online school programs. There are two types of cyberbullying: direct attacks, which are messages or posts sent directly to the person, and cyberbullying by proxy, which is using others to help cyberbully the victim. What would you do if you overheard students in your class talking about a group of students who are sending cruel messages to other students? You are not sure if this is bullying or if the teenagers are having relationship issues. Should you look deeper into this situation? What are the first steps you should take? If this is a case of cyberbullying, what procedures and organizations are available to help you and the student before the situation develops further?

2. Quality Online Education

Due to the amazing growth of K-12 online education, there are many types of organizations, businesses, and school districts offering K-12 online school programs. Many parents, teachers, and administrators have a shared concern about quality online education in the eLearning environment. This is a valid concern and one you should think about when determining where you might teach. Parents of your students are probably confused as well about the choices regarding online learning. As a current or future teacher of online courses, how can you assure parents they are choosing the right school to help their child both love learning and be successful? Of course you know you must research any topic, but where do you start? What types of accreditations does the virtual school have? Describe the advantages and disadvantages of learning online in the K-12 environment. Tell how you can communicate this information to parents of prospective online students.

3. Lack of Social Interaction

In the fast paced world we live in — where technology is the preferred mode of communication, many experts are revealing that individuals might be losing basic communications skills. Lack of real-world classroom interaction is often listed as a contributing factor in the lack of social and communications skills. There is a growing body of research on the issues surrounding the social interaction and social presence in online learning. With more students completing classes online rather than in a traditional face-to-face setting, teachers should be assisting their students in developing appropriate social skills. Teachers can help ensure that students are still interacting and developing social skills by teaching students to use other forms of communication and create assignments that require students to interact. What activities requiring social interaction do you have students complete in your classroom that you could do as an online activity?

4. Students' Authentic Work and Online Classes

Since lessons, activities, quizzes, and tests are given and completed online, the authenticity of student work is an ongoing and valid concern in online classes. Schools and educators must determine effective ways to ensure that students are completing their own work. For example, what if your students are taking a biology quiz online, what could you do to ensure your students are not copying each others answers? One option, often used in blended courses, is teachers can give some quizzes and tests in a F2F setting, which allows teachers to ensure that the scores are accurate. As a teacher, what solutions would you suggest for this very real area of concern? What steps do you think educators and programs need to take to ensure the authenticity of students' work?

Apps Corner

INSTRUCTIONS: Apps Corner provides extensive ideas and resources for integrating technology into your classroom-specific curriculum. To display this page from the Web and information on numerous education apps, visit the Computer Concepts CourseMate Web site at www.cengagebrain.com, and then navigate to the Chapter 6 Apps Corner resource for this book.

Apps Corner is designed for teachers and other educators who are looking for innovative ways to integrate apps into their content-specific curriculum. Apps Corner not only provides great apps with current information but also shows how other educators are using and integrating education apps. As a result, Apps Corner is designed with all educators in mind, regardless of their interests or subject area. You can use Apps Corner to expand your resources by reviewing apps outside your curriculum area; remember many apps associated with one curriculum area can be adapted for use and added to lesson plans in a wide variety of other curriculum areas.

Use Apps Corner as a springboard for collaborating and sharing the successes and hurdles of integrating apps in a classroom or an entire school system. Consider Apps Corner a place to locate app integration ideas and resources. Information on educational apps are organized in four Corners (Early Childhood, Elementary, Middle School, and Secondary), and different apps are available for each chapter. Many apps are free, others cost from $1 to $5. Inexpensive site licenses for classrooms, schools, and school districts are available for many apps.

Shown below are two highly rated Apps. The first is one for students to learn and then test their knowledge of English grammar concepts. The second is an interactive math app, MathBoard, for elementary students to learn numbers, master multiplication, solve basic algebraic equations, conquer beginning statistics, and more.

Software Corner

INSTRUCTIONS: Software Corner provides information on popular software programs. Each numbered segment discusses specific software programs and contains a link to additional information about these programs. To display this page from the Web, visit the Computer Concepts CourseMate Web site at www.cengagebrain.com, and then navigate to the Chapter 6 Software Corner resources for this book.

1. Blackboard Collaborate

As an educator, you know that all students are different and most of your students are at various performance levels and require varying amounts of support for differentiated instructional strategies. Some students need step-by-step guidance, while others need higher level activities to be challenged. Sometimes students in online classes need clarification on the LMS tools or need assistance in a particular concept about which they are lost, confused, or simply do not understand. Combining the capabilities of the popular programs Wimba and Elluminate, Blackboard Collaborate provides a comprehensive learning platform designed specifically for education. Blackboard Collaborate offers an interactive learning experience that helps keep everyone engaged. Blackboard Collaborate helps you create virtual classrooms, which open exciting new approaches for peer-to-peer learning and instructor-led help while involving each student on an individual level. Blackboard Collaborate helps you accommodate different learning styles or instructional needs and saves time with dynamic whiteboard content. Check out the free 30-day trail.

2. Second Life

Second Life is an online virtual world developed by Linden Lab and it is accessible on the Internet. Individuals, educators, schools, and universities have found many uses for the Second Life virtual environment. This virtual world is not specifically for education, but it can be a great tool for educators. This virtual environment creates a virtual world where teachers can hold classes or lectures, have guest speakers, or go over lessons and activities, while, at the same time, students can interact in real time from the comfort of their homes. Second Life uses Avatars, which allow instructors and students to be virtually in the class environment interacting with other students or the teacher. Avatars can raise their hands to ask questions, collaborate in small groups to work on team projects, and much more. As we know digital students love video games, Second Life creates a learning environment with a video game feel to it. How could you use Second Life with your students?

3. My Access!®

My Access!® from Vantage Learning is a Web-based program designed to assist in developing and enhancing student writing. This program supports what all educators know — strong literacy skills are crucial for all students to be successful. Teachers can make timely, data-driven decisions for successful differentiated instruction and motivate students to write more frequently by providing them with innovative prompts that use a variety of media like video and audio. There also is the ability to create lessons with immediate feedback. My Access! promotes students' learning experiences by making the writing process fun by encouraging students to choose writing prompts from a variety of topics. In addition to the writing prompts that come with My Access!, teachers can create their own prompts. As students begin the writing process, they are given a selection of prewriting tools, such as graphic organizers, to help them plan their essays. What is really great about this program is, once the student submits the essay, the program analyzes the writing and provides a holistic essay score. While this feedback is helpful for the students, it is also very helpful for teachers because it helps teachers narrow down which areas of instruction the students are having difficulties with.

4. GIZMOS

GIZMOS by ExploreLearning is a great example of an eLearning software program that provides hundreds of interactive online simulations for grades 3-12 in math and science. Students find GIZMOS fun and easy to use and, at the same time, the software helps students develop a deep understanding of challenging concepts through inquiry and exploration. This program allows teachers and students to explore and understand concepts virtually. Gizmos can be used for individual, small group, and whole group exploration and experiments. GIZMOS lessons are correlated with state curriculum standards, which makes it easy for teachers to ensure they are meeting all their lesson objectives and state standards. For example, if you are completing a unit on animal dissection, students can accomplish the concepts virtually and without the smell, instead of conducting real dissections.

Digital Media Corner

INSTRUCTIONS: Today's K-12 digital students need their learning to be meaningful and relevant to their lives. Digital Media Corner provides videos, ideas, and examples of how you can use digital media to enhance your teaching and your students' learning. To access the videos and links to additional information, visit the Computer Concepts CourseMate Web site at www.cengagebrain.com, and then navigate to the Chapter 6 Digital Media Corner resource for this book.

1. Digital Storytelling and Storyboarding

How do you teach your students to understand a story? With today's digital world, students are more inclined to use digital tools to create a script rather than spend hours working with a pencil to get the script just right. Creating digital stories and learning the skill of storytelling takes a lot of planning and creativity. One of the first steps in the creation of a story is creating a storyboard. A storyboard is a pre-planned series of panels that can include all aspects of the story such as scenes, scripts, camera angles, and effects. One of the true values of digital media in education is its ability to empower teachers and students to develop various forms of self-expression through story creation. Kidsvid is a Web site created for teachers and kids with step-by-step techniques for storyboarding, scripting, video production, and is full of tutorials to teach your students how to create better stories.

2. Interactive Digital Presentation Tools

To enhance PowerPoint or Keynote presentations, there are a number of Web 2.0 tools that let you create and present online digital presentations in order to engage students in new and exciting ways. Popular tools include SlideShare and VoiceThread. SlideShare uses any of your presentations created in PowerPoint or Keynote and allows you to share them on the Web. VoiceThread is an online visual and audio presentation collaborative, multimedia slide show tool that stores images, documents, and videos. It allows people to navigate through a presentation and leave comments using voice, text, audio file, or video. Essentially, it creates a thread of all the comments from within picture presentation and adds the thread automatically to the slide.

3. TV on Your Computer or Smartphone — Anywhere in the World

Slingbox, produced by Sling Media, is a device that enables you to view any program that plays on your TV or on a computer with a broadband Internet connection, which is a technology known as place shifting. Place shifting products and services can redirect up to four different audio and/or video signals simultaneously from a cable box, a satellite receiver, or personal video recorder to any computer in the world as long as that computer has a broadband Internet connection. This way of accessing content is available in standard or HD formats. Software loaded on a user's computer connects to the Slingbox and provides the user interface for viewing the video stream and for changing channels. There are numerous versions of Slingbox for PCs and Macs. When using smartphones and tablets, you can access your Slingbox from anywhere with the SlingPlayer app.

4. Web Adventures

Many schools are using digital media applications and the Web to help students better understand the past or gain a greater appreciation of other cultures. For example, by using digital media Web applications, students are able to immerse themselves in the content. This happens through Interactive Web Adventures — such as Amazon Interactive, a project focusing on the people and geography of the Ecuadorian Amazon, or Cyberchase, an interactive and fun math adventure by PBS. Lessons using these types of digital media applications and Web adventures can be created for all grade levels. How does their use compare with traditional approaches to instruction and learning? How could you use these types of resources in your classroom? What supplemental materials would you need?

Assistive Technologies Corner

INSTRUCTIONS: Assistive Technologies Corner provides information on current hardware, software, and peripherals that will assist you in delivering instruction to students with physical, cognitive, or sensory challenges. To access extensive additional information, visit the Computer Concepts CourseMate Web site at www.cengagebrain.com, and then navigate to the Chapter 6 Assistive Technologies Corner resource for this book.

1. How can a hearing or visually impaired student benefit from the use of a tablet computer, like the iPad?

Students who are hearing or visually impaired often become frustrated with the inability to do certain actions. Thankfully, for an increasing number of individuals the iPad has changed this and revolutionized the way they see or hear the outside world. iPads and other tablets have quickly become tools that can pave a fresh path to learning. Tablet computers have universal access features, such as built in text-to-speech, voice command, auto text, video chat, and magnification, that can assist the disabled. The screen's size and ability for zooming makes the tablet easily accessible for students with vision problems. Additionally, iPad users can use the VoiceOver function, which describes the item verbally when the user touches the screen. The White on Black feature can also be added to any application for those individuals who are color blind. In addition, Mono Audio also allows users with a hearing loss to reroute the audio channels from both the left and right ear to the preferred ear. Students can use Skype and talk on the phone, lip-read, or use FaceTime which is a new HD-quality video tool. FaceTime makes it possible for students to converse with other students anywhere in the world as if they were face-to-face, which allows students who are hearing impaired to sign real time using the Internet.

2. How could tablets help special needs students with their fine motor skills?

Using traditional computers can be challenging for some students with disabilities, particularly for students with fine motor skills deficiencies. These students often have a hard time typing, holding a pencil, or writing with any type of writing utensil, which can cause them to become frustrated since they take longer than the average student to complete a task. Some students with these difficulties find the touch screen offered by the tablets much easier to control. Students who are unable to write on paper can use their fingers to write on the touch screen. There are apps such as Dexteria, which help both students and adults improve their fine motor skills. This app uses a variety of therapeutic hand exercises. There are also many applications that can help students with their motor skills, while entertaining them at the same time.

3. How is a tablet more accessible than a traditional notebook or desktop computer?

A student with disabilities faces many obstacles to completing everyday tasks. With the use of assistive technologies, tablets open up a new world of possibilities for them. Although many previous devices before the tablet have been bulky and often expensive, the iPad and similar BlackBerry and Android tablets offer easy and inexpensive solutions for students with disabilities. A tablet's touch-screen design allows the users more agility than a desktop computer with a mouse or a laptop with a touchpad. Since there is no mouse or track pad, students simply touch the screen and it responds. For some students with disabilities, using a keyboard in the traditional manner can be a difficult task just as the mechanics of handwriting can be a challenge. Tablets offer numerous alternatives with their easy and functional touch screens, and their on-screen, touch screen keyboards. In addition, tablets offer hundreds of apps created specifically for use on tablets. Laptops and desktops can often take five minutes or more to boot up completely and get set up properly, which can take away from valuable teaching/learning time, but tablets turn on within seconds and are ready to go. In addition, tablets, with their 10-hour battery, last much longer than a typical laptop. Students can also move around with their tablets, which is impossible with desktop computers and which can be difficult for some students with heavier and bulkier notebook computers. Probably, most importantly, students can take their tablets home with them, which was often impossible with other hardware and software programs used by schools. Additional information on accessibility features standard on all tablets and information on accessibility apps are covered in this chapter's special feature, *A World without Wires — Tablets, Apps, and More.*

Follow the instructions at the top of this page to display additional information and this chapter's links on assistive technologies.

In the Lab

PRODUCTIVITY IN THE CLASSROOM

Introduction: Learning new technologies is essential in today's educational world because they are providing new and exciting pathways for both educators and students to follow. Being in the know about these new digital tools, such as wikis and blogs, and then integrating them into your curriculum allows your students to have a more enriching learning environment. Furthermore, many of these tools, once considered peripheral, have become essential instructional tools, especially as traditional learning environments have shifted to new learning environments. Tutorials can provide you with new and innovative teaching skills, such as setting up wikis and blogs. The following are some links to help you develop, process, or improve your wiki and blogging skills: building a wiki and building a classroom blog.

1. Creating a Class Wiki

Problem: You are trying to find ways to actively engage your students and so you ask your 7th grade students to help you build a class wiki. Your plan is to have your wiki consist of some of the topics that your students will be covering throughout the school year, which you hope will add enrichment to your curriculum and your students' learning. You have heard how students can engage and immerse themselves in a wiki and you have decided to try it out. As you create your class wiki, personalize it for either your current or future teaching position. If applicable, follow any specific content requirements for your wiki provided by your instructor. Use the sample wiki in Figure 6-47 as a guide. The first step is to sign-up for a wiki at a site of your choice, such as www.wikispaces.com (this is just one of many sites that you can use to create a wiki). The following general steps provide an overview of how to create your class wiki. You will need to follow the on-screen directions, which might differ from those listed next, in order to create your class wiki. While the steps are unique to each wiki development site, the general idea as discussed below is the same.

Instructions: Perform the following tasks.

1. Type www.wikispaces.com in your browser. Scroll to the bottom of the page and click Create a free K-12 wiki in the right pane. (Use a different wiki development site if you prefer.)

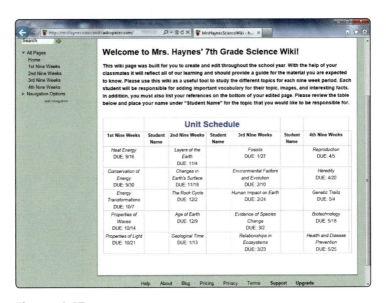

Figure 6-47

In the Lab

2. When you create your wiki, you should provide your name and the title of your wiki (note that the title you choose will be part of your wiki's URL). Personalize your wiki to your subject matter and school name or your name, such as Mrs. Smith Science Wiki; in this case, the URL would be: MrsSmithScienceWiki.wikispaces.com.

3. Join the wiki and spend some time reading the Getting Started directions to familiarize yourself with some of the many available wiki features. When you are done, close the Getting Started directions and begin creating your wiki.

4. Click the Edit button in the upper-right corner of the title bar in order to edit the current page. Write the title in the space provided, delete the existing text, and then write an introduction paragraph explaining the purpose of the wiki.

5. Next, add a table to your wiki page that outlines the topics that will be covered, the due date for each topic, and any other pertinent information. Later you can have each of your students sign up for a particular topic.

6. Save your wiki and write down your wiki information, including the URL, username, and password.

Enjoy your wiki and let the learning begin!

2. Creating a Class Blog

Problem: You are trying to increase classroom communication between your different periods for your 7th grade Language Arts class. You have never worked with blogs before and have heard that they may be a great way to encourage different class period communications while still supervising what is said. You know that there are many blog creation sites, but you decide to use Blogger to create a basic blog. As you create your classroom blog, personalize it either for your current or for a future teaching position. If applicable, follow any specific content requirements for your blog provided by your instructor. Use the sample blog shown in Figure 6-48 as a guide and follow the general directions below to create your class blog.

Instructions: Perform the following tasks.

1. Type www.blogger.com in your browser (or a blogging site of your choice). Note: These steps cannot be followed exactly because the instructions on each blogging Web site vary. These steps are intended to provide a general idea of how to create a blog. You should follow the

Figure 6-48

In the Lab

on-screen instructions specific to the blogging Web site you elected to use in order to create your blog.

2. Select the link to create an account. The link might say something like: Create Your Blog Now or Try the template designer.

3. If you plan to use a template, browse through the different templates and select a template that matches the purpose of the blog and type in appropriate class information.

4. Follow the on-screen directions to begin working with the template and to fill in the form with the information as requested. Note: You will probably be asked to type the blog title, the blog address (and check the availability of that address), type a Word Verification sequence if requested, and then continue to follow the on-screen directions. You will want to personalize your blog by creating a title using your name and the blog URL. Be sure to make the title meaningful to your class such as "Mrs. Smith's Class Blog." You could also use this title as part of your URL: www.mrssmithclassblog.blogspot.com.

5. You have just setup your very own blog. You can start blogging.

6. In your first blog entry, welcome your students and clearly outline your expectations for your class blog. Next, post a discussion thread that you would like your students to comment on.

7. Share your blog URL with your students and start working on your class online discussions.

8. Follow your instructor's instructions for handing in this assignment.

INTEGRATION IN THE CLASSROOM

1. You have been looking into ways to create social collaborations with your students, so you decide to integrate a wiki in your classroom instructional strategies. Wikis are a great tool to help enrich instruction and increase communication and collaboration among students. There are many free wiki-hosting sites for educators, like Wikispaces, PBWorks, and Wiki Educational Community that provide unlimited storage for digital materials including audio, photos, videos, screencasts, presentations, and more. Have your students create a class documentary video based on the content you chose. Students can use the wiki as a place to share resources, make decisions, and discuss before they start the process of creating the video — planning is very important and this helps your students to develop higher-order thinking skills while working with other students to create a consensus. The wiki gives all students the opportunity to participate and reflect on the learning process as they work on the project.

2. Students taking online classes do not have the same social and communication interaction with their classmates as they did in their F2F classroom. They need a place, like a class wiki to share and communicate with their classmates on a multitude of topics from sharing ideas about student organizations and clubs, field trip opportunities, and thoughts and questions about class assignments. By integrating a teacher classroom wiki, students can submit not only weekly homework but also journal reflections. They can also generate conversations about class tasks and formal assignments. This is also a great location to post reminders of due dates and online assignments for students. Each student should be required to make additions to the wiki and create discussions on particular content areas. At your classroom wiki, students can create and store projects for a classroom ePortfolio. Since all students have different levels of skills, this is a collaborative way for students to learn from one another on topics such as how to design a wiki or Web site, how to showcase projects, how to create writing samples, how to make videos, and much more.

3. You decide to incorporate journaling techniques into your Social Studies classroom and choose to authenticate this by integrating blogs into your classroom curriculum (this activity can be adapted for almost any grade level). The blogging activity can be linked to your curriculum resource page. The blog can be as simple or as detailed as you would like your student's responses to be on the topic. You can choose a blog site host like BlogSpot, Weebly Blogs, or Blogger just to name a few. Have your students enter a blog entry every other week about a current event issue (make sure it is within the last month, so that each entry remains recent). By asking your students to describe historical events in their blog entry and to follow your guidelines for proper writing you are also increasing literacy skills.

Learn It Online

INSTRUCTIONS: Use the Learn It Online exercises to reinforce your understanding of the chapter concepts and increase your computer, information, and integration literacy. To access step-by-step online tutorials, videos, practice tests, learning games, and more, visit the Computer Concepts CourseMate Web site at www.cengagebrain.com, navigate to the Chapter 6 resources for this book, and then click the link for the resource you want to review.

1. At the Movies

Click the At the Movie link to review a video about creating your own classroom blog. Click the At the Movies 2 link to review a video about turning your iPad into a movie studio for your students, using Apple's iMovie app.

2. Expanding Your Understanding of Apple's iPad Operating System

Click the iOS link to learn more about the latest operating system software that is the heart and soul of your iPad or iPhone.

3. Expanding Your Understanding of Cloud Computing

Apple's iCloud is changing the way users save and access their documents, photos, movies, and other files. Click the iCloud link to learn more about how iCloud is seamlessly integrated into your apps, so you can access your content on all your devices.

4. Practice Test

Click the Practice Test link. Answer each question. When completed, enter your name and click the Grade Test button to submit the quiz for grading. Make a note of any missed questions. If required, submit your score to your instructor.

5. Who Wants to Be a Computer Genius?

Click the Who Wants to Be a Computer Genius link to find out if you are a computer genius. When you are ready to play, click the Play button. If required, submit your score to your instructor.

6. Wheel of Terms

Click the Wheel of Terms link to reinforce important terms you learned in this chapter by playing the Shelly Cashman Series version of this popular game. When you are ready to play, click the Play button. If required, submit your score to your instructor.

7. Crossword Puzzle Challenge

Click the Crossword Puzzle Challenge link. Complete the puzzle to reinforce skills you learned in this chapter. When you are ready to play, click the Play button. If required, submit the completed puzzle to your instructor.

Special Feature: A World without Wires — Tablets, Apps, and More

Each time you use your smartphone or tablet computer, tune your television to a soccer game being played on another continent, or listen to satellite radio in your car, you are enjoying the benefits of the world of wireless communications. New wireless computers and mobile devices with wireless Internet access, including tablets, netbooks, notebook computers, and smartphones, simplify and expand your communications abilities. In addition to impacting computers and mobile devices, wireless technology is changing many other hardware devices, such as printers and video projectors, which traditionally needed wires to transmit data.

Wireless communications technology is not new. More than 100 years ago, Guglielmo Marconi sent the first wireless teletype message by using radio waves. Today, Marconi's discoveries allow you to enjoy the benefits of wireless technology, including such ways as connecting peripherals to your desktop computer without using wires and building a wireless home network. You also can keep in touch with family and associates from

anywhere in the world by phone or e-mail using a variety of wireless products.

Wireless technology has transformed the way people work, communicate, and learn. As a result, wireless technology has won enthusiastic worldwide use in a very short period. Even the casual observer notices dramatic changes in the way computers and mobile devices are used in homes, schools, and businesses, such as to send e-mail, communicate, access the Internet, share photos, text messages, and exchange files. Today's teachers and students are part of this wireless revolution — a revolution that is fundamentally changing the way students and teachers communicate and collaborate with each other.

Although Marconi laid the foundation for wireless technology more than a century ago, today's wireless products and standards represent an evolution of his original discoveries. Each day, the number of wireless devices increases as the price of connectivity decreases. Experts estimate that billions of wireless devices are in use worldwide and that close to a billion wireless devices are sold every year. As the world has gone wireless, Asia and Western Europe have emerged as leaders in wireless device use.

This special feature looks at a variety of wireless products, especially tablet computers, and illustrates how various segments of society, including PK-20 education, use wireless technology.

Wireless Connectivity — Any Place, Any Time, and Any Path

As technology advances and as the Internet has become fully integrated into the personal lives of students, this new "wireless generation" demands *always-on* access. Students need to access instruction in meaningful learning environments, and they need this access from any place, any time, and any path — in the classroom, on the school bus, in the library, in a car, playing soccer and other sports, hanging out with friends, or at home (Figure 1).

Figure 1 Today's students demand *always-on* access to the Internet, their families, and their friends, in other words, students want to be always on in their world.

Wireless Networks and Terminology

Several years ago, Nicholas Negroponte, founder and director of MIT's Media Lab, predicted what has come to be known as the Negroponte Flip. Negroponte predicted that communications media that formerly were wireless would become wired and media that formerly were wired would become wireless. Evidence of the Negroponte Flip can be seen today in the emergence of cable television (wireless TV antennas to wired cables) and the explosion in voice and data services over wireless networks (wired telephones to wireless smartphones).

Wireless networks can be characterized generally by the area they cover and the technologies they use. The following sections briefly describe the geographic coverage of wireless networks and wireless technologies.

Wireless Personal Area Networks (WPANs)

A **wireless personal area network (WPAN)** is a short-range wireless network often based on Bluetooth technology. **Bluetooth** technology uses short-range radio waves to transmit data between two Bluetooth devices such as smartphones, headsets, microphones, keyboards, mice, digital cameras, fax machines, printers, desktop computers, tablets, notebook/netbook computers, and many other wireless devices (Figure 2). Bluetooth-equipped devices *discover* each other and form *paired connections*. Examples of paired connections include a smartphone and a headset, or a keyboard, mouse, or printer and a desktop, notebook, or tablet computer. To communicate with each other, Bluetooth devices should be within approximately 10 meters, or 33 feet, of each other; although, some Bluetooth devices will work up to 100 meters or more from each other.

Many devices that traditionally have required wires to connect to other devices, such as printers, keyboards, scanners, digital cameras, cellular phones, microphones, headsets, interactive whiteboards, and notebook computers are now manufactured with integrated Bluetooth technology. Both Mac OS X and Windows 7/Vista/XP have built-in Bluetooth

Figure 2 Bluetooth technology allows users to connect devices wirelessly in a multitude of ways.

support that allows users to configure Bluetooth communications easily. For computers and devices not Bluetooth-enabled, you can purchase a mini Bluetooth wireless port adapter that will convert an existing USB port into a Bluetooth port (Figure 3). Using Bluetooth technology, your computers and mobile devices can connect wirelessly to a variety of devices. You can even transfer files easily from a PC to a Mac and vice versa using Bluetooth technology.

Wireless Local Area Networks (WLANs)

A **wireless local area network (WLAN)** is a network that uses wireless technologies, such as radio waves, to connect computers and

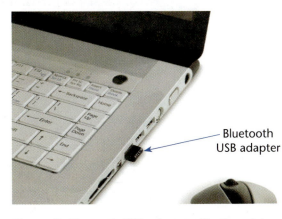

Bluetooth USB adapter

Figure 3 Bluetooth USB adapters, like the mini adapter shown, can be used to create Bluetooth connections with any Bluetooth-enabled device, in this example, a mouse.

devices in a limited space, such as a home, a classroom, an office building, or a school. Wireless LANs are based on the Institute of Electrical and Electronics Engineers (IEEE) 802.11 standard. The term **802.11** refers to a family of specifications developed for wireless LANs that allows computers and other devices to communicate via radio waves. **Wi-Fi**, short for *wireless fidelity*, is a popular term used when referring to any type of 802.11 network. Wi-Fi networking hardware is standard equipment on notebook, netbook, and tablet computers, eBook readers, and other wireless devices. The Wi-Fi Alliance certifies products that meet 802.11 specifications (Figure 4), as well as provides extensive information and resources regarding wireless networks.

WLANs are found in many public locations, people connect their computers or mobile devices to the Internet wirelessly through a hotspot. A **hotspot** is an area, such as a public WLAN, with wireless Internet connectivity. Hotspots are created using Wi-Fi standards and a **wireless Internet access point**. Users can connect to the Internet using a hotspot if their computers or mobile devices have an appropriate network card. Some hotspots provide free Internet access, some charge a per-use fee, and others require users to subscribe — in which they pay a per access fee, a daily fee, or a monthly fee.

Wireless Mobile Hotspot and Wireless Cellular Networks

Instead of using a fixed hotspot, such as at a public location, some users elect to create their own **mobile hotspot** or **personal mobile hotspot**, which is a hotspot that users take with them. In fact, users increasingly are using mobile devices that are 3G- and 4G-enabled to connect wirelessly to the Internet through **3G** (third generation) and newer **4G** (fourth generation) **wireless cellular networks**. 3G and 4G wireless cellular networks use **cellular radio technology** to provide users with highspeed wireless Internet connections, as long as they are in the network's range. A 3G network usually includes most major cities and airports.

To capture some of the expanding consumer mobile market, several major communications companies have worked together to develop a nationwide 4G network that is 10 times faster than 3G. At this time, 4G networks are more commonly available in large urban areas.

All smartphones connect to either a 3G or 4G network, depending on the service associated with the smartphone and the cellular

Figure 4 In addition to certifying 802.11 products, the Wi-Fi Alliance provides extensive information and resources regarding wireless networks.

network available. Some tablet computers include Bluetooth, Wi-Fi, and 3G or 4G capabilities, while others include only Bluetooth (for short-range connections) and Wi-Fi (for hotspot connections).

While smartphone users can use an app that allows their phones to become a mobile hotspot by connecting to a cellular network (discussed next), another option is for users to carry a mobile hotspot device with them, which some refer to as "the Internet in your pocket." Figure 5 shows a mobile hotspot device that allows users to connect up to five Wi-Fi-enabled computers and mobile devices to the 3G/4G cellular network, providing hi-speed Internet access from just about anywhere.

Figure 5 Shown is an example of a mobile hotspot device that allows you to connect up to five computers and mobile devices wirelessly to a 3G or 4G network, depending on the device and which network is available.

Some users are replacing their wired home network routers with a mobile hotspot device. Users like that they can use the device at home for home networking and also take the device with them for use wherever they are — for example, at a park, at a doctor appointment, at a basketball game, on a cross country car trip, on vacation, or even fishing offshore if cellular service is available. Some users use a mobile hotspot device with their notebook, netbook, or tablet computers to connect to a wireless cellular network.

One disadvantage to this is that the Wi-Fi device must be in proximity of the devices

using it. So, if one user on a home network takes the Wi-Fi device with him or her, the rest of the home network users cannot connect to the Internet while the Wi-Fi device is gone. As a result, instead of using a mobile Wi-Fi device, some users are using routers with wireless capabilities to create a wireless home network, discussed next.

Wireless Home Networks

A **wireless home network** connects your home computers and peripherals without the use of wires. Family members simultaneously can collaborate on projects, share digital files, print photos and documents, and access the Internet. Tablet, netbook, and notebook computer users can roam around the house or backyard and still connect to the home network if they are within 150 to 1,500 feet from the wireless access point, depending on the type of wireless home network installed.

One disadvantage of wireless networks is that they are affected by interference. Walls, ceilings, and electrical devices, such as cordless telephones and microwave ovens, can disrupt wireless network communications. In addition, the wireless router should not be placed on the floor or near walls and metal objects. If you experience slow wireless network connections or frequently lose the wireless network connection in your home, you may need to change the location of the wireless router. Also, make sure that the antennas (in externally installed routers) are fully extended from the wireless router.

Many home networking products are based on Wi-Fi standards and are becoming more affordable, abundant, and easy to use and install. Even in a wireless home network, one desktop computer often connects to the router/wireless access point using a cable because many older desktop computers do not contain a wireless card. Figure 2-4 on page 58 shows a typical home network and shown here again in Figure 6 for reference.

Earlier, we talked about the Negroponte Flip where technologies that were wireless become wired and vice versa. We are seeing this flip again as some users are cancelling their wired cable Internet service and instead using

Web Info

For more information about mobile hotspots, visit the Computer Concepts CourseMate Web site at *www.cengagebrain.com*, navigate to the Chapter 6 Web Info resource for this book, and then click Mobile Hotspot.

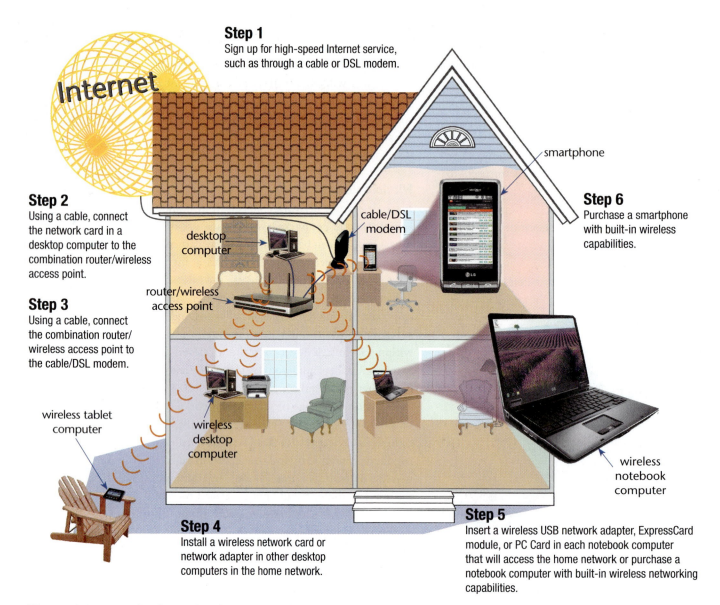

Step 1
Sign up for high-speed Internet service, such as through a cable or DSL modem.

Internet

smartphone

Step 2
Using a cable, connect the network card in a desktop computer to the combination router/wireless access point.

Step 3
Using a cable, connect the combination router/wireless access point to the cable/DSL modem.

Step 6
Purchase a smartphone with built-in wireless capabilities.

desktop computer

cable/DSL modem

router/wireless access point

wireless tablet computer

wireless desktop computer

wireless notebook computer

Step 4
Install a wireless network card or network adapter in other desktop computers in the home network.

Step 5
Insert a wireless USB network adapter, ExpressCard module, or PC Card in each notebook computer that will access the home network or purchase a notebook computer with built-in wireless networking capabilities.

Figure 6 An example of a wireless home network.

mobile hotspot wireless devices, as discussed earlier and shown in Figure 5 on the previous page, as the device used to connect their home network. To make their home network 100 percent wireless, users can also use Bluetooth technology to connect to a wireless Bluetooth-enabled keyboard or printer. Thus, some home networks use all three wireless technologies: cellular, Wi-Fi, and Bluetooth.

Some experts predict that mobile hotspot devices using 4G and new fifth generation cellular technologies being developed could replace cable connections in many homes. Users will simply stream movies (including premium channels), TV shows, sporting events, and more from their tablet computers to their HD TV and/or their TVs will connect wirelessly to their personal mobile hotspot.

People around the world now have many choices and can use a number of different technologies when accessing the Internet wirelessly, which means users, including students, having *always on* access (Figure 7). As a result, people are able to take advantage of this new technology — a world without wires. One of the latest mobile devices to fully embrace wireless computing is the tablet computer, which is covered in the next few sections.

Figure 7 Users today expect *always on* access regardless of where they are or what they are doing.

The Tablet Revolution

As stated earlier, experts are predicting that approximately one billion tablet computers will be sold worldwide by 2015. Tablets already are impacting and they will continue to fundamentally change virtually every aspect of our lives, including of all levels of education.

There are currently numerous tablet computers that are available and they vary in price from around $100 to over $600. Tablet PCs using Windows software have sold mainstream since 2001 but the input device was a stylus, not a user's fingers. The current tablet computer revolution (based upon multi-touch screen technology) did not start until January 2010 when Apple introduced the iPad tablet computer. The iPad uses Apple's iOS software, which is the same operating system used on iPhones and the iPod Touch. The introduction of the iPad brought the dawn of the mobile tablet revolution.

Current major competitors to the iPad run either Google's Android or BlackBerry OS software, which were discussed in Chapter 3; although, some manufactures use other operating systems, such as HP OS. Finally, companies are creating tablets and other mobile devices with multi-touch screens to address the needs of specific groups. For example, shown in Figure 8 on the next page is the **LeapPad**, a $100 tablet from LeapFrog that was created specifically for kids ages 4–9 and uses its own propriety operating system.

Tablets are as popular globally as they are in the United States. In fact, companies in other countries have or are creating tablets for their domestic markets. For example, WiPro, one company located in India, is marketing a very inexpensive tablet to India's rural poor and school children.

As you read through the remaining sections of this special feature, use your imagination and creativity to explore how you can integrate tablet- and app-based technology into your classroom curriculum in order to teach and, more importantly, reach all of your students.

Web Info

For more information about the LeapPad, visit the Computer Concepts CourseMate Web site at *www.cengagebrain.com*, navigate to the Chapter 6 Web Info resource for this book, and then click LeapPad.

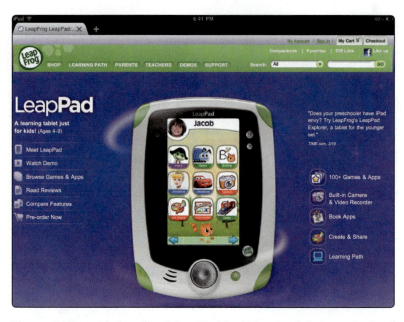

Figure 8 Shown is LeapFrog's LeapPad for kids ages 4–9, an example of a touch screen tablet created for a specific audience.

Tablet Software

Recall that **applications** or **apps** are the software used on tablet computers and other mobile devices. Some apps come preloaded on tablet computers, and others are downloaded from app stores. For example, apps can be downloaded from iTunes for use on traditional computers or from an app store, such as from the Apple App Store for use on an iPad. Many apps are free and most apps that do charge a fee, sell for less than $5, and often extensive discounts for teachers and schools are available. There are hundreds of thousands of apps that are available for the many different types of tablet computers sold worldwide. Thousands of these apps were created specifically for or are appropriate for PK-20 education, and they are being used by administrators, teachers, and students (Figure 9). Many virtual and blended schools and programs are creating apps to supplement their content.

Web Info

For more information about curriculum-specific apps, visit the Computer Concepts CourseMate Web site at *www.cengagebrain.com*, navigate to the Chapter 6 Web Info resource for this book, and then click Curriculum-Specific Apps.

Figure 9 Teachers can choose from a vast array of apps to integrate into their curriculum regardless of their grade level or curriculum area.

The following sections will showcase the Apple iPad tablet and some of the apps created specifically for the iPad. Remember, as you read through these sections, most of the information, integration ideas, and apps apply to other tablet computers that you or your students might be using.

A Closer Look at one Tablet — The Apple iPad

The iPad is a flat, rectangular computer with a 9.7-inch touch screen on its face. It is approximately 1/3 inches thick, weighs a little over one pound, and comes in different models based upon storage and wireless capabilities. The iPad comes with two cameras that are capable of taking still pictures or recording HD video. With two cameras your students can film their lives in HD, using the front facing camera for personal shots and the rear facing camera to film the world around them. The iPad has a 10-hour battery, supports over 30 languages, and is an *instant on* mobile device. The iPad uses **multi-touch technology** that allows users to manipulate objects on the screen simply by using their fingers (Figure 10). The iPad is **multi-directional**, which means that the screen can be viewed from any direction, and it contains many of the features of a traditional notebook computer and much more. And, if you are wondering — yes, an iPad is a computer; users can do most of what they can do on a notebook or desktop computer on an iPad, as well as many more things that are impossible to do on a traditional computer. Next, we will review a few of the important features, capabilities, and built-in apps of the iPad that have significance for education.

Tablet Features with Implications for Education

Tablet computers are being used in virtually all levels of education, as an instructor resource for curriculum integration, as a presentation and demonstration tool using a projector or HD television, as a tool to help students with special needs, and so much more. When used as a student resource, the possibilities are endless as thousands of new apps are specifically being

Figure 10 Tablet computers use multi-touch technology. Shown here is the Apple iPad, where users use their fingers to manipulate on-screen objects rather than a pointing device, like a mouse.

developed to increase student motivation to learn, increase student achievement, and provide for group collaboration. Finally, tablets are opening the world to you and your students like never before. The following sections cover just a few of the many standard features found on tablet computers.

Tablets and Video Conferencing

Tablet computers include extensive video conferencing capabilities that are possible because of their wireless capabilities. **FaceTime** is a built-in iPad feature that uses its two cameras so you make video calls from your iPad to your students' or their parents' iPad, iPod touch, iPhone, or Mac (Figure 11 on the next page). With just a tap, you can meet with your students, their parents, or collaborate with educators around the world. In addition to FaceTime, there are apps that expand the teacher-to-parent, teacher-to-student(s), and student(s)-to-student(s) video capabilities of tablet computers. For example, one free app called **fring Video Calls + IM** allows up to four people to video conference at the same time, even if they are using mobile devices from different manufactures. Think of the power of being able to involve parents and guardians in real time not only to discuss issues that require parental involvement but also moments to celebrate students' successes.

Web Info

For more information about FaceTime, visit the Computer Concepts CourseMate Web site at *www.cengagebrain.com*, navigate to the Chapter 6 Web Info resource for this book, and then click FaceTime.

Figure 11 FaceTime is a built-in iPad feature that has the potential to revolutionize the way teachers, parents, and students communicate in face-to-face, blended, and online environments.

Tablets as an Image and Video Projection Device

Anything displayed on a tablet computer can be shown on an interactive whiteboard or an HD television, as well as projected on a classroom wall screen. For example, iPad's **video mirroring** capabilities allow an iPad to connect directly using a cable (Figure 12) or wirelessly using many different accessories and Apple's AirPlay feature (see Figure 4-40 on page 176).

This means that you can display whatever content you have on your iPad and then the iPad can be passed around a class so students can show their work, projects, and more all instantly accessed by students from their cloud storage locations. Providing students with the ability to showcase their work by projecting it via a tablet is a constructivist instructional technique designed to engage students in their own learning.

Figure 12 Teachers can use iPads in so many different ways to project videos, presentations, instructional content, and more. Shown is one option to connect an iPad to a HD TV.

Tablets and Bluetooth (Wireless Printing, Keyboards, and External Speakers)

Tablet computers allow you and your students to print wirelessly from anywhere in a classroom using built-in wireless technology. iPads, for example, use a feature called **AirPrint** that allows you and your students to print effortlessly. In addition to wireless printing, users can enter input wirelessly using a built-in touch screen keyboard or a wireless Bluetooth keyboard. In the case of iPads, most newer Apple keyboards can be used with the iPad — simply turn on the keyboard, place it near the iPad, and the two devices will find each other. This allows your students to use a tablet computer with a traditional keyboard. You can also use wireless speakers with a tablet computer, which allows you to place the speakers strategically anywhere in your classroom to maximize the students' ability to hear output.

Tablets and Cloud Computing

Because tablets do not have a traditional hard drive, they are designed to be used as cloud computing and cloud storage devices. Many tablet manufactures allow users to store their documents, presentations, and other files in cloud locations they maintain, including Apple, Google, and others. Often, this service is free. For example, Apple's **iCloud** storage service allows each user to have up to 5 GBs of free cloud storage, and Microsoft's Windows Live SkyDrive allows a user to have up to 25 GBs of free cloud storage. Cloud storage allows you and your students instant access to all files stored in the cloud. Tablets and cloud computing allow all students to work collaboratively on their assignments and projects. No longer will your students be able to use excuses such as, "my dog ate my homework," "I forgot to bring my homework to school," or "I left my flash drive at home." The cloud allows all students to work collaboratively on their assignments and projects from any place, any time, and any path.

Tablets as a Resource Tool

Like all computers, tablets allow users to explore the world of knowledge, only now it literally is at their finger tips. For example, **iTunes U** is an expansive resource available to all users regardless of the type of computer they are using. It contains hundreds of thousands of free videos, lectures, books, presentations, podcasts, and much more from institutions all over the world, including Yale, Harvard, MIT, University of Tokyo, and broadcasters like PBS. As a teacher, you can integrate any of the iTunes U resources into your classroom curriculum (Figure 13). And, if you are using an iPad, simply tap the iTunes app, and then tap the iTunes U icon to access iTunes U.

Figure 13 Shown are some of the videos available at iTunes U that teachers can download and integrate into their classroom curriculum.

Tablets as a Teacher and Student Productivity Tool

All tablet computers have productivity apps that allow you and your students to create and work on all types of files, individually or as a group. For example, iPad production tools include Apple tools like Pages (word processing), Keynote (presentation), Numbers (spreadsheets), GarageBand (audio), iMovie (pictures and videos), and hundreds of other productivity apps available for use by you and your students. All students can now work collaboratively on their assignments and projects, take quizzes and tests, review instructional content, and so much more during school and just as importantly after school. They can then turn in or demonstrate their work and accomplishments either virtually (online) or in real time (F2F).

Web Info

For more information about Apple's iCloud storage service, visit the Computer Concepts CourseMate Web site at *www. cengagebrain.com*, navigate to the Chapter 6 Web Info resource for this book, and then click iCloud.

Tablets as an Administrative Tool

While the many concepts and ideas covered in this special feature also apply to administrators, tablet computers are also being used extensively by administrators as administrative tools. They can be used to keep track of meetings, calendars, events, lunch menus, attendance, and much more. One app administrators find invaluable is the one that helps keep track of school-owned computers. In the case of the iPad, this built-in app is called **MobileMe**, which uses the **Find My iPad** technology. Administrators think of this important feature as a LoJack anti-theft program for schools; they use it to protect their technology investments and minimize the issue of lost or stolen school-owned iPads. Find my iPad allows administrators to locate any lost, misplaced, or stolen school-owned iPad by using GPS technology (Figure 14). This is an important feature because it means school districts can allow students to take their school-issued iPads home and still feel confident the iPad will not be lost. In addition, the app allows administrators (and any owner of an iPad or iPhone) to remotely delete any personal or sensitive information as soon as the device is lost. Just as importantly, if the iPad has just been misplaced and not actually lost or stolen, the app allows the owner of the iPad to reinstate all deleted information after the device is located.

Tablets as an Interactive Textbook and Document Viewer

All tablet computers have eBook capabilities and can hold thousands of books, including student textbooks. Users can also download a number of eBook apps to expand the capabilities of the basic eBook features of tablet computers. For example, the **iBook** app on iPads has a full color screen using Apple's Multi-Touch interface that allows users to turn pages with a flick of their finger. Students can use bookmarks, highlight text, use the dictionary by tapping a word, take notes, conduct exploration learning, and much more (Figure 15). Users can download free or purchased books at the **iBook Store**, which is accessible via the iBook app. Tablets also allow students to read your PDFs and other files, including Microsoft Office documents, as digital handouts. While digital textbooks have been available for college-level students for some time, digital K-12 textbooks are being loaded on tablet computers in school districts across the country, and as a result, it has become mainstream to find PK-20 students reading and interacting with digital textbooks.

Web Info

For more information about Find My iPad technology, visit the Computer Concepts CourseMate Web site at *www.cengagebrain. com*, navigate to the Chapter 6 Web Info resource for this book, and then click MobileMe.

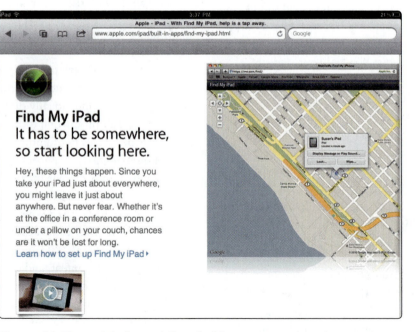

Figure 14 The anti-theft capability of tablet computers is an important security issue for school districts. Shown is the Find My iPad feature of iPads.

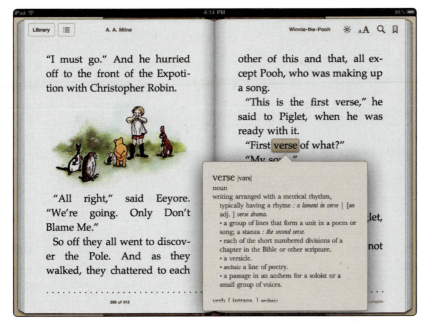

Figure 15 An example of a digital textbook using the iPad app iBook and some of its interactive features, in this case the built-in dictionary feature.

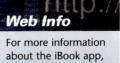

Web Info

For more information about the iBook app, visit the Computer Concepts CourseMate Web site at *www. cengagebrain.com*, navigate to the Chapter 6 Web Info resource for this book, and then click iBook.

Tablets as a Note Taking Tool

Since the beginning of the written word, note taking involved writing devices like a pencil and a surface like paper. Note taking has remained basically unchanged for thousands of years, that is, until Apple introduced the Multi-Touch iPad tablet computer in January 2010. Today's tablet generation can use their fingers to write on a pad of digital paper, make notes on their digital textbook, highlight text with their digital highlighter, study their handwritten notes using digital flash cards, and so much more. The Apple iPad and its Multi-Touch technology has changed the process of note taking forever (Figure 16).

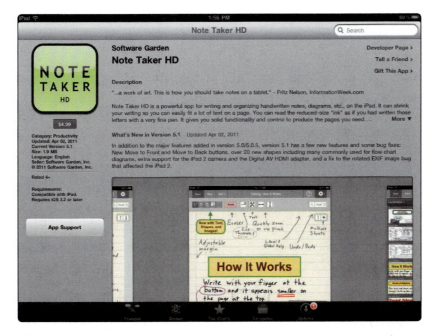

Figure 16 Shown is an example of an app that students can use to take notes using their fingers.

Tablets and Accessibility

Tablet computers are fundamentally and profoundly changing the way parents, caregivers, teachers, and administrators assist and teach students with special needs. Many of these people understand that tablets have immense potential to impact children and adults in many positive ways. A tablet's intuitive design, versatility, mobility, and ease of use means it can be used to help all children with special needs, even those with significant limitations. Tablets have many built-in accessibility features, for example, iPad users can activate the various accessibility features by tapping the Settings icon, tapping the General icon, scrolling down, and then tapping the Accessibility link (Figure 17).

Educators are just beginning to explore the full capabilities of tablets and the thousands of specialized apps available at the various app stores (Figure 18). Because many districts allow their students with special needs to take their school-issued tablet computers loaded with needs-specific apps home, parents are actively involved in helping their children at home and in ways not possible before. As you explore the incredible accessibility features of tablet computers, you will understand why the slogan, *Touched by an iPad,* is being used by parents and educators to describe their experiences when using tablet computers with kids with special needs.

Figure 17 Tablet computers contain many built-in accessibility features. Shown is information about one accessibility feature available on an iPad.

Figure 18 Shown are just a few of the thousands of special education apps that are available for administrators, teachers, parents, and other caregivers.

Wireless Summary

Your pockets, purses, book bags, and backpacks may be overflowing with small electronic devices, but the wireless revolution is making headway to combine some of these products and simplify your life. Wireless networks are growing throughout the world, driven by convenience, cost, and access, and they are changing forever the ways people communicate, learn, and work at home, at school, or in the office. At one time, computing abilities were limited by the length of wires; now communications and computing have no physical limitations. Wireless communication and tablet computers have opened the door to any place, any time communications and connectivity — creating an *instant on* world without boundaries and a world without wires that will forever change the way you teach and the way your students learn.

Evaluating Educational Technology and Integration Strategies

Objectives

After completing this chapter, you will be able to do the following:
[ISTE NETS-T Standards 1 a-d; 2 a-d; 3 a-d; 4 b,d; 5 a-d]

- Identify sources of information for evaluating educational technology and digital media

- Outline the considerations and tools used to evaluate software, including apps

- Describe and explain the key criteria used to evaluate Web resources

- Describe the tools for evaluating the effectiveness of technology

- Compare and analyze the methods used to evaluate student projects

- Identify different technology integration strategies by classroom layout and design

- Define and describe the value of a curriculum resource page

- Describe ways to integrate technology into specific curriculum subject areas

- Describe authentic assessment tools for student projects

- Identify and compare possible sources of funding for classroom technology

As you learn about the various types of emerging technology and methods of integrating them into your F2F or online classroom curriculum, undoubtedly, you will be called upon to evaluate the appropriateness of this technology and the effectiveness of its integration into the learning process. This chapter presents an overview of how to evaluate the many different types of technologies that are available today. It also offers specific strategies on how to integrate technology in your classroom based on the number of computers and other devices available to you and your students. Also provided are several subject-specific examples of curriculum integration activities. Finally, this chapter suggests several ways you can raise funds to pay for state-of-the-art technology in your classroom to enhance the teaching and learning experience.

Integration Strategies

To learn more about evaluating video games for use with your students, visit the Computer Concepts CourseMate Web site at *www.cengagebrain.com*, and then navigate to the Chapter 7 Education Issues resource for this book.

FAQ

How can teachers access reviews?

Teachers can access evaluations at state-sponsored Web sites or they can request them in printed form. Teachers can also review users' comments when evaluating apps at the various app stores.

Evaluating Educational Technology

Evaluating the appropriateness and effectiveness of educational technology is an important aspect of integrating current technologies into your classroom curriculum. To **evaluate** an item is to determine its value or judge its worth. Evaluating educational technology involves determining if the technology is appropriate and enhances the teaching and learning process. To be considered **appropriate**, educational technology must be suitable for the educational situation, must be motivational, and must promote learning at the correct levels of student ability and academic achievement. It also must address curriculum standards and related learning objectives.

Evaluating educational technology before instruction begins, during the instructional period, and after instruction has taken place is important (Figure 7-1). Before using software, apps, or Web sites for example, teachers should determine if this technology meets their curriculum needs and if the product or content is developmentally and age appropriate for their classroom learning situation. Information from many sources helps teachers evaluate the appropriateness of educational technologies. Teachers should continue to evaluate the technology while it is being used, as well as after the instruction using the technology is complete.

SOURCES OF INFORMATION

Finding the right educational technology can be difficult, especially for new users of technology because each year, developers create hundreds of new educational software programs, including apps, and Web sites for K-12 classroom use (Figure 7-2). To avoid confusion in this important task, teachers might rely on a variety of resources to help them identify and evaluate the appropriateness of educational technologies. These resources include material from school districts, state Departments of Education, professional educational organizations, recommendations of colleagues, published evaluations (including app reviews), technology conferences, and Web sites. When talking about software reviews throughout this chapter, we are also talking about apps reviews.

SCHOOL DISTRICTS AND STATE DEPARTMENTS OF EDUCATION Many school districts compile software evaluations that provide guidance on subject-specific software, including apps. In addition, many state Departments of Education provide lists of software, including apps, that are recommended and evaluated by educators.

To assist you in locating these sources of information from your school district and state Department of Education, contact your technology facilitator, curriculum resource specialist, media specialist, technology committee, or other teachers.

The Evaluation Cycle

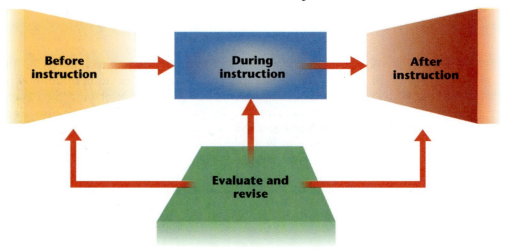

Figure 7-1 Successful technology integration requires evaluation during all phases of instruction.

Figure 7-2 Numerous high-quality educational software programs, including apps, are available for classroom use.

PROFESSIONAL EDUCATIONAL ORGANIZATIONS Many local, state, regional, national, and international educational organizations provide extensive information on how to evaluate educational resources (Figure 7-3). Many of these groups provide Web sites with information and feedback on software program levels, content, and pricing.

APPS REVIEWS There are thousands of apps that either are appropriate or were specifically created for PK-12 education. Apps are evaluated by users and their reviews are listed with other information about the corresponding app. The user reviews are a great starting place to determine if an app is appropriate for your specific needs. Often these reviews include integration ideas from teachers who are using the apps in their classrooms. Blogs that evaluate education apps are another great resource.

COLLEAGUE RECOMMENDATIONS A good way to identify software, including apps, and other technology that has potential for your classroom is to talk to other educators. Colleagues can offer advice about outstanding products as well as about which products to avoid — advice that often is based on firsthand experience.

PUBLISHED EVALUATIONS Departments of Education, professional organizations, and other educational groups publish evaluations of new products. Numerous software developers include evaluations completed by educators on their Web sites. Many educational publications and journals also have sections dedicated to reviews of educational technologies. In addition, many online publications, journals, and other Web sites provide educators with comprehensive evaluations and reviews of educational software, including apps, and hardware.

CONFERENCES Every year, dozens of national and state organizations host education and technology conferences (Figure 7-4). A **technology conference** is a meeting dedicated to providing a vast array of information and resources for educators. This gathering might be large or small and includes workshops and presentations by educators and vendors on hundreds of technology topics. In addition, software and hardware vendors usually have booths staffed by representatives to provide teachers with demonstrations and information about their products.

THE WEB By far, the Web is the most comprehensive source of tools and resources

---

FAQ

How can teachers find out about technology conferences in their state or across the country?

Access education conferences at *www. allconferences.com/ Education* and search by catagory or curriculum.

Figure 7-3 Many local, state, regional, national, and international educational organizations maintain Web sites that provide educators with evaluations of educational technologies.

Figure 7-4 Technology conferences provide teachers with valuable resources, information, and opportunities to discuss educational technology issues with other educators and vendors.

to help you evaluate educational technology. Teachers may visit thousands of Web sites dedicated to educational topics. Mailing lists, forums, newsgroups, discussion groups, listservs, wikis, blogs, and Webinars available on the Web also provide vast sources of information.

One of the larger well-known discussion listservs is EDTECH. The **EDTECH** discussion listserv allows educators from many different areas — teachers, administrators, technology coordinators, media specialists, and university faculty — to exchange information, comments, and ideas on educational issues. If you have never subscribed to a discussion listserv, a link on the EDTECH site provides subscription help and procedures (Figure 7-5).

Web Info

To learn more about EDTECH, visit the Computer Concepts CourseMate Web site at *www.cengagebrain. com*, navigate to the Chapter 7 Web Info resource for this book, and then click EDTECH.

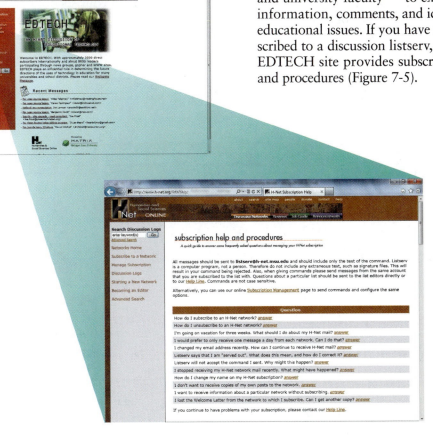

Figure 7-5 The EDTECH H-NET discussion listserv is a tool used and moderated by educators to share ideas, research, and other areas of interest dealing with educational technology.

Web Info

To access app reviews, visit the Computer Concepts CourseMate Web site at *www. cengagebrain.com*, navigate to the Chapter 7 Web Info resource for this book, and then click App Reviews.

Web Info

For more examples of evaluation rubrics for students, visit the Computer Concepts CourseMate Web site at *www.cengagebrain. com*, navigate to the Chapter 7 Web Info resource for this book, and then click Rubrics.

EVALUATING SOFTWARE PROGRAMS

When you identify a software **program** or an app as potentially suited to your curriculum needs, you should evaluate the software for appropriateness, review the accuracy of the content, and consider its relevance to the curriculum performance standards and related benchmarks. A cost-effective way to evaluate software is to download a free trial copy from some of the many software companies that offer these trial versions at their Web sites (Figure 7-6). You can then use the trial version for the specified period to determine its suitability for your curriculum. Some app developers provide free "lite" apps for you to evaluate before you purchase the full app.

A rubric is a great tool for evaluating software and apps. A rubric is a detailed scoring guide for assessment, based on stated criteria.

A **software/app evaluation rubric** is an assessment tool that provides a number of important evaluation criteria, including content, documentation and technical support, ability levels and assessment, as well as technical quality and ease of use to help assess the quality of the software and apps. Software/app evaluation rubrics help you and your students evaluate educational software and apps. A two-page Software/App Evaluation Rubric is shown in Figure 7-7 (on the next two pages).

Many school administrators develop software/app evaluation rubrics for teachers to use; while in other schools, teachers create the software/app evaluation rubrics. In addition, the Web is a great resource for locating rubrics. Many different software evaluation rubrics are available on the Web for you to use or alter to fit your specific needs.

CONTENT When evaluating educational software (including apps), content is the most important area to consider. When examining software content, you need to determine if the software is valid. **Valid** means the software has well-grounded instructional properties, meets standards, provides appropriate content, and teaches what is intended.

Most software companies and distributors provide a description of the content and learning skills addressed by their software program or app; most software companies match the skills the software teaches with specific curriculum standards and related benchmarks or instructional outcomes. When evaluating the content of a software program or an app, always relate the content to your school's and state's specific curriculum performance standards and related benchmarks or instructional outcomes.

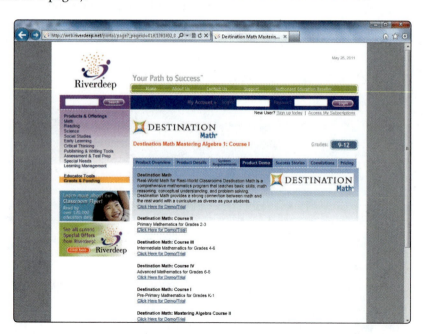

Figure 7-6 Many software companies allow you to download free evaluation copies of their software.

Rubric

Software/App Evaluation Rubric

Application Title: _____   Subject Area: _____

Version: _____   Producer/Publisher: _____

Date Published: _____

Curriculum Standard(s): _____

Learning Objective(s): _____

Technology Standard(s): _____

Prerequisite Skills: _____

Configuration

Hardware/System Requirements: _____

_____

Delivery Type: DVD_____ App _____ Network _____

Hard Disk Space Required: _____ Memory Required: _____

Program Categories: (Check all that apply)

☐ App   ☐ Drill and Practice   ☐ Educational Game
☐ Authoring   ☐ Simulation   ☐ ILS
☐ Problem Solving   ☐ Tutorial   ☐ Distance Learning

Other:_____

Skill/Ability/Grade Levels: _____

Use the following system to rate the software

1=Strongly disagree; 2=Disagree; 3=Agree; 4=Strongly agree; NA=Not applicable

Content

	1	2	3	4	NA
1. The content is accurate and factual.	1	2	3	4	NA
2. The content is educationally appropriate.	1	2	3	4	NA
3. The content is free of errors.	1	2	3	4	NA
4. The content meets your learning goals and objectives.	1	2	3	4	NA
5. The content is age appropriate.	1	2	3	4	NA
6. The content is free of stereotypes and cultural bias.	1	2	3	4	NA
7. The content meets district and state standards.	1	2	3	4	NA

Comments: _____

Documentation and Support

	1	2	3	4	NA
1. The teacher/instructor manual is clear and thorough.	1	2	3	4	NA
2. The software has an 800/888 support number.	1	2	3	4	NA
3. Online technical support is available.	1	2	3	4	NA
4. Help and tutorials are clear and easy to use.	1	2	3	4	NA

Comments: _____

Figure 7-7 A software evaluation rubric helps teachers evaluate educational software programs, including apps.   *(continued on the next page)*

Rubric

Software/App Evaluation Rubric
(1=Strongly disagree; 2=Disagree; 3=Agree; 4=Strongly agree; NA=Not applicable)

Ability Levels

1. The ability level can be set by the teacher.	1	2	3	4	NA
2. The ability level automatically advances.	1	2	3	4	NA
3. The software covers a variety of ability/skill levels.	1	2	3	4	NA

Comments: _____

Assessment

1. Software has built-in assessment and reporting tools.	1	2	3	4	NA
2. Assessment methods are appropriate and suited to learning objectives.	1	2	3	4	NA
3. Software documents and records student progress.	1	2	3	4	NA
4. Teachers can assess students' progress easily by evaluating progress reports.	1	2	3	4	NA

Comments: _____

Technical Quality

1. Animation and graphics are used well.	1	2	3	4	NA
2. Audio (voice input/output) is used well.	1	2	3	4	NA
3. Feedback and prompts are appropriate.	1	2	3	4	NA
4. The application allows branching and chunking.	1	2	3	4	NA

Comments: _____

Ease of Use

1. Directions are clear.	1	2	3	4	NA
2. Students can exit the program at any time.	1	2	3	4	NA
3. Students can restart the program where they stopped.	1	2	3	4	NA
4. The software is reliable and free of disruption by system errors.	1	2	3	4	NA

Comments: _____

Recommendation

☐ Purchase Immediately   ☐ Review Further   ☐ Do Not Purchase

Comments: _____
_____
_____

Evaluator: _____   Date: _____

Figure 7-7 A software evaluation rubric helps teachers evaluate educational software program, including apps. *(continued from the previous page)*

DOCUMENTATION AND TECHNICAL SUPPORT

When evaluating software (including apps), consider the technical support and documentation that comes with the software. **Documentation** is any printed or online information that provides assistance in installing, using, maintaining, and updating the software. You should review the documentation for readability and depth of coverage. **Technical support** is a service that hardware and software manufacturers and third-party service companies offer to customers to provide answers to questions, repairs, and other assistance (Figure 7-8). Companies usually provide technical support over the telephone or via the Web (often as a live chat or a blog). Some firms even provide on-site support.

In addition to reviewing the available documentation and technical support, you also should determine if any other support is available, such as clear, easy-to-use tutorials. Some software companies, for example, provide instructor resource guides and lesson plans to assist in integrating their software into curriculum areas.

ABILITY LEVELS AND ASSESSMENT

Educators need to evaluate whether the software or app can be used with more than one ability or academic level. An **ability level** refers to a student's current competency level or the skill level the student can achieve for a specific learning objective. The **academic level** is based on the grade level with increments to determine if a student is performing at the appropriate level. Several software applications, such as math and reading software, adjust the ability or grade level as students successfully move through specific skills. Numerous software applications allow you to set the academic level or the ability level at which you require students to work.

TECHNICAL QUALITY AND EASE OF USE

Technical quality refers to how well the software or app presents itself and how well it works. Items to evaluate are the clarity of the screen design; appropriateness of student prompts and feedback; and use of graphics, animations, sound, and other media elements.

Ease of use, or user-friendliness, refers to anything that makes the software or app easy to use. Software and apps should be easy for both teachers and students to use,

Figure 7-8 Many software manufacturers and app developers provide technical support for their products via the Web.

while at the same time maintaining the students' interest.

Student opinions also play an important role in successfully integrating any technology. Teachers need to be open and embrace the fact that today's digital students may be very technologically savvy. After you complete your evaluation, you might want to obtain feedback from students by allowing them to use and test the software. If students have a difficult time working through exercises, they might dislike the program and get frustrated. If students dislike the software, they will not enjoy using it even though they may learn. This dislike will limit the effectiveness of the software in classroom use. Make sure the software is easy to use and appropriate for your students' academic and ability levels.

EVALUATING WEB RESOURCES

The Web is an incredible resource for teachers. Not all of the information on the Web, however, is placed there by reliable sources. Web page authoring software has made it easy for anyone to create, or publish, a Web page or Web site that contains personal opinions, ideas, and philosophy. In contrast, before a book is published, the content is reviewed for accuracy and objectivity and the author's credentials are verified. After being published, the book's copyright date

Web Info

For more details about evaluating Web sites, visit the Computer Concepts CourseMate Web site at *www. cengagebrain.com*, navigate to the Chapter 7 Web Info resource for this book, and then click Web Site Evaluation.

and table of contents allow users to determine the currency of the information and the book's depth of coverage. A Web site offers no such safeguards.

Because Web sites often contain inaccurate, incomplete, or biased information, evaluating Web resources presents a unique challenge. Teachers must know how to evaluate Web sites and teach their students how to do the same. When evaluating a Web

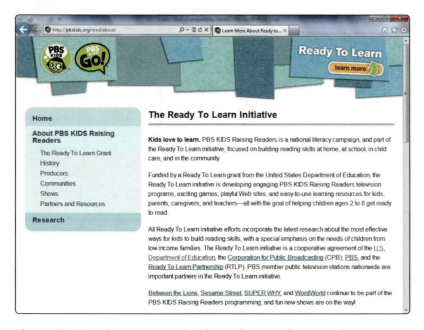

Figure 7-9 Teachers can consider this Web site authoritative because it is based on the latest research and the Web site is developed and maintained by a number of credible public and private organizations.

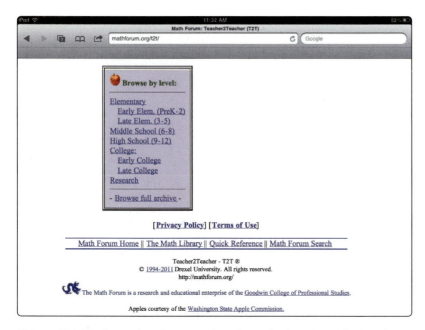

Figure 7-10 Information documenting the authority of a Web site often is found at the bottom of the Web site's home page.

site as an instructional source, you should consider criteria such as authority, affiliation, purpose, objectivity, content, learning process, audience, currency, and Web design.

AUTHORITY When evaluating Web sites (including blogs), **authority** refers to the credibility of the person or persons who author and maintain the site. Determining authority is the first place to start in the evaluation process. If the author is not a credible source for information, the information on the site might be unreliable or biased. A Web site on asteroids by a distinguished astronomy professor, for example, has more authority than an astronomy Web site created by an amateur stargazer. When reviewing a Web site, answer the following questions:

- Is the author or organization associated with the Web site clearly identified? If you cannot identify the author of or the organization associated with this Web page, you might want to avoid this Web site.

- Examine the credentials of the author of or organization associated with the Web site. What evidence indicates that the author qualifies to publish on this topic? The authority of the Web page shown in Figure 7-9, for example, is based on the credibility of several organizations and corporations.

- Has the author or organization listed experience, position, education, or other credentials? The bottom of the home page often provides additional information about the author's or organization's affiliation. Can the author or someone in the organization be contacted for clarification? Listing an e-mail address and other pertinent information is important for establishing authority.

AFFILIATION **Affiliation** refers to the professional organization, school, school district, university, company, or government office with which a particular Web site is associated (Figure 7-10). Well-known sources of information such as the U.S. government, universities, school districts, newspapers, and non-profit organizations usually have reliable facts on their Web sites. Also, it is good to examine the credentials and reputation of the organization or organizations affiliated with the Web site.

A simple way to determine a site's affiliation is to examine the URL and domain name to identify what type of organization maintains the Web page. A site with a .com domain, for example, is operated by a commercial business; a .edu domain is maintained by an educational institution (Figure 7-11).

PURPOSE AND OBJECTIVITY   **Purpose** is the reason the Web site was created or the intent of the Web site. As you evaluate a Web site, you must ascertain if it is being provided as a public service, if it is free from bias, and why the author or creator is providing this information.

Objectivity is the process of determining or interpreting the intent or purpose of the Web page and if it is free of bias. If the purpose is not clearly stated, you must attempt to determine the purpose or intent of the Web page. Is the primary intent to provide information or sell a product? Does the author want to make a political point or have fun? Determining the purpose or intent of the Web site plays a critical role in the evaluation process.

CONTENT AND LEARNING PROCESS
Content is the information a Web page provides. Web pages use a variety of media to convey facts, opinions, and news. As you evaluate the content of a Web page, consider the following questions:

- Is the content valid and appropriate? Is the content popular or academic, satiric or serious?
- Does the information on the page relate to your curriculum standards and related benchmarks?
- What topics are covered? Is the information clearly labeled and well organized?
- For what level is the information written? How thorough is the information?
- Do the links within the site add value and assist you in meeting your instructional goals?

As you evaluate the content of a Web page, keep the learning objectives and curriculum standards of the classroom in mind. Also, take the time to check the links to ensure they work and are appropriate

Figure 7-11 The .edu domain verifies the Web site is affiliated with an educational institution, in this case, the University of Central Florida (UCF).

for your intended audience and learning process.

Learning process is when the content engages students to use higher-order thinking skills to go beyond the simple acquisition of knowledge and become participatory learners. This is accomplished when the content challenges students to think, compare, reflect, hypothesize, and discuss.

AUDIENCE AND CURRENCY   The **audience** is the individual or group intended to view and use the Web page. You should review the Web page to determine if it is suitable for an audience such as your students. Is the content appropriate for your students? Can you use this Web page in your classroom? Again, keep your learning objectives in mind as you examine the Web page. **Currency** is the measure of how up to date, or timely, the Web page content is and how often it is updated. A good Web page states clearly when the page was last revised or updated.

DESIGN   The **design** of a Web site is the way it is arranged — that is, the way it uses instructional design principles to deliver content to the user. A well-designed Web site makes it easy and enjoyable for viewers to access the site's content and information. A poorly designed site, for example, where links or elements are organized in a confusing way, can frustrate viewers because they cannot find the information they want.

An effective Web page loads in a reasonable amount of time, has a pleasing visual appearance, is easy to navigate, and has links that are well organized, clearly marked, work properly, and lead to related materials.

Both in and out of the classroom, teachers and students should evaluate Web sites critically to maximize the value of the Web. To assist in the evaluation of Web sites, teachers often find rubrics useful. A **Web evaluation rubric** is a detailed scoring guide for assessing the value and content of Web sites. As shown in the examples in Figure 7-12 and Figure 7-13 on the next page, Web evaluation rubrics typically provide a number of important evaluation criteria for specific areas such as content, learning process, and authority of the author, and then present rating levels with specific standards for each. Students and teachers benefit from using rubrics. Figure 7-12 illustrates a user-friendly, engaging Web site evaluation rubric that might be used by young students. Figure 7-13 shows a more detailed Web evaluation rubric that might be used by a teacher. No matter which method you choose, the key is to have a predetermined way of effectively evaluating Web sites.

Rubric

Student Web Site Evaluation Rubric

Student team members:_____

DESIGN			
Users can move easily from page to page.	☺	😐	☹
Use of graphics (pictures and color) is good.	☺	😐	☹

CONTENT			
Information is useful.	☺	😐	☹
Content is as good or better than that of similar sites.	☺	😐	☹

TECHNICAL ELEMENTS			
Pages load quickly (within 5 seconds).	☺	😐	☹
All links work.	☺	😐	☹

CREDIBILITY			
Contact person is stated with his or her e-mail address.	☺	😐	☹
The name of the host school or organization is given.	☺	😐	☹
Date this site was last updated is provided.	☺	😐	☹

page 1 of 1

Figure 7-12 Young students enjoy rubrics that are fun and user-friendly when evaluating Web sites.

Rubric

Web Site Evaluation Rubric

Title of Web Site: _____

Curriculum Area: _____

URL: _____

Learning Objectives Supported by this Site: _____

_____

	Level 1	Level 2	Level 3	Level 4	Level
Authority	No author is listed and no e-mail contact is provided.	No author is listed but an e-mail contact is provided.	An author is listed with no credentials and you cannot tell if the author is the creator of the material.	An author is listed with appropriate credentials and is the creator of the material.	
Affiliation	It is unclear which institution supports this information.	A commercial Internet provider supports the site, but it is unclear if the author has any connection with a larger institution.	The site is supported by a larger institution, but some bias is apparent in the information from the institution.	The site is supported by a reputable institution without bias in the information.	
Purpose	The purpose is unclear or cannot be determined.	The Web site has more than one purpose but meets only a few of my objectives.	The purpose is somewhat clear and meets most of my objectives.	The purpose of the Web site is clear and meets my objectives.	
Objectivity	The Web page is a virtual soapbox.	The Web site contains some bias and a great deal of advertising.	The Web site contains minimal bias and some advertising.	The Web site is free of bias and contains little advertising.	
Content	The information on the Web site does not relate to my objectives.	The information relates to my objectives, but many of the links do not work.	The information relates to my objectives, links work, but the site is not well organized.	The information relates to my objectives, the links work, and the site is well organized.	
Learning Process	The information will not challenge learners to think, reflect, discuss, compare, or classify.	The information will not challenge learners to think but does provide interesting facts for resource information.	The information at this Web site will provide some challenges for the learner to think but does not relate to my objectives.	The information challenges learners to use higher-order thinking skills, effectively engages the learner, and meets my learning objectives.	
Audience	The Web pages are not appropriate for my audience.	The Web pages are written above the level of my audience, but some of the information is useful.	The Web pages are written at an appropriate level for my audience and some of the information is useful.	The Web pages are written at an appropriate level and the information is suitable for my classroom.	
Currency	Information on the site has not been revised in the last 18 months, or no date can be located.	Information on the site has not been updated in the last year, but the information still is of good quality.	Information has been updated in the last six months and seems to reflect currency.	Information has been updated in the last three months and is accurate.	
Design	The Web site design is inappropriate for my audience.	The Web site loads slowly and the general appearance is poor.	The Web site loads well, but the site is not easy to navigate.	The Web site loads well, is easy to navigate, visually pleasing, and easy to read.	
				Total	

Figure 7-13 A rubric is helpful in evaluating the educational value of Web sites.

Integration Strategies

To learn more about integrating and evaluating technology with your special needs students, visit the Computer Concepts CourseMate Web site at *www.cengagebrain.com*, and then navigate to the Chapter 7 Assistive Technologies Center resource for this book.

Evaluating the Effectiveness of Technology Integration

Integrating technology effectively into the curriculum requires planning, time, dedication, and resources. Because it is important to determine whether integration strategies are working, teachers, schools, and school districts should take steps to evaluate the effectiveness of their technology integration.

Evaluating the effectiveness of technology can be challenging; no simple way exists to evaluate what works in all situations — all students, all technology, all schools, and all classrooms. Nor do any standard types of evaluation show the relationship between the technology and student achievement.

The first step in evaluating educational technology's impact on student achievement is to develop indicators that measure a student's performance, skills acquired, and academic and ability levels obtained. Test scores are not the only, or even the best, indicators of the successful integration of technology. The types of learning best supported by technology are those not easily measured by traditional assessments, such as standardized tests. Due to the nature of technology and the way the learning environment is changing, educators must create and use different types of evaluation tools.

ASSESSMENT TOOLS FOR EVALUATING THE EFFECTIVENESS OF TECHNOLOGY INTEGRATION

Evaluating the effectiveness of educational technology can help you assess whether the technology is appropriate for the learner, meets learning objectives, and enhances the learning process. Traditionally, teachers use many different evaluation techniques in the final stage of instruction or when assessing **student performance**. To ensure that students meet the learning objectives, teachers must use many forms of assessment to evaluate student performance. **Assessment** is any method used to understand the current knowledge a student possesses; it can range from a teacher's subjective judgment based on a single observation of a student's performance to a state-mandated standardized test.

Reliable assessments accurately estimate student performance, permit appropriate generalizations about the students' skills and abilities, and enable teachers or other decision makers to make appropriate decisions. **Traditional assessments** include testing in the form of multiple choice, fill-in-the blank, true/false, short answer, and essay questions. Traditional assessments can be used to evaluate the effectiveness of technology.

Just as technology opens many new and exciting doors for teaching and learning, technology also opens new doors for evaluating student performance. When integrating technology, some teachers and schools move toward a nontraditional approach of student assessment, known as alternative assessment.

Alternative assessment uses nontraditional methods to determine whether students have mastered the appropriate content and skill level. Authentic assessment, project-based assessment, portfolio assessment, as well as checklists, rating scales, and rubrics, are alternative ways to evaluate students' performances. These assessment tools can be used to determine how well and in what ways they meet curriculum standards and related benchmarks.

AUTHENTIC ASSESSMENT **Authentic assessment** can be formal or informal and aims to present students with tasks that mirror the objectives and challenges typical of their instructional activities. Students answer open-ended questions, create questions, conduct hands-on experiments, do research, write, revise and discuss papers, and create portfolios of their work over time. Authentic assessment is based on a method of learning called authentic learning. **Authentic learning** presents learning experiences that demonstrate real-life connections between students' lessons and the world in which they live.

Authentic assessment measures this learning by evaluating a student's ability to master practical benchmarks. Using authentic assessment, for example, a student may be asked to discuss historical events, generate scientific hypotheses, solve math problems, create portfolios or presentations, or converse in a foreign language.

Authentic assessment helps students not only understand concepts and subject matter, but also develop real-world skills, which they can apply outside the classroom and beyond the school environment. For

Web Info

To explore technology assessment further, visit the Computer Concepts CourseMate Web site at *www.cengagebrain.com*, navigate to the Chapter 7 Web Info resource for this book, and then click Assessing Technology.

example, teachers might look for evidence of good collaboration skills, the ability to solve complex problems and make thoughtful decisions, and the ability to develop and make effective presentations. Authentic assessments reflect student learning over time and provide a better view of student performance, instead of measuring student performance based on just one item or one test. Using authentic assessments, a teacher has documentation of the student's progress throughout the entire project, which provides the teacher with evidence of growth and learning.

PROJECT-BASED ASSESSMENT Project-based **assessment** is an innovative approach to assessment that focuses on assessing student projects. It is based on a type of authentic learning called project-based learning. **Project-based learning** is a model for teaching and learning that focuses on creating learning opportunities for students by engaging them in real-world projects where they have an active role in completing meaningful tasks, constructing their own knowledge, solving problems, or creating realistic projects. Project-based learning transforms the teacher into the facilitator and the students into the doers or participants in the task at hand.

PORTFOLIO ASSESSMENT Another popular form of alternative assessment is portfolio assessment. **Portfolio assessment** evaluates student assignments or projects over a period of time. Portfolios are an effective way to match assessment with learning goals. Some educators call this **embedded assessment** because assessment tasks are part of the learning process. Through the process of creating their assessments, students improve their abilities to assess their strengths and weaknesses and are able to apply these skills to other areas of study to become better learners. Because portfolio assessments are usually associated with long-term assignments, students have the opportunity to fix or learn from their mistakes and do a better job on future portfolio assignments or projects.

For portfolio assessment to be successful, students must learn how to interact effectively with their teachers to ensure that they fully understand the teacher's, as well as their, assessment of each portfolio assignment or project.

When students receive guidance and support from their teachers and parents and gain an understanding of themselves as learners, they can experience amazing growth and powerful learning opportunities. The disadvantage of portfolio assessment is that creating and assessing portfolios takes longer to evaluate than a quick test and requires a great deal of work by both the student and the teacher. The results reveal, however, that portfolio assessment is well worth the investment.

In this digital age, electronic portfolios are starting to become more commonplace in K-12 and higher education. Recall that an **electronic portfolio** (also called **e-folio, eFolio, ePortfolio,** or **e-Portfolio**) is a collection of electronically created assignments and projects. Electronic portfolios offer a powerful way for students to create a variety of projects that contain digital media, reflective writings or narratives, drawings, audio, photos, and videos based on predetermined criteria that teachers can evaluate to assess learning.

CHECKLISTS, RATING SCALES, AND RUBRICS When using any authentic learning technique, many teachers use a checklist, a rating scale, or a rubric to evaluate the learning process. A **checklist** is a predetermined list of performance criteria used in project-based and portfolio assessment. See Figure 7-14 on the next page. After a student has met a criterion, the criterion is marked as complete. Checklists usually consist of yes and no questions used to determine if the item or items are present. Checklists allow you or your students to keep track of the items.

The benefit of a checklist is that you can use this tool quickly and students understand quickly if an item is or is not met. When creating a checklist, you should include items that clearly show if benchmarks are being met. Another effective option is to have students create checklists or add to yours.

A **rating scale** is a more complex form of a checklist that lists a numerical value, or rating, for each criterion. Assessment involves rating each student on her achievement for each criterion and specifying the total based on all criteria.

Another very popular form of alternative assessment is the rubric. As you recall, a rubric is a detailed assessment tool that

Integration Strategies

To learn more about alternative assessment, visit the Computer Concepts CourseMate Web site at *www.cengagebrain. com,* and then navigate to the Chapter 7 Education Issues resource for this book.

Web Info

To learn more about portfolio assessment, visit the Computer Concepts CourseMate Web site at *www. cengagebrain.com,* navigate to the Chapter 7 Web Info resource for this book, and then click Portfolios.

Checklist

Project Evaluation Checklist

Date: _____

Student Name(s): _____

Project Title: _____

	YES	NO
CONTENT		
The project meets all learning objectives (See project criteria for list).	☐	☐
The project is original and creative.	☐	☐
Mastery of subject is evident.	☐	☐
Use of higher-order thinking skills is evident.	☐	☐
Information is accurate and the subject matter is appropriate.	☐	☐
Information is presented in a logical sequence.	☐	☐
A variety of reliable sources are used.	☐	☐
Sources are properly cited.	☐	☐
Words are spelled correctly and sentences are grammatically correct.	☐	☐
LAYOUT		
The project is visually appealing.	☐	☐
The project is easy to navigate.	☐	☐
The text is easy to read and follow.	☐	☐
Digital media features are used effectively.	☐	☐
Color and design scheme are appropriate.	☐	☐
ORGANIZATION		
Student completed a project storyboard.	☐	☐
Planning is demonstrated.	☐	☐
Project flows smoothly.	☐	☐
Project was completed.	☐	☐

ePortfolio Idea

page 1 of 1

Figure 7-14 Teachers often use alternative assessment tools such as checklists (shown here) and rating scales or rubrics (see Figure 7-16 on page 368) to evaluate student performance.

makes it easy for teachers to assess the quality of an item, such as a student project. Rubrics help students understand how teachers will evaluate their projects by providing a range of criteria with information about how to meet each one. Rubrics describe specific and measurable criteria for several levels of quality against which teachers and students can evaluate completed projects. Rubrics can help students and teachers define the quality of completed assignments. Rubrics also help students critique and revise their own assignments before handing them in. For example, rubrics help students make sure they have included all required elements and have met each criteria for grading. Although a rubric is similar to a checklist and a rating scale, it describes the criteria that must be met in greater detail.

TEACHER OBSERVATION   When evaluating technology integration or curriculum integration, one of the more widely used authentic assessment techniques is teacher observation. **Teacher observation** (Figure 7-15) is the result of teachers actively observing their students during the learning process.

Teachers notice whether students are highly motivated during the learning process, that is, they observe the impact of technology used, how long the students work on

a given objective, and the length of time students continue working on a task to master its content and skills. Teacher observation is a powerful assessment tool, and often it is used in combination with other assessment tools. All of these tools can be used to evaluate individual and group projects.

EVALUATING TECHNOLOGY-SUPPORTED STUDENT PROJECTS

Today, technology skills are essential for students to learn. Technology-based student projects help facilitate integrating technology into the curriculum. In the process, students learn how to use, manage, and understand technology, as well as how technology is used to synthesize and present information on a variety of subjects. Although it might seem like a good idea, you should avoid teaching technology as a separate subject. Instead, you should integrate it into your curriculum.

Some software programs, such as those provided with integrated learning systems (ILS), automatically track student progress. Others, such as Inspiration, iMovie, and PowerPoint, do not provide assessment components. These applications, however, are ideal for students to use to create projects that are innovative and motivational. Teachers who use these software programs for technology-based student projects need to develop effective assessment tools to measure student achievement related to these tools.

Before a teacher presents a project's requirements to students, he or she should create an assessment rubric. Figure 7-16 on the next page illustrates a student project evaluation rubric that helps students understand how they will be evaluated on a project. Rubrics are excellent for evaluating all types of student projects. They provide an authentic assessment of project-based learning activities. To determine the criteria to include in the rubric, ask yourself what the students should learn and how this learning will be evidenced in their projects. In the rubric, be sure to specify what students need to include in their projects and clearly inform the students how they will be evaluated.

Checklists, rating scales, and teacher observation also are valid assessment tools for technology-based student projects. Your curriculum standards and benchmarks should define and guide the selection and creation of your assessment tool.

Figure 7-15 This teacher knows that teacher observation is critical when integrating technology.

FAQ

Is teacher observation really a powerful tool?

Yes! It is probably one of the most powerful tools that teachers use. A teacher needs to be aware of everything going on in the classroom, regardless of whether or not it relates to technology.

Rubric

Student/Group Project Evaluation Rubric

Team Leader: _____

Team Member(s): _____

Project Title: _____

	Beginning	Developing	Accomplished	Exemplary
Development Process				
Student(s) used quality reference materials and timely Web sites in gathering information.	0 1 2	3 4 5	6 7 8	9 10
Student(s) completed project outline/storyboard.	0 1 2	3 4 5	6 7 8	9 10
Student(s) obtained permission to use copyrighted materials.	0 1 2	3 4 5	6 7 8	9 10
Content				
Understanding of topic is evident.	0 1 2	3 4 5	6 7 8	9 10
Information is presented in a clear manner.	0 1 2	3 4 5	6 7 8	9 10
Information is appropriate and accurate.	0 1 2	3 4 5	6 7 8	9 10
Content shows understanding of the learning objectives.	0 1 2	3 4 5	6 7 8	9 10
Student(s) used higher-order thinking skills when analyzing and synthesizing information.	0 1 2	3 4 5	6 7 8	9 10
Important ideas related to the topic are included and an understanding of important relationships is evident.	0 1 2	3 4 5	6 7 8	9 10
Includes properly cited sources.	0 1 2	3 4 5	6 7 8	9 10
Design and Integration of Technology				
The content is presented in a logical, interesting sequence.	0 1 2	3 4 5	6 7 8	9 10
Video, 3D, and all enhancements are used appropriately.	0 1 2	3 4 5	6 7 8	9 10
Colors, images, animation, and sound enrich the content.	0 1 2	3 4 5	6 7 8	9 10
The project works and is technically sound.	0 1 2	3 4 5	6 7 8	9 10
Text is easy to read and students have followed rules of good screen design.	0 1 2	3 4 5	6 7 8	9 10
Accurate spelling and grammar are used throughout.	0 1 2	3 4 5	6 7 8	9 10
Presentation				
The student(s) maintains eye contact with class.	0 1 2	3 4 5	6 7 8	9 10
The student(s) speaks clearly and is easily heard.	0 1 2	3 4 5	6 7 8	9 10
The presentation is an appropriate length.	0 1 2	3 4 5	6 7 8	9 10
Technology is used well while presenting.	0 1 2	3 4 5	6 7 8	9 10

Total Possible 200   Total _____

page 1 of 1

Figure 7-16 A rubric helps students understand how they will be evaluated on a project. This rubric, for example, is designed to evaluate students' projects.

EVALUATING CONTENT   Your standards and benchmarks will help determine the content to include in student projects and how to assess this content. This should be the most important part of the project. For technology-based student projects, content may include factual information about a historical figure, key points included in a digital media math project, interactive PE presentation, biology lab data in a spreadsheet, and other pertinent information. In addition, evaluation of the content should include a review of punctuation, grammar, spelling, coverage of material, presentation of the material in a logical order, and specific information such as a title, references, and information about the author.

EVALUATING PLANNING   Effective presentations involve planning. Students also must plan a project before creating it, if it is to be effective. When assigning technology-based projects, establish how you want students to plan and what tools they will use. A software planning tool, such as **Inspiration** (Figure 7-17), helps students and teachers quickly develop and communicate ideas using flowcharts, concept maps, and story webs through visual learning techniques. **Visual learning techniques** are methods that present ideas and information through graphical webs. Inspiration lets you build visual diagrams to work through the process of thinking, organizing thoughts, revealing patterns, and prioritizing information.

Flowcharts are diagrams that show the step-by-step actions that must take place by plotting a sequence of events. Flowcharts are useful in helping students outline the individual tasks that must be performed to complete an action, a story, or an experiment and the sequence in which they must be performed. A **concept map** or **story web** helps students use flowcharting to understand the attributes and relationships of the main subject and provides a visual tool for brainstorming and planning (Figure 7-18). Another useful planning tool is a **storyboard**, which is a drawing that allows students to design and lay out a project or assignment before creating it on a computer.

EVALUATING CREATIVITY   When evaluating student projects, teachers should consider students' originality, imaginative and

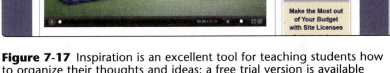

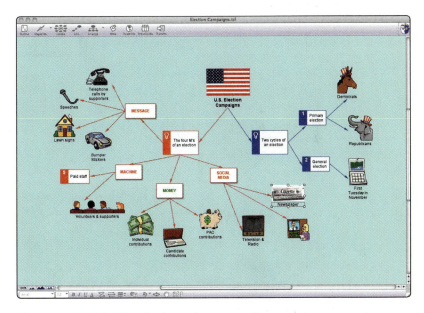

Figure 7-17 Inspiration is an excellent tool for teaching students how to organize their thoughts and ideas; a free trial version is available for download.

Figure 7-18 Using Inspiration software, students create a concept map to plan an undertaking such as this project on election campaigns.

innovative approach, and artistic abilities — all aspects of **creativity**. Creative student projects should be interesting and unique. Students should demonstrate an understanding of how to use the special effects offered by multimedia authoring software to enhance their projects, rather than distracting from their projects. Color, clip art, and artwork should strengthen content, not distract from it.

Integration Strategies

To learn about using peer evaluation of student projects, visit the Computer Concepts CourseMate Web site at *www.cengagebrain. com,* and then navigate to the Chapter 7 Digital Media Corner resource for this book.

PUTTING IT ALL TOGETHER — EVALUATING TECHNOLOGY INTEGRATION

Mrs. Vicki Osborne teaches social studies and other subjects at Fall Hills Middle School. She has one computer in her classroom and 26 students. Her middle school is on a **block schedule**, which is an alternative way of scheduling classes. This means the social studies class meets every other day for 90 minutes. Mrs. Osborne's curriculum requires that her social studies students learn about the electoral process, so she is having them research a recent presidential candidate and then prepare a digital media presentation to convey their findings to the class.

She has six goals for the lesson. The students are to do the following: (1) work cooperatively in groups with three or four students in each group; (2) use reference materials and Web resources to research their candidate; (3) identify three major campaign issues for their candidate; (4) provide personal facts about the candidate, such as education, occupation prior to politics, and military service; (5) create a group digital media presentation to present their research with PowerPoint, Photo Story, Movie Maker, or iMovie; and (6) use correct grammar, spelling, and punctuation in their presentation. She uses a rubric to evaluate the students' projects.

Mrs. Osborne begins her social studies lesson by displaying her PowerPoint digital media presentation using a projector for easy viewing by all students. The first step is to brainstorm with her students about the lesson and create a concept map about the election process and the candidates (Figure 7-19).

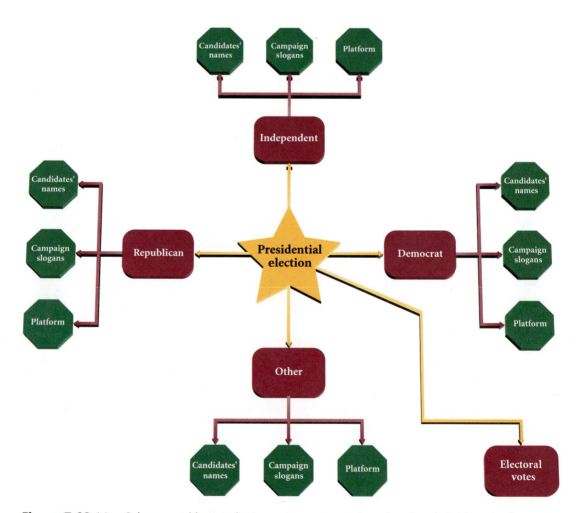

Figure 7-19 Mrs. Osborne and her students create a concept map showing their ideas on the election process and candidates.

She also hands out a copy of her evaluation rubric, discusses the rubric with her students, and answers their questions. Students then are divided into groups to complete their first task.

Students are required to create a flowchart or storyboard of their projects using concept mapping software, such as Inspiration. After Mrs. Osborne approves their flowchart drawings or storyboards, the groups are ready to begin creating their projects. Before starting the projects, Mrs. Osborne borrowed an additional computer from another teacher and arranged for two groups to use computers in the media center. This allows four groups to work on computers at the same time. Groups rotate through the four computers in 40-minute blocks.

When the groups finish their projects, Mrs. Osborne has each group present their project to the class in the media center. She also invites the principal, a local politician, the media specialist, and another social studies class to view the presentations. The students are very proud of their projects and enjoy showing them to their peers, teachers, and school administrators. The school newspaper plans to highlight some

of the projects. To make this an authentic learning experience, Mrs. Osborne's students created voting boxes and arranged for the students at Fall Hills Middle School to vote in a mock election. Her students created campaign slogans and ran the campaign just like a real-world political campaign.

To integrate technology successfully, teachers must continuously evaluate educational technology before instruction begins, during the instructional period, and after instruction has taken place. Technology not only changes the learning process (Figure 7-20) but also changes the teaching and evaluation processes. Teachers have the responsibility to evaluate and update assignments and activities continuously — on a daily, weekly, monthly, or semester basis — depending on the project or assignment.

To make learning more effective, often only minor changes and improvements are necessary. In other instances, however, teachers need to implement major revisions to reflect content, curriculum, or technology changes. The next few sections introduce you to other integration strategies, such as using technology in various classroom configurations and developing curriculum resource pages.

FAQ

Are there other software programs that teachers and students can use to create concept maps or flowcharts?

Yes, concept maps, flowcharts, and diagrams can be created easily in most word processing programs, such as Microsoft Word, by using the drawing tools.

Figure 7-20 Centers, such as the one shown here, allow students to work collaboratively in groups on student-centered projects.

Integration Strategies

To explore dozens of curriculum and grade specific integration strategies, visit the Computer Concepts CourseMate Web site at *www.cengagebrain.com*, navigate to the Chapter 7 Apps Corner resource for this book, and then navigate to your grade-level corner.

Integration Strategies

To help meet the constant challenge of motivating students to learn, teachers must change their traditional roles and become facilitators of learning. Technology plays a key role in easing this change because it allows teachers to use technology tools to enhance the learning environment, motivate students, guide students in a participatory learning process, and encourage them to learn. The most effective way to integrate technology is to place the technology at the point of instruction — the classroom. Because of the ever-increasing need to motivate students to learn, teachers have a mandate to use the powerful tools of technology to enhance the learning environment of today's digital students.

Many different technologies, availability of computer labs and media centers, and different kinds and numbers of computers in the classroom are found in schools today (Figure 7-21). The following instructional strategies describe techniques to integrate technology into a one-computer classroom, a multicomputer classroom, and a computer lab or media center.

ONE-COMPUTER CLASSROOM

Many classrooms are equipped with one digital media computer and are referred to as a **one-computer classroom**. Many strategies for integrating educational technology with only one computer in the classroom exist. As you learned in Chapter 5, the most common practice is to use the computer for classroom presentations and demonstrations. By projecting the computer's image on a projection screen or classroom wall, you can use the computer to supplement and enhance your traditional lectures to accomplish whole-class instruction of learning objectives. You also can use the computer to introduce new concepts, prepare students for a lesson, describe background information for assignments, and explain evaluation criteria.

Another strategy permits students to work on the computer in small groups to foster collaboration and cooperative learning opportunities. Students also can use the computer to present their assignments, projects, and research activities to the entire class. In addition, teachers can use the computer to maintain records, create presentations and projects, do research,

Figure 7-21 Technology can be integrated into many different classroom environments.

and communicate with other teachers (Figure 7-22).

To integrate technology in a one-computer classroom, follow these guidelines:

- Obtain Internet access. Use the Web's many educational resources, such as audio, video, and multimedia applications to enhance instruction and learning.

- Utilize educational software (including apps). Both teachers and students can make use of the abundance of educational software available on CD/DVDs, school networks, the Web, and app stores.

- Enhance lectures and presentations. Connect the computer to a projector, IWB, or document camera (a device used to magnify and project real objects, both 2D and 3D to a large audience), and then use the computer to enhance lectures, create and give presentations, and take students on virtual field trips.

- Use the computer as a teaching assistant. Tutor individual students by having them use drill and practice software, tutorials, simulations, and problem-solving software.

- Foster group and cooperative learning. Students can use the computer as an informational resource or a creation tool for group projects, such as digital media presentations.

- Write an ongoing story. Begin a story on the computer and invite student authors to add to it daily. Before you begin, explain the rules for acceptable behavior, the types of content to be included in the story, and the types of entries that are satisfactory.

- Create a class blog. Ask your students to evaluate the way we receive information today by reading and comparing two to three different blogs about a current event. Then, have them write a response in the class blog about the

Figure 7-22 Teachers benefit from using a classroom computer to maintain grades and other important files.

blogs they thought were most accurate and compelling.

- Start a class newsletter. Invite students to write articles and use word processing or desktop publishing software to create a class newsletter (Figure 7-23).

Figure 7-23 Students gain real-world skills by creating a class or school newsletter.

- Maintain a student database. Instead of having students fill out information forms, let them enter the information into a database on the computer. Students also can enter information on a variety of content-related subject areas, such as information on science projects, vocabulary words, historical places, and so on.

- Utilize the computer as a teacher productivity tool. The computer is an excellent medium for creating curriculum activities, lesson plans and tests, maintaining grades and attendance records, writing letters to parents, and creating achievement certificates. Purchasing gradebook or student information management software helps to streamline many daily management responsibilities.

- Supplement your one computer room by optimizing computer lab time. Use the computer to introduce students to various types of software and thus create learning paths before taking students to the school's computer lab. This will optimize the time students spend on computers while in the computer lab.

- Take advantage of emerging technologies that allow you to create an exciting learning environment; for example, you can roll a complete computer lab into your classroom. If your school has a wireless mobile lab, schedule time to use the lab. This is a great way to move the technology you need into your one-computer classroom.

MULTICOMPUTER CLASSROOM

Having two or more computers in your classroom fosters additional learning opportunities that allow flexibility in computer usage and make technology integration an integral part of the curriculum. Remember, one-computer classroom strategies also apply to a classroom with two or more computers.

One way to use two or more computers is to set up the computers as separate learning centers for student use. Teachers can divide the centers by subject area and then create activities that continuously change to match the curriculum or lessons being taught. A math center, for example, might include CDs, DVDs, apps, and network-based software to reinforce math skills. A language arts center might include word processing software or apps for creative writing projects; Movie Maker, iMovie, PowerPoint, and Photoshop to create digital media presentations; as well as reading and spelling software skill programs.

A social studies center might allow students to use the Web as a research tool and correspond with other classrooms via the Internet to learn more about the culture, language, history, and geography of other regions. Software programs, such as Oregon Trail and dozens of apps, help reinforce mapping and geography skills in relation to other curriculum areas.

Learning centers are an effective way to create a flexible learning environment with many options for students. Teachers can integrate technologies into learning centers to create specialized centers such as a video center, a listening center, and a digital production center.

To illustrate how one teacher is integrating technology into a science curriculum, consider the middle school classroom of Miss Julie Davis. At the beginning of class, she takes her students for a nature walk on school property to learn about trees, plants, changing seasons, and photosynthesis. During the nature walk, students notice a lot of trash on the school grounds. Students take their netbooks, smartphones, and tablets to enter data on a form Miss Davis created for them to fill out during their excursion. This way, the students enter their thoughts, explorations, and findings while they are in the environment, and not later, when they might have forgotten important information and findings.

She encourages her students to use digital cameras to take pictures of the trash, plants, trees, and other items of interest. In a follow-up discussion in class, the students decide the trash is a form of pollution — and they should do something to make the school cleaner. Miss Davis recognizes this as a teachable moment and asks essential questions to start the students thinking. She asks, "Can we make a difference? How can we help prevent pollution, starting at school?" The students begin brainstorming.

Following the discussion, Miss Davis shows the students a short CNN video on global warming.

The next day, Miss Davis continues the learning process by dividing the students into groups to begin their research projects on waste, environmentally hazardous materials, trees, plants, and air associated with the environment. Next, the students begin working on their KWLQS charts. A **KWLQS chart** is similar to the KWL chart discussed in Chapter 5, with the additions of Q, which stands for further questioning, and S, which stands for sharing (referring to the fact that students will share their projects with their fellow students). Miss Davis and the students decide to create a survey to examine all the environmental issues at the school. From the survey results, it is clear most students are aware that the school has to dispose of trash, but most of them have never focused on the hazardous products, such as cleaners, that need to be disposed. It is also clear that none of the students had thought about the school's various types of trash, or whether the school recycles, or whether the methods used for disposing of hazardous waste could harm the environment. Miss Davis places the students in groups and assigns each group different environmental issues to research.

Miss Davis is fortunate to have three new tablet computers and one notebook computer in her classroom. Two of the tablets are used as Web research centers, while the other one is set up as a creation center. To complete group projects, students rotate through the Web centers and use Miss Davis' curriculum resource pages. Miss Davis found resources on the Web (Figure 7-24) to help her create her curriculum resource pages. Students use the curriculum resource pages to locate resources from agriculture, environmental protection agencies, and other related Web sites. Then, they use the creation center to develop presentations that suggest ways to protect the environment. The students incorporate their digital pictures into digital media projects (Figure 7-25) via the notebook computer. While completing the projects, the students learn about citizenship and that everyone is responsible for protecting the environment.

As a result of their projects, students decide to start a schoolwide cleanup

Figure 7-24 Students can locate information dealing with pollution, global warming, and other environmental issues on the Web easily.

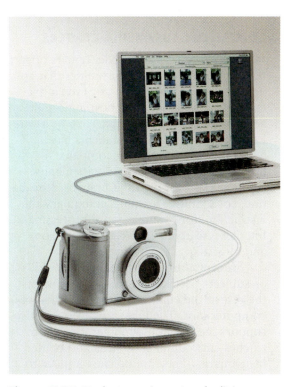

Figure 7-25 Students can import and edit images taken with a digital camera to enhance their projects.

project. The class creates flyers and posts them throughout the school so all the students and teachers will be aware of the environment. They also create a Web site, sharing what they have learned with the community.

As this example illustrates, using computers and other technologies in the classroom promotes participatory learning, involves the students, and provides a sense of ownership, or authentic learning, of the information being presented. Having two or more computers in the classroom — especially when they are used as learning centers — requires more planning and attention to detail than having just one computer. Before setting up a learning center or centers, teachers should consider how many computers will be in each center and what other technologies, if any, may be included in the center. After the centers are set up, teachers can work on managing and planning activities, scheduling rotation times through each center for the students as they complete projects and activities. Teachers can create a sign-up list or use a timing device so all students share time on the computers fairly.

COMPUTER LABS/MEDIA CENTERS

Computer labs and media centers offer teachers instructional opportunities that are not possible in a one-, two-, or even a five-computer classroom. The most important advantage of using a computer lab or a wireless mobile lab is that all students have hands-on experience using computer technology. Teachers may successfully use computer labs for drill and practice, remediation, collaborative learning, computer skill instruction (for example, word processing), Internet research, whole class instruction, and tutorials.

Students often learn technology skills or subject-specific skills in isolation from the rest of the curriculum while in school computer labs. The labs, however, can also support the technology integration that teaches curriculum standards and related benchmarks. They are not just a place to teach keyboarding, remedial math, and science drills. A lab with new computers, scanners, printers, Web access, and other technologies makes it possible to integrate computer-related skills into subject-directed curriculum areas. Teachers, for example, can integrate specific software applications into subject-area content.

Teacher-created activities, such as Web scavenger hunts and Webquests, also teach computer skills, while giving students direction. A **Web scavenger hunt** is an inquiry-oriented activity in which students explore the resources of the Web using discovery learning to find the answers to teacher-created questions (Figure 7-26). While searching for the answers, students use higher-order thinking skills. When teachers plan creative instructional activities in advance, the computer lab, along with other technologies and the Internet, can bring authentic excitement and enthusiasm to students who otherwise might be uninterested in their daily school work.

Curriculum Integration Activities

Many teachers already use computers and technology in their classrooms and computer labs to help meet curriculum standards. For curriculum integration to be effective, however, the curriculum should drive the technologies used in the classroom; that is, teachers should use the applicable technologies to enhance learning at the appropriate times.

As teachers use technology in the classroom, they are finding many different ways to integrate it into curriculum-specific learning objectives. Learning to integrate technology effectively, however, requires planning and practice. The more practice you have teaching with and integrating technology, the more you will discover innovative ways to use technology to facilitate all types of instruction.

CURRICULUM RESOURCE PAGES

One of the main technology integration challenges that teachers face today is determining exactly how to use the Internet in their classrooms. Teachers who integrate the Internet successfully are using it in ways that engage students in problem solving, locating research information, and developing higher-order thinking skills. Supervising students and controlling Web activities with curriculum resource pages are crucial to the successful use of the Internet in classrooms.

Roller Coaster Scavenger Hunt

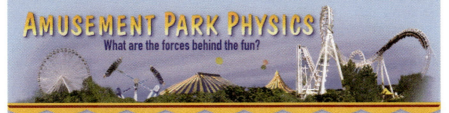

To learn more about the forces behind the fun, visit the Amusement Park Physics Web site using the following link:

www.learner.org/exhibits/parkphysics

Part A: Visit the site and read about roller coasters to answer the questions that follow.

1. Do roller coasters have engines? _____

2. What drives a roller coaster? _____

3. What is the difference between running wheels and friction wheels?_____

_____

4. How do roller coasters stop?_____

5. What is centripetal force? _____

6. What is gravitational force? _____

7. Name and explain three physics terms that relate to roller coasters. _____

_____

Part B: Follow the online instructions to design your own roller coaster and answer the questions that follow.

8. What hill height did you choose? Why? _____

9. What hill shape did you choose? Why? _____

10. Which exit path did you choose? Why? _____

11. What did you choose for the height of your second hill? Why? _____

_____

12. What type of loop did you add? Why? _____

13. Did your roller coaster design succeed or fail? Why? _____

_____

_____

On the back of this paper, list four additional facts that you learned. Good Luck!

Figure 7-26 A scavenger hunt is a great way to have students explore resources on the Web while, at the same time, using their higher-order thinking skills.

A **curriculum resource page** is a teacher-created document containing hyperlinks to teacher-selected Web sites that assist in teaching content-specific curriculum objectives. In addition, curriculum resource pages support learning objectives by providing students with quality Web resources, links to additional information, and opportunities to learn more. Because your curriculum resource page contains links that you have already researched and evaluated, students waste no time needlessly surfing instead of learning. A curriculum resource page can be a useful tool to ensure students spend your precious class time linking quickly to Web sites that you know will provide valuable information that is relevant to your lesson. Curriculum resource pages are easy to create and are a valuable teaching tool for students to use when accessing the World Wide Web.

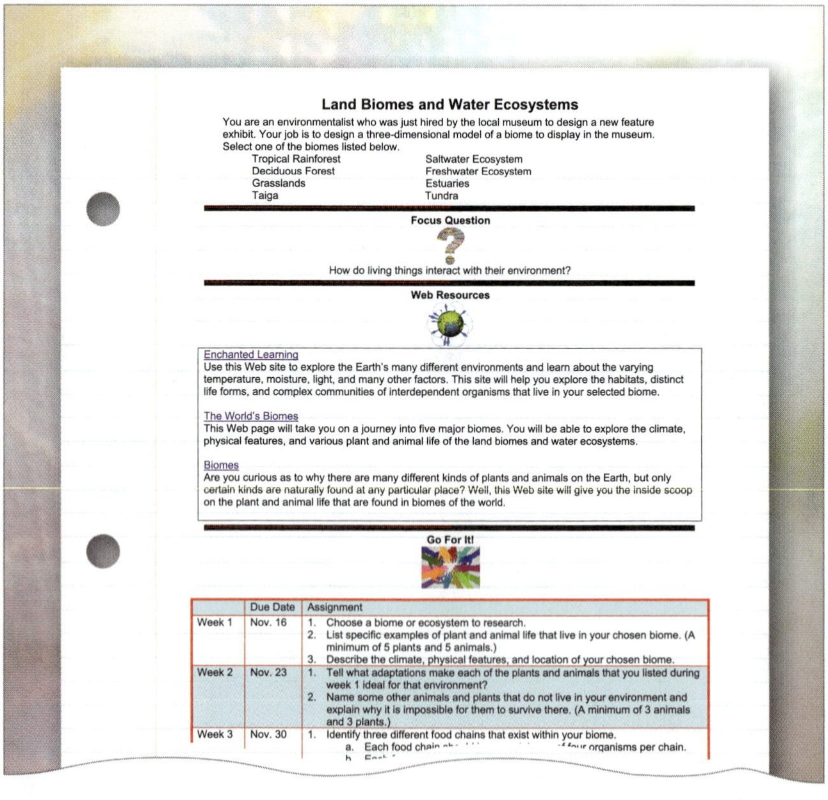
Land Biomes and Water Ecosystems

You are an environmentalist who was just hired by the local museum to design a new feature exhibit. Your job is to design a three-dimensional model of a biome to display in the museum. Select one of the biomes listed below.

Tropical Rainforest
Deciduous Forest
Grasslands
Taiga
Saltwater Ecosystem
Freshwater Ecosystem
Estuaries
Tundra

Focus Question

How do living things interact with their environment?

Web Resources

Enchanted Learning
Use this Web site to explore the Earth's many different environments and learn about the varying temperature, moisture, light, and many other factors. This site will help you explore the habitats, distinct life forms, and complex communities of interdependent organisms that live in your selected biome.

The World's Biomes
This Web page will take you on a journey into five major biomes. You will be able to explore the climate, physical features, and various plant and animal life of the land biomes and water ecosystems.

Biomes
Are you curious as to why there are many different kinds of plants and animals on the Earth, but only certain kinds are naturally found at any particular place? Well, this Web site will give you the inside scoop on the plant and animal life that are found in biomes of the world.

Go For It!

	Due Date	Assignment
Week 1	Nov. 16	1. Choose a biome or ecosystem to research. 2. List specific examples of plant and animal life that live in your chosen biome. (A minimum of 5 plants and 5 animals.) 3. Describe the climate, physical features, and location of your chosen biome.
Week 2	Nov. 23	1. Tell what adaptations make each of the plants and animals that you listed during week 1 ideal for that environment? 2. Name some other animals and plants that do not live in your environment and explain why it is impossible for them to survive there. (A minimum of 3 animals and 3 plants.)
Week 3	Nov. 30	1. Identify three different food chains that exist within your biome. a. Each food chain [illegible] four organisms per chain.

Figure 7-27 A curriculum resource page, in addition to hyperlinks, provides activities for students to complete at the selected Web sites.

Simple curriculum resource pages contain hyperlinks to teacher-selected sites. More detailed curriculum resource pages provide hyperlinks to Web sites and instructions for constructive and purposeful activities that students complete when they get to the selected Web sites (Figure 7-27). Using curriculum resource pages with these types of activities helps students find answers to teacher-created questions and helps them create and answer their own questions.

INTERACTIVE LESSONS AND ASSESSMENT

In a typical classroom, teachers deliver an assessment on Friday, grade the assessment over the weekend, and revisit the necessary content upon returning to school if there is adequate time. This does not always create a meaningful academic situation and does not address the needs of all students as the actual lesson progresses. Instead, it requires that educators wait until the lesson is complete to determine if students actually grasp the material.

Remember we learned about Interactive Whiteboards (IWB) in Chapter 5, IWB creators have developed a means for delivering ongoing assessment and collecting immediate student data by using a learner response system. A **learner response system** is made up of IWB software that is installed on a teacher's computer, a wireless receiver, and student hand-held infrared transmitters that collect student responses or data in real time. Then, this data can be used to determine students' needs on the spot, deliver necessary interventions, and provide enrichment opportunities to students who have mastered the content.

By using a learner response system, educators are able to create lesson assessments ahead of time or ask ad-hoc questions as the lesson progresses to formatively assess where students are in the learning process. Instruction then can be modified in real time according to student progress, and students in need of additional support can receive it when they need it most.

CREATING LESSON AND PROJECT PLANS

Planning is one of the most important variables for good instruction, and curriculum integration demands a great deal of planning. When first introducing technology into the classroom, many teachers try to incorporate technology into their existing lesson plans and activities. Because of the nature of the new technology tools, however, and because teaching and learning approaches must change, most teachers learn quickly this initial approach is only partially effective. To be successful in integrating technology, teachers must rethink and redesign activities and create new teaching and learning strategies as they actively integrate technology across their curriculum. In other words, new technology tools require new instructional lessons.

Teachers do not have to rely solely on their own resourcefulness to create technology-rich lesson plans and activities. Today, teachers may receive online advice from other educators by joining educational mailing lists, forums, newsgroups, discussion groups, bulletin boards, blogs, and vlogs. Teachers also may refer to the Educator's Reference Desk, which provides thousands of resources and services to the education community (Figure 7-28). In addition, numerous lesson plans and activities at thousands of educational Web sites are available for teachers to use (Figure 7-29 below). Many such sites provide search engines to locate curriculum-specific lesson plans and activities for almost any K-12 area.

The following sections provide examples of subject-specific and interdisciplinary teacher-created curriculum integration activities. Each of these lesson or project plans is centered on a focus question and uses a combination of learning processes and teaching strategies to assist in the delivery of the instructional process. The purpose of these curriculum integration activities is to provide a basic understanding of how to integrate technology into the classroom. You can adapt these examples to subject areas covered in your classroom or use them in other curriculum areas for thematic instruction.

Web Info

For more information about using computers as tools for learning, visit the Computer Concepts CourseMate Web site at *www.cengagebrain. com*, navigate to the Chapter 7 Web Info resource for this book, and then click Learning Tools.

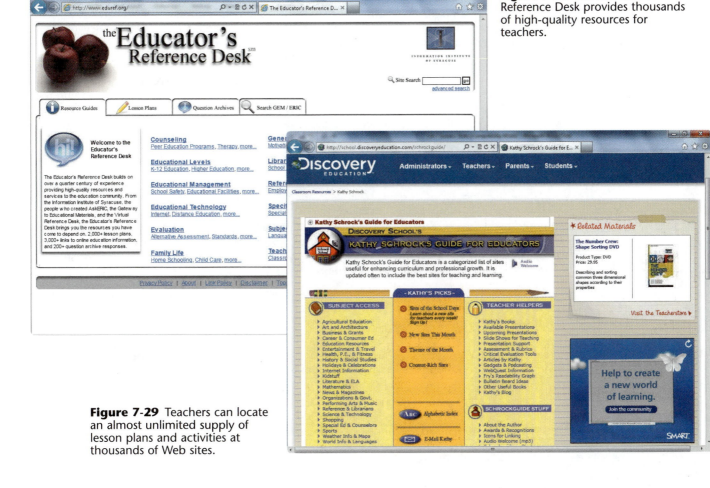

Figure 7-28 The Educator's Reference Desk provides thousands of high-quality resources for teachers.

Figure 7-29 Teachers can locate an almost unlimited supply of lesson plans and activities at thousands of Web sites.

LANGUAGE ARTS INTEGRATION Language arts curriculum usually includes instruction in reading, writing, listening, viewing, speaking, and literature. Figure 7-30 shows a curriculum integration activity, called *Word Wizards*, that integrates technology into the subject area of language arts, specifically vocabulary.

Language Arts

Curriculum Area:	Language Arts
Subject Area:	Vocabulary
Lesson Title:	Word Wizards
Suggested Grade Level:	2–5, could be adapted for any grade level
Equipment Needed:	Technology: Interactive whiteboard (IWB) connected to a computer, Learner Response System (such as ActivExpressions), classroom computers, digital video editing software, Publisher, or word processing software Software: ActivInspire (on teacher and student computers), Inspiration, vocabulary app Other: Teacher-created curriculum resource page on vocabulary resources, teacher-created Word Wizards vocabulary flipchart (lesson created in ActivInspire), vocabulary pre- and post-test
Focus Question:	Why is it important to determine meaning in vocabulary?
Learning Objectives:	■ Students will locate the definitions for each vocabulary word. ■ Students will work cooperatively in small groups to plan and create a Word Wizard activity. ■ Students will present their completed activities to teach their peers the vocabulary words. ■ Students will evaluate their peers' Word Wizard activities using a rubric. ■ Students will correctly define each vocabulary word.
Instructions:	Ask students why it is important to understand the meaning of words. Have students text in their responses using their ActivExpression (or other Learner Response System) devices and display their answers on the IWB. Discuss the various responses and ask students to explain their answers. Administer the vocabulary pre-test using the ActivExpressions. Be sure to save the data! Then, show students the vocabulary activities you have created in a flipchart to help students understand the meanings of various vocabulary words. Have students do a couple of the activities, and discuss how these activities might help students better understand the meanings. Explain the Word Wizard task students are to complete, and display the rubric that will be used on the IWB. Review the rubric components. Place students in small groups and provide each group with five vocabulary words. Model how to use the resources in the curriculum resource page to find definitions. Have students research and find the definitions for their five words. Direct them to the curriculum resource page for resources to assist in their search. Students will use Inspiration to create word webs for each word and its definition to assist in the understanding of its meaning. Students will work with their partners to plan the activity they will create to teach their peers the vocabulary words. Students have the choice to create any activity they choose, as long as it is interactive and teaches the vocabulary words (matching, fill in the blank, click and reveal, crossword, etc.). Be sure to provide each group with a copy of the rubric to assist in their planning. Once students have developed a plan, they will create their own interactive lesson teaching their assigned vocabulary words. Students work with their partners on a classroom computer to build their activity using ActivInspire software. Students then present their Word Wizard activities via the IWB, and their peers come up and complete the activities. It is the group's job to make sure their peers understand the meaning of the words. Teacher may scaffold as needed. Students evaluate each group's activity with the same rubric the teacher will use to evaluate student work. Once each group has presented their Word Wizard activity and their peers have completed them, administer the vocabulary post-test using student ActivExpressions. Compare the post-test data with that of the pre-test and discuss with students why the data has changed.
Evaluation of Content:	The evaluation rubric will be used to determine whether students met all intended criteria with the creation of the Word Wizard activities. The pre- and post-test data will represent student learning growth throughout the lesson and student understanding of the vocabulary.
Evaluation of Curriculum and Technology Integration:	Students will be evaluated on their ability to use the provided software and technologies to plan, create, and deliver content demonstrating their knowledge. Teacher observation and the teacher-created rubric should be used to evaluate student comprehension and motivation. The effectiveness of using the technology for students to teach their peers will be apparent in the project presentation.

Figure 7-30 A sample lesson plan for *Word Wizards*.

SOCIAL STUDIES INTEGRATION   Social studies curriculum usually encompasses instruction in history, geography, civics, and economics. Figure 7-31 shows a curriculum integration activity, called *What Wonderful Webs We Weave*, that integrates technology into the subject area of ancient Egypt.

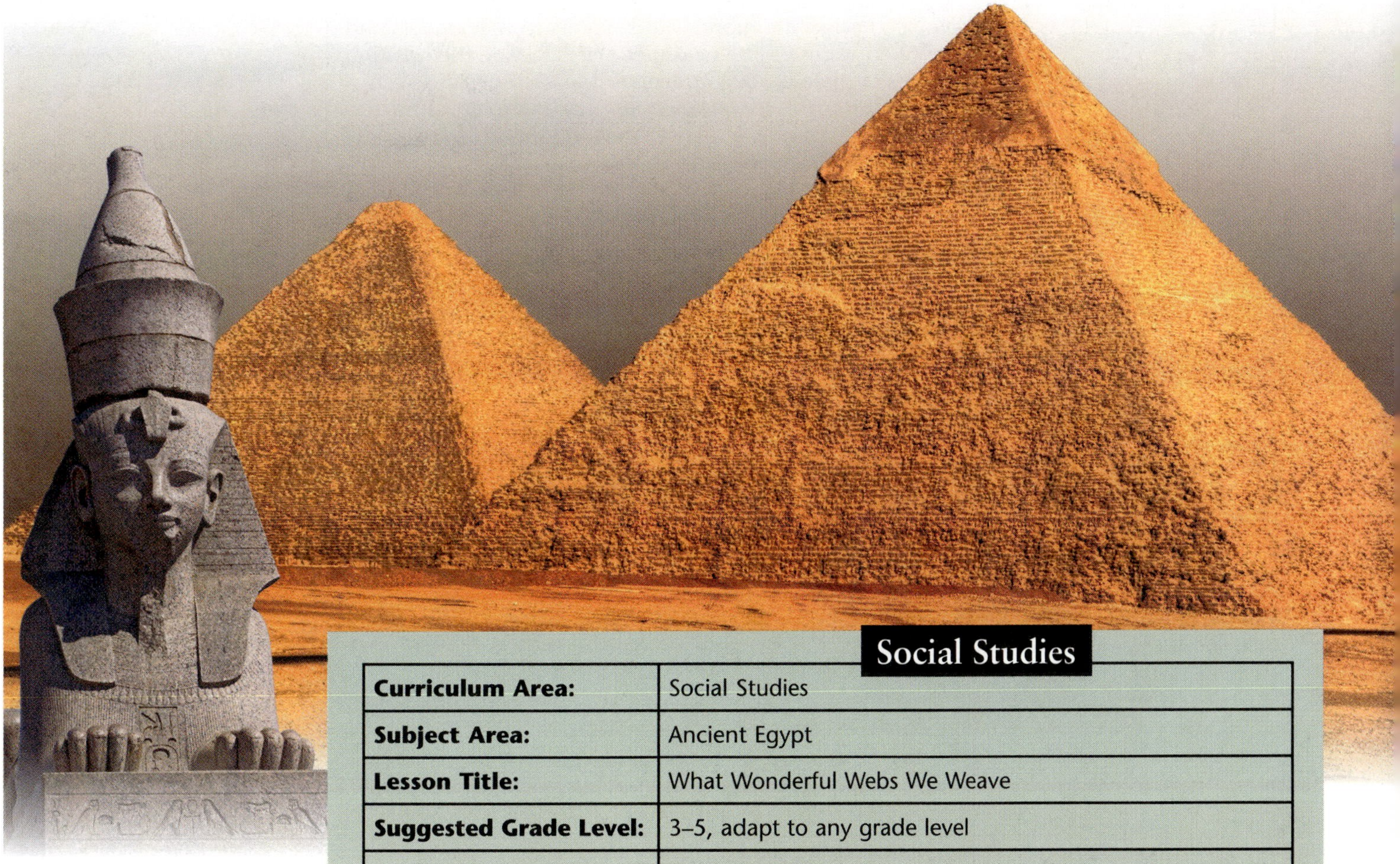

Social Studies	
Curriculum Area:	Social Studies
Subject Area:	Ancient Egypt
Lesson Title:	What Wonderful Webs We Weave
Suggested Grade Level:	3–5, adapt to any grade level
Equipment Needed:	Technology: Classroom computers, media center, or a computer lab, Internet access, and projector connected to a computer
	Software: Ancient civilizations CD/DVDs, apps about Egypt, electronic encyclopedias, and Web editors such as Web Blender, Microsoft Word, KompoZer, or Dreamweaver
	Other: Teacher-created curriculum resource pages related to ancient Egypt, books, magazines, and encyclopedias from the media center
Focus Question:	How are ancient Egyptian traditions reflected in our culture today?
Learning Objectives:	■ Students will describe what life was like in ancient Egypt based on class discussions and information found in books, CDs, DVDs, videotapes, as well as the Internet.
	■ Students will work cooperatively in small groups, create Web pages using a Web editor, and then publish their pages on the World Wide Web.

Figure 7-31 A sample lesson plan for *What Wonderful Webs We Weave*.

(continued on the next page)

| Instructions: | Introduce the activity to students by asking the focus question, then use student responses to create a KWLQS chart about ancient Egypt. As a class, decide on five or six broad topics of study relating to ancient Egypt: mummies, pyramids, Pharaohs, and so on. Connect a classroom computer to a projector and view teacher-created curriculum resource pages about ancient Egypt. Discuss what makes a Web site interesting, attractive, and relevant. Distribute an evaluation rubric for the students' Web page project. Review the rubric with students so they understand how their Web pages will be evaluated. Next, divide the class into small groups of three or four students. Have each group select one of the broad topics the class listed. Provide time for students to research their group's topic. They may use the CDs, DVDs, Web sites, curriculum-specific apps, books, magazines, and encyclopedias from the media center, and the teacher-created curriculum resource pages.

After students finish their research, have them complete a planning worksheet. Students plan their content, Web page layout, background, attention-getting titles, animated GIFs, pictures, and links to related Web sites. After students have created their Web pages on paper, have them use a Web editor to create their Web pages. When the Web pages are complete, they can be posted on your school's server or on a free Web server site. |
| --- | --- |
| **Evaluation of Content:** | Teacher observation along with the project rubric will be used to evaluate this activity. In addition, students' planning worksheets will be used for assessment purposes. Quality of research, the information drawn from Web sites, and the extent to which the students answered the focus question also will be assessed. |
| **Evaluation of Curriculum and Technology Integration:** | Teacher observation will be used to assess learning based on students' ability to access, analyze, and apply information from different resources. How well students locate information, determine what information is valuable, and apply that information will be examined. Student motivation and enthusiasm when creating a Web page also will assist with evaluating the technology. |

Figure 7-31 A sample lesson plan for *What Wonderful Webs We Weave.*

(continued from the previous page)

MATHEMATICS INTEGRATION   Mathematics **curriculum** usually includes instruction in basic number concepts, measurements, geometry, algebra, calculus, and data analysis.

Figure 7-32 shows a curriculum integration activity, called *The Business of Professional Sports*, that integrates technology into the subject areas of measurement, problem solving, and data literacy.

Math

Curriculum Area:	Math
Subject Area:	Measurement, Problem Solving, and Data Literacy
Lesson Title:	The Business of Professional Sports
Suggested Grade Level:	6–12
Equipment Needed:	Technology: One computer or more and a projector or document camera connected to the computer
	Software: Any presentation software (such as PowerPoint), spreadsheet software (such as Excel or InspireData), Inspiration, and math software such as Geometer's Sketchpad or appropriate apps
	Other: Teacher-created curriculum resource pages, sports reference books, newspapers, magazines, and media center
Focus Question:	How are math concepts used in athletic activities?
Learning Objectives:	■ Students will identify how math is used in sports. ■ Students will use geometry to build a scale model of their playing field. ■ Students will identify and explain the duration of a game for their sport. ■ Students will identify and explain the scoring system for their team sport. ■ Students will demonstrate how statistics are calculated for their team. ■ Students will determine ticket prices using range and central tendency to compute their findings. ■ Students will work cooperatively to create a project presenting information outlined above using presentation software.

Figure 7-32 A sample lesson plan for *The Business of Professional Sports*.

(continued on the next page)

Instructions:	Have students list all the team sports they know. Create a concept map using Inspiration, projected to the class on the television monitor with Math as the center. Brainstorm with the class on how math is used in each of the sports they named, and then add these ideas to the concept map. Invite students to select their favorite team sport and then group students according to interest. Distribute an assessment rubric and discuss how it will be used to evaluate students' projects.
	Students will use the rubric and follow the learning objectives to determine what elements to include in their projects. Encourage them to use the Internet for research, as well as any resources from the media center including newspapers to calculate statistics. Provide each group with a designated time to use the computer. When groups are not using the computer, they may be using other resource materials to develop their projects.
	Coordinate with the media specialist students' access to other computers or schedule time in the computer lab when the groups are working on their presentations. Have students use Geometer's Sketchpad to enter data and evaluate team statistics. Create graphs in Geometer's Sketchpad and compare. Have students create graphs using any spreadsheet software application or InspireData to include in their projects. When groups have completed their projects, share them with the class.
Evaluation of Content:	The evaluation rubric will be used to determine the extent to which students used the learning objectives to answer the focus question. Teachers will determine the extent of student learning by the level of student motivation and a demonstrated understanding of statistics.
Evaluation of Curriculum and Technology Integration:	Evaluate problem-solving skills based on the concept map students created to visualize their brainstorming responses. Furthermore, assess technology skills and problem-solving skills acquired through the use of software applications. Evaluate the use of software to learn how to organize information and see graphical representation of that information. Evaluate student presentations to determine if this process reinforces skills in communication, organization, problem-solving skills, and critical-thinking skills.

Figure 7-32 A sample lesson plan for *The Business of Professional Sports.*

(continued from the previous page)

SCIENCE INTEGRATION
Science curriculum usually contains instruction in physical sciences, earth and space sciences, and life sciences. Figure 7-33 shows a curriculum integration activity, called *Let's Think as a Scientist*, that integrates technology into the subject area of life science.

Science

Curriculum Area:	Science
Subject Area:	Life Science
Lesson Title:	Let's Think as a Scientist
Suggested Grade Level:	K-12
Equipment Needed:	Technology: One computer and a projector/IWB connected to the computer Software: Thinkin' Science or any appropriate science app. This lesson can be adapted with other software-specific products. Other: Student computers if available
Focus Question:	Why is it necessary for scientists to have good observation skills?
Learning Objectives:	■ Students will practice observation and problem-solving skills. ■ Students will demonstrate understanding of content. ■ Students will interpret data. ■ Students will determine cause and effect between two events.
Instructions:	Begin this activity with a whole class discussion; use the focus question to guide the conversation. Thinkin' Science explores the earth, life, and physical sciences. Connect the computer to a projector/IWB. For this activity, use the Thinkin' Science Animal Tracking activity. Students will need to observe animals and then apply problem-solving skills. Students will explore animal behavior and then interpret data that is presented. Guide students by asking questions and drawing their attention to important events. To provide further practice of observation skills and to increase problem-solving skills, use the Thinkin' Science activity, *What Did You See?* The students will be presented with a scene. The scene will disappear and students will have to recreate the scene. All students should tell you what needs to be placed in the scene. After you have used the Thinkin' Science software with the whole class, you can set it up in a learning center. *Note:* the software comes with a Teacher's Guide and reproducible activity sheets. You can place these in the learning center to support the students.
Evaluation of Content:	Students will be quizzed on content provided to determine if problem-solving skills and observation skills were mastered. The number of correctly answered questions from each student will determine attainment of content.
Evaluation of Curriculum and Technology Integration:	Teacher observation will be used to measure student motivation. An additional evaluation will be identifying how many students utilize the software in the learning center.

Figure 7-33 A sample lesson plan for *Let's Think as a Scientist*.

PHYSICAL EDUCATION AND HEALTH INTEGRATION Physical education and health curriculum usually includes instruction in basic health and physical education literacy. Figure 7-34 shows a curriculum integration activity, called *Eating Healthy!*, that integrates technology into the subject area of nutrition.

Physical Education and Health

Curriculum Area:	Physical Education and Health
Subject Area:	Nutrition
Lesson Title:	Eating Healthy!
Suggested Grade Level:	2–5, could be adapted for any grade level
Equipment Needed:	Technology: Three computers, at least one with Internet access Software: PowerPoint or Keynote, database and drawing programs such as Microsoft Office, iWork, Microsoft Works, Photoshop Elements, Photo Story, and Microsoft Paint Other: Teacher-created curriculum resource pages, books, nutrition brochures (from hospitals/health departments), and the Dole Web site (*www.dole.com*)
Focus Question:	How do food choices affect your overall health?
Learning Objectives:	■ Students will create five recipes that include at least one serving of fruits/vegetables in each recipe. ■ Students will enter one of their recipes into a class cookbook database. ■ Students will work cooperatively to locate facts about their assigned fruit/vegetable using the Dole Fruit and Vegetable Encyclopedia and other resources. ■ Students will use PowerPoint or Photo Story to create and present a multimedia project on their fruit/vegetable.
Instructions:	Individually, students will go to the Dole Web site to take the Nutrition Challenge and to discover how food choices affect their health. Students will be given time to browse the Web page to learn more about why it is so important to eat at least five fruits/vegetables per day. Students will use the information from the Web site and nutrition brochures to create five recipes for their 5-day menu. Students will select their favorite recipe and add it to the class cookbook database. Students will create a creative cookbook cover using a desktop publishing or drawing program. They will print copies of the recipes to share with their families. Students will work in groups of two or three to create a digital media presentation on an assigned fruit/vegetable. Students will use books, nutrition brochures, and the Dole Web site to collect the information that they need to complete their projects.
Evaluation of Content:	Each student's menu item will be evaluated using a rubric (spelling and grammar included). Group projects also will be evaluated using a rubric (spelling and grammar included). Teachers will observe students as they work to determine whether students understand how food choices affect their overall health.
Evaluation of Curriculum and Technology Integration:	The effectiveness of the technology will be evaluated by testing students' content retention in a culminating quiz. Effectiveness will be apparent in student presentations. Students will gain valuable experience exploring Internet resources and learning how to use them to complete an assignment.

Figure 7-34 A sample lesson plan for *Eating Healthy!*

ARTS INTEGRATION Arts curriculum usually incorporates instruction in the visual and performing arts, including drawing, painting, dance, music, and theater. Figure 7-35 shows a curriculum integration activity, called *The Theory of Color*, that integrates technology into the subject area of color theory.

Art	
Curriculum Area:	Art (integrates Reading, Writing, and Math)
Subject Area:	Color Theory — Reinforcing Basic Reading, Writing, and Math Skills
Lesson Title:	The Theory of Color
Suggested Grade Level:	3–6, easily adapted to higher levels
Equipment Needed:	Technology: Requires access to a student computer lab, requires computer connected to projector or IWB Software: PowerPoint and any paint program or paint app
Focus Question:	How does the world around you reflect colors?
Learning Objectives:	■ Students will increase understanding of color theory. ■ Students will increase use of reading, math, and writing in the art classroom. ■ Students will demonstrate abstract conceptualization of written materials. ■ Students will demonstrate skills using paint software or a paint app.

Figure 7-35 A sample lesson plan for *The Theory of Color*.

(continued on the next page)

Instructions:	Students are given a brief introduction explaining the goals of the lessons. They are told that an important part of the lesson is their ability to demonstrate their reading and writing skills. A simple pretest is given to allow students to demonstrate any pre-existing knowledge of the content area.
	Color mixing: Using basic math skills and written directions, students prepare a series of diagrammatic color charts that teach basic color mixing and theory. The blank charts are prepared with the paint software. The color formulas will be written in a mathematical or fractional way (for example, Orange = 1/2 Yellow + 1/2 Red). Students will use eyedroppers in their software programs to mix tempera paints to the proper proportion and paint samples as a permanent record in their portfolios.
	Relating reading and color theory: Based on the belief that students should be taught to visualize color as described in books or stories, students will read a series of excerpts from stories that include written descriptions of colors. Students will create color samples that show an understanding of the written excerpt and the colors described.
	Relating color to written descriptions: In contrast to the previous activity, students will be given blank lined pages for writing text. Each blank page will have a preprinted block of color. Students will be directed to create brief descriptive paragraphs that relate to each of the preprinted colors.
	Integrating technology: This lesson will be spread over time to allow adequate computer access time.
	Students will create a drawing with the paint program. The requirement for this piece of art will be that it clearly shows three primary colors, three secondary colors, one tint, and one shade.
Evaluation of Content:	A rubric will be used that the students easily can understand. Students will engage in critiques of each other's work. Critiques will be consolidated, and students and instructors jointly will discuss the results of the exercises. The teacher also will assign individual student work. This will be based on the rubric to ensure consistency and reliability of results. Final results are compared with the pretest, where marked improvement in the students' understanding of color and color theory should be identified.
Evaluation of Curriculum and Technology Integration:	Teacher observation and a teacher-created rubric should be used to determine the quality of the projects. Higher levels of complexity or variance in the final projects can be evaluated.

Figure 7-35 A sample lesson plan for
The Theory of Color.
　　　(continued from the previous page)

EXCEPTIONAL EDUCATION INTEGRATION

Exceptional education curriculum, or **special education curriculum,** usually contains instruction in all curriculum areas with adaptations made for students with unique characteristics or special needs. These students include those who are gifted, learning disabled, physically disabled, emotionally disabled, or mentally disabled. Instruction for regular-education students and exceptional-educational students is merging as teachers find that many of the technology resources and integration activities dramatically enhance the instruction of students with special needs. Teachers can modify many of the integration activities illustrated in Figure 7-30 through Figure 7-35 on pages 380 through 388 to meet the needs of exceptional educational students easily. Figure 7-36 shows a curriculum integration activity, called *Rain Forests Are in Trouble,* that integrates technology into the subject area of current events and can be used for all students, including students with special needs.

Special Education	
Curriculum Area:	Science, Social Studies, Math, and Language Arts for special education students
Subject Area:	Current Events
Lesson Title:	Rain Forests Are in Trouble
Suggested Grade Level:	6–8 (This project has been developed for grade levels 6 to 8 special education students. This lesson can be used with 3rd to 12th grade students with appropriate adaptations.)
Equipment Needed:	Technology: Computer and a projector/IWB, Internet access, and use of the *PBS Journey into Amazonia* Web site and Wikipedia Web sites
	Software: Electronic encyclopedias, iMovie, Movie Maker, PowerPoint, and appropriate apps
	Other: Teacher-created curriculum resource pages on rain forests around the world, audio device, closed caption software, 3 × 5 index cards, notebooks, pencils, pens
Focus Question:	Why are rain forests worth saving?
Learning Objectives:	■ Students will collect and analyze information about the rain forests.
	■ Students will describe a Web expedition to the Amazon using the Internet.
	■ Students will explain current research efforts on tropical rain forests.
	■ Students will demonstrate knowledge gained of tropical rain forest issues, and explore plant life cycles.
	■ Students will create a digital media research report.

Figure 7-36 A sample lesson plan for *Rain Forests Are in Trouble.*

(continued on the next page)

Instructions:	Start the activity by asking students what they know about rain forests. Use their responses to create a KWLQS chart with the students. Make sure print is large and colorful depending on needs.
	Students will work in groups of three or four. They will be given a list of Web sites about rain forests. They will access at least three different sites and take notes (3 $\times$ 5 index cards) about five different aspects of the rain forests. If an e-mail address is listed, students will write a short e-mail asking a specific question they have about the rain forest, and then send the e-mail.
	Students will work with their same team members and visit one of the Web sites, such as the *PBS Journey into Amazonia* Web site and others. While at the site, they will become an Amazon explorer and look for information on life on the land, in the water, and in the canopy, as well as investigate the different types of plants and butterflies. Students will create their own story, such as explaining the different butterflies and their migration patterns. Then the teams will create a journal of their discoveries. They will include details in their story about the migration patterns, location, the temperature, photographs with descriptions, and a narrative of the team's perceptions and opinions concerning the information they gathered.
	Students continue to work in their cooperative teams taking turns at the computer, using visual aids when needed. Each student plays the role of a scientific expert, chemist, ecologist, botanist, or taxonomist using student reference apps, books, and other resources. Students will create a research-based video production project on the computer with drawings, maps, and so on. Consider assistive technologies for the keyboard and mouse if needed.
Evaluation of Content:	The projects the students complete will indicate whether they grasped the concepts indicated by the preceding objectives. Students will be evaluated on their ability to analyze and present factual details This project could be used as an additional or follow-up assignment.
Evaluation of Curriculum and Technology Integration:	Teacher observation will help to verify if the technology assisted in meeting various learning styles and needs of special education students. Teacher observation will determine if technology assisted in student attention and motivation. Students will be evaluated on time on task and length of time students work to master content and technology skills. An additional evaluation will be looking at each student and his individual needs throughout the lesson.

Figure 7-36 A sample lesson plan for *Rain Forests Are in Trouble.*
(continued from the previous page)

INTERDISCIPLINARY INTEGRATION   An **interdisciplinary curriculum** usually includes two or more academic disciplines or curriculum areas to form a cross-discipline or subject-integrated lesson. A **cross-discipline lesson**, also called a **subject-integrated lesson**, is a lesson that integrates multiple skills, such as speaking, reading, thinking, and writing with multiple subject areas such as math, science, and language arts to create a more holistic learning experience. An interdisciplinary curriculum can combine various skills or disciplines to make a lesson more fully integrated for authentic and inquiry-based learning. Figure 7-37 shows a curriculum-integration activity, called *Natural Disasters Occur Everywhere*, that integrates technology in the subject areas of writing, research, science, social studies, health, and art. Figure 7-38 on pages 393 and 394 shows an activity, called *GeoMotion Learning Activity*, that integrates technology in the subject areas of physical education, science, math, and geography.

Interdisciplinary Integration

Curriculum Area:	Interdisciplinary — Integrates Writing, Research, Science, Social Studies, Health, and Art
Subject Area:	Natural Disasters
Lesson Title:	Natural Disasters Occur Everywhere
Suggested Grade Level:	5–8, can be adapted for any grade level
Equipment Needed:	Technology: Classroom computers or a computer lab, Internet access, and a projector/IWB connected to a computer Software: Inspiration, word processing program, database or spreadsheet program, digital media software, and appropriate apps Other: Curriculum resource pages, newspapers, journals, magazines, and books
Focus Question:	How can a brief moment in history affect the lives of many people for years?
Learning Objectives:	■ Students will use a variety of media resources, including magazines, newspapers, books, multimedia encyclopedias, and the Internet to gather information for research topics. ■ Students will determine the causes of a chosen natural disaster. ■ Students will describe the effects that natural disasters have on people and the environment. ■ Students will calculate the cost of disaster relief. ■ Students will list ways to prepare for natural disasters. ■ Students will interpret photographs of natural disasters. ■ Students will create a digital media presentation.

Figure 7-37 An interdisciplinary lesson plan for *Natural Disasters Occur Everywhere*.   (continued on the next page)

Instructions:	Introduce the task by asking the focus question. Allow several students to respond. Introduce the term natural disaster. Create a KWLQS chart to determine what students know about natural disasters and what they want to learn. Divide the class into groups of three or four and have each group go to *fema.gov/kids/dizarea.htm* to select a natural disaster that they want to research. Distribute a predetermined assessment rubric and cover the evaluation procedures for the final project.
	Students will use the Internet and other resources to collect data on their chosen natural disaster. Students will use Inspiration to organize their data into a concept web; students should include information such as the type and cause of the natural disaster, where the disaster occurred, the effect on people and the environment, and the type of aid currently being sent.
	Students will find and save photographs that depict the effect the natural disaster had on people and the environment.
	Using the knowledge that they gained from their research, students will determine what type of aid they could put into a relief-care package for a family of four with a $100 budget. Students should also use the food pyramid as a guide to help choose healthy food items to include in their care package. Students will gather the prices of each item using newspaper ads, the Internet, and other available resources. They will use a spreadsheet program to calculate the cost of the care package with appropriate sales tax.
	Using the computer lab or classroom computers, students will create a culminating multimedia presentation to present their research findings and their plans for aiding the victims. Groups will share their projects with the class.
Evaluation of Content:	Teacher observation along with the project rubric will be used to evaluate this activity. Students will be evaluated on usage of the Web and other technology tools. The quality of research and information utilized and the extent to which the focus question was answered also will be assessed. Students also will peer review projects.
Evaluation of Curriculum and Technology Integration:	Students' ability to access, analyze, and apply information from different resources will be observed. Students' motivation and enthusiasm when creating the digital media presentation also will assist with evaluating the technology.

Figure 7-37 An interdisciplinary lesson plan for *Natural Disasters Occur Everywhere.*   (continued from the previous page)

	Interdisciplinary Integration
Curriculum Area:	Interdisciplinary — Physical Education, Science, Math, Geography (N,S,E,W)
Subject Area:	Exercise, Heart Rate, Geometric Shapes, Math Computations, Distance in Miles, Directions
Lesson Title:	GeoMotion Learning Activity
Suggested Grade Level:	Grades 3–5, easily adaptable to 6–8
Equipment Needed:	Technology: One computer or more, projection system, Internet access, pedometers, and heart rate monitors (optional) Software: GeoMotion's Hip Hop or Learnercise DVDs, or similar exercise apps Other: GeoMotion Mats, calculators, pedometers
Focus Question:	Why is exercise so important for your heart?
Learning Objectives:	■ Students will learn about the heart and be able to take and then record their resting and exercise pulse. ■ Students will perform and analyze three different physical activities, comparing heart rates and number of steps (with use of pedometer) recorded for each five minute activity. ■ Each student will have a GeoMotion Mat and follow along with the DVD, performing step patterns, directional movements, and jumping to increase their heart rate and perform meaningful movement, while reinforcing cognitive learning. ■ Students will use a calculator to convert steps to miles.
Instructions:	Students will learn about the heart and how it functions using a curriculum resource page created by the teacher. Students will learn to take a pulse and understand that exercise with an increase in heart rate is needed to strengthen the heart. The teacher will introduce students to the pedometer and discuss how all student steps (miles) will be logged into a Web site to show how many miles were completed by the class and the distance traveled on a map at the end of the lesson. Students will wear a pedometer to gather data for three different activities. They will record their heart rate and number of steps after each activity on a worksheet. Students will follow along and perform the activities on the DVD. Each student performs each activity for five minutes with a five minute rest in-between to allow heart rate to lower to pre-exercise rate. 1. Geometric Shape Activity: Students will perform step patterns on the GeoMotion Mat named after geometric shapes and other symbols (square, rectangle, triangle, X, etc.) to music to increase their heart rate. 2. Geography/Directions Activity: Students will perform movements to the East, West, North, and South on the GeoMotion Mat to increase their heart rate. 3. Math Activity: Students will jump to the correct numbers on the GeoMotion Mat to solve addition, subtraction, multiplication, and division problems while increasing their heart rate and performing meaningful movement to learn math. At the completion of the three activities students will log all results and complete the worksheet. They will use a calculator to convert steps to miles. Students will create spreadsheets that keep track of their steps, miles, and calories they burned during the activities.

Figure 7-38 An interdisciplinary lesson plan for *GeoMotion Learning Activity*.

(continued on the next page)

Questions for Discussion:

Describe what happened to your heart rate for each activity.
Does stepping or jumping elevate your heart rate more? Why?
In which activity did you log more steps on your pedometer? Why?
How did activities help you learn directions, geometric shapes, and math?

Other Resources:

<u>Information about GeoMotion DVD's and GeoMat</u>

GeoMotion Group, Inc.
www.geomotiongroup.com

<u>Pedometer and Physical Activity</u>

PE Central Log It
http://www.peclogit.org/whatsnew.asp

Web Walking USA
http://www.walk-usa.com/

Step Up To Health
http://www.nrpa.org/Content.aspx?id=587

Walk 4 Life Pedometers
http://www.walk4life.com/

Walk Smart America
http://www.walk4life.com/ws/ws.about.aspx

Evaluation of Content:	By using teacher observation, students will be evaluated on correct movements on the GeoMotion Mat based on shapes, symbols, and math answers. Students will be evaluated on the data they enter in their worksheets for heart rate and number of steps. Student worksheets will be evaluated for the following information: miles logged, heart rate, and answers to questions. Students will be evaluated on their ability to use a calculator to convert steps walked to miles.
Evaluation of Curriculum and Technology Integration:	Students will be evaluated on their ability to use various resources to access, analyze, and apply information to different situations. The effectiveness of technology will be evaluated by students successfully logging data and completing their worksheets.

Figure 7-38 An interdisciplinary lesson plan for *GeoMotion Learning Activity*.   *(continued from the previous page)*

Finding Funds to Support Classroom Technology Integration

One of the more difficult aspects of implementing technology in schools is finding and obtaining the funds for new technologies and the associated ongoing expenses. At present, many school districts do not have sufficient funding to incorporate technology at all levels throughout the district. For this reason, a classroom might not contain all the hardware and software to fully integrate technology and digital media into the curriculum.

Although the continued drop in computer and educational software prices lessens the problem, obtaining funding for classroom technology is still challenging. Many teachers, however, find that persistence often produces dramatic results. To increase the quantity and quality of technology in a classroom, a teacher first should ask the principal and other district administrators for additional classroom equipment and software. If you still need to obtain additional technology funding, you can turn to numerous other sources, including local school districts, public and private businesses, and government agencies.

FUND-RAISING DRIVES AND ACADEMIC CONTESTS

Class car washes, bake sales, and other activities can help raise money to purchase additional computers, hardware components, and software for classrooms. Local businesses such as banks, car dealerships, grocery stores, and department stores often respond to solicitations to improve the educational quality of the schools in their areas with donations. Corporations frequently are eager to become involved in active school technology programs — whether it is to contribute equipment, funds, or expertise. Teachers regularly write letters to local school business partners stating the school's needs to enlist their support. Even relatively small amounts of acquired funding can make a difference in the availability of technology in your classroom. Raising $100 will fund a new all-in-one printer, numerous educational CDs/DVDs/apps, or a color scanner; $1,000 will allow the

purchase of two multimedia computers or several tablets loaded with curriculum-based software/apps or several digital cameras with software and accessories. Another way to obtain hardware and software for the classroom is to enter academic contests. Teachers can locate information about hundreds of academic contests on the Web and in educational journals. Teachers should always get permission from the school's administration prior to raising funds.

Teachers should involve the community, especially parents, in fund-raising. The local school community holds its schools accountable for everything that goes on in the classroom, so enlisting the help of parents and business partners will broaden the base of support for the school's educational technology efforts. In addition, parents might have contacts or affiliations with local businesses or be able to provide further information on how to obtain funding. Another avenue for locating potential technology-funding sources is to showcase your students' use of technology for parents, business leaders, and school board members at your school's Parent Teacher Association (PTA), Parent Teacher Organization (PTO), or Parent Teacher Student Organization (PTSO) meetings.

Schools also should consider asking for volunteer services from the community in addition to or instead of asking for funds to pay for services. If funding for equipment maintenance is not available, for example, a local consultant might be willing to donate services. Many schools find that a combination of financial and volunteer support demonstrates the community's commitment to technology integration and strengthens the long-term community-school partnerships.

GRANTS

The majority of outside funding sources for technology fall under a general category called grants. **Grants** are funds provided by a funding source that transfers money, equipment, or services to the grantee. The **grantee** is the teacher, school, or organization that the grant funds or supports. Grants can be obtained from school districts, state Departments of

Education, federal sources, foundations, and corporations. Grants range from a few hundred to millions of dollars. Many corporations maintain or support foundations that provide grants, both large and small, for creative projects.

To obtain a grant, a school district, school, or teacher must submit a grant proposal in response to a request for proposal (RFP). A **request for proposal (RFP)** is a document provided by the grant source that details the information teachers and schools need to provide in order to write a successful grant proposal. A **grant proposal** is the document the potential grantee sends to the funding source. Grant proposals vary from a simple one-page application to an extensive multipage document.

When writing a grant, schools can take one of several approaches. A single person might write the grant proposal; teachers might write grant proposals with other teachers, media specialists, technology coordinators, curriculum resource specialists, and school district personnel; or if the proposal is extensive, the school districts might even employ a grant-writing specialist or consultant to write the proposal to increase the availability of technology in their classrooms.

The principal, curriculum resource specialist, and technology coordinator usually receive notification of grant opportunities. In addition, teachers can locate many grant opportunities on the Web (Figure 7-39). Teachers should always receive approval from school administration before applying for any grant.

Summary of Evaluating Educational Technology and Integration Strategies

Technology will not make a difference in the quality of students graduating from K-12 schools unless teachers learn how to integrate the use of technology into their curriculum and use it as a tool to enhance learning. This chapter first introduced the various tools and resources teachers use to evaluate the appropriateness of educational technology and the effectiveness of technology integration. Next, a number of strategies were presented for integrating technology into one-computer classrooms and other K-12 instructional settings along with subject-specific curriculum and technology integration activities. Finally, the chapter provided information on how to obtain funding to increase the availability of technology in your classroom.

Figure 7-39 Many Web sites provide teachers and administrators with current and extensive information on grants for education.

Key Terms

INSTRUCTIONS: Use the Key Terms to help focus your study of the terms used in this chapter. To further enhance your understanding of the Key Terms in this chapter, visit the Computer Concepts CourseMate Web site at www. cengagebrain.com, and then navigate to the Chapter 7 Key Terms resource for this book. Read the definition for each term and then access current and additional information about the term from the Web.

ability level [359]
academic level [359]
affiliation [360]
alternative assessment [364]
appropriate [352]
arts curriculum [387]
assessment [364]
audience [361]
authentic assessment [364]
authentic learning [364]
authority [360]

block schedule [370]

checklist [365]
concept map [369]
content [361]
creativity [369]
cross-discipline lesson [391]
currency [361]
curriculum resource page [378]

design [361]
documentation [359]

e-folio [365]
e-Portfolio [365]
ease of use [359]
EDTECH [355]

eFolio [365]
electronic portfolio [365]
embedded assessment [365]
ePortfolio [365]
evaluate [352]
exceptional education
    curriculum [389]

flowchart [369]

grant proposal [396]
grantee [395]
grant [395]

Inspiration [369]
interdisciplinary curriculum [391]

KWLQS chart [375]

language arts curriculum [380]
learner response system [378]
learning process [361]

mathematics curriculum [383]

objectivity [361]
one-computer classroom [372]

physical education and health
    curriculum [386]
portfolio assessment [365]

project-based assessment [365]
project-based learning [365]
purpose [361]

rating scale [365]
reliable assessment [364]
request for proposal (RFP) [396]

science curriculum [385]
social studies curriculum [381]
software/app evaluation rubric [356]
special education curriculum [389]
storyboard [369]
story web [369]
student performance [364]
subject-integrated lesson [391]

teacher observation [367]
technical quality [359]
technical support [359]
technology conference [354]
traditional assessment [364]

valid [356]
visual learning technique [369]

Web evaluation rubric [362]
Web scavenger hunt [376]

Checkpoint

INSTRUCTIONS: Use the Checkpoint exercises to check your knowledge level of the chapter. To complete the Checkpoint exercises interactively, visit the Computer Concepts CourseMate Web site at www.cengagebrain.com, and then navigate to the Chapter 7 Checkpoint resource for this book.

1. Label the Figure

Instructions: Read each description in the grid that follows. Then identify the criteria category used to evaluate Web sites that the description describes.

1. _____	2. _____	3. _____
No author is listed and no e-mail contact is provided.	It is unclear what institution supports this information.	The purpose is unclear or cannot be determined.
4. _____	5. _____	6. _____
The Web page is a virtual soapbox.	The information on the Web site does not relate to my objectives.	The information will not challenge learners to think, reflect, discuss, compare, or classify.
7. _____	8. _____	9. _____
The Web pages are not appropriate for my audience.	Information on the site has not been revised in the last 18 months, or no date can be located.	The Web site design is inappropriate for my audience.

2. Matching

Instructions: Match each term from the column on the left with the best description from the column on the right.

_____ 1. curriculum resource page

_____ 2. request for proposal

_____ 3. checklist

_____ 4. evaluate

_____ 5. concept map

a. to determine the value or to judge the worth

b. provides a visual tool for brainstorming and planning

c. teacher-created document that contains hyperlinks to teacher-selected Web sites

d. predetermined list of performance criteria

e. a document provided by a grant source that details the information needed to write a grant

3. Short Answer

Instructions: Write a brief answer to each of the following questions.

1. Describe four resources where teachers can find information about how to evaluate educational software. Why is it important for teachers to evaluate software before using it in the classroom?

2. Should teachers evaluate Web resources for instructional value in the same way they evaluate print resources? Why or why not?

3. Describe three techniques for evaluating student technology projects.

4. Briefly describe three uses of technology in a one-computer classroom. Why does having more than one computer in a classroom allow for more flexibility and greater integration of technology?

5. Briefly describe grant funding for K-12 schools. Why are grants so important for many K-12 schools? Describe three ways in which teachers can obtain funding for classroom technology.

Teaching Today

INSTRUCTIONS: Teaching Today provides teachers with integration strategies and ideas for teaching and, more importantly, reaching today's digital generation. Each numbered segment contains one or more links that reinforce the information presented in the segment. To display this page from the Web, visit the Computer Concepts CourseMate Web site at www.cengagebrain.com, and then navigate to the Chapter 7 Teaching Today resource for this book.

1. Parent Teachers Organization

The Parent Teachers Organization (PTO) at your school has raised money to purchase tablets and apps for all classes in your grade level. Your principal asks you to work with other teachers in your grade level to make recommendations for app purchases to enhance the curriculum. The school has a list of approved tablets, so you don't have to research those. However, your principal asks you and the teachers to supply a wish list with seven to ten different apps, a detailed evaluation of each app, and pricing for each. Based on what you have learned in this chapter, what would be your next step in identifying appropriate apps and then evaluating each? Where can you find app reviews? To what extent are these reviews helpful? What type of information can you gather about the apps from these reviews? What kind of site-licensing and pricing are available for each app?

2. Integrating Blogging and Digital Teaching

So, you have heard about blogging. In fact, you may even have been doing it for personal fun, but not in your classroom. Well, why not? Your students will love it! Teachers are aware that students write better when they are engaged in authentic learning experiences — not just getting feedback from their teacher. Blogging can give your students excellent opportunities to read and write, provide effective conditions for cooperative learning, collaboration, and discussion, and be a powerful tool to enable communication skills to develop. Blogging can be highly motivating to students, especially those who otherwise might not participate in classroom discussions. Research suggests students are interested in blogging because they enjoy communicating with their peers and they are comfortable using this form of communication. How can you integrate blogging into your curriculum? What benefits do you think this communication can provide the students? How can you and your students use the 5Ws and 1H to create productive blogs?

3. More Than One Curriculum Area

You teach students with special needs in a middle school. You want to integrate software applications into your curriculum to enhance your students' learning. You are looking for software applications that can be used in more than one curriculum area. You are familiar with programs such as PowerPoint and iLife and already are using them in different curriculum areas. Describe the ways in which two other applications described in this chapter can be used in more than one curriculum area. Test drive SimCity, on your PC or Mac or download the SimCity app on your tablet computer. How would you integrate this type of software into your curriculum? What curriculum standards and related benchmarks could it help teach?

4. Evaluating Student Work

As you begin to integrate technology into your curriculum, you need alternative ways to assess student performance. In this chapter, you read about the rubrics that teachers use to assess performance. Itemize the key points to remember when evaluating student work. What alternative assessment tools can you use in your classroom? When is using alternative assessment tools most appropriate? When are other types of assessment tools most appropriate?

Education Issues

1. Video Games — Good or Bad?

There has been a lot of attention regarding whether video games are actually promoting aggressive behaviors in younger players. Studies have shown that many of today's youth spend up to 4–5 hours per day on computers. According to the Kaiser Family Foundation, 92% of American children play video games for 20 to 33 minutes per day. In his book, *What Video Games Have to Teach Us About Literacy and Learning*, James Gee is an outspoken advocate for the use of games to teach meta-learning principles. His research reveals even the so-called "shoot-em up" games can teach skills. On the other hand, there are those like Canadian psychology professor David Grossman who compares soldiers in training to children watching television. Grossman feels that both situations teach individuals to reject traditional values and create the illusion that the world is a dark and dangerous place. Grossman suggests that video games are increasingly desensitizing viewers — particularly children — to violence, and he has led a campaign in Canada to force media companies to become more accountable to this threat. Grossman is convinced that not only are media companies teaching violence but they are also teaching children to like it. What do you think? What implications might Grossman's campaign have on technology in education?

2. Evaluating Content

One of the extraordinary stories of the Internet age is that of Wikipedia, a free online encyclopedia that anyone can edit and everyone can use. Many teachers and professors feel that Wikipedia is not an acceptable resource to use for research and exploration. Researchers are now saying that Wikipedia, based upon research studies, is as accurate as Encyclopedia Britannica! Why? Because Wikipedia has many checks and balances in place to make sure the information is accurate. Should students be allowed to use this resource? Are you concerned about the accuracy of the information since anyone can check and update it? What should students do to verify the information? Should teachers and professors reconsider the accuracy of Wikipedia? Have you checked out the Wikipanion app?

3. Grants for Training

You locate a request for proposal (RFP) to fund a grant for tablet computers for all the teachers in your school. The grant will provide the tablet computers, but the school has to provide the teacher training. You want to develop the proposal with the help of the technology committee. You recognize this is a great opportunity to get technology into the hands of all teachers through the use of their tablet computers. You think your school has an extremely good chance of being funded. The principal immediately says, "NO!" She feels the teachers should write grants only to obtain student computers. She also states that no funds are available for teacher training. Do you see a solution to this dilemma? What should you do? Where can you go to obtain more information and creative ideas for writing the grant and solving the training issues? How will you convince the principal that putting a tablet computer in each teacher's hands is an important initial step toward technology integration?

4. Alternative Assessment

Your first teaching job is at a very progressive new school that has technology in every classroom. During your college education, you learned a great deal about assessing student achievement through testing. You learned how to create appropriate traditional tests for subjects. This new school, however, has no traditional testing program. It has implemented an innovative approach to learning that uses only alternative assessment. No grades are assigned and all assessment is based on mastery learning. Do you think this is a good strategy? Support your position with reasons based on educational research. What alternative assessment tools can you use to meet the school's standards? Describe the advantages and disadvantages of this type of assessment.

Apps Corner

INSTRUCTIONS: Apps Corner provides extensive ideas and resources for integrating technology into your classroom-specific curriculum. To display this page from the Web and its links to approximately 100 educational Web sites, visit the Computer Concepts CourseMate Web site at www.cengagebrain.com, and then navigate to the Chapter 7 Apps Corner resource for this book.

Apps Corner is designed for teachers and other educators who are looking for innovative ways to integrate apps into their content-specific curriculum. Apps Corner not only provides great apps with current information but also shows how other educators are using and integrating education apps. As a result, Apps Corner is designed with all educators in mind, regardless of their interests or subject area. You can use Apps Corner to expand your resources by reviewing apps outside your curriculum area; remember many apps associated with one curriculum area can be adapted for use and added to lesson plans in a wide variety of other curriculum areas.

Use Apps Corner as a springboard for collaborating and sharing the successes and hurdles of integrating apps in a classroom or an entire school system. Consider Apps Corner a place to locate app integration ideas and resources. Information on educational apps are organized in four Corners (Early Childhood, Elementary, Middle School, and Secondary), and different apps are available for each chapter. Many apps are free, others cost from $1 to $5. Inexpensive site licenses for classrooms, schools, and school districts are available for many apps.

Shown are two of the hundreds of available life sciences apps available at all grade levels. The first one is a free and interactive game app for younger students appropriate for any unit on butterflies. The second is an award winning and inexpensive Frog Dissection app.

Software Corner

INSTRUCTIONS: Software Corner provides information on popular software programs. Each numbered segment discusses specific software programs and contains a link to additional information about these programs. To display this page from the Web, visit the Computer Concepts CourseMate Web site at www.cengagebrain.com, and then navigate to the Chapter 7 Software Corner resource for this book.

1. Inspiration

Inspiration is a powerful software product that allows students to think visually through webbing, concept mapping, and more. Inspiration provides students in grades 4-12 and beyond with the ability to organize and develop their thoughts before creating reports, presentations, and video production projects. Language arts teachers will find Inspiration an awesome writing and literature tool. History and science teachers can use Inspiration to create timelines and to plan research reports and projects. Inspiration can be integrated into all areas of the curriculum.

2. Adobe Acrobat

Are you looking for a way to create professional documents that can be distributed electronically via various means including the Web and that can still maintain the integrity of images and formats that have been integrated using products like Adobe Photoshop, PageMaker, or other desktop publishing software? Adobe Acrobat is the perfect solution. Whether you are a novice just beginning to design formatted documents or a skilled designer, Adobe Acrobat helps you maintain control over how, when, and by whom your documents are accessed. Create and exchange documents, collect and compare comments, and tailor the security of a file in order to distribute your documents reliably and professionally.

3. Adobe Captivate

Adobe Captivate is a software program that you can use to create online demonstrations, tutorials, scenario-based instructional videos, and software simulations for F2F, blended, and online classrooms. You can easily publish to most Learning Management Systems. Captivate also can be used to build scenarios in which you can branch from one topic to another to create a controlled set of links and paths for users to follow. The software outputs to either Flash or PowerPoint files that can be used in podcasts. The software also lets you build interactive programs, demos, and lessons. Because it is based on several Flash technologies, the end product is a small file size that makes it very efficient to use on the Web. The ability to add links within the screen allows viewers to branch to other slides and sections of the presentation, providing an interactive lesson format.

4. LeapFrog

LeapFrog products are changing the way some children learn reading, writing, and arithmetic. LeapPads, a LeapFrog product, uses books embedded with NearTouch technology, which makes any part of a page touch-interactive. By using the special pen and touching it to words on the page, the voice program reads aloud the words. Students can write, draw, and paint using story-based games, the interactive touch screen, and the pen. LeapFrog products have multiple skill levels, tailored tutorials, and an entire system with features that meet the diverse learning needs of K-4 students.

Digital Media Corner

INSTRUCTIONS: Today's K-12 digital students need their learning to be meaningful and relevant to their lives. Digital Media Corner provides videos, ideas, and examples of how you can use digital media to enhance your teaching and your students' learning. To access the videos and links to additional information, the Computer Concepts CourseMate Web site at www.cengagebrain.com, and then navigate to the Chapter 7 Digital Media Corner resource for this book.

1. Edutainment Theory and Pedagogy

A key component to the effectiveness of using digital media is the term *edutainment*, more specifically, using the attractive qualities and aesthetics of entertainment media for learning purposes. The essence of edutainment as well as entertainment and traditional literature is, was, and always will be identifying with the story. This Web resource highlights how, why, and where implementing the benefits of digital storytelling can benefit your students' education and your lesson planning — everybody wins! If you need more information on edutainment, click the Edutainment Theory and Pedagogy link to learn more. After all, edutaining the youth of today about the invaluable information of the past by using the technologies of tomorrow and beyond is the future of education.

2. GameMaker

GameMaker, currently being distributed by YoYo Games, is a dynamic game development program that allows non-programmers the ability to make fairly robust computer games without the need to know how to be a programmer. You or your students can create professional looking games using drag-and-drop to place user-friendly actions in your game. The game software contains backgrounds, animated graphics, music, and sound effects. There is a built-in programming language for more advanced users that provides full functionality for creating a full array of game types and 3D graphics. The basic package is free but requires registration for access to full functionality of the programs. GameMaker comes preloaded with a collection of freeware images and sounds, making this a super media product for digital learners.

3. Evaluating Digital Media in the Classroom

As you have learned throughout this textbook, digital media is everything from QuickTime movies to graphic design software applications. With so much information and technology out there, choosing the appropriate form of digital media to integrate in your curriculum can be intimidating. Evaluating digital media for appropriateness and usability is just like evaluating software, Web sites, and other technologies. This textbook presents guidelines for evaluating Web sites that include examining authority, affiliation, purpose and objectivity, content and learning process, audience and currency, and design of the digital media. These guidelines are excellent for establishing the credibility of digital media as well. The tools you use to conduct an evaluation of a Web site, a software application, or a digital media piece can be very similar; including the elements you evaluate!

4. WatchKnowLearn

You Watch, You Know! You Learn! Today the Internet is full of video Web sites, but many are uncontrolled collections of unorganized media. WatchKnowLearn, created by the co-founder of Wikipedia, houses thousands of educational videos for students ages 3-18, as well as hundreds of videos for teachers and parents. Teachers and students can also add their own videos and edit how videos are organized on the site with keyword tags. Teachers and students can perform a quick search and select what they want to view. WatchKnowLearn.org aims to not only capitalize on the Internet as a learning environment but also provide some much-needed order to the vast clutter of free educational videos online.

Assistive Technologies Corner

INSTRUCTIONS: Assistive Technologies Corner provides information on current hardware, software, and peripherals that will assist you in delivering instruction to students with physical, cognitive, or sensory challenges. To access extensive additional information, visit the Computer Concepts CourseMate Web site at www.cengagebrain.com, and then navigate to the Chapter 7 Assistive Technologies Corner resource for this book.

1. How Can I Choose the Best Software for Students with Special Needs?

Many times, students with significant physical or mental disabilities will come to the classroom with a technology plan as part of their IEPs. When this is not the case, quality software will provide the best chance for success for a student with mild to moderate learning difficulties. To ensure a quality tool for a special needs user, the teacher might want to add some special considerations to the Software/App Evaluation Rubric (Figure 7-7 on pages 357 and 358) located in this chapter.

Technical Quality
1. Are captions available for video clips or audio files?
2. Will the software function using alternative input devices such as alternative keyboards?

Presentation of Information
1. Are directions presented using both visual and auditory means? Are directions intelligible with the sound turned off?
2. Is sufficient time given for the user to read and comprehend directions?
3. Are directions clear and are examples of user tasks provided?
4. Is text clear and easy to read? Does the user have control over text size?

Content
1. Is content presented dependent on color, or only by a single mode (auditory or visual)?
2. Does content provide logical structures for information and is the information presented using different structures?

2. How Can I Integrate Technology in the Special Needs Curriculum?

Integration activities for students with special needs enhance learning for all students. Exciting activities for learners with special needs may include some of the following.

Using **graphic organizing** tools (Inspiration, Kidspiration), students may
- Create a flowchart or timeline to plan their learning activities
- Create a similarities/differences chart for any new concept
- Create a concept map to demonstrate understanding

Using **digital video editing software** (iMovie, MovieMaker, and others), students may
- Create video clips to illustrate and share experiences
- Title or caption the video clips

Using **digital media tools** (Keynote, PowerPoint, and so on), students may
- Author and illustrate multimedia books to retell a story
- Prepare and illustrate researched information for presentation

Using **database tools** (Microsoft Works, Microsoft Office), students may
- Collect and organize information such as a Zoo Animal database
- Create database reports or tables based on information for alternative presentation of information

3. Does Technology Enhance Learning for Students with Special Learning Needs?

Technology is a tool, not a cure for learning disabilities. Used with clearly planned learning goals and appropriate instructional strategies, almost all technology tools can help level the field for students with disabilities, providing equal access to the curriculum and opportunities for success.

Follow the instructions at the top of this page to display additional information and this chapter's links on assistive technologies.

In the Lab

INSTRUCTIONS: In the Lab provides curriculum resource page development exercises that are divided into two areas, productivity and integration. To access the links to tutorials, productivity ideas, integration examples and ideas, and more, visit the Computer Concepts CourseMate Web site at www.cengagebrain.com, and then navigate to the Chapter 7 In the Lab resource for this book.

PRODUCTIVITY IN THE CLASSROOM

ePortfolio Idea

Introduction: As you have learned, many kinds of curriculum resource pages exist. For example, a curriculum resource page can serve as a guide, assisting students in locating quality information on the Internet. Teachers easily can create curriculum resource pages using a variety of software programs and Web editors. You can use Microsoft Word to create Web pages, and Word is available on many home and school computers. Microsoft Publisher also can be used to create Web and curriculum resource pages. Some popular stand-alone Web editors used by educators include WebBlender and Adobe Dreamweaver.

Teachers can use curriculum resource pages in a variety of ways. One type of curriculum resource page is a list of annotated links focusing on one area of the curriculum or supporting one particular project. A curriculum resource page also can present students with a learning task, provide guidelines for how the task will be evaluated, and provide preselected Web sites that support the task.

Utilizing curriculum resource pages in the classroom provides many benefits. Students develop independent thinking and reading skills, as well as higher-order thinking and problem-solving skills. Furthermore, preselecting Web sites maximizes the time students spend on the Internet and helps teachers to better supervise their students. Students also can create curriculum resource pages to provide evidence of their learning. This can be a powerful and exciting way for students to demonstrate their newly acquired knowledge and skills.

1. Creating and Formatting a Dental Health Curriculum Resource Page

Problem: You are beginning a unit on dental health in your fifth grade classroom as part of a health unit. You want to create a curriculum resource page to use with and read to the class to enhance the students' learning experience. Also, by using a curriculum resource page, the students will be able to go back and review Web sites after the unit is finished. A curriculum resource page is shown in Figure 7-40 on the next page. Open Microsoft Word or any Web editing software and create the curriculum resource page as described in the following steps. (*Hint:* Use Help to understand the steps better and Google "free clip art" to locate a similar image to the tooth image in Figure 7-40 or use any other appropriate image.)

Instructions: Perform the following tasks.

1. Change the page color, or if you prefer, insert a background image.
2. Display the first heading line, Let's Learn About Teeth, in 24-point Times or Times New Roman dark blue, bold font.
3. Display the second heading line in 18-point Times or Times New Roman dark blue, bold font. Personalize the curriculum resource page by inserting your name instead of Ms. Yoshimura's name.
4. Insert a table with one row and two columns. Format the table to display as shown in Figure 7-40.
5. Insert an appropriate picture, image, or clip art graphic in the left column.
6. Type the paragraphs and the bulleted list in the right column; apply 14-point Times New Roman dark blue, bold font to the text.
7. Type the line and the bulleted list following the table; apply 14-point Times New Roman dark blue, bold font to the text.
8. Link the words About My Teeth to http://www.adha.org/kidstuff/index.html. Link the words Healthy Teeth to http://www.healthyteeth.org. Link the words Colgate Kids World to http://www.colgate.com/app/Kids-World/US/HomePage.cvsp.
9. Save the curriculum resource page to the location and with a filename of your choice. Print the curriculum resource page and then follow your instructor's directions for handing in the assignment.

In the Lab

Let's Learn About Teeth

Ms. Yoshimura's Fifth Grade Class

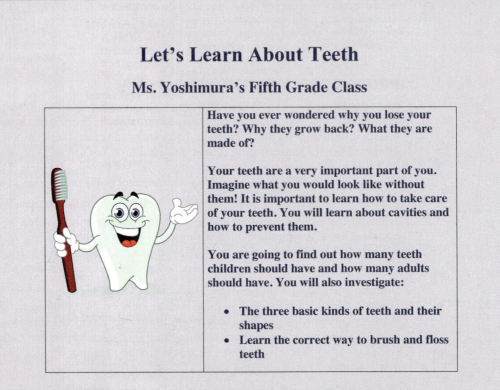

Have you ever wondered why you lose your teeth? Why they grow back? What they are made of?

Your teeth are a very important part of you. Imagine what you would look like without them! It is important to learn how to take care of your teeth. You will learn about cavities and how to prevent them.

You are going to find out how many teeth children should have and how many adults should have. You will also investigate:

- The three basic kinds of teeth and their shapes
- Learn the correct way to brush and floss teeth

Let's start our investigation!

- <u>About My Teeth</u> – This Web site helps you learn the names of the parts of a tooth and what teeth are made of. Then, you learn about when your teeth come in, how many baby teeth you had, and how many permanent teeth you have. This Web site will help you find all this information.
- <u>Healthy Teeth</u> – The Healthy Teeth Web site helps us learn more about how to care for your teeth. We will learn some tips on brushing, flossing, and visiting the dentist. You will find out how often you should brush your teeth and how often you should floss your teeth.
- <u>Colgate Kids World</u> – Now that we know more about your teeth, you will learn even more about how to keep your teeth healthy! Plus you will get to play games like Toothpaste Tower, Attack of the Plaque Monsters, and Lost Tooth Corner.

Figure 7-40

In the Lab

2. Creating and Formatting a Science Curriculum Resource Page

Problem: Your eighth-grade science class has been studying the weather. As a final project, students must gather research and create a digital media presentation. You create a curriculum resource page to facilitate their research. A curriculum resource page is shown in Figure 7-41 on the next page. (*Hint:* Use Help to understand the steps better and Google "free clip art" to locate a similar image and background image as shown in Figure 7-41.)

Instructions: Insert the background image. Enter the first heading line in 24-point Times or Times New Roman bold font. Insert your name in place of Mr. Pawliger's name. Enter the subheading The Weather in 18-point Times or Times New Roman bold font. Insert a table with one row and two columns and format the table as shown in Figure 7-41. Insert a graphic in the left column of the table. Type the text and bulleted list in the right column; apply 12-point Times New Roman bold font to the text.

Type the line immediately below the table; apply 12-point Times New Roman bold font to the text.

Insert a table with two rows and two columns to help organize the links. Format the table to display as shown in Figure 7-41. Type the text and bulleted lists; apply 12-point Times New Roman bold font to the text. Insert graphics and create the hypertext links using the Web site addresses (URLs) listed in the table below.

Linked Text	Web Site
Atlantic Oceanographic and Meteorological Laboratory	www.aoml.noaa.gov
The National Hurricane Center	www.nhc.noaa.gov
NOAA Photo Library - Tornadoes	www.photolib.noaa.gov/nssl/tornado1.html
Twister: The Tornado Story	whyfiles.org/013tornado/index.html
National Severe Storms Laboratory	www.nssl.noaa.gov
Storm Prediction Center	www.spc.noaa.gov
Federal Emergency Management Agency	www.fema.gov
The Weather Channel	www.weather.com

After you have typed and formatted the curriculum resource page, save the curriculum resource page to the location and with a filename of your choice. Print the curriculum resource page and then follow your instructor's directions for handing in the assignment.

In the Lab

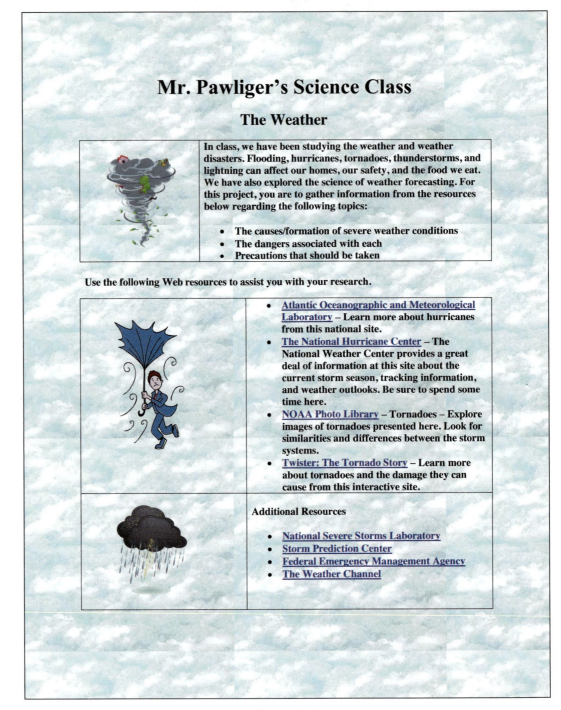

Mr. Pawliger's Science Class

The Weather

In class, we have been studying the weather and weather disasters. Flooding, hurricanes, tornadoes, thunderstorms, and lightning can affect our homes, our safety, and the food we eat. We have also explored the science of weather forecasting. For this project, you are to gather information from the resources below regarding the following topics:

- The causes/formation of severe weather conditions
- The dangers associated with each
- Precautions that should be taken

Use the following Web resources to assist you with your research.

- **Atlantic Oceanographic and Meteorological Laboratory** – Learn more about hurricanes from this national site.
- **The National Hurricane Center** – The National Weather Center provides a great deal of information at this site about the current storm season, tracking information, and weather outlooks. Be sure to spend some time here.
- **NOAA Photo Library** – Tornadoes – Explore images of tornadoes presented here. Look for similarities and differences between the storm systems.
- **Twister: The Tornado Story** – Learn more about tornadoes and the damage they can cause from this interactive site.

Additional Resources

- **National Severe Storms Laboratory**
- **Storm Prediction Center**
- **Federal Emergency Management Agency**
- **The Weather Channel**

Figure 7-41

In the Lab

3. Creating and Formatting a Subject-Specific Curriculum Resource Page

Problem: You want to create a curriculum resource page to support a concept you are teaching in your classroom and to provide students with preselected Internet resources.

Instructions: Create a curriculum resource page similar to the curriculum resource page illustrated in Figure 7-41 on the previous page. Use appropriate layouts, font types, font styles, font sizes, and clip art images. Include your name and the subject area you teach. After you have created the curriculum resource page, save the curriculum resource page to the location of your choice using an appropriate filename. Print the curriculum resource page, and then follow your instructor's directions for handing in the assignment.

ePortfolio Idea

INTEGRATION IN THE CLASSROOM

1. While studying the 50 states, you have your elementary students work in pairs to design and create a curriculum resource page about the state of their choice. They are to include their names and the name of the state at the top of the curriculum resource page. They also will include a graphic of either the state or the state flag, a brief paragraph about the state, and a bulleted list that includes the state capital, state bird, and state flower. The students then will include three links to Internet resources that provide additional information about their state. Create a sample curriculum resource page for your students using the state of your birth or the state in which you currently live. Include your name on the curriculum resource page.

2. To help your middle school language arts students develop reading, vocabulary, and writing skills and increase their awareness of community and global issues, you begin a unit using newspapers in your classroom. You arrange for local newspapers to be donated to your classroom so each student has a copy. You also have students explore local newspapers and news sources online. You direct students to select an article from either a local newspaper or an online news source and create a curriculum resource page that summarizes the news item and contains at least three links to Internet resources that support or give further information on their selected topic. Students will present their curriculum resource pages to the class and you will have them posted on your school's server so all students can access the information. Create a sample curriculum resource page for your students. Include your name and school at the top of the curriculum resource page. Include your e-mail address and the current date at the bottom of the curriculum resource page.

3. Your music class has been studying famous composers. To prepare for the end-of-unit exam, you divide the students into five groups and have each group research one composer. The groups then create a curriculum resource page that other students use as they study. On their curriculum resource pages, students are required to include a graphic image, a brief paragraph about the composer, a bulleted list of the titles of at least five famous pieces, and at least four annotated links to Web resources. The curriculum resource pages will be placed on the computers in the classroom, media center, and computer lab. In addition, you will post the curriculum resource pages on the Web to assist the students in studying at home. Select a famous composer and create a sample curriculum resource page for your students. Include your name on your curriculum resource page. Include your e-mail address and the current date at the bottom of the curriculum resource page.

Learn It Online

INSTRUCTIONS: Use the Learn It Online exercises to reinforce your understanding of the chapter concepts and increase your computer, information, and integration literacy. To access dozens of interactive student labs, practice tests, learning games, and more, visit the Computer Concepts CourseMate Web site at www.cengagebrain.com, navigate to the Chapter 7 resources for this book, and then click the link for the resource you want to review.

1. Integrating Apps

As you have learned throughout this textbook, tablet computers and apps are fundamentally chang-ing the landscape of education. Click the Integrating Apps link to review an article about integrat-ing apps into PK-12 education. After reading the article, write a one page summary of the article and list five ways you might integrate tablet computer apps in your current or future classroom.

2. Rubrics

Designing effective evaluation tools to assess student learning requires thought and preparation. One popular assessment tool is an assessment rubric. Click the Rubrics link to complete an exercise on how to create effective rubrics.

3. Expanding Your Understanding

Concept maps, flowcharts, story webs, storyboards, and other graphic organizers assist students with visualizing concepts and organizing information. Click the Expanding Your Understanding link to learn more about these concepts.

4. Practice Test

Click the Practice Test link. Answer each question. When completed, enter your name and click the Grade Test button to submit the quiz for grading. Make a note of any missed questions. If required, submit your score to your instructor.

5. Who Wants to Be a Computer Genius?

Click the Who Wants to Be a Computer Genius link to find out if you are a computer genius. When you are ready to play, click the Play button. If required, submit your score to your instructor.

6. Wheel of Terms

Click the Wheel of Terms link to reinforce important terms you learned in this chapter by playing the Shelly Cashman Series version of this popular game. When you are ready to play, click the Play button. If required, submit your score to your instructor.

7. Crossword Puzzle Challenge

Click the Crossword Puzzle Challenge link. Complete the puzzle to reinforce skills you learned in this chapter. When you are ready to play, click the Play button. If required, submit the completed puzzle to your instructor.

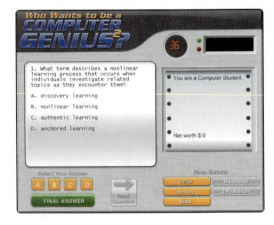

Security Issues and Ethics in Education

Objectives

After completing this chapter, you will be able to do the following:
[ISTE NETS-T Standards 3 c; 4 a-d, 5 a-d]

- Identify security risks that threaten home and school computers

- Describe how computer viruses and malicious software programs work and the steps you can take to prevent viruses

- Describe different ways schools safeguard computers and networks

- Explain why computer backup is important and how it is accomplished

- Define what is meant by information privacy and its impact on schools

- Identify the components of copyright that impact education

- Describe the ethical issues related to Internet usage and steps schools are taking to address them

- Identify safe and healthy uses of technology resources

Every day, businesses, schools, and individuals depend on computers to perform a variety of significant tasks, such as tracking sales, recording student grades, creating reports, searching the Web, and sending e-mail. People increasingly rely on computers to create, store, and manage critical information, so it is important to ensure that computers and software are protected from loss, damage, and misuse. School districts, for example, must take precautions to guarantee that student information, such as grades, attendance rates, personal and family data, and special needs accommodations, is protected from loss and kept confidential.

This chapter identifies some potential risks to computers and software, and it describes a number of safeguards that schools, businesses, and individuals can implement to minimize these risks. The chapter also discusses information privacy, including the current laws that keep certain data confidential. The chapter then reviews concerns about the ethical use of computers and which activities are right, wrong, or even criminal. Next, the chapter covers security, privacy, and the ethical issues that relate to how teachers and students use the information they find on the Internet. Finally, the chapter concludes with a discussion about computer-related health issues in education.

Web Info

For more information about computer viruses, visit the Computer Concepts CourseMate Web site at *www.cengagebrain.com*, navigate to the Chapter 8 Web Info resource for this book, and then click Viruses.

Computer Security: Risks and Safeguards

Any event or action that has the potential of causing a loss of computer equipment, software, data and information, or processing capability is a **computer security risk**. Some of these risks, such as viruses, unauthorized access and use, and information theft, are a result of deliberate acts that are against the law. Any illegal act involving a computer generally is referred to as a **computer crime**. The following sections describe some of the more common computer security risks and the measures that you and your school can take to minimize or prevent their consequences.

COMPUTER VIRUSES

At 4:30 in the afternoon, Mrs. Vicki Reamy of Ridgedale High School is in her classroom making last-minute adjustments to the Excel spreadsheet she plans to use in tomorrow's third-period Business Education class. As she opens the spreadsheet file to make one last change, the top of the spreadsheet displays the message, "Something wonderful has happened, your PC is alive." Dismayed, she realizes that a computer virus has corrupted her spreadsheet and she has lost all her work.

A **virus** is a potentially damaging computer program designed to affect your computer negatively without your knowledge or permission by altering the way it works. More specifically, a virus is a segment of program code that implants itself in a computer file and spreads systematically from one file to another. Figure 8-1 answers frequently asked questions about computer viruses.

Computer viruses, however, do not generate by chance. Creators of virus programs write them for a specific purpose — usually to spread from one file to another, to

Figure 8-1 A virus spreads from one computer to another as illustrated in this figure.

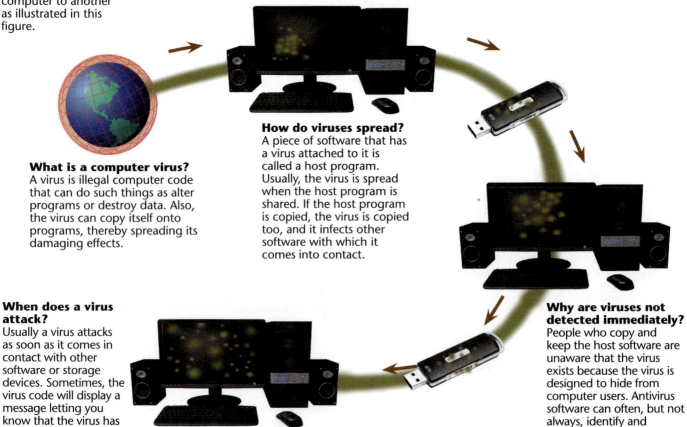

A COMPUTER VIRUS: WHAT IT IS AND HOW IT SPREADS

What is a computer virus?
A virus is illegal computer code that can do such things as alter programs or destroy data. Also, the virus can copy itself onto programs, thereby spreading its damaging effects.

How do viruses spread?
A piece of software that has a virus attached to it is called a host program. Usually, the virus is spread when the host program is shared. If the host program is copied, the virus is copied too, and it infects other software with which it comes into contact.

When does a virus attack?
Usually a virus attacks as soon as it comes in contact with other software or storage devices. Sometimes, the virus code will display a message letting you know that the virus has done its damage.

Why are viruses not detected immediately?
People who copy and keep the host software are unaware that the virus exists because the virus is designed to hide from computer users. Antivirus software can often, but not always, identify and quarantine viruses.

trigger a symptom, or to cause damage. Many viruses, for example, are designed to destroy or corrupt data stored on the infected computer. The symptom or damage caused by a virus, called the **virus payload**, can be harmless or it can cause significant damage, as planned by the virus creator. Figure 8-2 outlines some common symptoms of virus infections.

Unfortunately, Vicki Reamy's experience is not unusual. Although viruses are a serious problem for all computer users, the majority of virus programs are intended to infect PCs. Currently, more than 300,000 known viruses or variants exist, and hundreds of new viruses or variants are identified every month. The increased use of networks and the Internet makes the spread of viruses easier than ever. Viruses commonly infect computers through e-mail attachments. Figure 8-3 on the next page shows how a virus can spread from one computer to another through an infected e-mail attachment. Before you open or execute any e-mail attachment, you should ensure that the e-mail message is from a trusted source and you should scan the attachment using antivirus software.

Although numerous variations are known, three main types of viruses exist: boot sector viruses, file viruses, and macro viruses. A **boot sector virus** replaces the boot program used to start the computer with a modified, infected version of the boot program. When the computer runs the infected boot program, it loads the virus into the computer's memory. Once a virus is in memory, it spreads to any

storage media inserted into the computer. A **file virus** inserts virus code into program files; the virus then spreads to any program that accesses the infected file. A **macro virus** uses the macro language of an application, such as a word processing or a spreadsheet program, to hide virus codes. When you open a document with an infected macro, the macro virus loads into memory. Certain actions, such as saving the document, activate the virus. Macro viruses often are part of templates, which means they will infect any document created using one of the templates.

Two common variations of computer viruses, also known as **malicious software programs**, are worms and Trojan horses. A **worm** is a program that copies itself repeatedly in a computer's memory or on a network, using up resources and possibly shutting down the computer or network. Creators of worms often play on user psychology to entice people to download and run them. As a result, a number of well-known worms have hijacked e-mail systems and sent copies of themselves around the world in a matter of hours. The notorious Melissa worm quickly spread around the world causing serious harm to millions of computers. A **Trojan horse** (named after the Greek myth) is a malicious software program that hides within or is designed to look like a legitimate program.

Some viruses are relatively harmless pranks that temporarily freeze a computer or cause it to display sounds or messages. For example, when the Music Bug virus is

FAQ

How long is an unprotected computer safe from intruders?

One security expert maintains that an unprotected computer could be compromised by an intruder within 20 minutes. Slammer and Nimda, two devastating worms, wreaked worldwide havoc in 10 and 30 minutes, respectively.

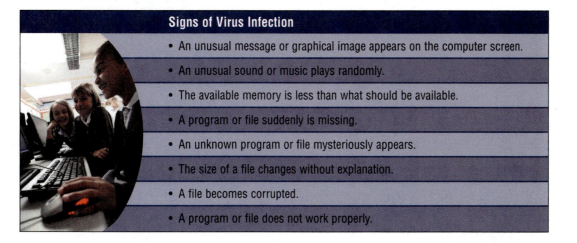

Signs of Virus Infection
• An unusual message or graphical image appears on the computer screen.
• An unusual sound or music plays randomly.
• The available memory is less than what should be available.
• A program or file suddenly is missing.
• An unknown program or file mysteriously appears.
• The size of a file changes without explanation.
• A file becomes corrupted.
• A program or file does not work properly.

Figure 8-2 Viruses attack computers in a variety of ways. Listed here are some of the more common signs of virus infections.

Step 1
Unscrupulous programmers create a virus program that deletes all files. They hide the virus in a word processing document and attach the document to an e-mail message.

Step 2
They send the e-mail message to thousands of users around the world.

Step 3a
Some users open the attachment and their computers become infected with the virus.

Step 3b
Other users do not recognize the name of the sender of the e-mail message. These users do not open the e-mail message — instead they immediately delete the e-mail message and continue using their computers. These users' computers are not infected with the virus.

Figure 8-3 One way a virus can spread is through an e-mail attachment.

triggered, the computer plays a few chords of music. Other viruses cause extensive damage to computer files and spread quickly throughout a network. For example, if a state administrator sends an e-mail message with an attached Excel spreadsheet infected with a macro virus to every school district in the state, the virus could quickly infect hundreds of computers.

Some viruses are considered logic bombs or time bombs. A **logic bomb** is a program that activates when it detects a certain condition. One disgruntled worker, for example, planted a logic bomb that began destroying files when his name was added to a list of terminated employees. A **time bomb** is a type of logic bomb that activates on a particular date. A well-known time bomb is the **Michelangelo virus,** which destroys data on your hard disk on March 6, the date of Michelangelo's birthday. Although technically not a virus, hackers have been using

rootkit technology to help spread viruses. A **rootkit** is a program that hides in a computer and allows someone from a remote location to take full control of the computer. The World Wide Web is a great source for finding information about viruses and malicious software programs.

VIRUS DETECTION AND REMOVAL

Completely effective ways to keep a computer or network safe from computer viruses simply do not exist. You can, however, take precautions to protect your home and classroom computers from virus infections. Viruses normally are spread between computers by inserting an infected storage medium (such as a CD or USB flash drive) in a computer or downloading an infected file from the Internet or via an e-mail attachment. Figure 8-4 lists some tips to help you minimize the risk of viruses.

Safe Computing Tips

- **Purchase and install reliable antivirus software.** Most programs offer free virus definition updates. Update antivirus software virus definitions every week. The cost of antivirus software is much less than the cost of rebuilding damaged files.

- **Scan all removable media.** USB flash drives and other removable storage devices are common culprits for carrying viruses from one computer to another and spreading viruses throughout networks. If someone hands you a removable storage device that has been used in another system — scan it.

- **Scan all files downloaded from the Internet.** The number-one source for viruses is downloaded files. To be safe, download all files into a special folder on your hard drive and scan them for viruses immediately after downloading.

- **Scan all attached files before opening them.** It is possible to transfer a virus to your system by opening an attachment.

- **Turn off e-mail preview.** Although it is not likely that you will get a virus from reading your e-mail, many e-mail programs allow users to preview an e-mail message before or without opening it. Some sophisticated viruses and worms can deliver their payload when a user simply previews the message. Thus, users should turn off message preview in their e-mail programs.

- **Scan all software before using it, even if it is shrink-wrapped.** Viruses have been found in manufacturer-supplied software. Scan before installing software.

- **Do not use pirated, illegal copies of copyrighted software.** Not only is using them illegal, but they are a favorite source of viruses.

- **Never start your computer with removable media in the drives,** unless you are sure that the media is uninfected.

- **Install a personal firewall program to help protect against unwanted incoming attacks.** As a minimum, make sure that your operating system's firewall is activated.

- **Back up your files often.** Even with the best antivirus software, realize that your computer's files can be infected. Be prepared to deal with the problem.

- **Set your antivirus program to scan automatically.** Most antivirus programs can be set up to scan the system automatically when booted and to check removable media devices whenever they are accessed, such as to open files.

Figure 8-4 Teachers can follow these simple steps to practice safe computing and minimize the risk of viruses.

FAQ

Can mobile devices be infected with a virus?

Yes. Mobile devices such as mobile tablets and smartphones can be infected. Be sure to install antivirus software on your mobile devices and keep the software up to date.

FAQ

Can multimedia files be infected with a virus?

Yes. The increase in popularity of media sharing Web sites provides a great opportunity to distribute malicious programs. Last year, approximately 500,000 people downloaded what they thought was a media file from the Internet. In fact, the file was a Trojan horse that infected many computers with spyware. For this reason, it is important to scan all media files using antivirus software before playing them.

Web Info

For details about anti-virus programs, visit the Computer Concepts CourseMate Web site at *www.cengagebrain.com*, navigate to the Chapter 8 Web Info resource for this book, and then click Vaccines.

Using an antivirus program is one of the more effective ways to protect against computer viruses. An **antivirus program** is designed to detect, disinfect, and protect computers and networks from viruses. Antivirus programs, also called **vaccines**, work by looking for programs that attempt to modify the boot program, the operating system, or other programs that normally are read from but not written to (Figure 8-5).

In addition to providing protection from viruses, most antivirus programs also have utilities to remove or repair infected programs and files. If the virus has infected the boot program, however, the antivirus program may require you to restart the computer with a rescue disc. A **rescue disc** is normally a CD that contains an uninfected copy of key operating system commands and start-up information that enables the computer to restart correctly. After you have restarted the computer using a rescue disc, you can run repair and removal programs to repair damaged files and remove infected files. If the program cannot repair the damaged files, you might have to replace or restore them with uninfected backup copies of the files. Later sections in the chapter explain backup and restore procedures.

To help protect against viruses, most schools install antivirus programs on their networks and on individual computers throughout the school. Popular antivirus programs used in schools and homes include Norton AntiVirus (shown in Figure 8-5) and McAfee AntiVirus.

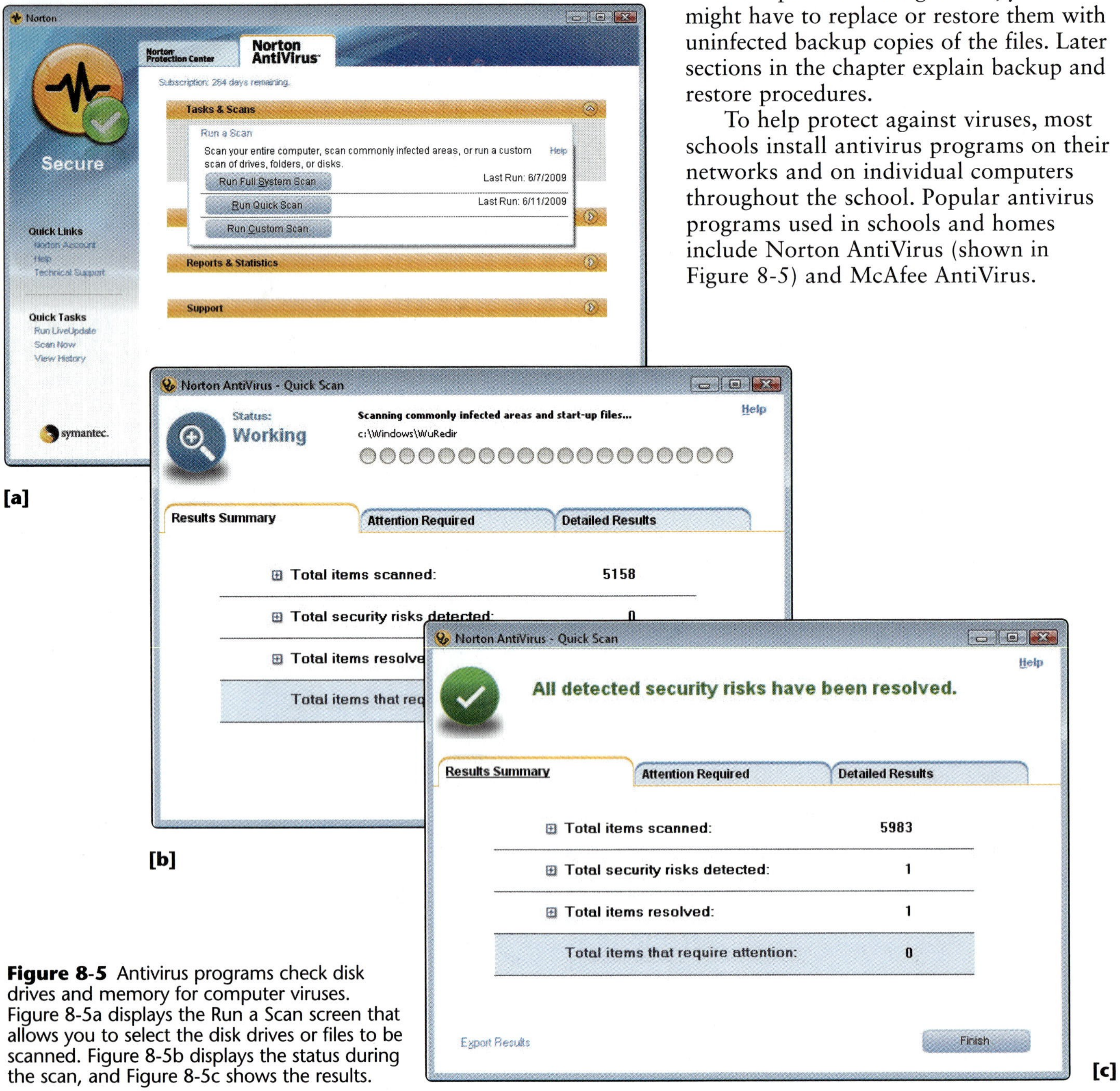

[a]

[b]

Figure 8-5 Antivirus programs check disk drives and memory for computer viruses. Figure 8-5a displays the Run a Scan screen that allows you to select the disk drives or files to be scanned. Figure 8-5b displays the status during the scan, and Figure 8-5c shows the results.

[c]

When you install an antivirus program, you should set up the program to monitor the computer continuously for possible viruses, including continual scans of all removable storage media and files downloaded from the Internet (Figure 8-6). You also should set the program to update virus definitions automatically every week.

False warnings about viruses often spread via e-mail and over the Internet. Known as **virus hoaxes**, these warnings describe viruses that are not actually known to exist. Given the damage viruses cause, however, you should take the time to research the validity of any virus warnings you receive, in the event the warning is real. The Symantec Security Response Hoax Web page regularly releases new virus hoax names. If you think you have received a message about a false virus, you can verify it at the Hoax Web page.

UNAUTHORIZED ACCESS AND USE

Unauthorized access is the use of a computer or network without permission. An individual who tries to access a computer or network illegally is called a **cracker** or hacker. The term, **hacker**, although originally a complimentary word for a computer enthusiast, now has a derogatory connotation because it refers to people who try to break into a computer, often intending to steal or corrupt its data. Crackers and hackers typically break into computers by connecting to the system via a modem and logging on as a user. Some intruders have no intent of causing damage to computer files; instead, they want to access data, information, or programs and use what they access for illegal purposes. Other intruders leave some evidence of their presence with a message or by deliberately altering data.

Unauthorized use is the use of a computer or data for unapproved or possibly illegal activities. Unauthorized use ranges from an employee using a company computer to send personal e-mail or to track his or her child's soccer league scores to someone gaining access to a bank system and completing an unauthorized transfer of funds.

One way to prevent unauthorized access to and use of computers is to implement **access controls**, which are security measures that define who can access a

computer, when they can access it, and what actions they can take while using the computer. To prevent unauthorized use and access to sensitive information, schools install different levels and types of access controls. Schools set up their networks so that users have access only to those programs, data, and information for which they are approved. Most schools and businesses provide authorized users with unique user identification (often called **user ID** or username) and a **password** that allows them to log on to the network to use e-mail, to transfer files, and to access other shared resources (Figure 8-7). When a user logs on to a computer or network by entering a user ID and a password, the operating system checks to see if the user ID and password match the entries stored in an authorization file. If the entries match, the computer or network grants access.

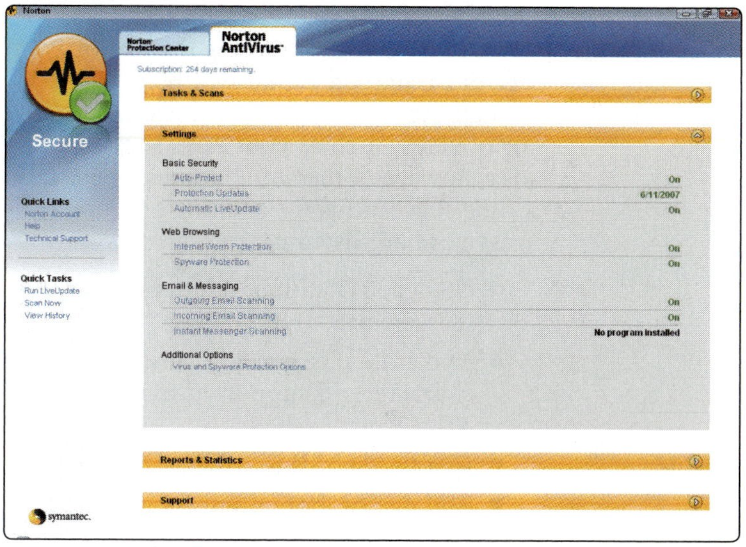

Figure 8-6 Using Norton AntiVirus Auto-Protect, users can opt for several different virus protection options.

Figure 8-7 Many schools require administrators, teachers, staff, and students to log on to the school's network with a unique user ID (or User Name, as shown here) and password.

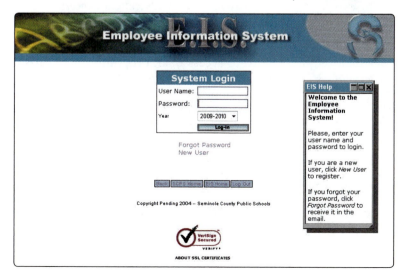

Often, you are asked to select your own password by choosing a word or series of characters that will be easy to remember. If your password is too simple or obvious, such as your initials or birthday, however, others might guess it easily. Some suggestions for creating a strong password are listed next:

- Use a combination of letters, digits, words, initials, and dates.
- Make the password at least eight characters (if supported by the software).
- Join two words together.
- Add one or more numbers at the beginning, middle, or end of a word.
- Choose words from other languages.
- Choose family names far back in your family tree.
- Choose a password you can type without looking at the keyboard.

Generally, the more creative your password, the harder it is for someone else to figure out. Even long and creative passwords, however, do not provide complete protection against unauthorized access. Some basic precautions to take include the following:

- Do not leave written copies of your passwords near your computer.
- Use a password that is easy to remember, so that you do not have to write it down.
- Change your password frequently.
- Do not share your password with anyone, especially telemarketers.

Following these guidelines helps to ensure that others will not use your password to access data, programs, or sensitive information stored on your computer or a school network.

At many schools, each user ID and password is associated with a specific level of computer and network access. A brief description of basic access levels that schools use to prevent unauthorized access and use of sensitive information follows:

- Students usually can access only instructional materials and software.

Although many schools also provide student access to the Internet and Web — many schools install filtering software on the networks to prevent students from viewing inappropriate Web sites. Students do not have network access to grades, attendance rates, and other sensitive and personal information.

- Teachers typically have access to all the programs, data, and information to which students have access; they usually have access to selected information about their students, such as grades and attendance. Teachers normally do not have access to information about other teachers, students, or any administrative files.
- Principals and assistant principals normally have access to all information that pertains to students enrolled at their schools; they may not access information about students attending other schools in the district.
- School district administrators and superintendents usually have access to all information stored on their districts' network servers.

POSSESSED OBJECTS AND BIOMETRIC DEVICES

A **possessed object** is any item that you must carry to gain access to a computer or computer facility. Examples are badges, cards, smart cards, and keys. The card you use in an automated teller machine (ATM) is a possessed object that allows access to your bank account. Possessed objects are often used in combination with a **personal identification number (PIN)**, which is a numeric password that provides an additional level of security.

Biometric devices authenticate a person's identity by translating a personal characteristic, such as a fingerprint, into a digital code that is compared with a digital code stored in the computer verifying the personal characteristic. If the digital code in the computer does not match the personal characteristic code, the computer denies access to the individual.

FIREWALLS

Despite efforts to protect the data on your computer's hard disk, it still is vulnerable to attacks from hackers. A **firewall** is a security system consisting of hardware and/or software that prevents unauthorized access to data and information on a network. Schools use firewalls to deny network access to outsiders and to restrict both student and teacher access to sensitive data (Figure 8-8). Many schools route all communications through a proxy server. A **proxy server** screens all incoming and outgoing messages.

If you are using Windows or Mac OS X, you already have a personal firewall that protects your computer from unauthorized access by monitoring all incoming network traffic. If you use a router, you also have a hardware firewall. Hardware firewalls stop many intrusions before they break into your computer.

For enhanced firewall protection and added features, some home and business users purchase stand-alone personal firewall software. A **personal firewall** is a software program that detects and protects your personal computer and its data from unauthorized intrusions. These products constantly monitor all transmissions to and from your computer and inform you of any attempted intrusions. These easy-to-use products are definitely worth their expense, which usually is less than $40. Figure 8-9 lists popular personal firewall products.

HARDWARE THEFT AND VANDALISM

For schools, hardware theft and vandalism present a difficult security challenge. To help minimize the theft of computers and associated equipment, schools can implement a variety of security precautions. In addition to installing security systems, many schools also install additional physical security devices such as cables that lock the equipment to a desk, cabinet, or floor (Figure 8-10). Schools also normally install deadbolt locks and alarm systems to protect the equipment in their computer labs.

With the increasing use of portable equipment such as notebook and tablet computers, iPods, smartphones, and other mobile devices, hardware theft poses a more serious risk. Increasingly, K-12 schools and colleges are providing notebook computers

Figure 8-8 A firewall restricts unauthorized intruders from accessing data, information, and programs on networks and individual computers.

Firewall Products
BitDefender Internet Security
McAfee Internet Security
Norton Internet Security
CA Personal Firewall
ZoneAlarm Pro

Figure 8-9 Popular personal firewall products.

Figure 8-10 Using cables to lock computers can help prevent the theft of desktop and mobile computer equipment.

Web Info

For more information about notebook computer security, visit the Computer Concepts CourseMate Web site at *www.cengagebrain.com*, navigate to the Chapter 8 Web Info resource for this book, and then click Security.

for teachers and loaning them to students for short periods. Some universities and colleges even require that each entering student purchase a notebook or netbook computer. Users must take special care to protect these portable computers. The size and weight of these smaller computers make them easy to steal, and their value makes them tempting targets for thieves.

Common sense and a constant awareness of the risks are the best preventive measures against theft of notebook computers, netbook computers, and other portable equipment. You should never, for example, leave a portable computer or any portable equipment unattended or out in the open in a public place, such as the cafeteria or on the seat of a car. Some schools install physical devices such as cables that temporarily lock notebook and netbook computers to a desk or table (Figure 8-11). As a precaution in case of theft, you should back up the files stored on your portable computer regularly.

Figure 8-11 The size and weight of netbook and notebook computers make them easy to steal, and their value makes them tempting targets for thieves. Schools and teachers need to take special precautions to prevent the theft of their notebook and netbook computers.

Some schools purchase insurance policies to cover their notebook, netbook, and desktop computers, as well as other computer equipment. In addition, schools can purchase a service that actually tracks down a stolen portable computer. This unique system often is called by its nickname, *the Lojack of the Computer World*. As soon as a person who has stolen a notebook computer uses the computer to access the Internet, the software on the

computer sends a message regarding the location of the stolen computer to the school's system network administrator, who then notifies the police.

In addition to hardware theft, another area of concern for K-12 schools is vandalism. **Computer vandalism** takes many forms, from a student cutting a computer cable or deleting files to individuals breaking into a school and randomly smashing computers. Schools usually have written policies and procedures for handling various types of vandalism.

SOFTWARE THEFT

Like hardware theft and vandalism, software theft takes many forms — from a student physically stealing a CD to intentional piracy of software. **Software piracy** — the unauthorized and illegal duplication of copyrighted software — is by far the most common form of software theft.

When you purchase software, you actually do not *own* the software; instead, you have purchased the right to use the software, as outlined in the software license. A **software license** is an agreement that provides specific conditions for use of the software, which users must accept before using the software. Manufacturers usually print the terms of a software license on the software packaging, or in the case of software downloaded via the Web, a page at the manufacturer's site. The same agreement generally displays on a licensing acceptance screen during the software's setup program (Figure 8-12). Installation and use of the software constitutes the user's acceptance of the terms.

The most common type of license agreement included with software packages purchased by individual users is a **single-user license agreement** or **end-user license agreement (EULA)**. An end-user license agreement typically includes numerous conditions, including the following:

- Users may install the software on only one computer. Some license agreements allow users to install the software on one desktop computer and one portable computer.

- Users may not install the software on a network, such as a school computer lab network.

Web Info

For an overview of software and technology law, visit the Computer Concepts CourseMate Web site at *www.cengagebrain.com*, navigate to the Chapter 8 Web Info resource for this book, and then click Software Law.

Figure 8-12 Software usually includes a licensing agreement, which is displayed during installation of the software and which the user must agree to before the program can be installed.

- Users may make *one* copy for backup purposes.
- Users may not give copies to friends and colleagues.

Unless otherwise specified by a software license, you do not have the right to loan, rent, or in any way distribute software you purchase. This means you cannot install the software on both your home and classroom computer or on more than one classroom or home computer. Doing so is not only a violation of copyright law, but also a federal crime.

Software piracy introduces a number of risks into the software market: it increases the chance of viruses, eliminates your ability to receive technical support, and significantly drives up the price of software for all users. Experts estimate that for every authorized copy of software in use, at least one unauthorized copy is made. One recent study reported that software piracy results in worldwide losses of billions of dollars per year.

Software piracy continues for several reasons. Some countries do not provide legal protection for software, while other countries rarely enforce laws. In addition, many buyers believe they have the right to copy the software for which they have paid hundreds, even thousands of dollars.

Newer Microsoft Office and Windows products contain software-based product activation technology, which means you need to activate your Office and Windows products to use them. **Product activation** is an antipiracy technology designed to verify that software products have been licensed legitimately. Microsoft states that product activation is quick, simple, unobtrusive, and that it protects customer privacy.

Product activation works by verifying that a software program's product key, which you must use to install the product, has not been used on more personal computers than intended by the software's license. Software companies take illegal copying seriously and prosecute some offenders (including school districts, school administrators, and teachers) to the fullest extent of the law. Penalties include fines up to $250,000 and up to five years in jail.

Most schools have strict policies governing the installation and use of software and enforce their rules by periodically checking classroom and lab computers to ensure that all software is properly licensed. Teachers who are not completely familiar with their school's policies governing installation of software should check with the school's technology coordinator before installing any software on a classroom computer.

Two additional types of software, shareware and freeware, also require license agreements and are protected under copyright law. **Shareware** is software that is distributed free for a trial period. If you want to use a shareware program beyond the trial period, the developer (person or company) expects you to send a small fee. **Freeware**, by contrast, is software provided at no cost to a user by an individual or company. You should carefully read the license included with any shareware or freeware to familiarize yourself with the usage terms and conditions. Some shareware licenses, for example, allow you to install the software on several computers for the same fee, whereas others allow you to install the software on an unlimited number of computers in the same school for a minimal additional fee. Always scan shareware and freeware programs for viruses before installation and use.

To reduce software costs for schools and businesses with large numbers of users, software vendors often offer special discount pricing or site licensing. With discount pricing, the more copies of a program a school district purchases, the greater the discount. Purchasing a software **site license** gives the buyer the right to install the software on multiple computers at a single site. Site licenses usually cost significantly less than purchasing an individual copy of the software for each computer; many school districts, in fact, purchase software site licenses that allow for use on computers throughout the district, thus gaining substantial savings.

Network site licenses for many software packages also are available. A **network site license** allows network users to share a single copy of the software, which resides on the network server. Network software site license prices are based on a fixed fee for an unlimited number of users, a maximum number of users, or per user.

A **community/state site license** gives an entire region or state the right to install an unlimited number of educational copies of a particular software program on individual computers or a network. As with other site licenses, a community/state site license provides substantial savings. Figure 8-13 summarizes the various types of software licenses used in education. A number of major software companies, such as Microsoft, provide site licenses for some of their software to K-12 schools at drastically reduced rates.

Type of License	Characteristics	Use in Schools
Single-user	Software can be installed on only one computer. Some license agreements allow users to install the software on one desktop computer and one notebook computer.	Used when a school needs only a few copies of a particular software. Commonly found in small schools and when purchasing specialized software programs.
Multiple-user	Software can be installed on a set number of computers, typically 5, 10, 50, or more. Cost varies based on number of computers.	Cost-effective method to install software on more than one computer. Most commonly used in schools.
Network License	Software is installed on the school's network. The license will specify and the software will control a specific number of simultaneous users, such as 50, 100, 250, or 500. Cost varies based on number of computers.	Cost-effective method of allowing students and teachers throughout the school to have access to an application software program. As schools continue to install networks, network licenses are becoming more common.
Community/State License	Frequently used with software distributed on CDs/DVDs. Any number of programs can be purchased for either Macintosh or PC platforms.	Very cost-effective method for school districts or states to purchase large quantities of software. Savings can be significant over individual CD or DVD pricing.

Figure 8-13 A summary of the various types of software licenses used in education.

INFORMATION THEFT

As you have learned, information is a valuable asset to an organization, such as a school district. The deliberate theft of information causes as much or more damage than the theft of hardware. Information theft typically occurs for a variety of reasons — organizations steal or buy stolen information to learn about competitors and individuals steal credit card and telephone charge card numbers to make purchases. Information theft often is linked to other types of computer crime. An individual, for example, may gain unauthorized access to a computer and then steal credit card numbers stored in a firm's accounting files.

Most organizations prevent information theft by implementing the user ID controls previously mentioned. Another way to protect sensitive data is to use encryption. **Encryption** is the process of converting readable data into unreadable characters by applying a formula that uses a code, called an **encryption key**. The person who receives the message uses the same encryption key to decrypt it (convert it back to readable data).

Both the sender and receiver computers use the same encryption software. Any person illegally accessing the information sees only meaningless symbols (Figure 8-14).

School networks do contain a great deal of important and confidential information about students, teachers, and staff. Although information theft is not a major problem in schools, the potential is taken seriously. As a result, schools implement many of the security precautions described in this chapter.

SYSTEM FAILURE

Theft is not the only cause of hardware, software, data, or information loss. Any of these can occur during a **system failure**, which is a malfunction of a computer. System failures occur because of electrical power problems, hardware component failure, or software error.

One common cause of system failures in school and home computers is an abrupt variation in electrical power, which can cause data loss or damage computer components. In a school network, for example, a single power disturbance can damage multiple computers and their associated equipment. Two more common electrical power variations that cause system failures are undervoltages and overvoltages.

[a]

The Gettysburg Address

Four score and seven years ago our fathers brought forth on this continent, a new nation, conceived in liberty, and dedicated to the proposition that all men are created equal.

Now we are engaged in a great civil war, testing whether that nation or any nation so conceived and so dedicated, can long endure. We are met on a great battle-field of that war. We have come to dedicate a portion of that field as a final resting place for those who here gave their lives that the nation might live. It is altogether fitting and proper that we should do this.

[b]

Figure 8-14 The first two paragraphs of the Gettysburg Address in plain text [a] and after the text is encrypted [b].

An **undervoltage** occurs when the electrical power supply drops. In North America, electricity normally flows from the wall plug at approximately 120 volts. Any significant drop below 120 volts is considered an undervoltage. A **brownout** is a prolonged undervoltage; a **blackout** is a complete power failure. Undervoltages cause data loss and computer crashes but generally do not cause serious equipment damage.

An **overvoltage**, or **power surge**, occurs when the incoming electrical power increases significantly above the normal 120 volts. A momentary overvoltage, called a **spike**, occurs when the power increase lasts for less than one millisecond (one thousandth of a second). Spikes are caused by uncontrollable disturbances, such as lightning, or controllable disturbances, such as turning on a piece of equipment that uses the same electrical circuit. Overvoltages can cause immediate and permanent equipment damage.

To protect your computer equipment from overvoltages, you should use surge protectors. A **surge protector** is a device that uses special electrical components to smooth out minor voltage errors, provide a stable current flow, and keep an overvoltage from damaging computer equipment (Figure 8-15). Schools should use surge protectors for all classroom and lab computers and printers.

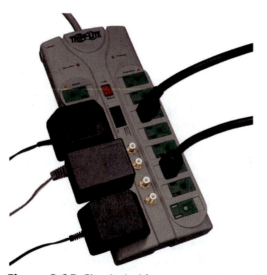

Figure 8-15 Circuits inside a surge protector safeguard equipment against overvoltages.

You will also want a surge protector for your home computer, and if your home computer connects to the Internet, you need to have surge protection not only for your computer, but also for your modem, telephone lines, DSL lines, and other Internet cables. Many surge protectors include plug-ins for telephone lines and other cables (Figure 8-16). If your surge protector does not have these plug-ins, you can purchase separate devices to protect these lines. Overall, surge protectors provide an inexpensive way to protect computers and associated equipment. Surge protectors range in price from about $15 to $35.

in-out network and phone line connections

Figure 8-16 Home users should purchase a surge protector that includes an in-and-out connection for telephone lines and other network cables.

Although a surge protector absorbs a small overvoltage without damage, a large overvoltage, such as that caused by a lightning strike, will cause the surge protector to fail to protect the computer components. Surge protectors also are not completely effective; large power surges can bypass the surge protector and repeated small overvoltages can weaken a surge protector permanently.

For additional electrical protection, many home and school users connect their computers and printers to an uninterruptible power supply, instead of a surge protector. An **uninterruptible power supply** (UPS) is a device that contains surge protection circuits and one or more batteries that provide power during a temporary or permanent loss of power (Figure 8-17). The amount of time a UPS allows you to continue working depends on the electrical requirements of the computer and the size of the batteries in the UPS. A less expensive UPS provides enough time for users to save their current work and properly shut down the computer after a power outage (about 10 minutes).

Figure 8-17 If power fails, an uninterruptible power supply (UPS) uses batteries to provide electricity for a limited time. A UPS also contains circuits that safeguard against overvoltages.

To ensure that their networks will continue to operate in the event of a power loss, most schools and businesses install UPSs to protect their network servers. Home users also should consider investing in a UPS, especially if they live in an area prone to power surges, power failures, and lightning strikes. For home users, the $30 to $75 investment in a UPS can prevent user frustration associated with most power-related computer problems, crashes, and loss of data. Some UPS manufacturers pay for any damage your computer sustains from power surges, including lightning strikes.

BACKING UP — THE ULTIMATE SAFEGUARD

To prevent data loss caused by a system failure or a computer virus, many schools, businesses, and home users back up their important files. A **backup** is a duplicate of a file, program, or disk that can be used if the original is lost, damaged, or destroyed. When a file is corrupted or destroyed, the backup copy is used to **restore**, or reload, the file on a computer or network file server. Schools and home users often overlook storing backup copies at another location, called an **off-site location**, as an additional precaution. This simple precaution prevents a single disaster, such as a fire, from destroying both the primary and backup copies of important files.

Most schools have a **backup procedure** that outlines a regular plan of copying and backing up important data and program files. At many schools, the backup procedures cover only essential school programs, information, and data, such as student grades, attendance, and other personal information. Schools normally do not back up the files individual teachers or students create on their classroom computers. If your school does not provide backups for the files you create in your classroom, you should make backup copies of your school files periodically and store them on a portable hard drive or CD/DVDs. Likewise, you should back up the files you create on your home computer. Whether at school or home, backing up your important files prevents loss of lesson plans, curriculum resource pages, handouts, tests, and more — files that represent years of work. Teachers also should teach their students how to back up their homework, projects, and other files.

Creating backup copies of your files is not a difficult procedure. The easiest way is to copy your important files from your hard disk to a CD, USB flash drive, or portable hard drive. In addition, most personal computer operating systems include an easy-to-use backup utility program (Figure 8-18). Such utilities not only allow users to back up their important files, they also compress the backed up files so they require less storage space than the original files.

Web Info

To learn more about Microsoft Backup, visit the Computer Concepts CourseMate Web site at *www. cengagebrain.com*, navigate to the Chapter 8 Web Info resource for this book, and then click Backup.

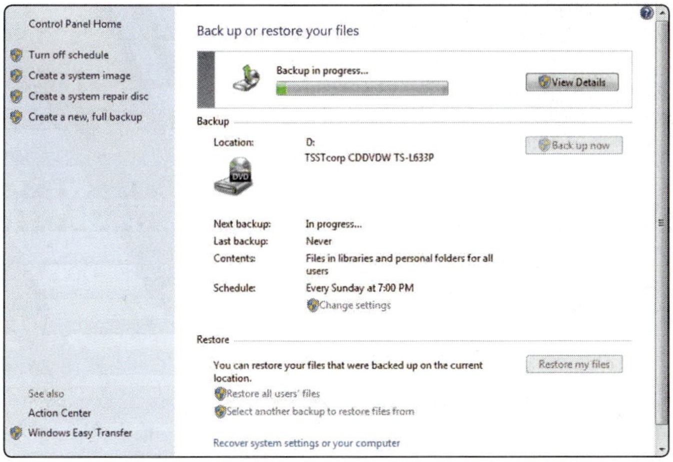

Figure 8-18 Microsoft Backup is a utility program that comes with Microsoft Windows and is an easy way to back up your important computer files.

Ethics and the Information Age

As with any powerful technology, individuals can use computers for both good and bad actions. The standards that determine whether an action is good or bad are called **ethics**. **Computer ethics** are the moral guidelines that govern the use of computers, networks, and information systems (Figure 8-19). Five areas of computer ethics frequently discussed are (1) unauthorized use of computers, (2) hardware, software, and information theft, (3) information privacy, (4) copyright, and (5) the existence of objectionable materials on the Internet.

Unauthorized use of computers and hardware, copying software, and information theft were discussed earlier in this chapter. The following sections present the issues surrounding information privacy and copyright. The ethical issues related to objectionable materials on the Internet are discussed later in this chapter.

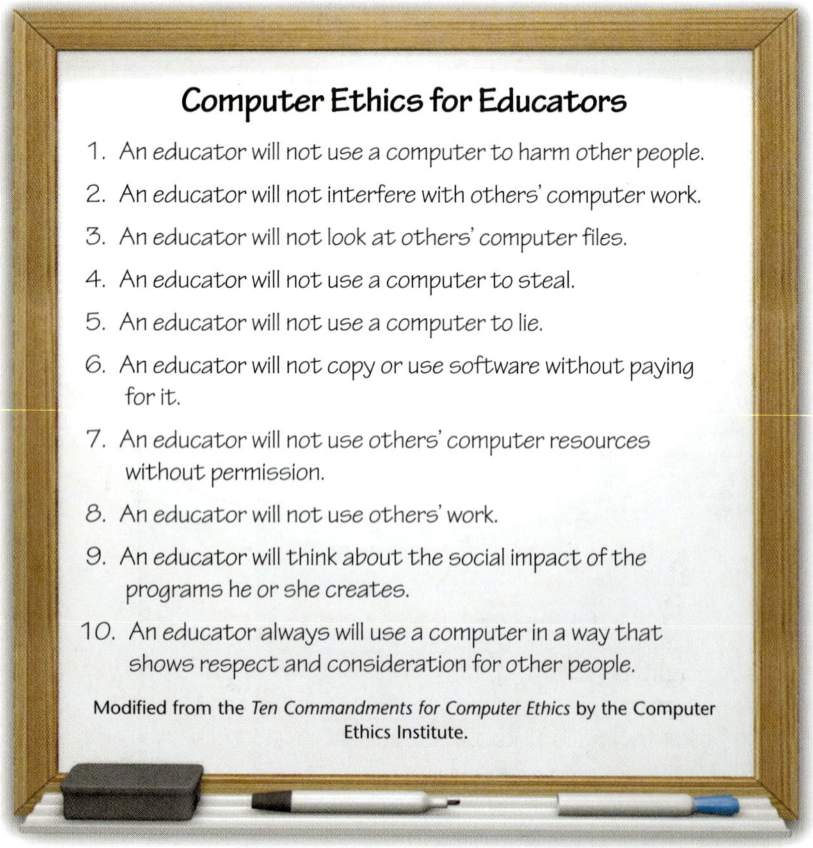

INFORMATION PRIVACY

Information privacy is the right of individuals and organizations to deny or restrict the collection and use of information about them. In the past, information privacy was easier to control because information was kept in separate locations, individual schools in a large school district maintained their own files, individual stores had their own credit files, government agencies had separate records, doctors had separate files, and so on.

Now it is feasible, both technically and economically, for schools, businesses, and other organizations to store large amounts of related data in a database or on one network server because of the widespread use of networks and increased storage capacity. These organizations also use computers to monitor student and employee activities. As a result, many people have concerns about how the unauthorized collection and use of data and monitoring affects their privacy. Figure 8-20 lists actions you can take to make your personal data more private.

UNAUTHORIZED COLLECTION AND USE OF INFORMATION   Most individuals are surprised to learn that national marketing organizations often purchase the information individuals provide for magazine subscriptions, product warranty registration cards, contest entry forms, and other documents.

By combining this acquired data with other information obtained from public sources, such as driver's licenses and vehicle registration information, national marketing organizations create an **electronic profile** of an individual. The organizations then sell these electronic profiles to organizations that distribute information on a product, service, or cause to a specific group of individuals (for example, all sports car owners over 40 years of age living in the southeastern United States).

Direct marketing supporters say that using information in this way lowers overall selling costs, which, in turn, lowers product prices. Critics contend that the information contained in these electronic profiles reveals more about individuals than anyone has a right to know. These same individuals believe that, at a minimum, companies should inform the individuals whose personal information they intend to sell or release and give the individuals the right to deny such use.

Computer Ethics for Educators

1. An educator will not use a computer to harm other people.

2. An educator will not interfere with others' computer work.

3. An educator will not look at others' computer files.

4. An educator will not use a computer to steal.

5. An educator will not use a computer to lie.

6. An educator will not copy or use software without paying for it.

7. An educator will not use others' computer resources without permission.

8. An educator will not use others' work.

9. An educator will think about the social impact of the programs he or she creates.

10. An educator always will use a computer in a way that shows respect and consideration for other people.

Modified from the *Ten Commandments for Computer Ethics* by the Computer Ethics Institute.

Figure 8-19 Computer ethics are the guidelines that govern the use of computers and information systems. This figure lists computer ethics for educators.

How to Safeguard Personal Information
Fill in only required information on forms, both in print and on the Web.
Do not preprint your telephone number or Social Security Number on personal checks.
Have an unlisted or unpublished telephone number.
Find out how to block your telephone number from displaying on the receiver's system if Caller ID is available in your area.
Do not write your telephone number on charge or credit receipts.
Ask merchants not to write credit card numbers, telephone numbers, Social Security Numbers, and driver's license numbers on the back of your personal checks.
Purchase goods with cash instead of credit or checks.
Avoid shopping clubs and buyers' cards.
Find out why merchants want personal information before releasing the information to them.
Inform merchants that you do not want them to distribute your personal information.
Ask, in writing, to be removed from mailing lists.
Obtain your credit report once a year from each of the three major credit reporting agencies (Equifax, Experian, and TransUnion) and correct any errors.
Request a free copy of your medical records once a year from the Medical Information Bureau.
Install a cookie manager to filter cookies.
Clear your history file when you are finished browsing.
Set up a free e-mail account, and then use this e-mail address for merchant forms.
Turn off File and Print Sharing on your Internet connection.
Install a personal firewall.
Sign-up for e-mail filtering through your Internet service provider or use an antispam program such as Brightmail.
Do not reply to spam for any reason. It might not be a good idea to unsubscribe to unsolicited spam; by sending back a message, you might only confirm that your e-mail account is active.
Surf the Web anonymously with programs such as Freedom Websecure or through an anonymous Web site such as Anonymizer.com.

Figure 8-20 Techniques to keep personal data private.

PHISHING **Phishing** is a scam in which a perpetrator sends an official-looking e-mail that attempts to obtain personal and financial information from the recipient. Some phishing e-mail messages ask the recipient to provide personal information in the reply; others direct the recipient to a phony Web site that collects the information. To help deter phishing scams and spam (discussed next), Microsoft and others are developing standards that will require e-mail messages to contain sender identification so recipients can verify the legitimacy of messages.

SPAM **Spam** is an unsolicited e-mail message or newsgroup posting sent to many recipients or newsgroups at once.

The content of spam ranges from selling a product or service, to promoting a business opportunity, to advertising offensive materials. One study indicates the average e-mail user receives more than 1,000 spam e-mail messages each year. Spam sent through an instant messaging system, instead of through e-mail, is called **spim**. Spam sent via Internet Telephony is called **split**.

You can reduce the amount of spam you receive using several techniques. Some e-mail programs have built-in settings that delete spam automatically. Other e-mail programs, such as Outlook Express, allow you to set up message rules that block all messages from a particular sender or subject. You also can sign up for e-mail filtering from your Internet service provider.

Integration Strategies

To learn more about teaching your students about monitoring software and related issues, visit the Computer Concepts CourseMate Web site at *www.cengagebrain. com*, navigate to the Chapter 8 Software Corner resource for this book.

E-mail filtering is a service that blocks e-mail messages from designated sources. You can block unwanted e-mail messages by using an **antispam program** that attempts to remove spam before it reaches your inbox. The disadvantage of using e-mail filters and antispam programs is that sometimes they remove valid e-mail messages.

PRIVACY LAWS The concern about privacy has led to federal and state laws regarding storing and disclosing personal data and other computer-related issues (Figure 8-21). Common points in some of these laws include the following:

- A business or government agency collecting data about individuals should limit the information collected and only store what is necessary to carry out the organization's functions.

- After it has collected data about individuals, an organization must make provisions to restrict data access to only those employees who must use it to perform their job duties.

- An organization should release an individual's personal information outside the organization only after the individual has agreed to its disclosure.

- When an organization collects information about an individual, the organization must inform the individual that it is collecting data and give her the opportunity to determine the accuracy of the data.

Schools and school districts have a legal and moral responsibility to protect sensitive information, whether it is in printed form or stored electronically on school computers. Just like any other business, school districts must follow state and federal laws concerning storage and release of personal information about students, teachers, and staff personnel. For these reasons, school districts generally restrict access to sensitive information stored on their networks and in printed materials on a strict need-to-know basis.

Teachers also must follow federal and state laws concerning the storage and release of information about their students. Teachers should carefully read and make sure they understand all school district

Web Info

For a crash course on copyright basics, visit the Teachers Computer Concepts CourseMate Web site at *www.cengagebrain. com*, navigate to the Chapter 8 Web Info resource for this book, and then click Crash Course.

policies concerning the release of sensitive information related to their students.

EMPLOYEE AND STUDENT MONITORING
Employee monitoring uses computers to observe, record, and review an individual's use of a computer, including communications such as e-mail, keyboard activity (used to measure productivity), and Internet sites visited. A frequently discussed issue is whether an employer has the right to read an employee's e-mail messages. Actual policies vary widely, with some organizations declaring they will review e-mail messages regularly, whereas others state they consider e-mail private and will protect it just like a letter sent through the postal service.

Most schools usually have very specific rules governing the use of e-mail and school networks by teachers, administrators, staff, and students. Some schools randomly monitor e-mail messages and the Internet sites visited by teachers, administrators, staff, and students, whereas other schools do not. Some schools also randomly monitor files stored on the school network.

Teachers should become familiar with all school policies concerning e-mail and computer and Internet usage. To ensure that individuals understand these policies, most schools require that teachers, students, staff, and parents sign an Acceptable Use Policy (AUP) that provides specific guidance for using school computers, networks, and the Internet. Teachers also should ensure that students fully understand that school personnel or their future employers might monitor their use of the organization's computer resources.

COPYRIGHT LAWS

As discussed earlier in this chapter, copyright laws cover software programs to protect them from piracy. Copyright law includes many other aspects, however, that teachers need to understand. The Copyright Act of 1976 and its numerous amendments apply to all creative works. A **copyright** means the original author or creator of the work retains ownership of the work and has the exclusive right to reproduce and distribute the creative work.

Date	Law	Purpose
2006	Telephone Records and Privacy Protection Act	Makes it illegal to use fraudulent means to obtain someone's telephone records.
2003	CAN-SPAM Act	Gives law enforcement the right to impose penalties on people using the Internet to distribute spam.
2002	Dot Kids Implementation and Efficiency Act	Establishes the Dot Kids domain that lists only Web sites that conform to policies to protect children under the age of 13. It functions similarly to the children's section of a library. Ruled unconstitutional in 2004.
2001	Provide Appropriate Tools Required to Intercept and Obstruct Terrorism (PATRIOT) Act	Gives law enforcement the right to monitor people's activities, including Web and e-mail habits.
2000	Children's Internet Protection Act (CIPA)	Protects children from obscene and pornographic materials by requiring libraries to install filtering software on their computers. Upheld by the Supreme Court in July 2003.
1998	Children's Online Privacy Protection Act (COPPA)	Protects personal information for children under the age of 13.
1997	No Electronic Theft (NET) Act	Closes a narrow loophole in the law that allowed people to give away copyrighted material (such as software) on the Internet without legal repercussions.
1996	Computer Abuse Amendments Act	Amends 1984 and 1996 act to outlaw transmission of harmful computer code such as viruses.
1996	National Information Infrastructure Protection Act	Penalizes theft of information across state lines, threats against networks, and computer system trespassing.
1996	Health Insurance Portability and Accountability Act (HIPAA)	Describes how personal medical information can be used and disclosed.
1992	Cable Television Consumer Protection and Competition Act	Extends privacy of Cable Communications Policy Act of 1984 to include cellular and other wireless services.
1991	Telephone Consumer Protection Act	Restricts activities of telemarketers.
1988	Computer Matching and Privacy Protection Act	Regulates the use of government data to determine the eligibility of individuals for federal benefits.
1988	Video Privacy Protection Act	Forbids retailers from releasing or selling video-rental records without customer consent or a court order.
1986	Electronic Communications Privacy Act (ECPA)	Provides the same right of privacy protection used by the postal delivery service and telephone companies to the new forms of electronic communications, such as voice mail, e-mail, and cellular telephones.
1984	Cable Communications Policy Act	Regulates disclosure of cable television subscriber records.
1984	Computer Fraud and Abuse Act	Outlaws unauthorized access of federal government computers.
1978	Right to Financial Privacy Act	Strictly outlines procedures federal agencies must follow when looking at customer records in banks.
1974	Privacy Act	Forbids federal agencies from allowing information to be used for a reason other than for which it was collected.
1974	Family Educational Rights and Privacy Act	Gives students and parents access to school records and limits disclosure of records to unauthorized parties.
1970	Fair Credit Reporting Act	Prohibits credit reporting agencies from releasing credit information to unauthorized people and allows consumers to review their own credit records.

Figure 8-21 Summary of the major U.S. government laws concerning privacy. As technology changes so do the laws associated with it, either through amendments or new laws.

Web Info

To learn more about fair use, visit the Computer Concepts CourseMate Web site at *www.cengagebrain.com*, navigate to the Chapter 8 Web Info resource for this book, and then click Fair Use.

All educators need to understand how copyright laws impact the manner in which they and their students use information created by others. Such an understanding is important because the building blocks of education use the creative works of others: books; videos; newspapers, magazines, and other reference materials; software; and information located on the World Wide Web.

Three areas of copyright directly impact today's classrooms: (1) illegal copying or using copyrighted software programs; (2) fair use laws and their application to the use of both printed copyrighted materials and copyrighted materials accessible on the Internet; and (3) use of copyrighted materials on teacher and student Web pages. The first area (illegal copying or using licensed and copyrighted software) was covered earlier in this chapter; the following sections cover the other two areas of copyright.

FAIR USE The Copyright Act of 1976 established **fair use** and provided the guidelines that allow educators to use and copy certain copyrighted materials for nonprofit educational purposes. Figure 8-22 shows Section 107 of U.S. Copyright Law, which deals with fair use. Copyright issues are complex and sometimes the laws are vague. School districts often provide teachers with specific guidelines for using copyrighted materials in their classrooms. Schools can interpret copyright issues differently, so school policies concerning the use of copyrighted materials vary widely. Teachers need to read and understand school policies concerning copyright.

In addition to providing printed school policies on copyright issues, most schools provide teachers with information and answer questions about copyright issues. For information or answers to questions concerning software copyright issues, teachers should ask their school or district technology coordinator. For all other issues concerning copyright, fair use, and associated school district policies, teachers should speak with their media specialist. Media specialists receive training on copyright issues and deal with them on a daily basis. If in doubt, teachers should contact the creator of the work and ask for written permission to use his material.

Fair use guidelines apply to copyrighted material on the Internet just as they apply to a copyrighted article published in a magazine. Basically, Web sites include two kinds of information: original copyrighted information and information without copyright restriction. Web pages that contain original information generally include a copyright statement on the page; the copyright statement normally contains the copyright symbol, the year, and the creator's name (Figure 8-23).

U.S. Copyright Law: Fair Use

(U.S. Code, Title 17, Chapter 1, Section 107)

§ 107. Limitations on exclusive rights: Fair use

Notwithstanding the provisions of sections 106 and 106A, the fair use of a copyrighted work, including such use by reproduction in copies or phonorecords or by any other means specified by that section, for purposes such as criticism, comment, news reporting, teaching (including multiple copies for classroom use), scholarship, or research, is not an infringement of copyright. In determining whether the use made of a work in any particular case is a fair use, the factors to be considered shall include:

(1) the purpose and character of the use, including whether such use is of a commercial nature or is for nonprofit educational purposes;

(2) the nature of the copyrighted work;

(3) the amount and substantiality of the portion used in relation to the copyrighted work as a whole; and

(4) the effect of the use upon the potential market for or value of the copyrighted work.

The fact that a work is unpublished shall not itself bar a finding of fair use if such finding is made upon consideration of all the above factors.

Figure 8-22 The Copyright Act of 1976 provides the structure for the copyright law. Section 107 of the U.S. Copyright Law defines Fair Use.

If a teacher uses copyrighted materials from the Internet, she must follow fair use guidelines, school policies, and any restrictions listed on the Web site. If the information located on the Web site does not include copyright restriction, it does not mean the creator is waiving his privileges under copyright. To be safe, you should assume everything on the Web is copyrighted. Always follow fair use guidelines and school policies when using Web materials for educational purposes. In addition, always give proper credit and use citations if appropriate.

These guidelines do not apply only to text-based materials on the Web. The Web also contains a multitude of graphics, animations, and audio and video files teachers can download and use for educational purposes or classroom presentations. When teachers download and use these materials, they must adhere to fair use guidelines, school policies, and any other restrictions noted on the Web site.

TEACHER AND STUDENT WEB PAGES

Teachers and students in school districts all over the country are creating and publishing their own Web pages (Figure 8-24). As previously discussed, Web publishing is the development and maintenance of Web pages. When developing these pages, teachers and students must take care to respect copyright laws and follow the guidelines outlined in the previous section.

Copyright laws do protect all original materials created by students and teachers and published on the Web. To ensure that this is clear, however, teachers and students may want to include a copyright statement at the bottom of their home page.

The use of copyrighted materials (text, graphics, animations, audio, and video) on teacher or student Web pages requires permission from the creator of the materials. Most Web pages include an e-mail link to use when asking for permission to use copyrighted materials. To use the materials on the Web, simply send a short e-mail message to the creator of the work and explain how you will use her work on your Web page. Many authors are more than willing to allow teachers to use their original text or artwork for educational purposes as long as they receive proper credit.

copyright symbol
and statement

Figure 8-23 This education company's Web page has a copyright statement.

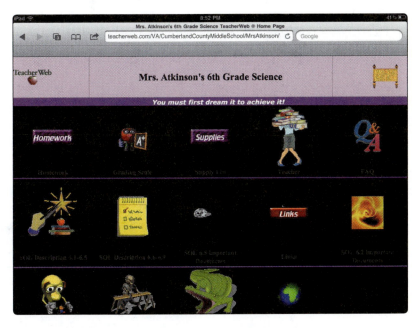

Figure 8-24 Teachers and students in school districts all over the country are creating and publishing their own Web pages.

Many school districts have specific guidelines that teachers and students must follow when publishing Web pages on school servers. Teachers should carefully read all school rules before publishing any teacher or student Web pages. Some schools, for example, prohibit using any copyrighted materials on Web pages. In such instances, students and teachers must use only original material or material that is not copyrighted. Generally, teachers may use materials from government-sponsored Web sites, which are considered public domain (Figure 8-25). Anything considered **public domain** — including software or creative works — is free from copyright restrictions.

Most school districts purchase or have access to CDs/DVDs containing copyright free material or they subscribe to services that contain thousands of clip art images,

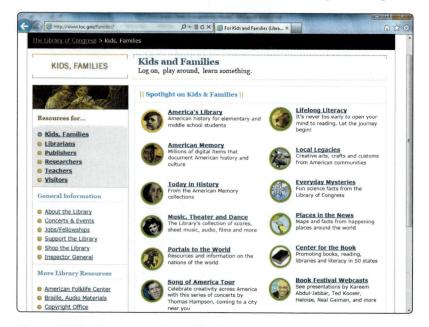

Figure 8-25 An example of a public domain government Web page. Government Web pages usually have a URL that contains or ends in .gov.

photos, graphics, and audio and video clips. Thousands of copyright-free materials are available on the Internet for teachers and students to use, such as the one shown in Figure 8-26.

In addition to respecting copyright law, teachers also must consider other issues related to Web page publishing. Teachers, for example, must protect their students from Internet users who might want to harm them by ensuring that no personal information about students is included on the Web pages. Figure 8-27 lists some basic guidelines that teachers should consider when creating Web pages.

Finally, a broadly interpreted issue known as intellectual property rights is beginning to play an important role in public education. The major intellectual property rights issue currently being discussed is who owns online content and courses, both in higher education and K-12 education. A recent survey found that most institutions of higher education see content as the property of the instructor. More than half also believe that the instructor owns the actual course. Currently, most K-12 districts handle ownership of items such as tests, lesson plans, and other teaching materials and these districts see ownership as a nonissue. Some districts are beginning to clarify the ownership of online courses.

Figure 8-26 This Web page for teachers provides links to dozens of Web sites that provide free graphics, animations, and more.

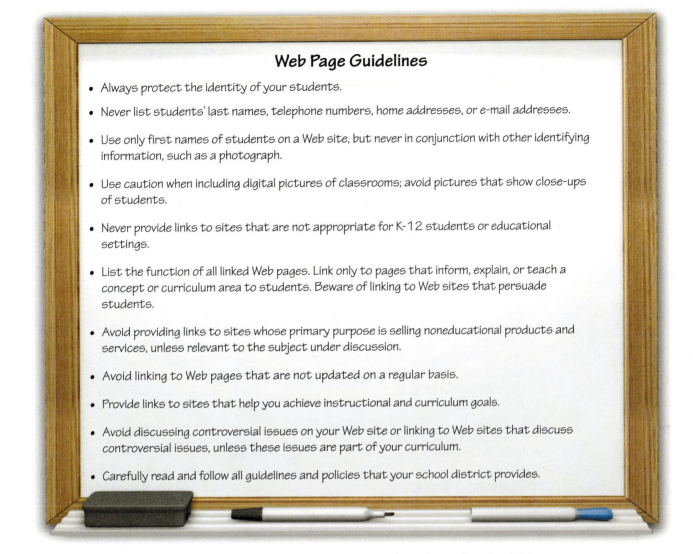

Web Page Guidelines

- Always protect the identity of your students.

- Never list students' last names, telephone numbers, home addresses, or e-mail addresses.

- Use only first names of students on a Web site, but never in conjunction with other identifying information, such as a photograph.

- Use caution when including digital pictures of classrooms; avoid pictures that show close-ups of students.

- Never provide links to sites that are not appropriate for K-12 students or educational settings.

- List the function of all linked Web pages. Link only to pages that inform, explain, or teach a concept or curriculum area to students. Beware of linking to Web sites that persuade students.

- Avoid providing links to sites whose primary purpose is selling noneducational products and services, unless relevant to the subject under discussion.

- Avoid linking to Web pages that are not updated on a regular basis.

- Provide links to sites that help you achieve instructional and curriculum goals.

- Avoid discussing controversial issues on your Web site or linking to Web sites that discuss controversial issues, unless these issues are part of your curriculum.

- Carefully read and follow all guidelines and policies that your school district provides.

Figure 8-27 Guidelines that teachers should consider when creating teacher and student Web pages.

Internet Ethics and Objectionable Materials

As you already have learned in this chapter, the widespread use of the Internet — especially in today's schools and classrooms — raises many issues regarding security, privacy, and ethics. Of all of these, one issue is of particular concern for teachers and parents: the availability of **objectionable material** on the Internet, including racist literature, obscene pictures and videos, gambling, and age-restricted items such as cigarettes and alcohol.

Teachers and other school personnel must be concerned with three different types of Internet materials that fall under the general term objectionable material.

The first area includes all materials that most people consider pornographic, such as obscene pictures, stories, graphics, articles, cartoons, and videos. The second area includes racist literature, controversial subjects such as gambling, and other similar materials. Teachers and parents usually can identify Web sites that contain materials in these first two areas easily.

Before the explosive growth of the Internet, it was difficult for most K-12 students to obtain and view objectionable materials, such as pornographic magazines. Today, anybody with Internet access can view a vast array of obscene and other inappropriate materials on the Web. Many people want to ban such materials from the Internet, whereas others would only restrict objectionable materials so that

Web Info

For more information about Web page guidelines, visit the Computer Concepts CourseMate Web site at *www.cengagebrain. com*, navigate to the Chapter 8 Web Info resource for this book, and then click Guidelines.

these materials are not available to minors. Opponents argue that banning any material violates the constitutional right of free speech. Opponents state that instead of limiting Internet access and materials, schools should teach students right from wrong. As you integrate technologies into your classroom, you must always be vigilant. Be sure your students do not encounter objectionable material, and if they encounter objectionable material, be sure your students know what to do.

The third area includes Web sites that contain incorrect material and thus are inappropriate for K-12 students. Identifying this type of Web page is more difficult than identifying the first two. Because anyone can create and publish a Web page or Web site, some people deliberately create and publish material on Web pages to fool unsuspecting people. Young students are extremely vulnerable to being fooled by these sites. These Web sites appear perfectly appropriate for K-12 students but contain information that is historically and otherwise inaccurate. Be sure your students know how to recognize if a Web site is from a credible source and if its content is accurate.

GOVERNMENT ACTIONS

Over the past two decades, many government actions have helped protect children from being exploited, including numerous Internet-related initiatives. One success story is the Children's Internet Protection Act, which is covered in the next section.

CHILDREN'S INTERNET PROTECTION ACT

Congress passed the **Children's Internet Protection Act (CIPA)** in 2000 to protect children from obscene, pornographic, and other information considered harmful to minors. CIPA requires that public libraries install filtering software to block Web sites that contain obscene images or content. As you learned in Chapter 2, filtering software programs prevent browsers from displaying materials from targeted sites or sites that contain certain keywords or phrases. CIPA was challenged by opponents who argued that this law would obstruct appropriate, nonobscene material from being viewed. In July 2003, the U.S. Supreme Court upheld CIPA, arguing that it does not

violate freedom of speech. As a result, all public libraries must install filters on their computers to block access to online pornography or lose federal funding.

Many K-12 schools and parents have proactively taken steps to protect their students and children from the negative aspects of the Internet. Although only a small percentage of the information available on the Internet is unsuitable for children at home or in K-12 schools, educators agree that such materials have no place in classrooms. Teachers and parents need to ensure that children understand that inappropriate materials exist on the Internet. Children also need to understand that some individuals might try to exploit them via e-mail messages or in chat room conversations.

A recent and emerging trend is a phenomenon called cyberbullying. **Cyberbullying** is the posting or sending of detrimental or cruel text or images using the Internet or other digital devices. Students are most often the victim of cyberbullying just as they are with traditional bullying. However, students are not the only recipients of cyberbullying; recently, teachers also have been victims of cyberbullying. Students have been known to post cruel information about their teachers. All teachers need to be aware of the actions and consequences of cyberbullying and teach their students that bullying either in person or in cyberspace is wrong. Teachers also need to make sure their students understand that they can and will be held accountable for their actions, including criminal prosecution, if appropriate.

The following sections cover what we can do both as parents and educators to keep our children and students safe from the negative aspects of the Internet and digital media.

PARENTAL CONTROLS

As a teacher, you can tell parents about parental controls — tools they can use to prevent their children from accessing pornographic and other objectionable materials on the Internet. One option is to use the parental controls available with the Windows and Mac operating systems. Figure 8-28 discusses some settings available when using Windows to help set limits.

Web Info

For more information on cyberbullying, visit the Computer Concepts CourseMate Web site at *www. cengagebrain.com*, navigate to the Chapter 8 Web Info resource for this book, and then click Cyberbullying.

Web Info

For more information on parental controls, visit the Computer Concepts CourseMate Web site at *www. cengagebrain.com*, navigate to the Chapter 8 Web Info resource for this book, and then click Parental Controls for Windows or Parental Controls for Mac OS.

Windows Settings	Additional Information for Parental Controls in Windows
Time limits	Use to set specific time limits on your children's computer use. Time limits prevent children from logging on during specified hours, such as afternoon homework time period. You can set different logon hours for every day of the week. If they are logged on when their allotted time ends, they will be logged off automatically.
Games	Use to prevent your children from playing games you do not want them to play. Allows you to control access to games, choose an age rating level (based upon the Entertainment Software Rating Board), choose the types of content you want to block, and decide whether you want to allow or block specific games.
Allow and block specific programs	Use to prevent your children from running specific programs that you do not want them to run.

Figure 8-28 Information on the various Windows settings (parental options) you can set when using Windows 7. To learn more, use Windows Help.

The first step when using Windows or Mac OS parental controls is to create a separate user account for each child and then set up the various controls, which can be different for each child and member of a household. For example, a seven year old probably should have different restrictions than a high school senior. To set up a new account for a child when using Windows, click Start, click Control Panel, and then click Set up parental controls for any user. Figure 8-29 shows the parental control options available when using Windows 7. Once parental controls have been set up, Activity Reports are available for review. To set up parental controls when using Mac OS, click the Apple menu, System Preferences, and then Accounts.

Parental controls and features available with Mac OS are similar to those for Windows users with a few additional controls: (1) Securing the cookie jar or preventing kids from many inappropriate computer issues; (2) creating a personal post office so a child can only exchange e-mail with people the parent identifies; (3) the don't talk to strangers feature that lets the parent decide who a child can chat with online.

Another effective approach to blocking objectionable materials is to install filtering software programs on any computer with Internet access. Many filtering software programs allow parents to filter harmful Web sites, restrict Internet access, monitor children's online activities, and prevent children from accidentally providing personal information in e-mail messages or in chat rooms (Figure 8-30).

Finally, the best way for parents to protect children is to monitor their

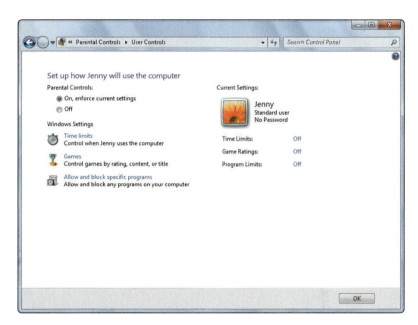

Figure 8-29 Shown are the various parental control options when using Windows 7.

Figure 8-30 Net Nanny is a popular Internet filtering software program.

children's activities while on the Internet both by direct and indirect observations. One technique is to keep the family computer in the family room or in an area where you can observe your children while they are working on the computer.

Because it is difficult to always monitor or observe children's Internet activities directly, you can check which Internet sites children are visiting by viewing the browser's history list (Figure 8-31). This simple but effective technique is useless, however, if children are allowed to clear the history list.

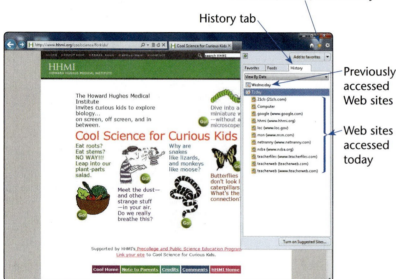

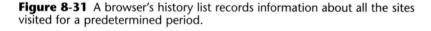

Figure 8-31 A browser's history list records information about all the sites visited for a predetermined period.

Web Info

For more information on filtering programs, visit the Computer Concepts CourseMate Web site at *www. cengagebrain.com*, navigate to the Chapter 8 Web Info resource for this book, and then click Filtering Programs.

EDUCATIONAL CONTROLS

As you have learned, businesses and parents have several available options to control access to inappropriate Internet sites. Most school districts also control student access to objectionable materials by implementing these controls and a few additional ones. For schools, attacking this problem requires a four-pronged approach: filtering software, Acceptable Use Policies, use of curriculum resource pages, and teacher observation, as discussed in the following sections.

FILTERING SOFTWARE As previously discussed, filtering software programs

prevent the browser from accepting material from targeted sites or material that contains keywords or phrases. A filtering software program is the first level of protection that many school districts use. Schools install Internet filtering software on their networks and then constantly update the software programs to keep them as current as possible. Although very effective, these filtering software programs do not prevent access to all objectionable and inappropriate materials. One drawback to using filtering software is that it also can block access to legitimate materials or research on controversial issues.

ACCEPTABLE USE POLICIES As discussed in Chapter 2, an Acceptable Use Policy (AUP) is a set of rules that governs the use of school and school district computers, networks, and the Internet by teachers, administrators, staff, and students. AUPs vary greatly from school district to school district. Many schools have separate AUPs for students, teachers, and staff. Many school districts require both students and their parents to sign the AUPs. Some schools publish their AUPs on their Web sites (Figure 8-32), which allows new students and parents to print, review, sign, and return them to the school. Schools normally will not allow students or teachers to access the school's network or Internet unless a signed AUP is on file. Many AUPs contain the following elements:

- A notice that use of school computers, networks, and the Internet is a privilege, not a right

- A notice that students should behave as guests when on the Internet — that is, they should use good manners and be courteous

- A list of rules and consequences concerning accessing objectionable Internet sites

- A list of rules and consequences dealing with copyright issues

- An outline of proper use of all networks and computers

- A list of rules covering online safety and release of personal information

- A notice that students who violate the AUP will face disciplinary action and possibly permanent cancellation of school network and/or Internet access privileges

CURRICULUM RESOURCE PAGES As you learned in Chapter 7, a curriculum resource page is a teacher-created document or Web page that contains hyperlinks to teacher selected and evaluated Web sites. Links on a curriculum resource page support learning objectives by providing students with quality Web resources and links to additional information about a specific topic. Using a curriculum resource page offers several advantages. Students quickly link to excellent sites, instead of the various locations they might find from searching the Internet for information. Because the teacher evaluates the linked sites for content and appropriateness, a curriculum resource page significantly reduces the chance students will view an inappropriate site. Furthermore, by providing links for students to click, a curriculum resource page eliminates the need for students to type URLs. Students often make mistakes typing URLs, which, in addition to wasting time, sometimes links them to inappropriate or incorrect sites.

TEACHER OBSERVATION Teacher observation or supervision permits teachers to monitor their students actively and continuously while they are on the Internet (Figure 8-33). Teacher observation is extremely important and, in most cases, the most effective step in preventing students from accessing objectionable and inappropriate materials on the Internet. For teacher observation to be effective, teachers must constantly and actively watch what their students are doing in the classroom and viewing on the Internet. Teachers should direct students that, if they access an Internet site that contains objectionable material, they should immediately click their browser's Back button to return to the previous page and if this does not work simply close the browser. Either is a quick-and-easy way to prevent objectionable material from displaying in the browser. You also might want students to notify you if such a situation arises so that you can add that site to the sites restricted by the filtering software. Some schools have installed software

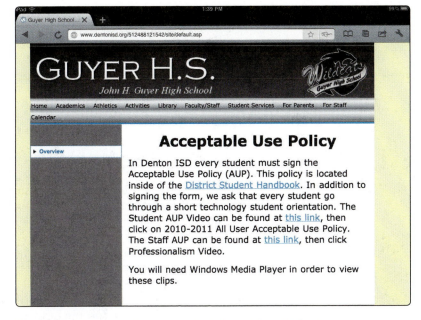

Figure 8-32 Many schools include AUPs on their Web sites so new teachers, students, and parents can print, review, sign, and then deliver the signed AUP to the school.

Figure 8-33 Teacher observations can prevent students from viewing objectionable or inappropriate material on the Internet.

programs on their lab computers, such as Apple's Remote Desktop for Mac computers, which enables teachers to keep an eye on all the computer screens in a classroom or lab.

As a final note, all educators should understand clearly the ethical issues covered in this chapter in order to model these concepts for their students and teach them to be ethical computer users. The questionnaire shown in Figure 8-34 on the next page will help you further understand these ethical concepts.

COMPUTER ETHICS QUESTIONNAIRE

	Ethical	Unethical	Crime
1. A teacher uses her computer at school to send e-mail to her friends and family.	☐	☐	☐
2. A teacher uses the Web at school to access stock market reports. He leaves the Web connection running in the background all day so that he can periodically check the market.	☐	☐	☐
3. A principal installs a new version of a word processing program on her office computer. Because no one will be using the old version, she installs it on her home computer so her husband and children can use it.	☐	☐	☐
4. While checking teachers' e-mail messages, the principal finds that one of his teachers is using the district's e-mail system to bet on football games and does nothing about it.	☐	☐	☐
5. A school technology facilitator has her students develop PowerPoint tutorials. When the projects are completed, she offers to sell the tutorials to another school.	☐	☐	☐
6. A principal tells a teacher to install a piece of software on numerous computers on campus. The teacher knows the software has a single-user license but, because the principal said to install it, he does.	☐	☐	☐
7. Personnel in the district's computer center occasionally monitor computer use in the schools. They monitor how often and for what length of time particular teachers are connected to the Internet, as well as what sites have been visited.	☐	☐	☐
8. The media specialist uses photo retouching software to put her school name on another school's logo.	☐	☐	☐
9. A teacher downloads a piece of shareware software. He uses it for the allotted time and when asked to pay for the software, he simply closes the window and continues to use it.	☐	☐	☐
10. An educational learning company contacts a principal requesting information about students, including names and addresses. The company offers to provide students with free learning supplements. The principal sends the company her student database.	☐	☐	☐
11. Your students are creating Web pages. They search the Internet for ideas. One of them finds a very cool home page, copies the page, changes the name, and uses it as her own.	☐	☐	☐
12. You use clip art from the Disney Web site for your curriculum resource page on famous cartoon characters.	☐	☐	☐
13. Two of your students have posted cruel and malicious information about a teacher you know from another school.	☐	☐	☐

Figure 8-34 Indicate whether you think each described situation is ethical, unethical, or a crime. Discuss your answers with other teachers; use this questionnaire as a springboard for a discussion about computer ethics with your students.

Green Computing

Green computing involves reducing the use of electricity and the production of environmental waste while using a computer. People use, and often waste, resources such as electricity and paper while using a computer. Society and schools have become aware of this waste and are taking measures to combat it. Figure 8-35 lists the ways you and your students can contribute to green computing.

Health Issues

Because users are the key component in any information system, protecting teachers and students is just as important as protecting hardware, software, and data. Many health-related issues concerning computer use can be minimized by teaching students at an early age how to use computers properly so they reduce their risk of injury. The following sections discuss health risks and preventions.

COMPUTERS AND HEALTH ISSUES

The Bureau of Labor Statistics reports that work-related musculoskeletal disorders account for one-third of all job-related injuries and illnesses. A **musculoskeletal disorder (MSD)**, also called **repetitive strain injury (RSI)**, is an injury or disorder of the muscles, nerves, tendons, ligaments, and joints. The largest job-related injury and illness problems in the United States today are repetitive strain injuries. For this reason, the Occupational Safety and Health Administration (OSHA) has developed industry-specific and task-specific guidelines designed to prevent workplace injuries with respect to computer usage.

Computer-related RSIs include **tendonitis** and **carpal tunnel syndrome (CTS)**. Tendonitis is inflammation of a tendon due to some repeated motion or stress on the tendon. **CTS** is inflammation of the nerve that connects the forearm to the palm of the wrist. Repeated or forceful bending of the wrist can cause either tendonitis of the wrist or CTS. Symptoms of tendonitis of the wrist include extreme pain that extends from the forearm to the hand, along with tingling in the fingers. Symptoms of CTS include burning pain when the nerve is compressed, along with numbness and tingling in the thumb and first two fingers.

Long-term computer use can lead to tendonitis or CTS. Factors that cause these disorders include prolonged typing and mouse usage, or continual shifting between the mouse and the keyboard. However, you can take many precautions to prevent these types of injuries both for yourself and your students. Take frequent breaks during computer sessions to exercise your hands and arms. To prevent injury due to typing, place a wrist rest between the keyboard and the edge of your desk. The wrist rest reduces strain on your wrist while typing. To prevent injury while using a mouse, place the mouse at least six inches from the edge of the desk. Finally, minimize the number of times you switch between the mouse and the keyboard, and avoid using the heel of your hand as a pivot point while typing or using the mouse.

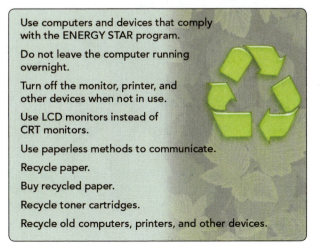

Use computers and devices that comply with the ENERGY STAR program.

Do not leave the computer running overnight.

Turn off the monitor, printer, and other devices when not in use.

Use LCD monitors instead of CRT monitors.

Use paperless methods to communicate.

Recycle paper.

Buy recycled paper.

Recycle toner cartridges.

Recycle old computers, printers, and other devices.

Figure 8-35 A few green computing tips.

People who spend their workday using the computer sometimes complain of lower back pain, muscle fatigue, and emotional fatigue. Lower back pain sometimes is caused by poor posture. Always sit and have your students sit properly in the chair. Take a short break every 30 to 60 minutes — stand up, walk around, or stretch.

Another type of health-related condition due to computer usage is **computer vision syndrome (CVS)**. You may have CVS if you have any of these conditions: sore, tired, burning, itching, or dry eyes; blurred or double vision; distance-blurred vision after prolonged staring at a display device; headache or sore neck; difficulty shifting focus between a display device and documents; difficulty focusing on the screen image; color fringes or after-images when you look away from the display device; and increasing sensitivity to light. Although eyestrain associated with CVS is not thought to have serious or long-term consequences, it is disruptive and unpleasant. Figure 8-36 outlines some techniques you can follow to ease eyestrain.

Techniques to Ease Eyestrain

Every 10 to 15 minutes, take an eye break.
- Look into the distance and focus on an object for 20 to 30 seconds.
- Roll your eyes in a complete circle.
- Close and rest your eyes for one minute.

Blink your eyes every five seconds.

Place your display device about an arm's length away from your eyes with the top of the screen at eye level or below.

Use large fonts.

Ask your doctor about computer glasses.

Adjust the lighting.

Figure 8-36 Tips to reduce computer-related eyestrain.

ERGONOMICS

Ergonomics is an applied science devoted to incorporating comfort, efficiency, and safety into the design of items in the workplace (Figure 8-37). Ergonomic studies have shown that using the correct type and configuration of chair, keyboard, display device, and work surface helps

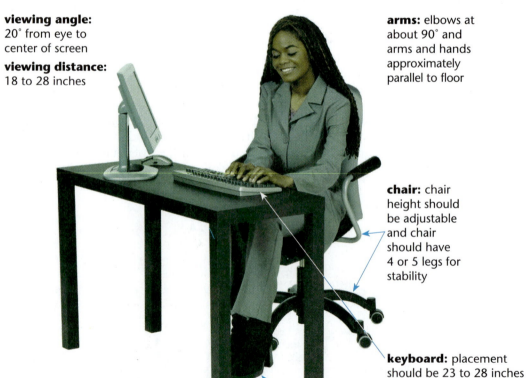

viewing angle: 20° from eye to center of screen

viewing distance: 18 to 28 inches

arms: elbows at about 90° and arms and hands approximately parallel to floor

chair: chair height should be adjustable and chair should have 4 or 5 legs for stability

keyboard: placement should be 23 to 28 inches depending on height of user

feet: flat on floor

Figure 8-37 A well-designed work area is essential to good health.

users work comfortably and efficiently, and helps protect their health.

Many display devices and keyboards have features that help address ergonomic issues. Some keyboards have built-in wrist rests and can be purchased from any computer supply store. Other keyboards are ergonomically designed specifically to prevent RSI. Display devices usually have controls that allow you to adjust the brightness, contrast, positioning, height, and width of images. Most monitors have a tilt-and-swivel base, allowing you to adjust the angle of the screen to minimize neck strain and reduce glare from overhead lighting.

The Changing Classroom

The classrooms and schools you attended throughout your PK-12 education probably were similar to the classrooms your parents attended. For some of you, the schools and furniture were exactly the same; you may even have sat in the same desk that your mother or father did. Even more striking, you and your parent's educational experience were probably very similar. Unlike society, which has changed dramatically, many schools and school curricula have been slow to change during the past few decades — *until now*.

Due to emerging technologies (primarily wireless technologies, tablet computers, and apps), public education is undergoing profound and fundamental changes. The one teacher to 18-26 students F2F model that has worked well for over two centuries is morphing into a combination of F2F with varying class sizes, blended, and online programs and schools. This morphing also is being driven by twenty-first century and worldwide economic and school budget realities.

Summary of Security Issues and Ethics in Education

The livelihood of businesses, schools, and individuals depends on the computers and networks in use every day. This increased reliance on computers and information sent over networks makes it essential to take steps to protect the systems and information from known risks. At the same time, employees, teachers, and students also have an obligation to use computers responsibly and not abuse the power computers provide. This responsibility presents constant challenges, which sometimes weigh the rights of the individual against increased efficiency and productivity. Schools have the added responsibility and challenge of protecting their students from unethical practices and people.

Educational technologies are tools, and their effectiveness is determined by the knowledge, skill, experience, level of training, and ethics of the user. The educational technology knowledge you acquire should help you participate more effectively in decisions on how to use computers and other educational technologies, and how to use the Internet efficiently and ethically.

Summary of Teachers Discovering Computers

To be effective in using educational technology in their classrooms, teachers must be computer literate, information literate, and most importantly, integration literate. This textbook provided you with knowledge and skills in all three areas. What you have learned is only a beginning. You must continuously update your technology and technology integration skills so you can use and integrate technology into your curriculum and in so doing influence future generations in immensely positive ways (Figure 8-38).

Figure 8-38 Teachers make a difference in the quality of their students' education when they integrate technology effectively.

access control [417]
antispam program [428]
antivirus program [416]

backup [425]
backup procedure [425]
biometric device [418]
blackout [424]
boot sector virus [413]
brownout [424]

carpal tunnel syndrome (CTS) [439]
Children's Internet Protection Act (CIPA) [434]
community/state site license [422]
computer crime [412]
computer ethics [426]
computer security risk [412]
computer vandalism [420]
computer vision syndrome (CVS) [440]
copyright [428]
cracker [417]
cyberbullying [434]

electronic profile [426]
e-mail filtering [428]
employee monitoring [428]
encryption [423]
encryption key [423]
end-user license agreement (EULA) [420]
ergonomics [440]
ethics [426]

fair use [430]
file virus [413]
firewall [419]
freeware [422]

green computing [439]

hacker [417]

information privacy [426]

logic bomb [414]

macro virus [413]
malicious software programs [413]
Michelangelo virus [414]
musculoskeletal disorder (MSD) [439]

network site license [422]

objectionable material [433]
off-site location [425]
overvoltage [424]

password [417]
personal firewall [419]
personal identification number (PIN) [418]
phishing [427]
possessed object [418]
power surge [424]
product activation [421]
proxy server [419]
public domain [432]

repetitive strain injury (RSI) [439]
rescue disc [416]
restore [425]
rootkit [414]

shareware [422]
single-user license agreement [420]
site license [422]
software license [420]
software piracy [420]
spam [427]
spike [424]
spim [427]
split [427]
surge protector [424]
system failure [423]

teacher observation [437]
tendonitis [439]
time bomb [414]
Trojan horse [413]

unauthorized access [417]
unauthorized use [417]
undervoltage [424]
uninterruptible power supply (UPS) [424]
user ID [417]

vaccine [416]
virus [412]
virus hoax [417]
virus payload [413]

worm [413]

1. Label the Figure

Instructions: Identify each type of software license.

Type of License	Characteristics	Use in Schools
1. _____	Software can be installed on only one computer. Some license agreements allow users to install the software on one desktop computer and one notebook computer.	Used when a school needs only a few copies of a particular software. Commonly found in small schools and when purchasing specialized software programs.
2. _____	Software can be installed on a set number of computers, typically 5, 10, 50, or more. Cost varies based on number of computers.	Cost-effective method to install software on more than one computer. Most commonly used in schools.
3. _____	Software is installed on the school's network. The license will specify and the software will control a specific number of simultaneous users, such as 50, 100, 250, or 500. Cost varies based on number of computers.	Cost-effective method of allowing students and teachers throughout the school to have access to an application software program.
4. _____	Frequently used with software distributed on CDs/DVDs. Any number of programs can be purchased for either Macintosh or PC platforms.	Very cost-effective method for school districts or states to purchase large quantities of software. Savings can be significant over individual CD or DVD pricing.

2. Matching

Instructions: Match each term from the column on the left with the best description from the column on the right.

_____ 1. filtering software
_____ 2. cyberbullying
_____ 3. Trojan horse
_____ 4. Web publishing
_____ 5. computer ethics

a. posting or sending detrimental or cruel text or images using the Internet or digital devices
b. moral guidelines that govern the use of computers, networks, and information systems
c. prevents a browser from displaying materials from certain Web sites
d. a virus designed to look like a legitimate program
e. the development and maintenance of Web pages

3. Short Answer

Instructions: Write a brief answer to each of the following questions.

1. What are computer security risks? What different types of security risks threaten school computers? What are some safeguards that minimize security risks?
2. What is a virus? Describe three types of viruses. Why are viruses commonly found in schools? What can teachers do to minimize the impact of viruses both at home and at school?
3. What are computer ethics? List and briefly explain five important areas of computer ethics. Describe two recent government actions that protect children while using the Internet.
4. What is an overvoltage? What precautions should teachers take to protect their computers and other electronic equipment from overvoltages, both at home and at school?
5. What is an Acceptable Use Policy (AUP)? Why are AUPs so important for K-12 schools? Describe two other ways to limit student access to inappropriate Internet sites.

Instructions: Teaching Today provides teachers with integration strategies and ideas for teaching and, more importantly, reaching today's digital generation. Each numbered segment contains one or more links that reinforce the information presented in the segment. To display this page from the Web, visit the Computer Concepts CourseMate Web site at www.cengagebrain.com, and then navigate to the Chapter 8 Teaching Today resource for this book.

1. Teachers Helping Parents

Using the Internet in your classroom can be an important and easy way to integrate technology; there are so many resources, Web sites, and online tools available for teachers to use in every grade level. Did you ever wonder how parents feel about their children using the Internet? What kinds of concerns do you think they might have? According to the National School Board Association (NSBA), most parents support the use of the Internet in the classroom. Parents also believe that using the Internet is an excellent resource for learning and communications. The NSBA reports that most parents who purchase computers for their children to use, do so to help their children with their education. Teachers need to help parents understand the benefits and pitfalls of their children's Internet and Web usage.

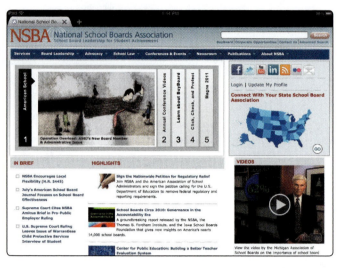

2. Acceptable Use Policy

You are an innovative teacher with three multimedia computers connected to the Internet in your classroom. You also have access to a wireless mobile lab and many other technologies. Your school has a schoolwide Acceptable Use Policy (AUP) for teachers, staff, students, and parents. You have been thinking, however, about having an additional AUP for your students and their parents, not only to protect the students, but also to have your students learn how to use different technologies responsibly and safely. What key components do you think your AUP should include? Do you think you should let your students help you create the AUP? Do you think this might be a good learning experience for the students? Why or why not? What are some consequences you think students should face for violating your classroom AUP? How will you enforce the AUP with students and parents?

3. Computer Viruses

Recently, you have been hearing a lot about viruses. You have two computers in your classroom and they are connected to the Internet. In the past, you have not worried about viruses because your computers have never been infected. Other teachers, however, have been discussing a new virus affecting their computers. Where can you get reliable information about viruses? What kind of support is available on the Internet? Can you get a virus from the Internet? How can you protect your computers from getting a virus?

4. Fair Use

Based on Section 107 of the Copyright Act of 1976, also known as fair use, teachers are allowed to photocopy and use a limited amount of copyrighted materials in their classrooms under specific conditions for educational purposes. With the advent of digital media, the Internet, and the World Wide Web, legislators have had to reexamine fair use. Many teachers and students wrongly think they can copy anything from the Web and it becomes theirs. Is using materials found on the Web different from using materials found in a copyrighted book? How can you determine if your use of copyrighted materials is governed by fair-use rules? Because it has become so easy to copy materials from so many different sources, how will you teach your students about copyright laws and fair use?

Education Issues

Instructions: Education Issues provides several scenarios that allow you to explore controversial and current issues in education. Each numbered segment contains one or more links that reinforce the information presented in the segment. To display this page from the Web, visit the Computer Concepts CourseMate Web site at www. cengagebrain.com, and then navigate to the Chapter 8 Education Issues resource for this book.

1. Essays, Research, and Term Papers

For years, the only way to write a paper was to visit the library and walk through shelves of texts and journals to find what you needed; however, things have changed — the most used source for locating information is now the Internet. Students can gather articles, books, and all types of resources using any computer; most resources can simply be downloaded. Today, several Web sites provide a searchable database of term papers gathered from college and high school students. Students can download a research or term paper, make any necessary changes, print a copy, and then turn it in as their own. How can instructors keep students from claiming the work of others as their own? Explain how using the Web for research differs from using it to copy someone's work. What should be the consequences for plagiarizing content from a Web site?

2. Teacher and Student Monitoring

Your school district maintains a policy that states classroom computers and Internet access are to be used for instructional purposes only. The district instructs teachers not to send or receive personal e-mail messages or instant messages (IMs), surf the Internet for fun, or play games on classroom computers. The district uses monitoring software to observe Internet activities. Some teachers feel they should be allowed to use the Internet or work on their personal projects during their lunch periods and after school. What limits, if any, should be placed on teachers' use of classroom computers? How closely should the school district be able to monitor teacher and student use? Why? Network specialists can see anything and everything on your computer. Should administrative personnel be allowed to monitor your e-mail messages and files on your school computer? Why or why not? Should you be allowed to monitor your students' e-mail messages? Why or why not?

3. Software Ethics

You recently purchased an educational multimedia DVD using your own funds for use on one computer in your classroom. Another teacher borrows your DVD so she can evaluate it for use in her classroom. A few weeks later, you find out that numerous other teachers in your school have a copy of the DVD. You ask the teacher about this and she says, "Oh, this is so cool. I have a DVD-RW on my home computer and it is so easy to copy DVDs. I am so proud of myself! I made one for everyone!" You know this breaks copyright laws, could get the school fined, and that it also is morally and ethically wrong. What to do? Should you tell the teacher, your principal, or technology facilitator? Could you be liable because you loaned her the original DVD? How will you solve this dilemma?

4. Software Piracy

Software manufacturers are watching school districts closely for evidence of illegal use of software. Recently, a major school district was fined $300,000 for having multiple copies of nonlicensed software installed on classroom computers. Teachers often illegally install multiple copies of single-user programs on their classroom computers. What are some of the ethical issues regarding software piracy? How does the software industry deal with violators of software copyright law? Describe several ways in which school districts can prevent illegal software from being installed on school computers.

5. Students, School Buses and Lunches, and Biometrics

A Florida school district requires that students provide a biometric thumbprint both as they enter and as they leave their GPS-tracked school buses each day. The school system cites both safety and financial (the fact that more accurate counting and tracking of the bus usage will result in more state transportation funds) reasons for using GPS. Many school systems now require students to use a biometric thumbprint to pay for their school lunches. The school board cites the need to keep better track of the number of free and subsidized lunches that the schools provide. Should children be required to provide biometric information to engage in common public school-related activities? Why or why not? What are the privacy issues involved and should parents be concerned?

Apps Corner

Instructions: Apps Corner provides extensive ideas and resources for integrating technology into your classroom-specific curriculum. To display this page from the Web and its links to approximately 100 educational Web sites, visit the Computer Concepts CourseMate Web site at www.cengagebrain.com, and then navigate to the Chapter 8 Apps Corner resource for this book.

Apps Corner is designed for teachers and other educators who are looking for innovative ways to integrate apps into their content-specific curriculum. Apps Corner not only provides great apps with current information but also shows how other educators are using and integrating education apps. As a result, Apps Corner is designed with all educators in mind, regardless of their interests or subject area. You can use Apps Corner to expand your resources by reviewing apps outside your curriculum area; remember many apps associated with one curriculum area can be adapted for use and added to lesson plans in a wide variety of other curriculum areas.

Use Apps Corner as a springboard for collaborating and sharing the successes and hurdles of integrating apps in a classroom or an entire school system. Consider Apps Corner a place to locate app integration ideas and resources. Information on educational apps are organized in four Corners (Early Childhood, Elementary, Middle School, and Secondary), and different apps are available for each chapter. Many apps are free, others cost from $1 to $5. Inexpensive site licenses for classrooms, schools, and school districts are available for many apps.

Shown are two highly rated education apps. The first one is an inexpensive and interactive app, Units — The Unit Converter, for students of all ages and used to supplement any lesson on unit conversions. The second, Shape-O ABCs, is an app for young students that encourages learning through play.

Software Corner

INSTRUCTIONS: Software Corner provides information on popular software programs. Each numbered segment discusses specific software programs and contains a link to additional information about these programs. To display this page from the Web, visit the Computer Concepts CourseMate Web site at www.cengagebrain.com, and then navigate to the Chapter 8 Software Corner resource for this book.

1. Antivirus Programs

Computer viruses spread faster than the common cold! When you and your students download files from the Internet, open e-mail attachments, or transport files between computers, you are at risk of getting a virus. Norton AntiVirus or McAfee's VirusScan will detect viruses in e-mail attachments, in files, on USB flash drives, and in your computer's system files. Both companies allow users to update their virus protection files online. These antivirus programs can be set up to scan your computer automatically on a regular basis. Their Web sites provide information about the latest viruses as well as news releases and virus tips to help consumers better protect themselves.

2. Ad-Aware

When using the Internet, problems are sometimes just one click away. Students are often lured by the "You have won!" pop-up ads that display on numerous Web sites. Unfortunately, many Web sites, including those with pop-up ads, install hidden files on computers that visit these sites. These hidden files cannot be removed by antivirus programs and, unfortunately, slow computers down significantly, sometimes even shutting down routers. One software program that can "sniff" out these files and quarantine or remove them from your computer is called Ad-Aware and it is free. This program allows you to scan and clean your computer's internal and external storage devices for annoying adware and spyware programs, allowing you to maintain a higher degree of privacy while you surf the Web.

3. Monitoring Software

Having an AUP is not always enough! Due to all the types of illegal activities that can take place using computers, many businesses, the military, and schools are purchasing software to monitor all activities on their computers. Spector Pro is one of the top-selling software programs for monitoring and recording every detail or keystroke of PC and Internet activity. Spector Pro provides the equivalent of a digital surveillance tape so that you can see everything students, teachers, or employees are doing on their computers. Spector Pro contains integrated tools that record the following: chats, instant messages, e-mails sent and received, Web sites visited, search activities, keystrokes typed, programs launched, and peer-to-peer file searching and swapping. In addition to monitoring and recording, Spector Pro has an advanced warning system that informs the system administrator when a PC being monitored has been used in an inappropriate manner.

4. Spyware Protection

Using the Internet can be wonderful because it opens your life to many different worlds. Unfortunately, it also opens your computer up to multiple security risks, making it important for you to protect it from invasion at all times. Windows Defender is a free program from Microsoft that protects your computer against multiple security risks. When used with other security programs, it adds to your computer's safety net. You can protect your computer from unwanted software attacks caused by spyware, pop-ups, viruses, and other security threats. A super feature of this software is the support for assistive technology for individuals who have physical or cognitive difficulties, impairments, and other disabilities. Another option is Spyware Doctor for Windows, recommended by PC World as one of the best spyware software programs.

Digital Media Corner

Instructions: Today's K-12 digital students need their learning to be meaningful and relevant to their lives. Digital Media Corner provides videos, ideas, and examples of how you can use digital media to enhance your teaching and your students' learning. To access the videos and links to additional information, visit the Computer Concepts CourseMate Web site at www.cengagebrain.com, and then navigate to the Chapter 8 Digital Media Corner resource for this book.

1. Mobile Learning and iTunes U

iTunes University (iTunes U) is a Web tool designed for higher education faculty, yet it has a global appeal by providing a centralized repository for storing courses, lectures, activities, presentations, video, audio, and more. Content is mostly tied to specific curricula and courses but it also contains other general information, which includes broad topics (such as geography, science, and technology) and specific topics (such as global warming and why baseballs have stitches). iTunes University is hosted on the iTunes Store and is devoted to education. Subscribers (enrolling free of charge) are given access to thousands of audio and video files. You also can access iTunes U directly on your iPad, iPhone, or iPod Touch by tapping the iTunes app and then tapping the iTunes U link. The popularity of iTunes U has grown and is a significant contributor to the schools without walls concept.

2. iWeb

Teachers are always looking for easy, user-friendly solutions to create Web pages for themselves and their students. Apple's iWeb, a template-based Web creation tool, is included with the iLife Suite. iWeb allows users to create and publish curriculum resource pages easily, Web sites, blogs, and wikis. It contains templates and themed design tools for those new to Web site creation, requiring very little previous knowledge. Once the theme is chosen, users can drag and drop photos, movies, and other media onto the pages in the placeholders provided.

3. Protecting Your Computer

You must protect your computer from many different security risks, such as viruses, unauthorized software attacks, and even spyware. Some programs install spyware when the program is installed, so you may be unaware your computer has spyware programs on it. Different types of spyware exist, such as keystroke recorder spyware and advertising spyware. There are videos on the Web that you can use to learn more about these threats; you also can use these video resources to teach your students about viruses and other programs that can harm computers.

4. Teacher Vlogs

One teaching technique that is being embraced by many educators and students is video blogging, also called vlogging. No longer do teachers have to depend solely on lectures and textbooks alone to convey the subject matter. Popular sites such as YouTube, SchoolTube, and TeacherTube have thousands of teacher vlogs posted that are accessible for anyone in the world to view. There are many reasons why teachers use a vlog in the classroom to supplement their curriculum. Some examples include videos for reviewing lessons, demonstrations, school events, student projects, and creating teacher professional development videos. The basic requirements to get started include a basic video camera, computer with video editing software, and an Internet connection.

5. Video Yearbooks

Video yearbooks are not a new idea but some schools are trying a new idea. At the beginning of the school year, selected seniors are designated as journalists who are asked to record their daily lives and activities their senior year. Using smartphones or small handheld digital cameras, these journals are recorded and uploaded as video blogs or vlogs to a senior class Web site. These informal digital journals are then released to the students who can follow along. At the end of the year, the vlogs are consolidated using video postproduction editing techniques so they can be saved to a DVD for distribution as a video yearbook or combined with the traditional paper version of the yearbooks.

1. What Is the Federal Accessibility Initiative?

In 1998, Congress amended the Rehabilitation Act to require federal agencies to make their electronic and information technology accessible to people with disabilities. Under Section 508, agencies must give all persons with disabilities access to technology that is comparable to the access available to others. In addition, the World Wide Web Consortium (W3C) has developed accessibility guidelines encouraging Web authors worldwide to create accessible pages.

2. What Are Accessible Web Pages?

Accessible Web pages are constructed to be usable by anyone, even if the person is using assistive technology to access the Web page. Examples of assistive technologies are screen readers, screen magnifiers, voice recognition software, alternative keyboards, and Braille displays. We speak of accessible Web pages as being Section 508 compliant, or meeting Web accessibility guidelines.

3. Do I Have to Make My Web Pages Accessible?

The Individuals with Disabilities Education Act (IDEA) of 1997 (with significant funding allocated under the The American Recovery and Reinvestment Act of 2009) guarantees access to curriculum for all users. Many school districts have accessibility policies in place and compliance with those policies is a professional responsibility. After a teacher-created Web page is posted, all should have access to it, including persons with disabilities.

4. So, How Can I Make My Pages Accessible?

An educator can consider the following issues when developing Web pages to meet accessibility guidelines.

1. **Use valid code.** WYSIWYG (What You See Is What You Get) programs for Web authoring, such as Dreamweaver, have means for checking that the HTML code in the pages is valid (correct). Use the option to check code validity in your program of choice.
2. **Use CSS (Cascading Style Sheets) when formatting pages.** In the preferences of your WYSIWYG program, choose anything that says, Use CSS.
3. **Provide text alternatives to images.** When you add an image to a page, write a descriptive phrase for the image, which a screen reader will voice.
4. **Make meaning independent of color.** "Click the red triangle" can be a difficult task for a color-blind person, but making each choice a different shape instead of a different color makes the task independent of color.
5. **Include visible text links** on a page for images that have hyperlinked hotspots.
6. **Use column-and-row tables for data only.** Put column and row headers in those data tables.
7. If you choose to use frames, be sure to **title each frame** you use.
8. **Do not depend on scripts** to make your Web site work. Some users (not only disabled users) may not be able to run the scripts.
9. **Caption video** before putting it on your site.
10. Provide users with an option to **skip repetitive links,** such as site navigation links.

Follow the instructions at the top of this page to display additional information and this chapter's links on assistive technologies.

In the Lab

Instructions: In the Lab provides rubric development exercises that are divided into two areas, productivity and integration. To access the links to tutorials, productivity ideas, integration examples and ideas, and more, visit the Computer Concepts CourseMate Web site at www.cengagebrain.com, and then navigate to the Chapter 8 In the Lab resource for this book.

PRODUCTIVITY IN THE CLASSROOM

Introduction: Effectively integrating technology in the curriculum allows students to demonstrate their learning using creative, motivating, and nontraditional means. Digital media projects and presentations, as well as other technology-oriented presentations provide students with authentic learning activities and require a different form of assessment. Rubrics can provide teachers with a more authentic assessment tool.

Chapter 7 introduced the use of rubrics as a means of alternative assessment. Rubrics assist students in understanding teacher expectations and provide a clear outline when creating projects. Students also can use rubrics as a self-assessment tool. This encourages students to be more involved with and responsible for their learning.

Teachers easily can create rubrics using numerous software applications, such as word processing, spreadsheet, Web editors, or other commercial products. Free online resources also are available that walk teachers through the process of creating a variety of rubrics and performance checklists.

1. Creating and Formatting a Problem-Solving Math Rubric

Problem: To encourage students in your sixth-grade math class to use higher-order thinking skills, you are beginning a unit on problem solving. Students will be given problems and have to write out how they solve the problem and their reasoning for selecting the approach they use. You design a rubric to guide your students through this process. The rubric is shown in Figure 8-39. Open your word processing, spreadsheet, or Web editing software and create the rubric as described in the following steps. (*Hint:* Use any appropriate clip art image and font to personalize the rubric. Use Help to understand the steps better.)

Instructions: Perform the following tasks.

1. Type the heading text shown in Figure 8-39.
2. Format the first heading line, Mrs. Georgiev's, in 20-point Times or Times New Roman bold font. Personalize the rubric by inserting your name instead of Mrs. Georgiev's.
3. Format the second heading line, 6th Grade Math Class, in 20-point Times or Times New Roman bold font.
4. Format the third heading line, Math Problem-Solving Rubric, in 18-point Times or Times New Roman font.
5. Insert appropriate clip art images.
6. Insert a table with six rows and five columns, then enter the table text as shown in Figure 8-39.
7. Center the row headings and format them in 11-point Times or Times New Roman bold font.
8. Format the remaining table text in 11-point Times or Times New Roman font.
9. Personalize the school name and insert the current date. Format the school name and date in 11-point Times or Times New Roman blue bold font. Insert your e-mail address instead of Mrs. Georgiev's. Format the e-mail address in 11-point Times or Times New Roman, blue bold font.
10. Save the rubric to the location file of your choice using an appropriate filename. Print the rubric and then follow your instructor's directions for handing in the assignment.

In the Lab

Mrs. Georgiev's
6th Grade Math Class
Math Problem-Solving Rubric

Task	Beginning 1 – 2	Developing 3 – 4	Advancing 5	Score
Student uses math language to explain the problem.	Used a few math terms in the explanation of the solution and the explanation was brief.	Used some math terms in the explanation of the solution and the explanation was adequate.	Used math terms correctly throughout the explanation of the solution and the explanation was thorough and complete.	
Student explanation demonstrates understanding of the problem.	Misinterpreted parts of the problem.	Solved the problem with minor interpretation errors.	Answer demonstrates complete understanding of the problem.	
Student articulates plan for solving the problem.	The plan for solving the problem is partially correct.	The plan for solving the problem is correct but may lead to minor errors.	The plan for solving the problem is accurate and will lead to a correct solution.	
Student correctly solves the problem.	The answer is incorrect or not solved.	Part of the problem is solved correctly.	The answer is correct and the work supports the answer.	
			TOTAL POINTS	

Woodrow Wilson Middle School
April 12, 2013
b_georgiev@tricounty.k12.ia.us

Figure 8-39

2. Creating and Formatting a Multimedia Research Rubric

Problem: You want to introduce your high school students to a systematic approach to research. The students will access, evaluate, and use information from a variety of sources on an assigned topic. Then they will write a research paper and create a digital media presentation to present their findings to the class. At the beginning of the unit, you hand out the rubric shown in Figure 8-40. (*Hint:* Use any appropriate clip art images and fonts to personalize the page. Use Help to understand the steps better.)

Mr. Hernandez
World History Class
Digital Media Research Project Rubric

Student Name: _____ Topic: _____ Date: _____

Research Process:	Level 1	Level 2	Level 3	Level 4	Self–Score	Teacher Score
Gathered information from books, journals, CD/DVDs, and the Internet	0 1 2	3 4 5	6 7 8	9 10		
Resources are current and reliable	0 1 2	3 4 5	6 7 8	9 10		
Extracted, synthesized, and applied appropriate information	0 1 2	3 4 5	6 7 8	9 10		

Writing Process:						
Organized information from resources to complete research paper	0 1 2	3 4 5	6 7 8	9 10		
Paper written following steps in writing process	0 1 2	3 4 5	6 7 8	9 10		
References documented using MLA citation style	0 1 2	3 4 5	6 7 8	9 10		

Multimedia Project:						
Presentation includes title slide, a minimum of seven content slides, and a bibliography slide	0 1 2	3 4 5	6 7 8	9 10		
Graphic images use a variety of resources are used appropriately	0 1 2	3 4 5	6 7 8	9 10		
Presentation is well organized, visually appealing, and flows well	0 1 2	3 4 5	6 7 8	9 10		

Presentation:						
Demonstrates good speaking skills	0 1 2	3 4 5	6 7 8	9 10		

TOTAL POINTS:						

Figure 8-40

In the Lab

Instructions: Refer to Figure 8-40. Type the rubric as shown in Figure 8-40, then format the rubric as directed in the text that follows. Format the first and second heading lines in 16-point Lucinda Sans Unicode bold font. Insert your name in place of Mr. Hernandez. Format the third heading line in 14-point Lucinda Sans Unicode bold font. Insert clip art or graphic images. Format the Student Name, Topic, and Date headings in 10-point Lucinda Sans Unicode bold font. Format the section headings in 10-point Lucinda Sans Unicode bold underlined font. Format the table text in 10-point Lucinda Sans Unicode font. Format the text in the last row with bold.

After you have typed and formatted the rubric, save the rubric to the location of your choice using an appropriate filename. Print the rubric and then follow your instructor's directions for handing in the assignment.

3. Creating and Formatting a Subject-Specific Rubric

Problem: You want to create a rubric to evaluate student learning of a concept you are presenting. The rubric also will serve as a guide for students as they create their end-of-unit project that demonstrates their learning.

Instructions: Create a rubric similar to the rubrics illustrated in Figures 8-39 and 8-40 on the previous pages. Use an appropriate layout; font types, styles, and sizes; and clip art images. Include your name and the subject area you teach. After you have created the rubric, save the rubric to the location of your choice using an appropriate filename. Print the rubric and then follow your instructor's directions for handing in the assignment.

INTEGRATION IN THE CLASSROOM

1. At the beginning of the school year, you want to establish classroom rules and criteria for positive behavior in your second-grade special education classroom. You decide to create a behavior rubric together with your students that will be used and sent home weekly to parents. You ask the students for their ideas about positive classroom behavior, and together, you and your students create a rubric on which you all agree. Create a sample behavior rubric for your students. Include your name, school name, and the current date on the rubric.

2. The students in your Earth Science class have been studying the environment and environmental hazards such as acid rain and oil spills. As a final project for the unit, students will work in groups and conduct a research activity. They will present their findings in either a PowerPoint presentation or a video. To encourage the students to take responsibility for their learning, you first assign each group to the task of developing a rubric that outlines the assessment criteria for their final project. You will assist the students as necessary; however, you believe they will have more ownership in their learning and be more motivated if they establish the majority of the criteria themselves. Create a sample rubric for your students to use as a guide. Include your name, subject area, project topic, and current date on the rubric.

3. To help your students understand rubrics, locate at least three different Web page evaluation rubrics. From your research, create a rubric to use as an example for your students. Include your name and class at the top of the rubric. Include your e-mail address and the current date at the bottom of the rubric. Then, ask your students to research Web page evaluation rubrics on the Internet. The students will work in groups to locate and print a minimum of five different Web page evaluation rubrics. They then will compare and contrast the different rubrics and determine what is important when creating a Web page. As a class, you will brainstorm, create a rubric, and then use this rubric to create Web pages. Include a column for self-evaluation. Share your rubric with the class and compare it with the class-generated one.

Learn It Online

Instructions: Use the Learn It Online exercises to reinforce your understanding of the chapter concepts and increase your computer, information, and integration literacy. To access dozens of interactive student labs, practice tests, learning games, and more, visit the Computer Concepts CourseMate Web site at www.cengagebrain.com, navigate to the Chapter 8 resources for this book, and then click the link for the resource you want to review.

1. At the Movies

Click the At the Movies link to review a video about computer viruses.

2. Free Virus Software

There are a number of free anti-virus programs that you can download and use to protect your computer from viruses, spyware, and more. Click the AVG Free Anti-Virus Program link to review one free program. After reviewing the AVG site, use Google to research the effectiveness of free anti-virus programs (including AVG), in addition, read user reviews and comments on AVG and other free programs. Write a one page summary of your research and reviewer comments and follow your instructor's submission instructions.

3. Using the Windows Firewall

When you use the Internet, data is sent both from your computer to the Internet and from computers on the Internet to your computer. A firewall is a barrier that checks information coming from the Internet and either turns it away or allows it to pass through to your computer, based upon your firewall settings. It also checks data being sent from your computer to the Internet to ensure your computer is not sending unsolicited messages. Click the Windows Firewall link to learn how to control the firewall usage on your computer.

4. Expanding Your Understanding

All states have content-specific accountability standards. To learn more about your state's content standards, click the State Standards link.

5. Practice Test

Click the Practice Test link. Answer each question. When completed, enter your name and click the Grade Test button to submit the quiz for grading. Make a note of any missed questions. If required, submit your score to your instructor.

6. Who Wants to Be a Computer Genius?

Click the Who Wants to Be a Computer Genius link to find out if you are a computer genius. When you are ready to play, click the Play button. If required, submit your score to your instructor.

7. Wheel of Terms

Click the Wheel of Terms link to reinforce important terms you learned in this chapter by playing the Shelly Cashman Series version of this popular game. When you are ready to play, click the Play button. If required, submit your score to your instructor.

8. Crossword Puzzle Challenge

Click the Crossword Puzzle Challenge link. Complete the puzzle to reinforce skills you learned in this chapter. When you are ready to play, click the Play button. If required, submit the completed puzzle to your instructor.

Appendix

References

This seventh Edition of *Teachers Discovering Computers* was created using information that was gathered, reviewed, and researched from various articles, books, Web sites, and other resources. You can review many of these resources by accessing the Computer Concepts CourseMate Web site for Teachers Discovering Computers at *www.cengagebrain.com*. The textbook Web site contains links to hundreds of resources, including many research articles and Web sites dedicated to educational theory, education practice, instructional models, and research-based integration solutions. The following are additional references that were used in the preparation of this textbook.

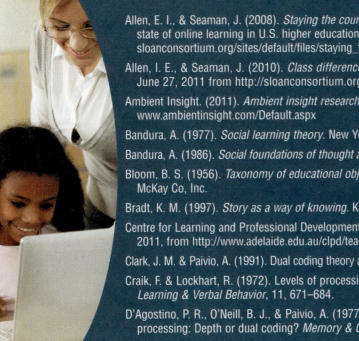

Allen, E. I., & Seaman, J. (2008). *Staying the course: Online education in the United States, 2008.* A report on the state of online learning in U.S. higher education. SLOAN-Consortium. Retrieved July 12, 2011, from http://sloanconsortium.org/sites/default/files/staying_the_course-2.pdf

Allen, I. E., & Seaman, J. (2010). *Class differences: Online education in the United States, 2010.* Retrieved June 27, 2011 from http://sloanconsortium.org/sites/default/files/class_differences.pdf

Ambient Insight. (2011). *Ambient insight research in the international news.* Retrieved April 20, 2011, from http://www.ambientinsight.com/Default.aspx

Bandura, A. (1977). *Social learning theory.* New York: General Learning Press.

Bandura, A. (1986). *Social foundations of thought and action: A social cognitive theory,* New Jersey: Prentice Hall.

Bloom, B. S. (1956). *Taxonomy of educational objectives, Handbook I: The cognitive domain.* New York: David McKay Co, Inc.

Bradt, K. M. (1997). *Story as a way of knowing.* Kansas City, MO: Sheed & Ward.

Centre for Learning and Professional Development. (2005). *Developing your teaching portfolio.* Retrieved July 8, 2011, from http://www.adelaide.edu.au/clpd/teaching/portfolio/t_portfolio.pdf

Clark, J. M. & Paivio, A. (1991). Dual coding theory and education. *Educational Psychology Review, 3*(3), 149–170.

Craik, F. & Lockhart, R. (1972). Levels of processing: A framework for memory research. *Journal of Verbal Learning & Verbal Behavior,* 11, 671–684.

D'Agostino, P. R., O'Neill, B. J., & Paivio, A. (1977). Memory for pictures and words as a function of level of processing: Depth or dual coding? *Memory & Cognition, 5,* 252–256.

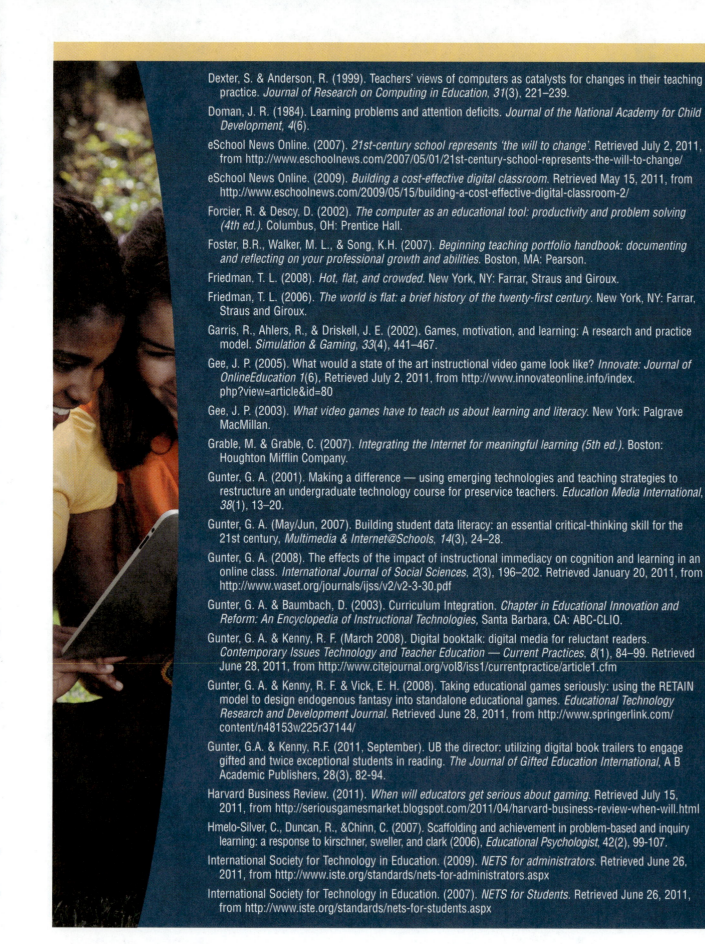

Dexter, S. & Anderson, R. (1999). Teachers' views of computers as catalysts for changes in their teaching practice. *Journal of Research on Computing in Education, 31*(3), 221–239.

Doman, J. R. (1984). Learning problems and attention deficits. *Journal of the National Academy for Child Development, 4*(6).

eSchool News Online. (2007). *21st-century school represents 'the will to change'*. Retrieved July 2, 2011, from http://www.eschoolnews.com/2007/05/01/21st-century-school-represents-the-will-to-change/

eSchool News Online. (2009). *Building a cost-effective digital classroom*. Retrieved May 15, 2011, from http://www.eschoolnews.com/2009/05/15/building-a-cost-effective-digital-classroom-2/

Forcier, R. & Descy, D. (2002). *The computer as an educational tool: productivity and problem solving (4th ed.)*. Columbus, OH: Prentice Hall.

Foster, B.R., Walker, M. L., & Song, K.H. (2007). *Beginning teaching portfolio handbook: documenting and reflecting on your professional growth and abilities*. Boston, MA: Pearson.

Friedman, T. L. (2008). *Hot, flat, and crowded*. New York, NY: Farrar, Straus and Giroux.

Friedman, T. L. (2006). *The world is flat: a brief history of the twenty-first century*. New York, NY: Farrar, Straus and Giroux.

Garris, R., Ahlers, R., & Driskell, J. E. (2002). Games, motivation, and learning: A research and practice model. *Simulation & Gaming, 33*(4), 441–467.

Gee, J. P. (2005). What would a state of the art instructional video game look like? *Innovate: Journal of OnlineEducation 1*(6), Retrieved July 2, 2011, from http://www.innovateonline.info/index.php?view=article&id=80

Gee, J. P. (2003). *What video games have to teach us about learning and literacy*. New York: Palgrave MacMillan.

Grable, M. & Grable, C. (2007). *Integrating the Internet for meaningful learning (5th ed.)*. Boston: Houghton Mifflin Company.

Gunter, G. A. (2001). Making a difference — using emerging technologies and teaching strategies to restructure an undergraduate technology course for preservice teachers. *Education Media International, 38*(1), 13–20.

Gunter, G. A. (May/Jun, 2007). Building student data literacy: an essential critical-thinking skill for the 21st century, *Multimedia & Internet@Schools, 14*(3), 24–28.

Gunter, G. A. (2008). The effects of the impact of instructional immediacy on cognition and learning in an online class. *International Journal of Social Sciences, 2*(3), 196–202. Retrieved January 20, 2011, from http://www.waset.org/journals/ijss/v2/v2-3-30.pdf

Gunter, G. A. & Baumbach, D. (2003). Curriculum Integration. *Chapter in Educational Innovation and Reform: An Encyclopedia of Instructional Technologies*, Santa Barbara, CA: ABC-CLIO.

Gunter, G. A. & Kenny, R. F. (March 2008). Digital booktalk: digital media for reluctant readers. *Contemporary Issues Technology and Teacher Education — Current Practices, 8*(1), 84–99. Retrieved June 28, 2011, from http://www.citejournal.org/vol8/iss1/currentpractice/article1.cfm

Gunter, G. A. & Kenny, R. F. & Vick, E. H. (2008). Taking educational games seriously: using the RETAIN model to design endogenous fantasy into standalone educational games. *Educational Technology Research and Development Journal*. Retrieved June 28, 2011, from http://www.springerlink.com/content/n48153w225r37144/

Gunter, G.A. & Kenny, R.F. (2011, September). UB the director: utilizing digital book trailers to engage gifted and twice exceptional students in reading. *The Journal of Gifted Education International*, A B Academic Publishers, 28(3), 82-94.

Harvard Business Review. (2011). *When will educators get serious about gaming*. Retrieved July 15, 2011, from http://seriousgamesmarket.blogspot.com/2011/04/harvard-business-review-when-will.html

Hmelo-Silver, C., Duncan, R., &Chinn, C. (2007). Scaffolding and achievement in problem-based and inquiry learning: a response to kirschner, sweller, and clark (2006), *Educational Psychologist, 42*(2), 99-107.

International Society for Technology in Education. (2009). *NETS for administrators*. Retrieved June 26, 2011, from http://www.iste.org/standards/nets-for-administrators.aspx

International Society for Technology in Education. (2007). *NETS for Students*. Retrieved June 26, 2011, from http://www.iste.org/standards/nets-for-students.aspx

International Society for Technology in Education. (2008). *Standards for global leanring in a digital age.* Retrieved June 26, 2011, from http://www.iste.org/standards.aspx

Iverson, K. M. (2005). *E-learning games — interactive learning strategies for digital delivery.* Upper Saddle River, NJ: Pearson Prentice Hall.

Kenny, R. F. & Gunter, G. A. (2006). Enhancing literacy skills through digital narrative. *The Journal of Media Literacy, 53*(2), 40–45.

Kenny, R. F. & Gunter, G. A. (2007). Endogenous fantasy-based serious games: Intrinsic motivation and learning. *International Journal of Social Sciences, 2*(1), 8–13. Retrieved April 20, 2011, from http://www.waset.org/journals/ijss/v2/v2-1-2.pdf

Kenny, R. F. & Gunter, G.A. (2008). Endogenous fantasy-based serious games: Intrinsic motivation and learning. International Journal of Social Sciences, 2(1), 8-13.

Kenny, R.F, & Gunter, G.A. (2011). Factors affecting adoption of video games in the classroom. *Journal of Interactive Learning Research*, 22(2), 259-276.

Ko, S. & Rossen, S. (2010). *Teaching online a practical guide (3rd ed.).* New York, NY: Routledge Press.

Koehler, M.J., Mishra, P., and Yahya, K. (2005). Tracing the development of teacher knowledge in a design seminar: Integrating content, pedagogy and technology. *Computers & Education*, 49(3), 740–762. Retrieved July 10, 2011, from http://www.sciencedirect.com/science/article/pii/S0360131505001752#implicit0

Kopler, E., Osterweil, S., Groff, J., & Haas, J. (2009). *Using the technology of today, in the classroom today: The instructional power of digital games, social networking and simulations and how teachers can leverage them.* Retrieved July 12, 2011, from http://education.mit.edu/papers/GamesSimsSocNets_EdArcade.pdf

Lewin, Tamar. (2009). *In a digital future, textbooks are history.* Retrieved from New York Times, July 12, 2011, from http://www.nytimes.com/2009/08/09/education/09textbook.html?pagewanted=all

Lynch, S. K., & Kogan, L. R. (2004). Designing online workshops: Using an experiential learning model. *Journal of College Counseling*, 7(2), 170.

Ma, W.K., & Yuen, H.K. (2011). Understanding online knowledge sharing: An interpersonal relationship perspective, Computers & Education, 56(1), 210-219,

Mitchell, D. & Gunter, G. A. (2004). The TIME Model: TIME to make a change to integrate technology. *Journal of Educational Media and Library Science*, 41(4), 479-502. Retrieved, July 1, 2011, from http://joemls.dils.tku.edu.tw/fulltext/41/41-4/479-493.pdf

Morgan, M. (2008). More productive use of technology in the ESL/EFL classroom. *The Internet TESL Journal, 14*(7). Retrieved May 25, 2011, from http://iteslj.org/Articles/Morgan-Technology.html

Nagal, D. (2009). Virtual school begins rolling out game-based courses. *T.H.E. Journal.* Retrieved June 28, 2011, from http://thejournal.com/articles/2009/06/02/virtual-school-begins-rolling-out-gamebased-courses.aspx

National Education Commission on Time and Learning. (1994). *Prisoners of time.* Report on Time and Learning Conducted to look at the status of education and time by the National Education Commission. Retrieved at archive on June 29, 2009, from http://www.ed.gov/pubs/PrisonersOfTime/index.html

O'Neil, H. F., Waines, R., & Baker, E. L. (2005, December). Classification of learning outcomes: Evidence from the computer games literature. *The Curriculum Journal, 16*(4), 455–474.

Ornstein, A. & Hunkins, F. (2007). *Curriculum foundations, principles, and theory (4th ed.).* Seattle, WA: Allyn & Bacon.

Paivio, A. (1986). *Mental Representations.* New York: Oxford University Press.

Palloff, R.M., & Pratt, K. (2009). *Assessing the online learner: Resources and strategies for faculty.* San Francisco, CA: Jossey-Bass.

Paquin, M. (2002). Effects of a museum interactive CD-ROM on knowledge and attitude of secondary school students in Ontario. *International Journal of Instructional Media, 29*, 101–111.

Partnership for 21st Century Skills. *Framework for 21st century skills.* Retrieved July 28, 2011, from http://www.p21.org/

Picciano, A. G., & Seaman, J. (2009). *K-12 online learning: A follow-up survey of U.S. School District Administrators, SLOAN-Consortium.* Retrieved July 18, 2011, from http://www.sloan-c.org/publications/survey/pdf/k-12_online_learning_2008.pdf

Picciano, A. G. & Dzuiban, C. D. (Eds.). (2007). *Blended learning research perspectives.* Needham, MA: The SLOAN Consortium.

Policy Information Center. (2000, October). How teaching matters. Princeton, NJ: Education Testing Service. *Media and Arts Association, 3*(1), 93–105.

Prensky, M. (2001). *Digital games-based learning.* New York: McGraw-Hill.

Read, D. & Cafolla, R. (1999). Multimedia portfolios for preservice teachers: from theory to practice. *Journal of Technology and Teacher Education. 7*(2), pp. 97–113. Charlottesville, VA: AACE.

Restak, R. M. (2003). *The new brain: How the modern age is rewiring your mind.* New York: Rodale St. Martins Press.

Richardson, W. (2010). *Blogs, wikis, podcasts, and other powerful web tools for classrooms (3rd ed.).* Thousand Oaks, CA: Corwin Press.

Schield, M. (2005). *Information literacy, statistical literacy and data literacy.* Retrieved July 12, 2011, from http://www.augsburg.edu/statlit/pdf/2005SchieldIASSIST.pdf

Schunk, D. (2008). *Learning theories: An educational perspective (5th ed.).* Columbus, OH: Prentice Hall.

Shelly, G., Gunter, G., & Gunter, R. (2010). *Teachers discovering computers: Integrating technology and digital media in the classroom (6th ed.).* Boston: Course Technology, Cengage Learning.

Shelly, G., Cashman, T., Gunter, R., & Gunter, G. (2005). *Teachers discovering and integrating Microsoft Office: Essential concepts and techniques (2nd ed.).* Boston: Thomson Learning — Thomson Course Technology

Shelly, G., & Vermaat, M. (2012). *Discovering computers 2010: Your interactive guide to the digital world.* Boston: Course Technology, Cengage Learning.

Shivetts, C. (2011). E-learning and blended learning: The importance of the learner — A research literature review. *International Journal on E-Learning*, 10 (3), 331-337.

Smaldino, S. E., Lowther, D. L., & Russell, J. D. (2008). *Instructional media and technologies for learning (9th ed.).* Columbus, OH: Prentice Hall.

Sulzen, J. (2011). Identifying evidence of reflective ability in preservice teacher electronic portfolios. *Journal of Technology and Teacher Education*, 19 (2), 209-237.

Tapscott, D. (1998). *Growing up digital — The rise of the net generation.* New York: McGraw-Hill.

Tapscott, D. (1995). *The digital economy: Promise and peril in the age of networked intelligence.* New York: McGraw-Hill.

Taylor, R. & Gunter, G. A. (2006). *The k-12 literacy leadership fieldbook.* California: Corwin Press.

Taylor, Sharon (2010). *Getting Started Teaching Online.* Retrieved June 27, 2011, from http://sloanconsortium.org/node/225451.

Tomlinson, C.A., & McTighe, J. (2006). *Integrating differentiated instruction* & *understanding by design: Connecting content and kids.* Alexandria, VA: Association for Supervision and Curriculum Development.

United States Department of Education. (2009). *Evaluation of evidence-based practices in online learning: A meta-analysis and review of online learning studies.* Retrieved July 4, 2011, from http://www.ed.gov/rschstat/eval/tech/evidence-based-practices/finalreport.pdf

United States Department of Education. (2010). *The elementary and secondary education act (The no child left behind act of 2001).* Retrieved August 3, 2011, from http://www2.ed.gov/policy/elsec/leg/esea02/index.html

University of Central Florida, College of Education. (2010). *LiveText Support.* Retrieved June 1, 2011, from http://education.ucf.edu/livetext/howto.cfm

Web-Based Education Commission. (2000). *The power of the Internet for learning: Final report of Web-based education commission.* A report to the president and the congress of the United States. Retrieved July 4, 2011, from http://www.ed.gov/offices/AC/WBEC/FinalReport/index.html

Welliver, P. (1990). *Instructional transformation: a module for change.* A report of the Pennsylvania regional computer resource center. University Park, PA: Pennsylvania State University.

Wikipedia. (2011). *Wikipedia: The free encyclopedia.* Retrieved June 30, 2011, from http://en.wikipedia.org/wiki/Main_Page

Young, J., Birtolo, P., & McElman, R. (2009). Virtual success — transforming education through online learning. *Learning & Leading with Technology, 36*(5), 12–17.

Index

curriculum-specific, 309–310
digital media, 127, 204–207
early learning, 131–132
educational. *See* educational software application
impact on education, 86
language arts, 132–133
math, 133
reviews as information source for evaluating educational technology, 354
science, 134
social studies, 134
tablet computers, 344–345
Web, 72, 120–121

app-based learning: The use of curriculum-specific apps on mobile devices to supplement online teaching and learning. Also called app-enhanced learning. 310, 323

app-enhanced learning: The use of curriculum-specific apps on mobile devices to supplement online teaching and learning. Also called app-based learning. 310

Apple. *See* MAC OS *entries*; Macintosh computer

Apple iWork: Contains word processing, spreadsheet, paint, and presentation software. 122

application evaluation rubric: An assessment tool that provides a number of important evaluation criteria, including content, documentation and technical support, ability levels and assessment, as well as technical quality and ease of use to help assess the quality of the software and applications. 356, 357–358

application program. *See* application software

application software: Programs designed to perform specific tasks for users; examples include educational, business, and scientific computer programs. Also called application program or software application. 102–107
categories, 102
communications, 102
starting, 103–104
voice recognition, 106
working with, 104–106

appointment calendar: Allows you to schedule activities for a particular day and time. 120

appropriate: Describes educational technology that must be suitable for the educational situation, must be motivational, and must promote learning at the correct levels of student ability and academic achievement. 352

Apps Corner, 31

ARCS Motivational Model: Developed by John M. Keller in 1983 and is applicable to learning in the digital age. 23–24, 274

arithmetic operations: Performed by the arithmetic/logic unit; include addition, subtraction, multiplication, and division. 159

arithmetic/logic unit (ALU): Another component of the CPU; performs the execution part of the machine cycle; specifically, the ALU performs arithmetic, comparison, and logical operations. 159

ARKive Education, 196

ARPA. *See* Advanced Research Projects Agency

ARPANET: A network that (1) would allow scientists at different locations to share information and collaborate on military and scientific projects and (2) could function even if part of the network was disabled or destroyed by a disaster, such as a nuclear war. 62

article: Message on a newsgroup. 81

arts curriculum: Curriculum that usually incorporates instruction in the visual and performing arts, including drawing, painting, dance, music, and theater. 387–388

ASCA. *See* American School Counselor Association

ASCD. *See* Association for Supervision and Curriculum Development

ASCII. *See* American Standard Code for Information Interchange

assessment: Any method used to understand the current knowledge a student possesses; it can range from a teacher's subjective judgment based on a single observation of a student's performance to a state-mandated standardized test. 364–365
alternative, 320, 364, 400
authentic, 364–365
eAssessment, 320
embedded, 101, 365
formative, 320
online, 320
peer, 320
portfolio, 365
project-based, 365
reliable, 364
self, 320
summative, 320
traditional, 364

assimilation, 268

assistant: An automated tool that helps you complete a task by asking you questions and then automatically performing actions based on your answers. Also called wizard. 110

Assistive Technologies Corner, 31–32

assistive technologies software: Designed specifically for students with physical impairments or learning disabilities to assist them in completing school assignments and everyday tasks. 135, 148
benefits, 252
choosing, 404
in classroom, reasons for, 197
definition, 40
Federal Accessibility Initiative, 449
fine motor skills deficiencies, 332
hearing impairment, 94, 332
input devices, 197
Microsoft and Apple built-in features, 40
reasons to learn about, 40
tablet computers, 350
technology integration in special needs curriculum, 404
uses, 252
visual impairment, 94
Web pages, 94, 449

Association for Career and Technical Education (ACTE), 45

Association for Educational Communications and Technology (AECT), 45

Association for Supervision and Curriculum Development (ASCD), 45

Association for the Advancement of Computing in Education (AACE), 45

ASSURE Model: Developed in the late 1990s by Heinich, Molenda, Russell, and Smaldino; a procedural guide for planning and delivering instruction that integrates technologies and media into the teaching process. 229–231

asterisk (*), search engine operator, 73

asynchronous: When communications occur at different times; it does not require that parties be present at the same time. 283

attention in ARCS Motivational Model, 23

Audacity, 39

audience: The individual or group intended to view and use the Web page. 361

audio: Any music, speech, or other sound. Any music, speech, or other sound that is stored and produced by the computer. 76, 173, 206
streaming, 76

audio input: The process of entering any sound into the computer, such as speech, music, and sound effects. 171

keyword: A special word, phrase, or code that a program understands as an instruction. 164

Kidsvid, 331

kilobyte (K or KB): Equal to 1024 bytes, but is usually rounded to 1000 bytes. 160

kiosk: A freestanding computer that provides information to the user. 170

KWHL chart: Alternative version of a KWL chart; an instructional planning tool, but adds an additional component - How students will learn. 227, 229

KWL chart: An instructional planning chart to assist a teacher in identifying student understanding of curriculum standards and related objectives by having students state what they already Know, what they Want to know, and then, based on that information recording what students Learned. 227–229

KWLQS chart: An instructional planning chart similar to a KWL chart, with the additions of Q, which stands for further questioning, and S, which stands for sharing (referring to the fact that students will share their projects with their fellow students). 375

label: Text entered in a cell that is used to identify the data and help organize the spreadsheet. 112

Laboratory School, 271–272

LAN. *See* local area network

landscape orientation: Printed page that is wider than it is tall, with information printed across the wider part of the paper. 176

language arts application: A type of software that supports student learning in the area of language arts, specifically in reading and writing. 132–133

language arts curriculum: Includes instruction in reading, writing, listening, viewing, speaking, and literature. 380

laptop computer, 8

laser printers: A high-speed, high-quality non-impact printer. A laser printer uses powdered ink, called toner, which is packaged in a cartridge. When electrically charged, the toner is transferred to the paper through a combination of pressure and heat. 178

law
  copyright laws. *See* copyright
  privacy laws, 428, 429, 434

LCD. *See* liquid crystal display

LCD monitor: A desktop monitor that uses a liquid crystal display to produce images. Also called flat-panel monitor. 175

LCD screen: The type of screen often used on mobile computers and mobile devices. 175

LeapFrog, 402

LeapPad, 343

Learn It Online, 32

learner response system: A type of system that is made up of IWB software installed on a teacher's computer, a wireless receiver, and student hand-held infrared transmitters that collect student responses or data in real time. 378

learning, 257
  app-based, 310, 323
  authentic, 219, 364
  blended. *See* blended learning
  collaborative, 270
  cooperative, 222
  curriculum-specific, 2–3
  differentiated, 298
  discipline-specific, 2–3
  discovery, 69–70
  distance. *See* distance education; eLearning
  distributed. *See* distance education; eLearning
  eLearning. *See* eLearning
  facilitator of, 216
  hybrid, 296. *See also* blended learning
  mastery, 266
  mixed mode, 296. *See also* blended learning
  mLearning, 35, 309
  online. *See* eLearning
  participatory, 219
  project-based, 365
  secondary, 219
  virtual. *See* eLearning

learning center: Provides the opportunity to break the classroom into many different types of learning environments without ever leaving the room; allows students to rotate around the classroom to complete projects or activities. Also called centers. 242–243

learning coach: A teacher or instructor who creates individualized lessons and engages with the learner through effective personal communication, feedback, and assessment, as well as provides support and encouragement. 295

learning environment
  integrated, creating, 241–242
  new, establishing, 2
  virtual, 25–27

learning expectation: A specific, measurable outcome or indicator that usually is tied to a curriculum standard. 211

Learning Management System (LMS): A secure, restricted, Internet-based comprehensive package that includes instructional tools for school administrators, documentation, student tracking, online courses and classes content, and training content. Also called Content Management System (CMS). 293–294

learning objective: A specific, measurable outcome or indicator that usually is tied to a curriculum standard. Also called benchmark. 211

learning process: Process of content engaging students to use higher-order thinking skills to go beyond the simple acquisition of knowledge and become participatory learners. 361
  technology integration and, 218–222

learning skill, 14

learning style: Refers to how individuals learn, including how they prefer to receive, process, and retain information. Learning styles vary among individuals. 216

learning theory, 244, 257–272
  behaviorist, 258–261
  cognitivist, 261–266
  constructivist, 266–272
  putting into practice, 277

Lee, Johnny Chung, 237

legal software: Assists in the preparation of legal documents and provides legal advice to individuals, families, and small businesses. 137

lesson planning, 227–229
  creating lesson plans, 379
  KWL charts, 227–229

Let's Think as a Scientist, 385

Library of Congress Web site, 50

life skill, 14–15

linguistic-verbal intelligence, 264

link: Allow users to navigate quickly from one Web page to another, regardless of whether the Web pages are located on the same computer or on different computers in different countries. Also called hyperlink. 68

liquid crystal display (LCD): Uses a liquid compound to present information on a display device. 175

LISTSERV: A popular software program used to manage many educational mailing lists. 81, 82

virus: A potentially damaging computer program designed to affect your computer negatively without your knowledge or permission by altering the way it works; a virus is a segment of program code that implants itself in a computer file and spreads systematically from one file to another. 412–417, 444
detection and removal, 414, 416–417

virus hoax: False warning about viruses often spread via e-mail and over the Internet. 417

virus payload: Symptom or damage caused by a virus. 413

visual learner: Individuals who learn concepts faster or retain a higher percentage of material if they see the information presented graphically. 206

visual learning technique: Methods that present ideas and information through graphical webs, used in planning projects. 369

VLE. *See* virtual learning environment

vlog: A blog that contains video clips. 72, 448

vodcast: A podcast that contains video and usually audio. 316

voice output: Occurs when you hear a person's voice or when the computer talks to you through the speakers on the computer. 180

Voice over IP (VoIP): Enables users to speak to other users over the Internet using their desktop computer, mobile computer, or mobile device. 83

voice recognition: A computer's capability of distinguishing spoken words. Also called speech recognition. 106, 171

VoiceThread, 195, 331

VoIP. *See* Voice over IP

volatile memory: Type of memory in which the contents are lost (erased) when the computer's power is turned off; example is RAM. 160

VR. *See* virtual reality

VR world: A 3D site that contains infinite space and depth. 77

VRS. *See* Sorenson Video Relay Service

Vygotsky, Lev, 269–271

Walden University: One of the leading fully accredited 100 percent online universities in the world. 286–287

WAN. *See* wide area network

WatchKnowLearn, 403

WBT. *See* Web-based training

Web. *See* World Wide Web

Web 2.0: Web sites that allow users to modify Web site content, provide a means for users to share personal information (social networking), and have application software built into the site for visitors to use; also called participatory Web. 68, 93

Web 3.0: When the semantics of information and services on the Web is defined, thus allowing the Web to understand and satisfy the requests of people to use Web content instantly; also called Semantic Web. 69

Web Accessibility Initiative, 94

Web application: A Web site that allows users to access and interact with software through a Web browser on any computer or device that is connected to the Internet. Also called Web app. 72, 120–121
applications and application software compared, 121–122

Web browser: A program that interprets HTML and displays Web pages and enables you to link to other Web pages and Web sites. Also called browser. 70–71

Web conferencing: Refers to a type of service that allows meeting events to be shared with individuals in different locations. 284

Web evaluation rubric: A detailed scoring guide for assessing the value and content of Web sites. 362–363

Web page: An electronic document viewed on the Web. A Web page can contain text, graphics, sound, and video, as well as hyperlinks to other Web pages. 68
accessibility, 94
copyright laws, 431–432
operation, 69–70
teacher's, creating, 310–312

Web page authoring software: Designed specifically to help you create Web pages, in addition to organizing, managing, and maintaining Web sites. 125

Web publishing: The development and maintenance of Web pages. 70

Web scavenger hunt: An inquiry-oriented activity in which students explore the resources of the Web using discovery learning to find the answers to teacher-created questions; encourages higher-order thinking skills. 376, 377

Web server: A computer that delivers (serves) requested Web pages. 69

Web site: A collection of related Web pages. 68
categories, 72
guide, 86

Web surfing: Displaying pages from one Web site after another. 70

Web-based course: A course or class taught completely on the Web, rather than in a traditional classroom. Also called eLearning course, online course, or virtual course. 283, 290

Web-based education: The delivery of education from one location to another; the learning takes place at a remote location. Also called distance education, distance learning, or distributed learning. 60

Web-based: Help Provides updates and more comprehensive resources in response to both technical and non-technical issues about software. 137–138

Web-based seminar: A presentation, lecture, workshop or meeting that is transmitted over the Web. Also called Webinar. 284–285

Web-based training (WBT): One approach to distance education that uses the technologies of the Internet and the World Wide Web. 284

WebBlender, 38

Webcast: A Webinar with mainly one-way communication from the speaker to the audience with limited audience interaction. 284

Web-enhance: Refers to adding Web tools, such as teacher-created Web pages, a curriculum resource pages, blogs, and wikis, to curriculum taught in a traditional face-to-face curriculum. 287

Web-enhanced course. *See* Web-based course

Webinar: A presentation, lecture, workshop or meeting that is transmitted over the Web. Also called Web-based seminar or online workshop. 284–285

Weblog: An informal Web site consisting of time-stamped articles, or posts, in a diary or journal format, usually listed in reverse chronological order. Also called blog. 72

Webmaster: The person responsible for developing Web pages and maintaining a Web site. 70

Welcome to the White House Web site, 52

Welliver's Instructional Transformation Model: Describes five hierarchical stages of technology integration through which all teachers must progress to integrate technology effectively; the stages are familiarization, utilization, integration, reorientation, and revolution. 217

Photo Credits